A STRANGE EVENTFUL HISTORY

Beside the Lives of Augustus John, Bernard Shaw and Lytton Strachey (which was filmed as *Carrington*), Michael Holroyd has written two volumes of memoirs, *Basil Street Blues* and *Mosaic* and is the only non-fiction writer to have been awarded the British Literature Prize. He lives in London and Somerset, with his wife, the novelist Margaret Drabble.

'Over thirty years Holroyd's books have revolutionised the intellectual standing of biography, and popularised it through narrative flair, witty and immaculate scholarship'

Richard Holmes, *Daily Telegraph*

'A wonderful book, wonderfully written'

Telegraph, Books of the Year

'One of the many extraordinary things about Holroyd's career has been his ability to push biography further and deeper into imaginative territory formerly occupied by the novel'

Hilary Spurling, *Spectator*

'It's possibly the most challenging work that Holroyd has ever attempted. It may also be the most successful . . . Holroyd evokes the mysterious world of the Victorian and Edwardian theatre, the hiss of the gas footlights, the coloured lights and smoke, with all the attention to detail of the star-struck fan seated in the front stalls'

Mark Bostridge, *Independent on Sunday*

'An epic, perfectly balanced by intimacies of setting and character'

New Yorker

'He writes with eloquence and clarity, sketching the broader context with a light but firm touch and incidentally providing a literary masterclass in the marshalling and sifting of detail'

Literary Review

MICHAEL HOLROYD

A Strange Eventful History

The Dramatic Lives of Ellen Terry, Henry Irving and their Remarkable Families

VINTAGE BOOKS
London

Published by Vintage 2009

2 4 6 8 10 9 7 5 3 1

First published in Great Britain in 2008 by Chatto & Windus

Vintage
Random House, 20 Vauxhall Bridge Road,
London SW1V 2SA

www.vintage-books.co.uk

Addresses for companies within The Random House Group Limited can be found at: www.randomhouse.co.uk/offices.htm

The Random House Group Limited Reg. No. 954009

A CIP catalogue record for this book is available from the British Library

ISBN 9780099497189

The Random House Group Limited supports The Forest Stewardship Council (FSC), the leading international forest certification organisation. All our titles that are printed on Greenpeace approved FSC certified paper carry the FSC logo. Our paper procurement policy can be found at: www.rbooks.co.uk/environment

Printed and bound in Great Britain by
Clays Ltd, St Ives plc

To Maggie
without whom
I could not have finished this book

'All comedy, is tragedy, if you only look deep enough into it.'

Thomas Hardy in a letter to John Addington Symonds,
14 April 1889

Contents

PART SIX

PART SEVEN

List of Illustrations

Endpapers

Front: Lyceum production of *Robespierre*, photograph, 1899
Back: *Hamlet*, Act IV, scene iv. Design by Edward Gordon Craig [EGC]; model by his son, Edward Craig © Helen Craig

Half-title and part-title illustrations

Decorative roundels from Cranach Press edition of *Hamlet*, EGC, wood-engravings, 1929–30

Text illustrations

Plates

Section One

Section Two

Section Three

Sources and acknowledgements

Back page endpaper, decorative roundels on half-title and part-title pages; illustrations on pages 146, 222, 306, 329, 338, 370, 372, 390, 435, 437, 467, 482, 513, 520, 556 and 573; section two, 10, 12, 13, 14, 15 and 16 © Estate of Edward Gordon Craig. Section one, 2, 3, 6, 7, 8 and 16; section two, 8 and 9; and section three, 1, 11, 12, 13 and 17, courtesy of the Collection of the National Trust, Ellen Terry Memorial Museum, Smallhythe, Kent. Section one, 4 and 9 © Estate of Julia Margaret Cameron, courtesy of the Science & Society Picture Library, Science Museum, London. Section one, 12, 21, 25 and 26; section two, 10; and section three, 2, 6, 8 and 14, courtesy of College Library, Eton College, Windsor. Section one, 13 © Getty Images. Section one, 14 courtesy of Gill Coleridge. Section two, 1 and 6; section three, 15 © National Portrait Gallery, London. Section two, 2 © Eastnor Castle Collection. Section two, 3 © National Galleries on Merseyside/ Walker Art Gallery, Liverpool. Section two, 4 © Tate, London 2006. Section two, 5, courtesy of The Metropolitan Museum of Art, Rogers Fund, 1910/Image © 2002 The Metropolitan Museum of Art, New York. Section two, 6 and 13, courtesy of the British Institute in Florence. Section three 19 © estate of David Lees/National Portrait Gallery, London. Section two, 11 © Mrs Lucy Dynevor/Mrs Michael Rothenstein, courtesy of V&A Images. Section three, 3 and 4 © Craig-Duncan collection, New York Public Library.

Notes on the text and acknowledgements

I have set out in this book to create a narrative that runs parallel to the course of several biographies, family memoirs and novels written during the twentieth century – the authors themselves often making dramatic appearances in a story that has its origins in the previous century. Despite alterations in the law, in accepted social and moral habits, and in our methods of recording history, the configurations of family life today still echo and reflect the concealed lives of a hundred years or more ago. It is a matter of human nature, rather than of prevailing fashion, which constantly changes, yet like Nature herself, does not change. As Claire Tomalin has written in her life of Thomas Hardy: 'The shifting feelings in a marriage, and in a family, are as complex and unpredictable as cloud formations.' I hope to carry readers back in time and convey a sense of adventure and intimacy with the past. A special debt of gratitude is owed to those owners, librarians, scholars and copyright holders who have helped me to find and allowed me to examine and quote from much hitherto unpublished material, enabling me to offer new interpretations of events. The telling of my interlinked stories avoids, I hope, too many anachronisms, though at the risk of falling into errors of 'appropriation' and what is currently considered incorrect usage (first names and gender specifics such as 'actress'). Not having the stamina of a Carlyle, I have not attempted to replace the bulky academic apparatus which disappeared between the operations and anaesthetics that interrupted my work. Such pedagogic business in books will in any case soon be made redundant, I am told, by the internet. It was unknown to most of my predecessors and the participants in this history who, well versed in Shakespeare, would have considered it 'wasteful and ridiculous excess'. So I find myself, like Edward Gordon Craig, inadvertently behind and ahead of the times and have tried to meet this anomaly by adding an Outline of Sources along with my Select Bibliography.

Among those who have given me help I must first thank John Irving, the great-grandson of Sir Henry Irving, and copyright holder in his estate as well as the estates of H. B. Irving and his son Laurence Irving. He has given me continual support during the research and writing of this book. In his twin roles as patron of the Irving Society and trustee of the Irving Foundation, he made extensive researches in the United States, particularly at the Folger Shakespeare Library in Washington, the Huntington Library, San Marino, California, the Harry Ransom Research Center at the University of Texas at Austin, the Honnold Mudd Library at Claremont, the Rush Rhees Library at Rochester and the Harvard Theatre Collection, all completed in time for the Henry Irving Centenary in 2005. This work was to prove a bonus for me.

I am most grateful to Ellen Terry Craig and her sister Marie Joy Taylor, both direct descendants of Ellen Terry and also joint copyright holders of the Edward Gordon Craig estate. Their enthusiasm for my project, shared by Marie's husband Tony Taylor, was strengthened with fortifying teas which helped to sustain me over the complicated years I was at work on this book.

Among the many people who gave me support and assistance were Pauline Adams, librarian at Somerville College, Oxford; Frith Banbury; Sue Bradley at the Folio Society; Anne-Elisabeth Buxtorf and Patrick Le-Boeuf at le Département des Arts du Spectacle, Bibliothèque Nationale de France, Paris; David F. Cheshire; Katharine Cockin at the University of Hull; Gill Coleridge; Helen Craig (who is the copyright holder in her father Edward Craig/Carric's work); John Craig; Tom Gordon Craig; William Dalrymple; Susan Doncaster; Christopher Fletcher at the British Library, London, and the Bodleian Library, Oxford; Richard Foulkes; Greg Gatenby; Victoria Glendinning; Veronica Franklin Gould; Jeremy Greenwood; Harvey Grossman; Susan Halpert at the Public Services of the Houghton Library, Harvard; Colin Harris, Modern Papers Reading Room, Bodleian Library, Oxford; Selina Hastings; Frances Hughes; Sarah Johnson; Deborah Kelley-Milburn at the Houghton Library Reading Room, Harvard College Library; Michael Kilgarriff, editor of *First Knight*; Andrew Kirk, assistant curator at the National Museum of the Performing Arts, London; Lorenzo Lees; Paul Levy; Fiona MacCarthy; Michael Meredith at Eton College Library;

Paul Meredith at Smallhythe Place; N. J. Milne, project archivist, Special Collections, University of Birmingham; Lindsay Newman; Suzanne O'Farrell; Richard Ormond; Christopher Phillips; Alyson Price at the British Institute, Florence; Marian Pringle at the Bram Stoker Collection, Shakespeare Centre Library, Stratford-upon-Avon; John Quentin; Kathryn Rawdon, Beinecke Rare Book and Manuscript Library, Yale University; Jeffrey Richards; Marcus Risdell, librarian at the Garrick Club, London; Denis Salter; Ilaria B. Sborgi at the Archivo Contemporaneo del Gabinetto Vieusseux, Florence; Sir Donald Sinden; Helen Smith; Virginia Surtees; David Sutton, director of research projects, University of Reading Library; Clive Swift; Bob Taylor, curator at the New York Public Library for the Performing Arts; Brian Taylor; Jo Watson; Tara Wenger and Richard Workman at the Harry Ransom Humanities Research Center, University of Texas at Austin; Emily White, archive curator at the Tate Millbank; Deborah Whiteman at the Department of Special Collections, University of California, Los Angeles; Aubrey Wilson; and Gwen Yarker, Museums Officer, Russell-Cotes Art Gallery & Museum, Bournemouth.

I also owe much to Alison Samuel, Clara Farmer, Juliet Brooke and Jenny Overton at Chatto & Windus in London, and to Jonathan Galassi and Courtney Hodell at Farrar, Straus & Giroux in New York, for steering my work so steadily towards publication; and to Richard Marston for the text and picture design, also Jane Robertson, my proofreader and Vicki Robinson, my excellent indexer.

The excerpts from Virginia Woolf's diary are taken from *The Diary of Virginia Woolf* edited by Anne Olivier Bell, published by Hogarth Press, and reprinted by permission of The Random House Group Ltd. The excerpts taken from Isadora Duncan's letters come from the Craig-Duncan Collection, 1901–1957, which are held by the New York Public Library's Dance Division.

A STRANGE EVENTFUL HISTORY

Rumours of a Death Foretold

On the night of 10 October 1868, after the curtain came down, a twenty-one-year-old actress left one of London's theatres, stepped into the dark streets and disappeared. None of her family knew where she was. In her bedroom at Kentish Town they came across a photograph of the artist G. F. Watts to which she had pinned a message: 'Found Drowned'. This was the title of a painting by Watts of a destitute young girl who had thrown herself into the river. Why had she left such a haunting message, if that is what it was, and what did it mean? Knowing how profoundly unhappy she had been, and feeling perhaps some responsibility for her unhappiness, her parents Ben and Sarah became acutely worried. They summoned her sister Kate's husband, Arthur Lewis, to help them look for her. He hired a detective and also sent an urgent telegram to the dramatist Tom Taylor. The Taylors were on holiday in the country, but Tom returned immediately to London and joined the search. 'We have been full of anxiety for you ever since you left,' his wife Laura wrote, 'and I long to hear from you of your safe arrival and that the great anxiety for poor N[elly] is partly relieved . . . The whole thing remains a mystery and a most painful one . . . Give my love and sympathy to Kate and also to the family, especially to the poor mother who is doubtless in great distress.'

Ben and Sarah had reported her disappearance to the police. A few days later the body of a young girl was found floating in the Thames. Ben was called to the morgue and he identified his daughter Ellen.

News of her death soon reached Ellen and she hurried back to Kentish Town to reassure her parents that she was still alive. She found them distraught and confused. The children had already been put into mourning clothes, though Sarah, who had followed her husband next day to the morgue and seen the body of the tall, fair-haired young girl drowned in the river, was convinced that this was not her daughter.

Ellen Terry omits this painful scene from her *Memoirs*, beyond saying that her parents were 'terribly anxious' and prepared to believe 'the first bad tidings that came to hand', knowing how miserable she had been. 'I had gone away without a word', she adds, forgetting the two dreadful words they had read as her message.

PART ONE

I

A Story in a Book

'The past is now to me like a story in a book', Ellen Terry wrote almost forty years later in 1906. It was a fairy story, her life; or perhaps one of those melodramas she had been playing onstage for as long as her admirers could remember. That June marked her fiftieth year in the theatre and the event was celebrated with wild delight in the streets of London. Crowds filled Drury Lane from midday till six o'clock in the evening – they would have stayed longer, singing, dancing, growing hoarse from cheering, but their rejoicings had to give way for Ellen's evening performance at the Court Theatre in Sloane Square. She was playing Lady Cicely Waynflete, a character Bernard Shaw had specially written for her, in Granville-Barker's production of *Captain Brassbound's Conversion*.

In the public imagination Ellen Terry had become an enchantress. Floating serenely across the stage, she was seen as a symbol of pure romance, virginal, unblemished, still in need of male protection: a 'wonderful being', the American actress Elizabeth Robins described her, 'with the proportions of a goddess and the airy lightness of a child'. She 'encompassed the age', wrote the theatre historian Michael Booth, 'in a way no English actress had done, before or since'.

Her beauty was not created by paint and lip-salve nor was it the illusory beauty of theatrical make-believe. She possessed a natural radiance and 'moved through the world of the theatre', Bram Stoker recorded, 'like embodied sunshine'. The artist Graham Robertson believed her to be 'the most beautiful woman of her time' and many people agreed with him. With the 'Hair of Gold' and 'Crimson Lips' celebrated in a sonnet by Oscar Wilde, and a mysterious smile which perhaps concealed no mystery, she was recognised as a Pre-Raphaelite ideal. Her reputation was extraordinary: not only was she a monument to female virtue, but also said to be the highest-paid woman in Britain. Virginia Woolf was to speculate as to whether the course of British history might have dramatically changed had she actually been queen, while Queen Victoria, meeting her at Windsor Castle in 1893, acknowledged her to be tall, pleasing and ladylike – everything a queen should be. Describing the scenes at Drury Lane as 'a riot of enthusiasm, a torrent of emotion', *The Times* dubbed her 'the uncrowned Queen of England' – though by now she had begun to resemble a Queen Mother.

Every Victorian gentleman who saw her at the Lyceum Theatre performing opposite the great Sir Henry Irving fell in love with her – and no Victorian wife objected. Some young men, it was said, would actually propose marriage to their girlfriends with the words: 'As there's no chance of Ellen Terry marrying me, will you?' Others, equally dazzled, reacted differently. 'I ceased to consider myself engaged to Miss King forthwith', wrote H.G. Wells on first seeing Ellen Terry walking one summer's day, looking like one of the ladies from Botticelli's *La Primavera*. He remembered being permitted to 'punt the goddess about, show her where white lilies were to be found and get her a wet bunch of forget-me-nots among the sedges . . .' She seemed to have the secret of eternal youth, to live beyond good and evil. In the opinion of Thomas Hardy, her diaphanous beauty belonged to a different order of being – a 'sea-anemone without shadow' or a miraculous dancing doll like Coppelia, apparently brought to life by the toymaker's magic, 'in which, if you press a spring, all the works fly open'. Even in her fifties she was still a marvellous child, delicious and fascinating.

Many people had expected her to marry Henry Irving – they were such a romantic couple onstage. It was rumoured that he secretly loved her – for how could he not have done so? Yet she was not regarded as a dangerous woman like the notorious Mrs Patrick Campbell or Edward VII's mistress Lillie Langtry. On the contrary she appeared an example of young motherhood as well as First Lady of the London stage. Her public image was all the more extraordinary since it conflicted dramatically with the facts of her life. And if those facts now seemed 'like a story in a book', this was partly because she had recently decided to write a book. She began her memoirs that year.

'I never felt so strongly as now', she said, 'that language was given me to *conceal* rather than to *reveal* – I have no words at all to say what is in my heart.'

When the book was published, it appeared to Virginia Woolf like 'a bundle of loose leaves upon each of which she has dashed off a sketch . . . Some very important features are left out. There was a self she did not know . . .'

'I was born on the 27th February, 1848', she wrote. After her death, when these memoirs were being prepared for a new edition, her editors loyally claimed that 'we have found Ellen Terry the best authority on Ellen Terry'. Yet there are potent omissions and genuine confusions in her writings which cover little more than half her adult life and grow ragged towards the end. As to the facts, she gives not only the wrong year for her birth but is also uncertain where it took place.

Alice Ellen Terry was born on 27 February 1847, at 44 Smithford Street, theatre lodgings above an eating house in Coventry, the city of three spires. On her birth certificate her father gave his occupation as 'Comedian'. Her earliest memory was of being locked in a whitewashed attic of some lodgings in Glasgow one summer evening while her parents and her elder sister Kate went off to the theatre. The Terrys were strolling players who travelled the theatre circuits and were then touring Scotland. But going further back, Ellen wondered, 'were we all people of the stage'?

2
The Terrys

Her maternal grandfather, Peter Ballard, was by profession a builder who worked as a master sawyer in the docklands of Portsmouth, a busy seaport and garrison town threaded with insalubrious cobbled streets and dark alleys where, like nocturnal animals, beggars, prostitutes and thieves lay in wait. He was also a Wesleyan preacher who spoke on Sundays in the smarter areas of the town with their muddle of demure Georgian houses and medieval churches. He disapproved of the town's theatre, a barnlike building in the High Street, which had been temporarily shut down in 1836 for 'unseemly and improper conduct'. But his daughter Sarah was to run off at the age of twenty-one with Ben Terry, the twenty-year-old son of an Irish innkeeper at the Fortune of War tavern in Portsmouth, a mere boy who had been picking up a meagre living working the drums in the theatre. In fact both Ben and Sarah kept their marriage secret from their parents. They were married on 1 September 1838 in the church where Charles Dickens had been baptised: St Mary's in Portsea, an area, near the docks, of taverns, shops and brothels that catered for the navy.

Their future was full of risk and excitement. They were a striking couple: he 'a handsome, fine-looking, brown-haired man' in peg-top trousers; she tall and graceful, with a mass of fair hair and exceptional large blue eyes. Ben seems to have taken it for granted that his wife would belong to the theatre and that all their children would be 'Precocious Prodigies' like the celebrated juvenile actress Jean Davenport. She had played at Portsmouth and was to become the original of Dickens's 'Infant Phenomenon' in *Nicholas Nickleby*, giving the theatre there a permanent place in stage history. The stage was everything to Ben, and Sarah was quickly caught up by his fervour and enthusiasm. As soon as they were married, they set off for whatever adventures might await them on the open road.

Ben had trained himself to be a competent supporting actor. As a teenager he hung around the stage door of the Theatre Royal where his brother George played the fiddle and got him casual work shifting scenery, painting and repairing props, and then playing the drums. He became mesmerised by what he saw: the frolics, farces and burlesques, the dissolving spectacles and nautical imitations, the scenarios with songs, the 'budgets of mirth and harmony' and juvenile performances in which the current child genius would dash round and about and in and out, playing all the roles, sometimes assisted by a 'marvellous dog'. When the professional season ended, the theatre was used for lavish balls and assemblies, or taken over by smart thoroughbred officers of the garrison and their well-groomed ladies who, under aristocratic patronage and to the beat of rousing marches from the regimental band, would put on ostentatious amateur performances, their playbills beautifully printed on pink silk. From watching rehearsals of the comedies and melodramas, Ben Terry learnt a good deal about the technique of acting – how to play the well-recognised roles of Heavy Father, Low Comedian, Walking Gentleman, Singing Servant, Character, Ingenu and so on. He was particularly fascinated by the expansive actor-manager of the stock company there. William Shalders appeared to be everywhere, doing everything, all the time. 'He painted the scenery, made the props, ran the box office', recorded the biographer Joy Melville, 'and even wrote pirated versions of London dramas in which his wife and daughter acted the minor roles, and visiting actors the lead parts.' He strongly influenced Ben Terry, who saw him as someone on whom he might model his own career.

'My sister Kate and I had been trained almost from our birth for the stage', Ellen wrote, '. . . our parents had no notion of our resting.' Usually she was bundled up and carried off to her mother's dressing-room in whatever town or village they had reached. 'Long before I spoke in a theatre, I slept in one', she remembered.

These days of travelling suited Ben's cheerful and impulsive nature. On him the sun always seemed to shine, though his family remained poor. It was a more worrying time for Sarah. Moving from place to place on carts and wagons, the children often slept on a mattress laid out on the floors of attics and played in the small areas below. To add to their income, Sarah would take on work as Wardrobe Woman or, under the name 'Miss Yerret' (an approximate reversal of Terry), play the role of Walking Woman to swell a crowd or decorate a chorus whenever she was not pregnant or recovering from a miscarriage. 'She worked hard at her profession', Ellen wrote, and she brought up all her children to be 'healthy, happy and wise – theatre-wise, at any rate'.

Six of her nine surviving children were to have careers onstage and Benjamin, who felt he had no dramatic talent, was obliged to work his passage to Australia and later seek employment in India so as to escape the force-field of his family destiny. Sarah, whose mother came from a respectable Scottish family socially superior to most theatre families, saw to it that her children were kept neat, clean and tidy. She was forever sewing, holding things together. The girls, she decided, needed little general education and only the boys were initially sent to school.

Ellen was soon being taught to read, write and speak properly by her parents. Ben was 'a very charming elocutionist', Sarah 'read Shakespeare beautifully' and they 'were unsparing in their corrections'. In the late Victorian and Edwardian theatre Ellen Terry and Johnston Forbes-Robertson were said to be the only actors who 'delivered the language of Shakespeare as if it were their natural idiom, and whose beauty of diction matched the beauty of the words'. In the opinion of her son, Gordon Craig, she 'was very much a daughter of Shakespeare, and when she spoke his prose it was as though she but repeated something she had heard at home – something said that morning'.

Ellen quickly learnt how to walk, breathe and cry onstage: in short, how to behave. She had a genius for pleasing people and even when she mixed up her lines or got caught in a trap-door, fell over onstage or laughed when she should have cried, they applauded her from the stalls and galleries. She was, as one critic called her, 'a perfect little heap of talent'.

Even so, she was not considered quite so talented as her elder sister. Kate Terry began her career at the age of four, dancing a hornpipe in a sailor suit, and was later to display what Charles Dickens called 'the very best piece of womanly tenderness I have ever seen onstage'.

The two little girls were born at a fortunate time in the history of the British stage. In 1843, a year before Kate's birth, a new Theatre Act was passed which finally broke the monopoly held by the Theatres Royal in

Drury Lane and Covent Garden. These had been the only two theatres in the country licensed by the Master of the Revels to perform 'legitimate' drama under letters patent granted in 1662 by Charles II – though these licences had been gradually extended to cities of royal residence and elsewhere through special arrangements. The bawdy, licentious wit of the late seventeenth century had reflected the amiable frivolity of Charles II's court, and would eventually lead to a severe reaction. In 1737, provoked by Henry Fielding's political satires and personal allusions, Robert Walpole took statutory powers to control dramatic performances by appointing an Examiner of Plays. On behalf of the Lord Chamberlain (who took the place of the Master of Revels), this examiner was to license all dramatic works for performance in public places. One consequence of this strict licensing system was that Restoration plays were largely replaced by rowdy entertainments that did not need a licence and that made theatres places of ill-repute: music halls and drinking dens at risk of being devoured by riots and fires, abominable places to which respectable people – people like Ellen's grandfather Peter Ballard – never went. The 1843 Act, which was to spread 'legitimate' theatre through the country, retained the Examiner of Plays, whose job was to encourage the staging of polite drama.

The Terry family belonged to a theatre that became dominated by a procession of famous actor-managers. They produced the great Shakespearean dramas, often in sentimentalised versions and with their parts adapted to suit the type of character-acting at which each excelled – the specialist eccentricities of John Hare, the graceful diction and classical good looks of Forbes-Robertson, the delicious light comedy performances of Charles Wyndham, Beerbohm Tree's luxurious decadence and genius for burlesque, George Alexander's aristocratic charm, the perfect deportment of Martin-Harvey, Gerald du Maurier's easygoing nonchalance. All these and others, following in the steps of Sir Henry Irving, whose speciality lay in exploiting the sinister components of romantic melodrama, were to reflect, with their glittering knighthoods, the genteel revolution that had taken place in the British theatre by the time of Ellen Terry's jubilee.

Though her attempted stage debut as 'the Spirit of the Mustard-Pot' ended in tears, Ellen was to remember her early years of travelling from one theatre town to another as being intensely happy. Like her father she had a naturally impulsive temperament whereas Kate seemed to have inherited her mother's carefulness. In 1852 the actor-manager Charles Kean, hearing of the eight-year-old Kate Terry's remarkable performance as Prince Arthur in *King John*, invited her to recreate the role at the Princess's Theatre in the West End of London. She went there with her mother and the younger children, and the following year Ellen, who (aged six) had been 'looking after' her father, travelled down with him from Liverpool to join Kean's company.

The morality of employing very young children onstage intermittently agitated the Victorians. There were those who, like Bernard Shaw, were to argue that 'dressing the stage' with enticing seven- and eight-year-olds, soliciting infants to make money for the proprietors of theatres, was an exploitation of impoverished families. How was it possible to justify this parading of prettily dressed boys and girls, who had not even reached their teens and had never been to school, so that adults might enjoy a repertoire of sensational entertainments? Why should theatre managers consider themselves exempt from the regulations that protected young children from being exploited in factories and workshops? Their descriptions of theatres as perfect schools of deportment, where the charges' characters were moulded by masterpieces of English poetry, were pure commercial bluff. But the Revd Charles Dodgson claimed that listening to the words of elevating plays – such as radically cleansed versions of Shakespeare – was an education in itself and kept children away from truly vicious pursuits on the streets. Besides, you had only to see these theatre children themselves to understand how they rejoiced in their work. 'They like it better than any game ever invented for them', Dodgson wrote in a letter to *The Theatre*. This passion for acting gave children 'a better average for straightness of spine, strength, activity, and the bright happy look that tells of health', he argued. 'The stage child "feels its life in every limb" . . . where the Board school child only feels its lessons.'

While writing her memoirs, Ellen Terry often wished she had been given some school lessons on grammar, punctuation and spelling to guide her through this task. They had worked her hard in Charles Kean's Company, so hard that on leaving the stage with the other children, sometimes in the middle of the night, her legs aching, she would creep into the green room and fall asleep. She hated the labour that led up to her performances, the wearisome learning of lines and the endless rehearsals lasting all day, sometimes without lunch or supper. Charles Kean, 'a short, thickset man' with 'chubby features', was a pedant of modest talent who liked to boast of the verisimilitude of his sets and properties. He enjoyed conducting rehearsals by ringing a hand-bell from the auditorium. His wife, a fine intelligent actress called Ellen Tree, 'parrot-beaked and double-chinned, moving solemnly within the periphery of her crinoline', would then ascend the stage and put everything to rights. 'I admired and loved and feared her', Ellen remembered. These were exhausting sessions, yet she would not have exchanged her life with anyone. 'My whole life was the theatre', she wrote, '. . . during my three years at the Princess's I was a very strong, happy, and healthy child.'

The Princess's Theatre was a narrow gas-lit building between a furrier's and a tobacconist's in Oxford Street. It had opened in 1840 and been used for concerts and operas until, following the new Theatres Licensing Act, a few plays began to be performed there. Charles Kean, son of the famous Drury Lane tragedian Edmund Kean (who had unsuccessfully tried to detach his son from the stage by sending him to Eton), took over the theatre in 1850 and gave his management there a reputation for extravagant productions of Shakespeare played against 'authentic scenery'. These were interspersed with rather tepid translations of French comedies and some swashbuckling historical dramas.

At the Princess's, Ellen learnt how to 'walk the plank', dance a minuet, draw her breath in through her nose and begin to laugh, how to produce her vowels correctly, tuck in her chin and puff out her chest when making an entrance, and also how to manoeuvre gracefully (not jumping like a kangaroo) while wearing a trailing flannel dress. It was 'heavy work for a child, but I delighted in it'.

She delighted especially in what she called 'the actual doing of my part'. She played important parts, small parts, dumb parts (the best of which was walking on carrying a basket of doves, agreeably aware of being regarded with bitter envy by the other children, and feeling as if this dove-bearer were the principal attraction in *The Merchant of Venice*). In *Richard II* she climbed a pole to a dizzy height during a street scene; in *Henry VIII* she was 'top angel'; and in a comedietta by Edmund Yates she played a tiger ('Tiger Tom') wearing a brilliant little pair of top boots. In another production she was 'a little boy cheering', but even in these tiny roles such opportunities for acting precocious boy-girls were exciting. In the Christmas pantomime of 1857 she played the blonde-haired good fairy Goldenstar, and the frightening bad fairy Dragonetta with flashing eyes and dark looks. It seemed as if she could be anyone and that everything was possible: changes of gender, character, appearance, species and identity. The world of the theatre was limitless.

Ellen's London debut at the age of nine was as the little prince Mamillius in *The Winter's Tale*. Increasingly aware of what she looked like, and getting to recognise the effects she created, she was able many years later to recall wearing a red-and-silver dress and oddly baggy pink tights for Mamillius, and a row of tight sausage curls arranged with perfect regularity by her mother. For two wonderful scenes (before she 'died' offstage), she propelled across the boards a splendid 'property' – a go-cart built like a toy depicted on a Greek vase in the British Museum. On the first night, with Queen Victoria and Prince Albert in the theatre, when told by Leontes (Charles Kean) to 'go play', she did so with such verve that she tripped over the handle of her go-cart and fell on her back. But it did not matter. *The Times* described her performance as 'vivacious and precocious' and the Revd Charles Dodgson noted in his diary on 16 June 1856 that he 'especially admired the acting of the little Mamillius, Ellen Terry, a beautiful little creature, who played with remarkable spirit and ease'. Ellen cherished this role so jealously that she did not miss any of the 102 nights of the run, and her understudy, Clara Denvil, a little girl with eager eyes, never got the chance to show herself.

In the autumn of 1856 Ellen was given the role of Puck in *A Midsummer Night's Dream*. She played it well, romping on the stage while putting a girdle around about the earth, full of mischief and vitality. Looking in her mirror she had been dismayed to see how gawky she was growing. But in the role of Puck she could escape this dismaying image for it was 'a part in which the imagination can run riot'. In Shakespeare's moonlight she entered a fairyland where every wish came true. 'I grew vain', she remembered, 'and rather "cocky".'

Ellen's last major role at the Princess's Theatre was as Prince Arthur in *King John* – the part in which her sister Kate had triumphed and which had been responsible for bringing the Terry family to London. It was the first really demanding character she had played and, aged eleven, she found the rehearsals miserably difficult. In a moment of exasperation, Mrs Kean slapped her face, unexpectedly getting from her the expression of mortification and tears she wanted when Hubert threatens to blind the little prince who pleads for his life.

Ellen was determined not to fail where her sister had succeeded. She would get up secretly in the night to practise her lines, experiment with her voice and examine her gestures in the mirror. For the first time she realised what perseverance and labour a successful career in the theatre would demand from her and 'all vanity fell away from me'.

Her Prince Arthur was judged a success. But at the end of the 1859 season Charles Kean gave up the Princess's Theatre and sailed to the United States. Kate and Ellen were earning good money for their ages, but the Terry family had been growing and, without a steady income, Ben had to leave London with his daughters and once more seek his fortune on the road.

3
Mirror, Mirror, on the Wall

Travelling the circuit was not so exciting as it had been when Ellen was very young. Then it had been all adventure and fun. This time she was made aware that many people in the provinces still regarded actors as they did the gypsies: travellers and vagabonds who lived beyond the law and were exiles from respectable society – what were called 'sturdie beggars' coming among respectable people in their poverty and snatching clothes from the washing-lines.

Over the next three years, as she moved from childhood into adolescence, Ellen began to feel a gradual disillusion with theatre life. It started during her last year at the Princess's as she began to notice rivalries between the actors. Of course there were sometimes moments of envy, feelings of unfairness, between the stage children, but the adults appeared to make a career of their resentments. Charles Kean and Ben Terry had never liked each other. Sometimes Ben was obliged to write obsequious letters apologising for outbursts of the 'Terry temper' and expressing gratitude for Kean's appreciation of his two brilliant little daughters. Kate, being more prudent than Ellen (or Nelly as she was called – her first name Alice having quickly disappeared), sought to distance herself from her sister's naughtiness which 'I hope will not occasion you to withdraw your kindliness and good wishes toward me', she appealed to Mrs Kean.

What sustained these actors through what one of them described as 'years of poverty, privation, sickness of soul and body, a constant sense of self-imposed beggary', was the 'burning desire for dramatic distinction' which could bring them deep pleasure from individual accomplishment and a sense of the mysterious lives they led in people's imaginations.

With several rapid changes of dress, Kate and Ellen played all the parts in their father's own theatricals – two domestic comedies *Home for the Holidays* and *Distant Relations* presented under the collective title *Drawing-Room Entertainment.* Ben's mother had recently died, leaving him a little money which he used to set himself up independently for a time. After a successful opening in the imitation caverns of the Royal Colosseum in Regent's Park, they set off on a long tour of England and Ireland, with Ben as stage manager and a young man, Sidney Naylor, as 'orchestra'. Sometimes they got lifts on wagons, sometimes they tramped the roads (walking all the way from Bristol through Somerset to Exeter – almost seventy miles). 'Each day a new place', Ellen remembered. 'It was great fun.' When their tour ended in 1861, Kate went to St James's Theatre in London. Here she understudied a Miss Herbert who, falling ill, gave her the chance to take the lead in an adaptation of a Victorien Sardou play. It was an important breakthrough in her career. 'No one knew', wrote the drama critic Clement Scott, 'that we had amongst us a young actress of so much beauty, talent and . . . dramatic power.' Having gained this success, she joined a well-known stock company at Bristol. Ellen meanwhile went to find work in London and was soon summoned for an interview with Madame Albina de Rhona, a petite Parisian dancer who had recently gone into management at the Soho Theatre, renaming it the Royalty Theatre. Ellen attributed her engagement there to Kate. 'At this time I was "in standing water", as Malvolio says of Viola when she is dressed as a boy', she wrote in her memoirs.

I was neither child nor woman – a long-legged girl of about thirteen, in short skirts, and feeling that I ought to have long ones. However, when I set out with father to see Madame de Rhona, I was very smart. I borrowed Kate's new bonnet – pink silk trimmed with black lace – and thought I looked nice in it. So did father, for he said on the way to the theatre that pink was my colour. In fact, I am sure it was the bonnet that made Madame de Rhona engage me on the spot!

Whatever Ellen did, her sister remained the principal actress in the family. While Kate took on several leading roles in Bristol, Ellen was being given more eccentric parts in London. In Eugène Sue's *Atar-Gull*, she made a harrowing entrance through a window dressed in white muslin and with a venomous snake coiled around her neck, repeating the terrible screams she had delivered when playing Prince Arthur. Everyone agreed that she had 'discovered the exact way a woman with a snake round her neck should scream' – it was a terrific piece of business. Madame de Rhona had been a successful performer at Drury Lane – and as far abroad as Paris and St Petersburg – but she had an uncanny knack for picking plays that had to be taken off after three or four performances. One result of this desperate repertoire was that, towards the end of 1861, while attempting to learn the lines of five different characters, Ellen suddenly had an attack of stage fright. 'Stage fright is like nothing else in the world', she wrote. She felt as if her tongue had been dislocated and lay powerless in her mouth. The muscles in her legs refused to work and an urge rose in her to plunge over the footlights into oblivion. Dragging herself offstage, she seized a book and, suddenly reappearing, ignominiously read her lines. She described the experience as 'torture'.

It was not only the quantity of lines she had to learn that prompted this panic, but also the loss of confidence she felt when she compared herself in the mirror with the exquisite Madame de Rhona. 'She was the first Frenchwoman I had ever met, and I was tremendously interested in her.' A quick-tempered, bright, energetic little woman with neat expressive ways, she danced exquisitely and drew all eyes to her. 'When I watched the way she moved her hands and feet, despair entered my soul', Ellen remembered. '... Her limbs were so dainty and graceful – mine so big and unmanageable! ... I was so much ashamed of my large hands ... that I kept them tucked up under my arms!'

Ugly was how Ellen felt when she was not wearing her sister Kate's clothes: ugly and stupid and of no interest to men. One night, overcome with curiosity, she peeped into the pretty little green room at the Royalty and saw Madame Albina – 'a wee thing, like a toy' – at an intimate supper-party with her admirers drinking champagne from her slipper. Ellen was almost fifteen now, on the verge of being an adult, yet as far as ever apparently from attaining this glamorous life – she who a few years earlier had thought she could do anything, go everywhere, charm everybody, be anyone.

In February 1862 she left London and joined Kate and the rest of her family in Bristol. While Kate continued playing the lead roles, Ellen took whatever she was given. Carrying a bow and quiver, she played her last male part, Cupid, the god of love, in an extravaganza called *Endymion*. But the scantiness of her tunic and the sauciness with which she danced, disturbed some of the audience who, though relishing the naughty jokes of the seasoned male comedian, raised their eyes at Ellen's suggestiveness. It was another instance of how difficult she was finding this transformation into womanhood.

Kate and Ellen were popular in Bristol. 'We were petted, spoiled, and applauded to our hearts' content . . .', Ellen recalled. 'We . . . had scores of admirers, but their youthful ardour seemed to be satisfied by tracking us when we went to rehearsal in the morning and waiting for us outside the stage-door at night . . . My mother was most vigilant in her role of duenna, and from the time I first went on the stage until I was a grown woman I can never remember going home unaccompanied by either her or my father.'

But there was one admirer to whose home the two sisters were allowed to go unaccompanied. Edward William Godwin was reputed to be a genius. The only matter in contention was what calling, of the many that presented themselves, he would choose to answer. His very indecision was impressive. From his Welsh mother he had picked up an ability to draw and been inspired on a journey by boat along the river Wye to Tintern Abbey. But in what profession could he best make use of this inspiration? Was he an archaeologist, an architect or a philosopher? Or might he turn out to be a Shakespeare scholar, a draughtsman or, as his father wished, an engineer – the new Isambard Kingdom Brunel? It seemed a pity to exclude any of these. But the multiplicity of his talents became entangled and made him cantankerous. Growing self-absorbed, given increasingly to grumbling, he needed a band of merry men – men such as the bohemian painter-playwright W.G. Wills and the scholarly Shakespearean actor Herman Vezin – to keep him in good humour. Like Dryden's fabulous Duke of Buckingham, he was

> A MAN so various, that he seemed to be
> Not one, but all mankind's Epitome.

Observing Ellen's 'winning ways', Godwin anonymously reviewed the Theatre Royal's productions in one of the Bristol newspapers – reviews that Ellen thought 'wonderful'. His theatre interests soon brought him into the company of Ben and Sarah Terry. Sarah did not like him. She could not precisely say why, but she thought him a sinister man. However, when he asked permission for Kate and Ellen to visit his home and take part in his celebrated Shakespeare readings, Ben gave his permission and Sarah did not object. In the early 1860s Godwin's life appeared uncharacteristically stable. He had recently married the daughter of a clergyman from Henley-on-Thames, a very presentable lady in her thirties whose respectability was to be enhanced by chronic invalidism. Godwin himself had harnessed his ambitions for the time being to architecture where his Gothic extravagancies were held in check by Mr Crisp, his partner, a kindly man with a strawberry-spotted face, who gave him a copy of Ruskin's *The Stones of Venice*. The future shone brightly. Besides local churches, schools and houses, he would design town halls and restore castles – in particular Dromore Castle for the Earl of Limerick and Castle Ashby for the Marquis of Northampton. Soon he would be spoken of as a possible architect for the new law courts in London and the Houses of Parliament in Berlin.

The Godwins' fine Georgian house at 21 Portland Square, in a fashionable area the other side of Bristol from the Terry family, reflected the strangeness of his tastes. He was in Max Beerbohm's words 'the greatest aesthete of them all', and as Ellen testified, he opened her eyes to 'beautiful things in art and literature'. Certainly his home was extraordinary – even the door-knocker which confronted you as you entered (a strange silver ball suspended from a chain) was unconventional. The walls inside, plain areas of colour on which hung an occasional Japanese print, appeared almost wholly undecorated by the cluttered fashions of the day. The floors too were bare except for some Persian rugs, and the furniture, some of which Godwin had designed himself, seemed by Victorian standards (which favoured deep carpets and rich upholstery embellished with many plump cushions) to be almost spartan in its simplicity. A final oddity, almost a sacrilege, was the organ Godwin had installed in his drawing-room.

Ellen was fascinated by Godwin. She had never seen anyone like him. He was a strikingly handsome man with penetrating brown eyes and expressive hands, still in his twenties when she met him. He appeared like a romantic lead for a drama in which something remarkable was about to happen. She described her visits there as 'a revelation'.

Oscar Wilde believed Godwin to be 'one of the most astute spirits of this century'. It was his conversation that initially impressed Ellen. She listened intently, thinking of things she had never thought of before. There was a strange excitement in being with him and she would come to mark their time together as a turning-point in her life. Recalling it many years later, she wrote:

> At the theatre I was living in an atmosphere which was developing my powers as an actress and teaching me what work meant, but my mind had begun to grasp dimly and almost unconsciously that I must do something for myself – something that all the education and training I was receiving in my profession could not do for me . . . I now felt that I had never really lived at all before. For the first time I began to appreciate beauty, to observe, to feel the splendour of things, to *aspire!*

What she aspired to was something beyond the theatre. She begins to tell the story of her developing friendship with Godwin, as she had told the story of her meeting with Madame Albina de Rhona, by describing the clothes she would wear. She had been cast as Titania in a new production of *A Midsummer Night's Dream*, opening after a recent fire at the Theatre Royal in Bath. 'Mr Godwin made my dress', she writes:

> He showed me how to damp it and 'wring' it while it was wet, tying up the material as the Orientals do in their 'tie and dry' process, so that when it was dry and untied, it was all crinkled and clinging. This was the first lovely dress that I ever wore . . .

Godwin's interest in the theatre was increasingly directed towards decor and costume design. He began to transform Ellen from the scantily dressed boy-girl in *Endymion* into a real woman. 'I learned a good deal', she wrote. But their relationship was interrupted when Ellen was summoned back to London.

4
Heaven and Holland Park

The Terrys had taken a house near Euston, in North London. Stanhope Street was a recently developed area of neat, red-brick, terraced houses designed for 'families of limited income but genteel pretensions'. The family home at number 62, flanked by a tavern and a pawnbroker's, was a narrow building with a steep flight of stairs leading from the hall, with pretty iron balconies at the front and a small paved yard surrounded by a brick wall at the back. For much of the time it was full of Terry children of various ages – besides Kate, Ellen and their brother Benjamin, there were George, Marion, Flossie, Charlie and now Tom, born just as Ellen returned from Bath. There was to be a family baptism at Old St Pancras on 1 February 1864, the year in which the Revd Charles Dodgson first came to visit them.

Ellen immediately resumed her career at the Haymarket Theatre. But she was not happy. She hated the malicious gossip of the green room and felt priggish when objecting to it and cowardly when she did not. She came to regard her engagement there as a series of lost opportunities. And had she not lost an opportunity by leaving Bristol?

Kate meanwhile was enjoying a spectacular success at the Lyceum. She was a 'stage divinity', as it was called. Two of the most popular dramatists of the day, Charles Reade and Tom Taylor, were writing plays for her – and would later do so for Ellen. They appeared an ill-matched couple – Reade so tall and thin, boisterous and bearded, Taylor so round and short – almost a pair of stage comedians. But they were close friends and had become friends of the Terry family. Charles Reade, a vice-president of Magdalen College, Oxford, was a successful novelist as well as a playwright, 'a strange, irascible man', Roger Manvell calls him, 'who combined the angry instincts of a social reformer with great kindness of heart, [and] had defied Victorian convention by living openly with an actress, Laura Seymour'. She, it was said, 'knew the male sex by heart' and had 'passed through the dark furnace of London life, and emerged from it a brave and benevolent woman'. Yet their relationship, in its fashion passionate, was reputed to be platonic, and this reputation, like a flag of convenience, allowed Kate and Ellen to visit their house in St John's Wood.

Reade's friend, Tom Taylor, famous for his social clumsiness and lapses of memory, was a middle-aged phenomenon – an 'institution' Ellen called him. He had begun his career as professor of literature at University College London, before becoming a civil servant at the Board of Health. In his spare time he contributed articles on art and drama to *The Times*, performed in amateur theatricals and campaigned vigorously for a national theatre in Britain – besides composing over seventy plays. A friend of Charles Dickens, he had dramatised *A Tale of Two Cities* and, with his spectacles tied on string around his neck, was said to resemble Mr Pickwick, being a small, fat, blinking, friendly character, somewhat dominated by his wife in Clapham Common.

Both Reade and Taylor acted *in loco parentis* to Kate and Ellen, introducing them to a wider circle of friends than those they met at Stanhope Street. Reade's favourite was the thirteen-year-old Ellen with whom he used to play 'blind man's buff' and who called him 'Papa' or sometimes even 'Daddy'. Tom Taylor she described as a 'sweet fellow', adding that he cared for Kate 'more than he cared for me'. Both of them took over from Ben Terry as the sisters' stage mentors.

It was Tom Taylor who was indirectly responsible for Ellen suddenly leaving the stage in the middle of one of his own plays. In 1862 he introduced Kate and Ellen to the painter George Frederic Watts, who had seen Kate act and given Taylor to understand that he would very much like to meet her.

Watts, then in his mid-forties, was a somewhat 'lukewarm' gentleman according to Bernard Shaw, rather 'bony and skinny' in Ruskin's words, but with a most luxurious dark brown beard falling down his chest (it 'could have been mistaken', G.K. Chesterton suggested, 'for a hair dresser's advertisement'). He was a prey to melancholia and needed the dramatic energy of someone like Kate Terry, with her vivacious charm and good looks, to rouse him to great work. 'I must have something to look forward to', he appealed to a friend. '. . . Every day I feel more and more the impossibility of living alone.' Would it be practical, he wondered, for someone to 'find me a wife'? He was too overwhelmed by the magnitude of this task to go about it himself, yet was prepared to reassure any young lady who might think of volunteering for the post, that it would not involve the unpleasantness of what he called 'violent love'. Matters were more complex, indeed more tepid, than that. What he needed was almost, and yet not quite, a sister or even perhaps a ready-made daughter, someone who could sit motionless while he went about painting her and who, as it were, acted as his muse. Yet he hesitated, and had gone on hesitating, not wishing to 'risk being deceived or disappointed'.

Kate was almost twenty and certainly ripe for marriage. She could not go on much longer living with her parents at Stanhope Street – and nothing could match being wife to 'England's Michelangelo'. She would have to be chaperoned, of course, should Watts desire to paint her. Sarah Terry, with so many young children to look after, could hardly be expected to visit Watts's studio. So it was Ellen who accompanied her sister.

When she came through the red baize door into Watts's studio, it seemed to Ellen that she was entering 'a paradise, where only beautiful things were allowed to come. All the women were graceful, and all the men gifted.' Indeed, she was made to feel beautiful herself. This was a similar impression, delightful and disturbing, to the one she had experienced when stepping into Godwin's house in Bristol. It felt infinitely preferable, this aesthetic world, to the world of the theatre as she was presently experiencing it, full of scandal, gossip, rivalry and hateful practical jokes.

Ellen told herself that she was without ambition – Kate was the ambitious one. In terms of the nineteenth-century theatre, it appeared as if she, and not Ellen, was to be 'the Terry of the age'. Ellen was often out of sorts and did not even try to do her best with some of the parts she was given. Her mind was full of delicious day-dreams from 'a world full of pictures and music and gentle, artistic people with quiet voices and elegant manners'.

This was the world she saw when Tom Taylor introduced her to Watts at Little Holland House in Kensington. It was like walking on holy ground where the object of adoration was the artist himself. The Signor, as he was called, seemed to sanctify the place.

It must have been a thrilling moment when Watts proposed painting the eighteen-year-old Kate and Ellen, then aged fifteen, together. *The Sisters*, as the portrait was to be called, is an unexpected work. Kate, at first glance, appears to occupy the superior position. She sits upright and is the taller of the two figures. But it is to Ellen that the eye is drawn. Kate's amiable, mild face is far less decisively painted than Ellen's, whose visionary expression, reclining on her sister's shoulder, fills the foreground and centre of the painting, giving Kate a largely supporting role. Ellen remembered being kissed by Watts. 'I'll never forget my first kiss', she wrote in her memoirs. She had never been kissed by a man before. 'Mr Watts kissed me in the studio one day, but sweetly and gently', she wrote. This was so unexpected, so significant, that she presumed the two of them were what people called 'engaged'. She described herself as being 'in Heaven for I knew I was to live with those pictures . . . and to sit to that gentle Mr W.. . . in wonderland'.

5
England's Michelangelo

Despite these happy premonitions, the year 1863 was a troublesome one for Watts. It was fortunate, perhaps, that he was so well schooled in trouble. From humble beginnings, he had grown up in frail health, a prey to asthma and migraines. His pious and consumptive mother died when he was nine, and his father, a piano manufacturer, passed much of his time failing to invent an ingenious musical instrument which combined the virtues of wind and strings, a device that, had it actually come into existence, might have financially rescued the family. Avoiding school and spending his adolescence in the company of two quarrelling stepsisters and a crippled brother, Watts nourished himself on 'large legendary literature' by means of which he rose, from time to time, above his troubles. But still the asthma afflicted him, and still the migraines. Sometimes he would lie in a darkened room 'thinking very seriously of prussic acid', he confided to a friend.

There were moments, however, of loftier speculation when images of allegorical and didactic compositions in the grand manner, similar to the heroic literature on which he gorged himself, would rise up promising a more elevated future. His urge to reveal himself as a Great Master was encouraged in 1847 when he won a premium of £300 with a cartoon showing the first-century chieftain Caractacus being triumphantly exhibited to the people of Rome.

With his prize money, Watts decided to make a similar journey himself and, arriving in Florence, was taken under the protection of Lord Holland, the British minister to the Court of Tuscany, and his eager wife Elizabeth. Both of them, especially Lady Holland, were moved by a need to help Watts. She saw him as a genius, locked in some internal prison, who must be released into the light. She wanted him to paint portraits – portraits of herself and her friends at the Hollands' villa, the Casa Feroni, near Florence. This was disappointing for Watts. 'Nature did not intend me for a portrait painter', he declared. Portraiture was the journalism of art when compared with the great emblematic masterpieces to which he must dedicate himself. But he bowed somewhat to this task in consideration of the valuable patronage offered by Lord and Lady Holland. 'Lady Holland, petite, attractive, with pointed features and wide eyes, sat for her portrait in a vast conical hat tied beneath her chin with a large neat bow', wrote Ellen Terry's biographer Roger Manvell.

She is shown staring out of the picture at the painter with that possessive stare which was to become only too familiar to Watts throughout the remainder of his life. Before he knew quite where he was, Watts had acquired the first of a succession of zealous patronesses who were to dominate his life.

'We have plenty of room', Lord Holland had written to him, 'and you must stay until you find quarters that you like.' But Watts never did find quarters that he liked so much as the Casa Feroni. He raised no objection to being called 'Fra Paolo', after Veronese, by Lady Holland who, though still longing to be his *femme inspiratrice*, began to feel more like a prisoner than a patron. It appeared as if her kindness of heart was actually deepening Watts's want of energy, his lack of initiative – those qualities that had initially intrigued her and eventually exasperated her. 'I have a strong and determined wish to break the spell', she asserted. But his lethargy was too potent. Finally, after two years, it was not Watts, but Lord and Lady Holland, who left. They invited their friend Lady Caroline Duff Gordon to take over their villa. She was a robust widow with two unmarried daughters whom Watts undertook to instruct in drawing.

Lady Caroline Duff Gordon greatly admired Watts, as did her young daughters – one of them to the point of imagining herself a Beatrice to his Dante. But Watts did not venture any amorous sentiments until this daughter had left for Rome, and then in so indirect a manner that it was difficult for her to know whom he had in mind. Meanwhile he had presented another pupil, a beautiful Italian lady, with some flowers which were understood by her to be a declaration of love.

And so, after some four years, Watts sailed away from this confusion back to England with four monumental canvases and dreams of creating a new

Sistine Chapel in London, a great House of Life magnificently adorned with his frescoes. Encouraged by another prize, he acquired a studio in Mayfair and began to paint – portraits. It was while he was painting the dashing Miss Virginia Pattle that his attention was diverted to her sister, Mrs Prinsep, who was in attendance as her chaperone and in whose expression he was able to observe a familiar possessive stare.

6

The Kingdom of Pattledom

Sara Prinsep was one of seven famous Pattle sisters born in India and, for the most part, educated haphazardly in France. Within the Pattle family might be read the imperial history of Britain. They had remarkable energy and made things happen wherever they went. It was a quality of which Watts stood much in need. Both the eldest sister, the rather sad and affectionate Adeline, 'prone to novel-reading' though increasingly in search of spiritual health (she was dramatically laid to rest in the Indian Ocean at the age of twenty-four), and the shadowy Louisa (whose nose – 'the dearest little nose in the world' – was eulogised by Thackeray), married well and soon became celebrated in Anglo-Indian society. Maria (who was the model for Dante Gabriel Rossetti's 'Virgin Mary' in his picture *Annunciation*) was a tall, long-lived invalid of tremendous refinement, famous in Hampstead as a connoisseur of rare maladies (she was later to become the grandmother of Virginia Woolf and Vanessa Bell).

Watts's sitter Virginia Pattle and her sister Sophia (whom he also painted) were the great beauties of this handsome family. Both married into the British aristocracy. Sophia became Lady Dalrymple, after marrying a good-looking baronet. Virginia, sick of being praised for her beauty and determined to spare her children similar embarrassment, married a peculiarly unprepossessing peer over whose better judgement she usually prevailed. She was especially ambitious on behalf of her two daughters, shielding them from education and the companionship of lesser children, and then, with disastrous results, planning advantageous marriages for them. The younger daughter married a withdrawn and solitary gentleman who became a duke and then died, leaving the childless dowager duchess to embrace charitable work. Her elder sister married Lord Henry Somerset who, after the birth of their son, ran off with his handsome young footman to Italy, causing such a scandal that Lady Henry was barred from society, including that of her sister, the dowager's, family.

The most remarkable Pattle sisters, Sara and Julia, shared a romantic enthusiasm for genius that was briefly but significantly to fall on Ellen Terry. Both of them married leading men in the Anglo-Indian administration. Sara's husband, Thoby Prinsep (known for his obedience as 'the dog Prinsep'), was an amiable giant of a man, devoted to the works of Horace. Julia's husband, Charles Hay Cameron, also a great six-footer and a member of the Supreme Court of India, was considerably older than his wife. During his retirement in England, he kept largely to his bed where he read Homer and dreamed of his exotic coffee estates in Ceylon. With his flowing snow-white hair, worn very long, a sleek small red face, little black eyes and no chin at all (an omission he concealed with a silvery beard 'touched', it was said, ' with moonlight') he had the appearance of a fabulous wizard. 'Behold the most beautiful old man on earth!' his wife was to introduce him to one of her guests, flinging open the door of his bedroom where he lay sleeping.

Of all these sisters it was Julia Margaret Cameron who appeared the most impulsive. The ugly duckling among them, short and squat and with a plump eager face, she was nevertheless 'a woman of noble plainness', as Thackeray's daughter Lady Ritchie described her. Queenly in carriage, imperious in manner, she would cause a house to shake as she made her entrance. 'We never knew what Aunt Julia was going to do next', remarked one of her great-nieces, 'and nor did anyone else.' Her devotion to great men was alarming. 'Mrs Cameron's enthusiastic and extravagant admiration is really painful to me', Watts eventually complained, 'for I feel as if I were practising a deception upon her.' Tennyson was another target for what he called 'her wild beaming benevolence'. Her favourite among men of genius, a far superior poet in her opinion, was Henry Taylor upon whom she showered hundreds of letters citing the magnitude of his virtues. 'Her genius is too profuse and redundant', he was driven to complain. '. . . She lives upon superlatives as upon her daily bread.' With her harsh husky voice, she was a terror to children. 'What a dreadful friend Mrs Cameron must be!' exclaimed Julia Wedgwood who had heard many stories of her. But this was not so. In a prim and strait-laced society 'her oddities were refreshing', wrote the botanical painter Marianne North. Her niece, Lady Troubridge, who had feared her tyranny as a child, nevertheless thought her 'compelling and even charming'; and Henry Taylor, too, for all the embarrassments she caused him, acknowledged her generosity of spirit: 'We all love her.'

The closest of Julia's sisters, Sara Prinsep, was a fine-looking woman with a rather dumpy figure, driven by the notorious Pattle energy. Watts was to be the most splendid of her artistic acquisitions. He had not long returned from Italy when the Pattle sisters cornered him. Julia (whom he also painted) was to elect him as a mentor in her career as a photographer. Describing herself as having 'wings to fly with' after his encouragement (he advised her to record ideas rather than facts), she went about fixing wings on children and transforming them into angels. But the chief Pattle sister in Watts's life was to be Sara Prinsep.

Before long she had uprooted him from his studio and repotted him at her house in Chesterfield Street. But these domestic arrangements did not altogether suit Watts. 'Often I sit among the ruins of my aspirations, watching the tide of time', he ruminated. How could Mrs Prinsep drive away such melancholy? It was Watts who came up with a solution. His old patron Lord Holland, he had heard, was prepared to lease a large, rambling dower house called Little Holland House, near his own great mansion in Kensington Park. Holland House itself had been made famous in the previous generation by the third Lord Holland and his wife. They had opened the library, dining-room and grounds to the great Whig statesmen of the day and the wits, poets and historians: Byron, Macaulay, Sydney Smith and others. Could not Mrs Prinsep, with her magnificent gift for bringing talented people together, achieve something equally spectacular at Little Holland House? Sara Prinsep rather thought she could, and so her husband bought a twenty-one-year lease on the place, eventually renewing it when this proved insufficient for Watts. For as Mrs Prinsep boasted with only slight exaggeration: 'He came to stay three days; he stayed thirty years.'

Little Holland House was really two houses joined together. The rooms were 'low and large and wainscoted', one guest remarked, 'and oddly placed in relation to each other, and then there are long passages, and out you come again into rooms where you don't expect them'. Many of these rooms were decorated in bold colours, greens and purples. But the most interesting room of all, a low-ceilinged dining-room, was painted by Watts himself with frescoes representing the history of civilisation. Here, under a dark-sky-blue ceiling interspersed with stars, pictures of the Pattle sisters were paraded dressed in bright flowing robes and ranged in sequence like the Elgin Marbles. The house itself was little more than two miles from Hyde Park Corner, but set in parkland and meadows – you could walk through fields all the way to the Thames. The garden, fringed with rose bushes, was rather overgrown with shrubs and mayflowers and, in the shade of elm and poplar trees, with many lilies of the valley. The scent of new-mown hay drifted into the rooms in the late summer. By day you could hear the lowing of cattle, the clucking of poultry; and after dark the songs of nightingales and blackbirds.

By the time Kate and Ellen Terry arrived there to have their dual portrait painted, Mrs Prinsep's artistic colony was well established. 'Mrs Prinsep has taken into her house and home a poor forlorn artist, with great talents and weak health', an American friend, the Hon. Mrs Edward Twistleton-Wykeham-Fiennes, had written to her family in 1853, '. . . and in consequence her house is full of his pictures.' Many visitors came to see these pictures, and to see Mrs Prinsep, her sisters too and their distinguished guests: Holman Hunt and Burne-Jones, Browning, Thackeray and Ruskin. Mrs Prinsep would welcome them all with fervour, seizing their hands, pulling them indoors and begging them, usually without success, to call her by her first name. But the intensity of her greeting sometimes provoked unexpected reactions. She was, wrote the Hon. Mrs Twistleton-Wykeham-Fiennes, 'so sweet to me, and overcame me so, with every kind of loving-kindness, that I was really upset, and fairly cried in Mrs Prinsep's face'.

It was inconvenient for the family having a name that approximated so closely with the indigenous Indian surname Patel since this gave rise to some dark stories (that an ancestor had married the daughter of a high-caste Bengali). Their father, James Pattle, reputed to be a man of unexampled wickedness – 'as big a scamp as you ever saw and a bad fellow in every way' as well as 'the biggest liar in India' (though some scholars maintain that it was his brother who had earned this title) – slowly drank himself to death on 'top-hole champagne'. He had left instructions for his body to be sealed in spirits, taken by sea to England and buried with the body of his mother which he believed, inaccurately as it turned out, to be waiting for him at a cemetery in Marylebone. His widow obediently placed his corpse in a barrel of rum (somewhat in the manner of Byron's and Nelson's bodies) next to her bedroom where one night it burst open with a tremendous explosion, revealing her husband's unbottled body in a semi-recumbent posture. The shock hastened his widow's death – she died on board the ship carrying the resealed corpse to England.

From such disasters the sisters had to make their individual recoveries. Sara Prinsep gathered in the lavender-scented rooms of Little Holland House 'everything that was gifted, amiable or admirable in the life of Victorian England'. Guests would exercise themselves over games of bowls and croquet in the garden, drink tea at long tables under the elms in summer, or stride in animated groups under the gabled roofs.

The atmosphere was curiously liberal. Surely it was not quite fitting that the guests, whatever their rank, should be treated as models for Watts's paintbrush or Julia Margaret Cameron's camera when she arrived humping her tremendous equipment across the lawn. The sisters were dressed very oddly – their sweeping gowns, richly coloured and held by gold cords at the waist, trailed across the ground as they walked. It was whispered, too, that they wore no corsets, which suggested a degree of hidden abandonment.

Watts himself, decked out in shades of velvet and wearing ornate slippers, reclined on a chaise-longue. The luncheons and dinners moved, as course followed course, from room to room, the calves'-head and lobster curries being taken along corridors and even out into the garden where various sofas and tables were carried. It was all most unusual. Then again, was there not a 'slight element of looseness', an aroma of polite lust, among these Pattles? Certainly the Hon. Mrs Edward Twistleton-Wykeham-Fiennes began to suspect that they harboured 'grave moral defects'.

The oddest feature of life at Little Holland House was Mrs Prinsep's exorbitant treatment of 'the Signor' who, though 'a grand fellow', had been worshipped 'till the manliness hath departed', George du Maurier thought. It had almost departed, but unfortunately not quite. Mrs Prinsep fed him special foods, arranged for soothing siestas, employed a woman with a soft voice to read to him, invited admirers to admire him, serenaded him with musical evenings and, to combat his lethargy, had him roused early from his bed each morning and escorted to his studio. Yet 'the slightest draught gave him excruciating pain', Ellen remembered and his life remained a burden. 'I am constantly so nervous that I am afraid almost of mounting the stairs and really quite alarmed at the idea of getting on my horse', he confided. '. . . I wish I were strong enough to go where deeds of heroism and daring are done, and privations suffered. The aspirations, even with the violence, of an heroic age would have suited me better.'

It was as if Ellen had been sent to him from this heroic world. 'Her face harmonised with his allegorical visions', her biographer Tom Prideaux wrote. '. . . She fitted into his circle of nymphs and nixes . . . [and] had a tonic effect on Signor.' He was dazzled by her beauty. She 'thrills all my being,' he wrote in a notebook. '. . . I know not why I am so tongue tied . . . why my hands are so weak.'

Watts's biographer, Wilfrid Blunt, believed him to be 'emotionally unstable, sexually frustrated, and probably sexually ignorant'. These were conditions beyond Mrs Prinsep's ministrations. When one day, at the end of a sitting for the dual portrait, Ellen fell ill, she was persuaded to pass her convalescence at Little Holland House. She already believed herself to be in love with this artist who had filled his studio with such beautiful pictures. What then happened – Watts's act of daring – she described years later in a letter to Bernard Shaw. 'He [Watts] kissed me – *differently* – not much differently but a little, and I told no one for a fortnight, but when I was alone with Mother . . . I told her . . . I told her I *must* be married to him *now* because I was going to have a baby!!!! . . . I was *sure* THAT kiss meant giving me a baby.'

7

A Marriage is Arranged and a Deed of Separation Signed

But could he secure Mrs Prinsep's approval? It seemed wiser to delegate a mission of such delicacy to a distinguished go-between, Lady Constance Leslie. The message with which Watts entrusted her emphasised the improving nature of this enterprise by removing Ellen from 'the temptations and abominations' of the stage and giving her an education. 'I can hardly regret taking the poor child out of her present life and fitting her for a better', he explained.

> . . . It is no light matter from any point of view, even the expense will be considerable as I shall have to compensate her family for loss of her services.
>
> . . . I should be v. glad if you would tell Mrs Prinsep and her family [and] so . . . give her [Ellen] a chance of qualifying herself for a good position in society . . . I shall want the sympathy and aid of all my friends.

Watts took upon himself the task of describing how the painterly stimulus of acquiring a child-wife as model would add lustre to his patron's artistic colony. It was hardly necessary to remind her – though equally a reminder could do no harm – that the myths and legends of his paintings were not simply aesthetic statements but what he preferred to call 'sermons' that would purify the young actress. For a time, apparently, he had considered adopting Ellen, but really at the age of fifteen was she not a little old for that? Besides, an adoption would not quite meet his requirements. A bolder plan was needed.

And so Mrs Prinsep, whatever her misgivings may have been, agreed, and between Watts's patron and Ellen's parents, a marriage was arranged.

In her memoirs which were written to please everyone, or at least give pain to no one, Ellen wrote that 'my parents were delighted'. But in a letter to Bernard Shaw, she admits that 'my people hated it'. Why then did they consent? There was, of course, the financial inducement which would give the younger Terry children their education and a start in the theatre in place of Ellen. And perhaps it was better that Watts should have chosen her rather than Kate who was realising so many of her father's dreams onstage. Also their good friend Tom Taylor helped them to see the social advantages of this arrangement. And perhaps there was another reason. Sarah Terry (of whom a chalk drawing was made in the 1840s by Archer Shee, later President of the Royal Academy) was proud of her great-great-uncle John Singleton Copley the elder, a famous American painter of portraits and great historical subjects. This was an imposing family precedent for her daughter's entry into the world of artists.

But the most compelling testimony must have come from Ellen herself looking as if she were 'in Heaven'. Certainly Little Holland House was the grandest 'theatre' she had ever played – and what a unique role she had been given! She was as ignorant of sex as Watts, probably more so, though she was not as troubled by her inexperience as he was. In her eyes he was a gentle man, almost a monk, certainly a genius. The romance of their relationship lay in the wonderful fact that 'my face was the type which the great artist who had married me loved to paint'. His paintings were more romantic than any mirror and could give her many wonderful changes of appearance. To go through that red baize door into his studio was to enter a magic place where Signor became the hero of a fairy-tale: a Prince Charming with Ellen herself his Cinderella. All the characters she had played so far had come and gone so easily. But Watts's paintings were permanent and conferred on the sitter, as well as on the artist, a form of immortality. So, in this new medium, whatever Kate achieved, Ellen could indeed become 'the Terry of the age'.

They were married on 20 February 1864 at St Barnabas's Church, Kensington. The witnesses were Ellen's father and her sister Kate, Mrs Prinsep's son Val, her sister Sophia (Lady Dalrymple), and the man who had introduced the bride and groom, the ever-ebullient Tom Taylor. Ellen wore a brown silk gown designed by Holman Hunt, a quilted white bonnet with a sprig of orange blossom 'and I was wrapped in a beautiful Indian shawl'. It was a cold day. She had spent the morning bathing her little sisters and brothers in Stanhope Street, and brushing their hair. Then she walked into another world. She had left Tom Taylor's *The American Cousin* in mid-run and insisted that 'I never had one single pang of regret for the theatre'. On the contrary: 'I was happy.' But as she moved up the aisle, 'a radiant child bride dancing up it on winged feet', and people saw the painful contrast with her 'atrabilious bridegroom', a hypochondriac almost three times her age and 'old for his age', old enough 'to be my grandfather', walking heavily back beside her, some sense of the poignancy of this misalliance must have touched them. 'I cried a great deal', Ellen remembered. The sight of these tears was distressing for Watts. 'Don't cry', he advised her. 'It makes your nose swell.'

Ellen's life at Little Holland House was to be divided into three compartments: her role as Signor's model in the studio; the part she played as his wife; and her place in Mrs Prinsep's drawing-room. Of these the happiest was her studio life.

Though she craved admiration, she was not an especially conceited or self-regarding girl. Violet Hunt described her as being a 'simple little innocent flirt'. Employing what Carlyle called 'much meestification', using many screens and curtains almost like a wizard in a story, Watts was becoming a potent maker of myths and legends for the Victorians – indeed, he was already something of a legend himself. In the magic laboratory of his studio, like a great alchemist, he transformed Ellen into one immortal character after another. She was recreated as Joan of Arc, as Shakespeare's Ophelia and Dante's Francesca, as Persephone, the sensuous wife of Pluto, and as a maiden protected from the abominations of the medieval world by her courtly knight. Her longings appeared to find their answers on Watts's canvases. 'I remember sitting to him in armour for hours', she wrote, 'and never realising that it was heavy until I fainted.' With the stimulus of these pictures, among the finest Watts painted, she would come to be worshipped as an idol for she had a face, as Henry James observed, 'altogether in the taste of the period'. Watts's most celebrated portrait of her, entitled *Choosing*, shows her wearing the wedding-dress designed for her by Holman Hunt, reaching out to an unscented camellia while holding a small bunch of fragrant violets near her heart – a metaphor, some critics have argued, for her *mariage blanc* (and perhaps the premonition of an unheralded romance).

Watts's marriage, together with Ruskin's attraction to the beautiful young girl Rose La Touche and the sado-masochistic ménage that formed around Swinburne, were all subjects for gossip in the offices of *Punch*. In the opinion of the photographic historian Colin Ford, George du Maurier (who was on the staff at *Punch*) 'based the poor put-upon artist's model heroine of his novel *Trilby* on her [Ellen], a victim of artists and the hypnotist Svengali (who must have owed something of his inspiration to both Sara Prinsep and Watts)'. There were many stories going the rounds that were eventually to find their way into books. According to Marguerite Steen, 'Nelly was discovered crying bitterly . . . outside the nuptial chamber' on the night of her marriage. Some twenty-five years later, Watts's second wife told a friend (as recorded by her son) that 'he couldn't do very much, but he liked to fumble about'. Ellen herself was said to have been alarmed by his impatience. Such stories were to send ripples of speculation down the years, earning Watts a place on the preliminary list of *Eminent Victorians* which Lytton Strachey prepared as examples of a 'Glass Case Age'.

> Themselves as well as their ornaments, were left under glass cases . . . it was simply the result of an innate incapacity for penetration – for getting either out of themselves or into anybody else . . . they were nearly all physically impotent . . . Matthew Arnold, Jowett, Leighton, Ruskin, Watts.

Virginia Woolf too, in *Freshwater*, the play she wrote for private entertainment, portrays Ellen as a prisoner of this glass-house world eventually released by a prince of lovers, the nicely named 'John Craig', whom the author generously invents for her. Escaping in this drama from Victorian respectability, Ellen becomes a fallen woman, 'painted, powdered, unveiled'.

Shortly after their marriage, Ellen and Watts, together with the Prinseps, visited Tennyson at his home, built like a miniature castle, on the Isle of Wight. He would go walking with her in the evenings over the fields, Ellen remembered, and 'point out to me the differences in the flight of different birds, and tell me to watch their solid phalanxes turning against the sunset, the compact wedge suddenly narrowing sharply into a thin line'. As he spoke to her about the barks of trees, the names of flowers, during these evening walks with the sea always on the horizon, Ellen felt quite at ease with him and thought that, though he was entirely free from romantic airs, he revealed himself to be a poet in everything he said. He was utterly different from Robert Browning 'with his carefully brushed hair, smart coat, and fine society manners', yet he could read Browning's poem 'How They Brought the Good News from Ghent to Aix' better than any of his own poems, preserving 'the monotonous rhythm of the galloping horses . . . [making] the words come out sharply like hoofs upon a road'.

But what Ellen really enjoyed was going off to play with Tennyson's sons, Hallam and Lionel, who, under Watts's influence, she saw as 'my young knights waiting for me'. She was a natural tomboy and loved 'jumping gates, climbing trees and running paper-chases'. Hallam and Lionel were aged twelve and ten, and the seventeen-year-old Ellen, rushing around the fields and woods with them, was like a schoolgirl playing truant. The adults indoors were so very old – it was good to get away and behave naturally. But she was called indoors to pose as a model, not for Watts, but for Julia Margaret Cameron.

They were staying with Mrs Prinsep's sister in Dimbola Lodge, her house at Freshwater, named after her husband's much-loved coffee estates in Ceylon. She had bought twin houses owned by a sailor and later joined them together with a crenellated tower to give the place an imposing entrance, covering the joined-up building with a blanket of climbing ivy from which its many gabled windows looked out to sea like a multitude of staring eyes. At the end of a path, a few hundred yards to the back of Dimbola, on higher ground, stood Farringford, the home of Alfred Tennyson and his wife Emily ('a slender-stalked tea rose' for ever 'lying on a sofa').

Mrs Cameron had only recently taken up photography. While her husband was visiting Ceylon and her children were all away, her daughter had presented her with a large wooden camera and plenty of darkroom equipment. 'It may amuse you, Mother,' she wrote, 'to try to photograph during your solitude at Freshwater.' And this is what Mrs Cameron principally continued to do for the next fifteen years. She was not afraid of disasters or impressed by professional photographers with their dull little cartes-de-visite. As an inspired amateur, she embraced accidents and made them her friends. She transformed her own fingerprints and smudges into the very artefacts of experience, added a provocative subtext of sexuality even for the children who sat to her, and became a connoisseur of light and shade – the drama of light and shade. She set out to ennoble photography so that her *tableaux vivants* ('my fancy subjects') would be the companions of Tennyson's poetry, Shakespeare's plays, biblical literature and Renaissance painting. As her biographer Brian Hill writes: 'She thought nothing of having to discard a hundred spoiled negatives to achieve one satisfactory result . . . she was determined to master this infuriating hobby.' She converted the coal house at Dimbola Lodge into a darkroom and the chicken house into a studio, and went to work, her dark dress stained with chemicals, as she summoned children, guests, her neighbour's cook and all manner of picturesque passers-by to sit for her. 'Her incalculable ways, brilliant words and kind actions had their fascination for everybody', recorded Mrs Burne-Jones, 'but her lens, when levelled at them, was merciless.' Roping in strangers she thrust them into wild costumes – the porter at Yarmouth was decked out as King Arthur, a parlour-maid transformed into a Madonna. She trussed Robert Browning up in complex draperies and left him helpless, and she assisted the astronomer Sir John Herschel in washing his hair until it stood out like a white fluffy brush – more like a soufflé than the intended halo. Tennyson complained that he had lost his anonymity and was charged double at hotels 'by reason of your confounded photographs', yet he nevertheless led his fellow poet Longfellow into her converted chicken house. 'You will have to do whatever she tells you', he explained. 'I will be back soon and see what is left of you.' Her sitters would have to stay motionless for seven to twelve minutes for each exposure (during which her husband, who modelled as Merlin, usually began giggling). But she was no respecter of persons and treated everyone as if she was conferring on them an honour. 'I have immortalised them.'

Of some seven photographs she took of Ellen Terry one has become well known. It was taken, so Ellen remembered, in the Tennysons' bathroom at Farringford and is, in the words of the historian of photography Helmut Gernsheim, 'among the most beautiful and remarkable pictures in the history of photography'. The picture shows Ellen leaning against the bathroom wall, bare-shouldered in her nightdress, fingering her necklace, her eyes closed as if concealing her thoughts from us – 'withdrawn behind the heavy eyelids,' J.B. Priestley wrote, 'the mystery, the challenge, the torment, the solace'. But then, as Julia Margaret Cameron's biographer Victoria Olsen reminds us, Ellen Terry 'was an actress and a photograph is not simply a reflection of reality'.

Ellen and the Signor seemed to be joint prisoners in Little Holland House. She was very much aware of her privileged status: among her husband's sitters and Mrs Prinsep's guests she met all manner of distinguished people in particular two Prime Ministers. She would remember being fascinated by the exotic figure of Disraeli on whom she felt peculiarly anxious to make a good impression. He wore a garish blue tie, she recalled, and his 'straggling black curls shake as he walks'. But in time this image would merge with that of Henry Irving's Shylock.

She preserved a more secure memory of Disraeli's political opponent Gladstone. 'Like a volcano at rest; his face was pale and calm, but the calm was the calm of the grey crust of Etna. You looked into the piercing dark eyes, and caught a glimpse of the red-hot crater beneath the crust.' Meeting such people was an important part of her education, she told herself, an education picked up from her surroundings which might prove superior to the schoolroom education she was so aware of having missed.

If Ellen's experience at Little Holland House was like that of a boarding school, then she must have seen Mrs Prinsep as a Dickensian headmistress who treated her as a disobedient child. 'I think she was pretty cruel, or stupid more like, to me', she later told her sister Kate. One afternoon at tea, Ellen unthinkingly loosened the pins from her hair and, shaking her head, let a waving mass of golden tresses tumble on to her shoulders. This exhibition of herself horrified Mrs Prinsep. It was one of many examples of her impossible behaviour. Her spontaneity drained the Signor too. One day, as he stood among some lilies, she actually threw a sponge full of water at him, putting all poetry from his mind. He braced himself to 'reconstruct Nelly's mind, character and habits'. But the task was beyond him. She seemed to have no control of herself, no proper sense of right and wrong. She was like a wild creature. Stories of her unseemliness were soon being passed among the town gossips: how one evening she had come down to dinner wearing an immodest stage costume (tights, according to some storytellers; her scant Cupid's outfit in another version – 'then with a merry laugh', this story ended, 'she turned and fled from the house').

Mrs Prinsep had no doubt she needed almost daily correction. Whatever her status in Signor's studio, she had absolutely no authority around the rest of the house. She was expected to be docile when in company and say nothing unless spoken to. It was a role for which she was ill-cast. And for once she found herself confronted by someone whom she could not charm or please. In this sense it was Ellen who was impotent at Little Holland House.

The stories that were being passed around the *Punch* offices and elsewhere by guests at Little Holland House – stories about Ellen's 'excitability' – were beginning to bruise Mrs Prinsep's reputation. There was one story, often retold, of her running naked around the bedroom and of Watts telling a friend: 'It frightened me' – at which some of the *Punch* staff, very jovial and bluff, protested that it would not have frightened them. Mrs Prinsep had never been especially conventional, but confronted by Ellen's impulsiveness, she became a martinet. It was as if the contrast between Watts's sensational pictures, conjuring up a gallant medieval world, and the moments of brittle decorum in Mrs Prinsep's drawing-room bewildered Ellen. Everyone wanted something from her – something different from her. In the studio, she was portrayed as a heroine; in the drawing-room she would sit 'shrinking and timid' in a corner. Her natural flow of spirits began to dry up, and one visitor remembered seeing her 'thin as paper and white as a ghost, with drowned eyes . . . like a broken-winged bird'. She had counted on her husband supporting her against Mrs Prinsep. But it became clear to Watts that the two women could not continue living in the same house and that Ellen was simply unsuited to domestic life. 'Such of us who live somewhat in the clouds', he wrote, admitting his inability to tame her, 'are particularly liable to fall into error.'

In her *Memoirs* Ellen attributes the sudden end of her marriage to the management of kind friends 'whose chief business in life seems to be the care of others'. She was proud of her marriage ring and makes it clear that but for this 'interference', she would not have been parted from her husband after a mere ten months. It was the manner of their separation she disliked. She was not so melodramatically unhappy as her friends believed. Though she eventually acknowledged the marriage to have been 'a natural, almost inevitable, catastrophe', she would have preferred to make an exit in her own time and on her own terms.

Despite her objections, the parties who had come together to arrange her marriage reconvened within a year to negotiate the terms of her separation. For Ellen, now approaching eighteen, it was humiliating to have everything taken out of her hands. She believed their judgement to have been warped by the 'manifestly absurd' stories they had picked up – though it was true that she had run away from Little Holland House one evening and spent the night at Tom and Laura Taylor's house in Lavender Sweep. 'I am astonished at the strength of her love for him [Watts] . . . too much love for one who has made her no return & I fear never can make her any', Tom Taylor wrote to Ellen's mother whom he urged to 'refrain from reproaching her husband or commenting on his conduct . . . you should treat Nelly with the utmost gentleness'. But Ellen felt guilty about Watts who, she told them, was '*really ill*'. At first she refused consent to the separation: 'I was miserable, indignant, unable to understand that there could be any justice in what had happened.' Mrs Prinsep had thought her rebellious, but 'I showed as much rebellion as a sheep'. Yet she *felt* rebellious and was so mortified by a sense of failure that she burnt many of the letters belonging to this period. It was a time of destruction – Watts himself, to Ellen's chagrin, destroying several portraits of her. 'I wish I could have made his sun shine, but I was so *ignorant*, so vulgar, & so young and he was so *impatient*', she wrote twenty years later to Stephen Coleridge, '. . . if he can hate he must hate me.'

Mrs Prinsep had been her enemy, but it was Watts who unforgivably let her down. 'I feel no love toward Mr Watts – He is to me now, as if he did not exist', she confided to a friend. She kept hearing reports of what he was saying about her: 'all most cowardly – and *most untrue*!!'

There is no shadow of doubt (for it has been *proved* to me) that *he* and not Mrs Prinsep only said these things!! (I cd have forgiven the spite and vexation of an *angry and* not good woman but not the *untruths* of one whose constant care was to make everyone *think me* untruthful . . .) I tried to make him fond of me by every power I cd think of, and for whom I wd *not* have left (if all the *world* had wished it) had *he* not desired it also – although I thought at the time it would be my death.

Watts became 'a source of the only unhappiness I ever had', Ellen wrote not long afterwards. It seemed that he had simply capitulated to Mrs Prinsep. 'God forgive her, for I *can not* do so.' But on hearing of her death over twenty years later, Ellen relented a little. 'She did treat me badly,' she wrote to her friend Mrs Rumball, 'beyond words once, but twas only through stupidity I do believe now . . . How strange that a vigorous woman like that should die before Mr W.'

The deed of separation, dated 26 January 1865, provided Ellen with an allowance of £300 a year while 'she shall lead a chaste life' and did not return to the stage. In fact, despite her breaking both these conditions, the allowance continued to be paid to Ben Terry for twelve years, ceasing only after a decree nisi was granted early in 1877. Watts claimed to be wholly ignorant of the circumstances of Ellen's life over this period (including the fact that she had two illegitimate children) but was possibly motivated by guilt. He had intended the separation to be more in the nature of an interruption in their marriage than an arrangement that would lead to a final parting. Returning her to 'life in a home of loving parents with means and time for many requirements', he later explained, 'would permit time for me to establish my own career' and give her an opportunity to gain maturity. He paid the money each year 'into her Father's hands always supposing the home still there & it was not till long after the event that I learnt with astonishment & great pain that home had been abandoned with terrible consequences'. Altogether the marriage 'has spoilt life for me', he maintained. But he let it be known that he would have prolonged it in the hope of a happy outcome. 'I never should myself have taken any steps for freedom, the wish never came from me.'

Watts did not accuse Ellen of immorality – a point she desperately clutches at when writing to her friends. 'He (Mr W) has *not* said I was *not* everything that was good to him, in fact he has not brought any charge against me *at all* that says I was not true to him in every way and that I didn't do my best to please him, but he simply says he *cd not live with me!*'

This was an ignoble rejection. She had done nothing wrong and was being treated as a wrongdoer. Who or what she was now, she hardly knew any more. She was certainly not a mother and no longer (except in name) a wife. It was a shameful condition, somehow identifying her as damaged goods. 'Her fall is certain', the connoisseur-collector Edward Cheney wrote to his friend Lord Holland, 'and it is idle to suppose that a pretty actress in her position can remain respectable.' Watts had promised before their marriage to rescue her from the 'temptations and abominations' of the theatre and to introduce her to a better life. But she had been found unworthy of that better life and, sent back in disgrace, condemned to do nothing beyond providing domestic help for her mother while living off the handouts of the Signor and probably Mrs Prinsep. That woman truly, she felt, was the dragon of this story – a dragon which had defeated a knight as ineffectual as the White Knight in *Through the Looking-Glass*.

As soon as Ellen returned to Stanhope Street, the Revd Charles Dodgson began calling there, hunting for subjects for his camera, eager to meet 'the beautiful little creature' whom he had first seen playing Mamillius and Puck half a dozen years ago. During those years he had been writing *Alice's Adventures in Wonderland*, transforming himself into Lewis Carroll and using Ellen as one of his collection of stage children to stimulate his imagination (Alice was her secret name, the name she had dropped, and Carroll, as it were, may have picked up). He made his first visit to the Terrys' home on 20 December 1864 and met Kate, whose acting he had also much admired. He thought her very natural and charming, but Mrs Watts, 'the one I have always most wished to meet of the family', was absent. He returned the following day and met Ellen for the first time. She appealed to both sides of his character, the children's writer and the clergyman. 'I was very pleased with what I saw of Mrs Watts, lively and pleasant, almost childish in her face, but perfectly ladylike.' This meeting took place a month before the deed of separation was signed, of which Carroll knew nothing. He was aware, however, of some social unease within the family and some tension between the two sisters. Ellen, it appears, was already taking refuge at Stanhope Street, and Kate seemed rather out of sorts. 'I fancy her gaiety yesterday, and Mrs Watts's to-day, were both partly assumed', Carroll shrewdly observed. Nevertheless these were red-letter days for him, his encounters with the two actress-sisters and some of their younger siblings – Polly (as he called Marion), Flossie (Florence), Charlie, Tom and Fred. Much delighted, he proposed returning there to photograph the family.

A delay of over six months before his return (when he brought copies of *Alice* with him) may have been caused by Ellen's difficulties. The Revd Charles Dodgson had to be careful not to tread on morally dubious ground. But eventually he came to the conclusion that she had been blameless. While she was 'scarcely more than a child', he wrote, a man three times her age had professed to be in love with her. The match was 'pushed on by well-meaning friends, who thought it a grand thing for her'.

From the first, I don't think she had a fair chance of learning her new duties. Instead of giving her a home of her own he went on living as a guest with an elderly couple and the old lady was constantly exasperating the poor child by treating her as if she were still in the school-room and she, just like a child, used to go into fits of furious passion.

This account, which presents Mrs Prinsep somewhat in the posture of Alice's Red Queen, shows how well acquainted he became with the Terrys' version of events. It was important to the Terry family that he be seen to resume his visits in order to show the world that Ellen had regained her respectability. Benefiting from Watts's £300 a year, they had by the summer of 1865 moved to a larger house with a garden, 24 Caversham Road in Kentish Town, and were living in a community of well-to-do actors. It was here that Dodgson took his series of photographs.

These photographs, taken in July 1865, are like exhibits presented as evidence of propriety (in one or two Ellen is wearing the wedding garment designed for her by Holman Hunt). They are unlike Julia Margaret Cameron's artistic images (of which Lewis Carroll disapproved). Though a few narrative pictures exist (Kate as Andromeda with her wrists in chains), they are for the most part family album pictures. The Terrys are conventionally grouped on a balcony, with the parents at each end, Kate dressed in white and Ellen in black at the centre of the group. In his single portraits of Ellen, she again appears in dark colours, her hair combed rigorously back, her expression demure, looking generally much older than she actually is, sometimes almost matronly. In one pose or another she embodies an image of rectitude, standing alone as if in mourning, like Queen Victoria following Albert's recent death, a figure of her times, a woman from whom childhood has departed.

Lewis Carroll was to make regular visits to the Terry family, playing castle croquet and card tricks, telling stories and taking the younger children off to pantomimes. He was an ardent playgoer and loved seeing Ellen onstage, recording her performances in his diary and sometimes sending her comments on them. He remained 'as fond of me as he could be of any one over the age of ten', she acknowledged. But, as the Revd Charles Dodgson, he continued to observe Ellen's moral condition. For there were difficult times ahead, shocking times, when he would have to suspend their friendship.

8
The Kate Terry Valse

'I hated going back to live at home', Ellen wrote in her *Memoirs*, '... I hated my life, hated every one and everything in the world more than at any time before or since.' She had been brought up to please everyone, had apparently pleased no one and was put to work darning her brothers' stockings. After the beauty of Little Holland House, the family home in Kentish Town dissatisfied her. She was frustrated, angry, deeply bored. Full of nervous irritation, she often lost her temper (the famous Terry temper) and on one occasion shut her terrified young brother Fred in a cupboard to lessen the sound of his screaming. 'I hated Nell ever after', he said in middle age. It was a relief to everyone when, carefully chaperoned, she went off for a recuperative holiday abroad.

'I paid my first visit to Paris', she wrote. '... [a] friend took me everywhere ... I often went to three parties a night; but I was in a difficult position, as I could not speak a word of the language.' She saw the Empress Eugénie driving in the Bois 'looking like an exquisite waxwork', went to the Comédie Française to see Sarah Bernhardt, marched through the galleries of the Louvre and altogether fell under the spell of the city's elegance. It was the tonic she needed and she lists almost everything she did there (meeting Tissot and Rosa Bonheur, drinking coffee at Tortoni's, visiting Meissonier's studio). She was accompanied by the Casella sisters, family friends of the Terrys, but she does not reveal the name of the 'friend' who took her to all these places. Since she liked listing the cast in such adventures, this omission may be significant. 'I've been treated very well indeed – have found more (new) friends, who *seem* anxious to love me and be of use to me', she wrote to Bertha Bramley in 1885. '... [I] am trying (I *feel* I shall *succeed*) to quite forget the one dark cloud which a little while ago hung over my whole life.' Some have suggested that her travelling companion was Charles Reade who still treated her like a wilful daughter (he had no children of his own). Theirs was an emotional relationship, complex, stormy on and off the stage. 'Dear, kind, unjust, generous, cautious, impulsive, passionate, gentle Charles Reade', Ellen described him years later, placing him at the top of her loving friends. 'Never have I known any one who combined so many qualities . . . He was placid and turbulent . . . inexplicable and entirely lovable . . . guileless and yet had moments of suspicion and craftiness worthy of the wisdom of the serpent.'

Reade himself believed Ellen to be equally paradoxical. In an early note he described her as 'yielding on the surface, egotistical below . . . always wanting something 'dreadful bad' today, which she does not want tomorrow especially if you are weak enough to give it to her'. She was soft, she was hard; she flirted and negotiated simultaneously; so innocent, so calculating. 'This is a charming character,' he noted on one of her letters pressing him for a larger salary, 'a really sweet loveable woman as false as hell.' Reade was proud of having fortified himself against female charm. But he needed all his strength to resist Ellen. Later, at a happier phase of her life, he observed that 'the hardness below is melting away'.

In good hands a very amiable creature but dangerous to the young. Downright fascinating . . . highly gifted with what Voltaire justly calls *le grand art de plaire* . . . Ellen Terry is an enigma. Her eyes are pale, her nose rather long, her mouth nothing in particular . . . her hair rather like tow. Yet somehow she is *beautiful*. Her expression *kills* any pretty face you see beside her . . . In character impulsive, intelligent, weak, hysterical . . . I see through and through her. Yet she pleases me all the same.

Ellen regularly saw Charles Reade whenever she took the horse-bus to Tom Taylor's house in Lavender Sweep on Clapham Common where she was always welcome. Reade was well known there for making himself weep while singing 'The Girl I Left Behind Me'. The two playwrights tried to persuade Ellen to go back to the stage. But she was reluctant.

She did, however, consent to make a single appearance as Helen, a figure noticeable for her décolletage, in Sheridan Knowles's *The Hunchback* on 20 June 1866. The play was staged as a benefit performance for Kate. It was not a happy experience and made no better by the Olympic Theatre's insistence on using her married name on the playbill. 'I was so nervous about the affair, that I got quite feverish about it', she wrote to a friend, begging her not to 'mix me up, in yr thoughts, with the character I am playing . . . [who] is not a very desirable person to *be*! . . . *although no harm in her*.'

But was there any harm in Ellen herself? Sometimes she thought there must be when she looked in the mirror. 'My old face looks like a tallow candle, only there's not much colour in it', she wrote, '– and I am in such bad spirits and can't account for it.' Sometimes she felt 'hysterical'. She had lost confidence in herself and onstage 'was *quite* the amateur' in comparison with Kate who, with her bright actress-smile, was an acknowledged favourite with the public.

But Kate's life was about to change. In the summer of 1867, at the age of twenty-three, she became engaged to Arthur Lewis, a tall sensitive young man with a handsome fortune. By profession he was a 'silk mercer' with a royal warrant. But by temperament he was a romantic, 'a princely fellow' as George du Maurier called him, who sang and painted and gave gorgeous entertainments at Moray Lodge, his 'splendid bachelor's paradise' with fine stables and beautiful gardens on Campden Hill, adjoining the estate of Holland House.

How then did Kate's engagement affect Ellen? In her *Memoirs* she wrote a characteristically benign summary. 'I was glad because he was rich, and during his courtship of my sister I had some riding, of which in my girlhood

I was passionately fond.' This childlike statement avoids all the adult complexities of the situation – for example, the strong objections of Arthur Lewis's widowed mother to her son's marriage to a common actress (objections that had been aggravated by the rumours circling around Ellen's own marriage). Ellen's notorious flirting was embarrassing for Kate. 'I hope Nelly will behave', she appealed to her mother.

It must have been galling for Ellen to see some of the same guests at Moray Lodge who had come to Little Holland House, and to contrast Kate's glittering performance as a hostess there – 'so tall and upright and with such bright, sweet eyes' – with her own humiliating role at Mrs Prinsep's gatherings. Kate had always outshone her and never more so than now. Many years later, in an unpublished letter to Bernard Shaw, whom she trusted not to misuse what she told him, Ellen wrote: 'As a quite young girl she [Kate] was full of asperity & we were all precious glad when she married and went away. She *did* play "the elder sister" & more!'

Ellen was soon '*driven* back to the stage' by the arguments of Charles Reade and Tom Taylor, in whose play *The Antipodes; or the Ups and Downs of Life* she appeared at the Theatre Royal, Holborn, in the summer of 1867. It was a poor play, and though she was eventually to concede that going back to the theatre was 'a good thing', at the time 'I hated it'. But then she also hated doing nothing at home. All life seemed hateful and 'I wish I were dead', she wrote to a friend.

Kate was to give farewell performances in London and Manchester shortly before her marriage on 18 October 1867. The last role she played in London, at the Adelphi Theatre, was Shakespeare's Juliet. *The Times* on 2 September reported that, at the end of each act, she was called before the curtain and at the conclusion of the play, she came on again 'in obedience to a thundering summons from every part of the house' and

> stood for some moments curtseying and smiling under the showers of bouquets and the storm of kindly greeting. Nor when she had retired with her armful of flowers – looking in the white robe and dishevelled hair of Juliet's death scene, as she used to look in Ophelia – was the audience satisfied.

After the curtain rose for the evening's farce to begin, the storm of voices 'grew into a tempest' and the name of 'Kate Terry' came from a chorus of a thousand stentorian voices until at last the fair favourite of the night appeared once more, pale and dressed to leave the theatre, and when the renewed roar of recognition had subsided . . . spoke . . a few hesitating words . . . 'How I wish from my heart, I could tell you how I feel your kindness, not to-night only, but through the many years of my professional life. What can I say to you but thanks, thanks, and goodbye!'

Then, to 'a still louder salvo of acclamation', she left.

There were similar scenes the following month in Manchester where Ellen was appearing in a supporting playlet. Between the two presentations, by command of the Prince of Wales, the specially commissioned 'Kate Terry Valse' was played by the band of the First Battalion of Life Guards. Retiring to her dressing-room, Kate was presented with a wide gold bracelet by her fiancé. On the outside was engraved: 'To Kate Terry on her retirement from the stage, from him for whom she leaves it'; and on the inside, in tiny letters, were the titles of a hundred plays in which she had appeared.

9
Found Drowned

Despite the tension between them in these last years, Ellen did not welcome her sister's leaving the theatre or see it as an opportunity for herself. She was lonely and losing interest in theatre life. 'I've been feeling lately I'd like to try *how drowning feels*!!!!!!!' she told a friend. '. . . I am so tired.' A week after Kate's marriage (at which Ellen was chief bridesmaid), she appeared with a new company run by a veteran actor-manager, Alfred Wigan, and his wife Leonora, a clever comedienne, very vain of her toadlike looks, who with much bellowing, taught Ellen how to 'stand still!'. The Wigans' Company occupied the vast New Queen's Theatre in Long Acre. Her one interesting play there in the context of theatre history was *Katharine and Petruchio*, David Garrick's sentimental short abridgement of *The Taming of the Shrew*, for this was the first time she played opposite Henry Irving. It is tempting to look for prophetic signals in this preface to their famous partnership. But as Laurence Irving writes in the biography of his grandfather:

Irving's Petruchio was a failure. The critics complained that he had made the shrew-tamer a good-humoured and rapacious brigand rather than a light-hearted gallant, and they commented severely that in his delivery of blank verse he had much to learn. Irving found little to admire in Ellen Terry except her natural charm. To one whose whole life was centred on his art there was something baffling about this frivolous girl . . . She, in turn, saw little to admire in Irving, a young actor, with a dull, heavy face, awkwardly self-conscious and lacking the technical proficiency which she had acquired in her cradle. She was, if anything, a little frightened by his fierce application and the earnestness of purpose . . . When at the end of the short run, she left the company, Irving hardly gave her a thought.

'I fancy neither of us played very well', Ellen wrote. Irving recalled Ellen as being 'rather on the hoydenish side', while she thought him a conceited and difficult man. She was feeling unwell again – one critic described her as behaving onstage like a spoilt child. Perhaps the story-line as well as the awkward fact that her character was called Kate, an amoral girl schooled by a superior gentleman, touched too painfully on her recent experiences. The play opened on a foggy Boxing Day and both the principal actors were not sorry when it was withdrawn in January 1868.

Later that year Ellen took the part of 'Kitty' in a slight but popular comedy called *The Household Fairy*. It was a trivial role and again she acted indifferently, 'caring scarcely at all for my work or a theatre, or anybody belonging to the theatre'. Her thoughts were secretly fixed elsewhere.

On the night of 10 October, after the curtain came down, she left the theatre and vanished. Only after her father had mistakenly identified a young girl found drowned in the Thames as his daughter, did Ellen return home. It is not difficult to imagine the family's happiness at seeing her alive – a happiness which may at first have overcome any anger they felt at the pain she caused them. But now she was obliged to tell them what she had done. It was a story her parents would have to pass on in some version to those who had been searching for her. In some people's minds she had embraced a fate worse than death.

10

Happiness For a Time

On 3 May 1865, after less than six years of a childless marriage, Sarah Godwin, the beautiful invalid-wife of Edward William Godwin, died in Bristol. She was thirty-eight and the cause of her death was given as 'Mania' leading to exhaustion. It was rumoured that she died in an empty house because brokers had carried off all the furniture from their home in Portland Square – though in fact Godwin claimed that, having opened an office so that his wife should not be disturbed by business callers, he had merely transferred some furniture and pictures there. Stories were also passed around about how, in answer to her last request, he played a Bach fugue at his organ, the sounds floating up to her as she lay dying in their bedroom. Though he may well have played to her during her illness, in fact she died in a nursing home nearby at Clifton.

A few months later Godwin came to London and took an office in Baker Street. He had much to occupy him: drawings for a town hall, an assize court, a theatre, several schools and also various industrial buildings. He was a man of great vitality and in addition to his office work he liked to study architectural history at the British Museum, regularly attend theatres ('plays were restful', he thought) and go for long walks, some of which, his biographer Dudley Harbron writes, 'ended at Little Holland House, where he renewed his acquaintance with the juvenile Mrs Watts'.

Some scholars have doubted whether Godwin was ever invited to Little Holland House. But several diarists and letter-writers could not resist conflating the Watts and Godwin chapters of Ellen Terry's life and creating a scandalous synthesis. So the story of her coming down to dinner one evening at Little Holland House wearing that outrageous Cupid's outfit from her disreputable theatre days acquired a dramatically romantic climax as she rushes out into the night – and into the arms of her lover, 'the wicked Earl', as Godwin was sometimes called by his friends.

In her group biography *A Pride of Terrys*, Ellen's friend, the novelist Marguerite Steen, revealed that 'during her lonely walks' around London, Ellen often 'dropped in' to see Godwin at his rooms above the office at Baker Street, to enjoy his conversation, look at his drawings and costume designs. Sometimes she would visit him with her husband, at other times she went alone – though 'she never made any secret of these visits'. This was not actually what Ellen had told her, but what Marguerite Steen had picked out of a book of memoirs, *Discretions and Indiscretions*, published four years after Ellen's death – though not cited in *A Pride of Terrys*. 'I was tremendously innocent,' Ellen had apparently confided, as well as being 'a very kind little girl'.

> . . . one evening I went to see him [Godwin] and found him very ill in bed, with terrible sickness and pain. I was so distressed for him that I never even thought of the conventions or the construction that might be placed on my actions. I spent the whole night with him, and only returned home the next morning when he was well on the road to recovery. To my dismay my husband was waiting there for me with my parents in solemn conclave. They accused me of infidelity and seemed utterly horrified at what I had done . . .

This story proceeds with Ellen protesting her innocence ('heating poultices' for 'a sick man') while her husband and parents accuse her of enjoying a 'night of love'. Godwin for some reason is not available to rescue her, and she is abandoned. The one plot-line of this tragedy not fully developed (though it is discreetly hinted at by Marguerite Steen) is that Ellen did in fact dispatch a message which was withheld by Mrs Prinsep, the villainess of the piece. This indeed is 'like a story in a book'. But it is not in Ellen's book.

Scholars have scorned such melodrama. Yet there is a letter from Godwin to 'Fair Mistress Watts' written in January 1865 – that is, while his wife was alive and before the deed of separation between Ellen and Watts was signed – which shows that the two of them had been in contact. It was this contact that was secretly to ripen during the following three years. For what Ellen told her parents when she returned from the dead was that her old life was altogether at an end and she had gone to live with Godwin at a house he had rented for them both in Hertfordshire.

Ben and Sarah had evidently not thought of Godwin when calling on their friends to join the search for her. She had kept her secret well. Had she confided the truth to her family before running away, they would certainly have tried to stop her. So she told no one. Not long before her disappearance she had been staying with Kate and her husband amid the 'singing and oysters' at Moray Lodge. That smart and expensive life she now renounced, for she would not be invited there again for many years – not even, along with the rest of the family, for the births and christenings of her nieces and nephews. 'I never go there now', she told a friend. But she did not mind, having 'got so hard lately that I've very little affection left in me'. Kate was evidently the 'good' sister, while Ellen had become the 'bad' sister. Yet she felt defiant. Her new life suited her – even in her childhood she had much preferred playing 'Dragonetta' the bad fairy to the good fairy 'Goldenstar'. If her character was compromised and her reputation drowned, then, like Thomas Hardy's 'The Ruined Maid', she would enjoy it (' "One's pretty lively when ruined," said she.').

Beyond the family there were few people whom Ben and Sarah told of their daughter's disgrace. When Lewis Carroll visited them at Kentish Town early in April 1869 and 'had a long chat with Mrs Terry', he was informed that Ellen was 'staying in lodgings, but had called at the house that day'. By then Ellen had been living with Godwin for almost a year and if she called at the house it was probably to tell her parents she was pregnant. They were anxious not to risk losing the allowance still being paid to them by Watts (Ben was later to find employment as a 'Water log collector' along the Thames to make up some of the family income).

Of course they had to tell close friends like Charles Reade and Tom Taylor, and could judge from their reactions how much their daughter had disappointed them. Reade had never liked Godwin (whom he called 'a blackguard') and Laura Taylor described the liaison as an 'unworthy affair . . . painful and disagreeable'. To some extent she blamed Ben and Sarah Terry for having left their daughter 'sadly too much to herself' after her painful separation from Watts, when she must have 'doubtless felt reckless and forlorn'. But she reserved her full disapprobation for Ellen herself. 'As to Nelly, I feel more sorry than surprised, though I should not have expected that she would have shown her vice in so hard and uninteresting a way.' Mrs Taylor must have seen how Ellen made up to men, openly flirting with them, and must surely have noticed their susceptibility to her. What particularly irritated her was the suspicion that her husband might somehow be implicated in Ellen's circle of seduction. 'Let me ask', she wrote to him, 'why *you* were supposed to be able to let any light upon it.' As to what she called 'the solution to the mystery', she reminded her husband that 'we never once thought of Mr Godwin! Certainly I did not . . .' And nor, it seems, did anyone else.

Among respectable people, Ellen's name was never mentioned, while Godwin took on the air of a conspirator in a play. When Beerbohm Tree's fiancée, Maud Holt, heard that Tree was seeing Godwin at the Costume Society, she pronounced herself '*disgusted*', adding that she would as soon share her dinner with a snake. She insisted that Tree cut all ties with him or she would break off their engagement. But so charming did Godwin eventually turn out to be, and such good company, that after her marriage she found herself inviting him to their home.

There is no doubt that Ellen passionately loved Edward Godwin. She was sexually attracted to him as she had never been to any man. That strange quality which her mother had thought sinister when she met him in Bristol, Ellen found exciting. He was naturally elegant, a man of middle height and slender build, with an emphatic personality, whose enigmatic air was enhanced by his hooded eyes. As for Ellen, if she had time now to regard herself in the mirror, she would have seen a slim young woman dressed in a blue linen kimono or loose clothes suggesting Grecian robes. At the age of twenty-one, she had attained that condition of womanhood she had longed for when, aged fifteen, she spied through the gas-light Madame Albina de Rhona's admirers drinking champagne from her slipper in a private room at the Royalty Theatre. But by now such a scene must have seemed stagy and artificial when compared with the rough and ready life she was living in the country with her lover.

'We seldom went to London', she wrote. There was no need. She was experiencing 'exquisite delight from the mere fact of being in the country'. She no longer valued a theatre that traded on dramatic trivialities. Nor did she miss Watts's painted melodramas. 'If it is the mark of the artist to love art before everything', she wrote in her *Memoirs*, '. . . then I was never an artist. I have the simplest faith that absolute devotion to another human being means the greatest *happiness*.'

That happiness was now hers. Unlike Watts (to whom Ellen was still legally married) Godwin treated her as an equal and his artistic interests appeared to come second to his 'absolute devotion' to her, indeed to depend on that devotion. One of his dreams was to build a house for her once they had a family. He was now in his mid-thirties, some fourteen years older than Ellen, an alert-minded man with a cavalier attitude to life rather like that of Whistler (whose ravishing White House in Tite Street, an arrangement in green slates and white bricks, he was to design). Liberating her from this suffering, he reignited Ellen's optimism.

She gives to her description of their life together at a cottage called 'The Red House', on the edge of Gustard Wood Common, a romantic glow that reflects the warmth of her happiness. But the conditions of her life were hard. Being hyper-active, she found it difficult to delegate work to her maid. She would rise at six each morning and begin work scrubbing the floors, lighting fires and feeding the animals – some two hundred ducks and chickens, a pony, a goat, a parrot and a bulldog which Godwin bought for her protection when he was away. In the afternoons she often worked under the fir trees in the kitchen garden and, studying Mrs Beeton in place of Shakespeare, began learning to cook. Behind the garden, over the common, was the village of Mackeray End to which she would sometimes go in the evenings for milk; and beyond that lay Wheathampstead where she travelled in the pony-and-trap to shop on market days. She had developed what she called a 'mania for *washing* everything and everybody', including the hair of her little servant girl whose mother eventually came up from the village to protest.

The Red House was an isolated cottage – they had no neighbours and almost no one came to visit them. To those whom Ellen did see in the village streets or at church she was known as 'Mrs Godwin'. She did not mind the isolation. This was an idyllic place. Downstairs there was a hall, two rooms with bay windows, at the back a bakehouse and kitchen and off the landing upstairs two bedrooms. Godwin soon gave the place his unique style, painting the rooms downstairs a pale yellow, hanging his Japanese prints on the walls, and introducing some of his own stern furniture. On most mornings Ellen would drive him in the pony-and-trap to catch the London train, and then meet him at the station in the evenings, which they would pass looking prophetically at his architectural plans, discussing some of the ideas that were to grow into a series of thirty-three articles on 'The Architecture and Costume of Shakespeare's Plays' and playing Bach's preludes and fugues together at the piano. He would take the bass and she the treble 'because it was too difficult for either of us to do alone', she later told her son. They began in 'such a stately way', she remembered, '& as the thing goes on & on the great pedal notes work it up & up' until he 'somehow got a thunderous finish . . . we managed it "quite awfully-frightfully well"'.

These early years were 'my *best* times, my happiest times' simply because, as she told her eldest grandson: 'He loved me Bobbie – & I loved him.' He filled her life but she did not quite fill his. He was a romantic, living off his nerves, seeing in her beauty an image of what he passionately desired, but never losing for long his mysterious discontent.

On 9 December 1869 Ellen gave birth to a daughter whom they called Edith, after Eadgyth, daughter of Godwin, Earl of the West Saxons, whom Edward liked to imagine his ancestor. Ellen was passing the village church when her labour pains came on. Hearing 'Rest in the Lord' being played and suddenly feeling 'frightfully ill and afraid', she made her way back to the Red House where the local doctor, Dr Rumball, delivered the baby. In a letter to Bernard Shaw she later described it as 'a bitter-sweet night': sweet because of Edy's birth; bitter because Godwin was not there with her.

He was not with her again for the birth of her son Edward Gordon in the midwife's home at Railway Street, Stevenage, on 16 January 1872. Once Godwin had caught up with events, he and Ellen mischievously registered the boy as being the son of 'Eleanor Alice Godwin, formerly Watkins'.

Godwin was often absent. Some evenings Ellen would harness the pony to the trap, go off to the station to meet him and find he was not on the train – and once, when coming back alone late at night, driving the pony through a dark wood, she had to use the whip to beat off a man who tried to attack her. There was no way Godwin could communicate his changes of plan to her and she began to feel neglected and anxious. She knew he had many engagements in London: meeting clients at Arthur Lewis's Arts Club; going to the Architectural Association; and attending council meetings of the Royal Institute of British Architects to which he had recently been elected a Fellow. He had plenty of work but was more aesthete than businessman, and on commercial matters he could be stubbornly evasive. He continually moved office and was harried by solicitors' letters complaining of leaking roofs and disputed bills. Such worries made him irritable.

Ellen herself was not very practical. Godwin gave her £2 or £3 a week which is more than her mother had received, yet she did not have her mother's carefulness. She was naturally extravagant. Besides, since the birth of Edy and Ted, their household expenses were rising. When they were alone, they had employed a maid-of-all-work at a mere £5 a year. But since Edy's birth, Dr Rumball's niece had come to them as the child's nursemaid; and after Dr Rumball himself died, his wife also joined the household – she was to stay with Ellen as her companion for the next thirty years. Dr Rumball had kept what was called a 'lunatic asylum' in a neighbouring village and on his death his widow 'tried to look after the lunatics herself', Ellen explained. 'But . . . they kept escaping, and people didn't like it. This was my gain . . . I was her only lunatic, and she my most constant companion and dear and loyal friend.'

Ellen regained the glow of her early happiness whenever she and Godwin went abroad. First they travelled to Ireland where he was investigating a troublesome castle; then in the summer of 1873 they went to France, leaving the infant Ted with his nurse but taking Edy in the care of Mrs Rumball. 'We went to Normandy,' Ellen recorded in her *Memoirs*, 'and saw Lisieaux, Nantes, Bayeux.' Godwin spent much of his time sketching and making notes while Ellen climbed the towers of churches and cathedrals. Left with Mrs Rumball below, hearing a choir practising and a boy's voice suddenly rising effortlessly above the others, Edy announced that she had seen the angels.

There seems to have been no serious thought of marriage. Divorce was still such a complicated, expensive and shameful business – and besides, Ellen's experience of being married had not been happy. As for Godwin, he was never extravagantly uxorious.

It was obvious, even in the early days of Ellen's second pregnancy, that the Red House would not be large enough for them all. But this acted as a spur to Godwin who began planning his dream house at Fallows Green, near Harpenden, a mile or two westwards from where they were living. This was a highly characteristic product of his Gothic imagination. Set in twenty acres of ground, the building rose up three unforgiving storeys above Ellen as she began planting the garden. It was finished, partly finished, almost finished, in a frantic hurry and amid much chaos: the sweeping of the tall chimney which emerged from a steep-pitched roof pointing to the sky like a slender periscope of brick; the scrubbing of the broad stone stairs and wooden floors which were to be covered with Chinese matting; the lifting of Godwin's organ into his studio; the hunting for Japanese paper curtains, blinds and shutters; and finally, like the assembling of a scattered army, the gathering of his surviving furniture. 'The house will be ready for habitation tomorrow night & I think you'll like the 2nd floor, our bedroom, dressing-room & Lady's Snuggery', Godwin wrote to Ellen.

Money and time were like hounds at his heels and there is a breathless, sometimes desperate tone to the notes he was sending Ellen.

> I am not up to fetching you although I should so like it, but the wet weather & the going about on my legs upstairs & down have told on me . . . so don't think me selfish if I ask you on your arrival to keep the chicks and Boo [Mrs Rumball] away from me & give yourself as a martyr altogether to me for a day or two . . .
>
> . . . I have tried to push on so as to get one sitting room and one bedroom finished and comfy for us, but the weather & other things have conspired against us & I may not be able to do it, so don't grumble more than you can help.

This letter, with its pleas and apologies, is evidence of how far Godwin's authority had diminished. He was not quite the man he had promised to be and Ellen could not avoid moments of disillusion. In a sonnet she later cut out (and which she believed to have been written about Godwin by Oscar Wilde), he is described as having been 'born to be a general king . . . the best of comrades, winning old and young, / With keen audacious charm . . .' Yet some of the charm had worn away and there were few comrades young or old in their country life, which was far from regal. The sonnet portrays him as a man with a visionary future but no actual present.

Fallows Green became a symbol of Godwin's unattained desires. Ellen and her two small children, their nursemaid (nicknamed 'Bo') and Mrs Rumball (called 'Boo') arrived at the house (which was heavily mortgaged) just ahead of the bailiff and his merry men. Ellen does not mention Fallows Green in her *Memoirs*. Perhaps the memory of it was too painful, and their time there too short. But despite this 'shadow of financial trouble', she remembered, 'I never thought of returning to the stage'.

11

All Change

One morning Ellen was out driving her pony-and-trap through the Hertfordshire country. In the distance she could hear the cries, the horns and thunder, of a hunt. She guided the pony into a narrow lane and was proceeding unevenly along it when suddenly there was a crack and the wheel of the cart was wrenched off. She got down, looked at the broken vehicle and saw it was beyond quick repair. What was she to do? Just then there was a crescendo of noise and volleys of horsemen in pink came flooding over the hedge and into the lane where she had halted. One of them, a bearded gentleman, stopped to enquire whether he could help. He came up to her and: 'Good God! It's Nelly!' Her knight in shining pink was Charles Reade. Ellen records their conversation in that lane as follows:

> 'Where have you been all these years?' he asked.
>
> 'I have been having a very happy time', she answered.
>
> 'Well, you've had it long enough. Come back to the stage.'
>
> 'No, never!'
>
> 'You're a fool! You ought to come back!'

At this point in the conversation, Ellen tells us, she thought of the bailiffs and the unpaid bills and heard herself say: 'Well, perhaps, I would think of it if some one would give me forty pounds a week!'

Forty pounds a week was a tremendous sum for an actress (equivalent to more than £3,000 a week today). But Reade could not resist the challenge, could not resist Ellen. 'Done!' he said. He explained that he needed someone to replace the leading actress in his play *The Wandering Heir* at the New Queen's Theatre in London. Ellen would, he added, never play any part that suited her better.

Barricaded by debts, Godwin was in no condition to refuse money. As for Ellen's parents, they did not speak to her these days. So she went ahead and, as in a film, we leave the conversation there in the lane, and cut to the playbills announcing that an eminent unnamed actress is taking over the lead in *The Wandering Heir* 'after a long period of retirement'. Then, in an atmosphere of great excitement, Ellen makes her entrance onstage to wonderful acclaim. Next day the newspapers are ecstatic and altogether, Ellen remembered, 'it was a tremendous success for me'.

This was the same theatre from which, one foggy night, she had walked out and gone to live with Godwin. Then it had seemed to her a hateful place, now everything was transformed by the athletic presence of Charles Reade in his 'wide-brimmed hats [and] a great blue jacket with brass buttons', striding through the rehearsals pouring forth volleys of ruthless encouragement. She 'revered & adored' the 'sweet, gentle-strong-brave splendid Charles Reade', she told a friend, because 'he taught me something' and 'made me a better woman' – by which she partly meant a better actress.

'Her acting is simply *wonderful*', wrote Lewis Carroll in his diary for 15 April 1874. Reade thought so too. But though he loved her 'a thousand times better' than anyone else, he did not hesitate to criticise her – indeed, he felt impelled to do so. During her absence she had forgotten, he noticed, how to breathe onstage. He reminded her too how to vary the pace of her speech, urged her to put more vigour into her words and showed her how to carry off a dramatic exit. He made her examine every line of her performance.

No great quality of an actress is absent from your performance. Very often you have *vigour*. But in other places where it is as much required, or even more, you turn *limp* . . . You should deliver a pistol-shot or two . . . I do not expect or desire to make a melo-dramatic actress of you, but still I think you capable of any effect, provided *it is not sustained too long* . . . Study to speak these lines with great volubility and fire, and settle the exact syllable to run at.

This tutoring was like that of Professor Higgins and Eliza Doolittle in Shaw's *Pygmalion* and it raises the same question: did anything more intimate lie within the master–pupil relationship? They were unusually close, sometimes quarrelling, then laughing and often marvellously happy together – like lovers. Reade was extremely susceptible to Ellen ('whether in movement or repose, grace pervades the hussy', he wrote). In her writings about him Ellen seems to imply that had he wanted more from their friendship, she would have been unable to deny him. 'I *love* him so', she told a friend. But 'he was a cautious silly-billy!!' He did not appear to want more than the fatherly role as her teacher onstage, and the happiness of her company. After all, he was more than thirty years older than she was, in his early sixties while she was in her late twenties. He would not make a fool of himself as Watts had done. He called his autobiography *Terrible Temptation*. Devoted as he was to the actress Laura Seymour, he did not give in to temptation, but he changed the course of Ellen Terry's life.

12
A Failure to be Proud of

One of Godwin's many interests was education. Now that he had a daughter and a son to practise on, he was able to put some of his theories to the test. He forbade all 'rubbishy picture books' and gave them volumes with charming illustrations by the designer Walter Crane (whose work was to lead from the Pre-Raphaelites to the art nouveau movement). He allowed them only proper wooden toys (when a friend injudiciously gave Edy a mechanical mouse, in which she showed a regrettable interest, it was confiscated). This severe training had its effect. Edy looked 'like a murderess' when, left alone with a vulgar pink doll, she smashed it to pieces. Her idea of hell was Madame Tussaud's house of waxworks.

Godwin did not subscribe to the theory that boys were boys – he saw no need for gender-segregation and a population of typecast men and women – and Ellen agreed with him. He was, she acknowledged, 'a man born long before his time'. Under his influence she set out to keep her son Teddy 'soft and gentle' and Edy, her daughter, 'hard as nails'. Teddy, 'a greedy little thing', always had a biscuit in his hand when he wasn't drawing with a pencil. Edy, who until the age of twelve seemed an uncompromising child, lacking 'sweetness and light', was nevertheless in her nurse's opinion 'a piece' (or, as Ellen called her, 'the pip of my heart'); whereas Teddy, 'fat and fair and angelic-looking', was dubbed 'the feather of England'. It was Edy's duty, as she understood it, to 'brace up' her little brother who was frightened of the dark, hitting him on the head with a wooden spoon as she exhorted him to 'be a *woman!*'.

Their upbringing planted deep differences between them which were to spread aggressively in adult life. But for the time being they were friends – partly because they had no other friends. It was a strangely secluded life the children led. They never saw their grandparents, Ben and Sarah Terry, or their many aunts and uncles, and they were never invited to meet their cousins, Kate's carefully brought-up children, at Moray Lodge. They appeared to inhabit a distant place beyond the confines of Victorian society. Edy, attired in a tiny kimono at the age of four and looking almost comically dour, resembled an infant cast for some future production of *The Mikado*; while Teddy in his minute white suit was like no other child. Ellen Terry's biographer Nina Auerbach, reflecting their mother's view, describes them as 'incomparably brilliant', got up as 'aesthetic prodigies' and referring to themselves 'like deities' in the third person: 'Miss Edy' and 'Master Teddy'. They regarded their unconventional life as a mark of privilege. On arriving at a railway station as the train was pulling out, Teddy was heard to shout: 'Stop the train – stop the train – this is Miss Terry's son.' And so, the story tells us, the train stopped. Marguerite Steen, historian of the Terry family, reflects orthodox Victorian opinion when she describes Edy and Ted as 'a couple of intolerable children' and concludes that this was largely their mother's doing.

'When my two children were born,' Ellen wrote in her *Memoirs*, 'I thought of the stage less than ever. They absorbed all my time, all my interest, all my love.' She had gone back to the stage partly to give them a more stable upbringing. Financially their childhood did become more stable, but emotionally there was greater insecurity. From now on they absorbed all her time that was not given to the theatre, all her interest that was not directed to the plays she was performing and all her love whenever she had an opportunity to show it.

Children, to Godwin's way of thinking, were in some respects like buildings – fascinating in theory, but peculiarly awkward in their refusal to behave theoretically. He was prepared to feel proud of 'the chicks', but felt like a martyr when left alone with them – even when they were being looked after by 'Bo', their nurse. Ellen was to remember his sudden rages and uneasy silences. 'He never was happy', she later wrote, '– he never will be.'

It cannot have been easy for Godwin to accept Ellen's money – money that she was being paid by Charles Reade. But it was necessary. It enabled him to rescue some of his peripatetic furniture and establish a London residence near the British Museum at 20 Taviton Street. Johnston Forbes-Robertson, then twenty-one and starting out on a brilliant stage career, went there to meet Ellen before taking the lead opposite her in Charles Reade's play. 'The floor was covered with straw-coloured matting, and there was a dado of the same material', he remembered.

Above the dado were white walls, and the hangings were of cretonne, with a fine Japanese pattern in delicate grey-blue. The chairs were of wicker work, cushions like the hangings, and in the centre of the room was a full-sized cast of the Venus of Milo, before which was a small pedestal, holding a little censer from which rose, curling round the Venus, ribbons of blue smoke. The whole effect was what art students of my time would have called 'awfully jolly'.

Presently the door opened, and in floated a vision of loveliness! In the blue kimono and with that wonderful golden hair, she seemed to melt into the surroundings and appeared almost intangible. This was my first sight of Miss Terry. I was undergoing a sort of inspection, but her manner was so gracious that it soon cleared away my embarrassment.

This handsome young actor, with his classical features and melodious voice (he had trained as a painter at Heatherley's and painted a picture of their house at Fallows Green), makes no mention of Godwin when he called at Taviton Street. He soon fell in love with Ellen – and the whole world, the world of the theatre, knew it. And Godwin must have known it too. He cannot have been pleased when Charles Reade gave Ellen £10 to leave London and go somewhere by the seaside to learn her lines. His diary shows him calling on Reade who was 'out'. But he could not be openly rude to him – indeed, he may have been calling on him for an advance on Ellen's salary.

Reade's melodrama, *The Wandering Heir*, was based on a notorious case of impersonation. In 1854 the heir to an ancient Hampshire baronetcy, Roger Charles Tichborne, had been lost at sea somewhere between Rio de Janeiro and Jamaica. Following a long search, the Dowager Lady Tichborne advertised for information as a result of which, on Christmas Day 1866, R.C. Tichborne, an impecunious butcher from Wagga Wagga in Australia, landed in England claiming to be the rightful heir. He was popularly received but finally identified, following twenty-two days of cross-examination in court, as a workman from Wapping, and was sentenced to fourteen years' hard labour for perjury. Reade took this story and married it to an updated version of Shakespeare's comedy *As You Like It*. Ellen, assuming the role of Philippa Chester, a 'kind of Rosalind part', is obliged to disguise herself as a boy,

Philip – an indelicate counterfeit condemned by law. Her breast is 'torn with . . . tremors and misgivings' when she falls in love with James Annesley (Johnston Forbes-Robertson) who confesses to being the Earl of Anglesey. The play had not been very successful on tour owing perhaps to the audience's inability to make out what was going on. But it promised to do better in London despite a noticeably lacklustre review by an anonymous critic in the *British Architect*.

It would be almost wearying to sit it out, even if every actor in it were equal to Miss Terry. So long as she is on the stage, notably in the fourth act, time passes quickly and pleasantly . . . Miss Terry is so well known and so highly appreciated by the old theatre-goers that it will be sufficient to say that her performance in this piece is one of the most graceful and natural effects it has ever been our good fortune to witness.

This review was written by Godwin. He was writing more for publication now – pieces on dramatic literature, feminism and architecture. It was not that he could make more money from journalism but that he stood to lose less.

His two main literary endeavours were to indicate the dramatic choice confronting him. The first was a commission from a magazine of sociology, *Women and Work*, whose editor, Emily Faithfull, invited him to contribute an essay on the prospects of women as modern architects. This he enthusiastically accomplished, welcoming young women into his profession because they possessed the desirable 'accuracy and repose', as well as 'that equipoise which is indispensable for the creation of beauty'. There was nothing in the charter of the Royal Institute of British Architects that excluded women from membership and no reason why ambitious architects should not employ lady pupils.

Godwin's second literary enterprise arose in part from the Shakespeare readings he had put on in Bristol. When young he had reputedly dressed in period costume at home when reading Shakespeare, and seems to have been something of an actor *manqué* with many parts in mind. His series of thirty-three articles was not confined to the buildings and clothes in Shakespeare's plays, but contained copious references to chivalric statuary, classical pictures, effigies on tombs and the authenticity of sets and scenes.

When audiences for *The Wandering Heir* at the Queen's Theatre fell away after six weeks, Reade replaced it with one of his melodramas and took the company across the river to Astley's (which, the usual company playing there being Sanger's circus, smelt strongly of horse). Finally, in the early summer of 1874, he took them all on tour. Godwin, left at Taviton Street writing his Shakespearean articles for the *Architect*, was not pleased. One of his difficulties was jealousy. 'He is apt to brood and imagine all kinds of ills that do not exist', Ellen wrote. It is not difficult to imagine the ills he brooded over while Ellen was travelling the country with a handsome young leading actor known to be in love with her.

Since Ellen had gone on tour her salary had been cut from £40 to £25 a week and though this was still a considerable sum, she was able to give Godwin less money. Nevertheless, having dispatched his children with their nurse to the country, he hired a housekeeper to look after him at Taviton Street while he looked after Shakespeare.

He also took on a lady pupil at his office.

Beatrice Philip, daughter of the sculptor John Birnie Philip, was a clever nineteen-year-old girl. She was described by some as 'handsome and French-looking' and by others as 'beautiful in a Latin style'. She had dark liquid eyes and a tea-rose complexion, and her bohemian temperament was nourished by potent ideals. She was much given to hero-worship and had, as it were, walked off the pages of Emily Faithfull's *Women and Work* into Godwin's life. In later years she would be given the name 'Trixie' and painted as a 'Harmony in Red' by Whistler who in 1888 was to marry her. But in 1874 her hero was Godwin.

It is not clear when Ellen first heard of Beatrice Philip. After she returned to London from her tour, Godwin suddenly went into hiding from his creditors, taking refuge on the Isle of Wight and leaving Ellen to open all his letters and 'detain' those that threatened legal proceedings. Meanwhile, their home at Taviton Street was plundered and left bare by the brokers – a mere shell of the aesthetic interior that a few months earlier had delighted Johnston Forbes-Robertson. When the actress Mrs Bancroft came to the house, she found the front door open. 'May I come in?' she called in her famous voice ('like a silver stream flowing over golden stones'). Ellen hurried to the door attired in what her daughter Edy used to call her 'frog dress' – a deep-yellow, woollen garment speckled with brown and cut by Godwin like a Viollet-le-Duc tabard. The two women standing by the door must have made a strange contrast: Ellen, painfully thin and so oddly got up;

and Mrs Bancroft, a petite figure, almost stout but fashionably dressed in a dark Parisian suit. She was shown into the drawing-room and, looking around, saw no cretonne hangings, no wicker chairs with their cushions, no prints on the walls, no pictures at all, simply an empty space, its floor covered with matting and, all the more obvious in its solitude, Godwin's colossal copy of the Venus de Milo (too heavy perhaps for the brokers' men). Having made her entrance on to this minimalist scene, Mrs Bancroft stopped dramatically, glanced around and as her eyes (those 'wonderful grey eyes') rested on the Venus de Milo, she raised her hands to her head – a gesture familiar to audiences who had made her the most successful comedienne on the London stage – and exclaimed: 'Dear me!'

And the two women burst into laughter.

Looking back at this time, Ellen described herself as being 'very miserable'. She gives two reasons: 'I was worried to death by domestic troubles and financial difficulties.' Her financial difficulties must have been evident to Mrs Bancroft as soon as she stepped into her home. As for domestic troubles – those which were not financial – they centred on her children and had begun circling around that young girl with the liquid eyes and tea-rose complexion who was Godwin's working companion. To make matters more complicated, Ellen's well-meaning friends, Charles Reade and Tom Taylor, were urging her to leave Godwin and make another great change in her life. 'Everything was at its darkest', she remembered. She felt no wish to entrust her future to her friends' pot-boilers. But what other kind of life was there? Mrs Bancroft, timing her entrance to perfection, had the answer.

Marie Bancroft had been responsible for a remarkable revolution in the theatre – a quiet cup-and-saucer revolution. In her teens she had, as Marie Wilton, played principal boys' parts, her acting being at once 'astonishingly impudent' and yet 'perfectly free from offence', according to Charles Dickens. Her burlesque performances in the Strand Theatre, saucy and audacious and brilliantly amusing, had gained her the reputation for being 'exactly like a boy'. She was 'the cleverest girl I have ever seen on the stage in my time', Dickens wrote.

In 1867 she had married Squire Bancroft, an actor-manager already renowned for playing 'swells'. He could hold a single eyeglass between his brow and cheekbone, flourish his moustache, and fill the theatre with his tremendous 'By Jove!' On his retirement from the theatre, he was to receive a knighthood and expand into something of a 'swell' himself. Marie Bancroft, always proud of belonging to 'one of the oldest Gloucestershire families', was already transformed from a burlesque comedienne with a precocious talent for breeches roles, into a lady of refinement and propriety living in Berkeley Square. Together they managed what had been an insalubrious theatre in Tottenham Court Road, known before their management as the 'Dust Hole'.

These premises had gradually changed over the years from a rowdy, smoke-filled den into what one playgoer described as 'the prettiest, most charming little house imaginable . . . upholstered in palest blue . . . [with] little antimacassars over the backs of chairs in the stalls, boxes and dress circle'. The Bancrofts placed the orchestra below the stage – a startling innovation – provided wardrobes for the actresses and saw to it that all the actors' wages (which no longer depended on benefit performances) were discreetly brought to their dressing-rooms instead of being handed out along a line of actors. The building itself, which they renamed the Prince of Wales's Theatre, was kept scrupulously clean and the drama put on there similarly cleansed. Violent blood-and-thunder pieces, composed in over-ambitious blank verse, littered with tremendous storms, bitter conquests and oratorical deaths performed by superbly voiced barnstormers in the 'Dust Hole', gave way at the Prince of Wales to civilised comedies played by smartly tailored members of the acting profession who could easily pass for real ladies and gentlemen. Their naturalistic style was set in carefully designed drawing-rooms full of genuine furniture and carpets, authentic books and china, edible bread and butter (replacing the pasteboard pies and wooden chickens), useful hats and sticks and real doors with actual door-knobs which became symbols of modern domestic drama. By making this commercially successful, the Bancrofts opened up the theatre to middle-class audiences.

The resident playwright at the Prince of Wales's Theatre was Tom Robertson, brother of the celebrated diva Madge Kendal (they came from a theatrical family of twenty-two children). He had been a child actor on the Lincoln circuit where he also wrote songs, painted scenery and adapted other dramatists' plays before developing a new genre of drama with credible dialogue and contemporary themes set in recognisable interiors.

His comedies, with their monosyllabic titles (*Ours*, *Caste*, *Play*, *School*) came as a refreshing change from the sham heroics that had dominated mid-nineteenth-century drama, and would later be seen as a step towards the theatre of ideas that was to be imported from Scandinavia as well as a precursor to the sophisticated romances of Noël Coward. But Robertson had died at the height of his success in 1871. Some four years later, as his attractive young lovers, so jolly and well dressed, became a little threadbare, the Bancrofts decided they must try something else, something classical perhaps.

Mrs Bancroft had not acted in any of Shakespeare's plays herself (though she once appeared in a burlesque of *The Winter's Tale*). Her style of acting was better suited to the topical comedies and extravaganzas based on nursery rhymes and legends composed by the confusingly named dramatist Henry James Byron. But she knew that Shakespeare was well regarded and judged him to be the right man to raise the status of the Bancroft management. She had come to Taviton Street to offer Ellen Terry the role of Portia in *The Merchant of Venice*. Mrs Bancroft explained that she could not take the part of the young heiress herself because she was recovering from illness and still something of a convalescent.

It was a long time since Ellen had acted in Shakespeare – nearly twelve years. But she knew the character of Portia well enough. What was especially appealing about Mrs Bancroft's offer was that it included a commission for Godwin as 'archaeological adviser'. Whether Mrs Bancroft originally made this suggestion, or Ellen herself came up with the idea, is not known. In any event, Ellen enthusiastically agreed.

Following a circuitous route from the Isle of Wight, Godwin arrived back in London. The proposal appealed to his many interests and needs. 'His aim was the apotheosis of Venice itself', writes Nina Auerbach. In his quest to represent the city as comprehensively as possible – its pavements and exteriors, the morning and evening light, the gardens, architectural plans and works of art depicting halls, palaces, staterooms and private rooms – he dispatched the principal scene-painter and his assistant to Venice itself. Meanwhile he went to look again at Titian, reread Ruskin's *The Stones of Venice*, Browning's Italian poems and Cesare Vecellio's *Habiti antichi et moderni di tutto il mundo* (1589). With such aids, he contrived to make the sets and costumes authentically gorgeous. 'Elaborate capitals of enormous weight', Marie Bancroft later recalled, '. . . were cast in plaster, and part of the wall of the theatre had to be cut away to find room for them to be moved by means of trucks on and off the stage.' These sets, designed in a diagonal scheme, were, Squire Bancroft wrote, 'beautiful beyond our hopes'.

They were also expensive beyond reckoning. No money was spared getting the arches of the windows framed, or the correct quantities of gold applied to cusps, carvings and the edges of the mouldings. Bright details of colour, just visible perhaps from the front row of the stalls, nestled in the background of the sunk work. Over the costumes too Godwin had gone into minute detail. He noted the 'marked difference' in dress between married women and maidens, examined the ways in which Paduan ladies of noble birth arranged their hair, and expounded upon the filmlike effect of their veils. A pouch 'worn at the girdle was not quite yet abandoned', he discovered. Equally useful were his observations on the seams of stockings, the soles of shoes, the perfumes used on gloves, the number of ostrich feathers that made up a fan, the size of pocket handkerchiefs, and the complexity of rings ('worn on the first, third and fourth fingers'). One of his speculations became a classic. 'Portia would do her shopping probably in Padua, and would therefore follow the fashions of the mainland.'

The Merchant of Venice opened at the Prince of Wales's Theatre on 17 April 1875 and closed three weeks later. 'I never saw so empty a pit at the Prince of Wales – not more than a dozen people', wrote Beerbohm Tree who had gone to see the third performance. The chief trouble was Charles Coghlan's feeble playing of Shylock. 'The perspiration poured down his face', Ellen remembered; 'yet what he was doing no one could guess.' Godwin's sets perplexed the critics. 'It all looked so unlike a theatre and so much like old Italian pictures than anything else that had previously been shown upon the stage', Squire Bancroft explained. '. . . It may be that it all came a little before the proper time.'

Despite its commercial failure, this production was to live in the minds of those who saw it as an aesthetic triumph, and was judged by Beerbohm Tree to be the first classical play 'in which the modern spirit of stage-management asserted itself'.

'I count it a failure to be proud of', Squire Bancroft wrote. Ellen Terry's performance, he added, though not of course quite what his wife would have managed, was to be the 'the foundation-stone' of her brilliant career.

Beerbohm Tree, too, acknowledged that her Portia made up 'with her art what others lacked. I cannot understand how she can smile so naturally. Her by-play was marvellous. She looked like one of [Frederic] Leighton's women, queen-like . . . Her genius was immediately recognised.'

No wonder she smiled so wonderfully. 'My work will, I feel certain, be joyful work', she had written to Mrs Bancroft, 'and joyful work *should* turn out good work.' In *The Merchant of Venice* she could enter a fairy-tale land of music and poetry. Each night, she was able to please everyone, banishing usury and its petty traffickers (like Godwin's brokers) and handing Antonio the news he most desires ('Sweet lady, you have given me life and living'). Above all, she could mend the tangled highways of love. It was a role in which she seemed prompted by nature to excel.

She was trying over these three weeks not only to rescue the play but also to revive her life with Godwin. She was comfortably at home with his large picturesque sets – had they not arisen from long, happy discussions during their evenings together? Besides she was 'the Painter's Actress' as her friend Graham Robertson used to say. 'Her charm held every one but I think pre-eminently those who loved pictures.' If she seemed a natural part of Godwin's scene-painting it was also because, as the drama critic William Archer noticed, such sympathetic adaptation was part of her special talent. 'Whatever her absolute merits in a part,' he wrote, 'she always harmonizes as perhaps she alone could with the whole tone of a picture.'

Characteristically Ellen tells the story of her success partly through the clothes she was wearing – the clothes Godwin had designed for her. When the curtain rose on the second scene – a room in Portia's house in Belmont – and the audience saw her that first night in a china-blue and white brocade dress with a red rose at her breast, the theatre filled with applause. 'In the casket scene I wore a dress like almond-blossom', Ellen wrote in her *Memoirs*. 'I played the part more stiffly and more slowly at the Prince of Wales's than I did in later years . . . The clothes seemed to demand it, and the setting of the play developed the Italian feeling in it . . .'

This was one of those rare nights in the theatre when everyone becomes aware that something special is taking place. It was not simply Ellen's beautiful diction but the intensely feminine way in which she conveyed the hesitations and perplexities of love. Her Portia was 'the very poetry of acting', wrote a reviewer in the *Telegraph*. In her *Reminiscences*, Alice Comyns

Carr recalled that 'her greatest effect was when she walked into the court in her black robes of justice, and I remember my young husband, who had rushed out between the acts to buy the last bouquet in Covent Garden, throwing his floral tribute at her feet amidst the enthusiasm of the audience'.

Over thirty years later Ellen singled out this production of *The Merchant of Venice* as a unique experience in her theatrical career. She would have many evenings of success, 'but never until I appeared as Portia at the Prince of Wales's had I experienced that awe-struck feeling which comes, I suppose, to no actress more than once in a life-time – the feeling of a conqueror . . . "What can this be?" I thought . . . "*This is different!* It has never been quite the same before." ' It was never to be quite the same again. 'And, while it made me happy, it made me miserable because I foresaw, as plainly as my own success, another failure . . . Short as the run of the play was, it was a wonderful time for me. Every one seemed to be in love with me!'

Everyone was in love with her except the man she loved. And while she attributes the misery that ran alongside her happiness to the commercial failure of the play, the real misery lay in her failure to win back Godwin into her life. Wearing a wide-brimmed hat and long black cloak, he appeared among the poets and aesthetes in the audience (which included Swinburne and Alfred Gilbert, sculptor of the winged Eros in Piccadilly Circus) and met for the first time Beerbohm Tree and Oscar Wilde. The play had ignited Godwin's interests but not met his needs – indeed, his sets had contributed greatly to the losses of the production which were so substantial that the Bancrofts dared not risk another Shakespeare play. Had *The Merchant of Venice* enjoyed a long run, then, Ellen believed, they could have resumed working and living together. But after the play closed, they parted. There was a flicker of hope that summer when Charles Calvert, manager of the Prince's Theatre in Manchester, offered her the parts of Juliet and Rosalind with Godwin as her artistic adviser. 'Darling . . . of course you can have *silk* for Juliet – pale red – pale blue – violet & a kind of vermillion were used mostly in 1300–10', Godwin wrote to her on 24 July. But Calvert's offer fell through and with it all hope of getting together again.

Godwin's letter was written at the Verulam Club in St James's Street. 'He went away and shut the door after him', Ellen wrote to a friend fifteen years later. 'It seems like that to me, but *he knows*.' Whatever he knew, she did not

July 8. 75
B
V.D.

wish to talk about it. 'Our separation was a thing agreed upon by *both* of us many weeks before it actually took place', she wrote when turning down someone's offer to mediate between them. 'The first steps were taken by *him* . . .'

It was not simply lack of money that drove them apart – poverty had been a companion for most of their lives together. 'He loved me, and I loved him, and that, I suppose, is the reason we so cruelly hurt each other.' She had not ceased to love him, but 'you cannot go on caring about somebody', she explained, 'in whom you no longer have faith'. She had lost faith in her ability to make him happy, and in his ability to sustain his love for her when they were apart – as they had to be whenever she went on tour. Alone, he became depressed – which was why he had taken up with that adoring young student, Beatrice Philip. Six months after leaving Taviton Street, he married her.

13
Men!

Ellen too left Taviton Street and went to live in lodgings at 221 Camden Road which had the advantage of a good garden where the children could play. But then something happened that temporarily extinguished her love for Godwin. It seems that in the discussions about their separation, Ellen offered him the custody of their son Teddy, but insisted on keeping Edy. 'Boys are not so much "in my line" as girls', she confided to Bertha Bramley. Godwin also wanted their daughter and not the son, and when Ellen would not agree to this, he made an attempt to 'kidnap' her. 'Part of our compact was that we should always maintain a kindly, friendly relation to one another', Ellen wrote shortly afterwards. 'He has since Tuesday last made this an *impossibility*. He tried by unfair means to get my little girl from me (I *had offered* to let him have the boy) and I now distinctly refuse to hold any communication whatever with him.' She did not soften her attitude when she heard that he was ill (he was always imagining illnesses), nor when she was told that he might 'lose his reason'. She knew his moods and how they drove others to lose their reason. She was determined to get 'stronger in health & purpose' and knew she must be hard to beat off her depression. But this 'hard behaviour', she insisted, had been brought about by Godwin's 'rash conduct'.

As if fearful of being abducted, Edy grew up disliking the idea of her father who, she let it be known, had left their home 'in a fit of pique'. Neither of her parents, she conceded, was 'an easy person to live with', but in a determined fashion, though with momentary lapses, she wished to live with her mother. Her brother Teddy, whom no one seems especially to have wanted, was to take an opposite line, designing for himself a surreal career in what he believed were Godwin's footsteps. If anyone was to blame for his parents' separation it had been trivial and officious men, he thought, like Charles Reade. In any event there was no fit of pique, 'no unkindness, no dissension – they were neither of them desertable people'.

Yet Ellen had been cruelly hurt. 'I could never suffer again as I have suffered', she wrote. Consequently she would only once risk falling in love with a man again, generally transferring her need for love to theatre audiences. She would still flirt of course – that was in her nature. But she kept on her guard. Ellen's friend Graham Robertson thought few people would believe that she 'loved (in the true sense of the word) one man only – and for ever' and that man was Godwin. Difficult as he was, and despite the suffering he caused her, there was simply 'no one like him'. She was continually reminded of him. 'With a *woman*', she explained to Clement Scott, 'it is the *Father of the children* who lives for her in the middle of her heart.'

Her son would later write of this time: 'E.T. worked on. Brave. Strange to realize now that she did not kill herself.' Paradoxically she had 'killed herself' by drowning (as her parents believed) at the beginning of their relationship, dramatically ending her unheroic role as Watts's abandoned wife and the dull domestic life she was living in Kentish Town. But now that Godwin had left her, she set about mending some of the injuries she had caused. 'Thank God, Mother is alive (& so fond of me) that I can atone a little to her for all the unintentional paining of her', she was to write. There was also the matter of her career. 'I am changed – oh dear oh dear – I am never anything now but in the depths of down-ness!!' she wrote to her friends the Casella sisters. Feeling 'an old woman', she forced herself to 'get over the feeling of wishing for "*thick veils*". You see I'm obliged to go to the theatre again – I'm once more public property.' So she went on working for the Bancrofts, taking omnibuses between her new home in Camden Town and the Prince of Wales's Theatre in Soho. She played a 'proud beauty' in a performance of Bulwer Lytton's *Lady of Lyons* – a performance that was hailed by the theatre critic Joseph Knight as 'the advent of genius' – and a more modern role in his comedy *Money*, which Lewis Carroll called 'a perfect treat'. She also took a small part in Reade's and Taylor's collaboration *Masks and Faces*, supporting Mrs Bancroft in the leading role. The greater the praise she received from the critics, the smaller the parts, it seems, she was given by the Bancrofts. Mrs Bancroft cannot have enjoyed being outshone by a younger actress whose entrances were greeted by wild cheering from her fans. She let it be known that Ellen Terry had been her *second* choice for Portia in *The Merchant of Venice* and would never have been offered the part had Madge Kendall been able to accept it. Squire Bancroft tried to quell the rumour that his wife was making Ellen play second fiddle to herself by saying that Ellen was only too pleased to play any part. But in his review of T.W. Robertson's *Ours*, Bernard Shaw noticed that Ellen Terry was not at her best, 'giving an appearance of waywardness; of not quite fitting into her part, and not wanting to'. That summer both she and Mrs Bancroft withdrew from the play because of ill-health.

What may have occasioned Ellen's illness was the re-emergence into her life of Watts. Her social position in her lodgings both at 221 Camden Road and 44 Finborough Road (near the Brompton Cemetery), where she moved with the children in 1877, was anomalous. Lewis Carroll might come to praise her performances onstage but he could never go backstage to see a married woman living separately from her husband and with two illegitimate children. Even Ellen's parents, though they too saw her in the theatre, did not visit her and their grandchildren at home. She increasingly felt a need to regularise her position. To be applauded in a make-believe world and shunned in real life had become a strain and could not be good for her son and daughter. She needed to be legally free from Watts.

The Marriage Act 1857 had made divorce in Britain a practical, if sometimes expensive, business (before this it had been obtainable only by a private Act of Parliament). When Ellen asked Watts for a divorce, he had no choice but to name Godwin as co-respondent, but generously paid all the costs himself. The proceedings started on their way in 1876 and slowly travelled to court where a decree absolute was granted on 6 November 1877. Watts's statement has been likened by the biographer Joy Melville to 'a schoolmaster's report on a pupil who has failed to live up to her promise'. He had 'hoped to influence, guide & cultivate' his young wife's 'very artistic & peculiar nature'. But soon after their marriage he discovered 'how great an error he had made'. She was not simply *restless*, by no means merely *impetuous*, but possessed of the most *sensational* and *exaggerated*, not to say *intolerable* fantasies. Though she was never actually immoral while living under his guidance, there was about her, he could not help but notice, 'an insane excitability indulging in the wildest suspicions, accusations and denunciations driving him to the verge of desperation and separation became absolutely necessary unless he gave up his professional pursuits'. This of course was 'out of the question'. He was dependent on his genius and had no means other than 'the professional aims his life had been devoted to'. Naturally, being 'considerably older' than his wife, he was 'willing to take the blame upon himself (excepting charges of immorality) . . .' But no such charges had been made – and indeed 'there could have been no sort of foundation for them'. Their ensuing separation, though inevitable, had 'pained him' so very much 'that he refused to go into Society altogether and gave himself up entirely to study and close pursuit of his profession'.

Mrs Prinsep, the patron who had brought Society to his door, could vouch for that last sentence, while Watts had evidently been guided by his lawyers through the earlier passages of his petition. Had he not painted his wife as Ophelia? His genius had penetrated to the truth of the matter and the lawyers, as it were, wrote the caption to his picture. Ellen was mad.

This petition briefly brought back to her all the frustration and sense of inferiority she had experienced at Little Holland House. Here, in Watts's statement, she was again cast as a maladjusted child whose wildness imperilled the Signor's artistic destiny. She had been 'given somewhat to hysterics when very young', Ellen admitted. But she later told an interviewer that 'all hysterical fits left me when I was quite grown ripe at 15'. In her *Memoirs*, she recounts that she saw Watts only once after their separation when they accidentally met in a street at Brighton and he announced that 'I had grown'. But early in the 1880s, she adds, when she was walking in a garden, Watts spied her through the hedge. Next day he sent over a note asking her to 'shake hands' with him 'in spirit'. 'What success I may have will be very incomplete and unsatisfactory', he declared, 'if you cannot do what I have long been hesitating to ask. If you cannot, keep silence. If you can, one word "Yes", will be enough.' 'I answered simply "Yes",' Ellen concludes her story, adding that she 'never came into personal contact with him' again.

But they did correspond. Both of them wished to set the past to rest, and each manoeuvred so as to gain moral ascendancy over the other. 'Let the past be, as you say,' Ellen agreed, 'a story in a book that we have both read.' It was as if they were reading different stories in this book, at least stories with different endings. Ellen was eager to reposition herself in the narrative and 'be an encouragement to you and a help to you in striving after real greatness as distinct from mere success'.

A year later, on 11 July 1883, she wrote again, reminding Watts how, for his peace of mind, she gave him that single word 'Yes'. His sacred request had 'made me dizzy with exquisite waves of feeling and gratitude and joy', but he had not allowed her words to convey all she felt. 'I am vexed and perplexed to think I can *say nothing*', she objected, for she was overcome with the wish to 'bless you'. This wish made it 'impossible for me to stay away'. However, she was in such popular demand as an actress that it was 'impossible for me to get a spare quarter of an hour' to meet him before the end of the month.

Watts, for his part, had been experiencing a desire to see his wife since their divorce. They could meet in secret maybe. 'No one need know', he assured her. But then, when she agreed, he modestly backed away from such 'unseemly' contact. His flickering aspirations spun uncertainly between awkward fact and sublime fantasy, and despite their newborn tenderness for each other, they did not meet. She praised his 'gentle goodness' and gave him her 'incessant gratitude'. He acknowledged her success onstage, but insisted that 'I have spoiled your life. I have never forgiven myself and never shall.' In recompense he offered to support her children 'should they ever need it' and invited her to confide in him whenever she felt miserable.

Then, having parted from Mrs Prinsep (who grew eager to obtain complimentary tickets for Ellen's performances), Watts married again: and his correspondence with Ellen ceased.

Tom Taylor, it was, who persuaded Ellen to leave the Bancrofts' company – a move made more urgent after Ellen (accidentally) stabbed Mrs Bancroft in the arm during a performance of one of Tom Robertson's plays. In the autumn of 1876, she began a new season with the Bancrofts' rival, John Hare, a famously irascible but scrupulously professional stage manager. His theatre was the Court, 'a suburban little bandbox in Sloane Square which had been a dissenting chapel', where Ellen was soon playing in yet another of Tom Taylor's plays, *New Men and Old Acres*, in which he had written the part of Lilian Vavasour specially for her. Lewis Carroll, who came to see it in January 1877, thought her 'unsurpassable', though he added regretfully that in her late twenties 'the gush of animal spirits of a light-hearted girl is beyond her now, poor thing! She gave a very clever imitation of it, but that is all.'

Ellen got on well with John Hare who gave her what she was to call 'the second great opportunity of my career'. This was the title role of Olivia in W.G. Wills's stage adaptation of an episode from *The Vicar of Wakefield* – a tale of temptation, a fall, and a miraculously happy end. 'You had better take a big handkerchief,' she told a friend, 'for it's a weepy play.' More than any character she had played, Olivia 'touched me to the heart', she later wrote. 'I cried too much in it . . . My real tears on the stage have astonished some people, and have been the envy of others, but they have often been a hindrance to me. I have had to *work* to restrain them.'

Olivia was a chamber work for an intimate theatre, the love story of an injured woman which seemed to release a stream of emotions from Ellen's own condition. People who would have been offended by her illicit affair with Godwin left the tiny Court Theatre much affected. 'When she repelled the further advances of the man who had wronged her, it [her performance] touched absolute greatness', wrote Joseph Knight. She was fortunate in playing opposite William Terriss, one of the most popular actors of his day, who made a speciality of melodrama and gave a brilliant performance as the villain. But for Lewis Carroll, who saw the play on 22 April 1878, 'the gem of the piece is Olivia herself, acted . . . with a sweetness and pathos that moved some of the audience (nearly including myself) to tears'.

Ellen had converted a great sadness in her life into a triumph onstage, and she wrote to Wills ('who is a dear kind old thing') to thank him. Suddenly photographs of her were on sale everywhere, and everywhere young girls were practising their demure but saucy Ellen Terry expressions. Newborn children were christened Olivia and, as Roger Manvell wrote, 'the milliners' windows filled with Olivia hats and kerchiefs'.

Two men entered Ellen's life while she was at the Court Theatre in the late 1870s. The first, and more surprising, of them accounts for her motive in asking Watts for a divorce. Charles Kelly was an actor in John Hare's company. Ellen had performed with him some years before at the Queen's Theatre, most memorably in a curtain-raiser by Charles Reade called *Rachael the Reaper*. To establish the verisimilitude of this piece, Reade had acquired a number of animals to swell the cast – '*real* pigs, *real* sheep, a *real* goat and a *real* dog'. His plan was to let them graze contentedly in his garden at Kensington while they were not performing, then bring them to the theatre in a four-wheeler to meet the actors and get accustomed to the stage where Reade could instruct them all, humans and animals, on the virtues of stage realism. The goat, however, did not get along very well with the pigs, especially when they were crammed together in the four-wheeler. On their arrival at the theatre, while Reade was attempting to pacify his goat, the pigs suddenly made off down the road. Then, while Reade was giving chase ('his loose trousers, each one a yard wide, flapping in the wind'), the goat scampered away in the opposite direction. 'That's a relief, at any rate', remarked Charles Kelly who was anxious not to be upstaged by these assorted flocks and herds. Nevertheless, on the first night, the dog bit his ankle and 'he kicked the *real* animal by a *real* mistake into the orchestra's *real* drum!'.

This misadventure appeared to fix Kelly as something of a comedian in Ellen's mind. His actual name was Charles Clavering Wardell. He had been a cavalry officer and was wounded in the Crimean War. Retiring from the army, he took up acting as a second career and with a new name. Ellen found him rather attractive: 'physically a manly bulldog sort of man', she described him, adding that as an actor he could show 'great tenderness and humour', though 'owing to his lack of training he had to be very carefully suited to a part'. In short, he was a minor actor with a limited range, but good at bluff manly roles, such as wounded cavalry officers. Unfortunately he was unaware of his limitations, and being passed over for William Terriss's leading role in *Olivia*, he sulked and refused to accept a supporting character he would have played well.

It was the look of distress on Kelly's manly face that touched Ellen so unexpectedly. She believed that he wanted the leading role so that he could play opposite her and share her success. He was enchanted with her – as the rest of the world appeared to be – but his need for her seemed especially poignant. He was an open-air man not really at home in the theatre, and he needed to be helped. After his failure over *Olivia*, Ellen made it up to him by arranging a tour for them in the provinces while the London theatres were closed during the summer of 1877. And he blossomed under her attention. Their tour was so successful that she agreed to repeat it the following two summers. He was very good company: a bon viveur with an appealing vein of unrehearsed humour and a wish to learn more about the craft of acting from her – to get an extra 'grip' on it all. She loved people being in love with her. Johnston Forbes-Robertson was of course more romantically in love with her than anyone, but he did not need her as Charles Kelly needed her and nothing serious came of it. And, in any event, Forbes-Robertson was now playing opposite Ellen's sister Marion who was about to achieve her first great success in a comedy by W.S. Gilbert at the Haymarket Theatre ('Nobody seems to remember', Marion plaintively remarked, 'that there was a time when *I* was the Terry of the age!').

Ellen's young brother Fred (whom she introduced to the stage in a popular play by Tom Taylor during one of these provincial tours, wickedly mimicking his voice when it began to break) spread a story that his sister Ellen had so many suitors at this time that she put all their names into a hat and asked him to pick one out. He put his hand in the hat and came out with Kelly's name.

Kelly is the name which Ellen was to use for him when writing her *Memoirs*, but it was Charles Wardell she actually married – she had visiting cards printed for herself bearing the name Mrs E. Wardell. This was to be her ticket back into society and a badge of retrospective legitimacy for her children. Wardell's father was a vicar, a friend of Sir Walter Scott, and he himself had been honourably wounded while in the service of his country. Yet he was more dangerous than she knew.

They were married in the autumn of 1877 at St Philip's, Kensington. Not long afterwards Ellen's parents came to visit the Wardell family in Longridge Road. This was the first time that Edy and Ted had seen their grandparents. Ellen told them both about her mother and father and when the doorbell rang, Edy in a voice of tragedy announced, 'That's Gran'mama.' A formal Victorian tea was laid out on the table, but when Ted, now aged five, tried to help the white-haired lady by politely moving her chair, he overdid it and she sat down suddenly on the floor. 'That *was* fun!' she said, and Ted burst out laughing. Ellen, seeing her mother so bright and tender with the children, and remembering, now that she was a mother herself, Sarah Terry's efforts to 'bring us up as beautifully as she could' (which had so often been taken for granted in the past) was surprised by how happy she suddenly felt.

In June 1879, after a cautious interval of twelve years, Lewis Carroll also renewed his friendship with Ellen. He had taken advice from a Canon in the

Church of England and been told that 'it would be the right thing to do', now that Ellen was legally married. 'She was as charming as ever,' he acknowledged, 'and I was much pleased with her husband. I also liked her two children, Edith and Ted.' He hoped nevertheless, he confided to Tom Taylor, that the 'poor little things . . . will never know their own sad history'. The children did not think much of him. Edy, who had drawn a picture of the devil with teeth, claws and a tail, and shown it to her brother, pretending it was their father, was suspicious of any man who called on her mother. As for Ted, 'I was not amused', he concluded after impatiently listening to Carroll tell a story, illustrated with matches, of how five sheep crossed a river in one boat. If there was to be a stranger in their home – and unlike his sister he longed for some male company in this house of women – he preferred the soldierly presence of his new stepfather: 'something large and heavy-footed' clumping and growling along the passages, someone who taught him practical things such as how to read a clock rather than silly things about sheep.

And yet, for all the solidity of this ex-soldier, there was, Marguerite Steen comments, an 'apocryphal flavour' to this marriage. This was partly because Ellen was 'not a marriageable person', as her son later wrote. 'How could anyone in his senses ask such a dear madwoman in marriage?' Ellen thought she knew the answer – for was Charles Wardell not madly in love with her? What neither she nor her son yet guessed was that he might be overtaken by a less sympathetic strain of madness.

Living directly opposite their house at 33 Longridge Road was the MacColl family. The art student D.S. MacColl and his sisters would regularly see Ellen taking leave of her children as she set off for rehearsals each day. Like an apparition of some legendary Greek Lady with a chorus of waiting women in a classical picture, she appeared upon the steps 'lifting wide eloquent lips, hooded eyes and breathless face to the light. She raised and kissed her two little tots . . . Her cushions were brought out, placed and patted in the open carriage; herself installed; the air became tender and gay with wavings and blown kisses; the wheels revolved, and greyness descended once more on Longridge Road.'

To the MacColl family the introduction of a very obvious Englishman into this classical scene did not seem right. 'We resented the conjunction', D.S. MacColl remembered. Ellen's daughter Edy quotes from his unpublished 'Batch of Memories' in the second edition of her mother's *Memoirs* in order to show that, even on a superficial level, Charles Wardell did not fit into their home. But though she did not welcome Wardell as a stepfather, Edy acknowledged that her mother was 'strongly attracted' to him. All through her life 'the man of brains competed for her affections with the man of brawn'.

But it was another species of man, a man apart, neither quite of brains nor simply of brawn, a man of strange countenance and with crablike gait, 'spare, and grim-jaunty in close-fitting short jacket, and tilted wide-a-wake', whom the MacColl family would soon see hurrying towards Ellen's home.

PART TWO

14
What's in a Name?

Samuel Brodribb came from a family of Somerset farmers but, having no interest in farming himself, he drifted into employment as a travelling salesman. On his travels into Cornwall he encountered the Behenna family near St Ives and in 1835 married the third of seven sisters, the twenty-seven-year-old Mary Behenna.

Their son, John Henry, was born in the village of Keinton Mandeville on 6 February 1838. The orchards, fields and farmlands around this Somerset village were a perfect playground for the boy, though he remembered the modest house in which they lived as a godforsaken hole – despite the regular visits there of the Methodist minister Mr Southey. By 1842 Samuel and Mary had grown so impoverished that they were obliged to make a drastic decision: moving to a room in Bristol and sending the four-year-old John to live with his aunt Sarah in Cornwall. 'My heart was breaking', he wrote, but 'I did not show half I felt.' Nor, he was sure, did his mother.

Cornwall in the mid-nineteenth century was cut off from the mainland of England. There were no railways, though the county could be reached by steamboat. This was Celtic country, half-foreign, a place of legends. 'We took the legends naturally', the boy later remembered. 'They seemed to fit with the solitude, the expanses, the superstitious character of the Cornish people and never clashed in our minds with the scriptural teachings, which were our daily portion at home . . . I remember the "guise dancing" when the villagers went about in masks, entering the houses and frightening the children.'

For the next half-dozen years the boy lived in the remote mining village of Halsetown, a clutch of small grey-stone houses, bare and desolate, in the brown hills above St Ives. 'It was a wild and weird spot,' he later wrote, 'fascinating in its own peculiar beauty', though disfigured by the slag heaps from the mines. Here he was looked after by his aunt, a woman whose severe simplicity of dress reinforced her primitive religious beliefs. Aunt Sarah 'frightened us by her terrible "iron-bound" Calvinism,' he remembered; 'her awful theories as to its being necessary to be "Elect" to be saved.' In her late eighties she was to write begging him to give up the stage and return to God. She had married a captain of mines, Isaac Penberthy, a giant of a man, ferociously bearded, with an explosive temper and a generous heart. 'He was a man born to command and to be loved. I can hardly describe how dominating was his personality.'

In later years it would be said that John Brodribb's interest in the stage was ignited by a Cornish impresario, Father Crink of Carbis Bay, whose company of actors, travelling from village to village, would anchor its tent in the lonely hills and re-enact blood-and-thunder melodramas, reverberating with hideous murders and deeds of terrible revenge, from which the villagers scuttled nervously back through the night along the precipitous unlit paths to their homes. Touring companies from the east too would occasionally sail into St Ives and give performances of Shakespeare's histories in the Assembly Rooms. The boy also remembered the celebrated lion tamer Van Ambrugh, whom he saw one summer in Bristol with his father, a glorious figure, exotically dressed, who entered 'a den of roaring but intimidated lions'.

'Acting is part of human nature', he was to write. The children in Cornwall had 'a passion for dressing-up' and pretending they were people 'quite different from themselves' – though this practice was frowned upon by some adults. One Christmas party near Bristol he later described as being a 'rehearsal for my professional life'. It took place in a long darkened room at one end of which, in 'a nice, uncomfortable ghostly light', the children paraded wearing the most fanciful costumes their parents could afford. Suddenly they were paralysed by the appearance from behind a curtain of 'an intruder from another world . . . an awful deathly face with heavy eyelids and a drooping face . . . the whole room gave a low long wail . . . I was terror-struck'. Later it was discovered that their host's son had borrowed a death mask from his father's study and 'frightened us to death with it' – for which he was severely punished. 'Such was my first ghost and the most successful I have ever known.'

Another dramatic influence may have been Isaac Penberthy himself.

Returning home unexpectedly one afternoon and finding his wife was out, he terrified John by suddenly smashing the chairs and even a table – anything he could find – in a volcanic rage before striding off back to the mines. When Sarah came back and saw the havoc, she quietly suspended the broken fragments of furniture along the walls of the kitchen, like a surreal exhibition of artwork. That night Isaac entered the house, saw this strange narrative of his temper displayed and exploded into laughter.

Isaac and Sarah had three children of their own, so John was never wholly alone. They were good enough friends, though he was naturally set apart, not being their brother. One day, at the age of seven, he rambled over the desolate hills down to the seashore and the rocks – 'the sea had a potent attraction for me' – and was lost for several hours. It was around this time that he began to develop a stammer. Once a year, in the summer holidays, he would take the hazardous paddle-steamer from St Ives to Bristol and stay there with his parents. His mother dreamed that one day he would enter the Methodist ministry and was pleased to hear that the small dame school which he was attending in Halsetown made use of the Bible to teach the children reading and writing.

At the end of 1848 Isaac Penberthy suddenly died. His widow could no longer afford to keep John in Cornwall, and so his parents, having recently moved to London, sent for him to join them.

John Brodribb was aged eleven when he arrived in London, a wiry youth with a pale freckled face, solemn expression, sloping forehead and penetrating eyes. He had by now a pronounced speech impediment that, like an echo from the interrupted rhythm of his childhood, made him an unpromising candidate for the ministry.This was a great disappointment to his mother. But his father had other plans. He had described himself as a linen draper at the time of his son's birth, but now lived rent-free at the top of a house in Old Broad Street, receiving an uncertain income as its caretaker. He was keen for his son to enter the business world and soon arranged for John to go to the City Commercial School nearby in George Yard. Its headmaster, Dr Pinches, was a beatific gentleman with silver hair and a small perpetually smiling face, whose theory of education rested in the belief that legible writing, correct grammar and spelling, reinforced by fine elocution, were the foundation of a successful career.

It was the elocution class that appealed most strongly to John Brodribb. At the end of each term Dr Pinches held a Speech Day at Sussex Hall. John, practising how to overcome his stammer, mastering the phrases he found most awkward by stubborn repetition, carefully prepared his speech. He wanted to deliver a long macabre poem chronicling a savage retribution, but was persuaded by Dr Pinches to try something less extreme. In the audience that Speech Day was an actor, William Creswick, who became aware that something about this boy, the intensity of his concentration perhaps, was out of the ordinary. After the performance, he went up and congratulated him – to the consternation of his mother who fiercely disapproved of her son's passion for play-acting. With Dr Pinches's encouragement, the boy begged his father to take him to a professional theatre, and his mother eventually gave her consent on the understanding that they went to a respectable play by Mr Shakespeare. The play they saw was *Hamlet*. It was produced at Sadler's Wells by Samuel Phelps, a tall, commanding, slightly ponderous actor of the heroic school. He had converted Sadler's Wells from a barbarous den of clowning and spectacle, where performances were nightly drowned by uproar and disorder, into a home for classic theatre. By sticking to his text, training his company, using fine scenery and creating grand effects, he hushed the audiences with powerful interpretations of Shakespeare. Modelling his declamatory style on the great William Macready, Phelps was rather more effective in comedy than tragedy (his rallying of Polonius and exchanges with the gravediggers were high points in his performance). That evening at Sadler's Wells held the boy riveted. 'He hung upon the lovely words so clearly spoken . . . [and] was thrilled to find the theatre an arena in which deadly rivals contended for popular favour, where loyalties and dislikes were loudly voiced and the atmosphere before and behind the footlights was charged with excitement and passion.'

To be part of this passionate world where his pent-up feelings might be eloquently released, his roughness of speech absorbed within rhythms of words he could not find himself, became a necessity. After he left school at the age of thirteen, his ordinary life had settled into Dickensian drudgery, working as a clerk first at a solicitor's office in Milk Street, Cheapside, and then at a firm of East India merchants in Newgate Street from half past nine until seven o'clock six days a week, and then every Sunday accompanying his mother to chapel. He had no wish to be a merchant or a minister. But what could he do?

Outside his hours of work he began to establish the regime he needed to liberate himself from his parents' ambitions. Each morning he rose at five and went swimming in the Thames to strengthen his physique. He also attended a school of arms in Chancery Lane where he learnt to handle the properties of romantic drama – swords, rapiers and daggers. In the evenings, still dressed in his clerk's uniform of black suit and Eton collar, he hurried off to the City elocution class to practise recitations. 'He was beginning to get the measure of his stammer,' wrote his grandson-biographer, 'and succeeded in hiding it entirely from his new fellow-students – only at the cost of hours of patient labour by himself, repeating each difficult syllable slowly, distinctly, and again and again.'

At the age of fifteen he was still extraordinarily thin, eating little beyond bread and butter and spending what money he earned on the fees and tickets of his self-enforced tuition. Some evenings, unknown to his parents, he would steal off to the Adelphi Theatre to witness its exciting melodramas and farces, or return to Sadler's Wells where Samuel Phelps was working conscientiously through what seemed to be the entire Shakespeare canon. Here he met one of the actors in the company, who gave him private tuition in comedy and pantomime after his swimming each day and who, impressed by the boy's determination, introduced him to the great Samuel Phelps. 'Sir, do not go on to the stage; it is an ill-requited profession', the veteran actor warned him. But John declared that nothing would stop him. 'In that case,' Phelps said, 'you'd better come here and I'll give you two pounds a week to begin with.'

Such an offer must have been beyond his dreams when, almost three years earlier, he had seen Phelps play *Hamlet.* 'He was the greatest actor I ever saw', the boy maintained, '– or ever shall see.' But then he politely turned down Phelps's offer.

Why had he sought this interview if it was not to join the Sadler's Wells Company? Possibly Phelps had indicated that there was an alternative route to success via the provincial stock companies. Perhaps, too, having been told so often by his mother that going to the theatre was entering the gates of hell, he knew that he must leave home before embarking on this career. Whatever the reason, it would be seen in later years as a wise decision. He came away, not with a contract from Phelps, but a letter of recommendation from his actor friend to the manager of a new theatre that was being built in

Sunderland – to be presented whenever he felt ready to take up a professional engagement there.

In the summer of 1856 he had a piece of good fortune – a legacy of £100 from an uncle. With this he was able to equip himself with some essential items: several spectacular wigs, an assortment of feathers and buckles, various pieces of stage jewellery, a dagger and three splendid fencing swords. To test some of these new properties, he purchased the part of Romeo in an amateur production of *Romeo and Juliet* at the Soho Theatre. For this performance he had to choose a stage name – a name which would protect his mother from public humiliation (he had by this time moved out of the family home and put up in lodgings at Romford in Essex). He rather favoured the name 'Barringtone' which struck him as having a good ring to it. But, shortly before the playbills were printed, announcing in bold black lettering his 'First Appearance', he changed his mind. 'I have determined on taking the name Irving instead of Barringtone and have accordingly ordered fifty cards', he wrote to a friend.

He chose Henry as his forename, and as 'Henry Irving' decked himself out with a red velvet costume, white cotton tights, some blue ribbons for his shoes, a black-feathered hat and at his side a glittering court sword. Then he applied the dry caking powder to his face giving himself a mask on which to paint his character – and experiencing a wonderful transformation as he stepped on to the boards that night and began to speak Romeo's lines, lines whose accents and inflexions he had studied so carefully in the secrecy of his bedroom.

The production soon fell into confusion – Irving lost his way in the wings, felt the new wig slide off his head, mislaid his dagger and waited endlessly for his fellow-actors to recover their lines. But he delivered his own lines, Shakespeare's lines, without hesitation amid the encircling chaos. 'I played Romeo in Shakespeare's *Romeo and Juliet* at the Soho Theatre here (London) very successfully indeed', he wrote with an understandable sense of triumph. Having emerged from this ordeal, he decided the time had come for him to be 'Henry Irving' for good. He had finally chosen to 'forsake the dull mechanical work of an office', he told a fellow clerk and 'try my fortunes in the Dramatic profession'. Giving in his notice, he returned home to tell his parents. He had prepared a treatise on acting and the stage. True actors, he believed, were 'created like poets'. He was born to be an actor, a true poetic actor who, if fortune favoured him, might become 'one of the companions of the master spirits of the age' and rank as a gentleman and scholar 'among Royalty and the aristocracy'. He had marshalled these rhetorical arguments like a barrister in court. But there was to be no appeal from his mother's judgement. His choice of career was an insult to her. She had become reconciled to the fact that his laboured speech made him unfit to be a Methodist minister – only to be told that he could find his tongue well enough for evil purposes. Though she would not cease to pray for him, she believed his soul was damned. She never forgave him for this wickedness and vanished from his life, dying of typhoid in April 1862 at the age of fifty-four before he had a chance to show his worth. But his father, who returned to Bristol to live with his brother, was to take pride in his son's career and keep scrapbooks of his performances.

Irving was now eighteen. In the face of such discouragement, what had given him his perseverance? It seems as if he had a deeply planted need to leave his parents, as they had left him when he was a child. His aunt, like his mother, had prescribed the Church for him and it may have been as a form of refusal, when confronted by their plans, that he developed his stammer. Only by abandoning himself, John Henry Brodribb, his parents' son, and becoming someone else – indeed, many other characters onstage – could he gain confidence and find coherence of speech. Having sent off his friend's letter of recommendation, he travelled up to the New Royal Lyceum Theatre in Sunderland, not knowing what would happen.

15
Entrances and Exits

'Here's to our enterprise!' These were Henry Irving's first words when, in September 1856, as Gaston, Duke of Orleans, in Bulwer Lytton's *Richelieu*, he made his professional entrance onstage. Over the next ten years he worked hard to learn his craft, developing a wide repertoire of roles from saints and devils to low comedians and heavy leads. Sometimes he was merely a Walking Gentleman, but he also played an imbecile in a farce, sang in opera and danced in burlesque. He became all sorts of villains and aristocrats in patriotic military and naval dramas, appeared as Scruncher, Captain of the Wolves, in *Little Bo-Peep*, then as an Ogre in *Puss in Boots*, also as the very wicked Venoma in *The Sleeping Beauty* and as one of the Ugly Sisters in *Cinderella*. He was an Irishman, a Frenchman and an Indian Prince who, in *The Relief of Lucknow*, had to contend with elephants, camels and bulls. Using the technique of applying water-colours with brushes (dark blue bones, red for the ears and a white countenance), which he never gave up for greasepaint, he gained cunning in the use of make-up. But there were many setbacks in becoming 'what I long wished to be – an actor' – failures and humiliations when, in moments of anxiety, his 'half-conquered speech impediment' broke from its secret prison to harass him. Audiences mocked the peculiar rhythm of jerky vowels and elongated syllables in his rural accent, mocked his disfiguring mannerisms, his short-sightedness, and the dragging gait on bent knees with which he unevenly perambulated the stage. In Dublin, he was met by 'a raging Irish audience, shouting, gesticulating, swearing volubly, and in various forms indicating their disapproval of my appearance', he wrote. 'Night after night, I had to fight through my part in the teeth of a house whose entire energies seemed to be concentrated in a personal antipathy to myself.' Elsewhere he was booed and hissed, met with a chorus of cat-calls and advised to give up his aspirations and return home. But he had no home and, cutting off his retreat, the bereft and loveless John Brodribb came to the aid of Henry Irving. His apprenticeship, and then his career, became an unending struggle to master his faults in diction, to manipulate the mobile features that were evolving from a rather ordinary face and, in short, to gain perfection. By the time this apprenticeship was over and he established himself in London, he had played more than 700 characters.

He travelled around the provincial stock companies from Sunderland to Glasgow, Dublin, Liverpool, Birmingham, Bristol and many other places in his long journey back to London. He was learning not only from practice but also from observation. In Edinburgh he saw the legendary Barry Sullivan, 'the prince of barnstormers' without an equal in bravura acting, whose resounding voice, magically rising and falling, held his audience in thrall. In Paris he observed the craftsmanship, deriving from Molière, of the Comédie Française. And in Manchester he came across the actor of his dreams, the great American tragedian Edwin Booth whose 'exalted treatment of Hamlet's mystery' became an inspiration to him. 'He was the star which floated across our horizon, bright, brilliant, buoyant, full of vigour and fire and genius', Irving remembered. 'An example to young actors.'

In 1866, at the Prince's Theatre, Manchester, Irving played an unscrupulous adventurer in Boucicault's *The Two Lives of Mary Leigh* opposite Kate Terry. The part suited him and he received an invitation from Louisa Herbert, the manager of the St James's Theatre in London, to join her company. At last he had won his way back to the capital, it seemed, but, as his wooden performance the following year with Ellen Terry in Garrick's *Katharine and Petruchio* showed, he was not ready yet for London.

The reviews he received measured a steady improvement in his acting. As a juvenile lead his 'good presence' and 'intellectual head and eye' had been noted as had his 'jerky walk and stiff neck and spasmodic elocution'. Critics observed how, when playing tragedy, for example, he sometimes found it 'difficult to avoid the gait and mien of comedy'. He was recognised as an accomplished light comedian with 'a gift for interpreting polished villainy'. But he had picked up some disconcerting tricks – 'licking his lips, wrinkling his forehead and speaking through his nose'. Not all critics welcomed the novelty of his acting which avoided the grand artificialities of the old school.

But Charles Dickens picked him out to be 'a great actor' one day, and G.H. Lewes, who saw him on his return to London play in Boucicault's *Hunted Down*, predicted that 'in twenty years he will be at the head of the English stage'. George Eliot believed he already was the best actor in the country.

Most of this time, earning between 30 shillings and £3 a week, he had lived in cheap lodgings, the cheapest he could find, along dilapidated streets all over the country. At Sunderland the only room he could afford was two and a half miles from the theatre and he walked to and from it each day carrying his costumes in a stage bag. He had been paid nothing during these first weeks and fell quickly into debt. On a freezing Christmas Day, he was invited to take dinner at the lodgings of a fellow actor who pointed with some embarrassment to a suit of warm underclothes hanging up above his bed. 'Upon my word, I think you'd probably better put them on', he said. 'It gets deuced cold.' Left alone, Irving sat down and burst into tears. It was an act of kindness he never forgot. His money troubles persisted and over these touring years he often had to borrow from moneylenders. He worked sixteen hours a day and was sometimes in desperate need, driven to accept odd half-crowns from fellow actors. He was haunted too by the fear that he might have overestimated his talent. But his insecurities evaporated when he was in the company of actors. He treated them as if they were his family. 'At the theatre you were surrounded by cheerful and happy faces who always greet you with a smile', he wrote in one of his letters on tour. Naturally there were rivalries, but for the most part these theatres were convivial places, while in his lodgings, a wet towel around his head, he went over his lines so diligently that he lost all sense of being lonely. 'I do everything in bachelor style and enjoy myself alone', he wrote. He was gaining extraordinary control of himself and great discipline over his emotions. He lived only for his work and in later years would allow himself one relaxation in *Who's Who*: 'acting'.

While in Manchester during the early 1860s, Irving fell in love with 'the sweetest and prettiest girl' he had ever met. She was a charming young actress called Nellie Moore. She had, we are told, 'a round face, with wide-set eyes, a fair complexion and a mass of golden hair which she wore with a fringe'. He wrote regularly to her after she went off to the Haymarket in London but, as he told his father, 'I have no engagement or prospect whatever of marriage'.

By the autumn of 1867, when he was playing at the St James's Theatre in

London, everything appeared about to change. He was still poor, too poor as yet to propose marriage, but he was happy to be seeing Nellie again and she appeared happy to be seeing him. Now in his thirtieth year Irving had become a striking figure, his pale complexion accentuated by raven-dark hair, and eyes 'beneath dark brows, glittering with the exaltation of success'. He was not conventionally handsome, but all the more fascinating for that: someone losing his rawness, growing more distinguished in manner, whose sensitivity was partly covered by a sense of power arising from the natural strength of his acting. Henry Irving had almost wholly replaced John Brodribb.

At Christmas 1867 Irving was invited by the drama critic of the *Sunday Times*, Clement Scott, to a party at his home and, turning up at the wrong address, was confronted by a distinguished-looking young woman, Florence O'Callaghan, who by coincidence had also been invited to Scott's party. He escorted her there and that evening she fell in love with him.

Nellie Moore, like Ellen Terry, came from a family of actors; Florence O'Callaghan's family were gentlemen and soldiers, some of 'the master spirits of the age' with whom, Irving believed, the exceptional actor could naturally keep company. Unfortunately Florence's parents thought otherwise. Exercising a far-ranging authority over his family from an Indian outpost of the empire where he was serving as Surgeon-General, Florence's father forbade her from seeing Irving for a year. But Florence treated any opposition as an incentive, employing her grandmother as go-between and making the affaire excitingly clandestine. She was all the more determined to have this actor for a husband. Her mother Elizabeth, who dreamed of her marrying into the aristocracy, was equally determined that she should not throw herself away on a mere mummer whose elevated roles onstage – as kings, dukes and emperors – seemed to mock these heady ambitions for her daughter. So Irving found himself caught between the fell incensèd points of mighty opposites.

The victim in this drama was Nellie Moore. She and Irving had lately grown rather self-conscious with each other, made so by the green room gossip of their fellow actors. An indefinable shadow fell between them and even before the entrance of Florence O'Callaghan their romance had been waning. Irving, feeling himself free to do as he wished, thought he saw in Florence another version of himself: someone of spirit and courage who needed to be rescued from an unloving family. When her mother appealed to him to be candid and declare himself as unsuitable for Florence's hand in marriage, he felt this as a spur. He must rescue his self-esteem and defend the respectability of the acting profession. The Surgeon-General, on his return from India, found to his surprise that this actor had perfectly good table manners, could drink a glass or two of punch well enough and come out with an amusing flow of conversation. He showed a peculiar stiffness in the drawing-room that was almost too correct. Since his daughter still insisted on marrying the man, he withdrew his objections and, to Elizabeth O'Callaghan's dismay (Irving having proposed to Florence at Hyde Park Corner) they became formally engaged in April 1869.

But as these obstacles disappeared, so other uncertainties rose up in their place. To Florence's consternation, Nellie Moore had joined the Queen's Theatre where Irving was then playing. Florence could not resist writing him a letter listing the derogatory stories she had heard about her young rival – pages that Irving read with anger. He knew that Nellie was naturally affectionate and, still only twenty-three, was winning a reputation as one of the most promising actresses in the theatre. They had played very happily opposite each other as Bill Sikes and Nancy in a dramatisation of *Oliver Twist* and then again with equal success in Boucicault's *London Assurance.*

In the spring of 1869, Nellie fell mysteriously ill. Some said it was typhus, others scarlet fever. The weeks passed and, knowing her family to be abroad, Irving asked a mutual friend, Laura Friswell, to call at her home and find out what could be done to help her. But when Laura arrived at the house, its blinds drawn against the light, she met Irving himself walking dejectedly away – and he told her Nellie was dead. What he did not tell her was his discovery that Nellie had been pregnant and had died as the result of an abortion. Her secret lover was apparently a fellow-actor, a married man and high comedian whom Irving considered his friend but who had helped to put an end to their romance. Nellie's brother, hearing this actor's stories, had told her that 'Irving would never be worth a bunch of dog's meat'.

The depression into which he descended led to a conviction that Nellie had been the true love of his life whom he should have married. Instead he was engaged to Florence. She loved him – he had no doubt of that – and she had been prepared to champion him against her parents. He had let poor Nellie down; he could not, with honour, let Florence down too. He was in his thirty-second year and had existed all this time without love. But his career was prospering and it was time to marry. Nevertheless, ostensibly for financial reasons, he postponed their wedding until the summer.

They were married at the parish church of St Marylebone on 15 July 1869, Irving giving his rank or profession as 'Comedian' and that of his father as 'Gentleman'. None of his family came to the wedding, and he had agreed with Florence beforehand that, though legally she would become Mrs Brodribb, their children should be given the surname Irving.

During the next three years Irving was to fulfil the great promise which critics had seen in him. He became recognised both as a grimly humorous comedian and as a character actor of wit and imagination. When he stood before the curtain at the Vaudeville Theatre, where he had given a wonderful performance as a Dickensian comic character, and recited Thomas Hood's terrible story of a conscience-stricken schoolmaster in 'The Dream of Eugene Aram', the audience was held in motionless silence by the power of his tragic acting. 'It was such acting as is now seldom seen', wrote a critic in the *Observer*.

Among those who rose to their feet and gave him a rapturous ovation was an American impresario, Hezekiah Bateman, who had recently taken a long lease of the Lyceum Theatre. He immediately offered Irving the position of leading actor there. It was, as Irving explained to his father, 'the most important business engagement I have ever made . . . I am engaged for three years at the Lyceum . . . at a weekly salary of fifteen pounds for the first year – £17 for the second and £19 for the third. The engagement to commence in September [1871].'

Bateman, known as 'the Colonel', was a hospitable family man as well as a passionate man of the theatre. He had married a playwright and given up acting himself to become a showman-manager dedicated to furthering the theatrical careers of his four daughters. His daughter Ellen, to his disappointment, had retired from the theatre on her marriage, but Virginia had married an actor and Kate was making a name for herself in a popular historical drama of doomed love between a Jewess and a Christian. Bateman hoped that his favourite daughter, seventeen-year-old Isabel, would rise to stardom beside Irving. But Isabel did not wish to be an actress and had gone on the stage merely to please her parents (after their deaths she entered a convent). Her range as an actress was narrow, but her limitations went unrecognised by her father who chose, as the first play in which she appeared with Irving, a French comedy that had been rewritten by his wife so as to enlarge their daughter's role beyond her capabilities. Equally ill-suited was their second play at the Lyceum, an unconvincing adaptation of *The Pickwick Papers*. 'Very bad indeed', noted the drama critic of the *Daily Telegraph*, E.L. Blanchard, in his diary, 'and I think Bateman must soon give it up.'

The Lyceum, which had a history of fires and bankruptcies, was regarded as an ill-omened theatre, and Bateman, now facing bankruptcy himself, was kept going with financial help from his daughter Kate. It was then that Irving stepped forward and reminded him of a promise he had made on engaging him: that he would be allowed to play the lead in an adaptation of a French melodrama called *The Bells*. Bateman, who had forgotten this agreement, was horrified. It would, he believed, be the end of all his ambitions. But Irving insisted, reminding him of what he had done on a bare stage before the curtain, without scenery, incidental music or dramatic lighting, when reciting 'The Dream of Eugene Aram'. *The Bells*, which told the story of an impoverished innkeeper called Mathias who murders a rich traveller and, with the victim's money, becomes a much-honoured civic dignitary, used the device of a dream through which a haunted conscience manifests itself and exacts retribution. There was something in this theme that strongly appealed to Irving, the echo of an unconscious guilt perhaps at having obliterated the very name of his family and grown successful by exploiting the impediments of John Brodribb, turning his defects into theatrical tricks for public entertainment. According to Gordon Craig, Irving 'existed as Mathias – gave it his life'.

It was unlikely that Bateman would have acceded to this proposal from anyone except Irving. The theatre man recognised in the actor someone who risked everything to attain excellence on the stage; the family man responded to someone who had lived so long without the support of a family – and whom he sought to integrate within his own family. So despite his forebodings, he reluctantly agreed to produce *The Bells*.

What Irving achieved during the late winter of 1871 was to raise a mediocre historical drama to the status of a dramatic masterpiece. Comparing the great French actor, Constant Coquelin, in the role of Mathias with Irving's interpretation of his character, the playwright Henry Arthur Jones saw

Coquelin as determined to prove a villain whereas Irving was any one of us, an innocent man who, of a sudden, gives in to temptation. The power of his performance held audiences in agonised suspense, and he became the talk of London. *The Bells* played to crowded houses for 150 performances and would gain increasing fame over the next thirty-five years as part of Irving's repertoire. His extraordinary achievement came from having grafted on to the role of the innkeeper-burgomaster something from within himself – something too that found an echo in the Victorian conscience. He had saved Bateman's fortunes and would soon be seen as a saviour of the British theatre.

But as Irving the actor prospered, so Brodribb the husband began to suffer. Florence had been attracted by his strangeness, by the courage and determination with which he walked alone towards what he believed to be his destiny. As his wife she wanted to draw him out of his loneliness and make good what he had suffered through the years. But he had no talent for domesticity and appeared locked in mysterious isolation. She could not reach him. He lived in what seemed to be an adjunct to a theatre rather than a home. She did not really enjoy the company of actors with their drinking and laughter and endless talk about this or that production of one play and another. Yet these gatherings seemed to give her husband more pleasure than all the time he spent with her. Florence was not someone who would accept such a situation meekly. But when she upbraided him for letting his work trespass into their home, he rented cheap lodgings in Drury Lane where he could study his roles without interruption. This was not the outcome she expected.

On 5 February 1870 Florence gave birth to a son whom they christened Henry ('Harry') Brodribb Irving, and this brought them closer for a time. But before the end of the year their arguments broke out again. By December they agreed to part and Irving found rooms for himself in Mount Street. His friend Henry Labouchere was not surprised. 'He [Irving] was in no way cut out for a married man', he wrote in a letter to Stephen Coleridge, '& I doubt whether the marriage would have been a success with anyone.' Florence had an allowance from her family of £500 a year which Irving agreed to supplement with an extra £4 a week whenever he was working. Once a fortnight his son Harry was brought to see him and they would spend the day together. 'It will be useless seeing the dear little fellow oftener *now* for he is but a baby and not at the most important age', he wrote.

Early in the New Year Florence came and asked for a reconciliation. Irving agreed and went off to look for a new apartment where they could restart their married life. Their letters to each other show a strong physical attraction. 'When I kissed you last night it gave me delicious ecstasy', Irving wrote to her. But the correspondence also reveals the incompatibility of their temperaments (Irving would issue instructions to her as if she were a servant). Nevertheless 'our married life is to recommence on, I think, a firm and happy footing', he told his father on 24 January 1871. He described Florence as 'an altered woman', and 'Master Henry is a perfect picture of health and beauty. He really is a magnificent fellow.'

A little later they took a three-year lease on a house in West Brompton for £52 10*s* a year. 'I have already been obliged to scrape together all I could for payments becoming due', Irving wrote on 6 June. One of his reasons for taking this lease was to calm Florence's financial worries. 'I know you're inclined to fidget about the future', he had written to her on 18 May 1871 while on tour in Dublin. 'Don't think I am so unmanly and cowardly as to leave you encumbered with debt.'

They moved into their new house and by September Irving was confiding to his father that 'Flo is very well and very happy and delighted to have me with her again and seems to have taken a new view of everything . . . Her devotion to our boy is extraordinary and a lovely noble-looking fellow he is.'

But Irving's instinct, so alert in theatrical affairs, was blind to the nuances of personal relationships. He simply did not know what Florence was thinking or feeling and could not pick up signs from how she looked or clues from her tone of voice. She was again pregnant, but her husband's time and energy were devoted to his work. The truth was inescapable: Irving loved the theatre far more than her, their son and their unborn child. He placed a world of bright lights above the needs of his family. She had come to realise that there was something fundamentally wrong with him and, with surprise and consternation, Florence found that she could not change him, could not penetrate that solitude he carried within himself or match his single passion for the stage. As she waited outside the Lyceum in her brougham after the first performance of *The Bells*, waited in mounting irritation for him to detach himself from the braying crowds within, and heard the chorus of fatuous adulation spilling out on to the street, her anger rose. Tired almost beyond endurance, anxious to get home, convinced that her husband had actually forgotten her pregnancy, she was nevertheless obliged to go on to a celebratory supper and hear him praised by people who had no knowledge of the real Irving. No one else knew what he was like. The boredom, injustice and mockery of it were too much for her.

Irving himself was wonderfully happy after his triumph. He noticed that Florence was not joining in the tributes, perhaps not realising that his success would lead to their financial security. Returning home late that night in the brougham, he remarked they might soon be able to afford a carriage-and-pair. They were crossing Hyde Park Corner (the very place where Irving had proposed to her) when Florence finally broke her silence. 'Are you going on making a fool of yourself like this all your life?' she demanded.

This was Mrs Brodribb addressing Mr Brodribb, Mrs Brodribb telling him to get rid of Henry Irving, return to reality, and come home. She had chosen a peak in his career at which to make her protest. After twelve hard years he knew what he had accomplished that night, and could at last feel confident of his future. It was John Brodribb, not Henry Irving, who must be abandoned. He had left the other Mrs Brodribb, his mother, for a similar offence and knew what he must do.

Irving stopped the brougham at Hyde Park Corner, got out and walked off into the night. Instead of returning to West Brompton, he turned up at the Batemans' family home in Kensington Gore. That December his second son, Laurence Sidney Irving, was born, but Irving, who seems to have been drinking heavily during this period, did not attend the christening. In March 1872, he wrote to Florence laying down the terms and conditions of their future life: 'I have determined to live apart from you . . . this course is imperative for my sake and for the sake of those relying on me . . . On this subject my mouth for the future will be closed to friend and foe. And now goodbye.' Intermittently, over their lives, they would communicate with brusque if 'kindly intended' letters. 'You always have my kindest wishes', he assured her. But when, some twenty-five years later, their son Harry announcing his marriage, Florence used the occasion to propose their coming together, Irving replied: 'The paths we have chosen we shall always keep. This I wrote sometime ago and now I am compelled to repeat it.'

16

Their Coronation

Over the next half-dozen years, Irving established himself as the most popular actor on the London stage. The public besieged him with gifts – scrolls, caskets, cups, pistols, medals. He was presented with the late eighteenth-century Shakespearean actor John Philip Kemble's dagger, with his predecessor, the romantic performer Edmund Kean's purse (given to him by Robert Browning), a walking-stick used by David Garrick, a circular snuff-box formed from wood believed to have been cut from Shakespeare's mulberry tree; and then, among more miscellaneous trophies, a blunderbuss, a fox which fortunately escaped, and a kangaroo which was escorted to the zoo. Less troublesome was the free membership of the Midlothian Swimming Club and preferential shares in the Henry Irving Silver Mine Company in New South Wales. He attracted people of all classes to the theatre, giving them a procession of historical pageants and melodramas that made the Lyceum a landmark in the romantic revival sweeping through the arts in Britain. Contemporary playwrights such as W.G. Wills, Bulwer Lytton and even Tennyson, he treated as tailors employed by a fashion house to cut their texts and redesign the facts of history to suit his acting skills and the wishes of his audience. One wit compared Wills to a traveller 'who uses a map of the Perthshire Highlands to find his way through the Swiss Alps', and characterised Bateman and Irving as his 'ardent fellow-travellers on this sentimental journey'. But Wills's adaptation of *The Vicar of Wakefield* had made Ellen Terry famous; and his *Charles I*, though bereft of dramatic ideas and a travesty of history, was a clever piece of stagecraft that depended almost wholly on Irving's gifts for its spectacular effect.

Irving enjoyed playing kings, counts, princes, noblemen. Bulwer Lytton rewrote *Richelieu* for him (modelled on the portrait by Philippe de

Champaigne) so that he could challenge Macready, or rather present a new style of acting that depended on expressiveness of feature and idiosyncratic gesture. His Cardinal was reported in the Paris newspaper, *La Presse*, as looking 'lean, worn, eaten up by ambition . . . His gait jerky, like that of a man shaken by fever; his eye has the depth of a visionary; a hoarse cough preys upon his frail body which is yet made of steel.' What appeared to exalt Irving was the paradoxical connection between frailty and strength, and also the overwhelming of innocence – the complacency of falsely-based innocence – by remorse: a tragic theme which he brilliantly portrayed in an adaptation of Balzac's story of misdirected revenge, *La Grande Bretèche*.

The best-known image of Irving at this period of his career is an 'arrangement' by Whistler, a glittering ghostly study in black and silver, showing him as the fanatical King Philip II of Spain in Tennyson's dramatic panorama *Queen Mary*. As Irving was beginning to match himself against the great actors of a previous generation – William Macready and Barry Sullivan – so Whistler used this opportunity to compare his portraiture with that of Titian who had painted the living Philip II. Indeed, Whistler would have liked to paint Irving in all his characters. 'It is ridiculous that Irving should not be painted – and who else shall paint him?' he demanded. Irving gave him a few sittings but there was no fire in the studio and the sessions were frequently interrupted by creditors demanding payment. Irving was not altogether comfortable with the artist (he would later use his famous laugh to blood-curdling effect when playing Mephistopheles). Nor did he particularly like the picture which was eventually knocked down to him for £30 following Whistler's bankruptcy. After Irving's death it was sold at Christie's for £5,000 and eventually found its way to the Metropolitan Museum in New York.

Ellen Terry had been horribly impressed by Irving's portrayal of King Philip. 'He never did anything better to the day of his death', she was to write. '. . . The horrid, dead look, the cruel unresponsiveness, the indifference of the creature! . . . It was the perfection of quiet malignity . . . I was just spellbound by a study in cruelty, which seemed to me a triumphant assertion of the power of the actor to create as well as to interpret, for Tennyson does not suggest half of what Henry Irving did.'

At the end of this successful season of 1874, Irving proposed reintroducing Shakespeare to the Lyceum stage. Of all Shakespeare's characters, he most resembled Malvolio at this point in his life: a high comedian, ambitious, needing yet incapable of comprehending love, pompous, poignant, who is brought to the bitterness of vowing revenge 'on the whole pack of you'. But, to Bateman's dismay, it was to the tragedy of *Hamlet* that Irving was inevitably drawn.

It was his bravest choice of role so far. He was comparing himself to legendary performers – Thomas Betterton, David Garrick, Edmund Kean – and demonstrating that there was a modern way of revealing Hamlet's character. Irving valued Shakespeare less as a dramatic poet than as an actor who knew how to provide opportunities for other actors, virtuoso actors, over all time.

Ellen Terry was taken by Tom Taylor to see the opening night of Irving's *Hamlet* on 31 October 1874. She noticed at once how pale his make-up made him look against the blue-black tone of his hair and how beautiful his haggard face appeared. Without any bombast, the first two acts were presented as a domestic drama. His Hamlet was a royal dilettante, unusually quiet, like a scholar thinking aloud. 'Henry Irving did not go to the audience', she wrote. 'He made them come to him.' This, she realised, was a far more skilful feat of acting than the antics he would go through when mounted upon such 'artificial high horses' as Bulwer Lytton's *Richelieu* and Wills's *Charles I*. In *Hamlet* he remained solitary on stage. He was courteous, even humorous, and evidently on terms of easy conviviality with Rosencrantz and Guildenstern – as Irving himself was with the Batemans and his fellow actors. He was not frightened by the ghost of his father, but exalted; for under his pleasant manner he was working out a devious strategy for revenge. He threw aside his assumed madness in the potent scene with his mother as he assaulted her conscience and appealed for her penitence – revelatory moments to which he brought a terrible earnestness. So, over five and a half hours (including the long intervals for change of scene and costumes) the tension mounted and, Ellen saw, 'attention gave place to admiration, admiration to enthusiasm, and enthusiasm to triumphant acclaim'.

The rest was theatre history. *Hamlet* ran for 200 nights and created a precedent for Shakespeare productions. It was magnificent: but was it really Shakespeare? Irving had cut 1,216 lines from the text (about 40 per cent), omitting Fortinbras, Prince of Norway, diminishing the roles of Rosencrantz and Guildenstern, weeding out some obscenities and simplifying the action by reducing Shakespeare's twenty scenes to thirteen. His acting edition, as the critic Alan Hughes observes, made Hamlet more lovable. When he was to play opposite Ellen Terry, he would restore some passages so as to emphasise Hamlet's longing for Ophelia (a longing he must resist), which he had taken out when playing opposite Isabel Bateman. So far as Bateman himself was concerned (despite some criticism from his daughter), these cuts proved, as with *The Bells*, the sureness of Irving's theatrical instinct. To honour his friend, and celebrate their wonderful partnership, Bateman hosted a great banquet at the Pall Mall restaurant, Haymarket, after the one hundredth performance. The following morning, as he was dressing, he had a heart attack and died.

Bateman had been Irving's one true friend and most generous companion, promoting his theatrical career and making up with the company of his own family at Kensington Gore for his lack of a home life. Though Irving would continue to pass much of his time with Mrs Bateman and her actress-daughters, he had recently 'pitched my tent' in lodgings at 15a Grafton Street, on the corner of Bond Street, in the dim light of which he was to remain for the next thirty years.

At the Lyceum, where Mrs Bateman assumed the managership, it was business as usual. After *Hamlet*, Irving took on *Macbeth*, *Othello* and *Richard III*, all of which wildly excited his admirers and gave fresh ammunition to his enemies. At this phase in his career, Henry James was the most percipient of his hostile critics. Among the strong points James noticed were his clever inventions of manner and movement, the picturesque 'colour' he often lent his characters, and above all his 'great skill in the representation of terror'. And yet, by the artistic standards of the Comédie Française, he struck Henry James's fastidious mind as being a very incomplete actor. His 'personal gifts' – face, figure, voice, enunciation – were meagre, and his declamatory powers flat and charmless. He succeeded best, James concluded, in roles where 'his defects positively came to his assistance'. Among these were Charles Reade's adaptation, *The Lyons Mail*, in which he played the dual roles of villain and hero. Henry Arthur Jones remembered his patting a horse as he murdered a postboy and being, as the critic Peter Thomson remarks, 'more terrifying in his gaiety than in his terror'.

Just as he bent Shakespeare to his purpose, so Irving made the work of lesser dramatists into one-man performances. But while he came in for criticism in London for putting on weak plays in which he could dominate the stage, he met with growing popularity during his tours of the provinces. He took criticism very seriously, treating hostility to himself as being an attack on the entire acting profession. 'I plead for the actors, not merely that their labours have honour but that their lives be regarded with kindly consideration', he retaliated after one personal attack. 'Their work is hard, intensely laborious – feverish and dangerously exciting. It is all this even when successful.'

He was not much interested in other people's acting – it was as if he could not 'see' them, though he was affronted by poor acting. Some of his friends, however, had made him realise that a weak supporting cast could influence the success of a production to the point of throwing a shadow over his own performance. 'No actor in the world can carry a bad play and a bad company', Henry Labouchere warned him. Looking around him, he saw that it was not quite business as usual at the Lyceum after all. Mrs Bateman was promoting her daughters' careers even more zealously than her husband had done. To this professional embarrassment was added a more personal problem. The demure Isabel Bateman had fallen unhappily in love with him. She could not stop herself. Her mother was delighted (her sister Kate furious). Mrs Bateman was fond of Irving. The prospect of her youngest daughter becoming his partner in success, the success she had helped to contrive, greatly pleased her. But it acutely embarrassed Irving. He liked Isabel, but knew that she was a reluctant actress whose performances were becoming more constrained as her love for him grew. Besides, he was married – in his fashion – with two sons.

He decided to take the initiative and come up with a professional solution to the problem. In the summer of 1878 he sent a carefully drafted letter to Mrs Bateman. The new season was to open with *Hamlet* in which, it was presumed, Isabel would again play Ophelia. But Irving now wrote that he must be free to engage his own leading lady to provide him with stronger support, someone who would bring with her the goodwill of the public. Mrs Bateman's reply took him completely by surprise. She could not, she wrote, overlook the injury his proposal would inflict on Isabel if the role of Ophelia was taken from her, leaving her to lag superfluous. 'It would be an endorsement signed by you – *the friend of the family* and me – her mother – of her entire incompetency. I cannot by any selfish consideration lend myself to such an act of injustice for to do this and retire her from the stage would take from her the means of a livelihood when I am dead or when my time at the Lyceum is over . . . I think it would be better for our association in business to end now.' She therefore proposed handing over to Irving the remaining three years' lease of the Lyceum, and relaunching her daughters' careers elsewhere.

This was a generous proposal and Irving immediately accepted it. On 31 August 1878 Mrs Bateman formally surrendered the lease and announced that the Lyceum had been 'transferred to Mr Henry Irving, to whose attraction as an artist the prosperity of the theatre is entirely attributable'.

Though Irving was to lose his adopted family, he had been building up another kind of family – a hand-picked company of supporting actors, comedians mostly, whom he had met on his tours in the provinces and whose fierce loyalty to 'the Guv'nor' or 'Chief' formed a protective ring around him. In addition there was his devoted and indispensable valet, dresser and wig-maker, the diminutive bespectacled Walter Collinson, who attended him each day at Grafton Street. Later on a clever wordsmith, L.F. Austin, who had been the Baroness Angela Burdett-Coutts's secretary, joined the team and drafted many of Irving's letters and speeches. During rehearsals, Irving relied especially on his faithful stage manager, the gentle Harry Loveday, originally a violinist whose father had been Edmund Kean's music director at Drury Lane; and also, more generally, on Bram Stoker, a civil servant from Dublin, who had been drawn to the Lyceum by Irving's magnetic personality, who was to serve as his business-manager and become famous as the author of *Dracula*.

It was characteristic of Irving to choose his leading lady last of all – and then leave the choice to someone else. He had not seen Ellen Terry onstage since their ill-matched performance together in *Katharine and Petruchio* over ten years before. But she was recommended to him by someone whose judgement he had come to trust. Juliet Pollock was the wife of Sir Frederick Pollock, a famous jurist, who edited William Macready's *Reminiscences*. Both husband and wife were ardent admirers of Irving. 'Your future may be such as will make you one of the highest reputations in Europe for you have the rare quality of resolution in conquering a fault and of unceasing energy in cultivating a beauty', she had written to him in the summer of 1875 after seeing his *Hamlet* for the twenty-first time. 'You have won from your deep voice harmonies such as few believed it to possess . . . you have gained dignity and power. All this you have done under the pressure of a labour which was extraordinary – and now, be proud of it.' She kept his letters in a special casket and each day she read them they became more precious; and every night she saw him onstage she grew more aware of his strengths.

Here was a critic to whom Irving could listen. He was peculiarly susceptible to the authority of older women as if in some way they occupied the vacant role of his mother. So when she advised him to enrol Ellen Terry as his leading lady at the Lyceum and to give her the part of Ophelia, he wrote to Ellen and arranged to visit her at Longridge Road in the last week of July 1878. He was now aged forty (Ellen was thirty-one). A great change had taken place in him, she observed, since they had last met. Then, with his unwrinkled face, a sloping forehead and wearing an experimental moustache, he had looked very ordinary to her eyes. Nor did he impress her as being sympathetic in his manner, but 'conceited and almost savagely proud of the isolation in which he lived'. Her memory of him was of a man stiff in his ways, given to odd exaggerations, encased in self-consciousness. He was not graceful. 'No rigid person was ever graceful.' The one remarkable aspect was his melancholy. She remembered hearing him sigh – 'the deepest, profoundest, sincerest sigh I ever heard from any human being'. It was like the expiring breath of John Brodribb from within. But ten years later, Ellen observed, 'he had found himself and lost himself' – lost Brodribb, lost his mother, left his wife and lost his children – and also lost his substitute family, the Batemans. Ellen knew almost nothing of his parents and his wife, but over Isabel Bateman, from whose banishment she was about to benefit, she reasoned that he 'had to be a little cruel, not for the last time in a career devoted unremittingly and unrelentingly to his art and his ambition'.

Irving's art and his ambition had made a new man of him, the Mr Hyde whom Dr Jekyll had manufactured. 'His forehead had become more massive, and the very outline of his features had altered', Ellen wrote in her *Memoirs*. 'He was a man of the world, whose strenuous fighting now was to be done as a general – not, as hitherto, in the ranks. His manner was very quiet and gentle.'

Yet he was still distant, someone with whom it was impossible to get on easy terms. What helped him over this first meeting at Longridge Road was his dog. He had brought this dog along with him and, it was said that, made nervous by the tense atmosphere, it had defecated on Ellen's carpet – after which the formalities disintegrated. But even in these relaxed conditions, it was awkward for Irving to make his intentions quite clear. To his old master Dr Pinches he wrote: 'I have engaged Ellen Terry – not a bad start – eh?' But to Ellen herself he wrote nothing and, on the advice of her 'hefty protector' of a husband, she was obliged to write herself, asking for 'some definite proposition' and assuring him that, should he want 'me to be with you at the Lyceum next season', then she 'for my part most earnestly desire to be with you'.

So it was agreed that, at 40 guineas a week and half the takings from a benefit performance, Ellen would join the Lyceum company and give her opening performance as Ophelia – the character in which Watts had painted her all those years ago. But first she went to see Irving give his *Hamlet* again while on tour in Birmingham. It was even more wonderful, she thought, than when she went with Tom Taylor to see the first night in London. He knew she was in the audience and she felt that he was playing it 'for me'. Irving was to describe Hamlet as 'the most intensely human of all Shakespeare's creations', and the play itself he believed to be the *magnum opus* of a man with whom he felt a special affinity – a man born like himself a poor country boy, who had risen to success by his hard work and irrepressible talent.

Ellen was not intimidated by Irving as so many actors were. She had enough confidence in her own abilities. But he fascinated her. In place of the melancholy in earlier days, she detected in him an acute vulnerability to criticism – indeed, this had become his most obvious human quality. Of course every actor dreads hostile criticism, but Irving seemed neurotically sensitive. He had been booed, hissed and laughed at by audiences in his early days, greeted with howls of execration by the public as well as attacked by critics for his curious looks, his odd walk, his very face – all that was natural in him. He had soldiered on and come through, acquiring some dramatic camouflage along the way – tricks and mannerisms that were almost caricatures, some of them, of his natural self. Ellen found she could soothe his apprehensions as few others could. When he revealed that people had jeered at his spindly legs, she told him that they were beautiful legs and that there was no reason on earth to want fat legs like a prize-fighter's. He came to depend on her tact and humour as useful assets – to value them almost as much as he valued her acting, which he appeared to take for granted.

Though Ellen had been to see his *Hamlet*, he had not troubled to go to her *Olivia* – it was enough that Lady Pollock had informed him (as if writing to a deaf person) that all London was talking about it. As Ellen was to discover, Irving was 'so much absorbed . . . in his own achievements that he was unable or unwilling to appreciate the achievements of others . . . *It was never any pleasure to him to see the acting of other actors and actresses*.'

Irving accepted that Ellen Terry was an actress of genius. She was rising to the top of her family profession with ease, whereas he, who lived for the theatre, had reached his high place with infinite labour. He did not feel resentment. He welcomed her natural ability largely because it meant that he would not have to trouble himself over her. She could find her own way.

She had to find her own way from the start. During the rehearsals for *Hamlet*, which began in December 1878, Irving read every part except her own. The power he put into these rehearsals was extraordinary, though the results were strangely disappointing. 'He threw himself so thoroughly into it that his skin contracted and his eyes shone', Ellen remembered. But he was drilling his actors to play their roles as he would have played them himself and this often led to feeble imitations. Ellen observed with irritation that he 'never got at anything *easily*' – and he never got to her part at all. Eventually she confronted him: 'Couldn't we rehearse *our* scenes?' she asked. But he shrugged off the suggestion: '*We* shall be all right.'

To avoid extra worries at the last minute, Ellen got on with her dresses and had them all finished early: a pink one for her first scene, one of pale gold and amber for the nunnery scene, and for the mad scene, one of midnight black. Irving solemnly asked her to put on these dresses. He was, she found, 'very diplomatic when he meant to have his own way'. His eyes hardly flickered when he saw the black dress. Later he called out to one of the old stagers, Walter Lacy, who was helping out with the production, and asked Ellen to describe her dresses to him. 'Pink. Yellow. Black.' At the word black Lacy gave a gasp and began to expostulate. But Irving interrupted him. 'Ophelias generally wear *white*,' he explained. 'I believe so,' Ellen answered. 'But black is more interesting.'

'I should have thought you would look much better in white,' Irving persisted. Then he dropped the subject and walked away.

Next day Walter Lacy came up to Ellen. 'You didn't really mean that you are going to wear black in the mad scene?'

'Yes, I did. Why not?'

'Why *not!* My God! Madam, there must be only one black figure in this play, and that's Hamlet!'

So she changed to a white costume, though later remarking: 'I could have gone mad much more comfortably in black.'

Ellen attributed the lack of rehearsals she was given to the enormous amount of additional work Irving had set himself for his first Lyceum production. He had arranged for extensive alterations to the building – the installation of more comfortable seats, the repainting of the auditorium in sage green and turquoise, also new scenery and new music as well as a new drop curtain for the play itself. He had already engaged a crew of 'salted actors' to join his company, actors whom he trusted and had put through their paces. The extra wages, together with the expense of rebuilding and redecorating the Lyceum and the new production costs of *Hamlet*, rose to a phenomenal £12,000 and Irving was given an overdraft for this amount by the London & County Bank. If this season of plays did not succeed, he was ruined.

The curtain rose at half past seven on 30 December and eventually came down at midnight. But at the end Ellen was not there. Convinced that she had played Ophelia poorly ('I am so unsatisfactory to myself as Ophelia,' she told a friend), she left the theatre immediately after her part was over and drove up and down the Thames Embankment in a cab before gaining control of herself and returning home. 'I have failed; I have failed.' She felt inclined to blame Irving for her failure. 'The only person who did not profit by Henry's ceaseless labours was Ophelia.' Irving, who was seldom at his best on first nights, had dragged his leg laboriously, she noticed, and in place of that perfection of grace she had witnessed in Birmingham seemed to become wooden and self-conscious. Obviously they brought out the very worst in each other.

What Ellen conveyed was the terrible spectacle of a normal girl, any girl, being driven into mental agony and madness. Not being in the theatre at midnight, she did not see the bouquets and laurel wreaths that were thrown upon the stage, or hear the prolonged cheering as Irving stepped before the curtain to announce that he had worked 'all his life for the result that the Lyceum had witnessed that night'.

Next day Ellen read the reviews praising her 'exquisite' Ophelia and pointing to the 'utmost importance' of her support for Hamlet. As for Irving, he already knew what she had achieved, and what they would achieve together. How delighted, he remarked to Bram Stoker, Shakespeare himself would have been to see Ellen Terry perform such an Ophelia. The pathos she conveyed was simply 'nature helped by genius'. And Bram Stoker too was pleased. Ellen's charm affected all the cast so that 'not even the darkness of that December day could shut out the radiant beauty of the woman'. At supper that night, though Ellen was not present, Irving appeared to shine with her reflected beauty. He had chosen well. As his grandson later wrote, neither of them could 'have wished for a more popular coronation'.

17

Our Lady of the Lyceum

'I *live* (& nearly die!) at the theatre . . . no time for reading & scarcely for *feeling*!!' Ellen told a friend. Acting, rehearsing, studying, eternally keeping everyone's spirits up, it seemed as if she was 'buried' inside the theatre walls.

The figure of Henry Irving loomed across these years, moving even her children into the shadows. Ellen had not realised before she began working with him quite how comprehensive his melancholy was. He knew only one way out of his isolation and that was by turning it to some use, even to grim enjoyment, upon the stage. 'The horrors had a peculiar fascination for him', she observed. He liked going to the police courts to hear the trials and study the expressions of the accused (innocent men, he told her, hesitated before answering questions and, except for their wide-open eyes, almost always appeared guilty). He too appeared guilty of some nameless crime and seemed to haunt the Lyceum in search of atonement.

In almost every aspect of their temperaments Ellen Terry and Henry Irving were each other's opposites. Her childish high spirits baffled him. Seeing her one day at the back of the theatre slide down some banisters towards her dressing-room at the foot of the staircase, he smiled, but seemed unable to acknowledge such a carefree spectacle or come to terms with it. Another time, she suddenly caught hold of a bit of scenery that was being hoisted to the flies and ascended forty feet above the stage until the astonished carpenters lowered her gently down – whereupon she performed an Irish jig to show how much she had enjoyed the flight. Her innocence was as mysterious to Irving as were his motiveless black moods to her. He admitted to being hampered when acting by the pent-up vehemence of his feelings, whereas she wore emotion easily, using its energy. Her apparent naturalness and charm were, in their way, as remarkable stage qualities as was the awful sense of apprehension he spread through audiences.

Irving was what Ellen called an egotist – 'all his faults sprang from egotism'. His aim was to make everything at the Lyceum above criticism. He employed some of the foremost artists of the day – Lawrence Alma-Tadema, Edward Burne-Jones, Ford Madox Brown – to design the sets and costumes and would spend unprecedented amounts of money (often on discarded scenery) on producing what seemed historically accurate and was visually dramatic.

Another component of Lyceum productions was the music. Music directors usually adapted well-known works by Mendelssohn or Weber, or supplied incidental music heavily influenced by such composers to serve as frameworks to the evening's entertainment – creating a pleasing atmosphere during the long intervals while the sets were being changed and the actors rerobed. But Irving 'saw the need for something better than . . . the sentimental hymn-like tunes which were being served up again and again in our theatres', wrote the composer Norman O'Neill. His first director of music was James Hamilton Clarke whom he had met at a hotel while touring Scotland. Clarke, whom he paid a handsome £600 a year, was a clever and prolific musician with several aliases, who had recently succeeded Arthur Sullivan as organist at St Peter's Church in Kensington. For *Hamlet* he composed a 'Danish March' that Ellen Terry thought was 'exactly right'; and then for *The Merchant of Venice* an overture, a song for the casket scene, some serenades and a haunting piece that accompanied a gondola making its way diagonally across the stage.

Irving made a practice of commissioning original scores – overtures, preludes, songs and incidental music – from contemporary composers. The German-born Sir Julius Benedict took on *Romeo and Juliet*; the Scottish musician, Sir Alexander Mackenzie, principal of the Royal College of Music, obliged over *Coriolanus* and *Ravenswood*; the Irish composer, Sir Charles Villiers Stanford, orchestrated *Becket*; and Sir Arthur Sullivan worked on *King Arthur* and *Macbeth* (for which he provided a score of over 200 pages for an orchestra of forty-six players and a chorus). The young, allegedly Welsh, Edward German was to make his reputation with an intermezzo, coronation march (later used for the coronation of George V), and three popular dances for *Henry VIII*. Irving himself sometimes played the piano but did not read music well. He knew nothing about orchestras but knew the sound he wanted, sometimes driving these composers frantic as they attempted to follow his instructions. It has been calculated that he spent almost £50,000 (equivalent to some £3 million today) on the Lyceum music during his reign there, raising a simple band into a professional orchestra of thirty-five musicians. Some of the compositions have the choreographic effect of ballet music and affinities with operetta, but they are essentially forerunners of film music designed to heighten the emotions of the audiences. In the view of the cultural historian Jeffrey Richards, we can see Irving's unmistakable features in two contemporary fictional characters he never played at the Lyceum, Sherlock Holmes and Dracula, 'the King of Detectives and the Prince of Darkness', though his true directorial heirs were to be found in the films of D.W. Griffith and Cecil B. De Mille.

Compared with him Ellen was an amateur. Behind the scenes she was notoriously unpunctual and often felt like a child caught giggling in church. She had little interest in theatre administration and her ambition never seriously conflicted with Irving's – indeed, their talents complemented one another's. Whenever her conception of a part jarred with Irving's – as over her black dress for Ophelia – she gave way and adapted her timing and tone to fit in with him.

Irving invented much new stage business for his actors, yet he 'never spent much time on the women in the company'. He would position them during rehearsals as a choreographer might, or an artist sketching in background figures – and for the most part leave it at that, having given them indications as to how he wanted their lines spoken during his initial reading of the play. Ellen would give them a few words of encouragement, but not much more. She had no wish to direct or produce plays.

As Tom Taylor's wife remarked, Ellen was 'an April kind of woman.' One would not think to look at her that there was such a strange moral obliquity in her. She felt everything very deeply but nothing very long. Though never losing her sincerity, her opinions were apt to veer rapidly one way or another, and she believed that only men (and few enough of them) had the settled convictions necessary to direct plays successfully. Besides, she would not have been easy in her mind ordering men around the stage. As for women's roles, except for that of the leading lady, they were often relatively unimportant – especially after Irving's editing of the text. It was either their fairly low status in the theatre, or possibly his own awkwardness in dealing with women, that persuaded him to leave them to themselves once he had given them their handwritten lines.

What Ellen brought to the Lyceum was an experience that lay outside the theatre in which Irving had for so long sealed himself. He came to rely on her aesthetic sense, the sense she had absorbed from Watts and Godwin. When, at some expense, he installed modern electric lights in the theatre, she persuaded him to restore the atmospheric gas footlights and limes, the thick softness of which bathed the actors in a more sympathetic atmosphere than naked electricity (among the Lyceum innovations, which included numbered seats and finely printed free programmes, was the lowering of lights in the auditorium as the curtain went up). Ellen would also make suggestions for the women's clothes and, as the biographer Laurence Irving wrote, she 'brought to the Lyceum a well-developed sense of colour and design'.

Irving's struggle for perfection was fed by anxiety. For long periods before his entrance cue, he would stand in the wings, tortured with nerves and making everyone else nervous, before Ellen persuaded him to wait more calmly in his dressing-room until the call-boy came to summon him. Like a political dictator, Irving 'never wholly trusted his friends', Ellen shrewdly observed in her *Memoirs*, 'and never admitted them to his intimacy, although they thought he did'. But in so far as he trusted anyone, he trusted her – at least she thought he did.

Ellen's radiance illuminated the Lyceum, reawakening some stirrings of emotion in Irving's life and easing his loneliness. It may have been (since Ellen's family often called her Nelly) that he associated her with Nellie Moore. In any event, according to his grandson, Irving came to feel that 'he had introduced an angel into the house, or perhaps a sylph – half-angel, half-imp'.

To follow *Hamlet*, Irving chose *The Lady of Lyons* by Bulwer Lytton – an inflated historical romance which, by the spring of 1879, was a good forty years old. Bulwer Lytton's plays and novels had been extremely popular with the public during a previous era. He was the man who invented midnight-blue evening dress for men and had boasted that 'the pen is mightier than the sword'. But his florid style had made him a figure of fun. As Desmond MacCarthy was to write, 'he cashed his cheque on fame for ready money'. Since his death in 1873 his reputation had been slipping into bankruptcy.

It may have been that Irving decided to stage this dated melodrama as much for Ellen's sake as for his own. She had already appeared in it when working for the Bancrofts, and he himself had first done so while in Edinburgh some twenty years before. But he had little idea of what roles best suited Ellen. Certainly she had difficulty coping with Pauline Deschappelles, a proud figure in pale amber, moving among her spinettes and then trembling with emotion in white satin and primrose ribbons when cruelly treated by her lover Claude Melnotte. 'Why Henry wanted to play Melnotte was a mystery. Claude Melnotte after Hamlet!' she irritably exclaimed. The reason, she decided, must have been that 'Henry was always attracted by fustian. He simply revelled in the big speeches.' And it was true that he loved heroic acting. After much difficulty he had acquired a marvellous virtuosity in bringing off the rhetorical style. Now aged forty-three, he judged it tactful to change Melnotte's youthful character of carefree irresponsibility into something darker, denoting indefinable tragedy. Ellen, manoeuvring around him on the mossy banks of an old chateau, found herself depicting a fragile and coquettish heroine – slipping into the role several delicate touches of emotion quite foreign to its traditions. The play had become a vehicle for virtuoso acting and magnificent productions. Irving hired 150 soldiers from the Brigade of Guards who, marching across the back of the stage, appearing through a window and an open door, and then, once out of sight, doubling back, suggested a mighty army – though this scene was not in the script. The audience loved this spectacle and, though the production costs were enormous, *The Lady of Lyons* made a profit. Nevertheless the play did not reappear in the Lyceum repertoire.

The rest of the season was filled with Irving's past successes. In *Richelieu* and *Louis XI* Ellen did not appear – though Irving loved her to attend his rehearsals. In *The Lyons Mail* she played the subordinate role of Jeanette, the mistress of a drunken villain, and in *Eugene Aram* (a dramatic version of Thomas Hood's poem supplied by W.G. Wills) she took the small part of Ruth Meadows. Only in *Charles I*, a play inspired by Frederick Goodall's picture *An Episode from the Happier Days of Charles I*, was she given a character, that of Queen Henrietta Maria, which offered her a sympathetic challenge. Here she was able to be 'exquisitely feminine', the critics wrote, while at the same time showing herself 'austerely regal' and generally bringing alive 'the prettiness and the pathos of the domestic scenes'. But she was once again playing a subordinate character to Irving, whose creation of Charles I, leaving not a dry eye in the house, became 'one of the classic performances of his repertoire'. Ellen admired his acting as much as anyone. 'I have lost myself looking at him and half-doubted its being Henry', she wrote in a privately printed copy of the play. 'It surely was the best Van Dyke portrait – moving and speaking – alive.'

By the end of this first season, though she had been given no very demanding roles, she had appeared frequently, was recognised wherever she went and was well on her way to earning the affectionate title, 'Our Lady of the Lyceum', which Oscar Wilde gave her. What audiences were discovering was that by seeing her move so gorgeously around the stage, responding with such charm to the authoritative figure of Henry Irving – simply witnessing her go through these actions – made them feel happy. As the sun and the moon contended in the skies while day followed night, so Ellen Terry and Henry Irving took their passage across the stage, and all seemed well. Like Polonius, audiences were convinced that they were seeing here 'the best actors in the world'. The Lyceum became recognised as a national institution, a cathedral of the arts that seemed to house the spirit of the age – the guardian spirit, as Nina Auerbach has suggested, 'of the larger theatre of Victorian society'. With the development of cheap public transport, London and its surrounding suburbs were growing enormously and with this growth came new audiences. Irving, who gradually increased the capacity of the Lyceum from 1,250 to more than 1,700 seats, helped to create their taste especially in respect to Shakespeare. His repertoire of plays represented British culture during the late nineteenth century in much the same way as Hollywood would represent the culture of the United States in the twentieth century.

In his *Life of Oscar Wilde*, the actor-biographer Hesketh Pearson reminds us that, although the elevation of actors was not uniform throughout the country, Irving had been steadily raising the social status of the London theatre to a point that would have been unbelievable a generation earlier. 'Princes, peers, cabinet ministers, judges and even bishops were constantly to be seen at the Lyceum, and they treated Irving as an equal, whatever their private feelings may have been', Pearson wrote. Wilde's own admiration for

Ellen Terry overflowed into three sonnets, the first of which was addressed to her Queen Henrietta Maria in *Charles I* which he saw at the end of June 1879.

> O Hair of Gold! O Crimson Lips! O Face
> Made for the luring and the love of man!
> With thee I do forget the toil and stress,
> The loveless road that knows no resting place.

Wilde had an ulterior purpose behind this serenading of Ellen Terry and his fulsome praise of Henry Irving (for whom he composed a sonnet with the stupendous line: 'Thou trumpet set for Shakespeare's lips to blow!'). A couple of years later he would send them each a privately printed copy, bound in dark-red leather, of his first play *Vera, or The Nihilists*. 'Perhaps some day I shall be fortunate enough to write something worthy of your playing', he added piously after Ellen Terry's name which appeared in gold lettering. Wilde championed Irving's policy of staging third-rate melodramas, arguing that this liberated the art of the actor. As for *Vera*, its 'literary merit is very slight', he explained by way of recommendation in a letter to the Lord Chamberlain's Examiner of Plays, 'but on an acting stage perhaps the best test of a good play is that it should not read well'. And it is true that *Vera* succeeds in reading very badly, and that it was, as his biographer Richard Ellmann wrote, 'a wretched play' – though it 'did not fall disastrously below the standard set by drama in a century when, as Stendhal said, plays could not be written'. Nevertheless this was a time when Irving pronounced himself 'satisfied' with the number of 'good plays' that reached the stage.

Wilde's attitude offended Henry James who also had his eyes focused on the Lyceum. He wanted to see an artistic revolution on the British stage which would enable him to present his own sophisticated chronicle of human behaviour. He was already an acute observer of London society and desired to be caught up and made more subtly integrated into the social scene he was recording – almost a participant as well as a watcher. Since childhood the theatre had enchanted him with its imaginative possibilities. Besides, he needed money to be a social performer as well as a conductor of performances and had fantasies of being able to throw off 'half-a-dozen – a dozen, five dozen' plays, he told Edmund Gosse, for a theatre that appeared to offer more popularity and applause than his publishers and the bookshops could. The prospect of becoming part of this dramatic world, semi-attached to smart society yet with its own secret tiers of moral behaviour, offered him another aesthetic viewpoint from which to observe human society – observe it with the passionate detachment of an anthropologist. Also, he seems to have felt, it might release him from his sense of solitude – at least make his existence more crowded. But what opportunity did he have of entering this theatrical arena and standing before the curtain while it remained so obdurately unsubtle and inartistic: in short, so thoroughly un-French?

James himself wished to dramatise the inverted values of human beings, put them through a complex obstacle course of ironies and paradoxes with little prospect of leading them beyond renunciation. What he saw at the Lyceum were pretty pictures, almost visual clichés, illustrating aspects of Victorian taste. It was because she was able to embody this taste so decorously, James thought, that Ellen Terry had been over-appreciated. 'She is greatly the fashion at present, and she belongs properly to a period which takes a strong interest in aesthetic furniture, archaeological attire, and blue china', he told American readers of the *Nation* at the end of the Lyceum's first season.

Miss Ellen Terry is 'aesthetic'; not only her garments but her features themselves bear the stamp of the new enthusiasm. She has charm, a great deal of a certain amateurish, angular grace, a total want of what the French call *chic*, and a countenance very happily adapted to the expression of pathetic emotion. To this last effect her voice also contributes; it has a sort of monotonous husky thickness which is extremely touching, though it gravely interferes with the modulation of many of her speeches. Miss Terry, however, to my sense is far from having the large manner, the style and finish, of a *comedienne.*

Yet despite Henry Irving's extravagances and Ellen Terry's girlishness, the Lyceum was, James reluctantly acknowledged, the greatest theatre London had produced.

18

Interval: Irving on Holiday

At the beginning of August 1879, their first season at an end and Irving having let the Lyceum for a month to the American actress Genevieve Ward (a heavy woman from the world of opera), Ellen and Henry went their separate ways: she with her husband Charles Kelly on a tour of the provinces, he as the guest of one of his patrons, the Baroness Burdett-Coutts, who had hired a steam passenger vessel, the *Walrus*, for a cruise in the Aegean.

Irving had never allowed himself a holiday and was not quite at his ease. While his body floated gently down the Bay of Biscay and into the Mediterranean, his mind remained actively at work with his colleagues in the Lyceum. 'My love to Stoker', he wrote to Henry Loveday; and via Bram Stoker he sent 'My love to Loveday'. He could congratulate himself on a most successful seven months since his new leading lady had joined the company. The receipts had come to almost £40,000 and he had been able to reduce his indebtedness by £6,000.

But he had little planned for the next season beyond a triple bill for the opening week – beginning with *The Bells* and ending with a new one-act comedy, *Daisy's Escape* by Arthur Wing Pinero, one of the young actors in the company who specialised in sublime conspiratorial roles. What should he do then? 'I hope Ellen Terry is doing well', he wrote to Loveday from Corfu. 'When can she be back at the earliest?' A few days later he is writing to Bram Stoker. 'As soon as you can, learn from Ellen Terry the first Wednesday she can act with me again.'

On board the *Walrus* he was naturally having 'a most delightful time in Spain, Tangiers and Tunis', as he told Loveday, 'and now we are in Greece or in its Islands – nothing short of fairyland . . . From here we go to Sorrento.' The sun shone perpetually, but he admitted to Stoker: 'I shall be glad to be back.' His letters to them both as he sailed towards Italy (the *Walrus* had auxiliary sails) were crowded with instructions about music, scenery and stage properties. Since Ellen Terry would not be back until the middle of October, he was obliged to go ahead without her, reviving an old warhorse of a melodrama, *The Iron Chest* (adapted from William Godwin's eighteenth-century propagandist novel *The Adventures of Caleb Williams*) and inviting Ellen's sister Florence to deputise for her. But her role was largely incidental, the piece having been chosen for Irving, in the character of a homicidal baronet, to display what one critic called 'the grimmer aspect' of his powers.

Angela Burdett-Coutts had presented Irving with David Garrick's ring (in which was mounted a miniature of Shakespeare) 'in recognition', she told him, 'of the gratification derived from his Shakespearean representations . . .' It had been David Garrick who, in the eighteenth century, ensured the survival of Shakespeare's reputation. 'Never let your *Shakespeare* be out of your hands or your Pocket,' he urged, '—Keep him about you, as a Charm.' This was what Irving, inheriting Garrick's vocation, was doing. So it was not surprising that he should be thinking of Shakespeare's plays on board the *Walrus*. He had it in mind, he confided to Loveday, to revive *Othello*, 'and then', he added confidentially to Stoker, '*Coriolanus*'. In fact he had come before the curtain at the end of *Hamlet* and announced a production of *Coriolanus* during the next season for which he had already commissioned Lawrence Alma-Tadema to design some Etruscan sets. Meanwhile Ellen Terry was informed that she would be playing in *Hamlet* again the moment she got back to London.

Then the *Walrus* reached Venice and everything changed.

19
His Shylock

'I am going to do *The Merchant of Venice.*'

Stoker was shocked, the gentle Loveday aghast – they had confidently expected to be given the Moor of Venice, *Othello*. Not once, in his letters to them, had Irving mentioned this play – surely one of Shakespeare's least appealing comedies. Yet now, on his return to London, he proposed going into immediate rehearsals and opening on 1 November. As for Ellen, she knew Portia's lines well – though the role she had played five years ago was full of painful memories of Godwin. Nevertheless she must have felt grateful not having to learn another fresh part in so short a time. But she soon found herself having to unlearn much of what she knew, for the play as realised by Irving differed considerably from the one she had performed with the Bancrofts.

Stoker and Loveday were the first to see how much thought Irving had given to the play over the late summer – and how much work everyone else would have to give during the autumn. He had invited them both up to a late supper in his newly restored Beefsteak Room at the Lyceum. Once it had been famous as the meeting place of the Sublime Society of Beefsteaks, whose aristocratic president, crowned with a hat of feathers and sporting a silver gridiron on his breast, would carve succulent cuts of meat for their solemn suppers. Then the place was used for some years as a lumber-room before Irving, hanging his theatre pictures on the panelled walls, introducing good lighting and a long dining-table, appointing a chef, installing a grill and laying down a cellar, was to make it famous again for his own splendid suppers. Stoker and Loveday climbed the tortuous series of narrow staircases to this dignified room one Saturday night in early October 1879. After they had eaten and were sitting back comfortably with their brandy and cigars, Irving pushed aside the plates and glasses, called for sheets of writing paper and made his announcement.

'I am going to do *The Merchant of Venice.*'

The sun had risen by the time the three of them had finished their discussion and emerged into the street.

When Irving summoned the cast to the green room for the first rehearsal, he had been studying the play for some three months. He had taken out almost 600 lines and removed what Alan Hughes calls 'the romantic impossibilities of the plot and the lyrical passages of verse [that] gave him trouble'. He had also 'cleaned up' Portia's dialogue so that she became the pleasant face (as Shylock was the unpleasant face) of judicial revenge in what by the end was a satire on legal justice. He read his version of the text out loud to the company, read it with mesmeric power, and then handed out the lines. It was as well for Ellen to listen carefully, for his interpretation of her character would necessitate 'an entire revision of my conception of Portia'.

It was said that while cruising in the Mediterranean, Irving had seen a remarkable Levantine Jew whose patriarchal dignity turned in a moment to picturesque fury over some small transaction, before, just as suddenly, he regained his composure and moved on. This spectacle gave him the idea of presenting Shylock as a sympathetic character in place of a malignant usurer replete with avarice and self-pity. So he set out to humanise him and suggest that this had also been Shakespeare's aim in reaction to the monstrous 'red-haired Jew' who inhabited Marlowe's *The Jew of Malta*. What Irving wanted to convey, as his biographer-grandson later explained, was 'a new conception of Shylock as a symbol of a persecuted race, a Jewish merchant in some ways more of a gentleman than anyone else in the play . . . a proud man, respected on the Rialto, the leader of his synagogue and conscious of his moral superiority to many of the Christians who baited him' – a concept that would later influence Laurence Olivier's playing of the role.

He was encouraged by Angela Burdett-Coutts, who put money into some of the Lyceum productions, to portray an injured man who was a prince of merchants (he was said to have imitated Tennyson's voice for the part). His austere Levantine costume – a dark brown robe and tunic with a striped sash, black cap with yellow bar, and a glint of gold from his earrings – set him apart from the other characters. It was an impressive uniform, worn as if to signify reparation for past injustices to 'my tribe'. Such an interpretation had the advantage of allowing Irving a greater variety of moods, from mournful nobility and meditative diplomacy to icy obeisance and bitter rage. But there was a corresponding reduction in Portia's role, a subduing of her high spirits. She was obliged to perform the trial scene loudly since Irving was delivering his lines quietly, and though some critics thought she was at her best when duelling with him, she believed that she had produced a more powerful effect *sotto voce*.

In adjusting Shakespeare from Elizabethan to Victorian taste, elevating his own part, extending and adapting it to match his strengths as an actor, Irving made several furtive omissions and grafted a number of short scenes on to other scenes, eliminating the silver casket and the Prince of Arragon along with Portia's speeches to him. He had conceived an original interpretation of Shylock's character but adapted the text uncertainly in support of it. In contrast to the eighteenth-century rewritings of Shakespeare by Colley Cibber and David Garrick, his violations of the text were relatively few. But his 'acting version' was, in the words of the British critic John Gross, 'the triumph of personal magnetism over plot-line'. During a conversation in 1879 with the journalist Joseph Hatton, Irving described Shylock as 'a strong lonely representative of an injured and humiliated race'. But when telling Shylock's story was he not also telling an actor's story, his own lonely tale and the injuries and humiliations that had attended his early years as the member of a despised profession? *The Merchant of Venice* was to remain in Irving's repertoire until he died and gradually, as the years of oppression and neglect receded and the status of the actor rose, a radical change came over his performance, making Shylock (in the words of the American critic William Winter) 'hard, merciless, inexorable, terrible'. Towards the end of his life he gave another incident as the source for his Shylock – that of seeing an old Jew rush threateningly forward to protect a young Jewish girl from the unwanted attentions of a Gentile. He never went onstage in *The Merchant of Venice*, he said, without recalling that memory. 'I seemed to see in its crushing enmity and disdain the history of the Jewish race.'

Shakespeare scholars were delighted by the Lyceum's achievement in making their dramatist so popular with the public. 'Up to that time', wrote the theatre historian Charles Hiatt, 'no play had been mounted with such astonishing care and completeness.' Ellen received 'more letters about my

Portia than about all my other parts put together', she wrote. 'Many of them came from university men.' The great Dr Furnivall, a prince among esoteric scholars, whose terrific whiskers and grave round face were to inspire Kenneth Grahame's creation of 'Ratty' in *The Wind in the Willows*, wrote to announce himself and declare his overwhelming admiration. An atheist, oarsman and vegetarian, Frederick Furnivall was primarily a founder of learned societies. Had he not set up the Early English Text Society and soon afterwards the Chaucer Society – not to mention the Ballad Society or even the Philological Society? But it was primarily as the creator of the New Shakespeare Society that he was writing to Ellen, a scholar who, taking time off from the teaching of correct grammar to working men, was preparing reprints of the First Folio and Quarto texts. Having sufficiently introduced himself, he felt able to confess that, like so many gentlemen in the audience, he had been entranced by Ellen's graceful manner and the way she wore her wonderful gold brocade dress, also of course by her fine delivery, above all perhaps by her striking beauty – and then her charming by-play with Bassanio (kissing her hand to him behind his back). He apparently overlooked the removal of the silver casket, the absence of the Prince of Arragon ('like pulling a leaf from a trefoil', Ruskin complained) and the fact that Ellen had been prevented from giving a grander reading of the part. Instead Furnivall rhapsodised over how 'pretty and natural' she appeared. 'Your whole conception and acting of the character are so true to Shakespeare that one longs he could be here to see you', he wrote in the one-volume Leopold edition of Shakespeare's plays (dedicated to Queen Victoria's son Prince Leopold). 'A lady gracious and graceful, handsome, witty, loving and wise, you are his Portia to the life.'

Ellen quotes Furnivall's encomium at a place in her *Memoirs* where it serves to uphold the integrity of Irving's Lyceum production in 1879–80. But Furnivall's Leopold edition, though undated, was published in 1877, and it seems far more likely that he was praising her celebrated performance as Portia at the Prince of Wales Theatre in 1875 ('I hope to say this in a new edition of "Shakespeare"', he wrote before sending her the inscribed Leopold volume).

Irving had known that Ellen's disarming 'genius was fatal to criticism', that it 'transformed her critics into lovers'. He calculated on her powers of enchantment bringing much advantage to the Lyceum and shielding him, as its actor-manager, from critical attacks. But when, in the early summer of 1880, he cut the final act of *The Merchant of Venice* and, for Ellen's benefit, staged in its place W.G. Wills's sentimental one-act adaptation *Iolanthe* so that she could perform contrasting roles – the indomitable Portia as against the pathetic character of a blind girl whose sight is miraculously restored – Furnivall erupted into one of his fabulous rages. In a letter to Irving, he inveighed against 'this treason' of reducing Shakespeare's masterpiece to a mere *lever de rideau* for *Iolanthe* and promised to bring an army of 'Shakespeare men' down upon him for 'this damnable barbarism'.

Irving appeared to make light of such attacks and would joke about having to be 'in robust health' when meeting academics and clergymen. He took the condemnation of newspaper critics rather more seriously and relied on a band of theatrical journalists such as Clement Scott to champion him. Since the Lyceum of the 1880s was virtually becoming a national theatre, John Ruskin believed that Irving had brought upon himself the responsibility for making it a place of imaginative education. 'You don't make money', he said, '. . . out of a church, nor should you out of a college, nor should you out of a theatre.' But this was not the way Irving saw his job. When asked whether there should be a subsidised theatre, he replied: 'Subsidies? Never!' Towards the end of his career, as things began to go financially off-course and he was absorbed into a private-enterprise consortium, he began to champion the support of municipal theatres by local authorities as well as state aid for a theatre that, in so far as it advanced education and encouraged enlightenment, was part of the public service. But in his prime he had little sympathy for such reforms, and was happiest when, the first nights over, his audiences were also happy, measuring his success by their pleasure and his profits. Shakespeare belonged to everyone, and almost everyone, it seemed, loved *The Merchant of Venice*. Breaking all records, the play ran for 250 performances. There was no opportunity for a production of *Coriolanus*.

To celebrate the hundredth performance in February 1880, Irving staged a party at 'Half past Eleven O'Clock in the Evening' for 300 guests. After the curtain came down, they gathered briefly in the Beefsteak Room, were given 'acting copies' of the play bound in vellum and decorated with gold, then descended the staircase on to the stage which had been transformed from 'The Avenue in Portia's House' in Belmont to a scarlet and white pavilion lit by chandeliers. Here, furnished with numerous supper tables bearing magnums of champagne, a five-course dinner was served.

The cost of this party was £600. But the receipts for the season came to almost £60,000, and the expenses (including the production costs of two new plays) were less than £50,000. With the profits that summer Irving could repay his debts and at last begin to put money into the Lyceum treasury.

20
Shakespeare's Lovers

The pattern of plays that would define the Lyceum Theatre in late Victorian Britain was now clear: blood-and-thunder melodramas, revivals of Henry's and Ellen's most popular roles from the past, and then Irving's new versions of all Shakespeare's 'actable' plays – there were, he calculated, at least a dozen. His repertoire accurately reflected the taste shared by all classes of society for picturesque history and patriotic pageantry, for tales of sentimental romance and a fascination with crime – its temptation and the inevitable retribution. Irving had good reason to feel satisfied with his success. But apart from a couple of one-act comedies by Pinero, the Lyceum was putting on no work by new dramatists. For the next season, he announced as an example of work by a living dramatist a two-act poetic tragedy, *The Cup*, based on a story told by Plutarch and adapted by the seventy-year-old poet laureate, Alfred, Lord Tennyson.

As in the previous summer, Ellen had gone off touring the provinces with Charles Kelly, leaving Irving to languish in another wretched holiday. He had already let her know that these summer truancies could not continue while she was employed at the Lyceum. This time she was taking the liberty of acting in a Shakespeare comedy, playing Beatrice opposite Kelly's Benedick in Leeds. Though Ellen reminded him that she had entered into this commitment before joining the Lyceum, Henry was upset. And Kelly was upset too by the increasingly intense involvement of his wife with Irving in London. It seemed impossible for her to please both these men.

Brooding over his anxieties, Irving retired for a month to Southsea with Stoker. Walking the streets, he could not hide his pleasure at the number of people who recognised him and came up to give their greetings. It was a very pleasant nuisance. Though he made a speciality of playing villains, it appeared that the public did not think of him as a villain, but responded with affection to someone who had given them so much entertainment. It brought home to him his duty to serve up a pleasing variety of plays for them, and he decided to add Hannah Cowley's popular Restoration comedy, *The Belle's Stratagem* (which both he and Ellen already knew well) to the coming season. It had slipped his mind how enthusiastic these provincial theatre-goers could be. Perhaps, now that Ellen was coming to her senses over her duty to the Lyceum, he could replace Kelly and go on summer tours with her himself – perhaps even go on tours abroad together. It was an enticing thought.

At Southsea it was growing difficult to escape the admiring crowds who recognised him from drawings and caricatures in the newspapers. Even when he and Stoker went sailing one day, people lined the shore, waving and shouting. It was almost embarrassing. Only at the sound of gunfire and the sight of a great column of water rising suddenly in the sea close to them, nearly overturning their boat, did they realise that they had drifted into a minefield laid for some naval exercises, and that those crowds gathered frantically along the shore had been trying to warn them. Their terrified boatman urged them to return immediately, but Stoker remained agonisingly quiet while Irving, retrieving his eyeglasses and lighting up a cigar, insisted on staying where they were until the excitement had abated. So they floated gently half a mile out to sea 'enjoying themselves', as Irving put it, amid the gunfire and water-spouts, surrounded by a widening carpet of dead fish. There was something in this curious experience that appealed to Irving as if it were an illustration of his own hazardous life with Hotspur's stammering words as its caption: 'Out of this nettle, danger, we pluck this flower, safety'.

But it was not of *Henry IV* or even *Coriolanus* he was thinking while in this naval storm, but of *Othello*, which he had decided should follow *The Merchant of Venice*.

During the autumn of 1880, the great American actor Edwin Booth, whose philosophical playing of Hamlet had so greatly impressed Irving when he saw him in Manchester twenty years before, returned to Britain. Though only four years older than Irving, he was then very much more the seasoned actor, coming as he did from a powerful theatre family in the United States (his father, Junius Brutus Booth, had been the American counterpart and bitter rival of Britain's Edmund Kean). But Edwin Booth's popularity was imperilled by his younger brother, John Wilkes Booth, an ardent white supremacist who had assassinated Abraham Lincoln during a performance of Tom Taylor's *Our American Cousin* at Washington in 1865. Some years later, when Edwin Booth was playing Richard II, someone in the audience fired a revolver at him twice, missing both times. Booth calmly completed his performance. 'I have been on guard,' he wrote, 'on the look-out for disasters . . .' Such dedication was very much to Irving's taste.

Edwin Booth was the first American tragedian to win popular success in Britain. But his season at the Princess's in London was a disappointment largely because of the poor management of the theatre. At the turn of the year Booth contacted Irving: 'I want to fix a day for a chat with you', he wrote. He asked Irving if he might present a series of afternoon performances at the Lyceum. But Irving came up with a bolder plan: to stage a production of *Othello* with Ellen Terry as Desdemona, while Booth and himself alternated each week in the characters of Iago and Othello. This was an imaginative proposal and Booth immediately accepted it. Observing his 'melancholy, quiet, unassertive' manner, however, Ellen wondered whether his pride had not been hurt, being so reduced by having to accept this generosity. He 'seemed broken and devoid of ambition'. But this was due to the serious illness of his wife who lay hovering between life and death in their rooms in London (she was to die shortly after their return to America).

An 'itinerant actor of the old school', Booth was used to playing with stock companies and, as an isolated figure at the front of the stage, delivering his lines facing the audience. He was happy to let Irving 'arrange the order of the programme to suit yourself', and curious to witness how his company demonstrated the English school of acting. 'Mr Irving is despotic on stage', he observed.

> At rehearsal his will is absolute law . . . From first to last he rules the stage with a will of iron . . . He sits among his players watching every movement, listening to every word, constantly stopping anyone – Miss Terry as well as the messenger – who does not do exactly right. He rises, explains the fault, and that part of the scene is immediately repeated . . . At the Lyceum one sees the perfection of stage discipline, and in Mr Irving the perfection of stage patience.

Both actors excelled as Iago, Booth giving a polished performance of cool precision, Irving bringing to it a peculiar stamp of treachery that, in Ellen's view, made Booth look almost commonplace by comparison. 'For the first time in his life', she wrote, 'he [Henry] knew what it was to win unanimous praise.' But his Othello was a sudden and terrible misjudgement which became 'one of the unspoken bitternesses of Henry's life'. In contrast to Booth's 'melancholy, dignified' acting, which was 'very helpful to my Desdemona', Irving 'screamed and ranted and raved – lost his voice, was slow where he should have been swift, incoherent where he should have been strong', Ellen remembered. 'I could not bear to see him in the part.' Irving himself hated playing Othello, angrily tore off his costume at the end of the production and never played it again.

As for Ellen, the most memorable moment in the play came when she was endeavouring to accept comfort from Iago ('Oh, good Iago, what shall I do to win my lord again?') and saw Henry's eyes grow luminous with tears. He tried to conceal this emotion – from her perhaps as well as from the audience – blowing his nose and turning his feelings into a display of hypocrisy. But Ellen knew. The man had momentarily overwhelmed the actor. 'One adored him, devil though he was.'

That year they took *Othello* on a sixteen-week tour of Britain, Bram Stoker arranging for a special train to carry fifty-four members of the company together with all the scenery, clothes, musical instruments and lighting for nine of their most popular productions. Though expenses were high, this turned out to be such a profitable expedition that these tours between London seasons became a regular feature of the Lyceum's calendar. Irving had been able to borrow money and buy a long lease on the theatre (he had, unwisely as it turned out, baulked at borrowing enough to buy the freehold) and while the company was on tour, the builders and decorators were at work making further improvements to the building.

Once again he postponed staging *Coriolanus* because there was no part for Ellen – no part he now wished to see her play. Instead he decided to put on *Romeo and Juliet* in the spring of 1882 and *Much Ado About Nothing* in the autumn. This choice is more easily explained in terms of his emotional life than his career. He was now in his mid-forties and looked older, while Ellen in her thirty-sixth year and with a daughter whose age approximated closely to Juliet's, had passed the time when most actresses have ambitions to play the part. They were both nervous and kept apart from each other while preparing their roles.

'This responsibility weighed on me', Ellen records. She studied the play in a cottage she rented at Hampton Court, 'cracking my brain' over the readings of her lines and 'making myself familiar with the different opinions of philosophers and critics'.

Equally absorbed, and alone in London, Irving went to see his friends Sir Frederick and Lady Pollock, and after supper read them his version of the tragedy neatly arranged into five acts and twenty scenes. This acting edition, like all his editions of Shakespeare, disentangled the main event-plot from the enriching subplots and poetic asides that held up the action of the drama. That evening he read Romeo's lines wonderfully well, bringing out the passion, the passing moods, all leading to the inevitable tragedy. Lady Pollock told him that the Lyceum production would be a triumph. But to her surprise, Irving disagreed. 'No, it won't,' he replied. She told him not to be silly. 'You are bound to have a great success.' But he was obdurate. He knew what he wanted to make of Romeo, and perhaps during this private reading in Ellen's absence had come close to achieving it. But, 'I know that on stage I cannot come anywhere near it – I should like to – but I can't.'

Of all his productions at the Lyceum until now, *Romeo and Juliet* was the most sumptuous and elaborate. 'I have availed myself of every resource at my command to illustrate without intrusion the Italian warmth, life and romance of this enthralling love-story', Irving wrote in the preface to his edition of the play. He employed two painters to give the sets what Ellen called 'a marvellous sense of pictorial effect'; and he commissioned Sir Julius Benedict to compose some charming incidental music. He also collaborated with Loveday in choreographing the street-gang warfare between the Montagues and the Capulets. 'I think half-a-dozen visits to the theatre could not do more than justice to the production – its infinite detail and wonderful wealth of colour', Pinero wrote to Irving after the first night. And the poet and statesman Lord Lytton (son of the playwright Bulwer Lytton) praised him for throwing 'the whole force of his mind creatively into every detail of the great play'. But these compliments skirted around Irving's and Ellen Terry's performances.

Ellen was not happy with her playing of Juliet. There were moments when she felt 'overpowered' by a sense of failure. She could not sustain the tragic intensity. But 'although I could not like it myself', she wrote, '. . . Henry himself liked me as Juliet'. And that, it seemed, was almost enough for her. How tenderly he wrote to her after the dress rehearsal. 'Beautiful as Portia was, Juliet leaves her far, far behind. Never has anybody acted more exquisitely the part of the performance which I saw from the front . . . the beauty of it is bewildering . . . Now you – we – must make our task a delightful one by doing everything possible to make our acting easy and comfortable. We are in for a long run.'

The emotional commitment in Irving's words seemed to burn away his melancholy. He was as vulnerable as ever, perhaps in some ways more so, and his imagination was still visited by mysterious anguish and horror. But Ellen appeared to have brought gleams of happiness into his life – a promise of happiness previously missing. Though he mesmerised everyone at the Lyceum with a power that seemed almost supernatural, he himself was mesmerised by Ellen. When he proclaimed that Shakespeare should be living to see her become his women, he spoke from the heart. This was not a language that others heard him speak. But onstage, like Orlando with Rosalind in the early scenes from *As You Like It*, Irving 'cannot speak to her' – cannot convey his feelings for Ellen. Romeo's passion seems to have unsettled him, stirring perhaps his own feelings too markedly – as Iago had briefly done.

When Ellen wrote of his Romeo it was in a very different tone, a tone of protectiveness. 'I am not going to say that Henry's Romeo was good', she wrote. But when he was abused, being likened to a pig that had been taught to play the fiddle, she became furious and ran to his defence, knowing how sensitive he was to these attacks ('I have determined not to see a paper for a week,' he confided to her, '– I know they'll cut me up'). She insisted that 'the worst thing Henry Irving could do would be better than the best of any one else'. For she knew that there were sublime moments in the play – at the beginning, for example, when, in pursuit of Rosaline he suddenly sees Juliet, and his face changes; and then at the opening of the apothecary scene when Balthasar tells him of Juliet's supposed death, the way in which his face, that extraordinary face of his, appeared to go white; and then again in the scenes of repressed emotion where his sadness shone through so touchingly. They said he was too old, but there were times when he looked old 'as only a very young man can look'.

Ellen Terry: aged nine (*right*); living with Godwin, 1873 (*below left*); as Ophelia, 1878 (*below right*)

Romance and Respectability: photographs of Ellen Terry by Julia Margaret Cameron, Isle of Wight, 1864 (*above*); and by the Revd Charles Dodgson (*below*), with her family at Kentish Town, 1865 (from left: Ben, Tom, Flossie, Ellen, Kate, Charlie, Polly and Sarah)

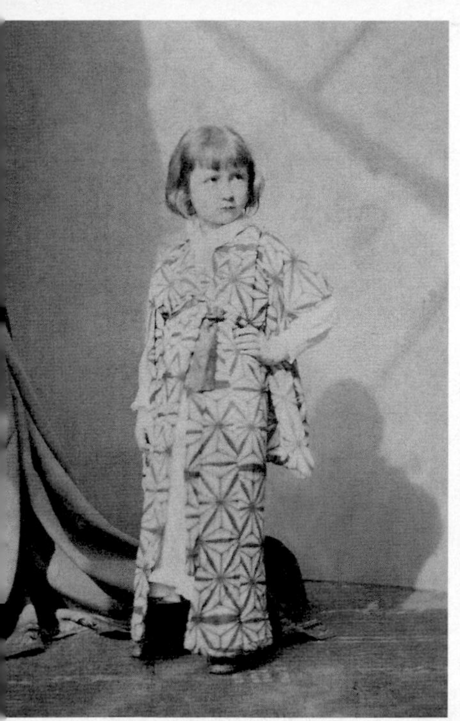

Edy Craig at home *c.*1874 (*above left*); Gordon Craig in *Much Ado About Nothing*, New York, 1885 (*above right*); Ellen with her children, 1888 (*below*)

Husbands and Lovers: G.F. Watts, E.W. Godwin, (*above*)
Charles Kelly, James Carew (*below*)

Charles Reade,
Stephen Coleridge,
Sarah Bernhardt,
Eleonora Duse,
W.G. Wills,
Tom Taylor

John Henry Brodribb (*above left*); Sir Henry Irving (*above right*);
Henry Irving on holiday at Winchelsea (*below left*); Elizabeth Aria (*below right*)

Henry Irving: 'making up' by Paul Renouard (*above left*);
as Hamlet (*above right*); as Becket (*below left*); as Shylock (*below right*)

On the SS *Arizona*, homeward bound, 1885 (Ellen and Henry seated left, Gordon Craig seated centre, L.F. Austin standing tall, H.J. Loveday standing right)

Florence Irving with her sons Laurence and Harry (*left*)

She knew he had chosen *Romeo and Juliet* for her – for both of them, so as to make their partnership 'a delightful one'. She believed, however, that this impeded him. In the Friar's Cell, as in the big emotional scenes of *Othello*, he failed because he could not act what he actually felt for the woman who had become so close to him. He could only recite such scenes rhetorically. But although 'it was one of our failures', audiences responded as if they sensed something disturbing and provocative between the lines: and the play ran for 150 nights.

The dramatic tension lay in the hidden subtext of their performances. To Henry James the production appeared an overweighted spectacle that obliterated Shakespeare's delicate poem. 'The play has thriven mightily', he wrote in *Atlantic Monthly*, 'and though people are sadly bewildered by what they see and hear in it, they appear to recommend the performance to their friends.' Irving himself, James thought, must have known how far his performance fell short of what he had sought, and yet 'there is something very touching in so extreme a sacrifice of one's ideal'.

When Irving heard people express their misgivings over his 'attempted youthfulness', he was apt to retort that it was an odd thing how 'every damn fool who's been onstage two minutes thinks he can play it' – possibly he remembered having done so himself when, as an amateur, he purchased the role at the Soho Theatre. He should perhaps have played Mercutio and would have done so but for his belief that 'in all London he could find no actor adequate for Romeo'. This implies that he rejected William Terriss (who was to play Romeo three years later opposite Mary Anderson) and overlooked Johnston Forbes-Robertson (who had already played the role successfully with the Polish actress Modjeska). A more likely truth was that he would not allow any man to be Romeo to Ellen's Juliet. But, irritated by his finicky slowness, Ellen had been obliged to modify her own natural timing and she quarrelled with Irving during rehearsals.

Irving informed the company that his reason for choosing *Much Ado About Nothing* had been the success of *The Belle's Stratagem*, which reminded him of the public's appetite for comedy. But privately he let Ellen know that he was reviving the play for her. 'It is only in comedy that people seem to know what I am driving at!' she said. She disliked being praised for her professional charm: 'There is something more to my acting than charm.' Nevertheless, as soon as they went into rehearsals the atmosphere in the

Lyceum lifted. A feeling of lightness permeated the theatre now that the tragedy of *Romeo and Juliet* was over and Ellen's and Henry's feelings for each other were being re-orchestrated as a cantankerous courtship between Beatrice and Benedick. Ellen was born to play Beatrice – not as a shrew but 'a "pleasant spirited lady" – all mirth and audacious mockery – a stranger to melancholy'. On the surface Irving's purpose was the same as Shakespeare's: to have a resounding commercial and aesthetic triumph, and this he seems to have achieved. 'The Lyceum production was a great success', Ellen wrote.

But Irving had another purpose: to eclipse Charles Kelly's production of the play, to usurp his character, better him, altogether to replace him by adding a spectacular wedding sequence in place of 'the *plain* form of marriage'. What Ellen could never tell him was that her husband's Benedick 'was in many ways a splendid performance, perhaps better for the play than the more deliberate performance Irving gave at the Lyceum'. As for herself, she was aware of not having played Beatrice so fluently with him. Perhaps these uncertainties were set off by other tensions in her life. For though Irving failed to act Charles Kelly off the stage, Kelly (or Charles Wardell, as he was known at home) was leaving 33 Longridge Road, and the MacColl family living opposite would soon become more familiar with the sight of Irving's grim-jaunty figure arriving at her house.

21

Children!

'Did H[enry] I[rving] offer Charles Kelly an engagement at the Lyceum Theatre?' Gordon Craig asked in a volume of memoirs he was to write. But Irving must have refused to do so. There can be no doubt that Kelly took this as an insult to which injury was added a year later when William Terriss was asked to join the Lyceum – the very man who had caused him unhappiness when chosen to play opposite Ellen in *Olivia* at the Court Theatre. His disappointment had been accepted then by Ellen as a mark of his love for her. But his resentment was later aggravated by jealousy. He hardly knew where to seek justice.

William Terriss had been a sailor, a tea-planter, and a sheep-farmer before becoming a 'darling of the gallery girls'. He had a sweet nature and seemed 'one of those heaven-born actors who, like Kings by divine right, can up to a certain point, do no wrong'. In other words he was like Ellen Terry herself. But very often, she noticed, he did not understand the character he was playing, did not understand in all probability the play itself or know where the plot was taking them. Yet by sheer instinct he made audiences 'believe in him the moment he stepped on to the stage'.

What Irving particularly liked about Terriss was the sheer entertainment he spread around the theatre. He was like a grown-up boy, full of fun and adventure, though actually rather modest. Irving 'never could be angry' with him. Surrounded as he inevitably was by sycophants and acolytes and what his secretary L.F. Austin called 'the contemptible littleness that seems to be fostered by the theatrical atmosphere', Irving allowed Terriss the freedom of a court-jester. On one occasion, while fighting a duel at a rehearsal of *The Corsican Brothers*, Terriss noticed that the limelight was being exclusively focused on Irving, loyally following 'the Chief' wherever he moved. Putting up his sword, he remarked: 'Don't you think, Guv'nor, a few rays of the moon might fall on me – it shines equally, ye know, on the just and the unjust.' Everyone expected a thunderbolt to fall, but instead there came the rare sound of Henry Irving's laughter – and he ordered the limelight man to spread the moon's beams more impartially.

With his dashing looks and the sheer attack of his performances, Terriss was becoming one of the best-loved actors of his day. Even in the roughest clothes – especially in the roughest clothes – he 'looked a prince' with his insolent gypsy eyes, his enviable athleticism and a 'beautiful mouth', Ellen added. 'That predisposed me in his favour at once!' As for her daughter Edy, she was 'simply *daft*' about Terriss.

Ellen could not help flirting with him, which was not very pleasing for her husband. Ever since his wife had gone to the Lyceum, Charles Kelly had felt an outsider at the theatre and sometimes even at home. After their marriage he had confidently expected to be acknowledged as Ellen Terry's leading man. He resented Henry Irving's influence over her and felt mortified by his subordinate position. Concerned by the course events were beginning to take, Charles Reade wrote an encouraging letter to Ellen during one of their early tours: 'Be assured nobody can appreciate your value and Mr Kelly's as I do. It is well played all round.' But Reade's approval had little force when it came up against Irving's hostility. While Ellen was at the Lyceum, Kelly took whatever roles he could get, sometimes acting with her sister Florence and also, less successfully, with her brother Fred. His confidence was fading and, as Ellen's friend the dress-designer Alice Comyns Carr noticed, he was increasingly 'given to reinforcing himself with stimulants'.

The disconsolate look that had so touched Ellen before their marriage was now distorted by anger. He wore an expression of ill-temper. Ellen's marriage had partly been undertaken for the sake of her parents. But in a letter to Bernard Shaw, she later confessed that she had married 'for her [Edy] and for Ted. A mistake I now know.' Her children had different stories to tell. Edy later acknowledged that her stepfather had been a 'good fellow in some ways'. Yet it was she who, in the notes added to her mother's *Memoirs* after her death, would make Kelly's resentment and bad temper known to the public. Ted had a memory of him brandishing a riding crop in the style of a lord of the manor as he clumped his way heavily around their house. It was a caricature of the male authority for which the boy longed –

like something unconvincingly learnt in a theatre and brought home. In retrospect, Ted blamed his mother for marrying him in the first place.

The more he thought of it, the more Ted came to resent the convention of blaming men for the break-up of marriages. If you looked carefully into such matters you could see that the women were often at fault. 'I was born loving my mama – she was so spoiling', he wrote in old age. She spoiled everyone – every man. But she was 'too passionately the servant of the stage'. How did she imagine that she could 'rock the cradle, rule the world, *and* play *Ophelia* perfectly, all in a day's work'? His poor mother 'could not give your evening hours to me', he lamented, addressing Ellen after her death. And there had been no need for her to marry Kelly. If she had stood firm with Godwin, they would have found a path to go along together – and the history of the theatre would have been revolutionised. '*I don't doubt it for a single minute!*'

So far as Ted remembered, Ellen said almost nothing about Godwin to him and 'I can't recall hearing my papa speak. I can't recall him at all, for I was seldom with him after the age of three.' Being two years older than Ted, Edy did remember something and whatever it had been, she did not like it. 'Edy was strong-minded!' her brother wrote. 'I was decidedly not.' She did not want a man in the house, any man coming between her and her mother. But Ted felt differently. 'Every other boy I knew had his mother *and* father. Not having mine – not hearing of mine – this grave sensation of *something being wrong* grew and grew into a fixed sort of small terror with me.' Why had Godwin abandoned them so completely?

When trying to understand the coming and going of men in his mother's life and her marrying that bear of a man Kelly, Ted came to the conclusion that she had tried to cover up the wrongs of her past with a cosmetic. 'I had become (by law!) Edward Wardell . . . and yet I was not, please God, Edward Wardell, but Edward Godwin Terry, later to become Edward Gordon Craig, and finally E.G.C.' If she had been 'trying to find a father for Edy and Ted' why did his mother separate from her husband so soon? There was only one obvious answer to that. 'She doubtless did so to please H.I.' These were bewildering times. As an understudy to Godwin, Charles Kelly was obviously inadequate. But Irving proved 'as kind as a father' and possessed that patriarchal authority which their family needed. He could not be bossed around, however lovingly, by Ellen or any other woman: 'A thousand blessings on the coming of H.I.'

Edy disliked being called Wardell as much as her brother did. In September 1883, while Ellen was on holiday with Ted, Irving and Bram Stoker off the Ayrshire coast in Scotland, she saw an island rock called Ailsa Craig. 'What a good stage name!' she exclaimed: 'A pity *you* can't have it, Ted. I shall give it to Edy.' And so, when Edy first went onstage as an adult she was billed as being 'Ailsa Craig', though she soon changed this to Edith Craig to avoid confusion with another actress called Ailsa Craig. In 1887, at the age of eighteen, she was christened and confirmed as Edith Geraldine (after her godmother Geraldine Coleridge) Craig; and the following year her brother was christened as Edward (after his father Edward Godwin) Henry (after Henry Irving his godfather) Gordon (after his godmother Lucy Duff Gordon) Craig. Upon that rock they would subsequently make their careers.

There was only one actor in the country of sufficient rank and magnitude to take Godwin's place as a father-figure. To Ted's mind, Irving's acting was 'child's play' – a phrase that points perhaps to the nature of his own need. In his imagination, the boy dreamed of 'the grace and discretion of H[enry] I[rving] and the knowledge of E[dward] W[illiam] G[odwin]' coming together in a vision of his own destiny. When in due course he entered the Lyceum and sensed Irving's 'powerful will', he felt at last that he had found a home from home. 'No actor ever dominated everyone else in the theatre world so easily as did H[enry] I[rving]', he wrote admiringly.

But in the early 1880s, it was Irving's 'careful attention' that appealed most to the boy, his generosity and patience – everything that Florence forbade him to show his own sons. Above all, Irving seemed to know 'what it might feel like having no father', though (unknown to Ted) it was a loving mother he had lacked. This loss of a father became a 'fearful strain' early in Ted's life. During the day he was lazy – far too fond of coloured sweets and warm cake. He had learnt what he called the grammar of eating: how to tackle soup, break bread and enjoy butter on it. But at night he grew afraid of the dark, would call out for company, and sometimes walked in his sleep. Over these early years, lulled by the voices of women from all sides, 'I was still in a sleepy dream'.

Though Ellen's children were eventually to see a good deal of Henry Irving, he never moved into Longridge Road. This seems to have suited Edy well enough. Her letters to 'dear, darling old "Harry"' from 'your affectionate little Edie' show how fond of him Ellen's daughter grew. 'Mother says I am a lucky girl', she told him, 'and I think I agree.' But Ted was disappointed that Irving did not live with them. He needed someone to direct him. Whenever he said something silly, his sister would tell him to 'Sit down and keep quiet'. Edy knew about keeping quiet. For the first twenty-five months of her life she had said nothing at all and was only spurred into speaking once she noticed her baby brother. But during his childhood and adolescence, Ted remembered that, despite her sternness with him, 'I was never happier than when with Edy'.

The two of them were sent while still very young to a coeducational school in Earls Court run by Mrs Cole, a lady of advanced ideas who believed that 'girls ought to have as good an education as boys'. Edy proudly remembered that when they first entered this school she and her brother 'were the most backward of the pupils in all but drawing, music and Shakespeare'. In 1883, the school having grown in size and reputation and moved to larger premises, Edy, then aged thirteen, became a boarder there, while her eleven-year-old brother was sent off to a boys' boarding school called Southfield Park, near Tunbridge Wells, in Kent. This was a solid house, presided over by a clergyman, set in fine grounds, and with an excellent tuck shop.

Why didn't Ellen put her children on the stage, Ted sometimes wondered, as Ben and Sarah Terry had done? In the old days Ellen had been happy as a theatre-child, but in her mid-thirties she was growing increasingly aware of lacking a formal education. If Edy and Ted were to choose careers for themselves, she reasoned, they must mix with other children at schools and colleges. Ted's unacknowledged humiliation was that Godwin never interested himself in his son and Ellen never thought it worth consulting him.

The person whose advice she did ask for was Ted's godfather. Irving 'saw very clearly the dangers of putting ideas about acting' into his own sons' minds. Such a decision was more clear-cut for him because Florence, though always accepting as of right a box at the Lyceum for her husband's first nights, held his acting up to ridicule before their children so that, on the few occasions he saw them, they appeared awkward and embarrassed.

Florence still found it hard to accept the fact that her husband had walked out into the night and never returned. She knew of course that she had provoked him, but had not reckoned on the terrible force of his reaction, or understood the vital significance which the theatre held for him. She felt both attracted to and repelled by him. For almost quarter of a century she drew in her diary, as if for a death, a heavy black-ink line around 15 July, the date of her marriage. It was St Swithin's Day, a day of rain and grief. Some years she writes a word or two within this dark rectangle: 'Alas, my wedding Day', 'Married 22 Years!!!!' or adds a comment: 'Appropriately not weeping for the mournful anniversary'. But she had wept and could not let it go. Open her diary on this day and you will feel this mark branded on her very soul. Otherwise she keeps little more than a social diary. She makes occasional references to Irving's trips abroad and utters a few exclamatory ironies: 'Irving's benefit!!!!' 'Ellen Terry ill. Did not act!' 'Irving at hotel with E. Terry!' She cannot endure finding their names together in the newspapers. After going to *Much Ado About Nothing* at the Lyceum, she writes: 'another case of "paranoia" '. There seemed no easing of this pain.

But there is one continuous stream of happiness in these pages, and this is her love for 'my darling boys'. She cannot take her eyes off them, chronicling all that they do and deriving constant pleasure from their company. In 1876 she moved her family from West Brompton to 10 Gilston Road, a good house with a pleasant garden in a green oval area called The Boltons in South Kensington. After much vacillation, Irving was to buy the lease for her in 1890. Here she created a secure home for Harry and Laurence. The two boys grew up much attached to the place. During their very early years, dressed in their sailors' suits and showing great affection for each other, they might have been taken for twins.

Florence installed a governess to provide them with an elementary education and engaged Walter Sickert (who had briefly walked the boards of the Lyceum) to give them drawing lessons – 'boys began holiday lessons with Mr Sickert', she noted in her diary on 26 December 1882. She herself saw to their manners, good health and social skills. For their summer holidays she would take them to the northern coast of France or Belgium where they swam and practised their foreign languages. 'We are so happy that I wish you were here with us', Harry wrote dutifully to his father from Dunkirk in 1879. But Irving never was with them. Despite their mother's continual denigration of their father, and though they loved her greatly, their quick intelligence and increasing awareness of Irving's fame as an actor, led them to some Machiavellian ways of expressing a dual loyalty.

Their mother did not want them to be actors, though she felt obliged to take them to the Lyceum first nights and special benefit performances once they were old enough. This exciting theatre-world occupied a separate place in their imaginations from the world their mother inhabited. 'We enjoyed ourselves immensely at your benefit', Harry wrote to his father. 'I particularly liked Charles I & want to know when The Corsican Brothers commences as mother has promised to take us both to London in time for the first night.'

Florence was careful to warn her sons of the teeming immoralities in theatre life. She had disparaged Nellie Moore, upbraided Irving for inciting Isabel Bateman's infatuation, and later accused him of conducting a clandestine affaire with his patron, Angela Burdett-Coutts. 'I am continually hearing the name of the Baroness Burdett-Coutts coupled with that of my husband, Mr Henry Irving, in a manner which I am sure and hope neither of them would like', she complained. 'My friends naturally remark "Can she possibly know that he is a married man with two children whom he has long since deserted?"' Such complaints subsided after the baroness married an American in the early 1880s. But by then Florence had found a younger enemy.

Meeting her with the Bancrofts one day, Bernard Shaw remembered how 'within a few seconds of our introduction she was abusing H. I. to me with a hatred of which only an Irishwoman could be capable'. Once the notoriously flirtatious Ellen Terry became her husband's partner at the Lyceum, any lingering notions of his returning to his family vanished. At home, and in front of her sons, she would call Ellen 'The Wench' and describe her association with their father as 'a gross and final insult'. When, in 1882, Irving and Ellen Terry went so far as to play *Romeo and Juliet*, she wrote in her diary: 'First night of *Romeo and Juliet* at Lyceum – jolly failure – Irving awfully funny.' Irving had taken the precaution of making it a condition of the generous allowance he gave her that she should stir up no public scandal. But he could not control what she said at home. Florence was one of the best-dressed women in London. Her lips were painted a delicate pink, her face touched with rouge, but she had a sad and selfish expression and, behind her dead-looking eyes, she was consumed with fury.

That Harry and Laurence should not be guided towards the professional stage seems to have been the single subject about which their parents were agreed. Florence certainly did not wish to see them moving any closer to their father, and he did not want them, simply because they were his sons, to be 'flattered and encouraged to believe in a talent which neither possessed'. Harry, it was thought, might one day make his way as a lawyer, while Laurence, who had a talent for languages, could enter the world of diplomacy. In any event, as the next step, the two of them were sent to an expensive public school. 'Boys to Marlborough. God bless them!' Florence wrote in her diary. Not turning up himself, Irving dispatched Bram Stoker there and he reported that they were enduring the rigours and privileges of school life with 'cheerful fortitude'.

The education Ellen provided for Edy and Ted was less conventional. In his memoirs, he has little to say about his schools. What he remembered was being brought up in a 'house of women'. Of these women Ellen herself was the least visible. 'Mother fades – has to.' Sometimes this fading felt like a rejection to her son. Turning to the theatre, so she 'turns away her face from a home', he wrote. Travelling with her son to the Lyceum, Ellen would often stop off to see her friend Audrey Campbell, an amateur actress and photographer. Audrey was never very happy and never very unhappy. She had steadiness – a quality that Ellen lacked and felt she needed. But Audrey had one fault: 'a jealous nature' which 'eats her up' and 'will poison her life'. She was very possessive of her friendship with Ellen. But Edy maintained that her mother's friend was 'stupid' and Ted resented these visits to her house. Their mother seemed so close to Audrey – she could speak more freely to her than to her children. Audrey was wonderfully attractive, but she took no notice of Ted. When the two women were together it was as if he ceased to exist.

Mrs Rumball, late of the lunatic asylum near Harpenden and still called 'Boo', had become the housekeeper at Longridge Road. She presided at the tea table and kept a watchful gaze on them all. 'Real lunatics she liked, especially when they took her for the Virgin Mary', Ted believed. But looking back at these years, he began to wonder whether their incessant 'Boo-ing' of her had not driven her mad. She settled down with the family, 'settled down and down', until she became 'a prisoner in a backroom downstairs'.

In his bedroom at the top of the house it was to a Miss Harries, who had put him and Edy to bed and taken away the light, that the nervous chubby Ted would call out in his terror. Miss Harries, a minnow of a woman, 'very church going' and with a fondness for small animals, was employed, under the general supervision of Mrs Rumball, to look after the house and its children. She had the keys; she saw to everything. In Gordon Craig's memoirs, she makes her appearance as a Victorian grotesque, a very tiny plain female with large feet, a long pointed nose, a slit of a mouth and no chin. Though given to baldness, she had sprouted a small area of stiff grey hair which stuck out sharply at the back of her head. Her manner was brusque and her voice brought to Teddy's mind the braying of a donkey.

Miss Harries did not attain the settled madness of Mrs Rumball, but was charged with a more active craziness that seemed to possess her as she scuttled all day around the house giving orders to tradesmen and children, and running incoherent errands between the other women, including the three maids whom Ellen employed.

The third woman at the tea table was Mrs Rumball's niece, Miss Bocking, called 'Bo'. Unlike the others, she was beginning to make a life for herself beyond Longridge Road, having acquired an admirer in the shape of a large patient man called Joe, by profession a blacksmith, whom she eventually married. They went to live at Brancaster, near the low-lying salt marshes along the northern coast of Norfolk. But Bo had not abandoned the Terry family. During the school holidays, while Ellen was on tour, Edy and Ted were sometimes sent singly or together to live in her big ugly house. Ted remembered being allowed to help with the blowing of the bellows as Joe hammered on his anvil, and then, the horse being harnessed, sitting beside him as he drove his trap to the fields. But most of his memories were solitary: walking along the great empty beach under an enormous sky, the sea creeping in with tiny waves like kittens stretching out their paws. He would pass the nets and hooks of the fishermen and the low slabs of rock where the crabs hid, and then, coming back inland, he would stop at the post office to ask if there was a letter from his mother.

'Our dear Bo looked after me and my sister', Gordon Craig was to write. But then he added angrily: 'A fatuous idea, for no one but the mother can look after a child.' For this fundamental piece of miscasting he never blamed Irving who actually took his mother away from home, but directed his anger towards lesser figures such as Stephen Coleridge, the son of the Lord Chief Justice, Lord Coleridge.

Stephen Coleridge was an 'intimate friend' of Ellen's, a 'bright affectionate boy', 'pretty' too she thought, whom she treated as what she called a 'toy boy'. In his early twenties he had become entranced by her, hiring a stage box on the prompt side of the Lyceum stage twice a week and always sending her a little bunch of stephanotis which she would fasten to her belt or her dress (throwing him a glance, he fancied, as she moved towards his side of the stage). After each performance he would secrete himself in a dark corner behind the scenes and wait – and one night she opened her dressing-room door slightly, put her hand out: and he kissed it!

This was the beginning of 'a beautiful love' on which, he declared, there fell 'no shadow of the flesh'. He soon got to know her dramatic story: how, as a child-bride, she had left the great Watts 'wounded and broken'; how she had then 'fallen prey to the clever unscrupulous Godwin' and how she made 'her last and most fatal error' by marrying a drunken actor. 'All this wretchedness and only 28!' he exclaimed. But now, 'stainless, she gave me her heart with both hands' – an operation carried out in the 'refined region of the spirit'. He swore to carry her off from this tempest into a place of quietness. And he asked nothing in return (unless it was the playing of his adaptation of *Jane Eyre* and his blank-verse translation of Schiller's *Don Carlos* at the Lyceum). His reward lay in the belief that he had taken 'permanent possession of the heart of one of the sweetest of all God's creatures, and the reigning beauty of England'.

For Ellen it was a game – a necessary game, harmlessly (as she thought) releasing her reservoir of natural affection, indulging her desire to be admired and show admiration. He wrote her loving letters and sent her many presents – flowers and jewels. She flirted with him, teased him and signed her affectionate letters back to him with the pet names of characters which she had performed onstage and which he adored. Their language derived from the theatre and touched on what Henry James described for American readers of *Scribner's* as 'this whole question of demonstration of tenderness on the English stage' and how it was spreading into social life. James found the spectacle of 'hugging and kissing that goes on in London in the interests of drama' highly displeasing. Ruskin too was shocked by Ellen Terry's intimate ways. 'Good heavens, she's touching him!' Fanny Kemble exclaimed when she saw Ellen's Portia stroking and patting Bassanio. *Blackwood's* magazine, too, chided her for holding Bassanio 'caressingly by the hand, nay, almost in an embrace'. Her 'coming-on disposition', which had once so dismayed Mrs Prinsep at Little Holland House, vulgarised several of her performances in Henry James's opinion; and even Lewis Carroll was moved to charge her with '*indelicacy*'.

The trouble was it did not stop inside the theatre. Whenever she felt emotion, Ellen knew that 'I should have *had* to touch somebody'. But were actresses to be permitted such freedoms and still be regarded as respectable? No wonder Charles Kelly had been so jealous. Ellen, it seemed, was changing the fashion of the times. 'We are not lovers – though I am very loving', she wrote to Stephen Coleridge. 'I could find it in my heart to love every *pretty* thing I meet.' But this overflowing of emotion embarrassed her children. And it had maddened her husband – the flowers Coleridge sent her, his visits to her dressing-room ('Come to the stage door any night you like', she had invited him) and the secret kisses that became common knowledge. On one occasion Kelly had insisted that she return an expensive set of Turner's prints. Feeling 'very ungrateful & rather shamefaced & a little cross', Ellen did so with a letter explaining that 'my husband is *generally* right'. Besides, physically 'he is a big man' and she was 'little'. Blinded by romance, and feeling he had surely been encouraged, Coleridge did not pick up the signs of danger, the danger of Kelly's fists, and he sent Ellen an amber necklace. She loved the young man's 'pretty beads', the provenance of which she had managed to conceal from her husband. In her letter of thanks, however, she warned him to 'read *between* the lines', and appealed to him to 'excuse her, forgive her, & forget her'. He had 'misunderstood' her circumstances. But he grew increasingly bewildered by her signals and subterfuges, now leading him on, now sending him away. When he was abroad she wrote to tell him 'how much I wish you could be here this moment' and instructed him to send her a white flower once he returned. But when he hurried back, Mrs Rumball (Ellen had arranged for her to write him coded letters) forbade him entrance. Unable to stop himself, he insisted on seeing Ellen at home and in some panic she warned him not to come 'on Monday or any other day' and not to write her love letters 'or you will bring dreadful trouble on poor *all* of us'. Nevertheless she was still excited by the attentions of this 'very naughty boy' and when he fell ill she insisted herself on 'running round to see you this evening – some time after 8. I cannot help it – to think of you being ill.'

In 1879 Stephen Coleridge went abroad for a year and came back with a wife. Ellen sent the two of them reservations for a box at the Lyceum and, by formally requesting Mrs Coleridge's approval of their friendship, gave her admirer a lesson on how he should have behaved. Coleridge could now see that, as he indignantly wrote in the margin of one of Ellen's letters, 'HER HUSBAND AT THIS TIME WAS NIGHTLY DRUNK & MIGHT HAVE MADE HIMSELF OFFENSIVE'.

It must have felt as if he had been granted the privilege of a troubadour, an extra-marital knight in a tale of courtly love, when Ellen invited Coleridge to accomplish a heroic task on her behalf. She wanted him to employ his legal skills and bring about a formal end to her marriage. So he set forth to discover whether Kelly's first wife (whom he had referred to as deceased on the marriage certificate to Ellen) was actually still living in New Zealand. This quest, in the manner of an epic medieval poem, might have lasted a lifetime, had not Ellen urgently appealed to him: 'I can't go on with this I'm afraid. I shall break down . . .' What she needed was a legal separation rather than some quest in search of a miraculous annulment. Henry Irving (referring to Ellen as 'my lady' as if she belonged to him – rather as Sir Lester Dedlock proudly refers to Lady Dedlock in *Bleak House*) then stepped forward to redirect Stephen Coleridge's energies. Would it not be better, he suggested, to 'draw up a form of guarantee embracing her Doctor's wishes and my desire – which is to keep "my lady" from any future anxiety or responsibility'. So, in this less romantic fashion, after some four years of marriage, Coleridge banished Charles Kelly with payments of £100 a month – a huge sum that was later reduced to £60 a month (after the 'Jackson Case' put an end to a husband's rights to his wife's property). Even then, Wardell lost so much money on tour that 'we had great difficulty with him continually', Coleridge complained.

Before their judicial separation, Kelly had managed his wife's money. Afterwards Ellen handed over her business affairs to Stephen Coleridge himself. 'I shall never be able to thank you enough for your constant care for us', she wrote. Her thanks took the form of making many demands on him and he responded by appointing himself her moral and financial guide. He could take credit for freeing her from what she called her husband's 'impudence and degradation'. As for Ellen, 'I should have died had I lived one more month with him', she confided to Bernard Shaw.

For two or three years she had been 'pitifully trying to hide her miserable home life from the curious world', Coleridge noted. She was also hiding it from her children. Edy was not unhappy to see her stepfather leave. 'One night in an awful passion', Ellen wrote to her son in 1896, '(I've never seen such an exhibition from her but twice before in her life) she [Edy] told me she loathed every friend I had in the world except Stephen [Coleridge]!!! – she was livid with rage . . .' Perhaps Coleridge was exempted from Edy's opprobrium because he was merely an imaginary knight and in some ways an additional child rather than a prospective lover.

But Teddy disliked him all the more. He did not want an outsider to come in and be treated as if he were a senior brother to himself – and when Coleridge was asked to act as his 'guardian' while Ellen and Henry were away, he rebelled: 'She [Ellen] was my real guardian, and if anyone else it was Irving, and both guarded and guided me.' Coleridge had the bad manners to walk around looking ill – made ill perhaps with his prim and hopeless love for Ellen. He was unmanned by her, a plaything, with responsibilities but no authority.

Ellen's children were happiest at Rose Cottage, a small house which she rented for weekends and holidays while she was playing at the Court Theatre and kept for five or six years. It was a bright, whitewashed, 'papered and painted little house of four to five rooms and a kitchen', Ted remembered, ' – in the Hampton Court Road, its back windows looking out on to Bushey Park, in which stags and deer could every day be seen daintily treading their way here and there against the background of many big trees'. The children would often sit on the window sill, straddling it, one leg in and one leg out, watching the animals. Sometimes, heads lowered, horns entangled, the stags fought one another (though maybe it was more playing than fighting) and Edy and Ted would later find pieces of their antlers on the grass to play with themselves.

Ellen Terry wrote of her 'little boy fat and fair' and her 'little girl thin and dark', both dressed in blue and white check pinafores and with hair closely cropped, running wild around the palace grounds. They were 'glued together' during these early years. Though Irving used to visit them at Rose Cottage, on the whole they had their mother to themselves. While she sat indoors reading her lines, they would rush out of the house, through the great Lion Gates to the palace gardens, and make them their playground. They liked inventing games together such as the Naming of Trees after the characters their mother was playing and the plays themselves. 'Come quick,' Edy would call, '– here's a squirrel on Charles I.' When they tired of inventing their own games there were plenty of other entertainments for them – the devouring of ice creams (and helping the shopman turn the handle of the machine that made them), and the finding of 'very great friends' such as the old soldier with a wooden leg who sold ginger-beer in cold brown bottles from his hut, and the gentleman who 'directed' the famous Hampton Court Maze and let them shout dubious instructions to the visitors. It was a gloriously idiotic time. 'Come along, Teddy, don't be a coward!' Edy would shout, and they were off on their next adventure. They would enter the palace itself where it was quiet and cool, and see from the windows the fountain playing in the square court below. Ted never forgot the sight of those lofty beds in the king's and queen's chambers, so impossibly grand and motionless, unslept in and standing as if themselves asleep – they entered his imagination and would reappear as the architecture for an imposing new stage.

In his memoirs Gordon Craig was to tell a story of how, at the age of twelve, he escaped the 'Serious Danger' of being 'kidnapped'. The would-be kidnappers were a sad-faced photographer and his kindly wife who lived in a big, comfortable, red-brick house in Brondesbury, surrounded by fields of oak and elm trees. Ellen would send Ted to stay with them from time to time – sometimes for as long as six weeks at a time – and Ted enjoyed eating their delicious plum cake. But the photographer had noticed how hard his mother had to work all the year round for the upkeep of her children and it troubled him. Having no father, he thought, was probably worse for the boy – in any event it was better to 'leave his sister out of it', Gordon Craig imagines him calculating. 'The sister – that was all negative.' But he had a positive proposal to make concerning the brother (of whom he had taken rather a good picture). He went to Ellen Terry and offered to adopt him, with the promise of leaving him his fortune, his house and the photographic business. Naturally Ellen turned down the proposal.

There is no evidence that Gordon Craig ever heard how his father had tried to kidnap Edy in the 1870s and how his mother had unsuccessfully offered him Ted. Understandably Ellen did not allude to this episode in her *Memoirs* and the letter she wrote revealing what had happened only came to light in the late 1960s when Gordon Craig's son, Edward Craig, was writing a biography of his father. But some rumour of these events with their bleak implications may have percolated through to him. For the narrative of his own kidnap-adoption – he uses several times the word 'kidnap' – is the reverse side of that earlier story and in essence a correction to it, showing how Ellen would never part with him. Had he been deprived of his mother as well as a father, he would simply have 'vanished'.

That he recounts this story at some length in his memoirs is a testament to his lifelong insecurity. This feeling was exacerbated when, in the autumn of 1883, his mother herself 'vanished' from the country, taking off with Henry Irving and the Lyceum Company on the first of several long tours of the United States. She was to be absent for seven months: a lifetime in Ted's imagination.

22
Our American Cousins

To mark the one hundredth performance of *Romeo and Juliet* a banquet was held on the tented stage of the Lyceum, and it was here that Ellen Terry met one of her heroines, Sarah Bernhardt. 'I noticed that she hardly ever moved, yet all the time she gave the impression of swift, butterfly movement', Ellen wrote. '. . . She was hollow-eyed, thin, almost consumptive-looking.' People said she was to the French stage what Ellen herself was to the English stage. Her admiration of '*ma belle et illustre amie*' Ellen Terry was founded on her interpretation of Juliet in which she entered '*vivante dans l'immortalité* '. Like Irving, Bernhardt did not appear to have the natural equipment of an actor. 'Her face does little for her. Her walk is not much . . . By what magic does she triumph without two of the richest possessions that an actress can have?' Ellen had seen Bernhardt act in Paris and London, and admired her miraculous stagecraft. To her irritation, Irving singled out her managerial work for praise. 'Of her superb powers as an actress I don't believe he ever had a glimmering notion', she complained. (Bernhardt considered Irving 'a mediocre actor, but great artist'.) What struck Ellen that evening (apart from Bernhardt's praise of her Juliet) was that 'while talking to Henry she took some red stuff out of her bag and rubbed it on her lips'. Such frank 'making-up' in the 1880s was astonishing – and at dinner in front of Henry Irving! She was a woman, after all, not merely a symbol, and 'I liked Miss Sarah for it'.

For Henry Irving the most significant guest at this banquet had been an American cornet-player, now turned theatre-impresario, Henry E. Abbey, who was to arrange the Lyceum Company's tour of the United States. Addressing Abbey in his speech after the dinner, Irving paid tribute to the importance of good audiences. 'Applause is well worth the trouble, for the audience gets the full benefit of it. I hope our American cousins, in the autumn of next year [1883], will consider it worth their while to try the experiment by applauding me.'

He had been preparing long and carefully for this journey. His generosity to Edwin Booth had provided the Lyceum with a fine ambassador. On his return to the United States, Booth told the *New York Times* that Irving was 'a very superior actor and is gifted with a remarkable talent for stage management . . . If he visits America he will be liked no less for his qualities as a man than for his powers as an actor.'

From many travellers' tales, he already knew the reputation of American newsmen – 'the toughest and least gullible in the world'. To soften them somewhat, he sent before him a young journalist, Austin Brereton (later to be one of his first biographers), to prepare the way. He also persuaded the *New York Tribune* to lend him its London correspondent, Joseph Hatton, to accompany the tour. When Edwin Booth's friend William Winter came over to London with the American romantic actor Lawrence Barrett, Irving invited them to a splendid luncheon in the Beefsteak Room and offered Barrett the use of the Lyceum during the opening three months of 1884, while he and the company would still be abroad. Winter himself was reputed to be the most powerful theatre critic in the United States – 'a loyal friend and an abusive foe' – and Irving took care to make a special friend of him, taking his advice as to which plays he should present at the many towns the company visited.

On 28 July 1883, when the fifth season ended, Irving made a short farewell speech before the curtain, confirming that the company would be in America for six months, and adding that he hoped everyone would give a friendly welcome to Lawrence Barrett next winter. To a thunder of applause he retired: then the curtain rose to show Ellen Terry and himself centre stage, framed by all the actors and staff. From all over London actors performing in other theatres had hurried to the Lyceum and now crowded the corridors and gangways, so that the place was packed with more than 2,000 people.

News of this splendid farewell reached the United States – and soon there was more for them to read about. 'The dinners he [Irving] had to eat, the speeches he had to make, and listen to, were really terrific.' The Prince of Wales had to be entertained as guest of honour at a supper on the Lyceum stage and given a command performance of *Much Ado* at Sandringham; 500 distinguished Londoners were to be addressed by Irving at a banquet in St James's Hall; he was invited also to Hawarden Castle by Gladstone, and on

Independence Day entertained by 100 American and British actors at the Garrick Club to which (after the initial embarrassment of being secretly blackballed) he was triumphantly elected. The newspapers were crowded with reports of his social appearances, together with many caricatures – one showing him reluctantly refusing an invitation from the Royal Family ('The fact is I am really so pestered with invitations to dinner that you really must forgive me!').

He sat, too, for his portrait by John Everett Millais, who depicted him as a handsomely dressed society man – a model of how to present oneself in the best company (though his hair perhaps is just a trifle long). This picture, which still hangs in the Garrick Club, came to represent his achievement in acquiring respectability. He was to reinforce his hold on respectability by becoming a freemason and joining several other London clubs: the Athenaeum, the Reform Club and the Prince of Wales's Marlborough Club among others. He preferred the Millais portrait to all other portraits: to Whistler's dark, bloodless image of him as Philip II of Spain (which Whistler had partly repainted); to Bernard Partridge's likenesses of him in his many roles from Mephistopheles to King Lear; to the lithograph by James Pryde; to William Nicholson's sombre woodcut; to Gordon Craig's ink and water-colour drawing; to the print by William Rothenstein; and many other images in all mediums. He even preferred the Millais to the brilliant oil portrait painted in 1880 by Jules Bastien-Lepage (which Ellen Terry later presented to the National Portrait Gallery). This sudden focus on the man at his desk as he turns to the painter with a quick knowing smile was conceived at a supper on 3 July with Ellen Terry and Sarah Bernhardt and painted in one or two sittings at Grafton Street. The least successful picture, in Irving's view, was to be a head-and-shoulders sketch of him in his early fifties by John Singer Sargent – 'white face, tired eyes, holes in his cheeks and boredom in every line'. But Ellen saw it as a remarkably true resemblance, though 'mean about the chin' and not the Henry she loved. It was exhibited at the Royal Academy, after which Irving hid it in a closet and eventually destroyed it. 'How Henry hated that picture', Ellen remembered.

Before embarking on their adventures abroad, Irving took the company on a tour of Scotland and the north of England to test the travel arrangements for their large stock of plays. This triumphant tour, with its enormous press coverage and the crowds (among them Lillie Langtry and Oscar

Wilde) which gathered to see them off for America at Liverpool docks on 11 October, gave these weeks the air of a national event, like the progress of royalty through the country. On board the *Britannic*, adjoining cabins had been set aside for Ellen and Henry – in fact each had a double (two converted into one) – while a quarter of the boat's drawing-room was reserved for Ellen's private use. The rest of the company (approximately eighty of them), together with several tons of scenery, hundreds of costumes and stage properties, were to follow in a slower vessel, the *City of Rome*. 'I have brought my company and my scenery', Irving was to tell the American journalists. '. . . And so I bring you – almost literally – the Lyceum Theatre.'

Throughout the United States and in Canada, Henry Irving and Ellen Terry were treated as very grand people indeed. At Staten Island they would not have to line up with the ordinary visitors, proceed through a wooden shed and submit themselves to a rather brutal examination by the Custom-house officers. Their examination was to be conducted by newspaper reporters.

Flying the Union Jack at her stern and the Stars and Stripes from her topmast, the *Britannic* anchored off Staten Island in the early hours of 21 October. Racing towards her from opposite directions came two vessels: a privately owned steam yacht, the *Yosemite*, with the romantic actor Lawrence Barrett and the powerful critic William Winter on board; and a larger river steamer, the *Blackbird*, on which their host Henry Abbey had quartered a troupe of a hundred newspapermen and thirty musicians from the Metropolitan Opera House. As they approached the *Britannic*, these gentlemen of string and wind could be heard above the rattle of cables and anchors, belting out 'God Save the Queen'. The *Blackbird* reached them first and as Irving appeared on deck flourishing his hat, a great cheer went up. From the paddle-box a plank was thrown between the two boats and Irving commenced his uncertain way across just as the *Yosemite* reached the other side of the *Britannic*. Seeing his friends boarding behind him as he almost completed his disembarkation, by now bareheaded and perilously balanced, he was obliged to turn on his heel and, while the band struck up 'Hail to the Chief!', walk the plank a second time. At the conclusion of this return journey, in a scene of 'peculiar and touching beauty', he and his American colleagues from both vessels embraced as the musicians on the *Blackbird* solemnly played 'Rule Britannia'. 'Men more intellectual have never graced the stage', William Winter was moved to record. '. . . I saw prefigured that cordial union of brotherhood and art which has since been established between the theatres of England and these States.'

Following a short conference on deck, it was decided to transfer the pressmen to the well-appointed saloon of the *Yosemite* where cold chicken, champagne and cigars were available. Leading the way, Ellen, a slight figure with soft gold hair and delicate complexion which, the reporters observed, 'caught a rosy reflection from the loose flame coloured red scarf tied in a bow at the neck', stepped with 'a pretty little shudder' over to the yacht where Irving, lighting up a cigar and poised as if for a fencing match, cried out to the assembly: 'I am at your mercy . . . Have at me!'

Ellen soon realised that 'the Americans *wanted* to like us', and that Irving was determined to give them every opportunity for doing so – there were rumours that one of his hosts, W.H. Vanderbilt, had built a room for him with wall-to-wall mirrors so that he could always see himself. He knew that these newspapermen would be sensitive to any patronising air of superiority from the British, such as 'the high and rather condescending tone' they were hearing from Matthew Arnold during his lecture tour of the States. They remembered too the frank insults they had received from an earlier visitor on the *Britannic*, Charles Dickens. (His likening of the continual spitting of Americans to 'ripping open feather beds and giving the feathers to the winds;' his description of their newspapers as 'more mean, and paltry, and silly and disgraceful than any country I have known' and their 'despicable trickery at elections'. In short, 'I do not believe there are, on the whole earth besides, so many intensified bores as there are in these United States.') It was the genial manner of a Dickensian character, the merry music-hall comedian Alfred Jingle from Dickens's *The Pickwick Papers* which Irving assumed at this first interview. 'In a minute,' Ellen observed, 'he was on the best of terms with them.' He paid tribute to the American theatre-men, from 'Colonel' Bateman to Edwin Booth, to whom his own career owed so much. When asked to what he attributed his success, he replied: 'To my acting' – and was much praised for his honesty.

Then it was Ellen's turn. Irving introduced her as 'one of the most perfect and charming actresses that ever graced the English stage' and whispered loudly in her ear: 'These gentlemen want to have a few words with you. Say something pleasant – merry and bright.' A reporter then asked her: 'Can I send any message to your friends in England?' at which, suddenly remembering her animals and her children, she answered: 'Tell them I never loved them so much as now!' and burst into tears.

For the sake of their reputations, Ellen and Henry had arranged to stay at separate hotels in New York. While he was taken off, bumping along the cobble-paved streets pitted with holes to the Brevoort in Union Square (more like an English country house than a hotel, clustered with pictures of Queen Victoria, the late Prince Consort and rustic scenes from the old country), Ellen was escorted from the docks uptown to the Hotel Dam, and was preparing to shed more tears when she noticed that her room was being filled with roses. 'My dear American friends', she later wrote, 'have been throwing bouquets at me in the same lavish style ever since.'

In the late nineteenth century the American theatre was in many ways in a similar condition to the British. A strict censorship existed and there were no serious contemporary playwrights at work. In addition to adaptations of Shakespeare and revivals of Restoration comedy, domestic plays were staged with comic scenes showing local differences in manners and customs, above which the simple virtues of American life shone forth. The method of acting was declamatory, the great actors advancing to the front of the stage to deliver their soliloquies and perorations.

The Lyceum productions, particularly the historical plays with their costumes taken from famous pictures by Van Dyck, Titian, Holbein and others, their clever lighting and gorgeous scenery, all this was a revelation. In place of the tremendous singular moments of the American school of acting, audiences were shown a series of images and effects leading to a cumulative experience. American audiences were quick to respond to the novelty, often taking up points that had been overlooked in Britain. They greeted Irving and his company as pioneers. This was new and, as Ellen remarked, 'to be new was everything in America'.

Even so, at the start they came up against many difficulties. They were to open at Henry Abbey's antiquated Star Theatre on 13th Street, an unfashionable area where a speculator was at work employing a platoon of men and boys to buy up as many tickets as possible, then reselling them to the public at more than six times their box-office price. They were to open with *The Bells*. When the music swelled to its climax, Irving, draped in fur sprinkled with flakes of snow, his hair flowing, burst through the door on to the stage and, standing before his first American audience as Mathias, announced 'It is *I*'. People rose to their feet and cheered, their ovation lasting several minutes. But watching the production from a box, Ellen saw that Irving was taking it too slowly. The audience watched in silence – except for the banging of doors by late arrivals. In the interval, Irving complained that it was like acting in a churchyard. What he did not know was that on first nights American audiences traditionally held back their verdict until the very end of the play – and when *The Bells* did end, the applause was thunderously long and loud. Alone onstage before this great reception 'I was filled with emotion', he remembered. '. . . Who could stand before such an audience and not be moved deeply?'

The following evening, Ellen made her American debut in *Charles I*. 'She possesses a sweetness that softens the hard lines of ancient tragic form and leaves the perfect impression of nature', wrote one critic. Ellen herself came to believe that 'it is in Shakespeare that I have been best liked in America'. When she played Ophelia for the first time in Chicago, 'I played the part better than I had ever played it before, and I don't believe I ever played it so well again'. But it was as Beatrice in *Much Ado About Nothing* that she was 'met with most enthusiasm'. At last she and Henry were outplaying Charles Kelly and herself on their provincial tour of England. From Boston, later on their travels, Irving reported that Ellen 'was even better than she ever was in dear old England and has had a glorious and brilliant success'.

It was her voice, that most sweet voice, half-whisper and half-sigh, which enchanted everyone: a soft, veiled, husky, intimate, thrilling sound, mysterious in its power, certainly not an English sound. But Irving's voice sometimes baffled the Americans, as it had British audiences. 'His voice is apparently wholly unavailable for purposes of declamation', Henry James had warned America. The audiences needed to be warned since the art of declamation was very dear to them and stood proudly at the centre of their theatrical tradition. Irving's pronunciation was littered with oddities – drawling grunts and ejaculations – to the very edge of incomprehensibility. He would say 'gaw' for go, 'naw' for no, and 'Gud' for God. 'He never spoke the great line of Shakespeare', Stephen Coleridge wrote in his *Memories*, 'as though it were anything but prose.' He had a light voice and sometimes chewed at the words. It was peculiar for an actor to possess such command over his audiences, rousing them to violent enthusiasm and even terror, without apparently the ability to communicate his words. 'M'Gud! Is that my voice?' he is said to have exclaimed on hearing a recording of it. Though the recording from *Richard III* he made on an Edison wax cylinder in the late 1890s shows that he was able to control some of these nervous tics offstage, the thick rs and his *rubato* are very marked. 'You speak into it and everything is recorded, voice, tone, intonation, everything', he wrote excitedly after the experiment. 'You turn a little wheel, and forth it comes, and can be repeated ten thousand times. Only fancy what this suggests. Wouldn't you have liked to have heard the voice of Shakespeare, or Jesus Christ?' To hear the voice of Henry Irving is to pick up only a little of what Henry James described to readers of *Scribner's Monthly*: eccentricities of speech 'so strange, so numerous, so personal to himself, his vices of pronunciation, of modulation, of elocution so highly developed, the tricks he plays with the divine mother-tongue so audacious and fantastic, that the spectator who desires to be in sympathy with him finds himself confronted with a bristling hedge of difficulties'.

But the Americans gamely scrambled over these bristling obstacles, reckoning Irving's words would have sounded quite natural to Shakespeare's contemporaries. 'We hear again the voice of that great age', the Bohemian Club of San Francisco informed its members. This belief added to Irving's air of authenticity. In Philadelphia, where he opened with *Hamlet* at the Chestnut Street Theater, playing before what was perhaps the most sophisticated of American audiences, his reception was said to have been without precedent. 'I have never seen an audience in this city rise and cheer an actor as they cheered Irving', wrote one reporter. '. . . Such enthusiasm is unknown here.'

At Washington he and Ellen were invited to the White House for supper with the President, General Chester Arthur, his senior ministers and their wives, and talked long into the night about the president's views on Shakespeare. Though their tour was spectacularly successful, it also turned out to be an arduous experience, made more exhausting by Henry Abbey's wayward arrangements (at Indianapolis they found themselves in close competition with a Two-Headed Pig, the Wild Man of the Wood, and the fattest of Fat Ladies). The company travelled thousands of miles during one of America's most bitter winters, stamping around in blizzards at railroad stations and waiting many hours in trains that were literally stopped in their tracks by huge banks of snow. They arrived at St Louis at three o'clock in the morning to find that they could walk across the frozen Mississippi; and steamed into Baltimore, where they played on Christmas Day, a few hours before the curtain went up, unpacking the folded-away fairyland of palaces and landscapes from the boxcars miraculously fast. For their journey to Chicago they were lent a private train by the president of the railroad company and given a militia of armed guards – Sarah Bernhardt's train having been attacked by desperadoes who had read of her fabulous diamonds and wounded one of the guards in a terrific gunfight.

Ellen enjoyed the travelling. She put on weight and blossomed in the invigorating atmosphere. Britain undoubtedly possessed more poetry rooted in the past, but 'the poetry of the present, gigantic, colossal, and enormous made me forget it'. The very sunlight appeared brighter than in Britain and was reflected in the greater optimism of the people. 'I saw no misery or poverty there. Every one looked happy', she recorded, adding that only the Italian, Russian and Polish immigrants 'washed in daily on the bosom of the Hudson' were poor. Yet even they had hope. 'The barrow man of today is the millionaire of tomorrow.'

'I liked *all* the American cities', Ellen was to write. She even remembered Pittsburgh as being beautiful – particularly 'at night when its furnaces made it look like a city of flame'. Chicago appeared to her like 'a fair dream city rising out of the lake' (she took care not to visit the notorious stock-yards); and she was impressed by New York's elevated railway, 'the El', which she described as 'the first sign of *power* that one notices after leaving the boat'. She loved too the old-world city of Philadelphia with its 'red-brick sidewalks, the trees in the streets, the low houses with their white marble cuffs and collars' and quietly dressed inhabitants revealing their Quaker origins. At the age of sixty she was to calculate that she had spent almost five years of her life in North America, making eight journeys there, seven of them with Irving. 'I often feel that I am half-American', she wrote. The place rejuvenated her. 'Something in this America makes me feel more sensitive', she was to write, '– I'm so much better in health here & don't get tired . . . Henry bears up quite marvellously well without his Garrick Club.'

When the company crossed the frontier into Canada and they arrived at Toronto, the final city of their tour, Ellen, now in her thirty-eighth year, went tobogganing like a schoolgirl. 'It was like flying,' she wrote, '. . . I felt my breath go . . . I shut my mouth, opened my eyes and . . . rolled right out of the toboggan when we stopped.' Then she climbed up and rushed all the way down again. 'Amazing!' Henry stood in the snow, watching her with a curiously forlorn expression. And behind him Stoker had positioned himself, hesitating between trepidation and desire until, unable to resist the iced toboggan chutes, he leapt forward, fell off the toboggan, and went somersaulting down the hillside, flapping his arms.

Ellen and Henry were very close during this long tour as if, on leaving Britain, they had given a Victorian chaperone the slip. Irving himself seemed to have been able, in part at least, to escape his shell of reticence, and show his emotions more freely. Both of them had brought their dogs to America. Irving's old dog, Charlie, was going blind and after his death Ellen was to give him her own fox terrier, Fussie. These dogs, and others which they shared over the years, were almost like surrogate children in their Lyceum family life. But after six months of travelling, they prepared to return to their more discreet English lives. It had been a 'voyage of enchantment' – one of Ellen's biographers was to describe it as being like a honeymoon. Later, when it was reported that someone in Philadelphia had made derogatory comments about Ellen's sexual morals, and scandal about her was rife, Irving instructed Joseph Hatton to offer up to £100 to find 'the scoundrel'. Ellen Terry, he said, had been much maligned, adding that were he free he would 'marry her tomorrow'.

On the way back they stopped at Niagara Falls. It was more wonderful, Ellen thought, than beautiful. Leaving the group of actors, she went and stood alone, staring down at the rapids and listening: but soon 'it became dreadful and I was *frightened*'. She was frightened not of falling, but of throwing herself down into the cascade of water. William Terriss actually did trip and almost fell to his death. 'Nearly gone, dear,' he gasped, clambering back up the slippery rockface. Irving himself was greatly impressed by the spectacle and how it might, with extra paintwork and lights, be improved. 'A great stage manager, Nature!' he exclaimed. It brought to his mind the young Englishman known as Captain Webb who, the previous year, following a quiet dinner and a siesta, had dived into the awful torrent and disappeared in the whirlpool. Perhaps there was a play in it. 'Imagine the coolness, the daring of it,' he remarked to Ellen. '. . . A great soul – any man who has the nerve for such an enterprise.'

They gave return performances in Chicago, Boston and New York. 'Honour goes before him and affection remains behind', wrote one critic before they left. 'The work has been heavy', Irving conceded. At every town the company visited, from Cincinnati to Detroit, he had made speeches, thanking his hosts for their unprecedented generosity and referring emotionally to Ellen as 'my sister in art'. At his farewell speech before the curtain of the Star Theater, he announced that the Lyceum Company would be returning to North America in the autumn. 'The seed we have sown I mean to reap,' he wrote to his secretary, Louis Austin, 'our work has been a revelation and our success beyond precedent.'

He had decided to dispense with the many carriages of heavy equipment which had encumbered their early travels, relying instead on simplified scenery augmented by the work of local carpenters and painters. They left New York at the end of April 1884 and were back in North America in late September, starting this time in Canada and opening with *The Merchant of Venice* at the Academy of Music ('a cross between a chapel and a very small concert room') in Quebec. Irving himself was reputed to be in 'the height of good humour' and all the company skipping around in the best of spirits. 'Never had our people played so well', Louis Austin wrote to his wife. Then suddenly things fell apart. Ellen collapsed from exhaustion and her roles were taken for ten days by a versatile understudy, Winifred Emery. When they reached Boston, the impossible happened: Henry Irving was laid up with rheumatic gout – and panic swept through the company. George Alexander (who had taken the place of William Terriss) played Benedick at short notice, but most of the burden fell on Ellen. 'She rose to the occasion magnificently, rousing the audience to positive enthusiasm', Austin reported. 'I never saw her play the scene in the cathedral when Beatrice tells Benedick to kill Claudio with such fire and energy.'

Another difficulty arose from the morbid rivalries among Irving's extravagantly loyal staff. Provoked by the continual 'flattering and scheming', Austin would sometimes voice his opposition so outspokenly that he shocked the mild-mannered stage-manager Loveday. But it was between 'that idiot Stoker', always so ferociously sentimental, and the arch-intellectual Austin that a serious feud broke out. Austin was employed to write the many speeches which Irving delivered in the United States, and which he took very seriously. Stoker resented the importance given to his rival and would sometimes try to substitute his own drafts on the various tables and lecterns at which Irving was to speak. 'Poor old Bram has been trying *his* hand,' Irving remarked to Austin, 'but there isn't an idea in the whole thing.'

These tensions in some ways strengthened the company. They came through intact, came through splendidly. Their two long tours were social as well as financial successes. Young American men worshipped Ellen's 'mischievous sweetness', while the young women were captivated by her dress sense (her feathered hats, billowing scarves 'dashingly cut top coats') in the French style. As for Irving, who gave his farewell speech at Harvard University, he was now regarded an honorary American.

During their last weeks in New York, despite playing amid the fever and scurry of a presidential election, they did good business and finally, after all the costs had been paid, made an enormous profit on these two epic tours – more than £20,000.

As he sailed back to England on board the *Arizona* in April 1885, Irving could look back on a phenomenal achievement. He had created what was undoubtedly the most celebrated and successful company of actors in the English-speaking world. But by now they were all suffering from a terrible weariness, and Irving himself was approaching a crisis in his emotionally charged relationship with Ellen.

23
From Malvolio to Mephistopheles

'America sends us back a better actor than the one who left our shores', wrote Clement Scott, greeting his old friend Irving. Nevertheless the new Shakespeare production put on during the brief interval between these two tours of Canada and the United States was one of the Lyceum's failures. *Twelfth Night* had not been performed on the English stage for some thirty-five years and Irving himself had never seen the play. He studied the text carefully and did what he could to cater for his audiences' sensibilities, plucking out some of the bawdy speeches and fanciful songs, and giving the comedy sixteen elaborate and costly sets. 'The seacoast of Illyria unfolded on a rock-bound promontory in the light of a red sunset after the storm', wrote his biographer Madeleine Bingham.

The Duke of Orsino reclined on a velvet couch, tied and tasselled in gold, and behind him in a dim mysterious alcove, dark with painted glass, minstrels played their soft melodies to the lovesick man. The noble palace of Olivia was splendid with columns, entablatures and sculpted friezes. Her garden was charming with clipped box and yew hedges, where she and her household basked all day on wide terraces bathed in perpetual sunshine. The kitchen fire, before which Sir Toby and his boon companions roared their catches, was warm and glowing in contrast with the ghostlike figure of Malvolio in his white nightshirt. But the last scene of all brought the play to a climax of adornment. The spreading portico of Olivia's house was flanked with branching palm trees beside a blue sea, the whole rendered more striking by the picturesque grouping of guards, pages, and ladies and gentlemen of the court.

Ellen's brother, Fred Terry, played Sebastian, brother to her Viola. The way he reproduced her voice and manner gave their performance a curious intensity. On the opening night she had to perform sitting down and wearing a sling, having poisoned her thumb (she played in only sixteen performances and her part was taken over by her sister Marion). But the main weakness of the play centred on Irving's miscasting of the comics, Sir Toby Belch, Sir Andrew Aguecheek and Feste the Clown. They simply were not funny. This may unconsciously have been Irving's intention. For by playing Malvolio as a Don Juan on stilts, a man more sinned against than sinning, he turned the comedy into tragedy and the fantasy into reality. His final curse, like Caliban railing against Prospero or Timon expressing his hatred of all mankind, rang out, shocking all who heard it, like a personal indictment against every one of them. It was as if he saw in Malvolio's ambition to better himself, for all its absurdity, some reflection of his own career, as if he heard in the ridicule filling Olivia's house an echo of his wife's contempt as well as those awful cat-calls which mockingly rang through his early career. That rejection sounded again in the booing and hissing that met him as he stood before the curtain at the end of the play. His speech to the malcontents was 'the only mistake that I ever knew him make', Ellen wrote ('an actor's opinion of his audience is better kept to himself', he later told Austin Brereton). He turned on them, rebuking the whole pack for their hostility. He was at a loss to explain how a company of 'earnest comedians – sober, clean and word-perfect' could have merited such treatment from a British audience. It was as if his extraordinary success in America had pulled him away from the native spirit of his country where he had positioned himself so perfectly. Then, at the last moment, he recovered himself with a touching appeal: 'In your smiles we are happy, prithee smile upon us.'

The production of *Twelfth Night* cost £4,000 and made a loss over the summer season in London – though it was to prove one of the Lyceum's more popular plays abroad. Ellen, who thought the production rather 'lumpy', judged Irving's Malvolio to be 'fine and dignified'. He had stepped outside what was expected of him and in doing so achieved something remarkable, his extraordinary bitterness being interpreted by the American critic William Winter as 'the cornerstone of his reputation'. Ted, too, who was later to have a walk-on part in the play (which was consequently one of the first Lyceum productions he remembered clearly), wrote that 'Irving was remarkable in the guise of Malvolio – not playing the buffoon, but solemnly comic, with great distinction, calm and dark'.

But Irving decided to avoid comedy in future and aim for high tragedy. For five years he had been pondering over Goethe's *Faust*. It was of course unactable for reasons of length and complexity and would remain unacted unless much simplified by someone who knew what was needed. He chose W.G. Wills, the Irishman who had revised *Olivia* for the Lyceum, and whose *Charles I*, composed in dramatic verse for Bateman, was still in Irving's repertoire. Wills was a bohemian character, enthusiastic and absent-minded, who lived (with several cats and a monkey) in great disorder – he once accidentally boiled his watch, it was said, in place of an egg. By preference he was a painter and hired a liveried footman to impress his sitters. But to earn a living he stayed in bed writing and adapting picturesque plays. 'I have lovingly worked up and diversified the character of Meph throughout,' he told Irving. His skill lay in creating great dramatic moments for the central characters – which Irving enhanced with enlargements of his own.

The most popular feature of *Twelfth Night* had been the scenery, and so Irving prepared for *Faust* what Ellen called their 'heaviest' production yet. He took her and the costume-designer Alice Comyns Carr (who spoke German), together with her husband and the principal Lyceum scene-painter Hawes Craven, to Germany, staying in Nuremburg and finding in the neighbouring town of Rothenburg the mediaeval atmosphere he felt the play needed. He was at his most beneficent, buying expensive presents for everyone, and bringing back numerous 'authentic' stage properties. When the main party returned to England, he and Ellen went off together to Berlin where they stayed privately with the German actor Ludwig Barnay – an appendix to their journey not mentioned in Ellen's *Memoirs*.

After what had been almost a year in America, the success of *Faust* was of more than usual importance to Irving. His behaviour during rehearsals shocked Alice Comyns Carr. 'Gone was the debonair, cheery holiday companion', she wrote, 'and in his place was a ruthless autocrat, who brooked no interference from anyone, and was more than a little rough in his handling of everyone in the theatre – except Nell.' Sarcastic to his fellow actors, he went about slapping and punching them as his rage boiled up. George Alexander who was to play Faust and who 'always acted like an angel with me', Ellen wrote, was 'sore all over' after the rehearsals.

This banging-about of the cast was in curious contrast to his eloquent public oratory on behalf of the acting profession, the charity he showed in creating the Provident and Benevolent Fund for Actors, and his generosity to those among his company who fell on difficult times. Everyone from carpenters to call-boys, baggage crews, cleaners, pageboys, ushers (over 400 staff worked at the Lyceum) were paid well above the average wage, while Irving gave himself the relatively modest salary of £60 a week. The dramatist Henry Arthur Jones was to accuse him of getting his plays 'on the cheap'. But although he did not value contemporary playwrights highly, he was generous to those who were loyal to him such as Tennyson, Sardou and especially Wills who was always making demands on him (on one occasion Irving handed him £800 for a play he never produced). He kept a list of forty retired actors to whom he gave weekly allowances, organised benefit performances for others and, on the spur of the moment, would hand out sovereigns or half-sovereigns to obviously needy people. Such was his reputation for generosity that his correspondence had become crowded with people wanting things – most often money. Characteristically he paid the cartoonist Carlo Pellegrini ('Ape' of *Punch*) £300 within hours of receiving a desperate request.

'I never cared much for Henry's Mephistopheles', Ellen wrote. She considered it a meretricious role – 'a twopence coloured part.' But she loved playing Marguerite. It was 'the part I liked better than any other – outside Shakespeare'. Her pathos was a perfect foil to Irving's diabolical power. Though she was now in her thirty-ninth year, she somehow managed in her resplendent yellow costume to look nineteen.

Wills had quickly boiled down the 1,200 lines that preceded the entrance of Mephistopheles to a mere 60 lines, so the audience did not have long to wait before Irving's dramatic appearance through the sulphurous smoke of Faust's book-lined study, a towering figure with a magnificent feather in his hood, apparelled entirely in scarlet, the vividness of which was 'intensified by the cold glitter of his pewter-coloured weapons and their harness'. He was no longer an ordinary villain: he was the devil himself. Yet it was not the daemonic Mephistopheles with his ominously swirling cloak, encircled by the blue fire that accompanied him everywhere, nor the beautiful young Marguerite, so pious and agonising in her remorse, that dazzled the audience so much as the amazing panorama of canvas and paint, the sonorous chords of Hamilton Clarke's incidental music on the newly installed organ, and the astonishing ingenuity of the stage machinery. Here was a masterpiece of stage decoration. 'The gloom is a good gloom', observed one critic. '. . . Seldom too have we heard better thunder.' Ellen recalled that there were some 400 ropes, each with a name, behind the scenes to induce counterfeit apparitions to spring forth and angelic visions to appear, trap-door vanishings to happen, and miraculous ascents heavenwards or descents into awful infernos suddenly to take place. The newest technology was employed to give spectacular effects with coloured lights and smoke – changing the atmosphere with the use of brimstone, calcium arcs, salvoes of limelight and, most extravagant of all, electrical pads and fluids (under the supervision of Thomas Edison's partner, Colonel Gouraud) which, during the duelling scenes, sent brilliant sparks flying hither and thither, astonishing the audience and terrifying the actors. The costs of manufacturing this spectacle were enormous, more than twice those of *Twelfth Night*. But, as Ellen remembered, 'it proved the greatest of all Henry's financial successes'.

The Royal Family took a box to witness the marvels; Gladstone wrote to congratulate Irving ('I do not know how much time had been given to preparing the mise-en-scene – but had it been ten years it could not have been done better'); and the Grand Duke of Saxe-Meiningen conferred on him the rank of a Commander of the Ernestine Order (Second Class). Journalists debated whether Faust could actually have married Marguerite; and throughout the country Mephistopheles hats, Marguerite shoes and postcards of Ellen with her golden hair braided down to her waist went on sale (her image was to be seen in magazines all around the country recommending everything from silk umbrellas to imperial furs). Irving's adulators, who had been uncomfortably muted after his Malvolio, greeted his Mephistopheles with a full-throated roar of acclaim as he skipped and jumped across the stage, uniting jokery with devilment and performing acts of cruelty with amazing glee. Behind a solemn mask, seductive and snake-like, there was galvanic energy.

Yet even now there were those still small voices among the literary and academic critics who disapproved of what they saw. 'I go to pantomime only at Christmas', retorted W.S. Gilbert when a friend asked him whether he had seen the production. Henry James warned readers of the *Century Magazine* that 'special precautions should be taken against the accessories seeming a more important part of the business than the action'. A great imaginative work of literature had been made trivial and vulgar. James attached little importance to the mechanical artifices with which the Lyceum sought to enliven what remained of Goethe's *Faust.* 'We care nothing for the spurting flames which play so large a part, nor for the importunate limelight projected upon somebody or something. It is not for these that we go to the great Goethe', he wrote.

That blue vapours should attend on the steps of Mephistopheles is a very poor substitute for his giving us a moral shudder. That deep note is entirely absent from Mr Irving's rendering of him . . . We attach also but the slenderest importance to the scene of the Witches' Sabbath, which has been reduced to a mere bald hubbub of capering, screeching, and banging, irradiated by the irrepressible blue fire, and without the smallest articulation of Goethe's text.

What troubled Henry James was the tremendous success of this banal exhibition, and the cheers with which the sheer immaturity of the Lyceum extravaganza was greeted. It reflected the philistine mind of the English that gave little opportunity for his own subtle work to find a place.

James's objections to *Faust* were to some extent echoed by William Archer, the forerunner of a brilliant new school of young critics that was to include Bernard Shaw and Max Beerbohm. 'A strange change is coming over *criticism*', Ellen warned her son. Archer ('that fool Archer' as Irving called him) had begun his career as a drama critic by contributing to a near-libellous pamphlet, *The Fashionable Tragedian*, which made fun of Irving's spasms and angularities and dragging perambulations (like 'trying to run quickly over a ploughed field'). He described his Hamlet as a weak-minded puppy, his Macbeth as Uriah Heep in chain armour, his Othello as an infuriated sepoy, his Richard III as a cheap Mephistopheles; and he argued that Irving's pretence of scholarship, combined with a drive for flashy effects, was becoming a menace to the British theatre. In 1884 he wrote a more moderate assessment, acknowledging that Irving's 'face and his brain' had 'made him what he is', and praising 'his glittering eye and his restless, inventive intellect'. But though he found something exhilarating in the 'histrionic romp' called *Faust*, 'I do think that Mr Irving might . . . omit Goethe's name from the programme', he wrote. '. . . The dead cannot defend themselves.'

Part of what Henry James and William Archer were protesting against was Irving's indifference to contemporary dramatic writing. The most powerful actor-manager in Britain never used his powers to fight the crippling censorship laws. 'Censorship is a very wise and necessary thing; most reasonable, I think,' he told a Select Committee of the House of Commons in 1892 (though the censorship laws obliged him to abandon plays about the Irish patriot Robert Emmett and the prophet Mahomet). He wanted to uphold respectability in the theatre and he did not value or sometimes even recognise genuine dramatic literature. He trusted to his sense of what mid-to-late-nineteenth-century audiences wished to see in their theatres rather than the quibbles from university men, dry scholars like Faust himself who was no match for Mephistopheles. What the public wanted was decency as a veil for shameful deeds and secret guilt: a contrast from which sprang his hypnotic power onstage.

A strong rebuttal of Henry James's and William Archer's criticism, and later the polemics of Bernard Shaw, was to be made by Ellen's son, Gordon Craig. Text-literature and the theatrical event might occupy adjacent territories but, he pointed out, they were often at war with each other. The pact which these literary men sought to impose between composition and performance, with the text always in command of the action, sprang from a false notion of what the theatre essentially was. No wonder they had dismissed Irving's *Faust* as pantomime, not seeing that it belonged to the genre of high tragedy. 'His [Irving's] performance (I made some notes on it in a copy of the play) was a great tragic performance – cynical – cold – dry and electrical', Craig wrote, '. . . it was high tragic and fearful to watch.' What these bookmen-critics lacked was the innocent eye. They looked down, as it were, at their conglomeration of notes and failed to witness the drama as an experience. Irving had presented the super-real and the super-natural in his extravagant productions. He went as far as it was possible to go – after which Craig himself would go further. Like a man crossing a time barrier, he was to break with pictorial realism, experimenting like a painter with a range of colours and shafts of light from above the stage, and creating an immense visionary architecture for the theatre of the future.

But it had been the spectacle of Irving at work during rehearsals at the Lyceum that finally woke Ted up to his destiny and enabled him, as Edward Gordon Craig, to 'spread my ideas out over the stages of Europe and America'. Irving was in his theatre 'what Napoleon was in the midst of his army', he wrote, '. . . sole ruler of the Theatre of England, from 1871 till his death'. It was his leadership which enthralled Craig. 'His will was all that mattered at the Lyceum Theatre.' This adulation, almost amounting to a fascist idolatry of power, was an illustration, Craig explained, of democratic dictatorship exercised for the benefit of his audience. '*Irving was a selfish man without a jot of self-interest.*'

Ellen Terry worshipped a different Henry Irving. 'People think they see everything on the stage', she said. 'Nothing of the sort.' It was his secret self that attracted her. The qualities that so allured her son, she found almost unintelligible. 'He [Irving] always put the theatre first. He lived in it, he died in it.' She had told him that if she suddenly dropped dead, his first emotion would be grief and his first question would be about the preparedness of her understudy – and he did not disagree. She admired him, but did not like some of the means by which he maintained his leadership: what she called his craftiness. 'I wish he were more ingenuous and direct.' She had a better understanding of literature than he did and sometimes 'I blushed for him'. He seemed to her a supreme egotist, seldom *without* self-interest. Yet she recognised all the same – who could deny it? – that he was a genius.

But it was what he concealed, what he lacked – the absence of 'homely qualities' and his awful isolation – that made him so unexpectedly lovable. He would spend hours in preparation, dressing up, painting his face, becoming someone else – and it was this 'someone else' the public applauded. But Ellen loved his unpainted face, that splendid face he wished to hide. She saw that he had no idea of 'his own beauty – personal beauty'. She doted on his looks: the unconscious grace with which he moved his hands – and what fine hands they were; then that refined Roman nose of his, curving and clean-cut; and also the firm line from his ear to his chin, so delicate and strong. She had never seen a man of such distinction. 'A superb brow', she observed; 'rather small dark eyes which can at moments become immense, and hang like a bowl of dark liquid with light shining through . . . His skin is very pale . . . and stretched tightly over his features. Under the influence of strong emotion, it contracts more, and turning somewhat paler, a grey look comes into his face, and the hollows of his cheeks and eyes show up clearly.'

These were the words of a woman who had found to her astonishment that she was in love. She makes it clear that it was the face she saw in private that was subject to these extraordinary changes. A few days before the opening of *Faust* in December 1885, Irving had sent her a note. 'No rehearsal this morning for you, my darling . . . It will be all right – of course – but it is a stern business . . . do not wear yourself out – & you shall not tonight either if I can persuade [you] to take it quietly. What a worry you are, you see. With all my love my dearest dearest.'

His concern for her was no longer just a matter of her performance onstage – she was 'more woman than artist'. Her feelings for him had never been exclusively tied to their theatre business, important as that was. 'To me it is perfectly horrible to be touched *in any way* unless by people I love', she wrote. All the world, it is said, loves a lover; but it is really a lover who loves all the world. When she was happy it seemed as if Ellen loved everyone. In her rehearsal notes for *Faust*, where Faust kisses Marguerite, she wrote: 'Startled! A little ashamed – happy.' Then, in large scrawling letters down the margin and, as it were, sliding off the page and into life itself, she went on repeating the word: 'happy, happy, happy, happy, happy . . .'

24

Death of a Husband, Death of a Lover

During her thirties, many of the men Ellen knew and loved made their exits. The first to go, in 1880, was Tom Taylor, who had been almost like a second father to her and Kate, giving them both much of their education in the theatre. Four years later her other stage mentor, Charles Reade, once almost her lover, was also dead.

Then, on her return from the second Lyceum tour of North America, she was told that Charles Wardell had died (Florence Irving sent her two sons like spies to his funeral). He had been drinking heavily since their separation and had become unemployable. The news of his death was brought to Ellen by a girl with whom he had been living and who took her to the room where his body lay. As she stood beside the bed, Ellen could not help thinking of Shakespeare's Juliet. It was a strange dramatic reflex, for she had never played that role with him and there was no love between them. But though he had bullied and sometimes assaulted her, she 'felt some kind of debt to this husband', having taken his name and given back less than he expected. He had expected something impossible and by the end she had paid her debt many times. On the surface all had been well – and that was important. By marrying the son of a clergyman, she had regained 'the position of a respectable woman', the Revd Charles Dodgson judged (even though he privately believed she had been married in God's sight 'without the ceremonial of marriage' to the father of her children, he had no choice 'but to drop the acquaintance' while she remained unmarried). Dodgson believed her husband had done 'a most generous act' by 'allowing the children to assume his surname', albeit one they were quick to cast off.

It was said by Dodgson and others that Ellen had fancied she could cure her husband of his drinking. But the truth was that it had been his jealousy of Irving, combined with her transcendent success onstage, that had turned this *bon viveur* into an alcoholic. 'I believe he drank himself to death', Dodgson concluded. 'So she is now a widow.'

She was also, at the age of thirty-nine, a free and independent woman again. And Irving too, having obtained a judicial separation from Florence granting her a very generous allowance, was as free as ever he would be. The collapse of his marriage had not left him sexless. One of his 'flames', the extraordinarily pretty actress Winifred Emery, who was to take over Ellen's role in *Faust* in the late 1880s, was obliged to advance the date of her marriage in 1888 so as to avoid Irving's sexual advances. Inevitably there were stories – stories 'that I am constantly hearing', Dodgson complained to his cousin Dorothea Wilcox, 'of the (alleged) immoral life of Miss E. T. and Mr. Irving'.

There is no doubt that Ellen and Henry were by now much in love. What little has been seen of their correspondence clearly indicates this, and the fact that almost all their letters eventually disappeared suggests that there was something that they and their families wished to conceal. They had to be careful. From time to time Florence still wrote complaining letters to her solicitor and made accusations against Irving to her sons. 'How dreadful it would be', her elder son Harry protested, 'if that about Irving and Ellen Terry was to come about in the divorce court. What a cad he is to bring all this disgrace on himself.'

Divorce proceedings would bring disgrace on all the family – Harry and his brother Laurence as well as on Florence herself. Her provocations were beginning to have rather less effect on the boys, she noticed, since they had gone to public school, though they were still loyal to her and, if she made the charges monstrous enough, still outraged on her behalf. When she saw signs of their softening towards their father, she would rally them to her cause by saying how sad she was feeling and they would reply that 'it makes us sad if you say you are sad'. But the truth was that her 'ever loving sons' were still her one source of happiness; and they knew this.

Florence, it was said, had read only one book, *Burke's Peerage*, but she read it all the time. 'It looks awfully as if you're going to be Lady Irving, doesn't it?' Harry wrote to her. 'There seems to be such a lot of knighting going about now . . .' But if Irving were to be knighted, Harry added, 'knighthoods won't be worth much'. It bewildered him to think that 'a drunkard who deserts his wife and children and does all he can to disgrace them', might be rewarded in such a way. Certainly the prospect of being a Lady, so ironically dangled before her by her son, placed Florence in something of a dilemma. On the whole, it was best to keep her position as a virtuous, wronged woman, sticking pins into the figure of Irving each day while urging her sons to pray for his redemption at night.

Everyone understood the rules. Actors, always with the flickering shadows of rumour and gossip playing around them, were still permitted a screen of privacy so long as they took care to protect it and let it protect them. To be found out was bad manners and 'what after all are good morals', asked the singer and comedienne Marie Tempest, 'but good manners?'

Nevertheless, from time to time there were 'scurrilous articles' and what Irving called 'press problems'. Reading these articles, the boys would complain of his 'orgies' to their mother. 'What a beast he is . . . his greatest sin (of which there are many) his marriage, the treatment of his wife and children, but men never get their deserts now from the public.' There was no actual scandal – had there been, it would certainly have found its way into the Revd Charles Dodgson's dossier. Biographers have been divided as to whether this was because, though Henry and Ellen certainly loved each other, they were not actually lovers; or whether they took care not to be discovered. Their families – including Laurence Irving, grandson and biographer of Henry Irving; and Ellen's grandson, Edward Craig, biographer of his father Gordon Craig – generally agreed that their grandparents were not sexual partners. Gordon Craig himself could never countenance the thought of Henry Irving being physically possessed by his mother, though Edy appears to have felt easier in her mind about their relationship. Ellen Terry's biographer, Roger Manvell, acknowledges that their feelings over-flowed from the theatre into their lives and that there was a degree of physical intimacy – though not sufficient for Ellen to be classed as Henry's mistress during her thirties and early forties. Contraception not being reliable, they had to be careful. Nina Auerbach, Ellen Terry's feminist biographer, describes them as having 'the look of intimacy and the feel of stability' while acting the conventional marriage 'that was so alien to them both'. And it was true that Ellen would go to the Beefsteak Room, framed by pictures and trophies of their theatrical careers, and before very grand guests be his partner there 'when I don't care in the least for the people, just to please Henry'. But this was a social rather than a sexual unease. The novelist Marguerite Steen, in her history of the family, *A Pride of Terrys*, writes that after Ellen's opening performance at the Lyceum as Ophelia, a role in which she believed she had failed, Irving turned up at Longridge Road at midnight to comfort her – and it was on that momentous night, 30 December 1878, Irving's biographer Madeleine Bingham adds, that 'she became his mistress'. Where Charles Wardell was that night she does not reveal.

The facts tell their own story. In 1880 Irving bought a 'fine Elizabethan house' called The Grange which belonged to Kate Bateman and her husband. It stood in the village of Brook Green (now part of Hammersmith), facing the green and being described as 'one of the prettiest places in the London suburbs'. But the property was run-down and during 1881, Irving spent much money and time preparing it as a handsome and comfortable retreat for him and Ellen, laying out the trees and arbours of the garden on the lines of Godwin's garden at Harpenden which he knew she had greatly loved before it was snatched away from her. This was at a time when the Lyceum was preparing its production of *Romeo and Juliet* and, according to Ellen, Irving 'felt like Romeo'. The Grange was intended to be their home where, in his fashion, Irving could take Godwin's place in her emotional life. He did not plan that they should live together out of wedlock as Ellen and Godwin had done, and when Charles Wardell died one great obstacle to their marriage was removed. Divorce, even if attainable, would ruin their careers and leave them bankrupt. Only Florence stood in their way – Florence whom Irving had married through duty not love. 'He had better have killed her straight off', Ellen burst out in a letter to Bernard Shaw. Irving called Ellen 'my own dear wife as long as I live'. His feelings for her were unique in his experience and he proposed marriage to her – and, like Romeo confronting the Capulets, to hell with the consequences! *Faust* appeared to have lent him magical properties and made him so wealthy that he seems to have felt invincible. He had enjoyed no life outside the theatre before he fell in love with Ellen, and she – 'the Queen of every woman' – had opened up a new kingdom for him. Their castle would be The Grange.

Years later, when Irving was dead, Marguerite Steen asked Ellen whether she really had been Irving's lover, and she promptly answered: 'Of course I was. We were terribly in love for a while.' But at earlier periods of her life when there were more people around to be offended, she said contradictory things. To Lucy Duff Gordon, for example, celebrated for her indiscretions, Ellen confided, while Irving was still alive: 'People always say that Henry is my lover, of course. He isn't. As a matter of fact he never sees further than my head. He does not even know I have a body.'

Laurence Irving has reasoned that his grandfather and Ellen Terry simply did not have the duplicity needed to carry on a sexual liaison. But Henry Irving did not need duplicity. He simply said nothing to anyone except 'my darling' Ellen. The best way of hiding their liaison was to make it known in socially acceptable language. The Victorians did not want to discover anything disreputable about him. He was a symbolic figure, someone who carried their honour on his shoulders. To expose him would be tantamount to revealing their own unworthiness. He never troubled to conceal his frequent visits to Longridge Road. Often he would find Ellen there with her circle of girls, sewing and talking. Into this queenly court Irving would make his entrance, a rather terrifying figure among the women. 'Once or twice I saw him in a towering rage,' wrote Lucy Duff Gordon, 'working himself up to fever heat over something that had happened at the theatre, but she could calm him in a moment.'

They found it easier to be alone together when they were abroad. Sometimes they stayed at separate hotels when in the United States and Canada, but were always invited as a couple to people's private houses. And there were other occasions abroad – holidays in Europe, the United States and Canada – that find no place in Ellen's *Memoirs*, but which her children sometimes discovered. 'Do you know that Henry is going to Berlin also !!!!!' Ted exclaimed to Edy in a letter of the late 1880s. Ellen's photograph album shows them together in Lucerne ('a dream'), Venice ('a wonderland'), Verona ('perfection'), Dublin, Paris and various places around Europe – 'Happy hours, a sweet place . . . in a cottage near a wood', Ellen noted. '. . . Beauty everywhere. To go away was cruel pain.' Once or twice they were unexpectedly seen together. 'Last week in Brussels my eyes were gladdened by a sight they little expected to see', wrote a journalist.

I had taken myself to an open air concert in the Waux-Hall and was listening to the music . . . when a loud ringing laugh from a neighbouring table attracted my attention as being strangely familiar. I turned round, and to my astonishment found myself rubbing shoulders with no less personages than Henry Irving and Ellen Terry . . . Here was genius relaxing indeed . . . She was in such buoyant spirits as would surprise some of the Lyceum patrons . . . Miss Terry wore a large black hat and a long brown wrap which the Lyceum manager solicitously adjusted about the shoulders of his leading lady. I did not wait to see or hear more as eavesdropping is hardly in my line . . .

On 1 August 1886, when the season was over, they took another holiday together. One newspaper reported that 'Mr Henry Irving and Miss Ellen Terry left Waterloo in a saloon carriage at 10.15am yesterday for Southampton.'

The train was met there by Herr Keller, the German consul, the party was conveyed to the North German steamship *Fulda* on which special accommodation has been provided. The Captain set apart his cabin as a sitting room. Mr Irving informed a representative of the Press that he proposes on reaching America to go yachting with a friend on the East Coast and he expected to be back in England in five weeks' time.

This must have been at a time when, Charles Wardell having died the previous year, and the refurbishment of The Grange having been long completed, their romance appeared to be leading towards possible marriage. Stephen Coleridge was so jealously agitated by all the talk that he felt bound to remind Ellen that, no longer having the cover of marital status, she was inviting disaster by travelling everywhere with Irving – especially on boats to America where some families were refusing to see her. His letter was so earnest that 'I couldn't help smiling', she replied and begged him 'not to trouble your mind' about this 'trifling' matter. 'I love you very much . . . (tho' you're a trying friend).' But other people, who did not speak to Ellen, were speaking to one another and thinking what Stephen Coleridge was thinking (there were even implausible rumours of a love-child, one candidate being a girl called Beatrice who became one of Ellen's companions, married an actor in Irving's company, and had a son who grew up to be an actor).

Then something happened which changed the course of their relationship.

One of Ellen's happiest memories of the Lyceum arose from the company's production of Tennyson's *The Cup*. In her *Memoirs* she was to write that the staging of this play had been 'one of the most beautiful things that Henry Irving ever accomplished . . . There was a vastness, a spaciousness of proportion about the scene in the Temple of Artemis which I never saw again upon the stage until my son attempted something like it in the Church Scene which he designed for my production of "Much Ado About Nothing" in 1903.'

Gordon Craig grew up believing that 'towards this production of *The Cup* my father contributed something'. There is no evidence that Craig, who was aged nine at the time, actually saw *The Cup*. But he remembered what his mother told him. It had been at her instigation that Godwin was invited to give advice on the stage decoration and ballet-effects of the play. The wonderful Temple of Artemis owed a great deal of its effect to the lighting, Ellen explained.

> The gigantic figure of the many-breasted Artemis, placed far back in the scene-dock, loomed through a blue mist, while the foreground of the picture was in yellow light. The thrilling effect always to be gained on the stage by the simple expedient of a great number of people doing the same thing in the same way at the same moment, was seen in 'The Cup', when the stage was filled with a crowd of women who raised their arms about their heads with a large, rhythmic, sweeping movement and then bowed to the goddess with the regularity of a regiment saluting.

William Archer went so far as to describe this temple scene as a theatrical masterpiece – unlike anything he had witnessed on the English stage. 'I doubt if a more elaborate and perfect stage picture of its kind has ever been seen and if so certainly not in England', he wrote. Upon its extraordinary architecture of richly sculptured pillars, out of the gloom, Diana of the Ephesians looked down, while her priestesses moved noiselessly among the sacred lamps. 'It almost seemed as if stage decoration could go no further', William Archer wrote. But Gordon Craig was to dedicate his career to taking his father's experiment further.

Godwin had also designed Ellen's dresses which, she remembered, 'were simple, fine and free'. After congratulating Irving on his showmanship in his paper *Truth*, Henry Labouchere went on to praise Ellen as the high priestess of aesthetes. 'She suits the dreams of idealists', he wrote. '. . . She is the embodiment of aspirations of modern art.'

This was the same picturesque praise that Henry James had been giving her. Ellen Terry was always pleasing; she always looked well in costume and was never less than graceful and refined. Her butterfly beauty so enchanted audiences and critics that, like Shaw, they lost themselves in dotage. She was a radiant figure, but she cast no shadow. Something was missing. Her pathos was the pathos of a child, touching but transient – and the public treated her as a child, indulging her tricks, spoiling her with injudicious petting of her limitations. Sometimes her inappropriate sweetness, her sheer playfulness, suggested that she was more concerned with her dresses than with Shakespeare's lines. No one complained about her technical faults: how she fell out of a play occasionally by failing to listen to others when not prominently placed onstage; how she allowed her mind to wander and broke the metre of the verse when memory failed her. But one theatre student, Agnes Platt, writing as it were from a more aggressive future in Dublin's *University Magazine* in 1898, was to express very trenchantly what others occasionally suspected. 'All the deeper human emotions are closed to her. She cannot command, she cannot defy, she cannot even despair.' Her brisk and sunny presence blinded people to a fatal shallowness. Nothing better was expected of her. Her talent lay poised between the old world and the new and she was awkwardly placed under the direction of an actor-manager who, by the 1890s, very decidedly belonged to the old world.

But in Tennyson's *The Cup* she represented perfectly the spirit of the age. It was as if she were bringing golden days from her past into focus with a play that united the two most significant men in her life, Godwin and Irving – all this under the benign patronage of Tennyson, a man who had been memorably kind to her in less fortunate times.

Perhaps Irving felt slightly uneasy working against Godwin's massive decorations and opposite Ellen dressed in costumes which her lover had designed. In any event his performance as Synorix did not please Tennyson. Ellen remembered his 'pale, pale face, bright red hair, gold armour and a tiger-skin, a diabolical expression and very thin crimson lips, Henry looked handsome and sickening at the same time. *Lechery* was written across his forehead.'

Godwin did not work again for the Lyceum. He was spending much of his time with one of Whistler's more troublesome sitters, the beautiful Lady Archibald Campbell, who was married to the second son of the Duke of

Argyll. Whistler was probably not displeased to see her time so taken up by his friend. She had suggested numerous improvements to his portrait, making so many changes to the clothes in which she wished to see herself painted that, when Whistler finally exhibited the picture at the Grosvenor Gallery in 1884, it was simply as an arrangement in black and yellow. Lady Archibald Campbell was instantly recognisable in this rather provocative portrait, yet 'every discretion has been observed that Lord Archibald could desire', Whistler politely reassured her. 'Your name is not mentioned. The portrait is known as *The Yellow Buskin.*'

Godwin possessed a mysterious fascination for women – mysterious, that is, to other men. In the company of Lady Archibald Campbell and several other discontented wives, he came alive. Back home with his own discontented young wife, he was often ill. Beatrice Godwin was obliged to lie sweltering beside him under six pairs of blankets as he shook with chills and fevers. If they could have afforded another room, or even another bed, they might have stayed together, for they remained friends. But they were miserably poor. Eventually Beatrice left him and went to live with Whistler, steering her way through a storm of violent quarrels with his previous companion, 'The Young American' Maud Franklin.

In 1884 Godwin helped Lady Archibald Campbell to produce the woodland scenes from *As You Like It* in the grounds of a 'hydropathic' institution near Kingston-on-Thames. He was made the 'Director General of Entertainments' among her Pastoral Players, a group dedicated to performances *en plein air*. The following year he adapted Tennyson's *Becket* for the group under the title *Fair Rosamund* and was to receive much praise from 'Lady Archie' in the first issue of Oscar Wilde's magazine *The Woman's World*.

Godwin was extraordinarily busy, extraordinarily poor. At the beginning of 1886 he produced a version of Euripides' *Helena in Troas* adapted by the Irish physician-playwright John Todhunter. Wilde wrote in the *Dramatic Review* that Godwin had 'given us the most perfect exhibition of a Greek dramatic performance that has yet been seen in this country'. The 'Prince of Wales was present', Gordon Craig later noted. But the contrast with Irving's spectacular *Faust*, which was being performed at the same time, was painful to him. 'It was no "success" ', he wrote, '– but a lasting victory for years after.' For the actual failure he loaded the blame on Todhunter, 'a one-legged soldier... overwhelmed by everything poor fellow', who should have 'asked E[dward] W[illiam] G[odwin]'s friend Wills to rewrite the piece, and had E.W.G. called in a good stage manager, the thing might have run for 250 performances and made many future efforts possible'.

That August, Ted went for a few weeks to stay with Irving in The Grange at Brook Green. It seems probable that Irving had been told that Godwin was seriously ill and that Ellen wished her son to be shielded from her obvious distress – she had loved no one so intensely as Godwin. 'Did my mother go to the hospital to see him?' Teddy did not know – did not even know at the time that his father was entering St Peter's Hospital for an operation to remove kidney stones. While he was playing with Irving's puppies and exploring his books at The Grange, Godwin was writing to his friend, the painter Louise Jopling: 'the next ward may be 6x4x2. I feel completely done with life.' He did not recover from the anaesthetic and, shortly before midnight on 6 October, at the age of fifty-three, he died. Beatrice Godwin, Whistler and Lady Archibald Campbell were with him in the hospital, and they accompanied the coffin by train to Oxford where it was placed on a farm wagon. The three of them clambered up beside it and as they jolted along the country lanes, they used the coffin as a table for a makeshift picnic (confident that Godwin himself would have approved). The burial took place 'in a corner of a field' near a church at Norleigh.

Whistler had asked Louise Jopling to call round at Longridge Road with the news of Godwin's death so that Ellen would not learn of it from the newspapers. On being told, she gave a great cry. 'There was no one like him!' During her recent holiday in America with Irving, the sun had shone on them and she felt extraordinarily happy. Now, suddenly, she fell into a depression and though 'the sun does shine for me, I am in the tight merciless grip of Melancholy for the first time in a very long life'. She had experienced nothing like it since 'the long-while-ago, through heavy sorrow and trial' after she had separated from Watts. But Godwin was unique, a man 'of extraordinary gifts & of comprehensive genius', she told Ted. In the depths of her grief she came to regret that they had ever parted. 'If only the dead could find out when to come back & be forgiven', she wrote in a book of photographs next to a picture of the house Godwin had built for her at Fallows Green. But he was gone: and the pain she had borne at the time of their separation returned. 'I'm wondering I don't die', she had written to a friend, Elsa Palmer. 'One does not get much love and he loved me most.'

Charles Wardell's death had brought her closer to Henry Irving, but Godwin's death defined the limits of their relationship. It was as if his faults had died with him and she could think of him only at his best. She had seen him at St Peter's Hospital and 'when he died he thought only of me', she wrote to one of her grandsons. This was certainly what she would have wished. But perhaps she had enjoyed too much happiness in those early days, she thought, been unkind to her parents and was paying for this with an intensity of pain. She would never risk such suffering again. 'I did not know how terribly it would alter me', she later wrote. Irving must eventually have come to realise that though he might have replaced the living Godwin, the posthumous being, like an immortal god, outshone everyone and was beyond reach. The 'dead past', she wrote, 'is the most living thing I have'. She could not express her grief openly – social conventions did not permit a public display. 'I think I've been a little mad since a few days', she told a friend. 'Nothing but rage & despair could find room in me, and I've been . . . unfit to be seen by any who didn't love me.' Her work at the Lyceum seemed meaningless. 'The last two months have been very cruel to me, full of disaster', she wrote to a friend on 27 November, '– and I seem to be fighting for power to *use* my life, not to enjoy it. People have a way of dying which makes "all the difference" to some others – I sometimes sit down and just wonder what it all means.' She tried to continue with her work at the Lyceum but suffered a breakdown and 'sent for Edy to be with me. Selfish and wrong', she admitted, 'but I couldn't help it – I think I should have lost my wits from misery.'

Irving seemed half-paralysed and could do no more than stand by and watch. Then, after she seemed to be recovering early in 1887, he did what he could, presenting her with the dramatic rights in a 'graceful trifle' called *The Amber Heart.* This 'pretty' three-act play, written by Alfred Calmour, an amanuensis of W.G. Wills, gave full scope to Ellen's powers of provoking tears in her audience. At the opening performance, a matinée on 7 June 1887, when she played opposite Beerbohm Tree, Irving was able to watch her, 'a dream of beauty', from the front of the house. 'You were very lovely, my darling', he wrote in a note to her. 'You yourself – alone – and there is nothing in the world beside you, *but* without you what a sad morning it would have been.'

The familiar pattern of work helped to establish a habit of normality. After the season was over, the company toured Scotland and the north of England; and then, from the autumn to the spring of 1888, they travelled again to the United States, carrying a huge quantity of folded scenery (including everything for *Faust*), but limiting their tour to four cities: New York, Philadelphia, Chicago and Boston. The production of *Faust* alone was to earn them £9,000, but perhaps their most successful venture was a hazardous journey through ferocious blizzards to play *The Merchant of Venice* at the Military Academy of West Point, where the soldiers, with thunderous cheers, threw their caps high into the air. 'The joybells are ringing in London tonight,' Irving announced at the final curtain, 'for the first time the British have captured West Point.'

With his profits Irving was to make more costly improvements to the theatre which had never seemed in a stronger position. Yet the truth was that since Godwin's death – indeed, since the opening night of *Faust* in December 1885 – Henry and Ellen had not appeared together in a new production. This reflected the state of their relationship, as if stuck in amber. For nine years Irving had held on to The Grange and then, at the end of the 1880s, he sold it and a few years later the house was demolished.

Knowing that they must stage a new Shakespeare production, he announced that their eleventh season would open with *Macbeth*.

PART THREE

25
Her Lady Macbeth

'What a combination!' Laurence Irving had exclaimed to his mother on hearing that his father was to play Macbeth with 'the Wench'.

'Mother in agony over it', Gordon Craig noted in his diary shortly before the play opened. But after the first night he told Edy: 'Macbeth was & is a perfect success in all ways . . . Best thing she's ever done.'

Irving's choice of plays had developed into a strange commentary on his relationship with Ellen. The two of them discussed several additions to their Shakespeare repertoire. It seemed possible that they would produce *The Tempest* – Henry would have made a superb Caliban, Ellen argued, and it didn't matter if for once there was no part for her (she was obviously too old for Miranda). But Henry disagreed. 'It would never do', he said. Of course there were occasional plays in which neither of them appeared, but Lyceum audiences expected to see them together in Shakespeare. Besides 'the young lovers are the thing in the play, and where are we going to find them?' If Irving had wanted to find them he could have done so readily enough, but the truth was that he wanted Ellen and himself to be the lovers.

Of all Shakespeare's characters, the one that Ellen should have played was Rosalind, daughter of the banished Duke in *As You Like It.* Rosalind combined comedy with romance, changed partners as she explored her own multiple identities and, in a perfect ending, tested and won the heart of Orlando. They discussed this play, and Henry indicated that the role for him must be Touchstone, the clown. Again, his dramatic instinct seemed right. As for Ellen, 'I was dying to play Rosalind'. But Henry gave his reasons so convincingly against putting it on that she was persuaded. Unfortunately by the time she came to write her *Memoirs*, she could no longer remember what they had been – only the inner conviction with which Henry had spoken came back to her (possibly he no longer relished playing clowns). He was, of course, convinced after *Twelfth Night* that the Lyceum should produce tragedy rather than romantic comedy – as Jacques says at the conclusion to *As You Like It*, 'So, to your pleasures: / I am for other than for dancing measures'.

Antony and Cleopatra possessed what Henry was looking for, but Ellen was adamant: 'I could not see myself as the serpent of old Nile.' So they moved on to other plays – to *King John*, *Timon of Athens*, *Richard II*, *Julius Caesar* – until all the talk 'left me cold', Ellen admitted. *Coriolanus* was put aside again with hardly a mention. Then, as if by a process of elimination, Henry arrived at *Macbeth*.

'Lady Macbeth interests me beyond expression', Ellen told Stephen Coleridge, '– how much I fear she will be beyond *my expression!*' Of what use would her celebrated charm, her gift for pathos, her natural vivacity, be in depicting the 'fiendlike queen'?

It was generally agreed that the great tragedian Sarah Siddons had given the definitive performance of Lady Macbeth in the late eighteenth century – a performance of such devastating power that some of the audience, overwhelmed by the atmosphere of evil they breathed in, had fainted away. William Hazlitt confessed that he could conceive nothing grander. 'It seemed almost as if a being of a superior order had dropped from a higher sphere to awe the world with the majesty of her appearance', he wrote. '. . . She was tragedy personified.' For Hazlitt, Mrs Siddons seemed a goddess who threw open the folding doors of imagination and let him see the pageant of life and death pass in gorgeous review before him. His famous verdict on her Lady Macbeth had been handed down through generations of actors, keeping her memory fresh. But what persuaded Irving to put on *Macbeth*, and gave Ellen guidance as to how she might find a new interpretation of her character, was an article, published on 12 August 1843, in the *Westminster Review*, which revealed Mrs Siddons's private thoughts about the play.

What surprised Ellen as she read this essay was the revelation that Sarah Siddons had apparently seen Lady Macbeth as a 'fair, feminine, nay, perhaps, even fragile' woman, 'captivating in feminine loveliness', whose power sprang from 'a charm of such potency as to fascinate the mind of a hero so dauntless, a character so amiable, so honourable as Macbeth'. This was very different from the virago she had portrayed onstage where Lady Macbeth's motivations appeared to spring from a hive of evil seething within her that destroyed her initially virtuous husband. In the theatre, Mrs Siddons's *Macbeth* had been the tragedy of power used as a substitute for love – she overwhelmed Macbeth's intermittent sense of the emptiness behind his ambitions. But on the page Mrs Siddons had written of *Macbeth* as a tragedy that evolved from a flaw in human nature.

Why then, Ellen asked herself, did Mrs Siddons 'write down one set of ideas upon the subject and carry out a totally different plan'? The answer must have been that she was a prisoner of her solemn talent, an actress who, in Leigh Hunt's words, could 'overpower, astonish, afflict, but . . . [whose] majestic presence and commanding features seemed to disregard love, as a trifle to which they cannot descend'. Ellen Terry possessed little of the stately genius of Sarah Siddons that had made her Joshua Reynolds's 'the Tragic Muse', but she had in a unique degree that 'trifle' of love and the potent web of charm that Sarah Siddons identified as being Lady Macbeth's essential qualities. Who would not murder for her husband? Ellen could understand such a question and perhaps achieve something that had eluded the legendary Sarah Siddons. Her Lady Macbeth 'pricks the sides' of her husband so that he will better attain his wonderful aspiration. She feels a joy in his presence and subdues everything to his dreams. Irving's acting version, which replaced the original twenty-nine scenes with nineteen, omitted Lady Macduff, leaving Lady Macbeth a more isolated figure like Macbeth himself. The two of them stand alone – and eventually stand apart from each other. Irving's Macbeth was 'a poet with his brain and a villain with his heart' who clothes his crimes in romantic glamour. His wife is deluded by this glamour until she sits 'wondering and frightened' as Ellen recorded, realising that Macbeth has 'no need of his wife now'.

Never before had Ellen prepared for a role so comprehensively. Irving presented the Lyceum players and technicians with some bound copies containing blank pages inserted in the text so that they could make annotations. Ellen filled two of the copies with her copious notes, trawling through the text for illustrations of Lady Macbeth's feminine nature and its effect on her husband. 'I *must* try to do this: 2 years ago I could not *even* have tried', she scribbled next to one of her speeches. In a letter to the playwright Alfred Calmour, she wrote: 'I have been absorbed by Lady Mac . . . She is *most feminine* . . . I mean to try at a true *likeness*, as it is within my means.' On the flyleaves of one copy of the play, she described Lady Macbeth as being 'full of womanliness' and 'capable of *affection*', adding: 'she *loves her husband* . . . and is half the time *afraid* whilst urging Macbeth not to be afraid as she loves a *man*. Women love *men*.'

Ellen was very aware of the fact that by inviting her to play Lady Macbeth – a character some people thought beyond her capability – Irving was paying her a compliment. He himself had acted Macbeth some fifteen years before when beginning his partnership with Bateman. It had not been one of his popular triumphs, though Bernard Shaw observed that he acted with great refinement, and Irving himself felt confident that he had judged Macbeth's character correctly – that of 'a barbaric chieftain entirely lacking moral fibre and the courage of his dark convictions'.

He had cut the text by approximately 20 per cent. 'The murder of Banquo, I have cut out as the scene is superfluous', he informed the designer Keeley Halswelle. But one important cut from the 1875 production he restored: the speech of the wounded sergeant in Act I, scene ii, which tells of Macbeth's extraordinary valour in battle – a valour which forms a juxtaposition to his moral cowardice. As Ellen observed in one of her annotations to the play, he was 'a man of great *physical* courage frightened at a *mouse*'. What this helped to define was the nature of Lady Macbeth's love for him: not simply an admiration for his exploits in the field, but a sense of what he lacked and she could make good.

Perhaps this reflected something in Ellen's feelings for Irving too. That she admired his achievements in the theatre he knew – many people felt this admiration. But she knew his weaknesses and doubts from which sprang those outbursts of bullying during rehearsals and his dictatorial methods of management. She had sweetened the atmosphere at the Lyceum and in this sweetness he could perhaps read a love of his whole nature, in particular some of those nerve-ridden traits he allowed her to see but that were hidden, he believed, from the rest of the world.

Macbeth opened at the end of 1888. The sonorous and supernatural music had been composed by Arthur Sullivan, who took his cue from Irving's various hummings and gestures. 'A drum, a drum, Macbeth will come', Irving had suggested, adding that a trumpet too might be useful – anything of a stirring sort. Sullivan got the orchestra to play him what he had written.

'Will that do?' he asked. Irving insisted that it was 'very fine' – but absolutely useless. Sullivan then asked for further hints, and Irving began swaying his body sideways, beating the air and making inchoate vowel sounds. 'I think I understand,' Sullivan said and turned back to his score. Presently the orchestra struck up some passages again and Irving cried out: 'Splendid! Splendid! That's all I could have wished for.' Sullivan completed his score in three days, working through the last night.

The sumptuous scenery, lit by flashes of lightning and shafts of moonlight that appeared to penetrate the thickest of castle walls, represented the awful depths in which *Macbeth* was shrouded: wide, desolate Scottish heaths, gloomy court interiors, a mysterious witches' cavern lit by uncanny radiance, and then the vast battlefield over which, to roars of thunder, Irving manoeuvred his army of actors.

He was fond of magnifying the sense of apprehension by 'leaving the stage in utter darkness', the American actor Arnold Daly observed. Sometimes he would light a set with 'a solitary lamp or dull fire which may be in a room; while he has directed from the prompt place or the flies, a closely focussed calcium . . . so that you can only see a lot of spectral figures without expression moving about the scene – and one ghostly face shining out of the darkness'. *Macbeth* was his most sombre production – the sets so extensively gloomy that when an outdoor scene was played in bright daylight there was a shout of relief from the audience.

Ellen's family came to the first night – Ben and Sarah occupying the centre box, Kate with her husband Arthur Lewis and their four daughters all dressed in white, their hair wreathed with white flowers. Speculation and excitement had been rising in the weeks before the opening night and queues outside the theatre began forming at seven o'clock in the morning.

But the critics were uncertain what to make of the acting. 'Nelly, dear, your performance of Lady Macbeth was *fine*,' her father reassured her. '. . . Don't allow the critics to interfere with your view of the part.' A young girl called Dolly, whose first visit to the Lyceum this was, came away feeling bemused by Irving's 'drawing-room Macbeth' and the 'inappropriate charm' of Ellen Terry. Yet Irving's ironic, semi-humorous speeches were peculiarly strong and, in recollection, Ellen Terry's interpretation of her role more memorable than it promised to be – the audience, as if hypnotised by her disordered figure, the haggard face, the straggling hair, had collectively seemed to hold its breath during the sleepwalking scene. It was not tragic acting but a masterpiece of pathos. 'There is more of pity than of terror in her end', Ellen wrote. '. . . She dies of remorse.' Her performance would lead to Dolly's own acting career and then (after being escorted to more Lyceum plays by the Revd Charles Dodgson) into Irving's family.

But was Macbeth really 'an Empire builder led astray by listening to bad advice from a parcel of witches who had lured him from his regimental duty'? Henry Labouchere could not resist poking fun at Ellen's soft-natured damsel who 'roars as gently as any sucking dove'. Nevertheless, he acknowledged that 'such a magnificent show as the new Macbeth has never been seen before'.

The play was an unusually controversial success for the Lyceum. 'Yes, it is a success,' Ellen assured her daughter,

> and I am a success, which amazes me, for never did I think I should be let down so easily. Some people hate me in it; some, Henry among them, think it my best part, and the critics differ, and discuss it hotly, which in itself is my best success of all . . . Oh, dear! It is an exciting time! . . . I do not do what I want to do yet. Meanwhile I shall not budge an inch in the reading of it, for that I know is right. Oh, it's fun, but it's precious hard work for I by no means make her a 'gentle, lovable woman' as some of 'em say . . . She was nothing of the sort, although she was *not* a fiend, and *did* love her husband.

This love was the ingredient Irving had been seeking to give his production its originality. 'The great fact about Miss Terry's Lady Macbeth is its sex', wrote a critic in the *Star*. 'It is redolent, pungent with the *odeur de femme*. Look how she rushes into her husband's arms, clinging, kissing, coaxing, and even her taunts, when his resolution begins to wane, are sugared with a loving smile.' Knowing how worried Ellen was growing over her part, Irving was tender and solicitous during the rehearsals, apologising for his customary moods of irritation. 'Your sensitiveness is so acute that you must suffer sometimes', he wrote. 'You are not like anybody else. You see things with such lightning quickness and unerring instinct that dull fools like myself grow irritable and impatient sometimes. I feel confused when I'm thinking of one thing, and disturbed by another . . . I do feel very sorry afterwards when I don't seem to heed what I so much value.' Before the rehearsals, as part of their research they had gone together to Scotland and also to Italy. He reassured her that 'things are going well' and after the dress rehearsal he sent her a confident note: 'You will be splendid in the part.' This was what he genuinely felt. 'Ellen Terry has made the hit of her life', he told the writer F.C. Burnand. 'She really begins to like her ladyship and plays it wonderfully.'

Macbeth ran until the end of the season. When the final curtain came down in June 1889 they had given 150 performances. The cost of the production had reached almost £7,000, but they still showed a profit of some £5,000. It was a climax to the Irving–Terry partnership. 'Henry could never have worked with a very strong woman', Ellen later wrote. 'I might have deteriorated in partnership with a weaker man whose ends were less fine, whose motive was less pure. I had the taste and artistic knowledge that his upbringing had not developed in him. For years he did things to please me . . .' And over these years she had pleased him with her Ophelia, her Portia, her Desdemona, her Juliet, her Beatrice, her Viola and now, perhaps above all others, her Lady Macbeth. She still had more of Shakespeare's women to create at the Lyceum, but sensed that her career was reaching a turning-point.

Weighed down, like an exhausted giant, by his suit of armour, Irving had been obliged to keep 'a tight rein on those peculiarities of gesture and expression which used to run away with him', observed William Archer. At the end, Ellen was haunted by his appearance, weak with fatigue and looking 'like a great famished wolf'.

But it was in the first act, when Lady Macbeth makes her entrance into the court at Inverness Castle reading a letter, that Ellen herself with 'blanched face and copper-coloured hair', and wearing a blue-green gown that shone with a strange metallic lustre, was to be best remembered. Among the audience on that first night was the American artist John Singer Sargent, who asked Ellen whether he might paint her in the role. A few days later he was writing to Isabella Stewart Gardner, Boston's great patron of the arts (in whose palatial house Ellen had stayed during her first tour of the United States), to tell her that Ellen Terry 'has not yet made up her mind to let me paint her in one of the dresses until she is quite convinced she is a success. From the pictorial point of view there can be no doubt about it – magenta hair!'

That costume in which Sargent painted her was made to look like soft chain armour 'and yet have something that would give the appearance of the scales of a serpent', Alice Comyns Carr wrote. She was assisted in creating this by a fine needlewoman, 'Mrs Nettles' as Ellen called her, wife of the animal painter Jack Nettleship, and before long to find herself cast in the unenviable role of Augustus John's mother-in-law. Mrs Nettleship 'bought the fine yarn for me in Bohemia', Alice Comyns Carr recorded, '– a twist of soft green silk and blue tinsel . . .'

When the straight thirteenth-century dress with sweeping-sleeves was finished it hung beautifully, but we did not think that it was brilliant enough, so it was sewn all over with the real green beetle-wings, and a narrowborder in Celtic designs, worked out in rubies and diamonds, hemmed all the edges. To this was added a cloak of shot velvet in heather tones, upon which great griffons were embroidered with flame-coloured tinsel . . . two long plaits twisted with gold hung to her knees.

Ellen was soon travelling by carriage to Sargent's studio in Tite Street dressed in this shimmering costume. A few yards off, from a house which Godwin had designed for him, Oscar Wilde would see her iridescent figure approaching. 'The street that on a wet and dreary morning has vouchsafed the vision of Lady Macbeth in full regalia magnificently seated in a four-wheeler', he wrote, 'can never again be as other streets: it must always be full of wonderful possibilities.' Sargent had begun with some grisaille sketches for a study in oil which showed her in an imaginary scene leaving the castle keep in a swirl of drapery, flanked by torches and bowing court ladies as she hurries off to meet Duncan. But he then decided to show her as a solitary figure with the 'rich stained glass effects' of her garments, the columns of magenta hair falling from under her veil beside the long green folds of her sleeves and, behind her, the great cloak embroidered with gold. Above her head she holds the crown, and in her face we can see an extraordinary expression, not so much of triumph as of aspiration. For this is a visionary portrait, a theatrical sublime, 'all that I meant to do', which gives us the emblematic presence of the actress herself rather than the image from an actual scene in Shakespeare's play. Over the next hundred years the picture would become familiar to many who never saw Ellen Terry onstage, taking its place with Thomas Lawrence's celebrated 'half histories' of actors.

On its first showing in 1889 at the New Gallery in Regent Street (previously known as the Grosvenor Gallery and owned by Alice Comyns

Carr's husband Joseph), the portrait became as controversial as the play. 'The picture is the sensation of the year', Ellen reported to Edy. '. . . there are dense crowds round it day after day.' But 'opinions differ about it'. *The Times* in London declared it to be 'without exception, the most ambitious picture of our time', and the critic at the *Magazine of Art* could remember no portrait of recent years 'which excels this in grandeur of pose, fineness of modelling, and magnificence of colour'. *The Athenaeum*, however, warned readers that the layers of stage paint shining in the glare of the footlights would make any refined visitor to the exhibition shudder. 'This is a painting for the pit.' The *Saturday Review* too described it as 'a *tour de force* of realism applied to the artificial' and concluded that Sargent's portrait had become 'the best hated picture of the year'.

Despite tiring at the number of sittings Sargent had demanded ('if I were *paid* for all the sittings, my face would be my fortune'), Ellen came to love the picture – '[he] has idealised me and of course I am delighted he has done so'. Echoing Mrs Siddons's verdict on Thomas Lawrence's portrait, she declared it to be 'more like me than any other'. And Irving, too, though destroying Sargent's sketch of himself, took pride in his portrait of Ellen. Here was his Lady Macbeth, raising the crown as if in tribute to her husband of the Lyceum – and he bought it for the Lyceum, hanging it in an alcove of the Beefsteak Room where she would preside over the festivities with the authority of (in the words of Edward Burne-Jones) 'a great Scandinavian queen'.

26

Ted and Edy and Harry and Laurence

Ellen had given Edy and Ted a taste for the theatre. Both of them had walked on in the production of *Olivia* at the Court Theatre when Edy was almost eight and Teddy nearly six. Then, when their mother joined the Lyceum Company, they were sometimes allowed to see the productions from the Royal Box. So that they should not be frightened by a ghostly apparition in *The Corsican Brothers*, they were taken backstage to see the men silently preparing the trap through which the actor, faintly illuminated by a supernatural light, ascended into the darkness above, calling to his brother for revenge. Ted 'could think of nothing else for days and wanted desperately to go back to the theatre'. Edy's attitude was different. Though she was 'audience shy . . . fearing exposure, judgement, comparison', she had quick and decisive opinions. 'That's not right!' she would sharply tell her mother when Ellen was practising her lines or her piano-playing at home. Ellen sometimes felt embarrassed by her daughter's eagerness to voice such criticisms. But Irving, she noticed, 'was delighted by Edy's independence', even when her frank opinions were directed at himself. During rehearsals for the Lyceum's production of *Olivia* in 1885 in which he was very piously playing the Vicar, Edy shouted out: 'Don't go on like that, Henry. Why don't you talk as you do to me and Teddy? At home you *are* the Vicar.' To his credit, Irving abandoned his pretentious manner, and on the first night gave a 'lovable performance', Ellen remembered. Edy, she added, 'was a terrible child *and* a wonderful critic'.

The death of their father had brought Edy closer to their mother but it filled Ted with bewilderment. He had been fourteen when Godwin had died, but had not seen him for ten years. How could you grieve over someone you had never known? It was more necessary perhaps to feel a need to blame someone. But, witnessing his mother's grief, he saw that she blamed no one. The fragments she let fall began to bring Godwin alive in Ted's mind. 'Until lately you have had so little understanding of the world, I have not been able to speak to you of many things', Ellen wrote to him in 1890. She promised him 'some nice quiet talks – and you will *understand*'. He was by then aged eighteen, yet these promises, promises, never matured into the discussions that would have given him this understanding. It was impossible for Ellen to speak of sexual matters to her son. So much lay hidden that Ted seemed stranded in a never-never land of unanswered questions. For example – and this was important to him – did Godwin know Irving? 'I am impelled to ask', he wrote seventy years later. But 'here I am brought to a full stop'. All he knew was that 'blind as most of us are, I only see loss'. Without Ellen, Godwin had floundered and sunk, whereas Irving would have survived without her and, in his solitary fashion, still prospered. As for Ted himself, he continued to feel impaired by the absence of a father, yet capable perhaps, with his godfather Irving's help, of prevailing over this loss.

Ted loved his mother but beneath the surface of his love moved turbulent undercurrents. Had she not made friends with his father's enemies – Charles Reade, Tom Taylor, the long-faced Johnston Forbes-Robertson (whom Edy and he had mockingly nicknamed 'Fluff')? And why had she turned to his sister for help when Godwin died – Edy who had drawn a picture of him as the devil? Did she prefer Edy to himself? Or could only women talk about these matters? Perhaps it was simply that Edy was older. Whatever it was, he never seemed to reach the right age or state of mind for anything. Ellen admitted that it had been 'selfish and wrong' to take Edy away from school after Godwin's death, but her instinct had been true. 'I am all right now', she wrote shortly before Christmas 1886. '*Edith did that.*' Ted had then been only fourteen. What seemed wrong to him was that his mother should have chosen this time to dispatch him to a public school. 'Be so good as to decide for me', she had written to Stephen Coleridge when he enquired after Ted's education. 'Mother tells me to write what I feel', Ted responded in a letter to Coleridge, 'but I cannot write what I feel.' It was on the advice of that 'tight-lipped piece of leather' (for this is what he did feel about Coleridge), that he was packed off to Coleridge's own school, Bradfield College. 'I learnt very little', he remembered. '. . . The whole attempt to push, pump and worry learning into me failed.' Bradfield specialised in subjects such as cricket, football and military drill at which, being short-sighted, he had no natural ability (he would later use a pince-nez in the manner of Irving). He did learn some rather coarse language from the boys at Bradfield which he tried out on his sister – and for which he was punished. 'I was not a credit to my learned tutors', he happily concluded. Indeed, it was pure debit: 'money thrown away'. This is what he remembered. But after the first two weeks there ('I feel so unhappy, Mother . . .'), his letters from school show that he was enjoying himself. 'We have fine larks now . . . I like the school *very* much. It is "Rare Jolly" – that is our word.' He seems to have felt that he belonged among his friends there – 'I don't want to know any "outsiders"', he told his mother. It was a feeling that, as the elemental outsider fifty years later, he could no longer comprehend. But when in 1929 he was invited to become Vice-President of Bradfield, he accepted on terms of extravagant gratification, writing that after years of neglect in England it should have been from his old school that recognition finally came.

While Ted was proceeding erratically through a conventional education, Edy had been sent for special tuition to Dixton Manor Hall, a sixteenth-century stone building, seven miles from Winchcombe station in Gloucestershire. She was described as 'an inmate' there, the house set in extensive grounds being 'sufficiently remote to have been owned by the Lunacy Commission'. It had been leased in the summer of 1882 to Frank and Elizabeth Malleson, retired teachers and educationists. Elizabeth Malleson, who had run the Working Men's and Women's College in London, was an egalitarian and nonconformist, dedicated to improving the educational standards of the working classes. Ellen had got to know her through her sister, Mrs Cole, the headmistress of the coeducational school in Earls Court which both Edy and Ted attended. Her house in Gloucestershire became for Edy what 'Bo's' home at Brancaster was for Ted: a place of safety and a refuge during times of difficulty. After Wardell and Godwin died, Ellen, overtaken by that 'fit of melancholy which I cannot conquer', wrote to Elizabeth Malleson acknowledging a debt of 'immense and endless gratitude' for her 'good services to me in a time of real perplexity of mind and pain of body', adding: 'You are always in my heart of hearts the best of the best.' Though Ellen did not often go down to Dixton

Manor Hall, Elizabeth Malleson's daughter Hope remembered 'brief flying visits – a whirlwind of gaiety, charm and affection'.

For both children the pattern of life was unpredictable. When Ellen sailed away for her first American tour, Ted went to stay with the Mallesons. 'It was a delightful time', he remembered. '. . . Edy and I there – on the roof, eating biscuits and fruit and chocolates . . . I see the window out of which we clambered to sit on the old red roof and look over the sloping ground . . .'

Ellen wanted Edy to go up to Girton College, Cambridge. 'Mrs Malleson's girls are Girton girls', she inaccurately informed Ted. But her difficulty, Ellen thought, was '*slothfulness*'. Edy, however, had her own ideas of what she wanted and easily succeeded in failing the entrance examination. 'I'm sure she can do it, if she tries again', Ellen persisted. But Edy had no intention of trying again. Instead of Cambridge, she went off to study music with the piano teacher Alexis Hollander in Berlin, travelling there with the Mallesons' daughter Mabel. 'No matter what the result is,' Ellen wrote to Alexis's wife, Anna Hollander, '. . . I know you have done everything – and more. Do not think her unfeeling or ungrateful – she loves you both – but it is so *natural* that young people kick up against steady work it's very naughty, but natural.' Edy also studied the piano with Alexander Mackenzie at the Royal College of Music. 'Do pass the Exam, please do so, Dear old girl', Ted encouraged her. But Edy's fingers were rheumatic and in 1890 she scored 76 per cent in the examination – not enough for a career as a concert pianist.

'I thought she played splendidly', her brother remembered. Even so he felt it was 'queer' that she had been preferred to himself as a music student 'for I think she was less musically haunted than I' (Ellen was to remind him that as a child he had been less responsive to music than his sister). Many years later he used his sister's piano-playing in a charming passage illustrating the comic incompatibility between Ellen and Edy. 'They often played together', he wrote.

When Mother attacked, she was resplendent, and Edy gave up. Duets they played – and Edy, despairing to improve my mother, took to arguing: and the fierce torrent of music ceased, and logic took its place. Edy utterly annihilated Mother with her logic: she explained that if a piece was written to be played slowly and with such and such emphasis, it was not being polite to the composer, especially if his name was Brahms, to . . . Here Mother peered at the music to see the name of this celebrated being: 'Yes – it *is* Brahms.' All this gently murmured while Edy's scathing logic marched on. At the end of the speech, Mother would say: 'Let's try it again' . . . And again Mother dashed in and on, and Edy came following after. Again a traffic jam. 'What's the matter?' 'Twice too fast,' said Edy . . . And the funny thing was that she was right and Mother couldn't believe her own daughter's ears . . .

But, he added, 'while Edy was right, Mother was not wrong'. His sister was of course literally correct, but his mother (though impulsive) had caught the spirit of the piece. At parties where Ted and Edy 'danced a dance always', she 'danced with me as though I mattered'. Too often Ellen did not treat him as though he mattered – at least that was how it seemed to him. But Edy 'fought my battles' and proved herself 'a deadly enemy' to 'anyone who put out their tongue at me'. When she transcribed his piano music for him, she made him 'as happy as anything'. She was 'a dream'. His early years were largely spent dreaming. But when he began to wake up he saw that he had more in common with Ellen's temperamental methods of attack than with Edy's neat efficiency.

After Bradfield College, Ted was sent to Germany – not like Edy as a music student in Berlin, but to Heidelberg College. Set in a valley of the River Neckar and bordered by little hills, it appeared at first sight 'a very jolly place', though the college was not connected to the university there and he resented being taken away from the theatre world – especially when Ellen and Henry went off on their third tour of America. He showed his resentment with a series of dramatic schoolboy exploits – burning sulphur matches under his desk, smoking cigars, missing lessons, having breakfast in town instead of in school and sliding down the wall from his dormitory window to go off on a night-time bicycle ride. He was constantly being punished with periods of confinement, and referred to the place as if it were a prison. When Ellen returned from the United States in late October 1888, she found a letter waiting for her from Heidelberg College, announcing that Ted was being expelled. 'You are aware that your son has tried our forbearance over and over again', she read. '. . . He has a very ill-disciplined nature with an impulsive temper. His actions are marked with utter disregard for consequences.' In a letter to Edy, Ted wrote that 'all the fellows at H. were awfully nice & jolly to me. The whole school sent up a written petition . . . but of course it was of no use.'

What had been so shocking as to merit expulsion seems to have been an episode one night with a local girl: 'a vulgar night's work', in Stephen Coleridge's phrase, though Ellen described it more romantically as 'the Karlsruhe affair'. She knew her son was 'terribly self willed'. Nevertheless, despite his bicycling adventure at Karlsruhe, 'he is such a good fellow'.

When Ted returned to England, Ellen having retired to Margate for a rest, he lodged for a time in London with his grandparents, Ben and Sarah Terry. 'Ted with me will be well looked after nothing serious', Ben wired Ellen. Towards his grandson he pretended to be 'rather angry', though he considered the episode 'idiotic'. Ellen reassured Stephen Coleridge that her father was making the boy 'do lessons regularly'. Coleridge, however, wrote to Ellen very sternly about Ted's morals, believing that Ellen was minimising the seriousness of the affair. 'Poor dear blind Nellie', he wrote on the margin of one of her letters. Ted's character, he thought, was contaminated by 'a stain of viciousness' that made him 'unfit to enter any other school'. This harsh verdict 'made me ill' to read, Ellen replied. 'I think you are SOMETIMES the silliest gentleman I ever met with and – SOMETIMES *appear* to be the most uncharitable . . . I know how earnest you are, & how with all your heart you serve me but you are so very unreasonable & – at least in manner & expression – so hard, that you often thwart the good that you intend.' Nevertheless Coleridge and his wife continued to be much exercised over the matter. 'I implore you to stop and consider how you are bringing them [Edy and Ted] up', Gill Coleridge wrote. The trouble, they both thought, sprang from Ellen's infatuation with Henry Irving. She was always putting his interests first, and neglecting the advice of her true friends. 'You used to let me say things to you sometimes, until Henry came and took your love away from me', Stephen Coleridge complained. He could not rid himself of this sense of injustice and went so far as to disclose this sorry state of affairs in a letter to Watts. Watts hoped that 'Henry will not act in an unworthy manner'. Coleridge called this a 'beautiful sacred' letter, adding '. . . The boy [Ted] is a villain!'

Ellen had not wanted to encourage her children to follow her blindly into the theatre, but how else could they be with her unless they joined the Lyceum? 'I do wish you were here or coming here', Ted wrote to her. There were times, happy intervals, when they all came together, Henry and Ellen, Edy and Ted – during the summer of 1888, for example, when they went on holiday to Switzerland. But nothing was settled, nothing secure. At the beginning of 1889, Ellen left Longridge Road. 'I hate the dull street, with its line of silly peering faces all along opposite, watching me as I come in & out & when I get up in the morning and go to bed at night', she wrote. She moved to 22 Barkston Gardens in Earls Court – quite close to where Florence Brodribb was bringing up her two sons, Harry and Laurence. Ellen's house overlooked the trees and lawns of a communal garden, and was itself draped in flowers from its many window boxes. She moved in some of Godwin's furniture from the old days and prepared separate studies for the children. Ted meanwhile was sent for a couple of months to Southfield Park under the special care of its headmaster, the Revd Ernest Wilkinson. 'I believe him to be a good boy – flighty, but good', Wilkinson reported to Ellen. '. . . Guided right I have every confidence in him.' But how was Ellen rightly to guide him? Edy she knew, though sometimes stern and critical, was 'very loving and clever' and people were sometimes tempted to spoil her a little. As for her brother, who had 'gone through much by way of shameful neglect', Ellen was convinced that he would eventually 'come out triumphant'. He was 'so merry & gentle & fat & satisfied', she told the Casella sisters.

Shortly after his seventeenth birthday, Ted found himself at Denchworth Vicarage, near Wantage in Berkshire, under the supervision of the Revd Mr. Gorton, who specialised in 'Shakespeare Readings'. For his birthday, Henry had given him the newly published first four volumes of *The Henry Irving Shakespeare* with an inscription: 'To the young Lord Hamlet from Henry'. The solitude of Hamlet was what they had in common. At Denchworth, Ted read many of the plays that were appearing in the Lyceum repertoire, reciting the lines of Malvolio, Shylock and Macbeth, as if he were in rehearsals for London productions. He was taking drawing lessons at Wantage from the daughter of Theodore Cook, editor of *The Field*, and a year later, when Sarah Bernhardt was playing *Hamlet* at the Adelphi, he made several sketches of her, selling them to *The Graphic* and *Sphere*, and reproducing them several years later in his own paper, *The Page*. But before he could be an artist deriving his inspiration from the stage, he felt that he must be an actor.

Ellen used the example of Henry Irving, whom she knew her son worshipped, to spur him into work. 'He [Irving] works so *very* hard, and *has* worked all his life', she wrote to Ted at Denchworth Vicarage, '– that's the meaning of such a brilliant record of success.' She had finally come to the conclusion that it would be better for both her children to join the Lyceum. They seemed interested in nothing but the arts – and Ted appeared otherwise unteachable. 'Nothing could make me quarrel with my children', she told Stephen Coleridge. Perhaps then she should not have cabled Coleridge, at a low period during her second tour of the United States, asking him to 'bring one of the children'. That had been at the end of 1884 when, to Edy's dismay, Coleridge and his wife had brought Ted. 'Am taken to America', Ted noted years later when scribbling out a chronology of his career. 'On board wish Edy had been chosen.' There seemed to be no pleasing them. Ted was allowed to walk on in several of the plays and in Chicago was given his first speaking role as Joey, the gardener's boy, in *Eugene Aram*. One of the American critics described him as 'a most beautiful lad'.

> His eyes are full of sparkle, his smile is a ripple over his face, and his laugh is as cheery and natural as a bird's song . . . This Joey is Miss Ellen Terry's son, and the apple of her eye. On this Wednesday night, January 14, 1885, he spoke his first lines upon the stage. His mother has high hopes of this child's dramatic future. He has the instinct and the soul of art in him. Already the theatre is his home.

He had been much 'gushed over' in the United States. 'All my friends love him', Ellen had written to Edy. The company thought him 'a peach' and in New York he had been 'pursued by all the little girls in the hotel'. Then, because her brother had gone to the States, Edy wanted to go. And Ellen, with her wish to keep the peace, recognised the justice in that. But justice, of course, had to be earned. Edy should be less selfish, less terrible to others. No one minded her arranging her hair like the famous Mrs Patrick Campbell's, but she should choose her friends more carefully. 'It must be the Theatre for her I suppose?' she queried in a letter to Ted. The manner in which Edy might pursue her theatrical career sometimes worried Ellen. But really what was the point in worrying? 'You *don't* suppose *she is not* going to have her bad & absurd times, & make mistakes, & all the rest of it', she wrote to Ted. '*Of course* she will. All one must do is *to help*.' Ellen helped Edy with advice: how she should give up drinking beer while in Germany and drink a little claret instead; how she must not write quite so freely to boys, and keep 'a little steadier' in shops and other places where there were strangers. 'And so America – the going to America is what you most desire? Well then, work away now', Ellen exhorted her. If she could have done all her mother advised her to do and 'been all she wanted me to be', Edy drily remarked, 'I should now be a very splendid and wise woman'. But she did enough to earn her passage to the United States during the Lyceum's short tour of 1888 and made her American debut in New York.

That she and Ted finally became members of the Lyceum Company was Henry's decision, his gift to Ellen. They had been quarrelling recently. But during 1888, Irving seems to have gone out of his way to show her kindness through his generosity to her children. During the summer of 1889, he invited Ted to stay with him at the Granville Hotel in Ramsgate where he was preparing his next season for the Lyceum. Ellen urged Ted to read *A Tale of Two Cities* since Irving had decided to present a popular melodrama, thought to be based on Dickens's novel, and to give Edward Gordon Craig (as his name appeared in the programme) a part in it. 'I have the *highest hopes* for you, & the *fullest trust* in you, that you will aim high & always endeavour to do your best in your new calling', Ellen wrote. 'You'll find temptations, but *with help* & determination . . . you *will* go right – will succeed – will remain a gentleman – & your mammy's own lad . . . I have had great experience in suffering . . . when I was young I was weaker than I am now – & suffering made me strong – but I've always found a helping hand, a loving helping hand . . . Now here's mine ready for you . . . never fear me. I love you & that means everything.' At the close of this homily, Ellen added a caution: 'Remember by the way to always say "Mr Irving" in the theatre – not "Henry".'

Soon Ellen was bombarding Ted over his misdemeanours. He must write her more letters, put dates on them, change his address less frequently, use cheaper writing paper and modify his handwriting so that she could read it. He should also learn how to keep money from slipping through his 'buttery fingers'. Moral questions were really quite simple. There was a straight path, the path of duty, which led to 'friends, money – honour among fine people – peace and sweetness'. And then there was the wrong path which meant 'dismal repinings, discontent, poverty and unrest' – in short: the career of a third-rate actor which was a very poor article indeed. Over time she began to wonder whether he was listening to her and she grew more assertive. 'Have a try, my Ted, at forgetting yourself', she recommended. '. . . the dreadful disease of "swelled head" is about & I warn you to avoid infection.' She saw with alarm that he was making 'many people miserable instead of making them happy'. These letters to her son were in a sense posthumously addressed to Godwin. She advised him to be less critical of everyone, begged him to honour his agreements, to avoid getting into debt and above all not to treat brutally any woman who truly loved him. He tortured her when he treated women inconsiderately and sometimes Ellen felt she could 'kill him' for taking everything so lightly. The truth was that he could cause her 'intenser suffering than I have ever experienced for myself', could do this because the suffering he caused revived her own past suffering. She warned him that he would 'tire out' love – then reassured him that 'you *could not* wear my love out, but that's because you are your Father's child, & because the blood being the same – yours and mine . . . You are all heart of my heart – breath of my body.'

Irving's generosity to Ellen's children was a reflection of his love for her. From his own sons he was cut off. Whatever he communicated to Harry and Laurence was filtered through their mother's unrelieved hostility. 'Harry received a nasty letter from his father – the dear boy did not mind it', Florence wrote. All his letters struck her as being nasty. So he wrote less than he should have done; and when he did write it was in formal rather than affectionate terms. Stoker's report that the boys were coping well with public school life at Marlborough was, it turned out, illusory. They felt it their duty to be seen to be doing well. 'We are very happy', Laurence reassured their mother, 'but of course nothing like as happy as if we were both with you.' Parted from her sons, Florence felt miserable. 'No news of boys. *So* disappointed', she noted after their first day at school. Within three days of their arrival at Marlborough, she had gone down to see them. She found them both 'stunned with home sickness' and in great despondency.

Built on the site of an eighteenth-century coaching inn, Marlborough was founded in the mid-nineteenth century for sons of the clergy and had developed into a notoriously rough school that excelled at outdoor sports. With their glaring athletic ineptitude, it seemed that the Irving boys could never fit into the rough and tumble of such a philistine place. 'They shrink from games which involve effort or violent exercise of any kind', the headmaster of their preparatory school had written. Certainly they had no interest in the mysterious game called football and no understanding of why other boys played it. 'I went to football,' Laurence wrote, 'it was beastly, the boys hit us because we didn't know what to do.' But he was quick to reassure his mother that football was 'really quite safe' and that he and Harry found it 'very jolly' to read her 'delightfully long letters' and that there was 'no need to trouble' about them – though they were 'mad with joy' at the prospect of coming home for the holidays.

Their mother's sudden appearance at the school agitated them and, searching around for someone to blame, they pointed to their father's spy, the 'blackguard' Bram Stoker. His turning up was 'a terrible mar to our happiness and we are rather wretched', Harry explained to his mother. 'I don't know what to do. I was getting on so much better before this cad came.'

What distressed him was that Stoker's enquiries opened up a painful division in him between his father's glamorous adult world and the domestic world he loved with his mother. How could he move without a sense of betrayal from one world to the other? It seemed impossible to negotiate this rite of passage without disloyalty. And yet there was something in him he had inherited from his father, something owed to him, which he was being made to deny. Why had his father not come down to speak to him? This was a question both boys asked again and again. They were 'really quite sick of writing to old H.I.' without an answer. 'I wonder why Irving avoids writing to us . . . Of course we have heard nothing from our affectionate father . . . It would be a good thing if we could make the old cab-horse take a little trouble.' In all these years, from 1882 to 1887, while the two boys were at Marlborough he visited them only once – and then it appeared he had come to see the new school chapel (he had made a generous donation towards its rebuilding) rather than to see themselves. Harry and Laurence felt they were excluded from their father's affection by his all-consuming business affairs – and, what was worse, by his disreputable affaire with Ellen Terry. He had banished their mother and exiled her children – all of them victims of his ambition and lust.

The headmaster told Stoker that Florence's appearance at the school, and her promises to visit them frequently, had made these first few awkward weeks more difficult than they need have been. So it was decided that Irving alone was to be sent their sons' reports. He paid the bills and was a valued benefactor: therefore all decisions must be his, and Florence should keep her distance.

As Irving explained in a letter to their housemaster, he wished his sons to be educated so that they might earn their living outside the theatre. On the stage their names would inevitably prove a drawback and it would be far better for them to have independent careers. This letter, as Harry shrewdly judged when it was shown to him, was probably drafted by Irving's secretary Louis Austin. But the pompous note which the boys themselves received could only have been written by Irving himself – it impressed Harry as being 'the most infantile and stupidest I should think a father ever wrote to his son' – more like 'a meteorological report' than a letter. It was almost better to receive nothing at all. Or was it? 'We would have written to you more in America,' Laurence wrote, 'only we got no answer and found it rather *uninteresting*.'

The boys held slightly differing attitudes to their father. Harry, who cultivated a cool sceptical manner, appeared the more rigid of the two brothers. He possessed more self-control from which only occasionally did his temper burst forth. He made no secret of wanting to act his father off the stage. 'The stage is what I like', he declared, '. . . and to nothing else will I give my full power and attention . . . nothing will deter me from it.' His father's attempts to discourage him merely spurred him on. He absolutely refused to be bullied. 'He [Irving] thinks to frighten me out of it by putting forward ridiculous arguments', he complained to his mother. '. . . He seems utterly to forget that there exist in the theatrical world other managers besides his mighty self who would be willing to give me an engagement . . . [I will] prove to him that there are others who can act quite as well if not better than the invincible Henry Irving.'

How could they find their balance between such a remote father and ever-present mother? Florence's long daily letters were becoming an embarrassment at school – particularly to Laurence whom she called 'Wee'. Each letter they wrote back protesting their happiness she logged in her diary: and the sun shone. She longed for their holidays, prepared for their birthdays, and dreaded their return to school. 'The boys have begun to humbug us somewhat because I get so many letters', Harry eventually explained to his mother. 'I should think one to both of us a week would be very jolly . . . I am sure you have a good reason for sending us so many letters considering you haven't (as most mothers have) a husband to be with you it is natural all your love should be given to your children.'

Such schoolboy analysis must have been hard for Florence to read. For fifteen years her boys had occupied all her thoughts and feelings, her energy and time. Now she began to fill the emptiness by going more often into society and to the criminal courts where there was always something to amuse her.

Laurence, her younger son, appeared more easy-going than his brother. He too had a passion for acting, but since this was to be denied him, he toyed with the notion of becoming an engineer and even joined the school cadet corps. But though he looked 'a very dapper little soldier' in his uniform, he simply did not fit in. 'The last thing I saw of him as the "troops" marched out of the court,' Harry reported, 'he was making frantic efforts to keep in step.'

At Marlborough Harry excelled at speaking in the Sixth Form Debating Society and performing at popular entertainments called 'Penny Readings'. The masters eventually persuaded him to study for the Bar since his debating and oratorical skills, they argued, could be used most powerfully in court. Crime was perhaps the only subject that fascinated his parents equally. So, in the autumn of 1888, Harry went up to read law at New College, Oxford.

Laurence's speciality was languages. He agreed to go up for an interview at the Foreign Office and to prepare himself for a career in the Diplomatic Service. At the age of seventeen his mother took him to St Petersburg where he was to lodge with a lecturer at the university. 'Started with darling Wee for Russia', Florence wrote in her diary on 9 September 1888. They reached St Petersburg a week later, and after assuring herself he was in safe hands she started back for home feeling 'very sad & lonely'.

Despite these manoeuvres, the theatre increasingly trespassed into both the boys' lives. Harry had become secretary and then president of the Oxford University Dramatic Society. But when he played one of the conspirators in a performance of *Julius Caesar*, the critics could not resist comparing him to his father. 'His face, figure and especially his walk', one of them wrote, 'are more or less those of his great father.' This was what Irving had warned him would happen – which made it none the easier for Harry.

Soon afterwards he received an offer from Lillie Langtry to play Orlando in her forthcoming production of *As You Like It* at the St James's Theatre in London. Learning of this offer, Irving made arrangements to see his son. 'The great visit has come off and was in a way of note', Harry wrote. It was of note because, instead of continuing to discourage him, Irving pledged his support should Harry decide to take up the invitation and play other *jeune premier* parts with Lillie Langtry's company. Perhaps his father's endorsement influenced Harry's decision. In any event he was able to assure his mother that he had declined the offer and would continue with his law studies.

But Irving was beginning at last to treat his sons more sympathetically, sending them hampers of food instead of meteorological letters, passing on comments in praise of their performances he had picked up from others, and even providing them with armour and uniforms from the Lyceum wardrobe for their productions.

While Harry was putting on presentations of Robert Browning's 'noble tragedy' *Stafford* and Shakespeare's *King John*, Laurence (who, now a disciple of Tolstoy, had grown 'a tentative moustache' and been converted to vegetarianism) persuaded the English colony in Russia to stage a palatial charity production of Tom Robertson's *David Garrick*. 'We shall wake up this old St Petersburg', he declared.

Irving could not help showing grudging admiration for his sons' initiatives. There seemed to be no quelling their passion for the stage. As a father, he felt that he had scrupulously done his duty. No one could have discouraged his children longer and opposed them more thoroughly. He had gone out of his way to provide them with a conventional, expensive and largely useless education. What else could any father do? 'I have seen, unfortunately, very little of them in their lives', he wrote. '. . . They say we see ourselves in our children. I have not realized that. I always had to leave – to fight my own way. Theirs has been too smooth. They are both clever and have good prospects – if they only strive to reach them.' But what should those prospects be? Having been given to understand that the boys possessed some genuine talent for acting, he finally gave ground. There was, too, another consideration behind his change of mind.

For a dozen years Irving had been making a profit at the Lyceum. But he had saved nothing. His money had been spent on tremendous banquets, spectacular productions, far-flung travel and large charitable donations; on buying and redecorating his empty house at Brook Green, and on the continual rebuilding and improvements he lavished on the Lyceum itself. He had bought the freehold on Florence's house in Gilston Road, made her a handsome allowance, and provided for her sons so that they would grow up as high-class young gentlemen. But at the beginning of the 1890s, after a year of loss at the Lyceum, Irving realised in what financial peril he stood. If Harry was to practise at the Bar and Laurence to enter the Diplomatic, they would need extra allowances for several more years. It was a worrying prospect and he wrote to Florence proposing that, since their sons seemed determined to prove themselves actors, it might after all be better for them to join the Lyceum Company – as Ellen's children, Edy and Ted, were doing.

Florence was profoundly shocked by this volte-face. Her first duty, as she saw it, was to direct a great tide of these shockwaves towards Harry and Laurence, and make sure they were as offended as she was. 'This last act of Mr Irving's seems to have opened all this matter again', she wrote to Harry (to whom she forwarded Irving's letter). 'I am certainly not going to submit to this sort of thing any longer.' She dreaded the prospect of her sons being taken from her and absorbed into the Lyceum family, with Ellen Terry as their adopted mother-figure and Ellen's illegitimate children their actor-siblings. This was the insult she read into her husband's letter, the insult she communicated to her sons.

Harry decided to trade insult with insult. Certainly he would be an actor, but on his own terms. He refused his father's offer to join the Lyceum and, taking a holiday from his legal studies, accepted an invitation from John Hare to play Lord Beaufroy in a revival of Tom Robertson's *School* at the Garrick Theatre. Unfortunately his performance was seized upon by the critics and brutally condemned. 'His delivery was monotonous, his manner stilted and . . . his love-making lacked even the pretence of ardour', Harry's son was later to record when summing up the reviews. It seemed, as Pinero advised him, that the wiser course would be to settle down, eat his dinners and become a barrister. He retreated to rooms in the Inner Temple and, as if inflicting a bizarre punishment on himself, set about writing a sympathetic life of the infamous seventeenth-century Judge Jeffreys, notorious for his 'Bloody Assizes'.

Laurence's response to his father's invitation was quite different. 'This of our father's is indeed a momentous and far-reaching proposal', he wrote to his mother from St Petersburg. But he saw it less as an offence than an opportunity. Harry, of course, being the senior brother, would have to take the lead. 'I do not well see how he can do other, as the offer is made, than appear at the Lyceum.' The wonder of it was that Irving 'with his selfish and egotistical nature' could 'stand the presence of a young and gifted actor' like Harry in the same theatre. The only objection was the contaminating presence of 'the Wench', Ellen Terry. But 'good might come of it,' Laurence explained to his mother, 'you must not forget it might be the means of ousting her from her place of infamy she fills and of reuniting your lives, if ever you find so much magnanimity in your heart to forgive the wrongs and insults that he has heaped upon you'.

This surreal proposal reveals the unhappiness Laurence had long felt over his parents' hostility. He wanted to play a part in their miraculous coming together. 'I feel certain that whatever I may be destined to do the stage has attractions for me that I cannot resist . . . The spirit is stirring within us. I must act . . . The diplomatic to the dogs!'

Laurence did not know when he sent this letter to his mother that Harry had decided to turn down Irving's proposal. Though he had enjoyed living in St Petersburg and spoke Russian quite fluently, he was 'not at all sorry' to be coming home. By the time he arrived back in London, his brother had already left the stage and when Laurence went to see his father, he learnt that Irving's original offer had been withdrawn – it having been given to both his sons or to neither of them. Laurence responded with bitterness. It seemed impossible to win his father's love now that 'he could not take us into his company whilst he's stuffing the goose with bastards [Edy and Ted] of the fell Terry breed'.

But Irving did promise to recommend Laurence to another actor-manager – one who never came to London. Frank Benson, who played Paris in the Lyceum production of *Romeo and Juliet* almost ten years before, had in 1883 formed the F.R. Benson Company, dedicated to bringing Shakespearean drama to all parts of Britain – a mission which was helped by the public's belief that he was somehow related to the Archbishop of Canterbury, E.W. Benson. 'I am sure you will be willing to give Laurence any chance that may rise for a display of the "spirited and graceful" attributes which he may possess', Irving wrote to Benson. 'An understudy perhaps or something in a new cast.' Benson responded at once to this request and invited Laurence to join his touring company in Scotland.

Benson's company was hugely popular in Britain, especially among school children who found its productions wonderfully enlivening after the tedious lessons of their teachers. It was true that they could not understand what was happening onstage, Benson's mouthings of the great tragic speeches being partly invented as he went along. But his deafening whispers and the general operatic delivery he gave his lines sounded magnificent. He possessed, it was said, 'nearly every fault of which an actor can be guilty'. Yet these bustling presentations, full of spontaneous energy and excitement, were 'thoroughly enjoyable . . . and the stage-fights were thrillingly realistic'.

Laurence was disappointed at not immediately being given any demanding roles. 'It's rather galling to see persons playing big parts feeling how much better I could do it', he explained to his mother. But he accepted for the moment that the company's senior actors must take precedence over him. 'The "boys" – Benson boys – of the company are really a very decent set of their sort', he reported. '. . . I rub along excellently well with all the company. I am at peace and goodwill with all men and women.' Yet their circus-like productions of Shakespeare were almost as unfathomable to him as the football matches at Marlborough.

As the weeks went by and the company travelled from one place to another, Laurence grew frustrated. He had been looking forward to 'cutting ourselves adrift from the old hulk [Irving] and very soon we shall not need to fear his hatred or win his love'. Yet he still desperately needed his father's help. 'Benson told me how well you had got on as Hortensio', Irving had written to him. 'I wish you could get more to do now. You must take it quietly for a while but it would be better soon if you had more important characters.'

This was what Laurence wanted. But Irving had struggled on without parental help and he felt that his son must do the same. 'I agree with you certainly that you must now be doing something better', he wrote to Laurence. 'The difficulty just now is *how* but I am thinking it over and shall be able to decide upon something to your advantage.' But what was that something? And when would it happen?

In November 1891, when the Benson and Lyceum companies were both playing in Manchester, Laurence and his father agreed to meet. It seems that Irving merely suggested that his son should speak to Benson and demand some major roles. He was anxious lest any success Laurence achieved should be seen as being due to nepotism. Laurence, who was still half-hoping for an invitation to join the Lyceum, was hurt by what felt like another rejection. He had dreamed of distinguishing himself rapidly onstage, discovering a means to peace and goodwill between his parents, and then casting out the serpent, Ellen Terry, from their lives. He had heard that Ellen and his father were having troubles. But in Manchester he 'saw no evidence of a rupture between H.I. and E.T.', he wrote to his mother. '. . . He was so icy and obnoxious. I was glad to leave him to himself.'

The Benson Company moved on from Manchester to Belfast where they were to stage a new production of *Othello*. Laurence pleaded with Benson to be allowed a significant character in the play, but when the cast list went up he saw that he was to be a Messenger and a Gentleman. It could hardly have been worse. He wrote at once to his father but received no answer. 'After our conversation this looks almost like an intentional insult', he complained to his mother. '. . . We cannot rely on Irving for anything. What cares he what happens to any of us?'

In Belfast, on the afternoon of 6 January 1892, after a rehearsal of *Othello*, Laurence and an actor-friend George Hippisley walked back from the theatre to their lodgings in Upper Arthur Street. Each then went to his room to study the play. But what was there for a Messenger or a Gentleman to study? At around teatime Hippisley heard the sound of a gunshot and hurried to Laurence's room. There he saw his friend lying unconscious on the bed, his chest covered in blood, a revolver on the floor.

27
All is True

The Prince of Wales, who enjoyed his suppers in the Beefsteak Room, was anxious for the Queen to emerge from her long mourning and resume contact with the theatre. In the years of her marriage, she and Albert had sometimes gone to Drury Lane and Covent Garden and, by inviting actors to perform at Windsor Castle, had revived a custom from the time of Shakespeare and the reign of Queen Elizabeth. Since the death of the Prince Consort, these entertainments had been discontinued. But in the spring of 1889 Henry Irving's company was invited to give a command performance before the Queen and the Royal Family at Sandringham.

Irving was careful to guard himself against the envy of his fellow actors. Though obliged to shut the Lyceum for three days, he refused to accept money for the performance (beyond travel expenses) and insisted that the honour was being granted through him to the whole profession. 'It is a tribute to the stage', he announced, 'which is not merely individual – it is collective.'

That April the company drove through the forests and green country to Sandringham where they erected new sets to fit a stage with a proscenium of some eighteen feet stationed in a room built to display the Prince of Wales's Indian trophies. There they performed *The Bells* and the courtroom scene from *The Merchant of Venice*. The Queen's and Prince of Wales's retinues which filled the room were instructed to display enthusiasm 'within the bounds of decorum'. Afterwards Irving and Ellen Terry were given an audience with the Queen, and then joined the royal guests at supper while the rest of the company were entertained by the equerries. The Prince of Wales presented Irving with a pair of gold cufflinks decorated with diamonds in the pattern of Her Majesty's monogram, while Ellen received a diamond brooch depicting two small birds (at the end of *Macbeth*, Princess Alexandra was to give her a diamond bracelet with their two names inscribed on a gold plate). In the early hours of the morning the company drove back through the darkness, reaching London as the sun was rising.

Ellen had begun to miss the country since leaving her cottage at Hampton Court. But by the beginning of the 1890s, she was less buried by work. Henry was experimenting with occasional readings around the country in place of some of the company's expensive provincial tours. He tried to present a few of these readings with Ellen, the two of them accompanied by music. But he was a Dickensian performer, happiest giving his performances alone.

At about the time she moved to Barkston Gardens, Ellen rented a cottage in a row of small pretty houses in the high street on the outskirts of Uxbridge. 'One had to go down a step or two from the street', wrote Gordon Craig, 'in order to reach the floor of the bar parlour, bare of all furniture, from which one passed into the kitchen and thence upstairs, where there were three very nice rooms and a big attic above them.' The Audley Arms, as it was called, had been a public house and Ellen was obliged by the terms of her lease to keep the bar open, though the cottage itself stood next to an inn. Only once during her tenancy did a customer turn up.

A little later she also rented a property at Winchelsea next to Alice and Joe Comyns Carr's home, Tower Cottage. It was a pretty place and by the town gate. 'I would very much like to end my days in Winchelsea', she told Stephen Coleridge. In April 1892 she instructed him to buy Tower Cottage for her. 'I want possession of it at once', she wrote. He bought it on her behalf for £900 (twice what Joe Comyns Carr had paid for it) and rented out the Audley Arms for £1 a week. On some Saturday nights, after the Lyceum curtain had come down, she would jump into a pony-and-trap (which she much preferred to the train) and drive herself through the night, arriving in Winchelsea at daybreak. Her holidays there initially provoked some gossip, partly on account of her fondness for dancing 'on the lawn in bare feet', Alice Comyns Carr remembered, 'clad only in the flimsiest of long white night-dresses'. As for Irving, 'he loves the place', Ellen told Stephen Coleridge. The rector's daughter, Blanche Patch, observed that Irving's visits during these summers 'did not lessen the doubts of those ladies who held fast to Victorian taboos about whether a London actress was the sort of person who should be "called on" '.

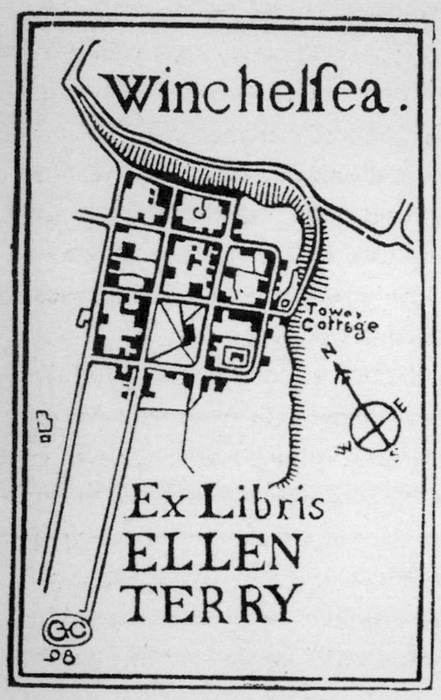

Irving often came to stay with her. 'I want to get to Winchelsea, my Nell, and be with you', he told her. A photograph of him there in the early 1890s shows him relaxed, smiling, looking positively happy, his hands not clenched as they usually were when going through the ordeal of being photographed. Next to this photograph Ellen has written: 'Henry having a real holiday!' Though he did not go around in bare feet as she did, 'we often caught glimpses of him in rather queer get-ups as he sat taking his ease in Nell's garden,' Alice Comyns Carr wrote. Sometimes, accompanied by their fox terriers, they would explore the countryside in the pony-and-trap. 'We drove to Cliff End,' Ellen wrote in her diary. 'Henry got the old pony along at a spanking pace – but I had to seize the reins now and again to save us from sudden death.'

They did not try to conceal the fact that they were living together. Their strange manoeuvres when rehearsing raised the eyebrows of some natives of Winchelsea. But such disapproval as there was quickly vanished once their dogs became better known. It proved to Henry that they need not worry much about what people thought. 'The longer we live,' he told Ellen, 'the more we see that if we only do our own work thoroughly well, we can be independent of everything else or anything that may be said.'

The fragile balance between Ellen and Henry, which had worked so well in *Macbeth*, was prolonged somewhat artificially over the next two years. 'Here I was in the very noonday of life,' Ellen wrote in her *Memoirs*, 'fresh from Lady Macbeth and still young enough to play Rosalind, suddenly called upon to play a rather uninteresting mother in "The Dead Heart". However, my son Teddy made his first appearance in it, and had such a big success that I soon forgot that for me the play was rather "small beer".' Irving must have known that for Ellen the sentimental role of Catherine

Duval was like striking a dumb note on a piano. But he believed that the public must be given the entertainment it loved – in this case a historical romance starring a beautiful wronged woman, an impoverished artist-hero, a virtuoso villain, and thrilling crowd scenes full of starving prisoners and soldiers in uniform. 'Irving was very noble', Edward Burne-Jones wrote. '– I thought I had never seen his face so beatified before . . . splendid it was.' As for Ellen, she was put 'in conceit with my part' by the casting of Gordon Craig as the Count St Valéry, Catherine Duval's son, whose life Irving saves with an act of supreme self-sacrifice at the climax of the play.

Knowing that Ellen did not think much of the play ('My part is too awful', she admitted), Irving allowed her in 1891 to buy the rights of one of Charles Reade's romantic comedies, *Nance Oldfield*, and to put it on as a curtain-raiser. Irving himself did not have a part in this comedy and it was produced so hurriedly that on their opening performance Ellen and her son, having little time to learn their lines, had to rush between the chairs and tables to retrieve the bits of paper on which they were written. Nevertheless it was 'a great evening for E.T.', Craig noted in his diary, and she was to make it into 'a marvellously attractive thing'.

Because of his stage-manager Loveday's illness, Irving was obliged to postpone his next Shakespeare production and put on *Ravenswood*, a truncated version of Walter Scott's *The Bride of Lammermoor* which had won additional fame through Donizetti's opera *Lucia di Lammermoor*. Ellen, cast as the lifeless heroine, seems to have found some relief in going insane like Ophelia and dying before a Turneresque landscape. Though the play gave Irving irresistible opportunities for bestriding the stage, it made no lasting impression on the public except for Ellen's riding tunic which 'set a fashion in ladies' coats for quite a long time'. By the end of the 1891 season the Lyceum had made another loss. Without Shakespeare, the Terry-Irving partnership was dissolving.

Shakespeare in the Victorian Age was a cornerstone, and one of the great exports, of the British Empire; illustrating in lavish pictorial settings the taste and values of the mother country. Irving was seen as an ambassador-at-large, using Shakespeare to establish a special Anglo-American trade, exchanging culture for wealth. He gave a lead to other actor-managers by helping to spread the plays through the dominions, displaying the benefits and privileges of belonging to this sceptr'd isle set in its silver sea. The very name Shakespeare conjured up the image of a blessed plot that never should lie at the proud foot of a conqueror. This was the hidden message that Irving brought with him on his extensive tours of Canada, and his son Harry would take to Australia, New Zealand and South Africa.

In 1890 Irving finally brought out the complete set of eight illustrated volumes of *The Henry Irving Shakespeare*, the donkey work having been done by 'a friend of my life', the journalist-playwright, Frank Marshall. The two of them had been brought together by 'the golden bond of a common love for Shakespeare', and Marshall's 'harassed and unwearying' life came to an end in 1889 when their work had almost reached completion. 'Light lie the earth over his honest earnest heart.' In his accompanying essay, Irving explained that 'in many plays of Shakespeare the omission of passages, the modification of certain words or phrases, and the transposition of some scenes are all absolutely necessary before they can be acted'. Of course, he added, any 'attempt to improve the language of our greatest dramatist is a hopeless task'. His aim was to assist groups of readers in English-speaking countries who wished to read the plays aloud and producers who needed acting versions. In the margins, he provided wavy lines beside passages that might be omitted without 'detriment to the story or action of the play'. In *Henry VIII*, which was to be his first Shakespeare production since *Macbeth*, there were not so many omissions because it was a short play – though some of Acts IV and V disappeared.

As a historical cavalcade, patched up and pulled together by Shakespeare from a work by John Fletcher, *Henry VIII* is only marginally in the Shakespeare canon. But since the Restoration, it had become one of the most popular stock plays, successfully revived by Macready, Phelps and Charles Kean playing Cardinal Wolsey – now Irving's role – while Ellen's part, Queen Katharine, had been taken by Sarah Siddons. As a theatrical showpiece recreating in fourteen splendid scenes the pomp and pageant of the Tudor court, it suited the Lyceum tradition well. Every sword-belt and headdress was checked by scholars, the costumes were matched against Holbein's pictures and Wolsey's specially woven silk robe was sent to the Cardinals' College in Rome to ensure it was dyed an accurate Italian blood-red. William Terriss and Johnston Forbes-Robertson were brought back to play Henry VIII and the Duke of Buckingham. Edward German was commissioned to compose the music ('In sweet music is such art, / Killing care, and grief of heart / Fall asleep, or hearing, die') and Alma-Tadema, the Royal Academician, employed to design the sets.

'Henry the Eighth will I think delight you', Irving wrote to one of his admirers. 'It will be a great thing.' Under his management, the Lyceum had become a palace of dreams. People came there to witness visions of themselves in, as it were, previous lives – lives of high romance in distant times. He manufactured magic spells with enticing music and imaginatively lit sets, suggesting a parallel world – a world of wonders – that fed a collective fantasy. He returned his audiences to their adolescence – even sometimes to their childhood. 'The plain truth is that for a good number of average modern Britons this is about the noblest kind of artistic pleasure they are capable of appreciating', wrote a critic in the *St James's Gazette*, '. . . the appetite for bright colours and lively action, for sonorous music and poetical rhetoric is as natural as it is blameless and it is one which ought to be indulged.'

The Lyceum production was a glorious indulgence. How noble Irving's austere and stooping Wolsey looked and with what depth of feeling, what terrible intensity, he delivered his famous farewell speech to greatness. 'When the curtain at last slowly descended on the retreating form of the humbled and sorrowing man,' wrote the *Saturday Review* critic, 'the deeply moved audience insisted on its being lifted again and again.' As Irving's grandson wrote: 'He dominated the play even when he was absent from the stage.'

Ellen acknowledged the sheer magnificence of the production and Irving's extraordinary visual impact – 'the very incarnation of evil' as Robert Peel called him. 'But I was not keenly interested in it, or in my part', she wrote. 'Henry's pride as Cardinal Wolsey was the thing, not my pride as the Spanish Queen.' To assume the character of a grey-haired matron while she was still in her early forties – a queen of whom the king wished to rid himself – was not an inviting task. Nevertheless, as Dr Johnson wrote, 'the genius of Shakespeare comes in and goes out' with Queen Katharine. She was acting once more with Ted who, equipped with a not very convincing beard, was playing Cromwell. 'He'll be a splendid comedian in time and a genial one', Henry had assured her the previous summer. This was his second year at the Lyceum and 'he is quite a success', Ellen wrote to a friend in the autumn of 1891, '. . . [he] has no end of offers and engagements and I must see he "gets on" . . .' As for Edy, she was more difficult to understand and there was no telling what she would eventually turn out to be. 'Edy walks on in some of our plays and now and then has a line or so given her to speak', Ellen wrote shortly before the rehearsals for *Henry VIII* began. '. . . I never should be surprised if she did something great some day, either as a writer, or an actress or a musician . . .' Tall and thin, with a strange brooding presence, she played one of Queen Katharine's ladies-in-waiting. But even the pleasure of having her children with her could not blind Ellen to the disparity that was developing between Henry's roles and her own.

Irving's 'piece of Tudor History' opened to a chorus of praise on 5 January 1892. Never, it seemed, had Irving won greater public acclaim. But then, as the curtain went up for the next evening performance, news was brought to him that his son had shot himself. Believing Laurence to be already dead, he 'went on the stage to play his part wonderfully', Ellen wrote to her friend Katherine Lewis, '– but oh you should have seen how he looked.'

28

After the Shooting

'All that is possible is being done', Frank Benson cabled Irving. He immediately summoned a Belfast doctor who saw that the bullet had pierced Laurence's lung and lodged in the muscles of his back.

Florence went at once, passing 'a terrible night' before reaching Belfast on 7 January 1892. By the time she arrived her son had regained consciousness. He was attended by two nurses and examined by an eminent surgeon whom Irving had dispatched from London. 'The darling not so well. Discharge from wound threatened . . . Anxious', Florence wrote in her diary. But once the wound was treated, Laurence's progress was good and by the end of the month he was out of pain, sitting up, and ready to leave hospital.

Rumours of this shooting quickly reached the press which came clamouring for more news. 'Poor darling,' Florence wrote to Harry, 'he has suddenly become most celebrated . . . Benson has been a perfect father to him.' Harry, the thankless messenger between his mother and father, arriving at the Lyceum with whatever information had been entrusted to him, observed how haggard and bent Irving looked.

But once they were certain Laurence would not die, an uneasy truce broke out. It was a truce based on a benign fiction that united all their wishes. 'I trust it was only an accident', Florence had written to Harry. However much she might fasten the blame on Irving, there was no easy escape from her own guilt while she believed that Laurence might deliberately have tried to end his life. Had he succeeded, the loss would have been unendurable. So after a few days watching him slowly recover, she went to his bedside and had what she called 'a very satisfactory chat' with him.

For years Laurence had repaid his mother's love by stoking up a loyal hatred of his father. But this prolonged hatred had done him damage. 'I wish both boys could understand how much their father cares for them', Ellen wrote to her friend Katherine Lewis. His remote temperament and apparent unhelpfulness made this impossible. It was an unhappy situation and Laurence had no desire to exploit it. So he readily agreed that his shooting had been a stupid accident. He was notoriously absent-minded, he reminded his mother, and had been examining this stage property, the revolver, when the damn thing suddenly went off. 'He tried to explain to me as far as he could without having a pistol in his hand how it occurred', Florence told Harry. 'So that sets all doubts at rest and forever – and my heart is much relieved because it broke my heart to think so good and noble a nature should be driven by disappointment and distress to commit such an act. Please convey this intelligence to your father and to all who impute any sinister motive to our darling.'

To what extent Irving himself believed this explanation he never revealed. In the index to his authorised biography, written by Harry's son, the event is listed simply as a 'shooting accident'. What Florence needed to quell her beating heart, Irving also needed for his peace of mind. Yet he had no peace of mind. The shock of this event, reviving memories of his own early miseries, persuaded him as no reasoned argument could have done to intervene and assist Laurence's career.

The only person who could not accept Laurence's story was his brother. Why would someone cast as a Messenger and a Gentleman need to rehearse with a revolver, a loaded revolver, in his hand? The two of them had always drawn strength from one another, but from this time onwards Harry felt he could no longer depend on Laurence quite so closely. Though they remained good friends, their companionship was fragmented.

In the spring of 1892, Irving appealed to the actor-manager John Toole on his son's behalf. Toole was the most popular low comedian of his day and had been encouraged to go on the stage by Charles Dickens. Irving had studied his technique in the late 1850s when he first saw him playing in Edinburgh. Drawn together by their common love of the theatre, they grew to be good companions. It was Toole who had consoled him after the death of Nellie Moore; who had interceded between him and Florence during their early separation; and who also helped to gain him his coveted membership of the Garrick Club. An ebullient and emotional man with a taste for practical jokes, in temperament Toole appeared at odds with the younger man's stern presence. Yet Irving trusted him.

Toole, who managed a theatre of his own in the Fulham Palace Road, had just returned from a tour of Australia when Irving went to see him. He was Laurence's godfather and he liked what he had seen of the boy. There was no one else from whom Irving could have asked such a special favour, and he did not ask in vain.

That spring Laurence joined Toole's theatre and by the summer, when the company went on tour, he took over the lead in a popular light comedy by a new playwright, J.M. Barrie. *Walker, London* told the story of a barber who poses as a man of substance. Laurence found that he fitted far better into Toole's company than he had Benson's and was soon enjoying himself. His performances were well received and he made good friends with some of his fellow actors – particularly with Seymour Hicks, a high-spirited, impecunious young man who appeared to live in a 'constant state of infatuation'. That summer the two of them began writing a dramatised version of Sheridan Le Fanu's novel of mystery and suspense, *Uncle Silas*. 'Bravo! Bravissimo!' Irving wrote to his son after reading the first act. 'You have both got on splendidly – you young dramatic authors. The dialogue is splendid and seems to be full of promise!' But when Seymour Hicks enquired whether he would finance a commercial production of the play, Irving found himself in difficulties. He was anxious to encourage Laurence, but wary of creating further mischief through misleading him. Although *Uncle Silas* 'is not suitable for the stage', he informed Hicks, '– I think you and Laurence have done your work very well indeed. I shall certainly look forward with pleasure to any other venture . . .' This balance between optimism and realism seemed to work and soon Laurence was writing more plays.

Time, Hunger and the Law, which achieved a single matinée performance for charity at the Haymarket Theatre in 1893, was described by his nephew as 'a turgid slice of Russian life in the Gorki manner with an uninviting title'. Still less inviting was his next play, *Godefroi and Yolande*. This was a one-act piece set in medieval times, partly inspired by Swinburne's poem 'The Leper', but also using R.L. Stevenson's recent defence of Father Damian, a missionary priest who, dying of the disease on a leper colony, was attacked by the Church. He made use too of Tennyson's poem 'Happy' (a monologue by a wife whose husband, returning from the Crusades with leprosy, she is grimly determined to love until death). Laurence's imagination seems to have been poised between his father's world of horror and retribution, and a new sense of social conscience which was advancing into literature. He piles on the agony by making Godefroi a lovesick scrivener's clerk, Yolande an ageing courtesan, and her mother a blind woman. He then introduces a dreadful goblin-like doctor who enters through a snowstorm, and adds a frantic hermit to lead a company of nymphs in the demolition of the polluted castle before casting Yolande outside the gates. Even with such exuberant stage directions as: 'Enter a chorus of lepers', this was, Irving decided, impossible for the Lyceum. But Laurence had sent it to him with an appeal for help. 'I dare to think that if I could get an opportunity of playing the part of Godefroi I might do much good for myself', he wrote. 'Will you put up the play at the Lyceum? . . . I turn at once to you, my dear Father. Your affectionate son, L.'

This was very awkward for Irving. His son really was an impossible fellow. When you failed to encourage him (for his own good) he went into a dangerous decline, and when you did put him in the way of an advantage he came back immediately asking for more than it was possible to give. So what should he do?

What he did was to hand the play over to Ellen who, to his astonishment, told him that she very much liked it. It showed, she said, that Laurence had natural talent as a playwright – by instinct he had done things right. There was something else in Ellen's mind that may have helped her come to this conclusion.

Six weeks after Laurence shot himself, Ellen's mother died following a difficult illness ending in six days of 'apoplexy'. Ellen was surprised by how grief-torn she felt, going back in her memory over so many incidents in their lives together. Sarah's death brought her more into the company of her family. 'We have all had to take our turn in watching with her & caring for her', she wrote. '. . . I am much stronger than either Marion or Flo.' Between Ellen and her sister Kate there were still embers of a rivalry, though nothing was so acute as the competitiveness of their handsome youngest brother Fred, soon to grow famous throughout the country as Sir Percy Blakeney in his swashbuckling production of *The Scarlet Pimpernel.* All of them loved Florence, the kindest and most obliging of the sisters. Now an amateur actress, she had gone on tours during her professional days with Charles Kelly and at difficult moments understudied both Ellen and Marion. Some people believed that Marion Terry, whose speciality was titled ladies, still ranked as the real 'Terry of the age' (she would create the part of Mrs Erlynne, the 'woman with a past', in Wilde's *Lady Windermere's Fan*). But her disciplined talent was largely put in the shade by Ellen's brilliance. In good times Ellen enjoyed teasing Marion whose self-control was sorely tried by her sister's boisterousness. But now, when the times were not good, seeing her and Florence by their mother's deathbed, Ellen wrote to a friend: 'My poor little Florence was so broken up – but she & Marion too – are magnificent in hard times – they are not only sunshine women.'

For several nights after Sarah's death Ellen was unable to go onstage. 'I pray we may never battle to live as she did, up to almost the last moment.' When she did return to the Lyceum, she found that Henry had filled her room with daffodils 'to make it look like sunshine', he said. It was one of those imaginative gestures that made her love him. The importance of family relationships was very much on Ellen's mind. She was especially worried over Ted who was so wild and unpredictable. Henry had been like a father to him – and so she decided to make Laurence 'my Irving boy'. She insisted that Henry take out an option on *Godefroi and Yolande* so that she could produce it herself – probably on one of their visits to America.

It was almost a year since Laurence's shooting, and Irving still had not seen his son. 'I have been so pressed with work', he explained to Seymour Hicks on 13 October 1892, 'that I have had to put everything else aside.' The work that pressed on him was *King Lear*. 'Irving sooner or later had to play Lear', his grandson was to write. 'Since Shakespeare's day every tragedian of any consequence played it.' Yet it was strange that he should have chosen this time at which to put on a tragedy which centred on the vicious ingratitude of children to their father and, 'omitting all superfluous horrors' such as the blinding of Gloucester (to use 'things vile and squalid and mean is a debasement of Art', he said), produce the play as a piece of family politics. Ellen, sensing him to be vulnerable, rushed to his defence. 'H.I. is hard at work studying Lear', she wrote. 'This is what only a great man would do at such a moment . . . The fools hardly conceive what he is.' To Ted she wrote that Henry was pegging away at his role 'wishing to Heaven all the time that he had studied the words 25 years ago at least – he says "I *never* had to study Hamlet. I've known the words, & *known him*, all my life." ' Ellen herself played Cordelia, the daughter whose love Lear in his vanity spurns – 'a wee part, but a fine one all the same', she noted. Yet it was a difficult role because there was 'so little to say, so much to feel'. Partly because there were so few words and the effectiveness of their final scene depended upon the illusion of hearing words that were never spoken ('What is't thou sayest? Her voice was ever soft, / Gentle and low, an excellent thing in woman'), the reconciliation between father and daughter – he brushing away her tears and tasting the salt – was the most moving part of the production.

Ford Madox Brown (whose painting *Cordelia's Portion* Irving much admired) designed the sets which showed the barbaric Britons camped amid crumbling Roman architecture – the huge temples and halls, with full-grown trees sprouting beside the pillars, towering over the actors. In his saffron robes, Irving's King Lear appeared among these ruins as a 'Priest-King, a David, ancient in mystery, the monarch from whom Merlin obtained his crabbed text'.

In her diary Ellen noted that 'H was just marvellous'. Marvellous he looked, everyone agreed; but to Ellen's eyes there was a terrible poignancy to his acting. Gordon Craig, who was given the part of Goneril's steward Oswald, observed during the rehearsals that Irving, though 'unique in certain scenes', looked 'rather tired'; and Ellen herself, in a letter written during the run of the play, mentioned that he had been experiencing severe trouble with his throat and was recovering in bed following an operation. He had also, it seems, added an artificial quaver to his voice (the word 'sterility' came out as 'stair-ril-la-ta-a'). Henry Arthur Jones, who usually admired Irving's performances, described his Lear as being 'slow, laboured, mannered, uninspired, screechy, forcibly feeble'. On the first night, when he stepped out before the curtain to pay tribute to Shakespeare's titanic genius, someone in the audience demanded: 'Why didn't you speak like that before?' and a murmur of assent spread through the auditorium.

Irving himself seemed baffled. 'He understands himself and thinks everyone else does', Ellen Terry explained to Stephen Coleridge. Was it really true that he had been so indistinct and, if he had been, why had no one told him? The truth was that no one dared tell him – no one except Ellen, whom he had rebuked for her interference. Now she told him again and, with a sense of shock, he listened and began to re-orchestrate his role, playing it quicker and speaking some lines more softly. 'He is perfectly intelligible *now*', Ellen wrote soon afterwards. Once he left out all the exaggerated grunts and groans, the play finished almost half an hour sooner. Later on, Graham Robertson was to describe his Lear as 'magnificent and terrible in its pathos'. But it was too late: the critics had delivered their verdict.

King Lear ran for just over seventy performances and was, Ellen acknowledged, 'one of our rare failures'. It 'broke down my physical strength after sixty consecutive nights', Irving wrote. '. . . I tried to combine the weakness of senility with the tempest of passion . . . [but] this was a perfectly impossible task.' It is doubtful whether the play could have been a commercial success. The tragedy envelops us all, rebukes us all, and allows no romantic flight of the imagination. The bare and barren sets, dwarfing the players with their imposing size, confronted the audience with the final loneliness of human beings which none of the Victorian virtues of family life, patriotism and religion could alleviate.

Some three weeks after *King Lear* opened, Seymour Hicks persuaded Irving to invite Laurence to his apartment in Grafton Street to celebrate his twenty-first birthday. Laurence was reluctant to go and had to be escorted by his friend to the front door. Suddenly alone together, father and son embraced, clutching at each other as if to remove all distance between them. Irving, with something of the incoherence of his Lear, tried to say how he longed for Laurence's affection. It was to be the beginning of a reconciliation that would eventually include Harry too.

As a coming-of-age present Irving gave his son a gold watch to mark not the unhappy years they had wasted but the time that still remained to them.

29
Counter Attractions

Gordon Craig was some four weeks younger than Laurence Irving. To mark his coming-of-age on 16 January 1893, Henry Irving presented him also with 'a massive gold watch'. In a circle around its edge were inscribed the words: 'To Gordon Craig from Henry Irving with love and remembrance'. This gift recorded a different nature of time from Laurence's watch – time happily remembered. The love that Irving added to his remembrance emphasised the hope that his godson – Ellen's son – would prosper at the Lyceum.

To gain acting experience and earn a little extra money, Craig had been acting in provincial repertory theatres during the previous two summers. He would send Ellen accounts of what he called 'things good and bad' – describing the 'mice, mice, mice' in his lodgings at Coventry ('I threw a pillow at one this morning and so stopped their manoeuvrings') and the elusive fleas that hopped around his bedroom in Tunbridge Wells ('when I requested them to go off, they the bugs waddled off down to the end of the bed & my bed was soon a mass of muddled up clothes'). From Oxford he reported that the theatre in which he had been performing the previous week at Cheltenham had been burnt to the ground; and at Margate where he was playing Ford, the native of Windsor in *The Merry Wives of Windsor*, Edy came to see him and judged that 'I was pretty good in it. This, from her, was high praise.' At Hastings, however, he fell ill and was looked after, not by Ellen who was away with Henry, but by the ever-kindly Miss Harries. 'She still ran about – seldom walked', he noticed. In her white cap, she 'looked like some of the people pictured by Edward Lear' – but was still 'one of my best friends'. Despite his illness, the fleas, fires and mice, his touring was 'such fun' that his letters brought back to Ellen her own early days on the road.

Irving had no objections to members of his company working elsewhere while they were not playing at the Lyceum, but the unevenness of Gordon Craig's performances was beginning to worry him. He was taking his work too lightly. He had 'a fine voice and a good presence' and was seen as possessing 'much of his mother's distinguished talent'. But 'in my bones, in my blood', Craig felt that he was an artist as well as an actor.

'There is a world of progress before him', a critic had written while he was on tour. But progress in which direction? Should he continue to act or become an artist or marry and become a father? Or do everything in a day's work? 'They say I was a genius', he recalled – a genius like his father. He would sometimes examine his face in the mirror and see that it was really 'far too pretty' (Oscar Wilde had exclaimed over his being 'such a beautiful boy'). Had he lived in Elizabethan times, he would have been cast as Viola, Imogen or Rosalind – characters that in Victorian times suited his mother.

This line of speculation somewhat displeased him – as did the minor roles he was being given at the Lyceum. Irving's sixteenth season there opened with Tennyson's romantic political history, *Becket*, in which Craig was down to play the youngest Knight Templar. On the opening night, in early February 1893, he 'fluffed my three lines'. Though he was officially to register his stage name, Edward Gordon Craig, by deed poll later that month, his career was about to change course.

Ellen had found that the easiest way of telling her son something about his father was to take him back to their cottage on the edge of Gustard Wood Common and on to Fallows Green where he had built the dream house for his family. She would sometimes take Edy as well as Ted on these pilgrimages, meeting neighbours she had known and spending the weekends nearby. The first time she appears to have taken Ted there was shortly after his eighteenth birthday early in 1890. They stayed with some friends from those early days, the Gibsons, at their beautiful home, Ashwell House, in a quiet part of St Albans. The Gibsons had a son and daughter, Edward and Helen, approximately the same ages as Edy and Ted, and were generally such good company that Ashwell House became a regular staging post on these journeys into the past. Ted would take Helen (whom everyone called May) to the theatre, and he was soon writing to his old nanny at Gustard Wood Common: 'You remember Mrs Gibson don't you – Mother's great friend: well, her daughter and I hope some day to be married . . . I thought you would care to hear this and perhaps from me.' But when Ellen picked up this news she was not pleased, fearing that May, so pretty but so conventional, would lure him away from the Lyceum. The thought of a separation from her son was 'equally startling & almost as shocking', she told Katherine Lewis, as Laurence Irving's shooting (though Edy made her laugh by describing her brother as being temporarily infatuated: 'a victim of the liberties of Leap Year!'). Ellen urged him to postpone this marriage and join her and Henry later that year on their tour of America. He would earn up to £300 and be in a much stronger position to marry (if he still wanted to) when he came back. It was his 'simple duty' to 'make some money for the first time in your life & bring it back to May'. But Ted did not seem to be listening. 'I have so much to make me happy', Ellen confided to Katherine Lewis, 'but a mother never leaves off loving her child – *unreasonably*.' And if Ted married she 'must miss all that'.

She turned to Henry for help, knowing how Ted venerated him. 'I have heard with regret that you do not think of going with us to America – Is this not a pity?' Irving wrote.

You have a prospect of playing some splendid parts, which would certainly give you great experience.

. . . I hope you will think better of it and come with us – but if you should be married (as this is not impossible) there would be nothing but to leave your wife behind in England.

The hard work and anxieties of such a tour as ours could be very great and to drag about a young wife on such an expedition would be positively dangerous – a responsibility *which* I would not undertake with anyone in whom I was interested . . .

Of the anxiety to (your) Mother I say nothing. Such a mother as yours has no peace when you are disturbed – or your interests are at stake . . .

I would very much like you to come with us as you told me you would – And I should not only like you to be with us for my sake but more for your mother's and your own – for I know it would be for your good. God Bless you old fellow . . .

This appeal should not have been addressed to an 'old fellow' but to a young chap of twenty-one who desperately 'needed a woman' and could not wait a year. As Gordon Craig remarked in old age, 'it is so easy to say, when one is seventy-two or eighty-two, what twenty-one ought to do'. Irving himself was then in his mid-fifties, Ellen in her late forties. His experience of marriage was no example of the wisdom and responsibility he was urging on his godson; while her marriage to Watts, as Ted sometimes reminded her, had been 'a ridiculous blunder' and her marriage to Wardell not much better. Ted must make his own mistakes and create his own experience.

Ellen had underestimated the determination of May Gibson. May knew that Ted had managed to save some £700 – enough for a couple to live on for a good three years – and she insisted that, now he had come of age, he must act on his own authority rather than his mother's. She knew that Ted was being pursued by other girls – for example, 'pretty Lucy Wilson' about whom he was always talking and Jess Dorynne, an attractive young actress with a far-away look in her eyes, whom Ellen very much liked. If May didn't marry him, and marry him quick, she knew that one or another of these actresses would snatch him – he was so handsome, so brimful of ideas, so unexpected and exciting, a young man in need of a young woman. So May made up her mind, made up his mind too, and they were married 'after the theatres closed for Holy Week' on Monday, 27 March 1893, when Ted sent his mother a telegram before going off for a brief honeymoon by the sea in Devon.

Ellen was devastated. For her it was a 'heart-breaking' business. 'I can't sleep – & I can scarcely do my work with all this worry.' Feeling bereft, she could merely sit by and watch. It was just as well she would soon be touring North America with Henry.

Looking back at this time from old age, Gordon Craig did not see his marriage as being so significant as two new friendships he formed that spring. He met the artist and designer James Pryde on a train and through him met his brother-in-law, the painter and engraver William Nicholson. May and Ted had moved into the Audley Arms at Uxbridge after their honeymoon. May immediately loved this half-timber-and-brick cottage next to a flour mill and beside a bridge over the River Colne; and Ted was delighted at the end of his train journey home to find that Pryde and Nicholson also lived in a converted public house, The Six Bells, close by at Denham, a very English village of six or ten cottages. The following day, he and May went over to see them there, and during the next four years 'I saw much of both men', Craig wrote. He saw them at work and 'I caught on to the woodcut idea'. He watched Nicholson working on wood, introducing a pattern of light on the dark background, adding minute details to the splashes of light, and finally modifying the block to gain the precise effect he wanted. Craig learnt much from him,* particularly a method of using photographs in which the highlights contrasted with the shadows, tracing them and transferring them on to a wood block, always keeping his work simple and bold.

James Pryde 'was a joy to be with' but 'never showed me how to do anything'. Yet the influence of his sinister architectectural pictures with their dramatic voids on Craig's stage designs is clear. Edward Craig's description of Pryde's pictorial world as 'a vast stage full of forms and shadows, enlivened by little figures here and there, suggesting that something dramatic was just about to happen', exactly fits his father's imposing theatrical scenes with what Max Beerbohm was to call their 'simplicity and austerity of surfaces, their effects of space and distance, the subtle use of cast shadows'.

The Six Bells was an enchanted place. Fresh air and sunlight filled the rooms that first summer, lighting up the drawings, cut-outs, areas of colour on the walls, and falling on the horizontal surfaces of the floors and tables scattered with pots of paint, with crowded stacks of brushes and stray chalks, sugar paper and engraving materials. Ted could not keep away and would charge up and down the one-street village with its surrounding tall trees, pretending to be a horse for Nicholson's young son Ben. William Nicholson's wife – Jimmy Pryde's sister – Mabel seemed to him a remarkable woman – far more remarkable, he could not help noticing, than his own wife May. This was unfortunate, and became more so after Ellen and Henry left the country on their extended tour of the United States – that tour he should by rights have been going on himself. It was difficult not to blame his wife. When Ellen returned, Ted and May went down to stay with her at the cottage in Winchelsea. She was overjoyed to see her son but 'his wife contrives to irritate me more I think than any other person *I have ever met with*', she admitted to a friend. However, 'she's Ted's wife and I'll do my best to keep from *spanking* her'. She saw that May was genuinely fond of Ted yet she was 'a marvellously vain, silly, and most aggressive girl – &

* Craig was to write introductions to William Nicholson's *An Almanac of Twelve Sports and London Types* (reprint from the original wood blocks, 1980) and also William Nicholson's *An Alphabet* (reprint from the original wood blocks, 1978).

mischief goes where she goes'. Ellen could not hide these feelings from Ted who began to think that May should never have insisted on marrying him – he had been a fool to oblige her. He had surrendered 'glory and money' for her; and by the beginning of April 1894 he had also given her a daughter, Rosemary, 'so funny & so musical' and full of the 'Terry temper'.

In his Lear-like old age, Gordon Craig would grant that his daughters 'were kind and loving to me. I had no kingdom to divide among them.' He might know little about daughters but he had picked up a good deal of knowledge about wives and mothers. 'No one but the mother can look after a child', he had once believed. But his own mother, he came to realise, had never been the right person to look after him and it was no surprise to him that she found 'it's bitterly disappointing being a Grandmother – and I thought it would be so lovely'. She possessed an untiring love for him and Edy and would help them out of muddles – but she never helped Ted, he believed, to avoid them. And the biggest muddle, more of a blunder perhaps, or even a catastrophe, was his wife. By the end of the year May told him that she was again pregnant. Rosie and now another child: it was really too much.

Between his mother and his wife Ted felt stretched. The world of art beckoned him, but he found to his surprise that he could not immediately produce designs and engravings as good as those by Nicholson and Pryde. They had awakened in him something that he longed for: what one of his sons would call a 'dormant artistic sense' inherited from his father. He knew that he was privileged, but it was extraordinary how people turned this privilege against him – his mother was actually charging him 5 shillings a week rent for the Audley Arms under the pretext that it was good for him. After Rosie was born, however, Ellen had been obliged to send him and May a weekly allowance. 'I could let you have £5 as easily as £3 – but my dearest darling you had better try the £3 . . . your father and I lived on only £2.'

It was not as if Ted had been idle. He had fallen back on what he learnt from Irving at the Lyceum: the great tradition of preparing a play for acting by cutting it to pieces, rearranging what remained and then adding some dramatic improvements. He found it much easier to work 'without any directions', he was to tell his mother when she offered him advice. He took the scissors to Shakespeare's *Henry IV*, adapting it so that a single actor (he had himself in mind) could play both Hotspur and Prince Hal. Then he turned his attention to Browning's *A Blot in the 'Scutcheon* and Ibsen's *Peer Gynt*. It was curiously satisfying work, this disembowelling of a writer's text, though so far there was no money in it.

While he was at work, a local vicar called to ask whether he would be prepared to give a recitation at the Uxbridge Town Hall to raise funds for charity. Ted responded enthusiastically, cutting and pasting a play by Alfred de Musset, persuading several actors at the Lyceum to join his enterprise, borrowing some damask hangings and props from *Louis XI*, sketching various costumes which were made up by the Lyceum wardrobe staff, and even getting hold of Edy's friend, the Baroness Overbeck – known as 'Jimmy' or 'Jo' on account of her pretty boyish looks – to compose the incidental music. 'We intend to give as *thorough* a performance as possible', Ted wrote to his mother. Being in control of everything was the greatest fun. And it was for a good cause too – 'the proceeds were given to the Building Fund of the Uxbridge National Schools', he remembered. But he had forgotten that there were no proceeds – there had been a loss.

After the birth of Rosie, Ellen had insisted that Ted must take a paid job. In the summer of 1894, he joined the W.S. Hardy Shakespeare Company which was touring England and Wales. 'It was an extraordinarily brave company, this', he remembered. Hardy himself had trembled and looked away from the stark modern poster that Pryde and Nicholson (soon to become famous for their 'Beggarstaff' posters for Henry Irving and others) had designed for his production of *Hamlet*. But he 'showed no fear' in handing over the roles of Hamlet and Romeo to Ellen Terry's son.

Hardy's company assembled at the Theatre Royal in Hereford where they found, occupying the stage on which they were to rehearse, a huge tank full of water which formed the chief attraction of the current show. 'Mr Craig, tell us exactly what you want and we will fit in,' the amiable Mrs Hardy invited him. And so, manoeuvring gingerly around this aquatic obstacle, they began.

Of his first two leading roles, Hamlet was the one Ted believed was better suited to his condition. Romeo's predicament he did not really comprehend. He had known no Juliets in his life and did not enjoy love-making on stage – nor, to judge from their cat-calls, did the audiences.

But there was joy in acting Hamlet. Here was someone who 'seemed to me if not to be myself – to be the nearest thing to me'. Irving had sent him his old costume with belt and sword for the performance and through the 'words, words, words' of Hamlet, Ted seemed to avenge his many mortifications – for surely he had more mortifications than most men. He felt himself misunderstood even by his loving mother, and raised the same piteous sighs over May as Hamlet did before Ophelia. He knew the play by heart – it was to be the inspiration for his most original stage production and a sustained series of engravings. Shakespeare's words 'are so inevitable & blood-on-fire', he later wrote to the Swiss stage-designer Adolphe Appia. 'I tremble with excitement whenever I read lines here and there.' Edy, 'bless her', came down on the first night, and William Rothenstein was to paint him in the role – a dark figure 'whose genius stood in the way of his talents'.

When Ted came back home at the end of the year, he noticed that his daughter looked rather larger than before and his heavily pregnant wife somewhat older. But, having to earn money for them all, he was soon off to join another touring company for the spring and early summer of 1895. On 5 May he briefly called back home to see his son Henry Edward Robert (often called Robin and sometimes Bobby) born.

Among the touring company he had been delighted to find his old flame, 'pretty Lucy Wilson'. He could not keep his eyes off her and 'accompanied her everywhere'. At the end of their tour that June he did not go home but accompanied Lucy to a theatre company in Scotland. 'I was still utterly puzzled by the problem of sex, I saw no solution', he wrote in his memoirs. He sent Lucy flowers and put to music some love poems by Heine for her. She remained as sweet as ever but would not have an affaire with a married man. That summer he noted in his diary that he was 'ill in bed – too much longing. Called a doctor in.'

When he eventually found his way back to Uxbridge, May looked 'hurt and aloof'. She saw nobody now except her two children and her parents in St Albans. Ted complained that he could not work with babies in the house and passed most of his time with the Nicholsons.

To add to his worries, Ellen was still sending him instructions on what to do and not do. He must 'give up dreaming of the future' and be a servant of his family. 'I cooked and baked, and washed and saved for you – and scrubbed for you, and *fainted* for you, and *got well again for you*, as my mother did for me – *You talk and talk*, and don't do.' This seemed peculiarly unjust. By the beginning of 1896 Ted had moved his wife and children up to

London so that May would feel less lonely and asked Ellen whether he might rejoin the Lyceum. She appealed to Brandon Thomas, author of *Charley's Aunt*, to help her find him 'steady work' in a London theatre. 'I don't want him to be at the Lyceum where he is spoiled', she explained. Nothing came of this and since Irving also believed that it was 'better for him not to come back to the Lyceum, at least for a while', Ted had no option but to set off on tour once more.

There were compensations: such as coming across Jess Dorynne again in a stock company he joined at Chatham. She was quite unlike May, a modern girl of vitality and independence. With her far-away look she appeared to see beyond Ted's marriage, and the two of them were soon talking of how they might keep in touch. Meanwhile Ellen, with one of her sudden changes of mind, renewed her appeals to Henry for Ted to come back under his protection. What did it matter if he was spoilt a little? 'What fools we are', she wrote to Bernard Shaw, 'in bringing up our children!'

30
One More Laurel Wreath

Tennyson had begun *Becket* in the late 1870s and finished it, so he believed, in 1879 when he handed it to Irving. Irving's response was an invitation for him to write a shorter play which would be less costly to mount (and which turned out to be *The Cup*). But Tennyson was still hopeful that Irving would stage *Becket* and, not wishing to 'take the bloom off it', postponed publication. 'My father', Hallam Tennyson told Irving, 'feels that so many alterations are needed to fit *Becket* for the stage . . . he would sooner that these alterations should be made for you under your guidance than of others.' But Irving prevaricated. The play was 'so good that I personally dare not touch it'.

Heartbreakingly eager to see it performed, Tennyson believed that he would bow to all Irving's suggestions. Irving wanted works by the Poet Laureate in his Lyceum repertoire and was fond of Tennyson. He feared that the proliferation of rewriting and rearranging which the play needed might wound Tennyson dreadfully – indeed, there was so much reconfiguration to be done that, practised as he was with the scissors and editorial pen, he hardly knew how to begin. So instead of beginning, he delayed, and the years passed. In 1884 Tennyson finally published *Becket* and the following year Lady Archibald Campbell's Pastoral Players gave a performance of the love scenes from it *en plein air* at Wimbledon, adapted by their Director of Entertainments, Edward William Godwin. Almost certainly Tennyson would have asked Irving's permission for this presentation, perhaps hoping that, after some six years, it might act as a reminder, even a spur. Another six years passed and Irving agreed that Tennyson should accept an offer from the American Shakespearean actor Lawrence Barrett to produce the play – only to see Barrett drop dead before the contract was signed. Irving had wanted Tennyson to dramatise his narrative poem *Enoch Arden* – an uplifting tale of misery which, ending with heroic virtue and self-sacrifice used as instruments of revenge, perfectly mirrored mid-Victorian sensibility. But nothing came of this and so he promised to stage Tennyson's pastoral entertainment *The Foresters*. But not finding it sensational enough (despite the late addition of a fairy scene) he withdrew it during rehearsals.

By this time he had examined the rearrangements that Lawrence Barrett proposed making to *Becket*, and thought he saw a way of constructing a practical acting version. But not quite liking to reveal the full extent of his reworkings, he sent down Bram Stoker to see Tennyson in the spring of 1892. When Stoker asked him whether Irving might in principle do whatever he thought necessary, Tennyson, who was ill in bed, agreed that 'Irving may do whatever he pleases with it'. 'In that case,' Stoker replied, 'he will do it within a year.'

Hallam Tennyson remembered his father and Bram Stoker going through Irving's draft, which had been made 'by cutting up two copies of the published play and sticking the pages on sheets of foolscap. In this way the reader could see the final result without having the actual omissions forced on his notice.' But Tennyson knew his play by heart. 'He did not look happy', Stoker observed. Indeed, he pleaded with Stoker for the restoration of one of his favourite characters, a cynical old churchman named Walter Map who comments on the action of the play, and Stoker made a note (though Map was never restored). Finally he signalled his acceptance and promised to draft a new speech that Irving had requested. He was evidently troubled, but five months later he told his doctor: 'It will be successful on the stage with Irving . . . I suppose I shall never see it.'

'I fear not,' the doctor replied.

'I can trust Irving,' Tennyson insisted, '– Irving will do me justice.'

Tennyson died on 5 October 1892, four months before the opening night of *Becket*. The play was mounted in the most handsome Lyceum style with a Gothic cathedral and wonderful bluebell woods. Tennyson's melodious verse was accompanied by incidental music composed by Charles Villiers Stanford, a specialist in church music who had composed oratorios for some of Tennyson's poems. There was a strong cast: Terriss as Henry II, with Genevieve Ward as Eleanor his queen and Ellen as his mistress Rosamund. But for the public, there was only one character: Irving's Becket, an immense figure, sweeping across the stage in his great cloak of scarlet. They heard the crescendo in his voice, harsh and terrible, as he refused the command to sign the king's document; and finally the awful pathos as he approaches the end of his struggle for life. 'You felt you were actually in the presence of this mighty man', the actress Lillah MacCarthy wrote.

Becket opened on Irving's fifty-fifth birthday – and something miraculous appeared to happen. He had played priests before – Richelieu and Wolsey – and played them well. Had his mother not dreamed of his becoming a great minister of the church? In Tennyson's dramatic poem he seemed in his fashion to fulfil her dream. The theatre was his church and he transferred his lofty habit of courtesy, his condescension and pride as head of his profession, to this priest. He spoke with absolute clarity and assumed a nobility of bearing, an inflexibility of will, a moral strength, unmarked by his usual eccentricities. 'Nature intended him for a prince of the church', William Archer observed. 'He was superb', Ellen told her friend Albert Fleming.

In an attempt to widen the play's appeal, Tennyson had introduced some scenes of romantic jealousy between Henry Plantagenet's wife and mistress. It was this theme that Godwin had extracted for his open-air presentation by the Pastoral Players. But Irving recognised that the real drama lay in the struggle for authority between the king and the archbishop, leading to Becket's assassination. The subsidiary romance sounded embarrassingly sentimental and did not blend well with the historical narrative.

Ellen wrote nothing about *Becket* in her *Memoirs* because she felt that Irving had given her nothing. The Fair Rosamund was worthless. 'I don't know what to do with her', she complained to Graham Robertson when she first read it. 'She is not there. She does not exist. I don't think that Tennyson ever knew very much about women, and now he is old and has forgotten the little that he knew. She is not a woman at all.' She was left with the feeling that she might no longer be a woman of any interest in Henry's life.

Irving attempted to atone for the unconvincing role he had given Ellen by paying out a great deal of money on her costumes – glittering crosses and rosaries with which to decorate her nun's habit, and the jewelled robes of the rich gown in which she made her first entrance – 'a wonderful, Rossettian effect of dim and glowing colour veiled in black, her masses of bright hair in a net of gold and golden hearts embroidered on her robe', Graham Robertson remembered. '. . . she looked her loveliest.'

Even in its adapted state, Tennyson's poem for the stage still remained episodic and undramatic. Yet Irving somehow managed to 'gather it round him' and make a wonderful tragic entertainment of it. On the first night, at the close of each act, the audience summoned him before the curtain; and at the end, to a roar of applause mingled with shouted congratulations on his birthday, he stepped out and made a brief speech saying that it had been a 'labour of love to add one more laurel wreath to the brow of the Master' who had so recently been laid to rest at Westminster Abbey.

Becket was to become one of the most admired plays in Irving's repertoire. On 18 March he was called to give a royal production-in-miniature before Queen Victoria in the Waterloo Chamber of Windsor Castle. 'It is a very noble play', the Queen told him. It was rumoured that she much preferred these beautiful words of her late Poet Laureate to 'the terrors of *The Bells* or the paroxysms of Shylock'.

'Tennyson's conception of Becket's character gave Irving the opportunity to portray a prelate utterly distinct from his Wolsey and Richelieu,' wrote his grandson, '– a statesman and soldier transformed by preferment and revelation into a saint and martyr.' No play influenced him so much as *Becket* and no character, Irving believed, had brought him so close to his public. For fourteen years, in one form or another, he had carried this play around with him, trying to discover its dramatic centre. On Tennyson's death he seemed to gain ultimate possession of it and become its very author. One night at supper in the Beefsteak Room he recited some of his favourite lines about 'a little fair-haired Norman maid' and said that he doubted if there was anything in Shakespeare to be preferred to them. When someone began to remonstrate, one of his lieutenants, Loveday perhaps or possibly Stoker, quickly restrained him, whispering: 'You don't understand how he feels about this play.'

It is doubtful whether Ellen understood how Irving's identification with 'this turbulent priest', who changed dramatically from a brilliant courtly figure to a zealous ascetic, might have marked a change in his own life. When a friend remarked that everyone knew how he had really made the play, Irving answered: 'No, no, the play made me. It changed my whole view of life.'

31
Mixed Fortunes

Despite the success of *Becket* the Lyceum was now losing money. The most practical way to recoup their losses, Irving realised, was to go on tours around Britain and Ireland and off to North America again where their productions were less well known.

Their first transatlantic tour ten years earlier had been in the spirit of a honeymoon. By taking a holiday together in Canada during the summer of 1893 (they were seen together, just the two of them, in a train on their way to Banff), it may have been that Henry and Ellen hoped to regain some of the romance that had been ebbing from their relationship.

'I never felt graver in my life', Ellen had confessed to Ted. '. . . The look forward for me is pretty blank. I don't mean in the *Theatre* – that's nothing – I care for that least of all . . . The dwindling of love is the only thing to be feared in this world. I'm sure of that.' But the peace of the sea seemed to make Henry so happy that Ellen, casting out 'hate from my heart', had the illusion of a new beginning. He was, she confided to Ted, 'very kind for awhile, & so it be I pray'. She suspected that whenever Henry was especially kind to her he had 'a new flame' hidden away somewhere. At one of the towns they visited Ellen was to receive from one of her ardent fans a serious proposal of marriage through the post which, Edy opening it by mistake, there was no concealing. So 'I told Henry,' Ellen wrote to Ted, '– thought it would not hurt him to know some living person regarded me – but he is too sure of my affection to be much disturbed. He was very nasty – said "Oh everyone thinks an Actress has plenty of money". I had to show him a few lines in which Mr J. said if I would marry him he should ask me to make a present of every farthing I have to my children – one for H[enry].' She was closest to him whenever he was ill and they stayed near each other in the same hotels so that she could look after him ('a great deal in the poulticing and Turpentine line'). Such times were reminiscent of the night when Godwin had been ill and Ellen, though married to Watts, was said to have stayed nursing him.

They had taken Edy with them. Henry also asked Ellen to invite her father Ben Terry over, though at the last moment he decided to stay in London to keep an eye on Tom, Ellen's younger brother, the black sheep of the family, who was in trouble with the police.

At the beginning of September, they joined the rest of the company in San Francisco, opening their tour at the Grand Opera House with *The Bells*, then working their way through the west and up to several Canadian cities where they could show their old plays to new audiences. In Chicago and Philadelphia, Washington and Boston, however, they tried out their newer productions among which the favourite turned out to be *Becket* (for which Irving added a harpist, chorus master and organist to their expeditionary force).

'Five years in a country of rapid changes is a long time, long enough for friends to forget', Ellen was to write in her memoirs. But they had not forgotten. 'This time we made new friends, too, in the Far West.' There were over ninety people travelling with the company now, and to their special palace cars were added ten baggage coaches carrying scenery and stage properties. Heading gradually north and then eastwards, they made many short stops – one night in Seattle, two nights at Portland (Oregon), three nights in Minneapolis and so on. Everywhere photographers stood waiting to snap Ellen as she alighted from the train 'as supple as a tigress', one reporter described her, her eyes 'like turquoise stars', and displaying a 'vast vintage of youth which mellows, not fades'. When, laden with flowers and 'looking like a fashion plate with a buttoned coat and jaunty toque', she returned to the hotel after her performances, young poets stood waiting to hand her their verses.

Leading this advancing army of actors, at a slight distance, rode the picturesque figure of Irving in his long fur-collared coat and soft hat, a solitary traveller among the ranks, with the air of a Don Quixote, Bram Stoker his unlikely Sancho Panza, and his ancient fox terrier Fussie in the role of Rozinante. 'A tall gaunt figure in dark clothes enveloped in a black overcoat surmounted by a tall, black silk hat with a wide rim', a journalist in

Boston described him, 'and attended by a queer looking dog with a small head and a barrel-shaped body and a stub tail strode on . . .'

Irving was an embodiment of the American Dream, the 'Knight from Nowhere' as Max Beerbohm was to call him, who had conjured success out of nothing. He loved Americans for their spontaneous applause, their generous spirit and never-ending hospitality. In San Francisco he was treated to the grandest of 'big feeds' and 'high jinks' by the Bohemian Club. As he mounted the steps to the great portals of this club, a deafening cacophony of bells rang out celebrating his first production in the town – everything from cathedral to dinner bells which gathered in volume and tumult until he reached the library where a bust of Shakespeare draped with the Union Jack and the Star-Spangled Banner awaited him. In the banqueting hall, the band played 'Ta-ra-ra Boom-de-ay', and massed sunflowers, yellow poppies and marigolds were laid out on silk draperies to represent Henry VIII's Field of the Cloth of Gold. It was a surreal experience, his American hosts having got themselves up to represent many of the characters he had played – Cardinal Wolsey, Mephistopheles, Shylock, Macbeth and others.

Ellen passed more of her time out of doors. In spite of the fruit and flowers, 'the marvellous Bay and the Golden Gates', she wrote, 'there is printed on the face of the people This-is-America-the-home-of-the-money-getter-Mammon-is-our-God and it spoils their faces and voices – although I *must* admit I don't think it spoils their *hearts*, for they are kindly to excess'.

At all the major cities they would advertise for supers and were overwhelmed with applicants who were quickly handed swords or spears and, many of them, had twirling moustachios fixed to their faces before being taken hurriedly through their routine of synchronised chanting and gymnastics. The company played to overflowing houses. In Chicago extra crowds swarmed in from the World Fair which was exhibiting Sargent's picture of Ellen as Lady Macbeth as well as several works by Watts, Whistler and Millais. 'The town has gone mad over itself and its fair', Ellen reported. The mood of gaiety was not overshadowed even by the murder and public funeral of the Mayor of Chicago. 'This is the first time Henry & I are staying in different hotels & we are both dull for that', Ellen confided to a friend. But, she added triumphantly: 'Henry was never so sweet & kind & unselfish as he is now to me. Long may it last!'

Finally they reached New York, playing in Henry Abbey's new theatre on Broadway and 38th Street to a eulogy from the press. Then, after a farewell dinner at Delmonico's, they boarded the *Majestic* on 21 March 1894 and sailed home – first to London for a short season of revivals, then on a provincial tour in the autumn.

Their American tour had shown the Lyceum a profit of over £20,000. But within eighteen months the company was once more in need of money, and in September 1895 they set off on what Irving planned to be their final transatlantic tour. 'I think Henry looks very ill – I wish for his sake we were not going to America this year', Ellen wrote to her son, '– it tells on him greatly.' But his financial difficulties had been made worse by his inability to cut costs. He kept an enormous company at the Lyceum and, never having forgotten his early years when he did not have enough to eat, he paid them handsomely. Though he often let the theatre while he was away from London, he seldom attempted to make much money from these arrangements.

This fifth tour, which began with a production of *Faust* at the Academy of Music in Montreal, lasted nine exhausting months and was the most gruelling of all their transatlantic journeys. 'I feel as if I'd been away from England for years already!' Ellen wrote to Ted after their opening night. They carried with them scenery and properties, orchestra and supporting staff, for fourteen full-length plays (including two new productions) as well as several curtain-raisers. And they went through the same procession of speeches and banquets, interviews and receptions, as they steamed about 'this unquiet galloping country', hurrying from one town to another. It was 'a *bewildering time* . . . quite distressing', Ellen told Ted. 'One wants extraordinary physical order to cope with America.' This time the company went south and visited some poorer cities. Ellen was particularly impressed by New Orleans, full of friendly people living in small houses – it seemed a different country from the grand mansions of the north. 'One sees tremendous Palm Trees in the streets & roses all over the walls of the houses . . . everywhere in New Orleans the water is found less than three feet deep & they can't bury their dead here, but have to take them away up to the hills.'

Towards the end of this tour Ellen was overcome by 'a dread' that she was 'going to break up'. Irving had been suffering from bouts of neuralgia aggravated by his anxieties over the ice, snow and floods that were threatening their progress, and he was advised to have a minor operation. 'Poor Henry', Ellen wrote. He 'bled frightfully' after a bone in his nose was cut away to relieve the pain. For weeks she had seen so little of him 'except in the confounded theatre'. But now, watching him sleeping peacefully following his operation, her true feelings declared themselves. There was a heroic quality to him. 'He is a wonderful person.'

The winter grew worse and their progress became more endangered. At one point where they were attempting to cross the Mississippi, the swollen water had swept away the tracks, and their carriage crept along a wooden trestle. Through the windows they saw a strange parade of wreckage rush past – chicken coops, fence-posts, snakes coiled around stray planks and upturned trees with roots pointing crazily to the skies. 'Hurry and dress yourself properly,' Ellen ordered Edy late one night as the floods almost engulfed the engine; 'we shall probably have to swim.' They were rerouted on to safer tracks and managed to come through just in time for their opening night. 'This rushing, tearing America, so full of hope!' Ellen exclaimed, 'but oh, so rough, so rough.'

For Irving the most memorable incident of this tour, fortifying him against its continual hazards, was a tribute from the great Italian actress Eleonora Duse. They were both playing at theatres in Philadelphia, and Duse sent over a letter signed by all the members of her company, the Città di Roma, thanking him and Ellen 'for having revealed, through your great talent, and by the proud flights of your genius, the sweet idioms of Shakespeare'. This he kept for the rest of his life.

For Ellen the 'chief incident' was to be the production of Laurence Irving's one-act leper play *Godefroi and Yolande*, which was put into rehearsals when the company reached New Orleans. 'I cannot tell you how deeply I felt all your generous enthusiasm over my play', Laurence wrote to her. This was the encouragement he had so desperately needed from his father. The irony of being so 'honoured' by someone whom he had loaded with blame for his mother's unhappiness and resolutely called 'the Wench' cannot have failed to strike him. But it did not inconvenience him. This was like the climax of a pantomime in which she had been miraculously transformed into 'the first of English actresses' – a miracle he was happy to accept. When he heard from his brother Harry that Ellen wished to play Yolande, the leper-courtesan of his medieval colony, he replied that such a consummation would be 'the making of my play . . . I know not how to thank you.' Characteristically he at once asked for something more. 'It now only remains to persuade my father to play Godefroi.'

But Henry would have nothing to do with the wretched thing and left it all to Ellen. 'We're rehearsing that filthy leper play every day,' one of the company complained, '[it] takes all our time, and it's such a muddle owing to the erratic Nell's stage management.' She herself could 'think of little else', she wrote to Katherine Lewis. 'Oh, I pray we may do it well & that it may be a success – for it's tremendously clever.' Edy devised the scenery, stitched together the costumes, arranged the lighting and organised the rather reluctant stagehands. She looked as 'jolly as 2 Sandboys', Ellen wrote to Mrs Rumball, 'working away like mad at Laurence's play for me. She is a great blessing . . . but at times a little too *vigorous.*' Working with a tiny budget, Edy ingeniously converted bits and pieces from other productions into what she needed – and even Irving at the last moment lent a hand. One of the actresses vividly recalled Ellen making her entrance at the world premiere of the play in Chicago. She walked slowly along a balcony at the back of the scene to a flight of steps where she stood clad in a crimson gown, her absolutely white face, haunting eyes and beautiful mouth set like a tragic mask. 'I, as a lady-in-waiting, had to follow, but I remember standing there transfixed by her strange loveliness, and the scene itself so rich, so beautifully composed.'

Chicago audiences 'received it splendidly', Ellen remembered. She sent off the good reviews to Laurence. But the play's success had partly been Edy's. Beside her radiant mother, and in contrast to her mercurial brother, Edy still appeared a shadowy figure. She had none of their easy charm and seemed to take pride in her awkwardness and belligerence, as if continually reminding Ellen of the difficulties in being an illegitimate daughter of an overwhelmingly famous mother. On the tours she did much sketching and, like the women around the guillotine during the French Revolution, knitted and needled fiercely away at her theatre costumes. She also took up photography, using her camera as if it were a weapon, snapping people in their most inelegant postures and at alarming moments ('she has the most outrageous collection of Kodak pictures', Ellen told Ted). She avoided newspaper reporters, though one of them from the *Chicago Herald* described her as 'rogueish', adding that her style was 'so vastly opposed to every color and turn in her handsome mother that there is not the slightest trace of resemblance between them'.

'Edy is enough to make one daft', Ellen had written to Ted the previous year. That she had talent, Ellen did not doubt, but she remained inexplicably reluctant to use it. She was now twenty-six and still 'she will *not work* at anything!' Ellen protested. '. . . She can be *taught* I think, but she's lost at sea, without a Pilot – & worst of all, the whole thing seems a supreme joke to her . . .' Her one difficulty was a slight lisp – but if Henry could overcome his stammering, surely Edy could deal with her lisp – even turn it to advantage in comic roles. But perhaps it was a sign that she wished to retreat into perpetual childhood.

Ellen criticised her daughter freely but she did not allow others to do so. She wanted them to animate Edy so that she would take acting seriously. But, unable to compete with her mother, she turned from acting to behind-the-scenes management of actors.

It was her attitude that troubled Ellen. Why did she sink into such stubborn silences, look so ill at times – and then so unaccountably happy? 'I think she has a terrific "temper" which she keeps a pretty tight hold upon', Ellen confided. But she remained a puzzle. 'I wish she'd fall in love – with a boot black,' Ellen suddenly exclaimed. 'But why do I say that, since she is very happy & as merry as a school boy!' Nevertheless Ellen could not help feeling that her daughter had no right to such bouts of happiness when she had achieved so little. She had been at the Lyceum now for some six years – and what was there to show for it? Then again did Edy really have much life outside the theatre? Ellen's thoughts grew muddled whenever she thought of her daughter – and she thought of her a lot, almost too much. 'At her *worst* & tryingest I dote upon her . . . poor little girl.'

Edy had assumed an indispensable role behind the scenes. A pallid companion, she accompanied Ellen to dinners and theatre-parties, seeing that she arrived on time and remembering people's names for her. 'She "bosses me" too much', Ellen wrote to Katherine Lewis, 'but that amuses me.' She would sort out Ellen's costumes, appearing to control everything with an air of brusque authority. 'Come on, Mother!' she would shout from the stage door, and Ellen, smiling sweetly, stopping to say something charming now to one stagehand, now to another, would look up and say: 'Oh, that's Edy. I mustn't keep her waiting!' But then something unexpected happened.

Amy Leslie, one of the actresses in the company, remembered Ellen saying to her: 'Wouldn't it be a fearful thing if some dear comfortless young gentleman should coax Edy to marry him? Two or three benighted youths have come to me praying to be allowed to pay attentions to Ailsa [Edy], but I have warned them of the fearful fate waiting for anybody bold enough to ask her. She won't have any of them – that's the only consolation.' It was a consolation for Ellen, though Edy did not like the caricature of her as someone consumed by ferocious arguments over 'laundry bills and dotted veils'. She appeared so solemn and isolated. 'Edy is going through a new & very strange phase', Ellen reported to Ted. '. . . I have scarcely *seen her on this tour* – and when I *most* of all wanted her she avoided me like the plague!!!' She seemed to believe apparently that 'she can do without *everybody so appallingly*'. But, Ellen insisted, she could not do without her mother.

Ellen needed the company of her daughter just then, having heard from England that her younger sister, the impulsive carefree Florence – 'darling Flossie' – had died suddenly of peritonitis at the age of forty-one while giving birth prematurely. 'I feel all is very black and cold', Ellen wrote to Ted, 'for the news of my dear little sister has pretty well done me in.' But why was Edy not there to comfort her? She was always vanishing. 'I hoped she might be in love! – but she scouts the idea – & it would be frightful chicanery.'

Yet Edy was in love and the chicanery lay in not telling her mother. Soon the whole company knew what was happening. 'She fell deeply in love with Sidney Valentine, who was married', one of them wrote. 'When Ellen Terry found out she reacted with violence . . . [and] threatened to send Edy home to England at once. It was an understandable way for a mother to behave, especially for this particular mother; but it did nothing to help Edy.'

Her son had left her to marry – Ellen was not going to let her daughter leave too. Edy never felt, as Ted sometimes did, that she lacked a mother's guidance – indeed, she received rather too much of it. In an odd reversal of roles Ellen even went so far to appeal to Ted for help in bringing his sister to her senses. 'My dear Edy,' he wrote, 'do let me help you about *things*. I could do so much better than Mother.' What he did was to tell her not to do what he had done. That is evidently what he intended to write, but as her pilot, lacking any clear sense of direction himself, he steered her into a fog of words. 'Dreams are nothing – & are best banished & impossible realities come to be dreams . . . I speak as I feel & know through experience . . . I know your ideal is in some one person very good & proper but make your ideal be ideal . . . I suppose you imagine you will never marry. Maybe – maybe not. I wish I were dead at the present moment. All seems going wrong . . .'

Ellen thought the Valentines a 'common & uninteresting' couple. Even if Sidney were unmarried he would not have been nearly good enough for her daughter. It was as if she wanted Edy to be a child eternal, her love child for all time. After their adult struggle and once Edy submitted to her wishes, Ellen took pity on her. 'I've just kissed her good night and tucked the dear thing up', she wrote to Ted, 'and she kissed me back so hard and I'm happy, too. So that's all right . . . Bless her old bones.'

The love-knot between mother and daughter was very strong. 'It wd be, I think, a very bad thing for her & for me too, if she were not with me – (unless of course she married happily)', Ellen wrote. '. . . when she gets ill & I have her with me she gets her old sweeter self . . . *she looks* so ill when she's away from me.' Ellen did not recognise her daughter's need to find independence or see the sickness of loving as a rite of passage. She places the notion of a happy marriage in parenthesis (where it now seemed to lie in her own life).

Ellen was about to enter her fiftieth year. Sitting alone in an American hotel on New Year's Eve and looking through her photographs, she had 'a long think' about her life. 'Your own till death', Henry had once written to her. But that was a long time ago. Despite their holidays together at the start of both these transatlantic tours, he was more distant. 'I think it is not quite right in him that he does not care for anybody much', she was to write. 'I think he has always cared for me a little, very little, and has had passing fancies, but he really *cares* for scarcely anyone.' This retrospective judgement was certainly unfair, but it accurately reflects her disillusionment. Had he really tired of her? Sometimes she almost wished he had and that he would find 'a nice clever young actress' for himself. 'I can enjoy nothing feeling so miserable, weak & ill', she confided to a friend. Irving was preoccupied by his sons but they too believed he had cared nothing for them. By encouraging Laurence with his play, Ellen had ensured that he would come knocking at the Lyceum door again, demanding to be admitted as a master-dramatist and actor of genius (he was already at work on a tragedy about Peter the Great). To Irving's mind it was typical of Ellen to shower her generosity among the deserving and undeserving so indiscriminately. She had even brought to America the script of an improbable one-act play on Napoleon by a brash young Irish troublemaker who had been flattering her, an impertinent puppy of a critic named Bernard Shaw who pretended to know more than anyone about everything. Irving no longer had time or energy for such vexations – the most pressing of which now came from his elder son Harry.

In his memoirs Gordon Craig was to lament not having been given so easy a passage into the theatre as Irving's two sons – Ellen's and Henry's children evidently knew almost nothing of one another's early lives beyond the misleadingly cheerful messages Ellen sometimes brought. Harry's difficulties were in some degree similar to Ted's: he appeared to have interests and qualifications for work outside the theatre, yet his sense of destiny kept pulling him back to it. Irving had felt proud when his son was called to the Bar. Like some general dreaming of a great military campaign, he calculated that the theatre needed well-placed friends in the legal profession to guard its interests and advance its position in society. But no sooner had Harry completed his legal studies than he returned to acting. His father went to the Comedy Theatre to see one of his performances – but left without going backstage to speak to him. Stubbornly refusing to abandon the profession, Harry left London to gain experience with one of the best-known touring companies in Britain, a ramshackle outfit owned by a famously gruff actor-manager named Ben Greet. Here, because he was his father's son, he was allowed to play a number of leading roles. But when a fellow actor, Ben Webster, wishing to ingratiate himself with Henry Irving, remarked on how pleasing it must be to read in the newspapers that Harry was appearing in the provinces as Hamlet, no sign of pleasure showed on Irving's face. 'Harr-y . . . hm . . . Ham-let . . . hm . . . Silly . . .' was all he said.

Harry's austerity, it was said, with its tantalising echoes of his father, attracted many actresses and 'he came to them like a child to his mother'. Foremost among them was a young girl whom the Revd Charles Dodgson used to escort to the Lyceum where she had seen Henry Irving and Ellen Terry in *Macbeth*. Dorothea ('Dolly') Baird was by now a 'pretty, rather plump' eighteen-year-old girl, naturally gregarious and easygoing. But her naïve self-assurance was ruffled on receiving a note from Ben Greet warning her 'not to encourage in any way what might end in being "attentions" from a gentleman in the company'. Dolly was offended and also frightened that 'I might get my dismissal', which would be very unjust because 'nobody has ever given me flowers or presents'. But she knew to whom Ben Greet was referring. She did not really like Harry all that much, though he had walked her home once or twice. He was a young man who, as it were, carried his weight around with him and impressed her as being rather 'stuck up'. But when a leading actress in the company fell ill, it was Harry who persuaded Greet to give Dolly her part as Rosalind in *As You Like It*. And it was while she was acting this role that Beerbohm Tree came to see the play.

Tree had recently been touring the United States and bought the British rights in an American stage adaptation of George du Maurier's sensational novel *Trilby* (in which Ellen Terry's name appears – she saw the American production and called it 'brilliant trash'). Tree's future as an actor-manager depended on the success of this play – and the success of the play depended on finding a sublime young actress to take on the difficult character of the artist's model who, at the Haymarket, would find herself dramatically mesmerised by Tree's impersonation of the sinister musician Svengali. The innocent candour of Dolly's Rosalind delighted him and he arranged to interview her together with George du Maurier. They were searching for an angel – someone angelic-looking to embody their tragic heroine. Max Beerbohm, Tree's half-brother, laid out the fictional dimensions of her character: 'a perfect head, a perfect foot, joyous youth and health, brown hair, blue eyes, the figure of a Venus de Milo and last and above all else an actress'. Du Maurier was much taken with Dolly when he saw her. 'You would love her', he wrote to Millais, '– 5ft 9ins – and made like a slender Venus.' As for Tree, he was enraptured by 'her beautiful golden brown hair, which hung down below her waist and clung in delicious little curls . . .' Dolly Baird (who had been earnestly slimming for her role as Rosalind) seemed to have come down from heaven in answer to their prayers. There was only one matter in doubt and that was her inexperience. She sounded far too prim for the 'phonetic acrobatics' of a part that Bernard Shaw was famously to reorchestrate for Eliza Doolittle in *Pygmalion*. Tree hired a voice coach who, like Svengali himself, tried to 'unteach her all she knew'. Gradually her gentility fell away. 'I am much vulgarer now', she reported happily. When *Trilby* opened at the Haymarket on 27 October 1895, almost everyone agreed that she had played the character to perfection. Harry himself marvelled at the transformation and even Shaw granted that her Trilby was 'a very pretty performance by a very pretty girl'.

'Do not altogether forget me', Harry appealed. He had been upset when she left Ben Greet to join Tree – and to her surprise she missed him too. They met on the few occasions when their two companies were performing near each other, Harry sometimes making the journey on a milk train rattling through the night. And they wrote letters all the time. Harry, who began formally 'Dear Miss Baird', was soon writing 'Dear Dorothea' and before long 'Dear Dolly'. By the end of 1895 she was 'My own dear darling'.

Reports of their impending marriage soon began appearing in the press, greatly embarrassing Harry who also had to come to terms with the fact that Dolly was now better known than himself. Not certain what to do, feeling unbearably tense, he went over to see Dolly at her home. Early in 1896, in the green room of the Haymarket Theatre, Dolly announced to the press that she and Henry Irving's son were to be married – and the news was reported almost as if it were a royal marriage. They had taken care that Irving himself should not hear of their engagement through the newspapers, sending a telegram to him in the United States asking for his blessing. Learning that he would not be back in London until June, they postponed the date of their wedding from May to July.

So Irving gave his blessing. But the future seemed hedged with awful complexities. Should he, after quarter of a century, be obliged to see his wife Florence again? He shuddered at the prospect. Watching him, as they continued with their travels together, Ellen realised that her own children's troubles had added to his family problems. Yet there must be something more to account for his awful solitude which was threatening to imprison her.

The most obvious explanation pointed not to any 'passing fancies' or a 'new flame', but to the knighthood which Queen Victoria had finally conferred on him in the interval between these two American tours. There had been rumours of a knighthood in the air for almost fifteen years – ever since he had met the Prince of Wales and begun entertaining him and his illustrious friends at the Beefsteak Room. In fact the first proposal had come from the Lord Chief Justice, Lord Coleridge, who in the summer of 1883 wrote to ask Gladstone: 'Would it be too audacious to offer Irving a knighthood?'

Gladstone frequently came to the Lyceum where, wrapped up in various shawls and protected from dust and draughts by a special velvet curtain, he had been given his own upholstered chair in the prompt corner so that, being rather deaf, he could follow the plots more easily. He enjoyed going backstage, sometimes discussing politics and plays with Irving in his dressing-room, and once or twice inviting him back to his breakfasts in Downing Street. It has been suggested that Gladstone, who like Irving had been expected by his mother to be ordained into the Church, learnt some of his oratorical techniques from studying Irving's performances.

No English actor had previously been granted a knighthood. Nevertheless Gladstone recommended that the Queen take this unprecedented step. Irving, however, cautiously refused because it would be improper, he explained, 'for an actor, while still actively pursuing his profession, to accept it'. Stephen Coleridge, who had been sent by his father to discover how Irving felt about such an honour, noted in his diary that he would not accept it because 'there was a fellowship among actors of a company that would be impaired by any elevation of one member over another; that his strength as a manager and power as an actor lay far more in the suffrages of the plain folk in the pit than in the patronage, however lofty, of great people; that he knew instinctively that large numbers of these same plain folk would be offended at their simple Henry Irving accepting decorations of a titular kind'.

That was the story which would later find its way into newspapers and biographies. But it was untrue. Gladstone had indeed unofficially offered Irving a knighthood (which Irving did not refuse) but found his offer vetoed by members of his Cabinet on the grounds that Irving had left his wife and established a questionable relationship with his leading lady. The matter was then handed over to Lord Coleridge. He proposed that if Irving could be persuaded to pretend that the offer had been unacceptable to him, then the government would be saved embarrassment. Irving agreed to this pretence. All relevant government papers were altered to support this 'refusal' story – all but one. This was the diary of the Cabinet secretary, Sir Edward Walter Hampton, which was not published until 1972 and which reveals how the proposal to confer a knighthood was abandoned after objections were made by Lord Granville and others. The significance of this is to show that actors were not seen as such respectable members of society in the early 1880s as to be worthy of this advancement.

Twelve years later, after Gladstone was succeeded by Lord Rosebery as Prime Minister, Irving delivered a speech (probably drafted by Louis Austin) at the Royal Institution. Painters and composers received honours – and was not acting also a fine art, he questioned, and therefore equally eligible for such preferment? 'In the face of the widespread influence of the stage today and its place in the thoughts and hearts of the people . . . we find that the records are deficient [and] we should, I think, endeavour to have them completed . . . Systems and courts, titles and offices, have all their part in a complex and organised civilisation, and no man and no calling is particularly pleased at being compelled to remain outside a closed door.'

He was speaking on behalf of his profession as he often did when addressing the public about his own work. Very shortly afterwards, on 24 May, a letter from Lord Rosebery (who appears to have known nothing of the previous aborted offer) was delivered to Grafton Street informing Irving that, in personal recognition and for his services to art, the Queen proposed to confer on him the honour of a knighthood. Stoker called round, and the two of them hurried off like schoolboys to tell Ellen the news. Her pleasure mirrored Henry's own. 'I'm delighted for some things', she wrote to Ted. 'He is *the first* (but he has a *knack* of being "first") . . . The dear old sweet was just as much pleased as he ought to have been.'

There were many at the Lyceum who believed that Ellen Terry should have been honoured too and who began calling her Lady Darling 'with which title I am well content'. Neither her children nor Henry's seemed particularly excited by the award, though they all sent him congratulatory messages (Harry in his telegram adding 'all congratulations from your wife' – Ellen imagined her hurrying off to the stationers to have new visiting cards printed bearing her title). When young, Irving had been 'full of animal vigour, never resting, never pausing, always rushing about and hardly ever seen to go upstairs at less than three steps at a time'. That, in the words of the novelist Hall Caine, is how Ellen first saw him. But now he was someone 'very solemn, distinctly intellectual, and with a never-failing sense of personal dignity', Hall Caine observed. '. . . He had done something which

I had never known to be done by anybody else – he had created a character and assumed it for himself.'

On the same day as the public announcement of Irving's knighthood came the news of Oscar Wilde's conviction at the Old Bailey. It was his dishonour that interested Harry and Laurence. 'Yes, Wilde is in the dust. Retribution has certainly overtaken him', Laurence wrote to his mother. '. . . I think old Queensberry's a brick.'

Henry and Ellen had been guests at Wilde's home, and Ellen considered him and Whistler – both Godwin's friends – to be the two most 'instantaneously individual and audacious' men she knew. One day, between Wilde's two trials, a veiled lady drove up to his house in Tite Street and left there a horseshoe with a bouquet of violets and a good luck card. This person was thought to be Ellen and the violets, Irving's favourite flower, to suggest he was the invisible partner in this gesture. Certainly when the artist Charles Ricketts met Wilde on his release from prison two years later, one of the few messages of welcome he brought with him came from Irving.

'The whole world rejoiced at the honour to Irving', Bram Stoker wrote. Hundreds of letters arrived saluting him as the first European actor to be honoured by his country. There were so many messages – from as far away as India and Australia – that Irving was obliged to employ five strong men to answer them all – after which Stoker had these 'hearty congratulations' bound up in a heavy folio with gilt edges. Even the brash new regiment of critics welcomed his award – Bernard Shaw characteristically explained why he should certainly have been offered the honour (though it would have been better had he declined it).

At the Lyceum, crowds gathered to witness the presentation of a congratulatory address signed by four thousand members of the acting profession. (It had been written by Pinero, placed in a gold and crystal casket, and read aloud from the stage by Squire Bancroft.) 'It made my heart thump to hear the public reception of Henry', Ellen wrote. To cheers from the audience, he received the tribute and stepped forward to reply: 'In olden times, our Britons showed their appreciation of a comrade by lifting him on their shoulders and I cannot but feel, and feel it with an unspeakable pride, that you, my brothers in our art, have lifted me on your shields. There is no more honour to come to the life of a man so raised.' This was, his grandson believed, 'the sublime moment of his life'.

On the morning of 18 July 1895, Irving caught a train to Windsor Castle where Queen Victoria was to confer the honour on him. Max Beerbohm happened to see him in a brougham on his way to the station. 'His hat was tilted at more than his usual angle and his long cigar seemed longer than ever', Beerbohm observed; 'and on his face was a look of such ruminant sly fun as I have never seen equalled. I had but a moment's glimpse of him; but that was enough to show me the soul of a comedian revelling in the part he was about to play . . . I was sure that when he alighted on the platform of Paddington his bearing would be more than ever grave and stately with even the usual touch of bohemianism obliterated.'

The ceremony took place in a small room at the castle. Irving was requested to take a few steps forward, then kneel before the Queen. She extended her hand 'which I kissed', he wrote, 'and her Majesty touched me on each shoulder with the sword and said "Rise Sir Henry", and I rose. Then, departing from her usual custom, she added "It gives me great pleasure, sir". I bowed and then withdrew from the room with my face to her Majesty. Walking backwards is unusual for me and I felt constantly as if I would bump into someone.'

Irving did not use his title during their most recent transatlantic tour – which at first disappointed and then, when they understood that he did not wish to set himself above them, delighted his audiences. But it felt to Ellen as if he were silently using the title in private, as if he were still walking backwards, moving away from her.

Unable to endure the loneliness of this long journey through Canada and the United States, Ellen began to take an interest in another member of the company, a rather wooden young actor with a distinguished provenance (he was a descendant of the Kembles). His name was Frank Cooper and according to Ellen he had 'a lovely voice, and never shouts' – a simple description that served to distinguish him from Irving. Bernard Shaw, who also fancied himself in love with Ellen, called him 'that stupid Cooper' and judged him to be a misfit in the theatre. 'Cooper is quite a pretty, amiable-looking chubby fellow off the stage,' he added, 'with a complexion as charming as wig paste.' In fact most people thought him a rather handsome fellow, manly and straightforward. His company came as a relief from Henry's subtle wiles. Ellen began flirting with him and encouraged him to send her flowers with anonymous cards 'from an admirer' written in his obvious handwriting. Whether through absent-mindedness or sheer mischief, she would sometimes call Henry 'Frank' – a habit that everyone in the company could see sent him 'livid with rage'. But Ellen enjoyed these love-games – they restored her confidence. 'No – I fear I can't snap up Frank Cooper and marry him', she later wrote to a friend, 'for he happens to have a wife.' She took no heed of the rumours because 'they marry me to every man I act with'. As for Frank Cooper's wife, she was 'a jealous little lady too, but *not* of me – and I'm fond of her'. Besides, she was back in England.

Ellen would bring Frank Cooper 'back to supper after the performance and insist that Edy should stay up – or get up if she had not been playing herself that night – in order to chaperone her', one of the actresses on their tour recorded. This was at the time when she had forbidden Edy to see Sidney Valentine, ostensibly because he was married. It seemed almost as if Ellen enjoyed provoking Edy, making her lose that brittle temper of hers and take to her bed where she could be comforted like a child. All this was threaded into the ties of love, possession and rivalry that bound mother and daughter so tightly together.

In May 1896, when the company finally disembarked at Liverpool, Ellen was handed a note telling her that her father had died. Irving, knowing how bereft she felt, finally agreed to let Ted back into the Lyceum, while he himself prepared to meet his own son's fiancée. 'I didn't go to meet him [Irving] at Liverpool', Harry wrote to his brother, '. . . as I don't think I have Mr Craig's craving for advertisement I stayed away.' So Irving met Dolly alone and was astonished by how much he liked her. Harry, who had been intensely nervous over this meeting, quickly recovered himself and sent his congratulations to Dolly. 'I told you the meeting would not be awful and it has turned out triumphantly.' He caught up with his father a few days later and 'I have never known him so friendly before. I mean in the sense of treating one more intimately and as a son.'

Unfortunately Ellen was also there. 'She is going to give you a miniature of my father which she values as one of her most treasured and sacred possessions', Harry warned Dolly. 'I can only say that it is much better in your hands than in hers. She was very cordial and well meaning, but she is a nonsensical creature.'

Harry's anxieties had now moved on to the actual wedding which was exercising his mother. Would Sir Henry, Florence wondered, use the occasion to perform a scene of reconciliation? And how, as Lady Irving, should she properly receive it? It depended, of course, on whether he had the effrontery to escort his mistress to the ceremony. The very thought of such an encounter sent spasms of outrage through her which she communicated to Dolly's family. 'I am sorry all this E.T. business is cropping up again', Harry apologised to Dolly. '. . . How wretched it is! I had hoped they would have spared you all unpleasantness . . . You will have to meet her [Ellen] as I met her and be rather bored by her, but she will not want to come to the wedding or our house or do anything that might be inconvenient.'

What Dolly may not have thought to tell Harry was that the Revd Charles Dodgson had taken her backstage to meet Ellen during a production of *Faust* and that they had greatly liked each other. She was not the empty-headed sentimentalist Harry described. This adult world of families was unexpectedly complex.

Harry had naturally hoped that his father would come to the wedding, but Florence's 'washing of family linen' somewhat changed his mind. He was relieved when Irving finally decided that a new Lyceum tour of the provinces made it impossible for him to attend. 'I am sorry not to be with you on what, I hope, will be the most auspicious day of your lives', he wrote to Dolly. '. . . I am told that brides like sometimes to wear their favourite flower – tell me yours and wear mine [violets] . . . my heart will be with you.' With this letter he enclosed a wedding present of £500 (equivalent in 2008 to £25,000).

Harry and Dolly were married at St Pancras Church on 29 July 1896. It was a fine day and crowds filled the streets nearby, many of them shouting 'Trilby! Trilby!' when they caught sight of Dolly. The presence of so many actors in the church, from Beerbohm Tree to Ben Greet, made Irving's absence all the more noticeable and Laurence cursed his father for being 'so unsatisfactory and insufficient' in missing what seemed to him a perfect opportunity for putting their troubled past to rest.

Visiting the bride and groom during their honeymoon, Irving noted that 'they are very happy – God bless 'em'. The more he saw of Dolly the more he liked her and the better he thought of Harry.

On Easter Day 1897, following a difficult delivery, the birth of their son was welcomed by the newspapers as being 'almost a national event'. *The Morning Press* predicted that 'the boy will probably carry on the acting traditions of the Irving family'. They named him after his uncle Laurence and he turned out (among other things) to be a biographer.

32
The Irish Pretender

Between their Atlantic tours, Irving added two one-act plays to the Lyceum repertoire. The first was *The Story of Waterloo*, adapted by Arthur Conan Doyle from one of his short war stories, 'A Straggler of '15'. In his *Memories and Adventures* Doyle was to recall, when a medical student in Edinburgh, paying his sixpence for the gallery night after night to see Irving: 'I had been a fervent admirer ever since', he wrote. His story evoked moments from the battle of Waterloo as remembered by an old soldier, Corporal Brewster, who expires as the curtain descends. Doyle knew instinctively that this veteran of the battle would appeal to Irving, but did not know whether his play was properly fitted for the stage. Before submitting it, he gave a copy to George Moore. 'I do not know if your play would act', Moore replied, '. . . but I do know that it made me cry like a child.' This was excellent news, Doyle himself having 'laughed and sobbed' while writing it (his laughter, when released from the tears, would go into the making of *Brigadier Gerard*, one of the most endearing comic figures in light fiction).

Irving saw at once that the play would act very well. Except for abbreviating the title, he made no changes and bought it outright for £100. 'Marvellous study in senility', Stoker noted in his diary. Once it became a popular stock piece, Irving gave Doyle an extra 2 guineas for each performance. 'I thank you with all my heart for having made my old veteran live', Doyle wrote to him.

The second one-act play, *A Chapter from Don Quixote*, which with Doyle's work and Pinero's *Bygones* was to make up a triple bill, had more convoluted origins. In need of a burlesque to satirise the glamour of war and balance Conan Doyle's military nostalgia, Irving retrieved an unsuccessful attempt by W.G. Wills to dramatise Cervantes' novel and amalgamated parts of his script with some images from Gustave Doré and paraphrases from Cervantes (there could be no objection from Wills himself because he was now dead). The main difficulty lay in securing a horse sufficiently well versed in theatre work to take on the role of Rozinante. Loveday made the mistake of sending for an almost dead animal from the north of England that, on its arrival at Euston Station, was arrested by the police and escorted to the knacker's yard. Its place was taken by a fitter animal which had acted with Beerbohm Tree and (though somewhat given to breaking wind) stood obediently through the dress rehearsals while signs of its emaciation were painted on its flanks and rib-cage.

The reviewers loved *Waterloo*. *The Times* drama critic A.B. Walkley was observed 'blubbering' all through it, and the critic of the *Daily Telegraph* W.L. Courtney declared that he had not experienced such a lasting mixture of pleasure and pain since witnessing Salvini's *Othello*.

But *Don Quixote* disappointed them, not so much on account of the extravagantly comic business behind which Irving tried to conceal the poverty of his text, but because, as when playing Malvolio in *Twelfth Night*, he introduced into the comedy moments of sadness and distress that unsettled his audience. He was the knight with the sorrowful countenance.

One reviewer, however, stood out from the rest. This was the Irishman, Bernard Shaw, recently employed as drama critic by the *Saturday Review*. Writing with a wit and eloquence quite different from the claque of coterie critics, he set down a challenging new agenda for the modern theatre.

In Shaw's account, *Waterloo* becomes a parody of the well-made play. The ready-made feeling and prearranged stage effects called for no original acting at all. All Irving had to do was to put on a dirty white wig, make himself up as toothless and blear-eyed, go through a hackneyed routine of hobbling and stooping and shaking at the knees, and perform a few mechanical exercises with a pipe, a firearm and a couple of chairs. But it was not the business, Shaw objected, of great actors and first-class theatres to rely on such pitiful stage tricks, let alone be praised for them by their friends in the press. Though he confessed to enjoying these stage-routines, their proper place, he concluded, was in the music hall.

Shaw also disagreed with everyone over *Don Quixote*, interpreting Irving's farcical excesses as a joyful release from the awful dignity, sustained over some half-dozen years, of performing King Lear, Cardinal Wolsey and

Archbishop Becket. Some terrific reaction to this series of tragedies was imminent and had come at last, Shaw judged, in the appropriate shape of the ingenious Don Quixote 'in which he makes his own dignity ridiculous to his heart's content'.

He rides a slim white horse, made up as Rozinante with painted hollows just as a face is made up; he has a set of imitation geese wriggling on springs to mistake for swans; he tumbles about the stage with his legs in the air; and he has a single combat, on refreshingly indecorous provocation, with a pump. And he is perfectly happy.

While Irving was ridiculously happy, Shaw rejoiced; when he put back his mask of solemnity, Shaw ridiculed him. He saw that this *Don Quixote* was an abortive vehicle for the modern stage, nevertheless 'there are moments in it when Wills vanishes', Shaw ended his review, 'and we have Cervantes as the author and Mr Irving as the actor: no cheap combination'. Such passages reveal, beneath the surface of his scathing criticism, Shaw's genuine admiration for an actor who had enchanted him as a boy in Dublin, but who now represented time past.

Ellen Terry had no role in these one-act events, but she was given the part of Queen Guinevere in the pageant play *King Arthur*, which opened at the Lyceum at the beginning of 1895, celebrating the ideal of chivalry that *Don Quixote* had satirised. Shaw's review of this production revealed what, in any other critic, would have been regarded as flagrant romanticism. He extolled Edward Burne-Jones, 'the greatest among English decorative painters', for having given audiences scenes of distant blue from the hills and the 'sunset gloom deepening into splendid black shadow from the horizons of Giorgione'. And against these 'deeply desired pictures', the mythical figures from the Round Table 'come to life, and move through the halls and colonnades . . . into the eternal beauty of the woodland spring acting their legend just as we know it, in just such vestures and against such backgrounds of blue hill and fiery sunset'. Shaw even went so far as to spare a few kindly words for the sugarstick orchestration of Arthur Sullivan ('the overture and the vocal pieces are pretty specimens of his best late work').

Irving had been at his most belligerent during the rehearsals, discomforting Burne-Jones who confessed that he had never wanted the *Morte d'Arthur*, a sacred text for him, 'to be dug up for public amusement'. Though some newspapers reported him making a bow between Ellen Terry and Henry Irving at the end of the play, in fact he did not turn up for the first night, preferring to sit at home 'playing dominoes – which is a game I like' – and it was Sullivan, in his evening dress, who shook hands with the heavily armoured Irving before the curtain.

King Arthur, Shaw declared, was 'a splendid picture' – indeed, more of a picture-opera than a play. There was only one thing missing: Irving had 'made a brave step' by resolving to 'get rid of the author and put in his place his dear old friend Comyns Carr'. For someone who had mutilated Shakespeare, travestied Goethe and rewritten Tennyson, it was perhaps a natural impulse to eliminate that awkward specialist, the playwright, and hand his duties to 'a jobber' such as Joe Comyns Carr. *King Arthur* was certainly a gorgeous pageant: 'but how am I to praise the deed when my own art, the art of literature, is left shabby and ashamed amid the triumph of the arts of the painter and the actor?'

Irving had handed Carr a rejected script by Wills based on Tennyson's poem 'The Passing of Arthur' which formed one of his *Idylls of the King* (Tennyson himself having turned down Irving's invitation to write a dramatic script of his poem). Carr, however, decided to go back to Malory's fifteenth-century cycle of Arthurian legends for his inspiration. But it was difficult to see what inspiration he found. His misogynist text, mixing Wagnerian motifs and grail imagery, presents the picture of a medieval empire in which Victorian gentlemen could easily recognise their own code of honour. As the theatre historian Jeffrey Richards observed, King Arthur was 'modelled on Prince Albert' and the Knights of the Round Table were 'prototype public school boys'. This romantic national myth became a pastiche of many cultural elements celebrating male supremacy (symbolised by the erect sword); and the drama springs from a struggle to resist the weakness of surrendering to female temptation (the sword sheathed in its scabbard). The visual beauty of the pageant is intended as a reflection of nature's inner truth. But Queen Guinevere's beauty is that of a poisonous flower and the effect of female degradation is to separate beauty from virtue. Carr's blank-verse adaptation, chronicling the ruin of the kingdom, 'is somewhat languid and lacks ginger', Irving conceded. But these missing qualities were to be provided by Burne-Jones's splendid costumes and scenery, Sullivan's charming music and Irving's own dynamic stage presence. Ellen's old flame, Johnston Forbes-Robertson, took the role of Lancelot. Wearing his plate armour most beautifully, he was proclaimed 'the hero of the piece', though Ellen could not help wishing he would not 'wave about' so much. His Lancelot and Frank Cooper's Mordred (another amorous knight of the Round Table) were considerably upstaged by the lofty courtesy of Irving's King Arthur, so erect in his suit of sombre black and gold armour. Edy appeared 'firm as a rock in The Spirit of the Lake', Ellen told Ted, but 'I am frightfully nervous about my part as Guinevere'. Spelt out in sorrowful iambics, the drama circled slowly around Guinevere's ill-directed love for Lancelot and the distress this caused her noble husband. Irving described her as 'wonderful' in the role of his queen and the American critic William Winter wrote that she displayed a 'profound knowledge of human love'. But Ellen's notes on her acting copy of *King Arthur* make clear that she was not happy with the play or her part in it. 'Hidebound', 'Not good', 'Useless', 'Dreadful' were some of the words she scribbled in the margins.

Shaw's gorge rose at seeing Ellen grovelling on the floor, her head within an inch of Irving's kingly toes, and he 'plainly conveying to the numerous bystanders that this was the proper position for a female who had forgotten herself so far as to prefer another man to him'. Shaw himself wanted to be that preferred other man, and to carry Ellen off from such infamous scenes. He regarded them both as being the victims of Irving's dictatorship at the Lyceum and dreamed of transporting her to a more invigorating theatre of ideas. Otherwise what sort of life was there for 'a born actress of real women's parts condemned to figure as a mere artist's model in costume plays which are foolish flatteries written by gentlemen for gentlemen? . . . What a theatre for a woman of genius to be attached to! . . . and all the time a stream of splendid women's parts pouring from the Ibsen volcano and minor craters, and being snapped up by the rising generation.'

This was a very Shavian interpretation of the fate of Ibsen's work and of his own – only one or two pioneering societies which could evade the censor's grasp were cautiously 'snapping up' Shaw's 'unpleasant' plays on prostitution, feminism and the financial exploitation of slum property for a few hole-and-corner performances. Nevertheless, it was true that Irving, while apparently in continual search for plays by contemporary dramatists, passed by Ibsen, Oscar Wilde, J.M. Barrie, Pinero, Sydney Grundy, Henry

Arthur Jones, Conan Doyle's Sherlock Holmes, his own theatre manager Bram Stoker and of course Bernard Shaw himself. None of them wrote the large-scale melodramas in which the Lyceum specialised. But all these writers were waiting in the wings. 'The old order changeth, yielding place to new . . .' says Tennyson's 'Arthur'. Shaw endorses this in his review of the play which, he wrote, had 'miscalculated the spirit of the age'.

The places of entertainment in London had greatly multiplied and diversified during the last twenty years, and Irving's 'market share', as Professor John Pick has observed, was declining in the 1890s, partly because his choice of plays was out of date, but also because his managerial style did not thrive in the competitive new business climate. Audiences were falling off in all the capital's theatres by the end of the 1890s when the Boer War began. 'I hear the theatres in London are doing terribly because of the war', Ellen wrote to Ted from America in 1900. But their provincial tours were still successful – 'the people run after us in the streets', Ellen wrote from Bradford in March 1900. '. . . we seem to grow in their affections.' But to avoid making losses in London, Irving was obliged to raise his advertising costs and – something he would regret – reduce his insurance premiums. There was a further problem: the range of parts that he and Ellen could play together was diminishing. 'It's all too late for Rosalind', Ellen wrote to Ted after she turned fifty in the late 1890s, '– so little pluck & "attack" left in me – a wearied machine is E.T.'

But Ellen had come to occupy a special place in Shaw's imagination. She 'invariably fascinates me so much that I have not the smallest confidence in my own judgement respecting her', he told his *Saturday Review* readers. He did not want to meet her for fear of breaking this spell, and she was touched by his idealism, content to remain a creature of fantasy which need never grow old. 'Ellen Terry is the most beautiful name in the world', he wrote to her: 'it rings like a chime through the last quarter of the 19th century.' In their private correspondence she became a superlative: 'my Ellenest Ellen'.

The last quarter of the nineteenth century, he believed, was a time for revolutionary new plays. Realism was surely more than a matter of real doorknobs, cups and saucers. It must embrace character, involve destiny, open its doors to comedies that sported with human folly, and to dramas that confronted real social problems – contemporary subjects such as slums and prostitution, finance and feminism. Ellen was only nine years older than

Shaw, yet he saw her in his mind's eye, from his heart's need, both as a contemporary and as a mother-figure, ageless and inspirational, who could carry his plays, almost like their offspring, into this new world of drama. So he laid siege to her in his published articles and private letters. While mocking Henry Irving whom he nicknamed 'His Immensity', he worshipped Ellen as someone who could create scenes and people onstage which 'become more real to us than our actual life'.

Like a depth-charge, Shaw had sent his one-act play *The Man of Destiny* – one of his deceptively 'pleasant plays' – to the Lyceum, and waited for it to explode under Irving's feet. Then he turned to *Cymbeline*, which was to open at the Lyceum in the autumn of 1896 (a production of *Coriolanus* having once more been announced and postponed). Shaw had damned Irving for giving Ellen useless parts. But now he had to change his tactics.

What could explain Irving's choice of such a florid fairy-tale with its dense and knotted plot? *Cymbeline* was an improbable romance that never touched firm ground but swung like a painted flag in the wind until, with a magic change of the barometer, the wicked suddenly become good and everyone embraces forgiveness. 'It is downright maddening to think of your slaving over Imogen', Shaw comforted Ellen. 'Of course you can't remember it: who could?'

Shaw cast himself as Ellen's secret director for this play, sending her a letter headed 'The Intelligent Actress's Guide to Cymbeline'. 'H. I.'s acting versions of Shakespear are past all bearing', he complained. For *Cymbeline*, Irving's cuts were designed (as he told William Winter) to remove the 'spirit and flesh problems'. And so, in their fashion, were Shaw's guidelines, as he attempted to take an intolerable load off Ellen's memory. Under the Shavian rodomontade, GBS worked with sensitivity, taking care to preserve the mysterious beauty of Imogen's lines. Throughout their correspondence he struck a tender note of exasperation against the bard for giving the actress he loved such trouble. And Ellen, with her wise heart, understood what he was doing. 'Now this is a real help! . . . Gods! How you seem to feel with one!' She began to read the scenes through his mind and felt instinctively that his intellect and her emotions were in accord. 'Bless you, and good night', she wrote after a day working at the text. He assured her that she would play Imogen beautifully: 'Be a mother to Shakespear . . . and make the most of his little scattered glimpses of divinity.' They developed a strange intimacy during their recreation of the play – an intimacy for which Shaw yearned and which Ellen missed in her partnership with Henry who 'has not the ghost of an idea of how anyone acts in his theatre, unless he's not in the play'. She had accepted her roles simply 'to please H. I.' for she was still a great draw at the Lyceum. 'They love me, you know! Not for what I am, but for what they imagine I am.' Shaw in some ways seemed to know who she really was, while Henry appeared to have forgotten. Working with him as her invisible director, learning Shakespeare's lines through their music, they were like two people on an imaginative journey together 'and we shall ride along over the celestial plains'.

When he came to write about *Cymbeline* in the *Saturday Review* Shaw hardly mentioned Ellen who was, he seems to have felt, beyond criticism, and it was left to that other critic of Lyceum productions, Henry James, to single her out for praise – not knowing that, in some degree, he was also praising Shaw. 'No part that she has played of late years is so much of the exact fit of her peculiar gifts', he wrote in *Harper's Weekly*. 'Her performance is naturally poetic, has delightful breadth and tenderness, delightful grace and youth. Youth above all – Miss Terry has never, without effort, been so young and so fresh . . . She is exactly the heroine demanded by an old-time story.' She was also the heroine he desired for a play of his own.

Shaw concentrated on the men: Shakespeare and Irving. He lambasted the poor foolish old swan – but could not help adding: 'I pity the man who cannot enjoy Shakespear. He has outlasted thousands of abler thinkers, and will outlast a thousand more.' In a true republic of art, he judged, Irving would 'have expatiated his acting versions on the scaffold'. Even so, Shaw did not try to hide his sheer enjoyment of Irving's new version of Iachimo – a goblin-like recreation of Iago as he explored the bedroom of the sleeping Imogen. 'I witnessed it with unqualified delight', he wrote; 'it was no vulgar bagful of "points", but a true impersonation, unbroken in its life current from end to end, varied on the surface with the finest comedy, and without a single lapse in the sustained beauty of its execution.'

It was in his letters to Ellen that Shaw most strongly assailed Irving. He had sent him his little Napoleon play, *The Man of Destiny*, in order to illustrate his corrupt business practices as a professional manager. 'H. I. quite loves it, and will do it finely', Ellen had promised him. Shaw however believed he knew better, and that Irving would offer him money for an option – buy him up, as it were – then lock the play away. Irving was not above purchasing the favourable opinions of his reviewers and manipulating his publicity. But how could Shaw, the unbribable critic of the *Saturday Review*, accept money except as a percentage of the profits on actual performances?

Ellen knew that his 'Strange Lady' in *The Man of Destiny* was a pen portrait of herself, but she did not quite realise that the play made fun of Irving as the outwitted Napoleon. After a year, Irving finally rejected *The Man of Destiny*, explaining that he had committed himself to producing Victorien Sardou's Napoleon play, *Madame Sans-Gêne*. This was at best a pyrrhic victory for Shaw, a paradoxical triumph that, in Ellen's eyes, was no victory at all. His cleverness was simply silly. But what did worry her were Shaw's assaults on Irving as an actor-manager who was wasting her talents at the Lyceum. If ever there were two artists apparently 'marked by Nature to make a clean break with an outworn past and create a new stage they were Ellen Terry and Henry Irving', he was to write. Shaw believed that Ellen was 'the woman who OUGHT to have played the Lady from the Sea – the woman with all the nameless charm, all the skill, all the force, in a word all the genius'. And in his fashion Gordon Craig agreed. 'Irving ought to have produced Ibsen', he wrote. '. . . *Ghosts*, *Peer Gynt* and *Borkman* would have suited him.' But when Ellen forced Irving to read Ibsen's plays, he merely shrugged and turned away. To involve oneself in such work would be to enter a madhouse. 'Has he ever loved you for the millionth fraction of a moment?' Shaw railed. It was the same devastating question Ellen had been asking herself.

Half a dozen years before, when she was convinced that Henry did love her, Ellen had written some 'Stray Memories' for the *New Review* in which she criticised Ibsen's heroines as 'silly ladies' who were attracting some young women because they were 'so extraordinarily easy to act'. Even now she felt that plays like *John Gabriel Borkman* made 'less hopeful some of us who long to dream a little . . . the theatre should gladden tired working people'. On the whole she felt grateful to have been 'called upon to act very noble and clear characters'. When she came to interpolate these 'Stray Memories' into her *Memoirs*, she omitted these passages.

Looking again at Irving she saw that he had become old-fashioned. He still took little notice of her during rehearsals, but Shaw more than made up for this lack of attention. He flattered her, of course, but for all his silliness wrote with a compelling conviction. 'You must advise me . . . You have become a habit with me', she told him. And again, after the opening of *Cymbeline*: 'You have been my sole delight for the last six weeks.' He made her smile by presenting himself as Childe Roland coming to the dark tower to rescue her from that 'ogre' Irving. When he told her that she would rank as 'the greatest actress in the world' if only she were not surrounded by 'people with heads like croquet balls, solid all through', she laughed. But she was also emboldened by his challenge. 'I want to act a modern part', she told him.

But what should she do? She had loved Henry as much as he allowed her to love him, and her love for him still lay dormant within her. She was also still flirting with Frank Cooper whose masculine presence she needed. And then there was this Irish pretender. In a sense he was like a boy and despite his cocksure attitude there was 'something deeply touching' about him. She took in his invigorating letters as if they were a tonic. 'I love you', he had written to her, and she knew that up to a point he did love her.

She was exhausted by the complexity of it all. 'Oh I'm ill. I'll just go back to bed', she wrote in the autumn of 1896. Having no character to play in the new Shakespeare production at the Lyceum, she set off the day after it opened for a holiday in France, hoping on her return to find some resolution to her problems.

33
Wishful Thinking

What about 'a Next Generation Theatre'? Shaw suggested in a letter to Ellen. Surely Edy and Ted, Laurence and Harry and his wife Dolly 'could make up a nice little repertory and go round the world with it'?

At the beginning of 1897, Henry Irving's and Ellen Terry's children were scattered around the theatres. Harry had joined George Alexander at the St James's Theatre in London. Irving earnestly warned Alexander against becoming an actor-manager, though in fact he was a shrewder manager than Irving himself and open to new work providing it centred on the world of aristocrats and peers of the realm. The St James's Theatre, it was said, catered for the dramatic taste of the upper classes 'much as the Savoy Hotel catered for their gastronomic taste'. Alexander successfully staged Pinero's 'problem play' *The Second Mrs Tanqueray* and Anthony Hope's Ruritanian adventure *The Prisoner of Zenda*; produced *The Importance of Being Earnest* when Wilde was under arrest (tactfully omitting his name from the posters and programmes); and experimented with Henry James's eighteenth-century period piece *Guy Domville.* Irving was pleased to see his son being given increasingly good roles by someone who had 'learnt his business' at the Lyceum.

But his younger son Laurence appeared to him to be going off the rails as he began rehearsing Ibsen's *The Wild Duck* at the Globe Theatre that spring. 'He should do well', Harry wrote reassuringly, '. . . and if he makes the people laugh at what is usually dreary enough they should be very grateful.' Laurence did make people laugh and Shaw joined in the laughter. It was a 'remarkable performance', he wrote, '[which] fairly entitles him to patronize his father who has positively never played an Ibsen part'.

Though he had 'many more faults than Harry', Laurence was still Ellen's favourite 'Irving boy'. He had sent her his historical epic *Peter the Great* – 'a wonderful play', she called it in a letter to Shaw, '(and if his father doesn't act it I give him up as they say)'. But Irving did agree to act in it, and father and son went off for a summer holiday in Cromer to work on the play. There was a big part for Irving as the Emperor and, in the 'judicial murder' of Peter's son Alex, a dramatic echo of his troubled relationship with Laurence. Unfortunately Ellen's character was 'horrid' and 'vulgar' – a version perhaps of 'the Wench' she had once been in Florence's house. But as they refashioned some of the plot, giving it a more sentimental climax, so the relationship between father and son prospered until, after the opening night on 1 January 1898, Laurence was moved to pay Irving a unique tribute: 'My father is great. I am proud to be his son.'

This was a time of reconciliation between Irving and both his sons. He was to invite Harry's wife Dolly, after the birth of her son, to join the Lyceum and began to comprehend just how much he and Harry held in common – an interest in criminology, an indifference to Ibsen and a positive hatred of Bernard Shaw. But Laurence's sudden closeness to his father was more remarkable. While in Cromer that summer they had worked and travelled contentedly around the country together. One afternoon they visited a new acquaintance of Irving's, a widow who was staying with her sister, the novelist 'Frank Danby', at a hotel nearby. Her name was Mrs Elizabeth Aria.

Ellen did not see so much of Henry that summer. She felt more awkwardly placed between him and Shaw after returning from her holiday in France. The warring between these two men had taken an ugly turn following the production of *Richard III*.

Irving had played Richard, Duke of Gloucester, twenty years before and Shaw remembered his performance with peculiar affection – a wonderfully impish character, it struck him, almost a buffoon from the pages of Dickens. But at the end of 1896, under the heading 'RICHARD HIMSELF AGAIN', he suggested that Irving had not been quite himself on the opening night. Ellen too, who watched this performance from a box before going abroad, noticed that something was wrong. 'I wish you would not write about Richard III until you have seen it again', she appealed to Shaw. The explanation she gave him for Irving's curious behaviour was that he always felt '"out of temper" when I don't act with him because I save him trouble, knowing exactly what he wants me to do to help him, and doing it, generally'. But Shaw attributed Irving's helplessness to another cause. His review nowhere uses the word drunkenness, but it seems to lie between the lines of several euphemistic passages.

He was not, it seemed to me, answering the helm satisfactorily; and he was occasionally a little out of temper with his own nervous condition. He made some odd slips in the text . . . In the tent and battle scenes his exhaustion was too genuine to be quite acceptable as part of the play .

Shaw maintained that he was innocent of the scandalous construction Irving put on these words. But the rumour spread. For it was true that Irving drank intermittently throughout his career, sometimes heavily. 'What a beast H.I. is to behave in that beastly drunken manner', Harry had written indignantly to his mother. But had he been drunk? 'Not being a man of insinuations, hints and stabs in the back', Shaw declared that, had he believed this, he would 'have said so unequivocally, or said nothing'. This was certainly true. So what could be the explanation? Ellen often represented herself as a mother to Shaw and sometimes he wished that he had been blessed with such a mother. His father had been an alcoholic and he may have unconsciously transferred his father's condition to Ellen's stage partner – it was she who had given him the phrase 'out of temper'.

The situation was made worse by what happened after the performance. At around midnight, Irving made off for a late supper at the Garrick Club with some friends, and then went on with one of them for a smoke and a chat in Albemarle Street. It was almost dawn by the time he arrived back at his rooms. 'On his way up the narrow staircase he slipped and struck his knee against a chest which stood upon the landing', his grandson wrote. 'He managed to reach his bedroom but at the cost of aggravating his injury.' Later that morning Walter Collinson, his dapper and meticulous valet, found him incapable of moving his leg. He had ruptured the ligatures of his knee and would be unable to go back onstage for a month.

The closure of the Lyceum appeared to confirm the suggestion of drunkenness. The Lyceum was 'losing £1000 a week and *that* must not go on', Ellen wrote. She began rehearsing *Olivia*.

Ellen's letters over 1897 and 1898 reveal her rapidly changing moods. 'I want nothing from you – nothing more I mean', she had written to Shaw –

though she still wished him to write 'some scrap for me'. She knew that he would probably marry a Fabian Irish woman, rather rich and clever (in any case quite different from herself). All the men she knew – Henry, Frank Cooper, and soon enough Shaw too – were married, and however much she pretended this made no difference to her, really it did make a difference. 'I think I won't be with you quite so much', she told Shaw. She admitted to feeling lonely and 'I'm not intrepid now'.

She decided to hold on to Shaw without disturbing Henry by redirecting his energy towards her children. 'I was going to say', she had written to Shaw, 'that if E[dward] G[ordon] C[raig] were given a free hand with *Peer Gynt* everyone else would believe in him, as well as his mother.' Shaw was curious: 'Is Ted a comedian?' he enquired. Ellen was unspecific beyond saying that he 'can act, or *will* act'. But here she was wrong. On rejoining the Lyceum in London, Ted had been pleased to find that he had been given two new roles: Arviragus in *Cymbeline* and Edward IV in *Richard III*. Staying with Ellen at Barkston Gardens to prepare for these parts, he had sent his wife and children to her parents' house at St Albans where, on 22 November 1896, their third child, Philip, was born.

Ted wanted to prove to Irving that he really could act. He worked particularly hard at Edward IV (whose death, after a brief early appearance, is reported in Act II, scene iii), obtaining a photograph of another Edward, his father Edward William Godwin, and making himself up to look like him. But after Irving's accident, *Richard III* was immediately withdrawn, and Ted was left with nothing to do. He wandered the country taking parts with touring companies – including Ben Greet's company with whom he played some of Harry Irving's roles. These were perilous times as he went about transforming himself from an actor into an artist. He still had the appearance of a romantic figure. 'Playing piano – leaping up – throwing back hair – flowing cloak . . . The Young Bacchus – His amours, almost mythological – pure type of artist – *Genius*', Max Beerbohm noted. But within himself he felt contaminated by failure: 'All seems agoing wrong', he confessed to Edy, '– work – affection – position – can't write a note of music – can do nothing.'

Part of this dejection stemmed from Irving's willingness to let him go. He did not know that Irving had decided to give preference to his own children over Ellen's – Laurence was to join the Lyceum shortly after Ted left. In his review of *Richard III*, Shaw had suggested that Craig was seriously miscast as Edward IV and 'wasted his delicacy' on a character which would have better suited the 'burly' Frank Cooper. If this were true he may have doubted the legitimacy of his acting career. 'Suspect nothing left but to retire from this splendid stage', he wrote in his chronology. '. . . Puzzled what to do – what direction to take'.

Shaw had ended his review on a teasing note, claiming that Edy, in the page's part, was 'the only member of the company before whom the manager [Irving] visibly quails'. Irving could not have known that the drama critic at the *Saturday Review* got many of his jokes from Ellen's letters. She had told him that Edy was really the best of all, though she 'never tried to compete for anyone' and would 'probably go to the wall unappreciated'. But she was not unappreciated by her mother who, in a strange phrase she used, adored her 'to the scaffold'. In some ways Edy was as impersonal as Shaw, but no show-off. 'Edy *looks* a tragedy and is about the most amusing, funniest, creature living,' Ellen wrote. '. . . She loathes emotional people, yet adores me. I hardly dare kiss her . . .' At the Lyceum she pretended to boss her mother who nevertheless believed she was still her baby – and 'such a baby'. She needed more work to complete her apprenticeship. 'Get Edy a chance some day with you', Ellen appealed to Shaw. 'That's the way to make me adore you in any blessed way you will . . .'

So he got her a chance with a small avant-garde society, the Independent Theatre, which was touring Britain during that summer of 1897. She played Mrs Linde in *A Doll's House* and in Shaw's mystery play *Candida* she took the role of Prossy, a secretary secretly in love with her clergyman-employer and described in the stage directions as 'a brisk little woman of about thirty', pert, not very civil, quick of speech, yet sensitive and affectionate. It suited her well, though she would need to 'work & use her head a good deal; for she is like a boy in her youth & virginity and cannot fall back on emotional effects'.

Irving had come to the conclusion that Ellen was actually in love with this mountebank Irishman. The news softened Shaw himself for a moment ('Did H.I. really say that you are in love with me? For that may all his sins be forgiven him!'). But this did not stop the battering ram that was his theatre criticism from thundering against the doors of the Lyceum.

And did she love him? Some days it almost seemed as if she must, though they were largely acting love. 'I've never been admired or loved (properly) but one-and-a-half times in my life', she had told him. Shaw did not occupy a place in her emotional life like that of Godwin or Irving. Yet he was unique. 'I have no lovers, only loves, and I have as many of those as I want, and you are the only one I don't benefit!' she wrote to him in May 1897. 'You do things for me. I do things for them.'

But when Shaw tried to do something for her by showing how 'unworthy of my Ellen' Irving was, she warned him: 'Don't quarrel with H. That would add to my unhappiness.' Shaw however could not help himself. 'I am like the madman in Peer Gynt who thought himself a pen and wanted someone to write with him.' So she rallied to Henry's defence ('Henry is not a *losing cause*. Folk crowd round his banner'). It was no surprise to her, seeing how silly Shaw had been, that in the late 1890s Henry gave him back *The Man of Destiny*. Again she warned him: 'if you worry (or try to worry) Henry, I must end our long and close friendship. He is ill, and what would I not do to better him?'

It was when he was well that Henry dismayed her. 'Ah, he makes me tired and sad and hopeless sometimes, and I do expect always the best of him.' She had been too gentle. 'I've spoiled him! I was born meek', she admitted. '. . . It makes me cry to know it.' Like a doctor writing a prescription, Shaw would soon set to work drafting a play for her in which her tenderness and humour grew overpowering. But this was not so at the Lyceum.

It should have been a relief to go onstage and 'be someone else for a few hours'. But Ellen's work was made arduous by the trouble she was having with her eyes. Was she slowly going blind? This was the terrifying thought which assailed her when she was tired. She hated the sentimental roles Henry was giving her. Victorien Sardou's and Emile Moreau's *Madame Sans-Gêne*, adapted by Comyns Carr, which the Lyceum staged in April 1897 to celebrate Queen Victoria's Diamond Jubilee, was a clever production. All the furniture was made higher, the door handles raised and the lower panels exaggerated so as to dwarf Irving's figure which was too tall for Napoleon. He surrounded himself too with the tallest actors in the company and, as Shaw himself acknowledged, 'made a part out of nothing – a Gladstonian sort of performance, and very clever'. But he had cut the play, leaving little of value for Ellen. 'Never have I had such a tiresome task', she complained. Those who had seen Réjane as Catharine in the original French production – one of her great performances – did not feel that Ellen compared with her.

There was nothing much for her either in *Peter the Great.* Was it merely an accident that Ellen's roles were now so uninteresting? Or did they signify Henry's declining interest in her? Her impulsiveness and spontaneity, which had been so entrancing when she was younger, had began to pall on him. She changed her mind from hour to hour, changed and changed again and still went on openly flirting with Frank Cooper, secretly corresponding with Bernard Shaw (or 'Pshaw' as Irving now called him) and generally behaving with an embarrassing lack of maturity. Now that he was entering his sixties and on good terms at last with his sons – also his enchanting daughter-in-law – Irving was finding emotional comfort within his family. Ellen was a woman who, Harry explained, 'speaks in moods and impressions', and who 'means what she says' at the time – but then, being overcome by a new sensation, does something quite contradictory. It was all instinct and no thought – and frankly it was growing tiresome.

She was aware of Henry's impatience with her and felt impatient with him for handing her yet another 'dreadful' part in the early summer of 1898. *The Medicine Man* was an unstable concoction commissioned from an editorial writer at the *Daily Telegraph*, H.D. Trail, and the music critic and novelist Robert Hichens, who had recently gained notoriety with *The Green Carnation*, his satire on Wilde's aesthetics ('the doubting disciple', Wilde called him, 'who has written the false gospel'). What Irving ordered from them was 'a Monte Cristo story in modern dress', and what audiences saw was a pale imitation of *Trilby* with Irving decked out as a wealthy West End doctor using hypnosis to practise social reform in London's East End. 'It "lunatics" me to watch Henry at these rehearsals', Ellen wrote to Shaw. 'Hours and hours of loving care over this twaddle! He just *adores* his absurd part.' The play itself was 'quite unworthy of us'.

In February 1898, the warehouse which held the great stock of their scenery and properties, all of it drastically under-insured, was destroyed by fire – some 260 sets for forty-four plays. 'He has had a long & bad round of ill luck, which, if it lasts much longer, will be grievous', Harry reported to his mother. It would take much time and cost over £30,000, Stoker calculated, to replace everything they needed. And until they had recovered from this catastrophe, Ellen knew she could not leave. As for Henry, he behaved wonderfully well over the fire. But then a rumour reached Ellen that he was relying on another woman for support – and a new tide of feelings rushed over her. She needed to find out more. 'But who is Mrs A[ria]?' she asked Shaw.

34
Choices

The aspirations of the Victorians were seen at their most resplendent in Moray Lodge where Ellen's sister Kate brought up her four daughters. She had given up the stage on the instructions of her mother-in-law and appeared to have become 'a sincere churchwoman'. Each morning she would assemble her servants – the Swiss butler, the Scottish gardener, the cook, and the ranks of maids, nannies and governesses – in the dining-room for prayers and inspection of uniforms. On Sundays she led her well-dressed and happy-looking flock of children to the service at St Mary Abbot's in Kensington. Sometimes she would read selected passages from the Bible to them (though they preferred *The Water Babies*, *Black Beauty* and Lewis Carroll's Alice books) and later on she introduced them to the novels of Walter Scott, Wilkie Collins and Bulwer Lytton. They were taught French and German as well as History, Geography and Literature, and attended the first Froebel kindergarten school in London.

'We spoke only when spoken to,' Kate's eldest daughter remembered, 'were not allowed to put our elbows on the table, nor our feet on the bars of our high chairs; their dangling obliged us to sit upright.' Though disobedience had naturally to be punished, the atmosphere at Moray Lodge was relaxed and prosperous. The children had plenty of animals and birds to play with in their spacious garden – ponies, dogs, a cat, canaries – and were taken for regular walks in Holland Park and to the Round Pond in Kensington Gardens (where a bell was rung to warn you that the gates were closing and you had to run and run so as not to be locked in). They were also taught to ride in Richmond Park and eventually joined the ceremony of fashionable people moving between Hyde Park Corner and the Albert Memorial in their barouches and landaus, their broughams, victorias, phaetons and coaches. They could recognise many famous people in this parade: Marie Corelli and Lillie Langtry and the Duchess of Westminster – once they almost collided with Queen Victoria herself! In summer they were taken to the Chelsea Flower Show, the Eton and Harrow cricket match at Lord's, the Henley Regatta; to the races at Sandown, polo at Hurlingham, the Royal Academy exhibitions at Burlington House, and to see the lions and bears in the Zoological Gardens ('the keeper of the pelicans was a crony of ours').

On Sundays their mother gave wonderful garden parties. The men would play fierce croquet matches and languid games of lawn tennis, while from another part of the garden a band struck up songs from Gilbert and Sullivan and the women in their vast hats and trailing skirts moved under their parasols to the huge ash tree where refreshments were being served. In winter the guests gathered in the billiard room before the fire and in all seasons there were dances to dream over: polkas and minuets and waltzes and the lancers.

The theatre was an essential part of this social calendar. Kate began taking her family to the Lyceum in the early 1880s and was given a 'stage box' at one corner on a level with the stage itself. All the elements of Victorian society were to be seen in this world within a world, and all were properly segregated. 'Boxes were for royalty and the favoured few, the stalls for wealth and culture, the dress circle for those not quite so well-to-do and for family parties; the pit was for the struggling intelligentsia, the upper circle and gallery for the less fortune-favoured. In boxes, stalls and dress circle evening dress was obligatory . . . there were no orderly queues then for pit and gallery, and these seats could not be booked beforehand.'

Only one of Kate's children became an actress, her youngest daughter Mabel, though some of the grandchildren took up the profession and Kate's eldest child was to be the mother of John Gielgud. But all the children were drawn into the dramatic stories as they unfolded and the characters developed, scene by scene. They were conscious, on account of their mother's distinction (and of course their aunt Ellen's), of being privileged spectators at the Lyceum. But it was Irving who commanded their attention. 'He bore himself as with a divine right to kingship', one of them wrote, 'but he bowed nightly to his audience as its "humble and grateful servant".'

They saw him first as Romeo battering wildly at the gate of the tomb, then bowing as he came down the dark steps to die at Juliet's feet; then as Hamlet, a sinister figure in black; and then again as the quick-witted courtier and lover in spite of himself in *Much Ado*; and after that they saw him as the slippered and night-capped Malvolio shocked by the indecorous behaviour around him; and of course Shylock, so cunning and so craven, suddenly swept into a frenzy of despair; and yet again with a huge sword over his shoulder, a hunted look on his tired face, Irving's Macbeth, leaning against the walls of the torch-lit courtyard; then more recently as Cardinal Wolsey (looking rather like the famous Cardinal Manning) in *Henry VIII*, remote, supreme and never more dignified than in his downfall. It was as if, enhanced by the mysterious gaslight against its coloured shades, many of the pictures they knew at the National Gallery and had seen in the art books which their father gave them, came to life in the theatre – and were indeed larger than life. How was it that Irving could transform himself from the grotesque and brutal into someone exquisitely tender, infinitely touching? They were enthralled.

By the mid-1880s Kate's family were sometimes invited to special midnight dinners in the Beefsteak Room and, a few times, to splendid candlelit banquets onstage. By then the children's hero Irving (and of course their aunt Ellen too) were invited to some of the formal dinners at Moray Lodge. From the children's point of view they were among the most glorious of their guests – as distinguished as Lewis Carroll who had been a regular visitor at a time when he felt unable to call on Ellen.

But in the forty years between the death of Prince Albert and the end of Queen Victoria's reign in 1901, the spirit of the age was changing. Though the reading public still bought the clerical-domestic stories of Anthony Trollope and tales of romance by Stanley Weyman, a new note of menace was entering imaginative fiction through R.L. Stevenson's macabre study *The Strange Case of Dr Jekyll and Mr Hyde*, H.G. Wells's unsettling science fiction, *The Island of Dr Moreau* and *The War of the Worlds*, and also the explorations of London's criminal underworld by Conan Doyle's drug-inspired detective Sherlock Holmes, accompanied by the innocent Dr Watson. In such an atmosphere of horror and fantasy, Bram Stoker's Gothic novel *Dracula* (published in 1897) found a natural place, and a dramatic version of it was given a copyright performance (in which Edy took part) at the Lyceum.

Count Dracula's crimes, which are committed in the darkness of late Victorian Britain, took their inspiration from the notorious Whitechapel murders of Jack the Ripper in August and September 1888. The Count's five 'brides' and the Ripper's five victims, all women, are sacrificed in a similar ritualistic fashion. Stoker had begun his Gothic fantasy early in 1890 and over the next six years took enormous trouble revising this famous book, and then adapting it for the stage. But the Chief refused even to take part in the copyright reading on 18 May 1897, and when Stoker asked him what he thought of the work, he pronounced it 'dreadful'. It has been suggested that this intense dislike arose from the fact that Irving was a freemason burdened with the awful responsibility of concealing the Masonic identity of the Ripper. But it seems more likely that he simply refused to accept Stoker as a writer, insisting that he remain the Lyceum's business manager. The irony is that, had he foreseen the extraordinary success of Stoker's horror story, he might have revived the ebbing fortunes of the Lyceum at the turn of the century.

He may have suspected that Dracula, a monster who came alive only by night, was modelled on himself (Stoker's later description of Irving's red eyes glowing in his marble face belongs to this fearful world of fantasy). Certainly there were physical similarities – the strong aquiline face, hollow cheeks and thin lips, the extraordinary pallor and vitality. And then what did this blood-drinking vampire suggest concerning his relations with women: his mother, his wife, Ellen Terry whom Stoker adored, and the greatest lady of them all, the Lyceum Theatre itself? In the opinion of Ellen Terry's biographer Nina Auerbach, it was Irving's Mephistopheles which 'gave Dracula his contours', though other scholars have likened his features to the famished, wolflike appearance of Irving's Macbeth. Whatever the actual inspiration, Stoker was desperately disappointed by the Chief's rejection of *Dracula*. His relationship with Irving was highly emotional, though not what is popularly understood by the word homoerotic. He had 'burst into something very like a violent fit of hysterics' after hearing Irving recite *Eugene Aram* in Dublin and after meeting him felt that 'soul had looked into soul'. The Chief became his god and in a peculiar way he identified with him, held him up as a model. He was not jealous of Irving's love of Ellen: he shared it, almost bettered it. Stoker was heterosexual. He was married, had a child and in later life went to prostitutes for sex – indeed, he may have resented his vulnerability to women (he was later rumoured to have died from tertiary syphilis). For two decades he had worshipped Irving: but now a coolness developed between the two men, with Irving turning for advice to Austin Brereton (who replaced Louis Austin as his confidential secretary), leaving Stoker 'not able to see so much of him as I had been in the habit of doing throughout the previous twenty years'.

Irving's misjudgement of *Dracula* showed decisively that he was not in tune with the times. It was as if people had grown surfeited by the decades of peace and prosperity presided over by the Queen in her black mourning clothes, and hungered for what they most feared: for danger, bloodshed, conflict and the unknown – even for war which was soon to erupt in South Africa.

'The happy years slipped by with strangely little change', Kate Terry's eldest daughter wrote. But then, in the late 1890s, change fell upon them as it fell upon Irving. They were obliged to let Moray Lodge one summer season and suddenly there were no more parties. 'I should say the relief of the big house off their shoulders would be grand', Ellen wrote to her son. 'Yet I suppose to poor old Kate it will be a wrench to leave the beautiful garden – & the place where all her children have been born.' Their father, so tall and upright, with such sweet bright eyes and a heavy beard that could never conceal his smile, all at once appeared tired and unsmiling. Arthur Lewis was like 'a good old Donkey' as Ellen called him. Each day he went to his office in Conduit Street, walking into town instead of being driven, and would come back looking ill and stern. Ellen instructed Stephen Coleridge to send him £5,000 – an immense sum (equivalent to £300,000 early in the twenty-first century) – and especially altruistic considering Kate's banishment of Ellen while she had been living with Godwin. But after her marriage Kate's asperity had faded and she became 'gentler & sweeter', Ellen confided to Bernard Shaw, until by the 1890s she was 'the sweetest kindest old thing living'. The downward drift in the family fortunes continued and by January 1899 Moray Lodge was sold. Kate, showing much fortitude, busied herself preparing a more modest residence in the West Cromwell Road where, two years later, she would nurse her husband through his last illness. 'Poor Kate', Ellen wrote to her son. 'She will be so lonely.'

Kate, then in her mid-fifties, was unknown to the younger generation of theatre-goers. But the actor-manager John Hare remembered her well and offered her a large salary to come back and appear with him and her daughter Mabel at the Globe Theatre. It was the money rather than the play – an improbable drama by Stuart Ogilvie called *The Master* – that persuaded her. As she made her first entrance a tumult of cheering broke out and filled the theatre, but at the final curtain there was only muted applause. 'Poor dear old Kate, I'll hold a wager she has stopped exactly where she left off 30 years ago!' Ellen ungenerously wrote to Shaw – and Shaw would use this, as he used so many of her letters, in his review of Kate's performance, though turning it to her advantage. 'She [Kate] apparently began, in point of skill and practice, just where she left off years ago, without a trace of rust', he wrote in the *Saturday Review*. But nothing could save the play itself which came off after a short run, and Kate did not act again. 'Yes, my dear old Kate would playact again if only they'd offer her an engagement', Ellen wrote. 'She is rather high priced . . . [and] says nobody wants her.'

Ellen too was beginning to feel that nobody wanted her. Her partnership with Irving 'looks as [if] it were at an end', Harry reported to his mother. The eighteenth season at the Lyceum, which finished in the summer of 1897, had shown a loss of £10,000, though some of this was made up on a tour of the provinces. They kept going with revivals of those plays whose sets were not destroyed in the warehouse fire, but on reaching Glasgow Irving fell seriously ill with pneumonia and pleurisy. Stoker, who visited him at his hotel, found him 'looking very old and weak – his hollow cheeks and cadaverous jowl bearded with white bristles; his nose, like that of the dying Falstaff, "as sharp as a pen"'. To Stoker's consternation, the Chief's daughter-in-law Dolly was called on to attend him – a task that should surely have been entrusted to Ellen. Everything was topsy-turvy. But Harry insisted that Dolly must nurse his father. 'Stick to your guns . . . What more natural than that you should look after him', he wrote to her. If Ellen was known to be at Irving's bedside then the public might come to believe they were closer than Harry wished.

'My present intention', Irving wrote to Pinero in December 1898, 'is to produce no more new work for some time – but to travel – to realise and not to speculate . . .' But while he was convalescing in Bournemouth early the following year, Joe Comyns Carr arrived with a speculative business proposal. His plan was to set up a syndicate with his two brothers, a solicitor and a financier. They would float a limited liability company and take over the last eight years of Irving's lease on the Lyceum. In exchange for his services (at least one hundred performances a year and four months of touring in Britain or America – as well as a guarantee of generous contributions towards the production costs) he would be paid £26,000, be given some shares in the company and receive a salary based on the net profits.

When they heard of this proposal, Loveday was obviously dismayed, Stoker really quite angry. But though he suspected all sorts of 'hocus-pocus', Irving was in no position to refuse. He had auctioned many of his theatre books and prints – yet was still obliged to borrow money from friends.

Visiting him in Bournemouth Ellen found him at his 'downest'. '*I had to come*,' she told her son. 'It must be just awful for him to be obliged to sit still, unable yet to get to work, or even go out in the evening.' The discharge from his lung continued to distress him and he would be left with a chronic inflammation of his throat. Now that 'poor old King H' was abdicating (he would, in his early sixties, be granted the title 'Dramatic Adviser' in the new company), he seemed to raise a shield of indifference to everything. But to Ellen he almost exulted in his tragedy. 'He wanted to tell me that not only was he broken in health but he was what is called "ruined".' For women ruin meant illicit sex and illegitimate children; for men it spelt bankruptcy.

What Irving was attempting to do at this meeting in Bournemouth was to give Ellen her natural exit from the Lyceum. There was to be only one new production during 1899, a political melodrama called *Robespierre* commissioned by Irving from Sarah Bernhardt's and Réjane's favourite dramatist Victorien Sardou and translated by his son Laurence. It was, Ellen decided, 'a bad play, but a wonderfully showy one . . . A one-man piece. Henry, and over 250 supers.' Only a very subsidiary role was available in it for her if she stayed on. 'Good God – my part!!!!! (but that is a detail)', she exclaimed to Laurence when she read it. It seemed that she herself was little more than a detail at the Lyceum now – she had been advised by Stephen Coleridge not to buy shares in the new company. Laurence had come to realise how she had helped his father 'over the Rubicon – a Rubicon over which, I might add, she did much to help me when I was severely in need of encouragement', he reminded his mother. But who was to help Ellen?

Irving liked to believe that Sardou was France's greatest scholar of the French Revolution – though his real authority lay in knowing exactly where Irving's strengths lay in performance. In fact he never came to England (he suffered from seasickness) and *Robespierre* was not performed in France. But the play was to be the Lyceum's last great success – it was said that anyone who had not personally witnessed the Revolution could see as much of it as was good for him in this play. The distinction of the piece lay in the vast choreographic movement of the crowds – the tumult of the convention scene, the rush of deputies, the struggle of the orator to be heard against what appeared to be the wild spontaneity of the actors – all drilled in their iconic gestures and controlled with the mastery of a ballet corps.

In 1899 Irving moved from his gloomy rooms in Grafton Street to a sunlit apartment at 17 Stratton Street near his old friend and patron, Angela Burdett-Coutts. Mrs Aria arranged the move. 'Crimson was to be the dominant note of his new dwelling', she decided, and she spread this cheerful colour over the walls of the entrance hall and down the corridor and on to the carpets. It was nicely interrupted by a stained-glass window 'with a sill bearing fine bronzes' – rather English in style. But then the drawing-room, with its pink brocade, was very definitely French; and the blue-and-gold embroideries of the large dining-room perhaps more Chinese. In one way and another, Mrs Aria concluded, it had a 'lordly air'. She positioned his bookcases and hung his paintings by Whistler and Bastien-Lepage and a dramatic water-colour by George Clint of Kean playing Hamlet. It looked delightful.

But who *was* Mrs Aria? According to Shaw she was a 'good sort' and in the opinion of Gordon Craig she turned out to be a 'gifted authoress' – though this is not borne out by her books. She was to call her autobiography *My Sentimental Self*, but her sentimentality was mixed with shrewdness and calculation. She had been born in 1860 or 1862 or 1864 – possibly later but probably earlier, for the date of her birth advanced as the seasons turned and the years progressed, keeping pace with her so that she seldom grew much older. She was the ninth and last child of Hyman Davis, a London photographer, and his wife Isabella. 'We were reared strictly in the Jewish faith', she wrote. At the age of about eighteen or perhaps twenty or even twenty-two, at the West London Synagogue of British Jews in Marylebone, she married a gambling man, David Borrito Aria, mainly to escape the desolation of being the only girl in the family still without a husband. 'I have always had the desire to spend money', she acknowledged. After five years of marriage, though gaining a daughter, she had spent all David Aria's winnings. Despite his dark southern eyes, slender figure, and gentle voice, there was 'little of real love between us'. Besides she suspected he was unfaithful to her. So they parted and he went away to South Africa to remake his fortune as a 'merchant' – she saw him off at the docks to make sure he caught the boat. For six years they wrote spasmodically to each other until one of her letters was returned, marked 'gone away'. Where had he gone? And would he ever come back? 'Don't make his return impossible', a friend advised her. 'You are young. You are attractive. You are in the thick of it.' She was careful to retain her respectability, doing exemplary work for charity, taking up refined journalism by writing fashion articles for *The Gentlewoman* and editing *The World of Dress* which, like her husband, went bankrupt. She also wrote two or three books, including *Women and the Motor-Car*, though it is unlikely that she made much money from them. How she kept 'in the thick of it', leading an expensive social life, was a mystery (when she died in 1931 her estate was valued as 'Nil'). But she was good at keeping secrets. Of her curious marriage she told people that nothing in her husband's life 'became him so well as his leaving of me for South Africa five years after I had driven with him from the Synagogue to hear his first rapture expressed in "I wonder what has won the Lincoln handicap?" '.

Mrs Aria had met Irving one evening at dinner. 'His personality overwhelmed me against his will', she recalled. '. . . The awe of him was very strong upon me.' He was so masculine, and she, in her early thirties (perhaps younger, maybe older), so filled with an 'absorbing love of the theatre' that her sister Julia immediately advised her to 'grapple him to your soul with hooks of steel'. But Eliza Aria's armoury was made of softer stuff: a fine noose of flattery, threads of feminine modesty, some measure of amiable humour and, under all these pliant materials, a firm resilient core. Speaking as a Jewess, she had thanked Irving for his dignified interpretation of Shylock. A little later she had been 'amazed at my audacity' in inviting him to tea when he and his son Laurence were staying at Cromer. Her sister Julia, who was gaining fame as the novelist 'Frank Danby' (author of *A Babe in Bohemia*, *Pigs in Clover* and *A Coquette in Crape*), urged her on, and Eliza pretended that her famous sister was the bait. She could see that Laurence was suspicious of her motives, though Harry when she met him was much friendlier. Soon she and Irving were going off on Sundays for rides through Richmond Park and Epping Forest. When, in December 1897, William Terriss was assassinated by a madman at the stage door of the Adelphi Theatre and Irving escorted his mistress, the actress Jessie Millward, to the funeral, Mrs Aria wrote: 'There was not a member of the theatrical world in the crowd which followed the murdered man to his last resting-place who did not fall in worshipful admiration of Irving when they noted the tenderness which went to his shepherding.' This passage, which recognises the social position a mistress may obtain if treated generously, and gives Irving the most prominent place in his fellow actor's funeral, is steeped in the 'worshipful admiration' she was to show him. But she was not Irving's mistress. Not quite. In later years, after Irving's death, she divorced her husband, but not being quite sure whether he was still alive (he died in 1913) she took a picture of him to court instead of the man himself. She was to model her later life on the Signora Vesey-Neroni, that fascinating invalid in Trollope's *Barchester Towers* who attracted the admiration of so many clergymen. Seldom leaving her chaise-longue and attended by a court of adoring men of letters, Mrs Aria (as she was still known) became celebrated in the literary world as 'the Récamier of Regent Street'. She flattered men but was not well liked by women, and united Ellen and Florence in opposition to her.

Though Ellen could not leave Irving while he was so much 'in the dumps', she refused to shed tears. 'As long as you and I have health', she said to him in Bournemouth, 'we have the means of wealth. We can pack a bag, each of us and trot round the Provinces. Yes, and go to America, Australia, India, Japan.'

Such loyalty was embarrassing. Irving was already making arrangements for a tour of Britain. 'What plays?' Ellen quickly asked. 'Where do I come in?'

'You can of course, do as you like,' Irving answered hesitantly.

But still she did not follow his directions and leave. Shaw tried to raise her spirits. 'Drive all worry from your brain, and be perfectly light of heart and happy', he counselled her. But when she pressed him to let her read his own most recent play, he was obliged to send her *Caesar and Cleopatra* – which she tactlessly put in front of Henry. 'He will never play anything of yours', she told Shaw. '. . . For he could have done *wonders* with that Play if he had done it.'

'I don't want you to do Cleopatra', Shaw replied. 'She is an animal – a bad lot. Yours is a beneficent personality.' Cleopatra had been tailor-made for Mrs Patrick Campbell. Soon afterwards he sent Ellen *Captain Brassbound's Conversion*, the beneficent play he had written for her. But she was not certain that she liked it.

Perhaps it was a malady of age, this feeling Ellen had of being deserted by everyone – most of all of course by Henry, but also by Shaw who had finally married his Fabian bluestocking; and then by her son Ted who was drifting away from the theatre and his family. She especially dreaded being deserted by Edy who had been invited to go to South Africa with a travelling company. 'If she is in any real difficulty she always sends for me, or comes to me, and we pick up her ends together', she wrote to Shaw. 'But when she is in Africa! Oh Lord, whom will she go to? And if she is ill too, she gets better quicker with me . . . However I know I am too anxious. I shall let her go. She is only sorry to leave me; else she delights in going.'

But Edy did not go to South Africa and by the early spring of 1899 she was back at the Lyceum where Irving had commissioned her to design the costumes for *Robespierre* ('crowds of dresses', Ellen wrote, '. . . and all excellent. She is a tremendous organiser, and a first-rate worker').

Ellen felt grateful to Henry for employing her daughter. At Bournemouth he had so bemused her with his cynical indifference that she could not be sure she had understood him. When he went on a tour of Britain without her, she retaliated by going on tour herself with Frank Cooper – rather as she had done in the old days with Charles Kelly. But now she had to make up her mind. Would she work for the horrid new syndicate and return to America in the autumn of 1899? Or would she grasp this opportunity and step into the new play-world of Bernard Shaw?

35
Confusions

Laurence Irving, it seemed, was an underperformed dramatist but an overemphatic actor with, according to Bernard Shaw, a narrow range of extraordinary abilities 'like a soldier who can do nothing but win the Victoria Cross'. He would make his entrance onstage as if he were 'a volcano smouldering with unutterable wrongs'. But when the moment arrived to burst forth with a tremendous flow of these wrongs the audience had acquired an 'indifference to lava'. His plays were considered violent and gloomy by the public and *Peter the Great* made another loss for the Lyceum.

Laurence sometimes found himself taking on his father's roles. He would also, to Bram Stoker's irritation, replace him at public functions. 'You have heard a great deal of my father', he announced at the end of one speech; 'but I assure you, you have not heard half enough about me.'

For years Laurence had been banging at the doors of the Lyceum demanding to be let in. But now that he was in, well and truly in, he found that 'the work I do is not very advancing or useful', and wrote to tell his brother Harry that 'I would prefer my independence'.

It was an unsettling time, especially since Laurence had lost his heart to one of a contingent of American players who, in the late 1890s, had come over to reinforce the Lyceum cast. Ethel Barrymore was a dark beauty with a bright wit who belonged to a famous theatrical family from Philadelphia, and who had been employed to play ingénues. Laurence was able to direct her during rehearsals and flirt with her in the intervals. She would play piano accompaniments to his sad Russian songs – after which it quickly became apparent to him that they were made for each other. So he proposed to her and she refused him. Since this was the wrong answer, he proposed again and went on proposing until, 'having been refused by Her Highness about half a dozen times', Ellen reported, they found themselves engaged to be married. In her *Memories*, Ethel records that Laurence rushed off to tell his mother, and this was followed by 'a terrifying visit I had to make to Lady Irving. I don't remember ever meeting anyone as frightening.' Fortunately the actor Gerald du Maurier also found himself engaged to Ethel Barrymore. Then, like a sorceress, she sailed away into the setting sun and the safety of her homeland.

By the summer of 1900 another new actress joined the Lyceum, a determined Welsh girl called Mabel Hackney. Laurence experienced no blinding infatuation this time, but a slow gathering of feelings brought them together. They were married before one of the Lyceum tours of America – and Ellen was delighted with her Irving boy. 'It is a *good match* I feel sure', she wrote to them both.

The pattern of Laurence's life, so his nephew observed, 'was wonderfully changed' by his quietly forceful wife who helped him 'gain mastery over his erratic and impulsive genius'. Irving himself appeared as pleased as Ellen, but Florence was not so pleased. She had gained a title and lost her two sons.

Harry and Laurence loved their mother and were made aware of the heavy obligation they owed her. But no longer was she the most significant woman in their lives and she did not take kindly to her daughters-in-law. More awful than anything else was this not-so-very-young widow, or divorcée, the Jewess whom they called Mrs Aria, who was bringing fresh scandal into their lives. A man could 'pay no greater compliment to a woman', Mrs Aria let it be known, 'than to ask her to be his mistress'. But that was a compliment, she quietly added, which Sir Henry had never paid her. Such was the disgusting tittle-tattle to which Florence felt subjected. She gave her house in Gilston Road to Laurence and his new wife, and retired from London to an apartment on the south coast where, an increasingly eccentric figure in a red wig, and with 'a penchant for the colour purple', her granddaughter remembered (purple ink, purple clothes and even purple ribbons on her underwear), she prepared to review at leisure a long life of grievances (she did not die until 1935).

She was pleased to receive a copy of Harry's book, *Studies of French Criminals*, which was much to her taste. But the public were more interested in his success when creating the title role (that of a radical butler) in J.M. Barrie's unsettling social comedy *The Admirable Crichton*. Florence learnt too that Laurence had, most unexpectedly, created the title role (that of a tragic-looking man of few words but much significance) in Bernard Shaw's puritan play, *Captain Brassbound's Conversion* – 'a brilliant part in a splendid play', he told her. At least, Florence was relieved to hear, the Terry woman was not acting with him. And then Dolly had made a sensible move and rejoined Beerbohm Tree's company at Her Majesty's Theatre playing Helena in *A Midsummer Night's Dream* – a production famous for its lively scampering rabbits.

Less satisfactory was the newspaper account she read of the wonderful gala performance and reception Irving gave on 3 July 1902 to celebrate the coronation of King Edward VII. Edward fell ill and the coronation had to be postponed, but Irving was not deterred – though it puzzled Florence how he got the money for such a sumptuous event. The theatre was filled with a rich cargo of visitors who had travelled to London from every quarter of the British Empire. There were resplendently dressed tribal chiefs, miraculously jewelled princes with their retinues, great men of science, the arts and the Church, splendid in their uniforms and medals, also 'grey and turbaned veterans from the Indian army', Ellen observed, 'broad-hatted Australians, and Negroes in buff and white shoulder belts'. 'Comrades all', Irving called them – and all were guarded by ace detectives dragged along the aisles by their dogs from Scotland Yard. Then, following performances of *Waterloo* and *The Bells*, a well-trained company of carpenters, cleaners, electricians and upholsterers swept in and, under Bram Stoker's supervision, rapidly transformed the entire theatre. They 'gutted the stalls and pit, hurling the seats into carts waiting at the exits', Irving's grandson wrote. They 'laid a field of crimson carpet' – Mrs Aria's favourite colour – 'while sappers bridged the orchestra with an imposing staircase, the florists planted a jungle of palms, exotic flowers and shrubs . . . Great chandeliers were hoisted aloft, and over the proscenium glowed a monstrous Union Jack surmounted by a crown in coloured lights . . . only forty minutes had elapsed when Irving took his stand, with a son to the right and left of him, to receive the thousand guests who filed through three entrances.'

Ellen was there that night. Joe Comyns Carr had told her that the syndicate which was being created to rescue the Lyceum (of which he was managing director) could not be completed unless she agreed to be part of it. 'I am a fool to do it', she confessed, 'but after all these years . . .' She had come to the conclusion that Carr was not 'at all nice. I have loved him, but my love shall turn to hate upon the spot!!!' she wrote to a friend. 'It should if it could, but it can't.'

So, in October 1899, she had set out with Irving on another tour of North America. They opened with *Robespierre* at the Knickerbocker Theater in New York and the audiences loved it. 'Public here support him more and more, and the tide is all in our favour, thank the Lord', Ellen wrote. 'He is pleased.' And because he was pleased, she was full of pleasure. 'New York is more marvellous than ever', she wrote to her son. 'They are the wonderfullest people – the Americans. We were knee deep in flowers – letters – gifts of all sorts before we had been here 6 hours . . . All seats gone at most extraordinary prices for the whole three weeks we are here. It will be a tremendous tour. This is the place to make money! (& to spend it unless one makes *terrific efforts to keep some.*)'

Laurence was travelling with the company and having trouble with his vegetarian diet (he ate chocolate mostly, calculating that eight bars a day equalled one pound of beefsteak). His father took little notice of him. 'Laurence does love his father', Ellen wrote. 'We both do, but oh Lord how he does try us.' He gave little help to his son's acting because, Ellen noticed, he 'fancies L. an inch or so too tall to act with, so down goes L. and up goes himself . . . Poor Laurence is getting *some* crushing notices.' Whenever he was not onstage, Laurence would bury himself in Tolstoy's novels – and write secret plays of his own.

When they reached Brooklyn Ellen went in front to watch Irving play Mathias in *The Bells* and observed how strangely altered his performance had become. 'Acts weakly, effeminately', she noted in her diary. 'He used to assume a rough, masculine vigour, but now he does odd things. Puts out a leg, elevates his chin. Goes for pathos of a *very* weak kind!'

They visited thirty American and Canadian cities during these six months. By the final month Irving was far from well. At the last seven places they came to, he took medical advice from a local doctor, but these seven doctors offered conflicting opinions and he tied himself in knots trying to follow their recommendations. Ellen felt both worried and angry with him. He was, she decided, 'singularly stupid in the matter of his health' – as men so often were.

One advantage of his illness was that he seemed to take her more into his confidence. 'I appear to be of strange *use* to H.', she wrote at the end of January 1900 while they were in Toledo, 'and I have always thought to be *useful*, *really useful*, to any person *is* rather fine and satisfactory.' Perhaps, as one got older, this special usefulness was as near to love as anyone could reach. Like a young girl, she had been living wholly in the present because Henry never revealed his plans. 'Now there is a glimmer of light and I can see plainly enough', she wrote to Bernard Shaw. After returning from the United States, she would tour Britain once more with Henry and complete their summer season at the Lyceum. Then 'never again with H.', she concluded.

Henry had given Ellen the chance to escape and she had not taken it. Now, his fighting spirit and sense of her worth somewhat revived, he used all his 'craftiness' to keep her with him. He was discovering that, however well they did, the syndicate seemed to absorb the profits. He knew that he had to keep on the move – and keep Ellen moving with him.

But outside the theatre everything was different. There were times when, following their return to England, Ellen felt 'certain Henry just hates me!'. Mrs Aria took him away on holidays to Norfolk, Derbyshire and Cornwall, and they also went together to Stratford-upon-Avon, always travelling like royalty, greeted by the stationmaster in his top hat, escorted by a company of porters and baggage-men, the convoy making its stately progress along the platform: a solemn procession, Mrs Aria usually accompanied by her daughter, some chaperone-companion, and her maid; and Irving by his faithful valet, his clever secretary and (to Eliza Aria's dismay) his favourite dog. He paid in her opinion excessive attention to his dogs. When Fussie, the terrier Ellen Terry had given him, fell through a trap-door on the Lyceum stage and died, it was difficult for Mrs Aria to conceal her relief. But Henry soon got another dog.

As for Ellen, the loss of intimacy, of actual companionship, 'has squeezed me dreadfully'. She blamed herself. 'All my fault. It is *I* who am changed, not him.' She had changed by twenty-five years – so had he of course, though she still thought of him at his best as the 'wonderfullest' of men. But suffering from rheumatism and poor eyesight, she knew that she herself was not so wonderful. 'My hair is getting nicely grey . . . I feel I can't look young.' She had not been able to accept his offer of marriage nearly twenty years ago when they were playing *Romeo and Juliet*, so it was no surprise to her that, as she confided to Marguerite Steen: 'Henry left me for Mrs Aria.' She still believed that given the right parts she could, if only for a time, turn back the clock and regain her beauty. But would Henry ever give her those parts?

Ellen made one stipulation when agreeing to remain at the Lyceum: that she must be given roles that maintained her position as an actress. If she was paid a salary simply for the use of her name on the Lyceum bill, she would accept offers from other actor-managers – there were several London theatres eager to capture her. 'I don't want a salary when I don't give services!' she told Bram Stoker.

For the first time she and Irving were both contemplating retirement. Mrs Aria took him on a convalescent holiday to the King Arthur Castle Hotel, near Tintagel in Cornwall. The hotel itself, a solitary, windswept, recently built Gothic edifice set on a rocky promontory overlooking the old castle ruins, was spacious and richly furnished, and from its formidable clifftop, like a bold piece of theatrical scenery, commanded a dramatic view over the Atlantic. Irving felt reinvigorated. Here was a place where he could retire and busy himself writing his memoirs.

Ellen had fallen in love with a dilapidated, sixteenth-century timbered farmhouse set in the water-meadows at Smallhythe, a village near Tenterden in Kent, which she had come across during one of her drives with Henry from Winchelsea in the pony-and-trap – perhaps one day he might join her there. She had wanted to buy it, but it was occupied by a shepherd who promised to let her know if it ever came up for sale. Towards the end of the 1890s, she received an unsigned postcard with a Tenterden postmark: 'House for sale'. Edy bicycled down with a friend and decided that her mother must indeed buy it. The farmhouse, which was in need of repair, was being sold together with two adjacent cottages, a large barn and some land – and Ellen, responding to her daughter's enthusiasm, went ahead and instructed Stephen Coleridge to pay £1,700 for the property and let out the sixty acres of land to a farmer.

But she could not yet afford to retire, and nor could Irving. He knew that he must add a spectacular new production to the repertoire. After some twenty-two years he finally chose Shakespeare's democratic tragedy *Coriolanus*.

G.F. Watts: *Choosing* (Ellen Terry), 1864 and *The Sisters* (Kate and Ellen Terry), 1862–3

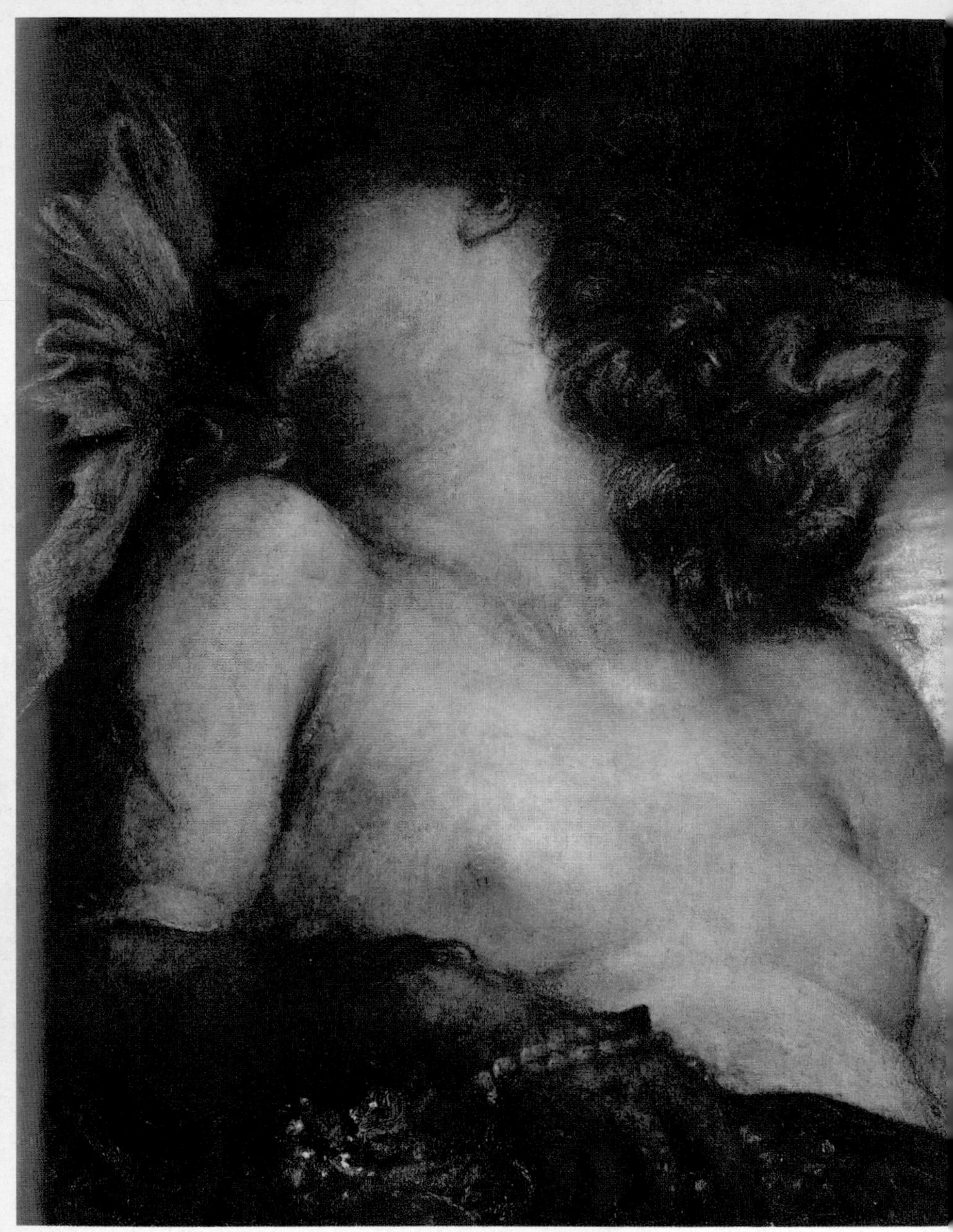

Ellen Terry as *The Wife of Pluto*, G.F. Watts, 1865–89

Ellen Terry as Lady Macbeth, John Singer Sargent, 1889

James McNeill Whistler's *Arrangement in Black No.3* (Henry Irving as Philip II of Spain), 1876, later reworked (*above left*); sketch by Henry Irving of himself as Don Quixote, 1895 (*above right*); Henry Irving at his desk by Jules Bastien-Lepage, 1880 (*below*)

Poster of Ellen Terry as Hiordis in Ibsen's *The Vikings of Helgeland*, 1903 (*left*); Ellen Terry in Laurence Alma-Tadema's costume as Imogen in *Cymbeline* (*below*)

Gordon Craig's painting of Elena Meo, 1902 (*above left*);
William Rothenstein's Gordon Craig as Hamlet, 1896 (*below*)

ACT IV SCENE V
LINES 56-74

THE TRAGICALL HISTORIE OF

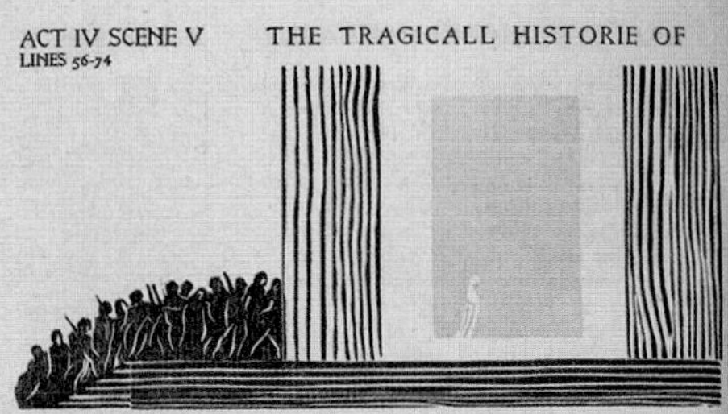

mesme, puis que c'estoit par luy, que j'avois perdu ce qui me lioit à telle consanguinité et alliance. Homme pour vray bardy et courageux, et digne d'eternelle louange, qui s'armant d'une folie cauteleuse, et dissimulant accortement un grand desvoyement de sens, trompa souz telle simplicité les plus sages, fins, et rusez, conservant non seulement sa vie des efforts et embusches du tyran, ains qui plus est, vengeant avec un nouveau genre de punition, et non excogité supplice la mort de son pere, plusieurs annees apres l'execution, de sorte que conduisant ses affaires avec telle prudence, et effectuant ses desseins avec une si grande bardiesse, et constance, il laisse un jugement indecis entre les bommes de bon esprit, lequel est le plus recommandable en luy, ou sa constance et magnanimité, ou la sagesse, en desseignant, et accortise, en mettant ses desseins au parfaict accomplissement de son oeuvre de long temps premedité. Si jamais la vengeance sembla avoir quelque face et forme de justice, il est bors de doute, que la pieté et affection qui nous lie à la souvenance de nos peres, poursuivis injustement, est celle qui nous dispense à chercher les moyens de ne laisser impunie une trahison et effort outrageux et proditoire, veu que jaçoit que David fut un sainct, et juste Roy, bomme simple, et courtois, et debonnaire, si est-ce que mourant il enchargea à son fils Salomon, luy succedant à la couronne, de ne laisser descendre au tombeau quelque certain, qui l'avoit outragé, non que le Roy, et prochain de la mort, et prest à rendre compte devant Dieu, fust

King. Pretty Ophelia.
Ophe. Indeede la, without an oath Ile make an end on't,
By gis and by Saint Charitie,
Alack and fie for shame,
Young men will doo't if they come to't,
By Cock they are to blame.
Quoth she, Before you tumbled me,
You promis'd me to wed,
(He answers.) So would I a done by yonder sunne
And thou hadst not come to my bed.
King. How long hath she beene thus?
Ophe. I hope all will be well, we must be patient, but
I cannot chuse but weepe to thinke they would
lay him i'th' cold ground, my brother shall
know of it, and so I thanke you for your good
counsaile. Come my Coach, God night Ladies,
god night, sweet Ladyes god night, god night.

126

HAMLET PRINCE OF DENMARKE

ACT IV SCENE V
LINES 75-98

King. Follow her close, give her good watch I pray you.
O this is the poyson of deepe griefe, it springs
All from her Fathers death, and now behold.
O Gertrud, Gertrud,
When sorrowes come, they come not single spyes,
But in battalians: first her Father slaine,
Next, your sonne gone, and he most violent Author
Of his owne just remove, the people muddied
Thick and unwholsome in their thoughts and
whispers
For good Polonius death: and we have done but
greenly
In hugger mugger to inter him: poore Ophelia
Devided from herselfe, and her faire judgement,
Without the which we are pictures, or meere beasts,
Last, and as much containing as all these,
Her brother is in secret come from Fraunce,
Feeds on his wonder, keepes himselfe in clowdes,
And wants not buzzers to infect his eare
With pestilent speeches of his fathers death,
Wherein necessity of matter begger'd,
Will nothing stick our person to arraigne
In eare and eare: O my deare Gertrud, this
Like to a murdring peece in many places
Gives me superfluous death.
A noise within.
Queene. Alacke, what noyse is this?
King. Attend,
Enter a Messenger.
Where are my Swissers, let them guard the doore,
What is the matter?

before by him sharpned, which served for prickes, binding & tying the hangings, in such sort, that what force soever they used to loose themselves, it was unpossible to get from under them, and presently he set fire in the four corners of the hal in such sort that all that were as then therin not one escaped away but were forced to purge their sins by fire, and dry up the great aboundance of liquor by them received into their bodies, all of them dying in the unevitable & mercilesse flames of the whot & burning fire which the prince perceiving became wise, and knowing that his uncle before the end of the banquet had withdrawn himselfe into his chamber, which stood apart from the place where the fire burnt, went thither, & entring into the chamber, layd hand upon the sword of his fathers murtherer, leaving his own in the place, which while he was at the banket some of the courtiers had nailed fast into the scaberd and going to Fengon said, I wonder disloyal king how thou canst sleep heer at thine ease, and al thy pallace is burnt, the fire thereof having burnt the greatest part of thy courtiers and ministers of thy cruelty, and detestable tirannies, and which is more I cannot imagin how thou sholdst wel assure thyself, & thy estate, as now to take thy ease, seeing Hamlet so neer thee armed with the shafts by him prepared long since and at this present is redy to revenge the traiterous injury, by thee done to his Lord and Father. Fengon as then knowing the truth of his nephews subtil practise, and hering him speak with stayed mind, and which is more, perceived a sword naked in his hand which he already lifted up to deprive him of his life, leaped quickly out of the bed, taking hold of Hamlets sworde, that was nayled into the scaberd, which as hee sought to pull out, Hamlet gave him such a blowe upon the chine of the necke, that hee cut his head cleane from his shoulders, & as he fell to the ground sayd, This

A strange revenge taken by Hamlet.

A mocke but yet sharp and stinging given by Hamlet to his uncle.

127

Gordon Craig's 'Dress of Rushes' for *Acis and Galatea*, 1901 (*above left*); 'Hoop-la!' from *Gordon Craig's Book of Penny Toys*, 1899 (*above right*); and his design for Act IV, Scene v in the Cranach Press *Hamlet*, 1929–30 (*below*)

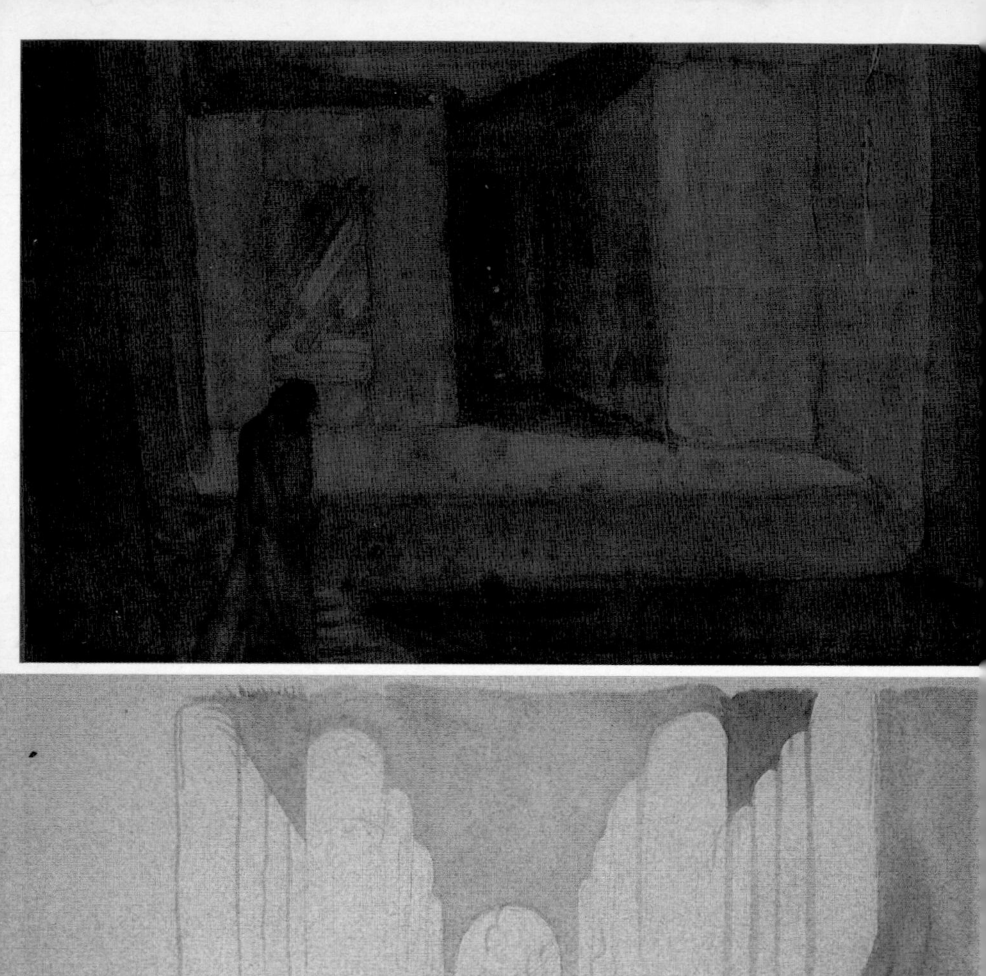

Gordon Craig's designs projected or realised for the closet scene in *Hamlet* (*above*) and Ibsen's *The Pretenders* (*below*)

'How he [Irving] will *live* through the rehearsals of "Coriolanus" Heaven knows', Ellen wrote to Ted. As a study in single-minded leadership, the character of Coriolanus suited Irving well enough. 'He kept throughout an attitude of disdainful pride,' Arthur Symons wrote, 'the face, the eyes set, while only his mouth twitched, seeming to chew his words with the disgust of one swallowing a painful morsel.' But Lady Gregory reported that his 'voice is quite gone, & sounds as if coming from a phonograph'. Volumnia, the mother of Coriolanus, who brings some more diplomatic touches to this harsh political tragedy, is one of Shakespeare's few major roles for older women and one to which Ellen could have no objection. But she made it clear that '[I] don't care for it much . . . the length, the exertion' – and also perhaps the knowledge that she has created such a brutal son whom she cannot save from himself. 'Mistaken all this while / Between the child and parent . . . There's no man in the world more bound to's mother.' The play itself (its designs by Alma-Tadema mostly made over twenty years before) seemed to be the work of an ailing dramatist performed by an ailing actor. The arrogance of Coriolanus and his diatribes against the many-headed mob leave no one guiltless. 'Speaking is for beggars; he wears his tongue in his arms.' The mood is one of universal condemnation, one of disillusion with the speeches of playwrights and performers, the stupidity of audiences, and with the empty pretences of the political theatre. Action is all, and it is usually all bad, though it is better than nothing. 'When blows have made me stay, I fled from words.'

Early in 1901, the gas-lights of the winter streets half dimmed and the London buildings hung with crêpe-de-noire to mark the death of Queen Victoria, Irving began rehearsals. Omitting the battles, he prepared the play as 'a tragedy of filial love', reflecting perhaps something of his own incompatibilities with his mother, his service in the theatre providing a parallel to Coriolanus's duty to Rome. His three-act version of the play opened on 15 April. But despite the introduction of a splendid triumphal procession, the public preferred the fashionable new musical comedies at Daly's and the Gaiety, and Beerbohm Tree's light-hearted entertainments carrying 'ornament to excess' at His Majesty's. 'C[oriolanus] is coming off', Ellen wrote to her son on 13 May. As for Irving, 'he preserves his usual apparent Stoicism', Harry reported to his mother. Only when the play was brought back at the end of the season and Irving discarded the heavy warrior beard that had muffled his voice and obscured his features would he perform the part with strength – and then it was too late (Alma-Tadema had advised him that a little beard would make him look younger, while the rest of the cast could wear bald wigs). Everything now depended upon the success of their tours.

36
For Love or Money

'I rather dread poverty,' Ellen admitted. She wanted what she thought of as enough corn to feed the famine of her old age and enough to feed her children ('I feed them all the while'). There had never been any doubt in her mind that 'what's mine is always Edy's'. It was always Ellen's hope and, despite some moments of revolt, Edy's expectation that they would live separately-and-together on the estate at Smallhythe. After the success of *Robespierre*, Edy had set herself up as a theatrical costumier in an atelier at Covent Garden, working for the Lyceum and other theatres, and always making sure, to a degree that might have pleased her father, that her costumes, unlike the plays themselves, were historically accurate.

Ellen was happy financing 'Edith Craig and Co.'. She knew where her daughter was and approved of what she was doing. 'Of course I shall support her a very long way on the road she wants to go', Ellen assured Stephen Coleridge who noted on one of her letters that Edy's business 'was conducted with hopeless irregularity & ended with thousands to pay up!' It was Ted, however, who worried Ellen more. His marriage apparently at an end, he led a wandering and distracted life. In the chronology he was to prepare forty years later, he noted at this time: 'Quite vague [about] what is going on . . . A nuisance to everyone – but chiefly to myself . . . Scraped a living. Forget how.' He had been over to see his wife May and taken the trouble to tell her that it was all over between them. His message was simple: she should no longer put up with him – to do so 'was extraordinarily kind of her – and extraordinarily stupid'. There was no denying that May was 'a kind, charming, pretty, buxom, vain, practical, far-too-good wife', and he had for her 'the natural, soft, cosy, liking that one rabbit has for another rabbit'. He never planned anything – whatever happened seemed to take him by surprise. So perhaps it was not surprising that by the time he had finished telling her that their marriage was a farce, she should find herself pregnant again, this time with their fourth child, a son not mentioned in his memoirs, whom May called Peter – and this despite the fact that he had politely explained to her that he had 'no time to see the children'.

Ted looked so 'dreadfully ill' that Ellen feared 'to make what is already bad – *worse*, by my interference'. She had no alternative but to interfere. Surely it was 'enough to make any man ill not seeing his children', she upbraided him. What most appalled her were the letters he was sending May – letters which May showed her. They were not only unnecessary, but also '*very* vulgar & very insulting, & cad-ish I'm quite ashamed of you', she told him, '– & it's quite likely that some day, earlier than you think, all the stuff you write to her may be in print . . . if you think that because you married a "very stupid" girl . . . you are justified in separating from her, & throwing up all your responsibilities concerning her, no one else will think so & all this unnecessary writing will bring great trouble to you & those you love one of these days.' Whenever Ellen got hold of such letters, 'into the fire like lightning they go'. Later Gordon Craig would keep many files of his letters marked 'Not Sent'.

But apart from paying some of his debts, what could Ellen do? What she did was to instruct her solicitor to settle a weekly allowance on May for herself and the four children. 'I have no words to speak severely enough about T[ed]'s conduct', she assured Stephen Coleridge, 'but M[ay] is enough to make one *mad* when you know her well.' She wanted above everything, it seemed, to live with her husband and yet everything she said was calculated to drive him away. 'Everything is terrible', she complained in an agony of incomprehension. When her divorce decree was eventually made absolute in the spring of 1905 and she was given custody of the children, she petitioned the court for permanent maintenance, but did not proceed once Ellen made her a new allowance of £478 a year. In 1913 (when Rosie was in her twentieth year and two of the boys had completed their public school education) this was reduced to £372 a year. The allowance was to cease in 1917 when all the children were of age and Ellen, aged seventy, was in financial difficulties herself.

'Oh dear oh dear I do think of you until my head bursts', she told Ted. 'Don't live with *anybody* male or female (unless you go back to M[ay] & the lovely babies).' But if he was to get on to what he called 'the right road at last . . . [and] begin to see light' such a move back into darkness was impossible.

What were these difficulties with women? In a note Ted had written: 'I wish to live until the evening of my mother's death, when I should wish nothing more enjoyable than to die before the next day waked.' But it was the dreamer who wrote this, the dreamer who 'had great, great fear in my dreams'. He was struggling to wake up, to grow from Ted into Edward Gordon Craig, and aware 'that mothers do keep little sons as hostages, taking certain situations in life as declarations of war instead of taking them for what they were'. The mothers of his own children, he came to suspect, often used them to imprison him. But he had to be free. 'I was in a state when I doubted everything – marriage, theatre – friends – career – money matters – all seemed to have cheated me.' To guard himself against this sense of being cheated, he manufactured what he called 'a vain little egotism', and in his loneliness 'called out to a girl I knew' to join him. In his memoirs he was to call her ABC, though she was in fact that girl with a far-away look, the actress Jess Dorynne. The day after he wrote to her, she arrived – followed a little later by an enquiry agent employed by his wife May.

This would finally be the end of their marriage. 'It must be a never ending disgrace to you that you leave your chix & your wife after such a *short* time of trial, & even now I consider you ought to put things straight for the children within a year', Ellen upbraided him. '. . . The mistake you made is in searching for Happiness – that never comes to any of us.' Behind these words lay the ghost of Godwin with whom Ellen had searched for happiness with more tenacity than Ted. She had prayed that he would avoid her mistakes, avoid his father's mistakes too – all her moral prescriptions were prepared with this in mind. But she could never 'put things straight' for her son. She had planted in him a sense of destiny – that of fulfilling his father's unachieved ambitions.

It was Jess Dorynne who rescued him from solitude and darkness and got him back on 'the right road'. Though several men had shown an interest in her, she never responded to them and was a virgin. She was waiting for someone to give her what she called 'a thorough, vibrating, intense Present, sound and happy – a living Present not a shifty undecided one'. In Craig she believed she had found this special man. But to sustain a sexual relationship was not easy. Her father was dead, but her severe and conventional mother throbbed with curiosity about her. Jess needed caution as well as courage for such a serious adventure. 'When we are together', she promised Craig, 'we will drift & leave it to the Gods to order our direction. I'm taking some of your advice in coming at all & risking Mamma's discovering it. If she remains ignorant – she – you & I will be happy . . .'

Her love was passionate and free: she did not want to trap him with a baby or imprison him in marriage. She believed in the value of his work and recharged his belief in it. Yet there was something missing in the story of ABC and EGC – perhaps the letter D, her own letter which he suppressed (and would encounter in another country as he would many letters in his alphabet of women). By day Jess was able to support him with her allowance. But he suspected her of having a different agenda at night. On their very first night together by the sea he was suddenly woken by her getting into his bed. What should he do, reader? What he did was to blow out the candle and give her a child. Actually they lived together for almost two years in a bewildering number of places before, many candles being blown out, she conceived. In his version of events she 'had got what she wanted, and like a wise woman she hugged it to herself'.

Her letters tell a different story. 'Our ideas of honesty differ,' she wrote. Though no heart loved him more than hers, a poignant atmosphere, strange, almost tragic, seemed to envelop the two of them. 'I feel as if I had witnessed some irresistible calamity', she confessed, '– murder, horror, death.' Craig too had similar nightmares. Jess had told him she did not

expect eternal fidelity. She insisted they remain 'personally independent'. But when he folded her along his body and kissed her throat and lips, such independence was hard to maintain, especially when he chided her for her caution, having none himself. So she threw away caution and in the spring of 1900 became pregnant. Then everything changed. 'I was always too sick, too ill – you were alone. I was alone – the hours became days, weeks & months . . . I should have been sleeping in your arms still, my head on your right shoulder, or sitting reading to you by the fire.' Feeling very vulnerable, it seemed to her that Craig 'mocked even my figure when, heavy with child, weighed down with grief . . . every step was an excruciatingly painful effort and contortion'. In November 1900, when their daughter Kitty was born, they were no longer regularly seeing each other. The horror of it was that 'this baby has separated us entirely – from what we were and might have been', Jess wrote to him. '. . . Kitty is very good & very sweet but she lies a dead weight on my heart & my life & even, in fact, in my arms – a bitter and sorrowful joy which I could not now be without.'

Kitty soon became a pawn in their negotiations. 'Kitty is sweet & would love to see you', Jess told him. '. . . [She] is adorable – & exactly like you . . . I think a young child's life should not be saddened by a father in one place & a mother in another – she will grow melancholy . . . You have scarcely ever come to see her.' Sometimes Craig did come, though more often he did not – and Jess never knew whether he would or wouldn't come. 'I count the hours . . . uncertainty is always a torture to me.' But was she using Kitty in order to see him? She wanted to see him and also feared seeing him – he was always more affectionate at a distance. Would there be danger, she wondered, in a single half-hour? 'Help me to make you happy,' she appealed to him. But he did not trust her. Once, like his mother, 'I trusted everyone', he wrote; 'now I trust no one.' She was so demanding and she contradicted him all the time. He sensed that she wanted to occupy his freedom, smother him. Though they were sexually attracted to each other, their love, he decided, must be 'an illusion'. Whenever they met 'what fearful shocks we give each other', he wrote, '– what dead spirits enter us – that is why it is hateful to meet'. She agreed. Yet when she did not see him 'a death-like stillness creeps through me', she confessed. The trouble was that 'I am so lonely, my Ted – there is nothing to counteract this horrible pain . . . Every fibre in me strains towards you.' So he promised to 'cheer you up' and a 'most painful afternoon' was followed by 'the sweetest night we've ever had'.

Then he left. It was as if he was testing her strength. He did not want to mislead her with easy sentimentality. He needed her to be strong and sympathetic if their relationship was to come alive and sometimes he shook with unexpected anguish when he contemplated the labyrinthine mysteries of their love. 'I do not understand it', he told her. 'Can you explain it? We seem to talk in two languages.' She wondered if 'money would have made you much fonder of me'. But he angrily denied this, seeing it as an accusation. She was no longer the woman whom he had once loved and promised to marry after his divorce from May. 'I am what I despise', she admitted. '. . . I have become bitter from gall . . . [and] am doomed to be one of the damned.' She had given Craig his self-confidence, then lost her own. In their early days she had sworn never to leave the stage – not for a million pounds: now she believed that she had no gift for acting. She despised jealousy but was sometimes consumed by it ('Who gave you the flowers on your table that you are so loth to throw away? . . . Who was the "Mrs Craig" who came?'). The girl who once attracted Craig so strongly had promised 'never to marry' or take on 'the duties of a wife'. Her ideal had been: 'no domesticity, no children, simple freedom & collaboration'. But after three or four years she was prepared against all these principles to settle into domestic life with a marriage certificate for Kitty's sake. 'When I say "where's Papa" she stares at your photo with a grin . . . Let me know clearly if you wish to marry me . . . I will wear a ring if you wish and keep your name after mine . . . it is not in the least a matter for us but merely a ceremony to give Kitty your name & an "honest" mother as I believe the term goes & your legal rights over the child – so that if I died my friends could not take her entirely from you, as they could otherwise . . . Kitty is yours.' But how could he be sure Kitty was his? In any event Ted persuaded himself he had no urge to see Jess.

But he still needed to see her occasionally whenever he sensed that she was falling out of love with him. When she appealed to him: 'God send you to me soon', he stayed away; but when she wrote saying that her love for him 'has been murdered . . . and now goodbye', he decided to see her and find out whether she was after all the woman for him. Determined to keep herself at arm's length, she begged him not to 'let me be weak again'. He took up the challenge and she melted in his embrace, risking another pregnancy. Then he left her once more. 'My lips are warm from your kisses. I cannot bear another separation.' She began taking laudanum – 'my precious morphia' – to stifle her misery. 'I die of grief – it comes in huge waves, one quick on the other till I am crushed.' Gradually, after half a dozen years, she came to terms with their unequal love. 'I must have been quite blind not to have seen you didn't love me . . . You admire the tilt of my nose, or my instep or a crinkle at the corner of my mouth . . . fascination not love was what you felt for me.' What a 'green fool of a girl' she had been. The two of them were like comic characters in a farcical tragedy which left her 'an entire wreck – heart – body – mind – morals'. Her love for him was dead, but 'my heart hugs tight Love's corpse and cannot bury it'. The ghost of this love kept haunting her and she wished she could 'kill dead the nerve of my life as one has the nerve of a tooth killed'. Trapped by a 'terrible hallucination', she reproached herself for becoming such a cooped-up, complaining, pitiful creature. She was lucky not to be in a madhouse and threatened to commit suicide if only to agitate Craig's conscience. But it was hopeless. 'I don't feel capable of any love again.' She would rather 'go to hell'. At any rate 'if I can go abroad, I shall'. But it would be Craig who eventually fled abroad.

'God send you the sort of woman you want', Jess wrote to him. He had not liked to tell her, but he had already met this godsend of a woman, someone ordained to share his life. It had not affected his decision to leave Jess – that, he believed, had been due to her own obstinate weakness. He thought of her now as a vampire, drinking his blood. So he had to leave her. 'I felt a steadily growing determination not to be interfered with by anyone on earth', he wrote. As for her, 'my life is blasted'.

The birth of Kitty, and Ted's parting from Jess, propelled Ellen back into her son's emotional life. She urged him to comfort Jess's 'anxious heart' and 'prove the integrity of the man' to whom she had given herself. 'I *ache to be proud of you*', Ellen told him. Where was that loyal and generous spirit which meant 'half the world to me'? When he was rough and unfeeling, Ellen wanted to curl up and roll into a ball. 'I would rather *kill* you than see you grow *systematically* exacting & dishonourable to women', she wrote:

. . . I believe in my soul you feel tenderly, but I have never seen you behave tenderly to any woman . . . You are so blind with jealousy, vanity, discontent &

obstinacy that you don't see . . . [what] your foolish obstinacy has done in simply driving Jess from you . . . She has done everything a woman can do for three years to prove her love for you – in spite of your *outrageous ungentleness* & selfish inconsiderateness – she longs for you to be with her – I can't get a word from her upon any other subject . . . I entreat you not to lose her – Heavens – she's not *granite* – you will wear all the beauty of her character out by your unreasonableness . . . You take everything so lightly & go on & on, & leave all the women you are connected with to bear the pains – & I am the one you make suffer most.

More important to Gordon Craig than anything now was the theatre. It had been his place of education, an old school of experience with Irving its headmaster. For many years he would carry around in him what he called 'the dead actor'. But he was becoming aware that there was much else to be done around theatres – there was writing and music and dancing and painting and sketching. He was never idle. He cut boxwood all day and devoted many hours to engraving. He went into publishing too with a charming book for children, *Gordon Craig's Book of Penny Toys*. Each of its twenty wood-engravings, which were hand-coloured (many of them by Jess Dorynne) and produced on thick dull-yellow sugar paper, was accompanied by a verse or 'jingle' printed in bold 'Elephant type' and had been composed by Ted (under various names), his sister Edy and Jess – almost a family book among whose first readers were his own children.

I am a Penny Pony,
Very like the Troy one,
  Made of Wood
  Misunderstood,
Buy your little boy one.

Between 1898 and 1901 he also edited an occasional magazine called *The Page*, sometimes issued 'At the Sign of the Cross – Hackbridge – Surrey', a cottage 'smothered in ivy and birds' where he lived with Jess before her pregnancy. The contents were miscellaneous: woodcuts and drawings; bookplates (including ones for Ellen and Edy and pretty Lucy Wilson); designs for posters, inn-signs, menus; illustrations for novels, a few songs and some disturbing verses for his and May's three-year-old son.

Robin with the dark brown eyes –
  Eyes that look us through with scorn,
What's the power you utilize
  That makes us wish we'd ne'er been born . . .

Ted pressed everyone he knew into making contributions – James Pryde, Will Rothenstein, Max Beerbohm, Burne-Jones and even Henry Irving (a flagrantly moustachioed figure done with grease-paint or a wash of red in his dressing-room as he was making up for Don Quixote). 'I wonder will *The Page* be my passport to Paradise?' he asked Edy. In later years he would be rather disparaging about this 'silly little magazine'. But it was playful and surprising, and held its freshness until his interests veered elsewhere and the editing became a burden.

He felt a need, partly an actor's need, to keep his work before the public. The circulation of *The Page* was tiny, but its continuing publication was vital to him. Despair never quite got its teeth into him, though 'I was a little bit surprised at times that I was never taken to a lunatic asylum'. He was aware of being considered 'a little cracked, but a clever fellow really' as his mother called him. But what haunted him was a suspicion that he was destined to share the fate of his father: that of a man, praised for his multifarious gifts, but remembered only as a might-have-been.

The turning point came through a new friendship. He had met Martin Shaw at Southwold, a picturesque seaside town in Suffolk, where the two of them, together with James Pryde and some local performers, put on an entertainment of songs, recitations and piano solos at an inn. Martin Shaw, then in his mid-twenties, was three years younger than Ted, rather gruff in manner, with a disfiguring birthmark on his face that, according to one witness, 'made sensitive people avert their eyes quickly'. He was 'a musician to his fingertips', Gordon Craig wrote. He 'made the piano sound like three, six, or ten instruments, and gave the music a swing which Southwold cannot have heard before or since'. It was this music that led him out of his uncertainties.

The inspiration for Shaw's music came from the English countryside, and it showed Craig the dramatic value of natural beauty as opposed to a reliance on melodrama and the preponderance of detail exploited by Irving at the Lyceum. 'He's practical, direct, I can't think of anyone better' – and certainly there was no one whose talent better complemented his own. 'Shaw – Shaw – Shaw – how I yearn for the stage again', Craig wrote. Though he venerated Henry Irving, he 'detested the state of the theatre' at the end of the nineteenth century. Irving was undoubtedly a great man of his time. Like a lion caged in a zoo, he found himself imprisoned by the suspect commercialism of his business syndicate. Ted had tried to find a syndicate himself to take on the responsibilities of *The Page* and realised how dangerous money and numbers were as guides to valuing the arts. Like a mythical creature, a unicorn perhaps which inhabits a make-believe world, he could not be caged by syndicates or marriages, and in company with Martin Shaw he began to feel 'like someone who has been released from a dungeon'. But in throwing off the yoke of the old theatre, he also threw off £8 a week and now earned (give or take a few shillings) 'nothing a month'. Always anxious, sometimes scolding, usually soft-hearted, Ellen reminded him of the necessity to 'make your *bread and butter for today*', while nevertheless enclosing large sums of money for him. 'This makes £500', she calculated. '. . . You must be careful dear not to lose cheques – it gives such a lot of trouble.' Ted believed that his mother still had 'lots and lots of money', but she had also spent lots of money, some of it on Edy, and for the first time in her career was overdrawn at the bank.

After purchasing Smallhythe, Ellen was preparing to leave Barkston Gardens and had employed Stephen Coleridge to busy himself over buying a house for her in Chelsea, 215 King's Road, into which she moved in 1902. 'It is *exactly* right for me', she wrote, giving him the wrong address and asking him to inspect it for her. It turned out to be quite a small house with a flagged courtyard in front and a little garden behind where she built a modern studio. It was not in perfect condition (from the treads of the tumbledown staircase you could see out into the garden), but it suited her better than Earls Court until the King's Road became too busy, obliging her to install special double windows on the first floor where she converted the drawing-room into her bedroom. All this was expensive. 'As yet I am not out of debt', she told her son who wondered whether she was not being too generous to Edy. But as Ellen explained, she gave her daughter nothing except what she earned 'by serving to the best of her ability in the way I want to be *served* – and she does not worry the life out of me beyond my bearing powers'. So she was pleased to learn that there was a Shaw in Ted's life as well as in her own and that Martin Shaw had raised several hundred pounds, formed the Purcell Operatic Society, and was planning a dramatic new presentation of *Dido and Aeneas* with Ted as its *metteur-en-scène*. At last he appeared to be earning what she gave him.

All that Gordon Craig had been doing seemed suddenly to have a purpose. The *metteur-en-scène*, whatever else he might bring to his work, 'must have been an actor', he reasoned. As for the designing of scenes, it was really 'child's play if you had been born the son of an architect and worked in Irving's theatre'. Why, he asked himself, had he spent so much time over that painfully slow craft of wood-engraving if it had not been 'to teach myself how to design scenes for the Drama' and 'how to delineate characters better'? It had given him an exceptional fund of patience ('not a natural virtue in me') and kept him from heartbreak over this long puzzled apprenticeship. Lying in bed at night, 'watching the shadows in the walls and ceiling', he saw how his dreams – those dreams that others had deplored as idle and immature – were part of his original vision for a new theatre. 'I woke up', he wrote, and recognised 'what I could do to serve the British Theatre'.

Without Martin Shaw, Gordon Craig's thoughts would never have turned to *Dido and Aeneas*; and without Gordon's Craig's imaginative energy Martin Shaw would have been too cautious to present the opera so dramatically. A bond of friendship grew up between the two men. During the rehearsals they worked together in what seemed to be entire freedom and happiness. When the music began, Shaw appeared to lose his timidity and, like an actor, become someone else. Listening to his playing ('I never liked piano playing to the extent that I liked his'), Craig was stimulated by ideas – how the singers should move, what they should wear, and how they might be lit to make a dance of white arms against a dark background. It was a perfect partnership.

The Hampstead Conservatoire of Music (later the Embassy Theatre) had no proscenium and nowhere to conceal the lighting. It was a concert hall with a series of unmovable platforms for sections of the orchestra. With ingenious scaffolding, Craig created a bridge from which lights shone down on the stage, then side-lights with changeable gelatines giving the unusually shaped frame a feeling of simplicity. And what the audience saw was a fusing of opera and ballet, dance and song, performed against a vast background conveyed by a sky cloth that went up far out of sight. Stimulated by what he had read of his fellow reformer Hubert von Herkomer's 'atmospheric backgrounds' (a method of giving a three-dimensional effect to a painted background by stretching a grey gauze on a frame at an angle tilted forward in front of it), he visualised a limitless sky against which his figures moved in a harmony of colours. Though a few of the critics made quickly for the bar, others reported on 'one of the most original presentations of opera ever witnessed'. Both Shaw and Craig were congratulated as 'bold pioneers of a distinctly new movement in stage production'. The *Review of the Week* placed Gordon Craig's representation as an alternative both to Irving's lavish productions of Shakespeare and to the non-dramatic readings reproducing the original sixteenth-century setting to which William Poel's Elizabethan Stage Society had dedicated itself in the 1890s. This *Dido and Aeneas* avoided both pedantry and superfluity, and its arrangement of illuminated colours applied to scenery, costumes and groups of leaping, crawling, swaying singers 'gave hopes of a third and better solution', the reviewer explained.

> The real triumph of the setting was, however, in the use of light and shade; it was as carefully considered as in a wood engraving, and added immeasurably to the tragic simplicity of the whole performance . . . The main principles acted on by Mr Craig can be applied to work on the scale as big as that of Covent Garden . . . why should we not see more of his work, and have other memories of harmony, of colour and form?

Gordon Craig 'always felt most grateful for praise' though 'we pretend not to care a damn'. Despite having to pawn the gold watch Irving had given him to help pay off a deficit of over £180 for the three performances, he was eager to move on to his next production. Martin Shaw suggested that Purcell's music for Fletcher's *Prophetess, or The History of Dioclesian* would give them a good opportunity to work together again, and by the summer of 1900 they had begun to plan what they called *The Masque of Love*.

Ellen came to see an early rehearsal and, much liking it, agreed to give seven performances of her one-act romantic comedy *Nance Oldfield* which, with *Dido and Aeneas* and *The Masque of Love*, would make up a triple bill during the last week of March 1901 at the Coronet Theatre in Notting Hill.

The Masque of Love 'proved (maybe) the best thing I ever did', Craig hazarded in his memoirs, '. . . or so I thought it'. Unaided apparently by instinct, it touched on something mysterious and released it like a creative stream: but when he looked back, he could not by any process of reasoning discover what had taken place. Because Ellen Terry was appearing, the audience was large and the critics who came to see her were also introduced to what Max Beerbohm described as her son's 'very serious and delightful experiment'. There was no painted scenery, 'just three walls of light grey canvas and a grey stage cloth', Edward Craig wrote in the biography of his father. 'The main colours were black and white . . . with pools of coloured light and the figures moved in and out of different fields of colour', leaving what Max Beerbohm called 'ineffaceable pictures in my memory'. W.B. Yeats sent his congratulations on the 'wonderful scenery at the Purcell Society, the only good scenery I ever saw', and Ted was particularly pleased to receive a letter from Walter Crane, the artist and illustrator whom Godwin had admired: 'Your staging is distinctly original and artistic and strikes quite a new note in the Theatre.'

'It was a lovely show', Ellen assured her son. '. . . I enjoy thinking of it.' He appeared to have made no money from this triple bill, but she was pleased with him. And since he hoped before long to produce Handel's secular oratorio *Acis and Galatea*, it was clear to her that he would soon need more investment. So it was fortunate that, in October 1901, she set off on what would be her seventh and final tour of the United States and Canada with Irving.

Ellen could not help looking forward to being in the United States again. 'I love the country!' she wrote. 'So many *nicer* happenings, than nasty . . . They spoil me.' The tour, which took in twenty cities, was another great success, Ellen receiving £300 a week and Irving himself making a profit over the six months of some £12,000. Since their first United States tour seventeen years ago, some American cities had risen in their fortunes, others gone noticeably down. Chicago, 'like a dream from morning to night', had risen spectacularly; New York, as seen from the Plaza Hotel, was 'more amazing than ever'; the whole of Los Angeles still 'like a garden'; but St Louis, Detroit and Toledo seemed desperately low. Ellen's own spirits were clouded by the increasing difficulties she was experiencing with her eyesight. 'My eyes are dreadful in America', she wrote, '. . . it even now may be found necessary to put me in the dark for a fortnight.' Fortunately this was not necessary, though she was obliged to employ a secretary to write letters for her.

On their return to London in April 1902, they discovered that the Lyceum Company had been overtaken by financial disaster. To enforce new safety regulations against the risk of fire, the London County Council had demanded extensive structural alterations to the building. They would have to close the doors for several months and pay out a good £20,000 – money that the company did not have.

In a desperate rearguard action, Irving set about trying to raise £50,000 to reclaim the theatre. 'I feel it to be my duty', he let Stoker know. The prospect of being associated with bankruptcy, the loss of all his shareholders' investments, and the handing over to the Receiver of what had become a national institution appalled him. He had fallen into the hands of 'rogues and incompetents', he told Loveday, and wanted to 'baffle the pack of daylight robbers' who had brought this humiliation upon him. The syndicate was seeking to reconstitute the Lyceum as a music hall – a plan that dismayed Irving. What a falling-off it would be. 'I have grave doubts as to the success of such a scheme', he wrote. 'Holding the view which I do regarding the possible good influence of a theatre on the community, I could not possibly acquiesce to such a proposal.' Instead he offered to help pay for the costs of keeping the Lyceum empty until a better scheme could be found. Nevertheless, if the shareholders were in favour of a music hall, he promised not to stand in their way. At an angry meeting of these shareholders, the directors of the company blamed Irving himself for the failure. But Bram Stoker had all the figures before him and was able to show that, besides handing over the lease, Irving had actually paid back to the company more than he had originally received from it, as well as giving more performances than he had been contracted to give. At the end of the meeting, Irving flung his own share certificates into the fire and was cheered. He had saved his reputation, but the shareholders still voted for a music hall.

Until recently he had not been attracted to Ruskin's ideal of the theatre as a place of national education – he was too much of a gambler, liking to accept private favours and negotiate secret deals. Besides, he had believed box office receipts to be the essential measure of success. Now he was on a losing streak and a victim of that belief. Looking at these events from another point of view, Gordon Craig saw this as a missed opportunity for establishing a National Theatre which Irving himself would have favoured. He had entertained the most influential people in Britain and was among 'the best-known and best-loved men' in the country. But they did not flock to his banner and no one came forward to help him. 'So the National Theatre never came into existence', Gordon Craig wrote in 1930, 'and Irving went out of existence . . .' It was 'a disgraceful business', the implications of which were to help redirect his own career elsewhere. But Ellen Terry disagreed. She believed that there had been much 'sentimental gush' and 'crocodile drops' over the Lyceum. They had been too firmly set in the past. 'They should *smash* the existing state of things', she told her son, '. . . the *actual facts are* that H. I. is better off by far (alas that it shd be so) now in a worldly sense than he was during the *glories* of the Lyceum & I cd . . . be in the same position.'

For their final performance at the Lyceum on 19 July 1902, Irving was to choose *The Merchant of Venice*. The two of them were almost in tears. 'I shall never be in this theatre again. I feel it,' Ellen said. After the stage was struck, the pieces put away, the lights extinguished and the actors made their exits, the two of them walked out into the evening and went their separate ways. 'The place is now given over to the rats – all light cut off', Irving wrote to her. '. . . Everything of mine I've moved away.'

PART FOUR

37
Made in Heaven

On 22 April 1958, a 'Series of 18 Autograph Manuscript Love Poems', attributed to Bernard Shaw and addressed to Ellen Terry, came up for sale at Sotheby's auction rooms in London. A dealer had apparently purchased them from the estate of Ellen's younger brother Charles. But the scholars who assembled to inspect these poems expressed doubts as to their provenance. Charles Terry had been dead for twenty-five years, so it was almost impossible to verify the ownership. They knew that he had been a wine merchant, an easygoing sort of character, some said rather irresponsible, who according to his brother Fred 'always got away with murder!'. Yet how he might have got away with fakes or forgeries, they could not tell. All the scholars who bent over these love poems, even the greatest of them all (a man famous for never agreeing with anyone), were in agreement over this: that whoever wrote them, it had not been Shaw. They showed, it was true, something of his lack of talent as a versifier, but bore no resemblance to his other bad verses, containing no humour and being deadly serious. Attaching Shaw's name to them, however, considerably raised their price and they were bought for £400.

This appeared to be an unpromising investment. Nevertheless, over twenty years later, the love poems, still 'attributed' to Shaw, were published under the title *Lady, wilt thou love me?* Then an expert in graphology was called in to examine the text and decided that, though the handwriting was disguised as a man's, these poems had been written by a woman.

Ellen Terry was a goddess to both sexes and all ages. They wooed her with flowers, presents, letters, poems. One particular admirer, who had been besieging the 'goddess of my youthful idolatry' with many adoring letters during the 1890s, cut out a poem printed in the *Pall Mall Gazette* dedicated to Ellen and sent it to her. The sonnet was published anonymously – so perhaps the infatuated letter-writer and the author of the adoring poems were one and the same person. Certainly it would be more satisfying to send your own verses to your goddess than those of some rival.

The name of this worshipper was Christabel Marshall. Later, when she published her own books, she was to use a man's name as her *nom de plume*. This *nom de plume* can be found in the index of Dan H. Laurence's great bibliography of Bernard Shaw, directing the reader to his entry on these misattributed verses – but her name does not appear in the entry itself. So, though no one can prove that she wrote these love poems, her presence continues to haunt them.

Christabel Marshall had first seen Ellen Terry onstage one autumn evening in 1890 at Bristol. She had recently left Clifton High School for Girls and for six years she would write ardent letters to Ellen, receiving back a 'few brief notes'. They did not say much, these notes, but the handwriting was so very beautiful that Christabel kept them all, staring at them, touching them, hiding them: and she was almost content. Through the illusion of the theatre she could escape what she called her damnation. 'I had always instinctively loved the theatre', she wrote. 'All the games that I played by myself as a child were dramatic art in its first stages. I represented the adventures of imaginary people, fought battles in which I acted both the victors and the vanquished, invented dialogues between the lover and the beloved.' So when she first saw Henry Irving and Ellen Terry in *The Merchant of Venice*, she was in a familiar atmosphere. 'His method was difficult, thorny and painful; hers as easy as the singing of a lark . . . His was the art of sorrow, hers of joy.'

In 1890 Christabel had won a scholarship to Somerville College at Oxford, where she was to obtain a disappointing Class III degree in Modern History. In 1895, after leaving Oxford, to her great excitement she received an invitation to see Ellen in her dressing-room at the Lyceum before a performance of the pageant play *King Arthur*. It was a brave and difficult pilgrimage towards this sacred room. She had to pass by the terrible soldier who kept the gate, Henry Irving's glowering multi-medalled Irish commissionaire Sergeant Barry; and then keep up with Ellen Terry's dresser, the nimble Sally Holland, who vanished up a narrow staircase in front of her; and finally she must not be misled by Ellen Terry's dark-eyed double, attired in the green and gold dress of Queen Guinevere, who swept past her to take her place as a vision of the queen in *King Arthur*'s prologue.

Each test she passed drew her deeper into the strange world of the theatre: the illumination of its gas-lights, its internal architecture of dangling ropes and spreading canvas, its pervading smells of greasepaint and glue, and the never-ending commotion of its backstage life full of carpenters and call-boys. Then suddenly Christabel heard the sound of running water: a door opened and there, in an old grey flannel dressing-gown, vigorously washing her face at a hand-basin and drying it on a rough towel, stood Ellen Terry. She ushered the young girl in, sat down at the dressing-table and, while they were speaking, began gradually to transform herself before her admirer's eyes into the ethereal Guinevere.

Fifty years later Christabel would say that she remembered little of what Ellen said to her that day. But at the time she felt mortified. In her letters she had laid her dreams at Ellen Terry's feet, only to be treated, now that she finally met her, like a child. She stood awkwardly in a corner of the dressing-room, twisting her hands, incapable of expressing what she felt. And what she felt was her inescapable lack of beauty. She wanted Ellen Terry to remember her – for surely she had an original face. She was almost in tears when Ellen handed her some violets – they were the very violets Christabel had sent her the previous day. 'I sent you those,' she blurted out. Ellen casually remarked that she thought they came from a man. She did, however, praise the cleverness of her letters, adding a warning: 'Don't wear your heart upon your sleeve. The world is full of daws.' No doubt this was sensible advice, but it struck at the very core of Christabel's confidence. 'Neither that night nor at any time', she later wrote, 'did she understand me in the least.' Then, flicking her towel at the young girl with a laugh as she sat with her little pots and bottles of ointment and washes and powders, Ellen finished recomposing the illusion of youth, stood up and became that queen over whom Sir Lancelot and King Arthur would soon fight their great battle.

It was impossible not to reveal your heart at such a tragic tale of courtly love as was played that evening or, if you were possessed of a religious temperament as Christabel was, remain unaffected by the queen's final repentance and transfiguration into a nun. Irving had what Christabel called 'a greatness which forced his audiences to reverence and their knees', while in Ellen Terry's acting 'there was a touch of spirituality, of aloofness from the common ways of women . . . which appealed to the desire in every human being to look up and away from ordinary experience'.

Christabel lived alone in London. During the mornings she would work as a secretary for Lady Randolph Churchill and occasionally her son Winston. But she passed her afternoons in a very different world as she experimented in her two attic rooms at 21 Great College Street with a sensational Nietzschean novel. *The Crimson Weed*, as she called it, was a crowded tale of Gothic happenings beginning with illegitimacy, pursuing lurid plots of decadence and revenge, and culminating in madness. It was still a pleasure to see Ellen Terry onstage, but she realised this infatuation could lead nowhere. The great actress, it seemed, had done her some damage. Every time Christabel received a rebuff from someone, she would remember her humiliating visit as if it had left an invisible bruise on her.

She was often rebuffed. 'I have been face to face with terrible things', she confided to Gordon Woodhouse. One of the terrible things had been her sudden passion for a dark young harpsichordist, Violet Gwynne. 'At every turn I long for you', she wrote to her. '. . . I feel like a fire when you are by my side.' Unfortunately Violet was engaged to marry Gordon Woodhouse. But she commissioned Christabel to find out if her husband would be content with a *mariage blanc* (he would eventually settle for a *ménage-à-cinq*). 'I enter into your wonderful love for Violet', Christabel confided in him. 'Our brilliant little Violet' belonged to them both. She was their 'little child', a 'fantastic soul', so original, unselfconscious, unaccountable. 'I know you may have a difficult time when you are married', Christabel assured Gordon Woodhouse. 'But I believe you will be strong enough to face the perplexity of it . . .' And he, who had little interest in women, responded by inviting her to join them during their honeymoon. But after her marriage, Violet distanced herself from Christabel, turning her attentions to the novelist Radclyffe Hall and the composer Ethel Smyth. So their romantic attachment, which Christabel hoped would supplant her hopeless love of Ellen Terry, began to fade. Writing a music column in *The Lady*, she tried to revive their passion with eloquent passages on Violet's performances. But 'she doesn't trouble about me'.

Christabel was the daughter of a prolific children's writer and novelist called Emma Marshall. As Christabel Gertrude Marshall, she had been born at

38 High Street, Exeter, on 24 October 1871, the youngest of nine children (her closest sister being called Edith). Her mother belonged to a Quaker family and her father was the son of a clerk in holy orders. The couple had moved from one cathedral town to another following Hugh Marshall's position as a local bank manager. But when the West of England Bank went out of business, he was left severely in debt. It was then that Emma took up writing books, wearing herself out over the years to pay off what he owed, educate their children and give them all a home.

Emma Marshall, it was said, had abominated the theatre until in the early 1880s she was taken to see Henry Irving and Ellen Terry in *The Merchant of Venice*. 'I lost myself completely, which has always been my dream of what the power of acting should be', she confided in her diary. The event signalled 'a new era in my life'. But according to her daughter Christabel, it had merely been 'the fashion' to see these two famous actors perform in one of Shakespeare's plays, and her mother always 'wished to be in the fashion'.

Emma Marshall loved 'the sunshiny presence' of 'my dear little Christabel'. Such love conferred on her daughter a 'pretty face' that was hidden from others. She had been brought up in Gloucester and Bristol, but after she came to work in London, her mother referred to 'three misfortunes' that befell her there. One was a fire at Great College Street which destroyed her 'books and many treasures'. Another was a serious bicycling accident in which, among other injuries, she fractured her kneecap. 'It will be a long time before she can be her wonted active self again', Emma wrote. With her broken knee in stiff leather manacles, Christabel was obliged to return home (her sister 'Edith's happiness was delightful to see').

Then, early in 1896, Emma Marshall experienced 'one of the greatest and most sudden shocks of my life'. She received a telegram telling her that Christabel was lying unconscious in Westminster Hospital suffering from an overdose of phenacetin tablets. As with Laurence Irving's shooting, the story was given out that this had been a careless accident, Christabel being at the time 'in agony from toothache and neuralgia'. Her mother, who presented a bright face of optimism before all adversities, readily accepted this story. She described her daughter, who was still in hospital, as 'bright and blooming as ever' and praised God that 'all is now well with her'.

But all was not well. This attempted suicide began a pattern of emotional crises in Christabel's life. Following the failure of her romance with Violet

Gwynne, she had given up hope of finding a loved one and had taken the overdose not long after her first, much-desired meeting with Ellen Terry at the Lyceum. She was desperately lonely. Her mother loved her of course, but wanted to keep her and her sister Edith as children. 'I hear their merry voices', she wrote in her diary, 'and how I long for the touch of my *vanished* children's sweet clinging arms as every night I bent over their pillows!' Not one of her nine children was to give her a grandchild.

The stiff leather manacles which Christabel wore in her mid-twenties when, following her bicycling accident, she temporarily returned to live at home, became a symbol of the restrictions that her mother's conventional optimism imposed on her. Emma Marshall could accept a child's problems, but had to censor her knowledge of their adult lives. 'My children's sweet infancy came before me, and they were real children once more', she wrote in her diary: 'the young men and women were the phantoms'. One of Christabel's letters to her mother during the 1890s contained 'the worst news she had ever received. She turned white, and for a while it seemed as if the blow would completely shatter her'. But within an hour her 'inextinguishable' *joie de vivre* returned and with it her 'power of detachment from cares and worries'. The content of this letter is not revealed: but it seems to have been either a message that her daughter had been accepted into the Roman Catholic Church – or possibly a declaration of her lesbianism.

Then one night, after seeing Ellen's 'lovely incarnation of Shakespeare's Imogen', all Christabel's past feelings revived. She sent off a sonnet from the *Pall Mall Gazette* (a paper for which she did occasional proof-reading) and received an invitation to come and meet her once more, this time at the Grand Theatre, Fulham. Wearing a red coat and a wicked little black three-cornered hat, and feeling a curious vibrancy, Christabel bicycled through the dangerously crowded streets to the theatre where she was met by Edy and given 'a welcome I cannot truthfully describe as cordial'. Edy had been instructed to look after this girl who 'knew nothing' of the theatre, the sort of task her mother often assigned her. Nor did she recognise the girl from that brief moment when, as Ellen's double in *King Arthur*, she had passed her by in a corridor of the Lyceum. 'I had no premonition of a great change in my life', Christabel recalled. But a great change, as miraculous in its fashion as anything she was describing in her novel, was about to happen. Edy had been mending some of her mother's clothes and, shaking hands with this visitor, suddenly pricked her skin with a needle – a stab that hurt yet was desired. 'Cupid's dart', Christabel divined. 'For I loved Edy from that moment.'

After the play was over, Ellen invited Christabel to join them both for supper at Barkston Gardens. In the dining-room she grilled some kidneys over the fire, and the three of them sat up late talking and drinking coffee. For Christabel this was an extraordinary night. It was as if, at the magic stroke of midnight, she had been absorbed into this exhilarating family. But it was not Ellen who brought about this transformation. 'A thought persisted in my heart that I was disappointed in her,' Christabel confessed, 'although I kept it inactive with great assurances that I was not!' She noticed, not without a pang of pleasure, that Ellen was growing rather fat. Even her acting in *Olivia* was not quite 'so virginal' as she remembered it, having become 'a little fussy and over-elaborate'. Also she seemed to make such 'harlequin leaps in her conversation' that it 'required some mental agility to follow her. If you had anything to tell her, you had to be very patient, for she was as slow in grasping a point as she was quick in making one.' It occurred to Christabel that she need not have felt so mortified at their first meeting for she was actually cleverer herself. On the other hand Edy, though limited in her acting abilities, possessed a curious distinction. She was a sphinx. People who loved Ellen's open-hearted ways were mystified by Edy's guarded tone, her indolent expression. 'Although the mother had the warmer manner,' Christabel wrote, 'I divined in a few minutes that it was possible that the daughter had the warmer heart.' In those few minutes Edy's antagonism seemed to evaporate and she arranged to see Christabel next day for lunch. 'I liked you at once', she later told her. 'You didn't seem like a stranger.'

The two women saw each other regularly that summer, and Ellen seemed pleased that Edy's new friend fitted so well into their lives. That autumn, while preparing her tour of America, she helped settle them into a house together. Number 7 Smith Square in Westminster was 'a lovely specimen of Queen Anne domestic architecture, panelled throughout and fortunately in perfect condition', Christabel wrote. '. . . There was a charming little Dutch garden at the back. Fig-trees flourished against the high brick walls. We planted carnations in the bed in the middle . . .' Even with Ellen's financial help, they were living 'recklessly beyond our means', and soon took in lodgers to help pay their way. One of these, the actor and director Harcourt Williams, then in his young twenties, remembered a Twelfth Night party in those panelled rooms beginning with a pungent mulled ale drunk in his bedroom, then the making of a circle around the fire while W.B. Yeats told enthralling ghost stories, 'his raven black hair and pale bird-like features caught in the firelight'. The house was said to be haunted, but whether the ghost would ultimately reveal itself as beneficent or malignant, who could tell?

In the opinion of Radclyffe Hall's lover Una Troubridge, Christabel was 'an interesting and rather tragic figure'. She was said to be 'ugly as few are ugly, to deformity' and without charm or attraction to men – her friendships were always with women. In *The Crimson Weed*, published (with crimson flowers, designed by Gordon Craig, stamped on the front board and spine; also in black as a tailpiece) while she was living with Edy in Smith Square, the surrender to forbidden passion leads to sexual anguish and awful guilt. But if love possessed a spiritual dimension, then, Christabel believed, it could act as a spell as in the fairy story *Beauty and the Beast*. It might release her from deformity, banish guilt and enable her to be reborn through the devotion of another woman. Edy appeared in moments of intimacy to be Christabel's other self, her ideal being. 'We saw the visible world through the same eyes', she wrote.

'Unwieldy' was the word that Vita Sackville-West would choose to describe Christabel's frame; whereas Edy was seen by Christabel as having 'a lovely slender figure' and a carriage that was 'perfect in its grace' – it was a pleasure to watch her walk across a room or simply relax in a chair. Christabel had a speech impediment so extreme that some people thought it was due to a cleft palate; Edy's voice, enhanced by her slight lisp, was mellow, deep, resonant – it 'was always a delight to hear her talk'. Searching for an arresting phrase for Christabel, Virginia Woolf hit on the words 'mule-faced harridan'; Edy had a fine face with beautiful 'brown eyes set far apart' and a mouth (not her best feature) resembling Ellen's. Finally Edy was illegitimate but also, in Christabel's judgement, 'a saint' – which showed that irregular liaisons and unconventional family structures did not necessarily lead to hell.

To become closer to Edy, Christabel confided that she also was illegitimate – what she called 'a waif and stray'. After the death of both her

parents in 1899, she embarked on a parallel life of the imagination. For this 'new era', almost a rebirth, she reassembled her name, changing gender, moving away from her family, ascending from the menacing world of Coleridge's unfinished medieval poem 'Christabel' into a place of supernatural expectations. She retained the syllable Christ, acquired nominal sainthood with an attachment to the Baptist who had proclaimed Christ's coming, and added to herself the Holy Virgin Mother of God. When Ellen Terry went off to America, she had left her daughter living with Christabel Marshall. When she returned, Edy was co-habiting with Christopher Marie St John, though it was not until 1910, after a pilgrimage to Rome, that she legally acquired this name by deed poll.

In later years Vita Sackville-West was to describe Edy as 'a tearing old Lesbian'. But at the beginning of the century she wore a prim virginal air, as if stationed in a no-man's, no-woman's, land of unrealised bisexuality. Outwardly the two women had a sensible working partnership, Christopher becoming a translator, adapter and writer of plays, a dramatic critic, one of Ellen Terry's early biographers and editor of her correspondence with Bernard Shaw. Their friends nicknamed her and Edy 'the Squares', which might be innocently taken as referring to their house in Smith Square, but which also indicated the fact they did not easily fit into the social round of late Victorian and Edwardian life.

At first Ellen was grateful that Christopher was helping to bring stability to her daughter's life. Homosexuality had been made a criminal offence in 1885, but the offence excluded female relationships partly because sexual attraction between women, which lay outside many people's knowledge, did not stir the moral revulsion that had risen following Oscar Wilde's conviction. Christopher admired Wilde. In *The Crimson Weed*, disguising her own lesbian feelings, she exploited the decadent attractions of men for each other, using surnames – Luke Gray, Richard Savile – that would have been familiar to readers of Wilde's writings.

None of this seemed to trouble Ellen. She was not ignorant of the emotional ties among women, but she was incurious about people's sexual habits and had, as Christopher noticed, 'a mind that was clean, innocent, and almost childlike in its simplicity . . . she simply could not see the point of a subtly improper story, or else she ignored it deliberately'. To some extent Christopher admired Ellen's propriety of speech; to some extent she pitied her. For a woman to be so ignorant of the undercurrents of sexual knowledge was surely a serious deficit. Perhaps this language of innuendo belonged to a later and more knowing generation of women. In any event, Ellen had been happy enough to leave 'Chris and Edy' together while she went abroad with Irving. But then she began to have doubts. To her son, who had an aversion to 'mannish women', she wrote: 'She [Edy] wants *better* people around her – she likes to roam – & she *should* – but to the right spot – to the right people . . . It must be the Theatre for her I suppose? Else I'd contrive she shd roam . . . far away from her inferiors – & yet Ted my dear "old boy" by pushing, she might light on worse things.' Certainly pushing had never been of much use to Ted.

On his return from America in the spring of 1902, Irving had decided to open his last season at the Lyceum with *Faust.* For Ellen's role as Marguerite he engaged a pretty music-hall performer, Cissie Loftus, twenty years younger than Ellen and said by *The Times* to come 'nearer to the magic charm and sunny vitality of Ellen Terry than any other actress of her time'. Feeling depressed, Ellen insisted that Edy come back home to cheer her up. But she wanted this 'because I have gone away', Edy reassured Christopher. 'When I lived at home I hardly ever saw her – partly because she was never there, and partly because she can never bear to be with any one for long at a time.' Besides, Edy explained, 'no one can look after my mother'. It was a prophetic statement.

Once Ellen was persuaded that Christopher would readily step aside, she no longer insisted on her daughter's return. Suddenly Christopher found herself treated almost 'as a son-in-law might have been treated'. They discussed Edy's health, Edy's talents, Edy's looks, Edy's clothes . . . 'I became the willing slave of both mother and daughter', she wrote. 'My life became most intimately bound up with theirs.'

That spring and summer season of 1902, before their final presentation of *The Merchant of Venice*, Ellen had only one other character to play at the Lyceum: Henrietta Maria in Wills's *Charles I.* Returning from playing

Queen Katharine with Frank Benson's company in a single performance of *Henry VIII* for Shakespeare's birthday celebrations at Stratford-upon-Avon, she suddenly felt rejuvenated, and asked Irving whether he would release her that summer to take the role of Mistress Page in Beerbohm Tree's production of *The Merry Wives of Windsor*. Irving had little choice but to agree, providing she continued playing Portia and Henrietta Maria at the Lyceum's matinées.

Theatre-goers that June were surprised to see Ellen Terry's name on the bills of both the Lyceum and His Majesty's Theatre. Some were to accuse her of disloyalty to Irving – particularly since Tree was regarded as his chief Shakespearean rival. As Irving's grandson was to write: 'Tree's hunger for the throne that Irving occupied was well-known; this apparent capture of his Queen seemed to herald the deposition of the reigning monarch.'

Tree was a romantic comedian, a joker with a permanently youthful appetite for theatrical extravagance. It was characteristic of him to have chosen this rough-and-tumble farce to celebrate the coronation of Edward VII. He did not dominate the theatre, even as an antlered Falstaff, with the mesmerising power of Irving, and sometimes risked being acted off his own stage through his habit of employing the very best actors he could find. The cast he found for *The Merry Wives of Windsor* contained no passengers: 'all rowed in the boat with precisely the right swing', Ellen remembered.

'Heaven give you many, many merry days and nights', Irving telegraphed her on the first night, and heaven was to grant this wish. *The Merry Wives of Windsor* ran for 156 performances and it seemed to Ellen that she had never acted in a more enjoyable comedy. In Gordon Craig's opinion, 'it was the best work of her career'. The sheer fun of Tree's production came as a relief from the doomed atmosphere that had filled the Lyceum. Ellen was fifty-five, Madge Kendal who played Mistress Ford fifty-three and Tree himself in his fiftieth year, 'but they romped through the play like children', wrote Tree's biographer Hesketh Pearson. Tree's wife Maud described her husband as standing 'between two ancient lights'. But they shone, these lights, with ageless brilliance. According to John Gielgud, Madge Kendal and Ellen Terry were implacable enemies, and it was this enmity that stimulated their 'extraordinary love-hate jinks when they played with Tree'.

Edy designed a costume that 'helped me enormously to be a real merry wife', Ellen wrote. In her diary, she noted: 'Edy has real genius for dresses for the stage'. After Ellen's dress was burnt at the theatre, Edy made her another 'more wonderful still' in a single day.

When Ellen agreed to go with Irving on a twelve-week tour that autumn, she knew that he was seriously ill. But acting was the only medicine that could restore him – without the theatre he might as well be dead. The accidents and illnesses of these last few years had made him an old man. 'But he did not give in. One night when his cough was rending him,' Ellen remembered, 'and he could hardly stand up from weakness, he acted so brilliantly and powerfully that it was easy to believe in the triumph of mind over matter.' But how long could this last? His feebleness sometimes frightened her, but 'his belief in himself is amazing', she told Stephen Coleridge, '– & splendid I think'.

While travelling together they spoke of the future. Irving had commissioned Sardou to write a new play for him about Dante. But hearing its sombre thirteen scenes read aloud in Laurence's translation, Ellen saw 'no possible part for me in it' – though she told Irving that Gordon Craig would produce it splendidly. 'Ah well that might be very good,' Irving answered politely. 'We'll see about it.' But he never did see about it.

38

A Sea of Troubles: *Helgeland* and *Hungerheart*

Before he found Martin Shaw, Gordon Craig had not, in his friend's reckoning, 'found himself'. It was the concerts Martin took him to and his own piano-playing that called forth his imaginative powers. As Martin played, Craig would sometimes cover the walls with images. The loyalty and enthusiasm of the singers, especially the chorus, in the Purcell Operatic Society – all unpaid amateurs employed because they could sing in tune and were willing to dance onstage – filled him with an enchanting confidence. Rising to each challenge he set them, unrestricted by professional pride, they were Gordon Craig's new model army, ready to follow him anywhere, do whatever he desired. Together they would do such things . . .

First he would produce Handel's *Acis and Galatea*. 'We both realised pretty soon that if a production was to be achieved we should have to concentrate on it to the exclusion of everything else', Martin Shaw remembered; 'so Craig joined me in my rooms in Finchley Road, Hampstead, and soon after that in [8] Downshire Hill.' They shared the rent which was cheap because, though 'the good old house [was] much admired – even the bailiffs liked it', as Gordon Craig explained, the building itself was in a terrible condition. From the summer of 1900 until late the following year he occupied the two lower floors, and Martin Shaw lived above him.

It was as if he had escaped the worries of London and was free. London might lie close to Hampstead, beat down on it from many directions, but the bustle of the West End was far away and the great heath, like a piece of ancient countryside with woods and meadows, hills and valleys, preserved its identity as a leafy village. On Downshire Hill stood a little church, and not far off there was the famous White Stone Pond where Shelley had sailed his boat, and in the houses lived philosophers and poets, artists and musicians.

They set to work preparing *Acis and Galatea* and all was well. But then Martin Shaw went off to visit his family in the country. Left alone, Craig grew painfully depressed. His guilt over abandoning Jess, kept vividly alive by his mother's letters, gave rise to paranoid delusions. Was she laying plots against him? Jess had threatened to 'arise in my wrath' if he ever forgot 'you are mine' and tried 'to make me vanish from your life'. She knew by now that 'men will have what they want' and realised that Craig was seeing someone else. 'I confess to feeling great contempt for the lady', she declared. So he began to suspect that the girls who came to his door asking to join the Purcell Operatic Society might well be her spies – a sinister company of women who meant the opposite of everything they said and were determined to destroy him. Only great men such as Henry Irving and Martin Shaw had the power to simplify life. Women confused it all. They must have no place in his theatre. 'No women in it boy,' he wrote to Martin Shaw. 'Only comrades!'

Desperate to escape, he persuaded Edy's friend, the Baroness 'Jimmy' Overbeck, to disguise herself as a boy and travel with him to France for an 'adventure – no lovemaking – sheer fun'. Speaking no French and meeting French people who spoke no English, he was cut off from human contact and felt purified. 'I am as a virgin in the land', he told Martin Shaw, 'and the land a vestal to me.' But as soon as he left this make-believe world and returned to England, he lost his way again. He was assailed by disturbing dreams of his father. 'Although I had never seen him whilst he lived I fancied in my dream that his face was as familiar to me as Mother's – But it was terribly sad', he wrote. 'We sat on boxes that floated on a calm sea.'

> At times he would rise from a sitting position and standing on his floating box would pour out a torrent of praise and love addressed to his lost lady, my mother . . . All the time his eyes would rain tears which ran down into the salt water and spread round him in rings of crimson, purple and black . . . and from the three circles of colour came thousands of voices all like drowned voices – a mixture of sobbing and laughter flung up from the deep.
>
> All the time I remained wonderstruck and a feeling of deep sorrow took hold of me.

He had lost hope of changing the sadness and tears, which were his inheritance, into beauty and delight, which were his quest. In a notebook he began keeping during this difficult time, he wrote: 'I shall be dead if I do not discover myself in the next three or four years.'

Then Martin Shaw returned, they resumed work on *Acis and Galatea* and Gordon Craig was himself again. This marked the beginning of an intensely active period in his life. All manner of original ideas for the production crowded in on him: how to use lengths of upholsterer's webbing and tape to convey the illusion of a transparent tent; how to suggest the haunting presence in a dark wood of the giant Polyphemus by cleverly adjusting the shadows that shone on a vast screen; and finally how to show Acis transformed into a fountain by employing an old pantomime trick – piercing the backcloth and revolving perforated discs before lamps concealed behind it so that spots of light continually moved as in a cascade of water.

They invested £300 in this new venture, and though their production of *Acis and Galatea* would not be expensive (there was no scenery in the ordinary sense), they needed money to pay all manner of bills from printers to wig-makers – not forgetting the rent of the theatre itself. But Gordon Craig's appeal for more financial help from his mother provoked a bitter reply.

> I have been paying your 'old bills' these ten years . . . you will be disgraced publicly by having the whole thing stopped by your creditors – meanwhile you are running up bills every day by speculating in a theatrical enterprise with *no means* – Do you call this anything but dishonest? . . . My patience is fast going.

A few months earlier, when he was suffering delusions of persecution, he might have seen this letter as proof of a female plot against him. But by now everything had changed and he exultantly described himself as 'the richest man alive!!!' In his memoirs he would announce the significance to him of the new century: 'It was in 1900 I first met Elena Meo.' It seemed as if he could not delay writing down her name, though they did not actually meet until September that year when, in his diary, using capital letters, he inscribed one word: 'ELENA'.

She was one of the daughters of Gaetano Meo, a landscape painter and mosaic artist, the friend of Rossetti and Burne-Jones, who lived down the road at 39 Downshire Hill. Martin Shaw knew the family because he sometimes accompanied Elena, who was a virtuoso violinist, at the piano. One September afternoon she ran up the hill and knocked at the door of number 8. But Martin Shaw was out and the door was opened by Craig.

They stood in the doorway 'very long . . . neither saying a word'. Then she came into the house and soon they were 'laughing like children' and talking excitedly about music. 'She has black hair – magnificent black eyes – a deep voice – noble brow and clear cut nose', he wrote in one of his confessional notebooks, and went on listing her aesthetic virtues: 'firm and good lips – strong and kind chin – clear white skin – and the manner of her ancestors – the grand and simple manner of the dead times – nobility and courage in every gesture – and generosity spread over all . . . This is a woman for whom kings might die, and to whom gods shall bow – I would live for her.'

Next day Elena called again, ostensibly to see Martin Shaw. And then, passing the house a day or two later, she saw in the window an enormous picture of a teapot with a question mark against it. So in she went and had tea with Craig. In his memoirs, he questioned whether 'all young men of twenty-seven' were as 'unaware of the difference between "love", attraction, liking, passion and LOVE' as he had been. In the past he had been attracted to May, felt passion for Jess, and liked plenty of other girls. But now he knew the difference.

Over tea at this, their third meeting, they discussed everything openly: the marvel of what had happened and the difficulties that lay before them. He would not be able to visit her at home because her father would not let him into the house. The 'grand and simple manner of the dead times' that he so admired was imprinted on all the family. They were strict Roman Catholics and would not tolerate Elena courting, let alone marrying, someone outside the faith. Though she was now almost twenty-three years old and could by law do what she wished, there was a higher law she had been taught to obey. Brought up in a convent school, she had contemplated becoming a nun before her musical talent carried her into another world. So all they could do for the time being was to write to each other and arrange clandestine meetings, sometimes chaperoned by Martin Shaw.

But he was less frank with her than she with him. Not wishing to pile extra obstacles in the way of their romance, he failed to tell her that he was married, had four legitimate children and one illegitimate daughter – all of which she learnt by accident one day from Martin Shaw. That he was looking forward to a divorce scarcely mattered. Only an annulment would clear the way and that was impossible. Yet she still believed that this man was the love of her life. What then should she do?

What she did, early in 1902, was to return to her convent school in Sussex where she could make up her mind in peace. They wrote to each other almost every day of the two months she stayed there. For Craig this was an agonising time. 'She has brought me new life new love new trust, and a *belief*', he wrote in one of his notebooks. Could all this suddenly disappear?

The decision Elena had to make was painful and perplexing. She 'believed in her Church like an Italian peasant', her son was to write, and she knew that, if she were to live in sin with Gordon Craig, she would 'suffer terrible punishment in her after-life'. Yet if she continued seeing him sexual intercourse between them would be inevitable. Could she banish him from her life? That seemed to go against nature itself.

On 10 March 1902 *Acis and Galatea* opened at the unfamiliar Great Queen Street Theatre. Martin Shaw had rented it cheaply from the owner, a charming singer and actor, W.S. Penley, who had become rich through creating the leading role in the phenomenally popular transvestite farce, *Charley's Aunt*. Graham Robertson described Gordon Craig's production as 'beautiful and imaginative'. He was spellbound by the vision of a dream-seller in the opening scene – 'a fantastic, childish figure' who, in the glaring heat of the summer meadows, wandered among the drowsy nymphs and shepherds, 'bearing many-coloured balls which hung suspended from a hoop, held high above her head. And to each dreamer she gave her wares, purple and green and red and blue – little bright dreams to be had for the asking . . .'

It seems possible that this childlike presenter of dreams was inspired by Elena Meo. She arrived back in London three days after the opening of the opera and met Gordon Craig secretly in Keats Grove. She told him that she had made up her mind: she would elope with him, live with him, have his children and love him for the rest of her life. That night, Martin Shaw came home to find a note from Craig telling him that he and Elena had run off together. During the spring, as they travelled the country, Shaw would receive notes from various stopping-places, asking him to pawn some of his friend's possessions and send him the money.

Why was Elena Meo's love preferable to Jess Dorynne's? Perhaps because Craig had taken the place of God in Elena's life and their relationship seemed divinely inspired. Her love was unqualified, forgiving and as continuous as a fast-flowing river. She uses the same words, the same sentences again and again over the years. All her letters are one letter.

How I do love you my sweetest, my dearest heart . . . sometimes you look at me & look so sad. You know I *love* you, adore you, worship you . . . do always love me – if you were to stop *I could not exist.* You know how to treat a woman properly . . . if anything goes wrong in *your* case it is the woman's fault pet. People are always too ready to blame the man & I won't have you my pet to be the one blamed. You are in my eyes *perfect.* When I get so frantically jealous it is not because I don't trust you but only because I love you so much. You will never love anyone else, will you pet? . . . You are my all, my heart, soul & my life . . .

It was almost as if he were playing back his father's elopement with Ellen – the similarity of Elena's name could not have failed to strike him and he often called her Nell and sometimes Nellie. But she was not like a mother to him, not yet, more like another kind of sister, a child who enabled him to regain his own childhood – reinvent it as a happier time. She was the single Nell who could grant him his dreams, someone to whom he acknowledged an obligation and owed his inspiration. 'By all that I love and honour I will raise myself up to her', he promised.

At the beginning of the summer they returned from their wanderings to what was now hostile territory. Gaetano Meo had disowned his daughter and was eager to kill the man who had 'stolen' her. Since 8 Downshire Hill was encircled by bailiffs, Gordon Craig struck camp, migrated to Kensington and then moved quickly on to Chelsea, very close at Trafalgar Studios in Manresa Road to his mother's new home in the King's Road.

And what of *Acis and Galatea*? Had it been a success? Gordon Craig believed it was 'as good as we could make it'. Writing in the *Saturday Review*, Max Beerbohm praised it as a pure success, untainted by commerce. It had come off after only six nights either because, Craig suggested, no one could find the theatre or else because those who did find it expected to see *Charley's Aunt* there. As to the profits from these six nights, Martin Shaw seemed vague, deducing from the fact that the broker's men were in the theatre on the last night searching the bags of the singers to make sure they made off with nothing valuable, that there was less profit than loss. But what an adventure it had been! So, 'in a blaze of glory', the Purcell Operatic Society expired.

In his new studio, with Elena Meo and Martin Shaw at his side, and Ellen Terry so near, Craig felt well placed to make a brilliant advance. Graham Robertson predicted that by making the Sister Arts of Music, Painting and Pantomime 'cast away their jealousies', he would 'create anew a Forgotten Art – the Art of the Theatre'.

But such was his debt-ridden reputation that no theatre would risk employing him. Ellen Terry procured him the job of designing three scenes for her brother Fred Terry's production of *Sword and Song* at the Shaftesbury Theatre, but the most interesting work he did over the rest of the year was to design and produce Laurence Housman's nativity play *Bethlehem*. For this he drew some sixty costumes which his sister Edy made in her Covent Garden atelier, departing from the traditional nativity scenes, borrowing images from Rembrandt ('a born dramatist') and adding to the solemn procession of the Magi a following of beggars, cripples, musicians and a murderer. He also used a few sheep-hurdles, sacks, some crystals and an indigo backcloth to reveal the shepherds under a starry night gathered in a pool of light among the shapes and shadows of their flock. Because the play depicted the Holy Family, it was refused a licence by the Lord Chamberlain and, being performed privately in the Great Hall of the Imperial Institute, was seen by few critics – one exception being Christopher St John who reviewed it favourably in *The Critic*. W.B. Yeats also came to see it and, taken backstage by Edy, wrote to Lady Gregory: 'I have learned a great deal about the staging of plays from "the Nativity".' Laurence Housman himself described it as 'a very beautiful production'. But 'it was not the play, or the music, which had been given him to produce', he wrote. 'Disembowelled, decapitated, dismembered, he shaped its broken fragments into a new identity of its own. The whole of the chief speaking-part was cut out, and replaced by a gesture, of the music only fragments remained . . . with my financial losses about twice what I had reckoned they might be, I crept out of the venture with an accompanying loss of temper.'

It was not surprising that West End managers were wary of Gordon Craig. Beerbohm Tree was now their favourite actor-manager – a 'charming fellow', Craig conceded. 'I could murder him with great pleasure.' He and Sir George Alexander and Sir Johnston Forbes-Robertson and Sir Frank Benson and Sir John Martin-Harvey and Sir Gerald du Maurier, all to be knights of their little kingdoms, prevailed over the long confusion of the British theatre during the early twentieth century with their poor imitations of Sir Henry Irving – 'a craven lot these white mice'. That at any rate was how it appeared to Craig. 'What a lot of harm they did do', he wrote.

Despite her success in *The Merry Wives of Windsor*, Ellen received no new offers of work. Like her son she was unemployed. But unlike him she had money in the bank (he had taken his fee for designing *Bethlehem* in florins and flung them high into the air, scattering them among the singers). Now at last Ellen decided to risk a financial experiment with the new drama. She had gone through the copyright-reading of Shaw's *Captain Brassbound's Conversion* with the Lyceum Company at the Court Theatre in Liverpool as early as 1899. 'H[enry] I[rving] never came near the place! Horrid of him.' The reading had not gone well. 'It's because I read it wrong', she apologised to Shaw. Somehow she had made the character of Lady Cicely Waynflete, described in the stage directions as 'tender and humorous', appear a tremendous moral humbug. Edy had explained all this to her. She 'says I could not read the lines other than I did', Ellen reported, 'but that it seemed to her you thought your Lady C. *one* sort of woman and have *written* another'. In her fashion Edy was telling her mother that Shaw did not understand her. Yet when Ellen read the play again to herself, she began to see its possibilities – even the germ of romance that lay within it. 'I love the whole thing and I am certain I could do it . . . I and H. would have been *perfect* in it', she lamented, overlooking the way in which Shaw had made Irving's character, in a Shavian reversal of their Lyceum roles, offer to 'take service' under Ellen.

For more than five years she and Shaw had been corresponding, but still they had not met. They feared to 'break the spell' which their written words created. For only on paper could such abiding love be achieved and no one hurt. In life itself there was always a day of reckoning. What would have happened had they met? She '*might* have thrown my arms round your neck and hugged you! I might have been struck shy', she speculated. And, though he loved her 'soulfully and bodyfully, properly and improperly, every way that a woman can be loved' in his letters, might he not have 'found me such an old thing, and so different from the Ellen you've seen onstage'?

Sometimes they wavered and Ellen longed 'just to touch you, to put my hand on your arm'. Shaw also wondered whether they had been mad not to meet each other: 'Don't let us break the spell, *do* let us break the spell, don't, do, don't, do, don't, do, don't . . .' But they didn't and the spell held.

Then on 16 December 1900, passing under the stage at the Strand Theatre on her way to Laurence Irving's dressing-room, Ellen met Shaw and they spoke to each other. And suddenly the spell was broken – at any rate they did not appear to correspond again for almost a year and a half. What they actually said no one heard. But some cruel gossip about what Shaw was supposed to have felt soon reached Ellen. 'They say you could not bear me, when we met, that one time, under the stage', she wrote to him two years after their meeting. '. . . you can't abide me! And no wonder! Can I ever abide myself!'

To this letter no answer was printed in the published volume of the Ellen Terry and Bernard Shaw correspondence, no explanation offered in the notes supplied by the editor Christopher St John. In her book *Bernard Shaw and the Actresses*, Margot Peters has suggested that Edy Craig herself was the messenger of scandal: Edy, who had watched this long epistolary affair with such a guarded eye, used Shaw's play to separate actress and playwright, destroyed a number of her mother's letters, and continued to police Ellen's relationships with men as fiercely as Ellen policed hers. Edy was 'a devil' Ellen conceded, and in a letter not included in their published correspondence, she warned Shaw that her daughter's gossip needed to be taken with some salt.

'I don't want to take the risk of a theatre on my shoulders', Ellen told Shaw at the end of 1902. '. . . I have saved for my old age, and in spite of my children pressing me to risk it, I cannot.' Then, at the beginning of 1903, with one of those swift changes of mind that had once so delighted Henry Irving, she took a short lease on the Imperial Theatre, a beautiful white elephant of a building created specially for Lillie Langtry, and went into management there. 'I'll venture some, but not *all* my pennies', she wrote. '. . . I'd like to include Brassbound in my list of plays, but at present I am hidebound. I can't move.'

She was made hidebound by her children, knowing that Edy did not approve of Shaw's play and that Ted positively disliked him. She dreamed of transforming the Imperial Theatre into an omnium gatherum for her extended family – Ted and his friend Martin Shaw and Edy and Chris and herself. There were no investors besides Ellen herself.

However unorthodox Chris and Edy's relationship might be it was still Ted who kept her awake at night with worry. He was so 'unwise and intractable'. It was a tragedy that he had removed himself from the discipline of the Lyceum, and come to wallow in a never-never land of theories. 'Anything better than theorize', Ellen thought. 'Talk – & not *do* – It's bad in a woman but terrible in a man.'

She had liked Jess Dorynne and understood the integrity of her love for Ted. That was why, when he left Jess and their daughter Kitty ('so pretty & *extraordinarily clever*'), Ellen had let forth a tirade of agonised maternal reproach on behalf of both women – both of them actresses, both mothers. 'We are two devoted women who long to be friends & show our friendship to you . . . [but] *nothing we do seems to have the slightest effect upon you* . . . You are all heart of my heart – breath of my body – *Mother*.'

It was untrue that this letter produced not 'the slightest effect' upon Ted. It tortured him, as he tortured her. But what could he do now that he had met Elena who, early in 1903, gave birth to their first child, a daughter said to resemble Ellen and named after her? (The characters in these families have names and variations of names, as abundant and confusing as any in Shakespeare's comedies.) Elena and Ted would walk through Hyde Park and up the Mall together as far as the Duke of York's Steps, and then at other times through fields of standing corn near Dunmow in Essex (near where their daughter was born), he 'full of a lot of feelings I can't express', watching her and making notes about the light, the rhythm of her walking or running up the steps, or simply standing among the waves of corn that moved around her like great armies, and the patterns made by groups of children who came up to speak to her.

For the best part of ten years Ellen had been negotiating with her son over women and the theatre. 'You have heaps of ability, & with a determination to *govern yourself a little*, to deny yourself *a little*, to use the present usefully instead of philandering, all will be well *I am certain* in a few years', she had written to him. 'Your desire for *instant* recognition is foolish – nobody gets anything *worth having* in a hurry . . . all the suffering is caused by our own faults.' She had rescued him from financial disaster (spending over £5,000 paying his debts) but achieved little else. 'You have fooled away your character so much in the theatre I almost fear you'll have a hard struggle to get in again', she warned him. 'I should have helped you do bigger things.'

Ted had been asking her to collaborate with him in the theatre. Their coming together at the Coronet Theatre had been a success. But he needed something more substantial and long-lasting. 'I fear it wd be quite impossible', Ellen told him because until 1902 her plans 'hang on the plans Henry [Irving] makes'. By the time she and Irving parted there was another difficulty. She was in her fifty-sixth year and 'to work at all under the very easiest circumstances is, at times, a tremendous effort now-a-days for me'. But he persisted and her refusals grew more desperate. 'I shd not feel at all inclined to be entirely in the hands of my dear old rash & inexperienced-in-business boy . . . I fear we cd not work together I am not at the *beginning of it at all*, and wd much rather furnish the where-withal, & turn you loose to run amock by yourself than topple down with you . . . If I am of no help to you it is my great misfortune . . . What can I do that I have not done?'

She had been in the United States when *Acis and Galatea* was produced but, hearing good reports of it, she suddenly decided to take 'a jump in the dark' and work with both her children.

Ted had told her that he was thinking of producing Ibsen's early operatic tragedy *The Vikings at Helgeland*, which had never been performed in Britain – and she agreed to stage it at the Imperial Theatre, employing Edy and her friends to make the costumes. They were to use William Archer's translation of the play – Gordon Craig, Ellen assured Archer, was 'an admirable worker – molten enthusiasm fills his every cranny' – and certainly he worked hard reducing Archer's script. As for Ellen herself, she was 'going at this business like a bull at a gate . . . it will be a great success'. Archer sent her his translation act by act and she was appalled by what she read. 'All Ibsen's women talk at *such frightful length*.' She was determined, however, to see it through. 'Anything is better than wobbling.' Archer himself felt dismayed by her reaction. 'Poor old thing,' he wrote to Elizabeth Robins, 'what *can* she do except make a hash of it.'

Henry Irving, too, who was then preparing to take his new Sardou play, *Dante*, to the United States, knew that Ellen's theatre management spelt disaster. 'It will be strange and rather sad without Nell', he wrote to William

Winter. '. . . Poor dear, she has been absolutely under the influence and spell of her two children – who have launched her on a sea of troubles.' Even Ibsen's champion, Bernard Shaw, would describe their production of *The Vikings at Helgeland* as 'a most unnecessary maternal extravagance'. And Gordon Craig himself eventually decided it was 'a bad choice'. In *Ellen Terry and her Secret Self*, published after his mother's death, he wrote: 'She agreed to it because her son wanted it – which is no good reason at all.'

And yet if Ellen could show the world that her son was a practical man of the theatre and have Edy as an essential part of his success, she would unite her family and keep them close to her. As for Gordon Craig, he believed that within two or three years it might lead to their establishing 'a permanent Theatre in London of value to the dramatic art and profitable to our family as well'.

Red are the rocks
White is the sand
Blue are the waters
Of Helgeland.

Everyone liked to cast Ellen Terry as part of his or her private world. For Lewis Carroll she had been an eternally adventurous child; and for Christopher St John a goddess. Henry Irving cast her as the new Lady Macbeth who transmuted power into love; Bernard Shaw refashioned her as an ideal Shavian heroine who prevailed through beneficent strength of character; Henry James gave her the character of a protagonist from the historical world of his imagination in his play *Summersoft* ('it's delightful', Ellen told Ted*); and James Barrie was beginning a play for her as a sentimental mother scandalously misjudged by her daughter. This tendency was to be passed on to her biographers for whom she became a paragon of the theatre, a feminist icon, a queen of romance. But in *The Vikings at Helgeland*, Gordon Craig wanted her to play 'a wicked woman's part'. The fierce warrior wife, Hiordis, denounces her weak son as a bastard, murders her husband and then drowns herself. This was 'a grievous spectacle' for her admirers to behold. Ellen was to be a more violent mother than Volumnia and, in her own words, like '3 Lady Macbeths'. Surely, she protested,

* Though when Ellen failed to stage the play she became, in uncharacteristically direct Jamesian language, 'a toothless chattering hag'.

'nobody would believe in me in such a part'. But her son was exhibiting to the public an Ellen Terry it did not know: the dominating mother who had overwhelmed both his and Edy's lives.

Ellen thought she saw a way of presenting the 'primitive, fighting, free, open-air' Hiordis more brilliantly than William Archer's weighty translation suggested. Helped by Martin Shaw's incidental music, she transformed herself into what Max Beerbohm called a 'genial Britannia'. She also made preparations for failure, asking Ted to prepare a production of *Much Ado About Nothing* using existing scenery and dresses, but giving it special lighting and adding a dance 'in which I dance too, during the scene with Benedick, & all going very merrily & then if "The Vikings" doesn't go, pop it on, as if we meant to all the time'. This he did.

At the Imperial everyone's strengths revealed everyone else's shortcomings. Compared with Edy's professionalism, Gordon Craig seemed amateurish; but measured against his imaginative vision, her work appeared limited. Ellen was used to having Irving as a commander-in-chief. At the Imperial, she was nominally in command herself, but her management was 'rudderless'. According to her son, she employed the wrong business manager, several inadequate actors and at least one hideous obstructionist – and failed to sack any of them. 'I gave my son a free hand', Ellen declared in her memoirs. But this was not what Gordon Craig understood he had been given. During rehearsals his mother behaved 'like an overanxious & kind prompter giving one the word when one hasn't forgotten it but is merely making a carefully considered pause'. He had been used to working with Martin Shaw who never criticised him and was 'a good sportsman'. Beset by worries, Ellen muddled everyone and listened to all sorts of ill-disposed whispers until her son lost his affection for the work.

Some of the actors complained that Gordon Craig had introduced obstacles which made acting almost impossible: for example, the strange Irish costumes they were obliged to wear ('no one can act in it', wrote Ellen of Sigurd's elaborate cloak). Then there were the bolts of light blinding them and making their faces invisible to the audience. And what of the massive, sharply angled rock structure which was wheeled on to the stage for the fight – how could they duel over it without falling off? (The solution was to employ the slow movements of samurai fighting with great flashes of their enormous swords.)

Despite these difficulties, the production marked a significant step in Gordon Craig's career. The sets were extraordinarily original and compelling, 'turning the stage', Theodore Watts-Dunton wrote, 'into a poem'. The American critic James Huneker praised the bizarre effects Gordon Craig used to escape 'the deadly monotony of London stage problems' – effects such as the sinister glow and mysterious shadows which gave 'purplish tones to the stony faces of the players' and conveyed an atmosphere of dread. He introduced a strange, supernatural element into every scene.

But difficulties flourished backstage. The actors felt reduced to stage props, mere items of scenery, and the atmosphere grew thick with ill-feeling and subversion. 'We will lose all unity', Gordon Craig warned, '. . . & so over goes the apple cart.'

Henry Irving had offered Ellen £12,000 to go with him to the United States with *Dante* – and now it looked as if she might lose a similar sum with *The Vikings at Helgeland.* The play opened on 15 April 1903 and after a couple of weeks the audiences were so thin that she decided to bring on *Much Ado About Nothing.* 'I never did believe quite in *The Vikings* although it has been a great artistic success, & a most honourable venture', she wrote somewhat defensively to Stephen Coleridge, '. . . a good company – nicely and picturesquely produced by Ted – *very cheaply.*' Early in May she closed the theatre for a fortnight while the company rehearsed *Much Ado.* 'It wd mean ruin to me if this Play don't succeed', she wrote.

Martin Shaw again wrote the incidental music and Gordon Craig created a great impression with the symbolist church scene. His father, he had been told, 'made a sensation' designing this scene for Henry Irving's production. He himself did not attempt to make an accurate recreation of the streets, houses and gardens, the prison and the church interior at Messina. 'That sort of labour was beginning to strike some of us in the theatre as rather ridiculous.' He created a simplified impression with curtains gathered like columns, and a raised platform on which, like an altar, were crowded giant candlesticks – a spectacle that dwarfed the actors. 'As usual Ted had the best of it', Bernard Shaw acknowledged in a letter to Ellen, '– I have never seen the church scene go before – didn't know it *could* go, in fact.'

But Shakespeare, Christopher St John noted, 'was no more popular' than Ibsen at the Imperial. It was agonising for Gordon Craig to watch the actors striving to make the comedy go down better with the public, adding more noise and 'a viler gaiety' to it. 'I cannot tell you how painful the operation is,' he told Martin Shaw. '. . . This is Hell – I know nothing more tormenting.'

Like shipwrecked sailors the company looked around frantically, each one blaming someone else for the failure. In *Ellen Terry and her Secret Self*, Gordon Craig focused his hostility on one of Edy's friends. He did not reveal her identity, but in quoting a slightly mocking letter by his mother he let slip that her first name began with the letter C and that she became a militant suffragette. There can be no doubt that he was referring to Christopher St John, who had joined Ellen Terry's company at the Imperial and would later heckle Cabinet ministers, chalk 'Votes for Women' on pavements, and during one suffrage demonstration, be arrested, it was said, for seizing the bridle of a police horse.

'I looked forward to the collaboration with my costumière sister', Gordon Craig recalled. 'I thought that when she and my mother and myself got to work, we would be able to defy all the intrigue of the theatre . . . But this obstructionist in the costume department had the devil in her, and managed so to upset Ellen Terry and to play people one against the other, that our fortunes and the fortunes of the Imperial venture began to look dark at once.'

This intrigue was not a matter of aesthetics. It was the warfare of gender politics. 'She saw women as angels', Gordon Craig claimed. '. . . She saw men as demons.' And the principal demon was Martin Shaw, who had astonished everyone by falling in love with Edy and proposing marriage to her.

In 1915 Christopher St John was to publish a *roman à clef* called *Hungerheart* in which she presents her version of events with a frankness that would have been impossible in a work of non-fiction. The early chapters on 'Infancy', 'Growth' and 'Juvenescence' teem with fanciful speculations over the protagonist's mysterious birth and unhappy adoption – plot-lines similar to some of the sensational melodramas she had found so compelling at the Lyceum. The 'foreign blood' of the central character, John-Baptist Montolivet (which combines John the Baptist with the Mount of Olives – the beginning and end of Christ's story on earth), is used as a metaphor for the author's lesbianism, and the story of his unsatisfactory adoption by a conventional family reflects the anomaly of homosexuals in British society in the years following Wilde's imprisonment.

After a hundred pages of androgynous make-believe, the story of *Hungerheart* adheres closely to the facts of Christabel Marshall's/Christopher St John's life. Though the chronology is sometimes adjusted and events conflated so as to make a neater shape and capture greater dramatic power, every happening that can be checked from independent sources is here: the fire, the bicycle accident, the attempted suicide, Emma Marshall's death, visits to the Lyceum, writing poems to Ellen Terry and then meeting Edy.

Describing their ménage at Smith Square, she wrote: 'We were as happy as a newly-married pair, perhaps happier . . . I used to wonder which was the husband and which the wife of the *ménage*! . . . We fought sometimes, but we loved – that was the great point. Even our fights were interesting, and our reconciliations bound us together more closely.'

Chris did not see the world as a pleasant place. She longed to unburden herself of her emotions – and Edy was not always 'patient with the romantic strain in me'. Edy chided her for never being content: 'You always want too much'. Chris wanted sexual love, whereas Edy seemed happy with a friendship. 'If I abstained from the sins of the body it was more from lack of opportunity than from horror of them', Chris confessed in *Hungerheart*. 'In my brain I often sinned.' She had denied in an early chapter of her novel being the 'man-hater' that Gordon Craig depicted. But after two years of living with Edy, 'I had lost all desire for the friendship of men', she admitted, 'and for their love I had never cared'. She felt 'a natural dislike' for the stereotypical man, but 'I envied them their prerogatives as lovers'. What was vital to her was the knowledge that she need never be alone again or feel the despair which had led her to attempt suicide. Then 'a bomb came hurtling through the serene air of my Paradise'.

She describes Martin Shaw as having 'nothing first-rate about him except his conceit, which was sublime'. In addition to his facial disfigurement, he was 'sickly' and 'stunted' and 'not sensitive about his affliction. He seemed to be proud of it, to brazen it out, to wear it as a panache, which made compassion for him difficult.'

Certainly Chris had no compassion – she felt outrage, panic, hate. This was how men behaved, taking whatever they wanted regardless of others. What exasperated her was that Edy should actually wish to marry such a man. In her novel she uses the word 'deformity' to describe him – the very word that Una Troubridge was to use when describing Chris herself. She did not know that the only other man for whom Edy had felt an attachment, Sidney Valentine, also had a facial blemish. 'What attracted her to me?' Chris wondered. 'She never told me.' But Edy seems to have responded emotionally to people whose marks of disadvantage were plainly visible.

Chris believed she had probably been the last person to find out that Edy was in love with this man. When she did so, 'I pressed my hands to my heart and ran out of the room. I was burning in the fire of my own wrath, and had a kind of ecstasy of desire for death . . . I remembered clearly a bottle of cocaine lotion in the bath-room . . . I went in and drank it without a moment's hesitation. The effect of the action was to put out my wrathful fire. I became weak, timid and sorrowful . . . I burst into sobs.'

She left the house, caught a bus and travelled aimlessly around London until she lost consciousness. Next morning she woke up in hospital. 'My dominant emotion was shame', she wrote. '. . . I was appalled at the monstrous selfishness of love, at the mortal hatred and cruelty that it conceals.' Edy came to the hospital and later on the two of them returned to Smith Square.

In her weakened state, Chris believed that she had come to accept Edy's marriage to Martin Shaw. But she could not utter his name without a shudder or think of him other than as 'a thing' of 'filth, stench, corruption'. For years she had restrained her own 'ignoble passion' and now Edy was to enter the 'grossness of matrimony'. As she recovered her strength so her resistance grew. 'It can't be. It shall never be.'

Edy never mentioned Martin Shaw's name when the two women were together. But 'I knew she saw him constantly'. They lived as before 'yet not as before'. She took heart from the fact that Ellen also opposed the match. 'Poor Chris seems to be having an awful time of it', she wrote to Ted. He and his friends appeared to like 'poor Martin Shaw' as she called him. But 'I want you to tell me what there is against him except his misfortunate personal appearance, his poverty . . . I'm sick at heart and cry my eyes out all through the night . . . I am just *mad* with Edy.'

In his memoirs Gordon Craig tells of his mother coming round to his Chelsea studio greatly disturbed and telling him that 'I must help her to prevent' the marriage. But he had his own problems and 'all I could do was to do nothing'. If Martin really loved Edy as he himself loved Elena, then he would elope as they had done. But his friend possessed a more diffident temperament. His only complaint was of a 'bodyguard' that prevented the relationship advancing. 'Is it an outer bodyguard or an inner bodyguard?' Gordon Craig asked. Was he alluding to Christopher St John? He did not say. In his own memoirs Martin Shaw never mentions Edy or his proposal of marriage to her, and his references to Ellen are particularly courteous. But she behaved ruthlessly, threatening to stop her daughter's allowance if she married and to let Edith Craig and Co. fall into bankruptcy. 'With no gilt on the gingerbread they will get sick of each other', she wrote to Ted.

Sometimes Edy and Chris would leave Smith Square and travel down to Smallhythe. 'A feeling of infinite repose came from our beloved marshes', Chris remembered. 'Human pain seemed powerless here.' Only once did she ask Edy directly whether she still intended to marry Martin Shaw. 'I suppose so', she answered – and Chris flew into a rage. 'One thing is certain', Edy remarked, 'you can always be trusted to behave badly.'

Eventually Chris and Ellen prevailed over Edy. 'How it ended I never knew', Chris wrote. '. . . She never spoke of it, she never explained.' Chris's state of mind is not difficult to understand. But what was the secret of Ellen's hostility? According to her grandson Edward Craig, 'she liked Martin'. But liking or not liking was immaterial to the game that mother and daughter were condemned to play: a game from which neither one could get up and walk away. All other characters were moved like pieces to be taken or sacrificed, but never to reach their destination and gain advancement. It was a loving battle for power and possession, dependence and independence: 'a theme for a dramatic poet', as Gordon Craig described it.

'This first phase of my long friendship with Edy cannot be epitomised as an idyll', Christopher St John admitted many years later. 'It came near to being a tragedy'. Of this too Edy never spoke – 'we did not break open the grave of a thing past which had threatened to separate us'. In her novel *Hungerheart*, Chris wrote: 'I still loved my friend, but my ideal of friendship had been tarnished. I saw that I was never to know a human relationship in which I was to be the "only one" to the "only other".' She hints that she was to have two or three flirtations or episodes with other women and then, as a convert to Roman Catholicism, embrace its ascetic ideal of surrender to the love of God.

*

These dramatic events on and off the stage changed all their lives. 'As soon as possible I shall get away from all responsibility & enter an engagement', Ellen told her son. She wanted to move back the clock, and appealed to Irving, offering to play 'anything' that was 'at all fair', and urging him to 'let me know quickly'. But he was no more able to help her now than Bernard Shaw had been. To Edy and Ted she made no secret of her disappointment – 'it is you two kids who have disheartened me terribly'.

So Ellen abandoned theatre management and would in due course hand over the managing of her career to Edy – and also to Chris, who wrote and translated plays for her, composed Shakespeare programmes which she delivered around the world and took the pen from her hand when completing her volume of memoirs. To this extent Chris appeared to gain authority over Ellen's life – though 'I have never read anything of mine in print yet without a sensation of disappointment', she confessed.

Edy's 'heart was not broken'. Throwing herself 'with immense energy into arranging a long tour for her mother', she appeared to take command of Ellen. But was she really in command? 'Did I tell you she is my right hand', Ellen wrote to Bernard Shaw in the summer of 1904, 'and still growing to be my left hand, and happy as a sandboy all the while? I fear to be too happy in her – I try to be very quiet with it all.' Perhaps the only happy solution to their game was for both of them to maintain an illusion of command.

Ellen's provincial tour during the winter of 1903 and 1904 with 'my delightful company of young people' including Edy and Chris was a success and, she told the drama critic W.L. Courtney, 'I am getting back the money I lost at the Imperial – I don't care in the least for money but one must have the bothering stuff to do & to do & to do'. But she did not retrieve all her money. For the first time in her career she played an old woman – a woman whose compliance with an oppressive and greedy shipping system in her fishing village proves disastrous for her husband and sons. *The Good Hope* was a tragedy, written by the Dutch playwright Herman Heijermans, a 'clever & most pathetic' drama Ellen called it, which shows the dangers of trying to please everybody. It had been 'dug out of the Dutch language', Ellen told Austin Brereton, by Christopher St John who 'took a whole month about one act', but who eventually came up with a 'simple and vigorous' English version in which there was a good small part for Edy. *The Good Hope* soon settled down as a moderate success, playing 'once or twice a week – &

we play it jolly well', Ellen reported to Ted. The news did not interest him. 'I have nothing in this', he noted. But Laurence Irving sent Ellen a letter of congratulation for putting on an essentially modern work in construction and development 'that deals with lives as they are lived . . . you are not going to let the times leave you behind them'. But she had staged it to please Edy (because it pleased Chris) as she had staged *The Vikings of Helgeland* to please Ted.

Ellen did not take Ibsen's play on tour with her. 'You and Edy quarrelling has finished me nearly', she wrote to Ted at the end of 1903. '. . . We are all standing on the brink of a height from which we shall assuredly topple and be useless any of us *to help the other* – unless something is done at once to avert the catastrophe.' Only Shakespeare could rescue them. Relieved to see their favourite actress in the familiar role of Beatrice, audiences would not leave until Ellen, coming before the curtain, announced: 'Ladies and Gentlemen, I am sorry, but the author is *not* in the house.' Her own relief was so evident that she appeared to be brimming over with fun.

Henry Irving came to see *Much Ado About Nothing* before the play left London. 'I sneaked into the darkened box which he filled with his dear lonely personality,' Gordon Craig wrote, 'and sat behind him, breathing as quietly as I could and saying nothing.' What he listened for in the dark was some illuminating word of encouragement. But Irving said nothing – no more than he had ever said to Harry or Laurence. Precision of speech, which he himself had struggled so hard to attain, was what he most liked to find. 'Talent, even genius, I think, mattered less to him', Gordon Craig wrote, '. . . except in my mother's case, for he was never tired of speaking of her "God-sent genius." My stuff must have irritated and bored him. He said not a word.'

While Ellen was away touring the provinces 'without me, but with my sister', Craig tried to start a theatre school in Trafalgar Studios. 'Nothing came of it', he wrote. This was partly because early in 1904 Beerbohm Tree opened a successful Academy of Dramatic Art – dismissed by Craig as a disguised 'theatrical agency'.

'Still no work for the stage . . . no work I would accept', he noted in January 1904. It was obvious to him that his mother 'could only carry on with one of her children' and that the chosen one was Edy. By making herself 'a willing slave' to Ellen, Christopher St John had manoeuvred herself into the position of a family insider, while Gordon Craig was 'one of the impossibles' – a member 'of the clan to which Hamlet belonged'. He saw foul play all around him. Ellen wrote to comfort him; wrote again to hold him to her. But he could not bear the oblivion of his work and did not believe she understood what it had meant to him. He was a man without a shadow, almost invisible, rejected by everyone: his family, his mother country, everyone. What could he say to his mother? 'You ask. I answer: and destroy my answer. Do you not know that sometimes there is no answer?' In this destruction lay his answer. 'Don't ask me ever again darling of all darlings for an answer, for the next one will be a cry which will be heard from one end of this creation to the other . . . I am the man who can save the theatre & shall do so *unaided*.' He was still her 'son of sons', but 'I have oaths of fidelity to the art . . . & I have heard them fade away . . . I have felt friends close to me & seen them go'. If he were not to die, and die soon, he must leave. That is what he told her. 'I never found the world so grey and cold before', she replied.

In the summer of 1904, to Ellen's great grief, her son 'left England broken & on my last pair of legs', as he told Martin Shaw. Though his mother would try to coax him back, he travelled further across Europe: from Germany to Austria, the Netherlands, Italy, Russia and France. For more than sixty years, Europe was to give him something of what England had denied him: the encouragement of vivid, active and imaginative people who valued what he did, and saw him as a man of vision able to make manifest our dreams.

39
The End of Irving

Henry Irving had often been told how strikingly he resembled Dante. Everyone agreed that Dante had a fine face and, glancing in the mirror, Irving could not help recognising that he was indeed destined for the role – increasingly so as he became older and the resemblance grew unmistakable. But there was an obstacle. As Max Beerbohm put it: 'There never lived a great man whose life would tempt a dramatist less than a life of Dante . . . not Maeterlinck himself could bring [him] into terms of drama.' Yet Irving coveted the role and had invited Tennyson to compose the play for him. 'A fine subject', Tennyson agreed. 'But where is the Dante to write it?' Victorien Sardou, with Emile Moreau, met the challenge by creating a romantic melodrama, with opportunities for fine swordplay, around the margins of his subject's life. He had written a moral rather than an historical portrait of Dante, he explained – what others would come to call an 'antidante' for whom, *The Times* drama critic suggested, a special circle of hell should be reserved. But Irving was set upon this course. There was something in Sardou's invented character that appealed to him: a harsh, narrow saint whose grim personality and high principles concealed a warm beating heart. He could make something of that.

He brought together some fifty actors and arranged to stage the play at the Theatre Royal, Drury Lane. 'You and I are too old to act in such a huge place', Ellen warned him. And to Stephen Coleridge she wrote: 'I fear it [*Dante*] will be his grave.' But during rehearsals, he 'read it wonderfully well', Stoker remembered. Everyone was impressed. No one, however, could quite make out what it meant. The production provided a spectacle rather than a philosophical exegesis – a parade of gorgeous and elaborate costumes, a chorus of spirits and demons, and some miraculous stage mechanics including an illusive Inferno and a moving panorama that gave the impression of Dante and Virgil speeding rapidly (though still magisterially) through Purgatory and Hell. All this was hugely expensive – Irving invested £12,000 in it – and though the play lasted through the season, running for eighty-eight performances, it was never popular. Max Beerbohm's hostile judgement in the *Saturday Review* recalls a similar objection made by Henry James to Irving's *Faust*. 'I am distressed by the cheapening of a great and semi-sacred figure', Beerbohm wrote. '. . . Dante's external life was prosaic . . . But his soul was the soul of a great poet and saint – a fiery and illustrious essence, a pure flame. And I do not care to see M. Sardou lighting his gas from it.'

Though Irving never revived *Dante* in Britain, he opened his next tour of America with it during the last week of October 1903 in New York. But the Americans warmed to the play even less than the British, and after a few performances he was obliged to withdraw it from the repertoire. His disappointment was intense – he wished to identify himself with Dante as he had with Becket, and the public had not allowed him to do this. He had not brought *Coriolanus* to America – it 'is an unprofitable play which the public doesn't want', he explained to William Winter. But the tour itself, which covered thirty-three cities in five months, was a success and everywhere Irving was given banquets and receptions – a triumphal progress crowned by a meeting with the President, Theodore Roosevelt. It was as if everyone sensed that this would be his farewell to the United States and Canada. At each city, the people rose to greet him and then to say goodbye to a long-shared past. 'Never before had an old actor of nearly sixty-six, playing parts he had created thirty years ago, attracted an audience whose enthusiasm seemed to be as great as ever', his grandson wrote.

'My boys both well', Irving had written to William Winter before setting out on this tour. 'Laurence's wife coming with me and Loveday and Stoker.' By the time he returned he had a new grandchild, Harry and Dolly's daughter, Elizabeth. Following his success in J.M. Barrie's *The Admirable Crichton*, Harry was soon invited to head a strong cast at the Adelphi Theatre in a production of *Hamlet*. 'Poor little H.', his father wrote in a notebook, '. . . he'll never make anything of Hamlet.' His ghostly message to Harry himself – 'I AM THY FATHER'S SPIRIT BROODING O'ER YE' – was disturbing; and when, accompanied by Mrs Aria, he went to see the production, his doubts were confirmed. He sank ever lower in his chair and began ominously muttering. This new style of acting, now the fashion apparently, reduced the audience to mere onlookers at something that was going on next door. It had no operatic value, no ballast or rhetoric: in short, nothing that the dramatic poet created for the skills of the performing actor. Irving had given his life to the classical theatre and he could not, with integrity, say a word of praise to Harry. The best part of it perhaps was that his son, now with two children, seemed financially secure – Dolly, his wife, was also in employment creating the part of Mrs Darling in a strange new fairy play called *Peter Pan* by J.M. Barrie. But few people thought it would last long.

Laurence's career had taken a turn for the worse, descending from the legitimate theatre into vaudeville. It was really his wife Mabel's decision to stage Charles Reade's and Tom Taylor's popular romance, *Masks and Faces*, as part of the music-hall programmes that were so popular around the country. Though Laurence's translation of *Dante* had been praised for its rough poetry, Mabel clearly saw during their recent tour of North America how little opportunity there ever would be for him to advance his own career as an actor or playwright in a company still dedicated to 'the Chief'. Mabel was not in awe of Irving, not afraid of being thought a renegade among the theatrical elite – providing she was confident of furthering her husband's interests. What Mabel had hit on was a method of earning enough money to make him independent of his father over the next year or two.

His friends had been shocked by Irving's appearance after he returned from the United States. He had difficulty breathing sometimes and was so overcome by weakness that he had been obliged to take a drink or two as a stimulant before going onstage. He knew that he could not continue like this indefinitely, but hesitated to call an end to it. Instead, he planned an extended farewell, lasting almost two years and taking in comprehensive tours of England, Scotland, Wales and Ireland, one last visit to North America, and finishing in London where, in 1906, he and Ellen Terry could celebrate their grand jubilees together. It would be a tremendous finale.

He was less gregarious these days – they hardly saw him at the Garrick Club. He preferred to spend his evenings with his old friend, Angela Burdett-Coutts, a few yards off in Stratton Street. That summer of 1904, Mrs Aria carried him away to Cornwall for 'a good rest' before his next tour began in September.

'The work has been hard', he wrote to a friend during rehearsals, '. . . but I think we are shaping well.' He was a wandering player again, the touring actor he had been in his young days. 'It's a pity', he remarked to one of his fellow actors, '– just as one is beginning to know a little about this work of ours – it's time to leave it.' He felt that time was running out. 'I hope to die in harness', he told his friend J.L. Toole.

At each town along the route he would make a short farewell speech before the curtain, and the audiences stood and cheered him. But the actress Lena Ashwell, who saw him towards the end of the year, noticed how very frail he was looking. 'It is cruel work for him', Harry told his mother. Arriving in Wolverhampton in a snowstorm that February, he caught a severe cold, struggled though performances of *Waterloo* and *The Bells*, then fainted. A doctor who examined him at his hotel the following morning told him that he was too ill to continue his tour on to the next eight scheduled towns. But Irving insisted that he must complete the two remaining performances at Wolverhampton and, the doctor reluctantly acceding to this, he was given injections of strychnine to get him through.

Harry and Laurence were so accustomed to their father's miraculous recoveries that they accepted his assurance he would soon be well again. Stoker and Loveday were more apprehensive, but there was little they could do beyond contending with Walter Collinson and others to nurse him – little except draft replies to the many letters of condolence that went on being delivered (drafts that Irving would praise but seldom consider quite good enough to post). He was experiencing difficulties in coming to terms with his infirmities. But the doctor explained that, after ten weeks or so of rest, he should be able to take the stage again. With this tentative encouragement, he made arrangements for a short season at Drury Lane in the late spring and early summer of 1905 and once these arrangements were made he felt better.

'He is best alone for the present', the doctor advised, '– even from his own people.' But Ellen Terry could not stay away. She went up to Wolverhampton as soon as she heard the news of Irving's collapse. First she saw the doctor, who informed her that Irving's heart was 'dangerously weak' and that he should never act again in *The Bells* – it was simply too great a strain. Then she went to the hotel and entered Irving's bedroom carrying a bunch of daffodils (the flowers he had given her after her mother died).

He was in bed, very pale, drinking a cup of coffee, an old dressing-gown hanging over his thin shoulders like some mysterious drapery, reminding Ellen of a 'beautiful grey tree that I have seen in Savannah'. He told her that two queens had been especially generous to him that morning. There was a telegram from Queen Alexandra – and now this visit from Ellen. They had not been alone for a long time. Both of them were moved, almost embarrassed, and fell into talking of their work. J.M. Barrie had come to see Ellen at Smallhythe and told her of a play he wished to write for her. She had been enchanted, but now that she came to prepare for rehearsals, *Alice-Sit-By-the-Fire* did not seem so good. She could see that Barrie had worked some of her ways into the character of Alice (Ellen's abandoned name) – her habit, for example, of carrying everywhere a large bag crammed with odds and ends. But she was used 'to broader work in a larger theatre' – Irving's theatre. She felt that she would burst at the seams in this neat little role Barrie had tailored for her. Though he had made his play to measure, he had not got her measure at all.

Had Henry ever got her measure? Yes and no seemed to be the best answer to that. When she thought of the blows he had received over the years – his awful marriage, that devastating fire, his crippling fall, a dreadful syndicate sucking the lifeblood out of the Lyceum, and now this sequence of illnesses – when she thought of this and how valiantly he had fought against it all, and was continuing to fight, never giving up, she was moved to tears. 'What a wonderful life you've had, haven't you?' she said. 'Oh yes,' he agreed, 'a wonderful life – of work.' They could look back on almost fifty years of work that had devoured their time. What, she wondered, had he got out of it? He hesitated. 'Let me see . . . Well, a good cigar, a good glass of wine, and' – here, with perfect timing, he took her hand and kissed it – 'good friends.'

'How would you like your end to come?' Only a good friend could have asked such a question. She knew he was a connoisseur of endings – so what would he answer? He repeated her question lightly, making his calculations. Then he raised his hand, snapped his fingers: 'Like that!'

Soon after Ellen left, Mrs Aria arrived.

Becket opened at Drury Lane on 29 April 1905. Loveday, Stoker and the diminutive Walter Collinson helped Irving to the theatre and on to the stage, and at the end of each performance they guided him before the curtain to say a few words and, one after the other, they returned him to his dressing-room and then home. Though he was occasionally incoherent, once he gained the centre of the stage and began to speak the lines of his character, the change that came over him was remarkable. Word soon travelled around London that something extraordinary was taking place at Drury Lane, something miraculous and awful. Henry Irving was dying, slowly, inevitably, night after night in front of his public. They rose to their feet and cheered him, went on cheering him, would not let him go, as he stood there supported by his team, gravely acknowledging them but too overcome to know what he said: 'Only my blood speaks to you in my veins.' Were they witnesses, these audiences, to his end, or could they stop time and keep him alive? Somehow he came through. He played Becket in the final performance. The knights, rushing to the cathedral in the play, had cried: 'King's men! King's men!' Then at the end a voice from the gallery shouted out: 'Irving's men!' and everyone stood chanting: 'Irving's men! Irving's men!' These cries of the people and their thunderous applause reached out to him, filling the theatre with an extraordinary barrage of sound which continued longer than seemed possible, continued until suddenly everyone was standing still and silent, as if before 'things too sad to realise'.

As soon as the season was over, Mrs Aria took him up to Yorkshire. He enjoyed relaxing, she believed, in solitary landscapes, watching strange birds and contemplating distant mountains. Irving himself disagreed. What was the use of all this resting? He could not get accustomed to it. He was determined to complete the tour he had been obliged to end prematurely. He felt the shame of letting his public down. The tour recommenced on Monday, 2 October, at Sheffield with *The Merchant of Venice*. Watching him fighting for his breath as he waited in the wings for his cue, Loveday felt greatly agitated, but when the cues came he always answered them. To Stoker's alarm, he had added *The Bells* to the repertoire and played it two days later. At the end he looked desperately tired. 'His fatigue was not for one part,' Madeleine Bingham was to write, 'but for hundreds of parts, and for a lifetime.'

The company moved on to the Theatre Royal at Bradford and again, on Thursday, 12 October, he played Mathias in *The Bells*. It was, his grandson wrote, 'an agony to watch him' and at the final curtain he collapsed. Only then did he recognise that he could not take on this play again, and acquiesced to the stage-sets being sent back to London. He even seemed to accept that he would never return to America. 'A kindly continent to me', he remarked to Stoker, 'but I would not leave my bones there.'

On Friday, 13 October, he played Becket. Perhaps because this was his favourite character, he seemed curiously light-hearted that day. During the performance he made several strange slips, but his final words rang out clear: 'Into Thy Hands, O Lord, into Thy Hands!' Then he died as he had died so many times before. But this time he did not quite recover himself. 'What now . . .?' he asked. He seemed bemused. Loveday supported him and, praising Shakespeare instead of Tennyson, Irving spoke a few halting words to the audience.

Back in his dressing-room he was more himself. He mentioned some detail to Stoker about Birmingham, the next stop on their tour and, grasping him suddenly by the hand, told him to muffle his throat against the night air. Walter Collinson helped him into his heavy overcoat, and Loveday put him into a cab back to the Midland Hotel. Entering the hotel he stumbled. 'That chair!' he called out and was escorted to a chair in the hall. He sat down, lost consciousness, slid to the floor, and was dead.

Stoker telegraphed Harry and Laurence and they went up to Bradford the next day. Their father's body, oddly shrunken, lay in a bedroom at the hotel. All that day members of the company arrived to say their farewells before the body was sealed up in a lead coffin to be transported back to London. The following morning it appeared as though the entire population of Bradford had turned out and was silently lining the streets, the men raising their hats in a final salute as the carriage passed by on its way to the railway station.

The newspapers were full of tributes to 'the greatest English actor of his generation', a man whose career, the obituary writer of *The Times* recorded, had 'restored the fortunes of the theatre and marked a turning-point in the history of the English drama'. He was seen as partly a product and partly a creator of the Victorian age, 'a fascinating but alarming figure' who, by reviving the art of tragic acting on the grandest scale, had dignified the nation. His method of acting, distinct and unborrowed, imaginative rather than physical, had won him the place as leader of a new school of performers who enlisted under his name. His greatness sprang from a source different from that of his predecessors. He was the champion of tragedy, regenerating it socially, morally and artistically by bringing together the skills of the scene-painter, the musician, the designer and the actor to convey a singular unity of purpose – a legacy which, in quite another form, he would hand on to Gordon Craig.

Irving's death was experienced as the loss of a legend. He had come to represent the entire English theatre and was 'the last of several symbolic figures', William Rothenstein wrote. 'He was *the* actor as Ellen Terry was *the* actress, Sir Frederick Leighton *the* President of the Royal Academy, Gilbert and Sullivan *the* authors of Comic-Opera.' In London the six large columns of the still empty Lyceum Theatre were draped in black, flags hung at half-mast and the cab-drivers (whom he had always tipped so generously) tied black bows on their whips. At the Garrick Club, Beerbohm Tree was given the message over supper and, after handing it around his friends there, the news travelling from room to room, everyone left the club in silence. The country was in mourning for 'the father of his people' – that family of entertainers of all kinds and conditions, who not so long ago had been no better than 'rogues and vagabonds' but whose status was so astonishingly raised during Irving's lifetime; and also for those generations of people who had crowded the stalls and pits, boxes and galleries throughout the land, whose secret dreams he had aroused and enriched over almost half a century.

The weight of Irving's death rested most obviously on Harry's and Laurence's shoulders. But it was also felt with intensity by the women in his life. 'I shall not come [to] Bradford', Ellen Terry had told Stoker. 'He is not there.' She felt 'ill all the time', she told her son, 'with never a gleam of "well" in it . . . just steeped in "ill" '. Gordon Craig knew his absence abroad was helping to make her ill, knew Irving's death had sent her off her head, and knew also that 'it is what will come to me some day too'.

Harry and Laurence agreed that their father's body should lie at Angela Burdett-Coutts's house, the large dining-room of which she converted into a *chapelle ardente*. Here, over the following few days, friends and colleagues came and tributes were delivered. In the middle of the room, Irving's grandson remembered, 'a huge mound of flowers and foliage surmounted by my grandfather's coffin reached nearly to the great crystal chandelier that hung from the ceiling . . . On the top of the coffin lay a cross sent by the

Queen; in front of it, raised on a table like a rock above the floral foams, was a cushion of rosemary bejewelled with carnations – Ellen Terry's parting tribute. Banks of wreaths rose high along the walls . . . The end of the room appeared to open onto a forest of dark green leaves . . . In a corner my grandmother, heavily veiled, held sad court.'

As soon as the news of Irving's death reached her, Mrs Aria had set to work designing an enormous pall, ordering two dozen florists to work thousands of leaves into its contrivance and mount it closely over a green foundation. This huge object hung ominously over all other offerings and cast a shadow over Florence herself, perched in her corner with a small group of mourners glancing nervously over their shoulders and murmuring formal words of sympathy.

Florence felt the awkwardness of her position keenly. She resented being placed in an inferior position in the Baroness Burdett-Coutts's house – but at least the baroness was a lady. It was inexplicable to her why a woman of any distinction would have allowed Mrs Aria's hideous jungle of leaves to be exhibited there.

In the newspapers she read the obituary columns praising Ellen Terry as Irving's inspirational stage partner but never mentioning Florence herself. After some complicated negotiations, it had been decided that Irving should be laid to rest in Westminster Abbey at the foot of Shakespeare's statue and next to David Garrick's grave. This was, as Squire Bancroft wrote to Austin Brereton, 'the greatest honour and memorial which can be bestowed upon an Englishman'. But Florence objected. She felt deeply injured by Irving's omission of her in his will and additionally insulted by the inclusion of Mrs Aria (to whom he had left a third of his estate – the other two thirds being shared by Harry and Laurence). She longed to take revenge. But what should she do? What she did was to appeal to Bernard Shaw.

Shaw had alienated Irving's family by publishing a controversial obituary. It had in fact been written for a Viennese newspaper, *Die Neue Freie Presse*, translated into German, and then rendered back into English for publication in Britain. In this mangled version Irving was presented as 'a narrow-minded egoist, devoid of culture, and living on the dream of his own greatness' (Shaw had originally written that Irving was 'interested in nothing but himself; and the self in which he was interested was an imaginary self in an imaginary world. He lived in a dream.'). But what Florence read persuaded her that this was the man to help her over what she called 'the intricacies of my most painful position'. How, she asked him, could she abort Irving's will and avoid this final indignity of a funeral service at Westminster Abbey? Shaw's reply was ingenious. As the widow of a famous man buried in such august surroundings, he explained, Florence might expect to receive a state pension. But if she challenged Mrs Aria in the courts and used their relationship to forestall the state funeral, then she would almost certainly lose this pension. While Florence felt obliged to accept this advice, it gave her little satisfaction. A few days after the funeral she instructed her solicitor to draft a letter for the press. 'Now that the excitement of Sir Henry Irving's funeral is over, it may not be amiss to inquire how it is that in the midst of all this enthusiastic display no mention that I have seen has been made of his wife . . . It may interest many of your readers to know that Lady Irving is in excellent health, notwithstanding the shock and excitement of the last few days.'

The day of the funeral was grey and windy. 'Slowly, imperceptibly, like shadows in their silence, the crowds gathered', Bram Stoker wrote in his ominously Gothic style. It seemed as if the entire nation had turned out. The muffled drums recalled both the dignity and loneliness of Irving's life – 'no man I ever met', wrote John Martin-Harvey, 'was so truly lonely as he'. People filled Whitehall and Parliament Square, waiting for his final performance. Inside the abbey the ushers – all fellow actors – showed people to their places. There were representatives not only from the English-speaking world but also from foreign-language theatres, including the Comédie-Française. It was a full house. The great coffin, mantled in Mrs Aria's skirt of leaves, was carried up the aisle by fourteen pall-bearers, among them Beerbohm Tree and Forbes-Robertson, Pinero and Alma-Tadema. Alexander Mackenzie's funeral march from *Coriolanus* filled the cathedral and a shaft of sun suddenly lit up the misty atmosphere as the coffin was lifted from its bier and manoeuvred towards Poets' Corner where Irving's family was gathered. 'I had, as it were, never heard such a stupendous silence', his grandson wrote. Peering through the adults, the boy suddenly saw what none of the general public had seen. It was not after all Sir Henry Irving's body that was being buried, but his ashes. Learning that there was no longer room for corpses in Westminster Abbey, Laurence had taken his father's to be cremated at Golders Green. The solemn burden which had passed laboriously through the streets of London and been carried up the aisle was a stage prop.

PART FIVE

40
Women!

Gordon Craig was in Amsterdam when news of Irving's death reached him. No one, he believed, who had not worked with Irving could measure his genius. He was quite simply the greatest figure Craig had ever met and he planned to write a book bringing him back to life – he had already begun making notes. 'The old Angel dead', he wrote to Martin Shaw. 'I cannot tell you the state I am in, unrelieved – may my immortal Henry float away and away where ever fancy allows.' But mixed in with his sadness was a sense of relief. He no longer lived in the shadow of 'my master'. The time was coming when he would be a master himself.

He could not return to London for Irving's memorial service – and for the same reason that he could not go back for his mother's jubilee the following year. It was ironic that his reason should be the commonplace one of work. Ellen had constantly chided him for not working, holding up Irving, who had died from overwork, as an example he should follow: and this was her profit on it.

The thought of his mother's jubilee disturbed him, for there would be no place at the feast for his father. Godwin seemed 'like Chaucer or Robin Hood', he was to write in one of his day books, 'one an outlaw, the other [who] wrote verse which few could read easily. He [Godwin] had to walk around and do different jobs . . . The most daring thing he ever did was to avoid becoming rich.' This figure still haunted him. 'My father, my master and I, all loved the same woman', he wrote in old age when recalling this time. He acknowledged that Godwin and Irving had done more for Ellen Terry than he had ever done: 'yet I believe she loved me most'. He pointedly left out Edy from these calculations and confined himself to the men. Ellen had loved him, not because he happened to be 'the least of the three, the weakest and the smallest', but because in loving him so much she also 'loved my father'.

But Ellen's love seemed to vex his relationships with women. The previous year had begun promisingly when, on 11 January 1904, Elena Meo gave birth to their second daughter whom they were to name Ellen Gordon Craig, known as Nelly. But soon afterwards their first little child, called Nell because she looked so like her grandmother, suddenly died.

Everyone that spring seemed miserable. Ellen did her best to help – in so far as the essential business of paying money to the three mothers of her six surviving grandchildren could help. But her son seemed curiously helpless, as if paralysed by emotional panic. It was not so much the solicitors' letters and the continual stream of debts that no amount of 'borrowing' from his mother appeared to stem. It was something which he confessed to no one: *he could not bear to contemplate being cast into wedlock with the woman he loved and their child.* Not quite admitting this, he had attributed his low spirits to lack of work. And for work he naturally looked to men for help, his collaboration with Ellen and Edy having demonstrated how disastrous it was to rely on women.

It was Will Rothenstein who, following his prediction in the *Saturday Review* that Gordon Craig would one day win 'the foremost place in the modern Theatre', introduced him to Count Harry Kessler. An influential patron of the arts at the Court of Weimar, Kessler had particularly admired his production of *The Vikings* with its Wagnerian costumes and was determined to bring him over to Germany. As a result of his recommendation, Craig was invited that summer to design the sets for Hugo von Hofmannsthal's adaptation of Thomas Otway's seventeenth-century, blank verse tragedy *Venice Preserv'd* at the Lessing Theater in Berlin. Though he felt anxious over working in a country where he did not speak the language, he seems to have been more 'horribly nervous' of the complexities at home. He had been very loving to Elena following the death of their elder daughter, but both of them recognised that he must begin to earn some money – particularly since Elena was again pregnant.

His collaboration with the new director of the Lessing Theater, Otto Brahm, was a bad omen. Craig's imaginative settings, designed to reinforce the poetic tragedy, did not appeal to Brahm's naturalistic temperament. Besides, both men wanted to control the production of *Venice Preserv'd.*

Brahm, who described himself as 'a fighter by nature', resented the imposition on him of this arrogant young Englishman; while Gordon Craig insisted that anything short of 'doing the scenes, costumes and lighting scheme' for the play, indeed almost everything, would be an intolerable insult to him. When the play finally opened in January 1905, just two of the scenes were based on his drawings and he had left for Weimar.

Here the welcome he received 'was of a different kind from any I had experienced up to then'. Kessler, a 'vivid person in the matter of the arts . . . and always very active', helped to arrange exhibitions of his drawings all over Germany, and introduced him to many people who 'found something good in what I was doing'. In a letter to his mother, he wrote excitedly that 'everything is alive', though these exhibitions, like shots fired with blanks, left a peculiar emptiness: 'thunder & lightning & laughter & then – silence'.

And it was true that his early reviews, though generally favourable, were short and somewhat superficial. What he was showing in these exhibitions were his past achievements and future hopes. He was also revealing what he believed to be a distinction between the interpretive and creative functions of the stage artist. As a designer, his feeling for proportion, line and colour conveyed the atmosphere of a play in which he immersed himself. But his rhythmic emphasis on movement, suggesting mime and dance, replaced the spoken word as the most significant element in the modern theatre.

His creative fervour and radical ideas excited his new patron. An admirer of Nietzsche, Kessler dreamed of creating a new culture in Germany and saw in Craig's revolutionary experiments for the theatre a means of fulfilling some of his dreams. Believing Craig to be 'the sole genius among living English artists', he appointed himself his patron. For over thirty testing and precarious years, like the pursuer of some phantom, Kessler hung on, refusing to be dislodged by all manner of shuddering disappointments. Initially greeted as Ellen Terry's son, Craig soon became recognised as a person in his own right who was proposing something original for the modern theatre. 'Here beauty is not held to be above the heads of their audiences', he wrote to Martin Shaw to whom, with all its unpaid debts, he had relinquished his studio in Chelsea. '. . . In Germany the creative spirits are honoured.'

*

He had planned to bring his new experiments back to England. But then he met the American dancer Isadora Duncan, 'the oddest and most unexpected person in the world', as W.B. Yeats called her. Craig had heard much talk of her (some calling her a genius, some a fool) and he pictured her as 'a sort of governess who had taken to dancing in an artistic manner'. In fact, as he later acknowledged, her rare gift had been 'brought to perfection by 18 years of persistent labour'. Growing up in a small house near San Francisco – from which her father soon disappeared and where her mother, a piano teacher, supported her four children – she lived beside the sea, endeavouring as a child to 'follow the rhythmic movements . . . of the waves'. Later she took small roles in Chicago and New York before, as the biographer Francis Steegmuller wrote, 'all five of the nearly penniless, semi-bohemian Duncans transferred themselves to England by cattle boat and for a time lived hand to mouth in London'. By the end of 1904, at the age of twenty-six, Isadora Duncan had achieved such astonishing success throughout Europe that, in the words of Martin Shaw, 'her name was a household word even among the ordinary public'.

Craig allowed himself to be taken one afternoon to her apartment in Berlin where he met her family. They were, he somewhat prematurely decided, 'a nice group', while Isadora herself he thought beautiful. It was not a classical beauty – her 'tip-tilted nose and the little firm chin' hardly qualified her for that. Nor was it what she said to him that spoke of her beauty – she uttered 'a lot of nonsense' so far as he could judge. It was her silence, her calm and natural ease that were impressive.

She seemed unlike anyone he had ever met, though in some mysterious way her face reminded him of every beautiful woman he had known – in certain lights Jess Dorynne as he had first seen her, and from some angles 'pretty Lucy Wilson' in her early acting days, and also his mother. Isadora had seen Ellen Terry at the Lyceum and thought she was a natural performer like herself – 'my most perfect ideal of woman!'

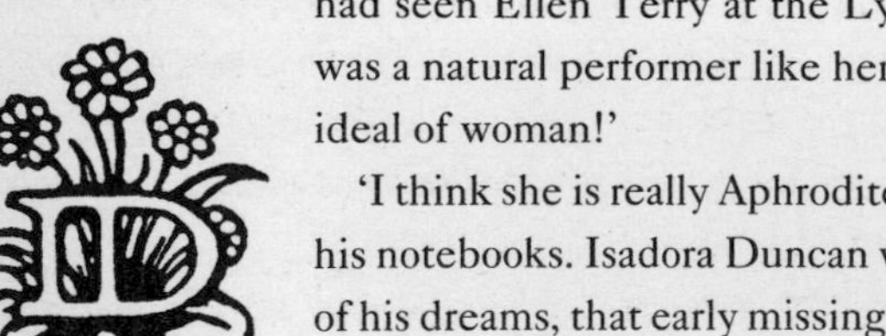

'I think she is really Aphrodite', Craig wrote in one of his notebooks. Isadora Duncan was to be the realisation of his dreams, that early missing letter in his alphabet of women, the D which had separated ABC from EGC.

He expected to be bored by her dancing. She was

performing a Chopin programme with a pianist in a Berlin concert hall. He went and watched her come through the curtains on to the stage and stand by the piano, listening to the gentle notes of the prelude, not moving at all. Then the music began again . . .

She started slowly, walking a few paces sideways and back, going before and after the notes, then suddenly flying up like a bird and floating lightly down as from the sky. There was an infinite charm about these lovely steps. She appeared to move as no one had moved before. Her whole body danced, bewitched by the music, bathing in its rhythms. Her feet and legs, so pale, so thin, were bare, and her scanty clothes – bits of stuff like torn rags, almost translucent – were hardly beautiful. But she made them beautiful. Everything was transformed by her skill as a conveyor of unspoken things.

As he watched, Gordon Craig's spirit seemed to dance with her. 'She was full of natural genius', he remembered almost fifty years later, '. . . speaking her own language . . . telling to the air the very things we longed to hear; and until she came we had never dreamed we should hear; and now we heard them . . . I sat still and speechless.'

After the performance he rushed round to her dressing-room and they went on to supper with her family. Next day, dressed all in white, she came to his exhibition of drawings. When she left, he went out to a café and wrote her a letter – a letter of love – and delivered it by hand that night. 'She is genius, & better than her it would be impossible to be.' Nothing could keep them apart. 'We sit together – she is just simple, lovely & we seem to be about *one*.' Then they drove somewhere, anywhere, from the day into night by motor car or carriage-and-horses – time plays such tricks when in love it is impossible to be certain of anything but love itself. Yet some things are certain. On 17 December they make up a bed on the wooden floor of his studio with two carpets, a sheet, and their overcoats as pillows and 'we sleep together'. This is their perfect time and all is as it should be. 'We were born to lie holding each other . . . We do not separate for 4 days & nights . . . she gives herself to me and reserves nothing.' Then she leaves to dance in St Petersburg. 'I will come Back *Soon Soon* and then', she writes, '. . . we may grow *gradually* to some Inspiration.'

Over the next year they were to travel together around Europe, she dancing and he 'being happy with her'. It was, he told Martin Shaw during the early months of 1905, 'a glorious time . . . I am in magnificent company

. . . I am not making money but living like a Duke. It's fearfully exciting . . . As you may guess I'm not paying my hotel bills & haven't a sou in the world – but am damned if I'll starve or sit on a stool & wait for things . . .' And he was no longer dependent on his mother.

Seeing each other almost daily, they could see little else. They were spellbound, partners of illusion, living a fairy-tale. 'I loved him with all the ardour of my artistic soul', Isadora was to write in her autobiography. He was her first love, the love of her life, and there was no one who understood her dancing as he did – 'I have seldom been so moved by anything', he confessed. '. . . Inspiration is given out by the thousand volts per second from Miss D. And I am alive again (as artist) through her.'

They were to discover many similarities – even an Irish ancestry. 'We were born in the same star', she had told him; and he saw her as 'a *sun* genius – horribly like me'. When this sun shone their mercurial temperaments rose and were exhilarated; and when their star lay hidden they were left in anguish. Craig admired Isadora's opposition to the dead formalism of classical ballet, which mirrored his own battle with the commercial theatre after the death of Irving. Her dedication to the beauty of movement, the flexible melodic movement of the human body, heralding a revolution in the art of choreography, had a profound effect on his theatre of the future where the interplay of light, sound, shadows, screens would replace the dry words of dramatic poets, the fancy games of foolish actors, and the vain calculations of producers whose pretence of historical scholarship belonged to museums and curiosity shops.

'We were indeed full of admiration for each other', Craig remembered. But below the brilliant gloss of this admiration lay many contrasting undercoats. She was an inspiration – and a distraction too. Ideas flooded into his mind by the hundred, but 'I cannot finish my thoughts – they are swept away by a name – Isadora'. Unlike most other artists he admired, Isadora was a woman; and this gave rise to all sorts of complications. 'I hope we'll have a dear sweet lovely Baby', she had written to him from St Petersburg, '– & I'm Happy forever.' Back in Berlin she told him over a bottle of vintage champagne not to fret over this possibility of a child. 'It's all right in Heaven.' He called her Topsy – perhaps after the lively slave girl in *Uncle Tom's Cabin* who grew and grew and claimed to have no parents. She believed their love was unique and would last for ever. He thought it a miracle which could not last. Her work had the same daring, he told Martin Shaw, as theirs when they put on *Dido and Aeneas*, but the difference was that 'these darned Americans make their attempts succeed'. As admiration gave way to resentment, he accused her of stealing his ideas, exhibiting a vein of paranoia that would gain on him over the years. He had revelled in this luxurious life of travel as they roamed their way through Europe, but eventually he grew restless. Isadora's brilliance put him quite in the shade – he was invisible next to her. He must fulfil the extraordinary potential Kessler and others had seen in him. Also he must 'rake in' some money. In short he needed someone to manage his career.

He saw the very man at an exhibition of his drawings in Berlin. The only son of an adoring mother, Maurice Magnus was a neat, fastidious, birdlike American with quick blue eyes and red hair, almost offensively polite in manner, who believed he was the illegitimate grandson of the Prussian emperor, William I. A connoisseur of pomades and powders and fine cambric handkerchiefs, he had grown up as a man of luxurious habits, an opportunist adept at evading the consequences of living far beyond his means. As the 'smart man of a shabby world', he wore his conscience lightly. Guided instinctively by his royal blood, he knew a short cut to all 'the right people'. But his sharp tailoring and decisive opinions were no more than confidence tricks. Yet he had natural charm and a dynamic spirit and he did not forget an act of kindness. Indeed, he expected kindness, generosity and forgiving spirits, for there seemed to be some shadow of tragedy within him reflected sometimes by his forlorn expression – which he cleverly exploited when soliciting loans. In business matters his watchword was optimism, his speciality chaos.

Magnus was twenty-nine when Gordon Craig first met him, a slender figure pacing lightly around the gallery and stopping before each drawing, examining it intently, closing his eyes as if listening ecstatically to music. Such was the sublime performance that before he knew what he was doing, Craig was telling this stranger of his and Isadora Duncan's careers and of their need for someone to conduct their business affairs. And Magnus knew just the man. With great generosity he offered to lay aside all his own projects, and put his experience at his new friend's disposal.

Confident that they were now in the hands of someone well equipped to make their fortunes, Gordon Craig and Isadora Duncan opened a joint bank account and waited for the money to accumulate. Magnus meanwhile invented a company with the telegraphic address 'Footlights Berlin' and, using his skills at obtaining credit, rented an office and employed a multilingual secretary. All the money that came in was from Isadora's dancing, and this was divided between her and Craig (who offered to redesign her programmes) and Magnus himself, who received a salary and commissions. Excluded from this financial equation was that 'nice group' of Isadora's dependent family (now Craig's rivals), and also the school of dance that she had started for children and that was to be managed by her sister Elizabeth. So Isadora went on dancing and for the time being there appeared to be enough money for almost everyone.

With this income temporarily assured, Gordon Craig found fewer opportunities for writing to his mother. For her jubilee in London he sent her a portfolio containing six reproductions of his drawings of Isadora dancing, prefaced by some rather blank verse. He was not good at drawing figures and perhaps one day they would not be necessary. He looked forward to a time when the theatre could dispense with actors, he told his mother. They were 'an insuperable difficulty and expense'.

His letters to Elena Meo and Martin Shaw teemed with the projects, plans and proposals that were careering around his mind. He gave them his thoughts on kinetic theatre, puppet shows and the use of movable screens; he communicated his hopes of founding a school for teaching the art of the theatre in Berlin and of directing the Dutch National Theatre in Amsterdam for Eduard Verkade; he mentioned the names of several exceptional people, including Max Reinhardt ('a first class man') and the 'magnificent' Eleonora Duse, 'wonderful and godlike', who were eager to support him; and he told them of his determination to start an international magazine that would make his ideas known throughout the world.

What these letters show is that his entry into Europe, and particularly his association with Kessler in Germany, came at a crucial moment in his career. 'The days at Weimar were always so full of happiness', Craig wrote, '– light free spirit days.' It was here he met many stimulating members of Kessler's circle, including the Austrian poet and dramatist Hugo von Hofmannsthal who, despite artistic differences arising between them, proclaimed: 'every pea-sized drawing or vignette by Craig shouts: Genius'; and also the impressionist painter Emil Heilbut who, in an interview for *Kunst und Künstler*, traced Craig's development from Aubrey Beardsley and the Beggarstaff Brothers, by way of the French symbolist theatre, to the stylised simplification he used to escape from conventional realism. We are shown him 'revelling in the fantastic and poetic'.

Before he left England, Ellen Terry had presented him with a copy of Roget's *Thesaurus*, a book which stimulated his wish to write. Between 22 April and 4 May 1905, in what he called 'seven days', he dictated a short book in the form of a Platonic dialogue between an omniscient Stage Director and a naïve Playgoer. *The Art of the Theatre*, as it was called, became his manifesto, his thesis and visiting card. It shows him, in the words of T.S. Eliot, 'wading through seas of theatrical blood to grasp his own crown'. Badly translated into German by Maurice Magnus and with a foreword by Kessler, it was quickly followed by English, Dutch, Japanese and pirated Russian editions. The book, which presented Craig's credentials as a reformer, claimed for the stage director-designer the autonomy that Henry Irving had won for actor-managers. The art of the theatre, he argued, was the work of one man who commanded the actors as a conductor did his orchestra. In the future such a man would create masterpieces of action, colour, line and movement. Such a man was himself.

What this meant in practice was to be experienced by both Max Reinhardt and Eleonora Duse. When Reinhardt turned up with suggestions for him to design the 'scene, costumes, lights, movements' for the premiere of Bernard Shaw's *Caesar and Cleopatra*, at his Neues Theater, Craig went into action, working extraordinarily fast, while slowly negotiating terms for his contract which, eventually arriving late in 1905, he turned down at the beginning of 1906. 'Whatever you think of Shaw's piece, it gives you an opportunity, at any rate,' Kessler had urged him. Craig appeared to agree. But he thought *Caesar and Cleopatra* a 'wretched vulgarity variety show', and found it impossible to unify this static library play by someone who championed the overall power of words with his own belief in the priority of movement. Besides, there was another difficulty. 'Reinhardt', he told Kessler, 'is a humorist.' He certainly must have been joking in so far as he led Craig to believe he might surrender authority in his own theatre – all the more unlikely since Craig spoke no German. Craig insisted that he alone 'be master of the stage, and that beyond me there should be no appeal'. Only then would success follow. In fact nothing followed from these negotiations, which may have come as something of a relief for Craig.

Intermittently over eight years, bedevilled by bewildering misunderstandings and financial discord, the 'international force' that was Reinhardt and the 'lonely pioneer' that was Craig persisted in their negotiations over one play then another, performing a complicated dance, moving backwards and forwards yet never quite coming together. It was, in the words of the Craig scholar L.M. Newman, 'reminiscent of farce'. Eventually Craig was left accusing Reinhardt of purloining his ideas, while Reinhardt unwittingly made Craig's work known to the public in what became a distant collaboration in spite of themselves.

He was to find rather more success with Duse, though their partnership had begun unpromisingly. In 1905 Craig created twenty-two 'utterly magnificent and *suggestive*' costumes (in Kessler's words) and one adaptable set for Duse's touring production of Hugo von Hofmannsthal's *Elektra*. They would, he believed, 'be a huge and wonderful success'. For this was probably his finest work for the stage up till now – and he had delivered it all on time. But it was never used, Duse eventually deciding not to add *Elektra* to her repertoire. This was a sad disappointment. To Craig's mind Duse was the 'perfect' actress. He admired her above all others. When he saw her 'godlike death' onstage, 'everything else seemed to die too. No fall, no noise . . . I could not applaud . . . I could only shake with tears.' So when she asked him to do 'something beautiful for Rosmersholm' he agreed, chiefly, as he later claimed, 'for the sake of Isadora'. He needed alibis and excuses in case anything went wrong. Whenever he was invited to work in the theatre a surge of anxiety would rush through him, exciting his imagination but making him highly unstable. From Duse he demanded the same absolute control as he had from Reinhardt. But speaking neither of her languages, French or Italian, he relied on Isadora's diplomatic translation of this demand as an expression of his total commitment. So 'a sort of unsatisfactory combination betwixt us' was arranged.

There was to be a single performance of *Rosmersholm* at the Teatro alla Pergola in Florence on 5 December 1906. In mid-November Craig and Isadora crossed into Italy. As they descended into the plains of Lombardy, 'the rising sun cast a great shadow across the landscape, and he felt', his son later wrote, 'that at last he had come home'. But during rehearsals he was erratic, ordering Isadora to 'keep Duse out of the theatre' and then complaining about her 'lack of co-operation'. In the street he had picked up a couple of young housepainters who, working night and day for over a week, using a secret formula containing powdered colours, covered several lengths of cloth and a huge rough-textured board with brilliant, graduated streaks of indigo, ultramarine and Russian green.

At the beginning of his play, Ibsen had given a detailed specification of the 'old-fashioned and comfortable' living-room at Rosmersholm with precise descriptions of its interior design – the tiled stove dressed with birch-branches, the folding door, the arrangement of flowers and plants before the window, the portraits of clergymen and officers. Gordon Craig dispensed with all this flim-flam (what he called 'the umbrellas and hats') and in his programme note referred to Ibsen's detestation of realism. 'The words are the words of actuality, but the drift of the words, something beyond this', he explained. 'There is the powerful impression of unseen forces closing in upon the place . . . We are in Rosmersholm, a house of shadows.'

When the curtain went up, the audience saw a single circular table and some chairs, above which a vast window, illuminated by strange light, seemed to reveal doubt and fear on one side, aspiration on the other. Over this scene towered a mystical architecture of exotic blues and greens suggesting 'the forces beyond'. Everyone was astonished, bewildered and finally impressed. Moving like an apparition between doubt and aspiration, 'Duse was magnificent – threw her details to the winds and went in. She has the courage of 25. She, Ibsen and I played our little trio out and came home happy', Craig reported to Martin Shaw. '. . . The pleasure I got from seeing

Miss Duncan watching my work with Duse was infinite.' Embracing him, Duse invited Craig to work with her 'in joy and freedom' at other plays, and he left Florence in a glow of happiness.

Back in Berlin this glow quickly faded as his income diminished and the complexities of his life multiplied. Duse's letters in garbled English outlining her many changes of plan were oddly confusing. In early February 1907 he received a request from her to visit Nice where their production of *Rosmersholm* was to be performed. Isadora, who was then dancing in Warsaw, urged him to put aside his impatience and go, though as she later wrote in her autobiography: 'I had a terrible premonition of what would happen to these two when I was not there to interpret and to smooth over their differences.'

Arriving at the Casino Theatre in Nice, Craig found that the stage-manager had cut two or three feet from the bottom of his set so as to fit it into the low proscenium opening. Suddenly he lost his temper. To save the theatre from destruction, he reminded Duse, actresses like her 'must all die of the plague – they poison the air, they make art impossible'. It did not matter that he was shouting in meaningless English – it was clearly the awful rage of a very large child. Duse was appalled. 'I have never seen such a man', she later told Isadora. '. . . He towered more than six feet, arms folded in Britannic furore, saying fearful things.' Pointing at the door, she ordered him to go. 'I never want to see you again.'

From his letters to Martin Shaw it appears that Craig somewhat regretted the volume of his abuse, transferring it in his mind to Duse herself and hoping for a reconciliation. But it would have been easier to pacify a bison than 'to tame the wild D'. Not being accustomed to women rejecting him for long, he predicted that 'I shall win'. But Duse never worked with him again. His theatre lay elsewhere. 'I want to fly far beyond all that haphazard work', he told Martin Shaw.

In moments of loneliness Craig felt very close to Martin Shaw. 'I have had – actually – the wish several times to witness your enjoyment of things I am enjoying', he wrote to him. He suspected success – though 'I also suspect failure. Both things are killing.' Perhaps Martin should help him aim for 'a little moderate restful success', he speculated. But soon he grew more ambitious. 'I'm getting awful, Martin', he confided. 'I see only one thing now – the seizing of opportunities – & the forcing them to fit my wishes.' He wished his friend would leave England and join him on his adventures. 'Why the devil aren't you here? . . . Come on at once.'

So Martin did come and helped Isadora Duncan with her music, 'which was in dreadful chaos'. Soon he was playing the piano and composing for her. 'I had never seen her before and the simplicity and beauty of her movements gave me deep enjoyment', he wrote. Craig, however, seemed strangely ill-at-ease. It was a time for discretion, Martin realised. His friend had been placed in a peculiarly sensitive position. In short, he was between two pregnancies.

Elena Meo had given birth in England to their son on 5 January 1905. She called the boy Edward (known as 'Little Teddy' while his father became for a time 'Big Ted'). Because of his flow of work – that same work which had prevented him from attending Henry Irving's memorial service – Craig was able to make only two or three brief visits to Elena over a couple of years. But he wrote to her continually, never mentioning Isadora but irregularly enclosing instalments of her money. He had wanted a son, and the son of such a woman as Elena 'might be the greatest man on earth' (he was to be Craig's biographer). All this work in Europe, he explained, he would deposit 'at the feet of my son and his mama' – he appears for the moment to have overlooked their daughter Nelly. As for his other four children, they were under May's custody and almost impossible to see except when they were visiting Ellen, while Jess's daughter Kitty now belonged to a vanished past. Sending him a photograph of 'sweet Kitty', Ellen begged him not to tear it up.

He had received his decree absolute from May, citing Jess Dorynne as co-respondent, in the early summer of 1905, but had not yet fulfilled his promise to marry Elena. Coming over to visit her for three days in July 1906 he was troubled by a sense of having let her down – which was awkward because he wished to unburden himself of other troubles. But Elena blamed him for nothing. 'I am true to those I love, true I love few [but] you are THE LOVE of my heart.' His letters to her, with their marvellous perceptions of the future, strengthened her faith in him. So he felt able to confide that he was being pursued by a dancing woman who had become infatuated with him. What he did not tell her was that Isadora was pregnant.

'At the time of which I am writing', Martin Shaw wrote tactfully in his autobiography, 'Isadora had no children of her own.' Nevertheless she was five months pregnant by the time Shaw returned to England. The doctor had told her at the beginning of 1906 that 'I must be careful but that I can dance until the end of May'. Helped occasionally by Maurice Magnus, she had taken on an extraordinarily busy programme around Germany, Scandinavia, Denmark and the Netherlands, for some of which Martin Shaw and Gordon Craig accompanied her. But to Craig's dismay, she was giving some of her money to her sister Elizabeth. 'I had to take on this tour because of the depleting expenses of the school', she was to explain. 'I had drawn upon my reserve funds and had no more left.'

Isadora may have believed that the birth of this child would strengthen their love. If so, it was a miscalculation. While Craig's thoughts were centred on the international theatre magazine he wished to start, Topsy's mind, he noticed, was fixed on baby clothes. The financial implications were serious. How was he to achieve anything? 'I try to do the best I can – although you don't seem to think so', she wrote. 'Chiefly you expect too much.' Although his initial reaction had shocked her, yet 'I *can't help it.* I have the most exquisitely happy feeling sometimes.'

She danced for as long as she dared, then, in late June, found an isolated house, the Villa Maria, at Nordwjick, near Leyden, on the sand dunes along the North Sea. Perhaps it reminded her of living near the sea as a child in California. 'It's pretty wonderful', she told Craig, '– & a garden full of white shells.' Here her child would be born. Here she waited for Craig to join her. Unfortunately he felt moved just then to visit Elena.

He had told Isadora of Elena when they first met – told her that he was destined to marry her, but not that she was giving birth to his son. Isadora cared little for marriage certificates – they were simply pieces of paper. Now, she felt apprehensive and, not realising perhaps quite how many people might be involved, made him an all-embracing offer. 'I am so glad you are well, and also glad you see your own dear Mother or see any that you love . . . if there is anyone you care for very much who feels unhappy and wants to come with you she can have half my little house with *all my heart.* It will give me *joy* – and Love is enough for all.'

Craig now found himself in a perplexing situation and fell to musing about it in one of his notebooks. 'I am in love with one woman only', he began confidently. But then he could not deny that he was 'keenly attracted to another woman, who may be a witch or a pretty child (and it really doesn't matter which) and I find it hard to be away from her'. The only way to solve this painful riddle was to accept that there was an essential link between sex and creative ability. If he did not quarrel with this notion, then he could be at peace with himself. But this was a philosophical solution and not the literal coming-together proposed by Isadora, which would be preposterous. As he explained in a letter to his mother – that Ellen-Terry-of-a-mother who had surely conditioned his relations with women: 'It is the same with plays as people, one does not love the same person and one cannot always love the same play, but to *renew* love – that is the secret, not to hang on to the past and dead things.'

As the autumn of 1906 approached it became easier to renew his love for Elena than for Isadora. Elena lived the life of a saint, making no demands on him, presenting him with a son, and showing absolute faith in his genius. Isadora, despite her divine gift, was no saint. Sometimes, when she spoke in an American accent about her own work, she bored him. At parties she earned his disapproval by drinking too much champagne and, perhaps to summon up his passion, flirting with men who, he could see, were 'equally attracted as myself – and I object to being equally anything in such matters'.

Isadora kept up a stream of cheerfulness in her letters, knowing how aggressively Craig reacted to bad news. She had invited the English artist Kathleen Bruce* to stay with her at the Villa Maria as she prepared for the baby to be born. These were uncertain days. Sometimes, when doing her yoga lessons or walking along the deserted dunes and watching the great waves come in or simply stitching tiny clothes for her baby, Isadora looked radiant. But there were painful hours and sleepless nights when she was wakened by fearful sea-storms. Some days the whole sky turned black and, her body stretched and deformed, an awful apprehension enveloped her. She had been upset to discover, perhaps from Martin Shaw, that Elena already

* A formidable character who had been a pupil of Rodin, Kathleen Bruce (1878–1947) was destined to wander through the indexes of many books under different names. In 1908 she married the Antarctic explorer Robert Falcon Scott, who perished in 1912. Ten years later she became the wife of Hilton Young, an old Etonian barrister and journalist who, entering politics, was made a baron – after which she was known as Lady Kennet of the Dene. Her *Self-Portrait of an Artist* was published posthumously in 1949. Besides Craig, the subjects of her portrait sculpture include Bernard Shaw, W.B. Yeats and several politicians, among them Lloyd George, Asquith and Neville Chamberlain.

had Craig's son. Her father's disappearance when she was a child may have made her all the more apprehensive that the father of her own child might leave. One night Kathleen Bruce suddenly woke up and, wandering around the rooms, found that the house was empty. She ran down to the sea and there, in the calm water, she saw a figure. 'As I neared it, calling, she turned round with a gentle, rather dazed look, and stretched out her arms to me with a faint, childish smile, saying, "The tide was low, I couldn't do it, and I'm so cold" . . . Isadora came from the water fully clothed.'

A few days later Gordon Craig arrived unheralded 'to stay we knew not how long', and everything 'turned to festival'. Kathleen Bruce knew how infatuated Isadora was with 'Ellen Terry's golden-haired little boy', now a handsome man in his mid-thirties whose beauty and genius had inflamed her love. She had spoken of his white, lithe, gleaming body and how it had first hypnotised her in his Berlin apartment. 'I had met the flesh of my flesh, the blood of my blood . . . As flame meets flame, we burned in one bright fire. Here, at last, was my mate; my love.'

To Kathleen, Gordon Craig had sounded like a monster. Yet now she met him, she began to understand how he had entranced Isadora's body and mind. 'He was tall and well-built', she wrote, 'with a mass of long, thick hair, just beginning to turn grey. He had good features, high cheek-bones, and a healthy colour.' He was not the voluptuary she had imagined, but a romantic figure with something feminine in his temperament. Isadora treated him 'as a Messiah'. In his chronology, Craig was to note that Kathleen Bruce made a 'remarkable statuette' of him. Then one day, as the date of his child's birth grew near, he 'bolted' (to use his biographer-son's word) and Isadora 'sank back exhausted into the monotony of the long wait'.

Isadora had thought that having a baby would be a simple matter. But when the labour pains began, she was convulsed by an overwhelming agony. 'There followed the most terrible hours that I had ever spent', Kathleen Bruce remembered. She sent a telegram to Gordon Craig in Rotterdam – and he immediately returned. The birth itself, which came suddenly, without opiates or ether, in the late morning of Monday, 26 September, was an 'atrocity of pain', causing an internal rupture and bringing into question whether Isadora would ever dance again. But the blue-eyed baby, a girl, 'was unhurt by it all . . . [a] miraculous object'.

As soon as their daughter was born, Gordon Craig hurried off in pursuit of work, leaving Isadora to lie long hours with her baby 'in my arms, watching her asleep; sometimes catching a gaze from her eyes, feeling very near the edge, the mystery, perhaps the knowledge of life'. Her letters to Craig proclaim her abiding love for him – 'You are the unique life-giver for me & without you it would be the Earth without the Sun.' She touched lightly on her worsening health – 'aches & pains, pains and aches . . . There is too much feminine in my composition.'

He had felt obliged to press on her the urgent need to earn money again and she started dancing too soon. That winter, while in Warsaw, she fell onstage and was carried back to her hotel. 'Darling Heart,' she appealed to him, 'don't let these things annoy you – don't let anything annoy you.'

In all this time their happiest hours together had been in Florence for the performance of *Rosmersholm*. Then it was his work that was onstage and she the spectator. She rejoiced in his success as much as he did, knowing how fretful and impatient he had been growing the previous year when he became 'horribly troubled' by his 'entire lack of genius or even talent'. But after the debacle in Nice, their relationship deteriorated.

In the summer of 1907 Craig returned to Florence, still 'not at all happy about my achievements or my discoveries or my setbacks'. But Florence itself, 'this sacred city of great artists dead and gone', restored him. Walking through the streets towards night-time, 'the great dead seemed to me to come to life – passing as shadows'. These ghostly beings, so marvellously congenial, gave him courage. They seemed 'solely purposed to do well' and he resolved to make them his future companions and exemplars.

'I wish I could just simply help your great work & stop everything else', Isadora had written to him from Amsterdam. But that was not what he wanted. This dancing girl had threatened to obliterate his own art and her all-absorbing love was devouring his very self. He had nothing more to learn from her. He needed fewer emotional outpourings and more simple facts and figures – especially figures. That summer, he drafted a curious document by which she was committed for five years to dance with his touring marionette theatre and pay him her earnings. In this fantasy, she renounced her human status, her dangerous feminine identity, and became a moving shadow in his illusory world of drama. And so desperate was she to hold on to him that she agreed to 'go forward with our great plan', as if she could bind him to her and dance her way into five more years of love.

In her autobiography Isadora retrospectively created her own romantic fiction. 'I adored Craig – I loved him with all the ardour of my artistic soul – but I realised that our separation was inevitable', she wrote. '. . . To live with him was to renounce my Art, my personality, nay, perhaps my life . . . and to give up my Art I knew to be impossible; I should pine away – I should die from chagrin. I must find a remedy.' And then, she added: 'the remedy came'. In this and other passages, Isadora appropriates Gordon Craig's arguments and makes them her own.

During the spring and summer, intermittently still using the business skills of Maurice Magnus, Isadora planned to dance around Europe and send Gordon Craig money so that he could employ a team of men in Florence to work for him. But she was ill for much of that spring and 'making money in summer is like trying to hold water in a sieve'. Despite this she tried to remain optimistic: 'I feel our plan is being accomplished – fearfully slow – but surely', she wrote to him. '. . . I am going to devote myself to one thing now, & that is – Bank account.'

But he did not write to her as he had before. 'Do be happy a bit', she had pleaded with him. But he was not happy. Though they travelled together to Heidelberg and Stockholm that summer, they saw much less of each other during the subsequent months and, as he went about creating a new life for himself in Florence, so Isadora became 'a sort of stranger' in his mind. He began to demonise her. Had she not *promised* to send him money and then failed to do so? She had left him in the humiliating position of having to rely once more on his mother. He sensed that 'my hour has struck', but Isadora was still trying to turn the clock back. He must resist her.

She came to Florence in the early autumn, stayed one day, and left in tears. He told her that their grand days as lovers were over and that there was no place for her in his new life. In private he was writing down many bitter denunciations of her so that he could learn them by heart, preventing her from taking possession of him. He knew that he might succumb to her 'if I did not remember that I was Gordon Craig'. So he remembered and insisted that she must forget. 'Think about me no more. I no longer exist for you.' Then he fell silent.

But he could not get her out of his mind. In later years he would explain that 'I deliberately made her think ill of me'. He felt an unendurable guilt and blamed her for causing it. She was like a flower whose petals he kept pulling off: 'I love you. I love you not . . .' He accused her of being incapable of love, confessed that he felt 'red hot with shame' when he thought of their relationship and then, in a letter he did not post, declared: 'Isadora I love you – and I ought not to say it – for it is almost ALL.' Looking back at this time in one of his notebooks, *Book Topsy*, written over thirty years later, he described their love as 'a big tormenting thing – so desperate a thing that we felt quite mad'.

It was to limit such madness that Craig tried to keep his relationships with women – Ellen and Edy and May, Elena Meo and Jess Dorynne and Isadora Duncan – in separate compartments. But as they got to hear of one another they broke through these compartments – Ellen and Isadora had already written to each other. This was one reason why he had bolted to Florence, vowing to work alone there. 'I'm afraid you needed someone a bit stronger than your poor Topsy to help you', Isadora had written to him. He used her letter to give himself strength. 'She was a strange, lovely, strong creature', he wrote in a notebook, 'but it seems I was the stronger. Perhaps she wished to see me at her knees, at her feet, and there she did not find me. I *stood*, no matter what the pain I may have felt, I stood.'

Isadora must have known this was the end. Yet how could it end on such a false note? 'Dearest Ted you have a funny effect on your Topsy', she wrote to him after leaving Florence. 'You fill me with a Longing & Pain that are terrible . . . I only want to fly into you & die.' But there was of course their living daughter. She sent him news of this 'most good natured & contented little Being' who at one time resembled Ellen Terry and at another 'is the image of you'. If these charming glimpses of their daughter were intended to revive his love, then Isadora had again miscalculated. He did not see his daughter, following her birth, for some six years. 'He never felt any responsibility for his children', one of his sons said. In her autobiography, Isadora wrote that 'Craig thought of a wonderful Irish name, Deirdre . . . beloved of Ireland. So we called her Deirdre.' Actually, until she was aged two, their daughter was called Snowdrop. 'Do find the child a name!' Isadora had pleaded with Craig. 'I shall call [her] Snowdrop', Craig replied, '– you may call her Artemis, Diana, Sappho Duncan Craig IF you like.' But among the many names he came out with had been Deirdre – and so she was given this ill-omened name, Deirdre of the Sorrows, from an old Irish tale revived by Synge and Yeats.

By the beginning of 1908, Isadora was dancing again in St Petersburg. 'I'm nothing but a silly old dancing dervish, always en route – I can't help it – it seems to be my cussed fate', she wrote to Craig, '& I haven't been able to help you much either for your life or your work, but Patience – perhaps I will be able to some day.'

In the margin of this letter Gordon Craig wrote: 'No – only in 1904–5'. He no longer wished to be encumbered with empty offers of help and had lost patience with the theatre she inhabited. There is a sense of relief as well as a note of protest in his claim that there existed 'a regular barrier against allowing me to produce as I like or write as I like'. He was struggling to start his school of theatre in Florence where he could experiment as he wished and launch an international magazine called *The Mask* in which he could write as he chose. 'If the productions are impractical,' he had written to Isadora, 'the writings are essentially harmless.'

But just as he was reconciling himself to the 'superhuman task' of creating a theatre of spaces, planes and curves, of mysterious heights and intimate corners, an abstract place where human beings revealed the unspoken strangeness of their lives: just at this point, everything changed.

Konstantin Sergeivich Stanislavski, director of the Moscow Art Theatre, had first seen Isadora dance when she performed a Chopin programme in the Moscow Solodovnikov Theatre early in 1905. At the end of her performance he rushed up to the footlights, applauding her frantically. But it was not until three years later that they met in St Petersburg where she 'continually mentioned the name of Gordon Craig', Stanislavski wrote in his autobiography, 'whom she considered a genius and one of the greatest men in the contemporary theatre'. She showed him some of Craig's designs and insisted that he must work in an atmosphere where his genius had the best chance of displaying itself – in short 'in your Art Theatre'.

Stanislavski, who did not speak much English, suggested that Isadora write to Craig on his behalf. 'I know that she wrote a great deal to him about me and our Theatre.' Against this sentence in his copy of Stanislavski's autobiography, Gordon Craig was to write: 'hardly a word'. He could not admit that she had behaved generously. But it was true. 'Mr Stanislavski, the regisseur of the Theatre, is a wonderful man', she wrote in the course of a long letter to him that February. '. . . I talked to him many hours about you

– He says he would love to have you come & be regisseur altogether, as he prefers to *act* . . . He says he would give you a perfectly free hand in the Theatre – that actors would follow your directions as to movements . . . he is great & simple & Beautiful – such a man one doesn't meet with once a century . . . I hope with all my heart that this can be arranged.'

And it was arranged.

But was it an opportunity or an interruption? It was both. 'It may be a dream, dear old chap,' Craig wrote to Martin Shaw, 'but it's like Heaven after Hell.' It was also a fearful nuisance, as he acknowledged in one of his notebooks: 'I do not want to waste time producing plays – for that is vanity . . . Moscow is old work, I have passed it all.' Nevertheless, perhaps it was necessary sometimes to go back: 'I had half turned the leaf – had glimpses of the next.'

In May 1908 he received a telegram inviting him to Moscow that autumn – an invitation that enabled him the more easily to turn down offers from Max Reinhardt and Beerbohm Tree. Stanislavski was spending part of the summer near Ostend where Maurice Magnus went to see him. 'He [Stanislavski] would like you (after you have seen the theatre and Moscow and feel you can stay there and work there) to become engaged to the theatre by the year', he wrote to Craig. The theatre proposed paying him 500 roubles (approximately equivalent to £3000 today) a month plus expenses and he would be asked to stay half of each year in Moscow producing a series of plays. 'It is the best proposition I have yet heard', Maurice Magnus concluded, 'and certainly one which is more dignified than any other, for you deal with first class people.'

In mid-October, Craig travelled to Moscow where he was welcomed even more enthusiastically than he had been in Weimar. 'I arrived here at 4', he wrote excitedly to Edy. '. . . 6 huge Russians seized on me and landed me in a red and gold motor car – I was with them till 6 next morning', all this time seeing gypsy dancers and singers who 'shrieked and wept and leapt for me'. It was 'ridiculously splendid', he told her. '. . . But oh god I'm lonely (ever been lonely?)' By the end of his three-week stay, photographing the theatre, meeting the actors and holding long discussions with Stanislavski, he agreed to design a production of *Hamlet*.

His loneliness dissolved in a romantic attachment with Chekhov's widow, the actress Olga Knipper. Neither tragic nor comic, her voice was a grand mixture of both tragedy and comedy. She brought to mind 'something from the woods . . . always something good, like the twigs, the brown fern'. He called her Temple. 'Dear Temple', he wrote early in 1909. '. . . You are so charming – and so much more – something so mysterious that I can say at once

I love you very much –
I fear you very much –

To preserve his love, guard against this fear, he presented himself as a Pushkin-like figure who 'dies a death once a week if he lives a life once a week' and who devours more time in an hour simply lying under a tree than most people do in a year. But he protected himself by making a game of their romance. 'I see such wonders in your face – I see the reflection of all the wonders you have looked at. When I look at you and see in your face . . . the gravity of great beauty, then with my eyes I try to tell you all about the Love for which I know we all care so little . . .'

There are pictures of them on picnics together and when they were apart his 'Darling Temple' sent him pictures of herself 'with a nice kiss'. Over twenty years, later when Craig returned to Russia, he was still her 'dear beautiful old friend', and she wrote to assure him that 'Temple has nothing forgotten . . . you must come to me'. Their closeness gave him happiness for a while. 'I have in Moscow a home for as long as I like', he wrote to his mother on an early visit. 'I wish to God', Ellen replied, 'I could be in Moscow . . . When you are in Russia you seem to be off the earth.'

Over three years Craig went to Moscow for rehearsals and continued working at the sets and costumes in Florence. The solitary figure of Hamlet, set on avenging his misfortunes, still seemed to mirror his own condition. Hamlet 'is no ordinary man; his words and looks and actions are so extraordinary, so superfine', he explained to Stanislavski's wife, Maria Lilina, '. . . so full of the intoxication of love that no one can understand him, not his mother nor the critics, to this day'.

His production opened with the Ghost – a vision of Craig's father – who has crept onto the stage unseen, a grey winding-sheet the colour of the castle walls covering his armour. A projection lamp suddenly illuminates him and then, as if startled by the shouts of the soldiers, he vanishes. We are in a 'phantasmagorical world', wrote the American critic Lawrence Senelick, '. . . Craig's concept of *Hamlet* as monodrama: everything that took place within the scene [Act I, scene ii] until the exit of the Court was Hamlet's nightmare'.

Though he recognised Stanislavski's courage and loyalty for testing his experiment in the living theatre, Craig came up against many frustrations while preparing this production – in particular those presented by the screens which he was trying out in his studio-workshop at Florence. These screens, silently sliding one way or another to reveal a castle platform, a churchyard, a view from the queen's apartment, though they would have been easily moved by twenty-first-century technology, were at this time so cumbersome that Stanislavski was obliged to dispense with Craig's theory of continuous imperceptible movement and use them only for simple manoeuvres. And even then they did not combine well with the thematic development of the play – it was as if Craig were unsuccessfully mixing abstract and figurative painting. Each day he changed his mind – changed it many times each day. The compromises which had to be imposed on the choreography, lighting and costumes during the final rehearsals, gave rise to another of his violent tantrums, similar to his fury with Duse. This time it was directed against his Russian assistant, Leopold Sulerzhitsky, whom he had previously described as 'a dear man . . . a rough diamond – full of intelligence and with natural talent'. He now insisted that his name should be taken off the programme. The Russians, nevertheless, refused to be balked by Craig's temperament. To them he had the licence of a great artist. Sulerzhitsky, who had worked over two years with him on *Hamlet* and knew that Craig would never have completed the production without his help, wrote: 'Craig the artist I respect, but Craig the friend no longer exists for me.'

Craig was in Moscow for the opening night of *Hamlet* in January 1912, and noted in his diary that it was an 'overwhelming success'. He had wanted to place Claudius and Gertrude upon high at the back of the stage with a great cloak that fell from their shoulders to cover the entire stage. 'Through gaps in this sea of material appeared the courtiers so that the court became an image of Claudius's power', wrote Peter Holland in an introduction to Craig's memoirs. 'The cloak flowed down the stage and into a trap where Hamlet sat, brooding, with the court behind him seeming like a monstrous dream of Hamlet's own imagining.'

But, as Laurence Senelick has explained, Craig could not achieve this effect with a single piece of cloth pierced with holes through which the smirking heads of the courtiers were to appear. One of the court ladies, Serafina Birman, remembered that 'the people were arranged on wooden platforms so as to represent symbolically the feudal ladder: at the top the King and Queen, the courtiers below; at the feet of Claudius and Gertrude assemble their more intimate henchmen . . . The actors were distributed at various levels, their mantles flowed out and gave the impression of a monolithic golden pyramid.' The reflection of their gold costumes on the gilt walls produced a splendid glow. Apparently separated from this by a barricade, and semi-recumbent on a bench, 'Hamlet sits facing the audience,' Senelick wrote, 'lost in reverie, isolated from the image of molten gold behind him'.

At the end of the play Craig was called before the curtain with Stanislavski and 'turning round, I find the stage packed – band and all – music strikes up and the company applaud me'. Then the theatre manager, Nemirovich-Danchenko, stepped on to the stage and delivered a eulogy: 'You, Mr Gordon Craig, came to us from England, from Shakespeare's native country . . . You come with new methods for our art, and you have put in them all your poetical genius. We bow before you . . .' Here were the scenes of vanity against which, in case they were not forthcoming, he was eternally on his guard, yet to which he remained susceptible. 'The whole theatre seems glad I should be with them', he told Kessler, '& this gives me infinite happiness.' But later, when the Russians invited him to 'stay for ever', a sense of desolation spread through him.

Hamlet was praised by *The Times* critic in Moscow as a 'remarkable triumph', and Craig himself described as possessing a 'singular power of carrying the spiritual significance of words and dramatic situations beyond the actor to the scene in which he moves . . . he is able in some mysterious way to evoke almost any sensation of time or space, the scenes even in themselves suggesting variations of human emotion'.

Gordon Craig's *Hamlet* was to go into the theatre's repertory and would eventually be given over 400 performances, during which time continual modifications were made to the production. Though he never again worked with Stanislavski, his ideas were to infiltrate the theatre's history. He left Moscow at the end of January. '"Hamlet" was a success – I can't say anything else', he wrote to Martin Shaw before leaving. And to Edy he sent a sketch of himself, hat triumphantly held on high, as he splendidly soars through Stanislavski's hoop.

Though he was later to take exception to Stanislavski's memories of the *Hamlet* production, Craig retained an affectionate admiration for his 'noble life given to research work'. He was to praise Stanislavski's 'research' in terms which, with a little modification, might be applied to his own lifetime of dramatic experiment. 'All the time he researches to discover how he can transform the body and its flesh and blood into pure spirit, the actor into divinity', he wrote in *The Mask*. '. . . You have gone far; not utterly useless has been your quest: for you have proved it impossible that flesh and blood shall be a *practical* spirit – a working useful divinity: proved it over and over again by refusing to be beaten . . . You will search to the end.'

41
Brothers

Gordon Craig's exile seemed to press sometimes on the bruise of his illegitimacy. 'I am as it were cut off from the Theatre,' he protested, '– I who possibly happen to be THE THEATRE.' He knew that many of his countrymen thought him a spoilt child – a spoilt child of genius perhaps who was conducting hidden experiments abroad. Occasionally he would pick up an English newspaper and marvel at 'the insularity of the old land'. He castigated those who, like Shaw's friend Harley Granville-Barker, tinkered academically with one or two new ideas – in all likelihood his ideas. 'Only H. B. Irving kept his head', he wrote. But of the two Irving brothers, it was Laurence who was importing the work of modern foreign playwrights such as Eugène Brieux and Ibsen, and picking up something of Stanislavski's methods of stage direction. Assuming his father's legacy, Harry on the other hand, was scrupulously reassembling the Lyceum sets and reviving the old melodramas.

Sir Henry Irving was dead: but the potency of his legend lived on and this was Harry's inheritance. Determined to honour his father's debts, he auctioned off many of his theatre pictures and costumes. It was believed that the old man had died with 'an empty purse' – all his biographers repeated this – but the gross value of his estate, when resworn, was calculated to be more than £20,000, and after every debt was settled, there still remained almost £15,000 – enough for Harry to secure a lifetime allowance for his mother.

He shouldered other paternal responsibilities too. His father's companion, Mrs Aria, became in effect one of his family at 1 Upper Woburn Place. She still looked remarkably young and made the air crackle with her stories of the old days. She was accompanied everywhere by Henry Irving's death mask which she would place reverently on a blue velvet cushion. Sir Henry's designated biographer, Austin Brereton, was another frequent guest at Harry's home. He also engaged Walter Collinson, his father's dresser (who had been left an annuity of £50) to be his own dresser. And he oversaw the arrangements for a public statue of his father, paid for by members of the acting profession, to be sculpted by a Royal Academician, Thomas Brock, and erected outside the National Portrait Gallery on the Charing Cross Road.

Most important of all, he offered employment in a newly formed touring company to many people from his father's disbanded troupe – character-actors, small-part players, carpenters, electricians, box-office managers, property men, wardrobe masters. Only two major characters were left out – as they had been from his father's will: the Lyceum's stage-manager Henry Loveday, and the business and acting manager Bram Stoker. Over many years Henry Irving had paid them both up to three times what managers in other theatres were receiving. After his two sons were married and Harry had two children, there was no occasion to make further provision, especially during difficult times. Besides, Loveday was happy enough to retire.

But Stoker was not happy. The loyalty he felt for the 'Guv'nor', its depth and sincerity, had been plain for everyone to see as his pushing form, burly and red-headed, filled the Lyceum with its ceaseless activity. Staunch and faithful, he seemed in a mortal hurry to serve Irving's interests. In the beginning, Irving's words to him in Ireland had been addressed 'with love', but this endearment soon gave way to formality once he came to the Lyceum. Quarter of a century later, Irving was a tyrant there, while Stoker, still his envoy and manager, obeying every trifle set on him, had become his Caliban. Was his profit on it to conjure forth that vengeful fantasy, *Dracula*? In her memoirs, Ellen Terry described Stoker as 'one of the most kind and tender-hearted of men'. He had virtually given up his life for Irving, and when Irving's life ended he himself suffered a stroke. He was left, it seemed, without an occupation except as Irving's biographer. Momentarily he regained his power as the man 'authorised to speak for Irving on all matters'. There were hardly even walk-on parts in these reminiscences for Harry and Laurence, to whom, at the end, he is seen reluctantly 'handing over such matters as were in my care'. It was 'by their own desire' that he was obliged to do this. But it was not by his desire. 'It was all so desolate and lonely, as so much of his life had been', Stoker wrote in his final chapter. 'So lonely that in the midst of my sorrow I could but rejoice in one thing: for him there was now Peace and Rest.'

To Harry and Laurence he handed over a dead man. The living man he had protected from everyone, even his sons. Little wonder then that he was to have no place in their careers.

Harry began touring the country with some of his father's actors in the summer of 1906. They travelled to the United States between September and February 1907, then came to London. Carrying on his father's business, adding to it, he was championing the role of the actor-manager, warning his colleagues against unforeseen ills that might arise from challenging the censorship laws, and tying himself to a theatre syndicate formed by Henry Irving's creditors. He was also reviving some of his repertoire – *The Lyons Mail*, *Charles I* and even *The Bells* – risking comparison by taking on roles his father had made famous. In New York, a critic from *The Stage* warned him that 'the popularity and regard of his late father's genius would avail him nothing'. But by the end of the tour, Harry's 'own colours [were] flying above the frayed standards of the Lyceum'.

The baton was also ready to be passed on to Harry's son. The H.B. Irving Company of players, the boy remembered, 'became my relatives'. The rhythmic transition from ordinary to theatrical life seemed to remove life's pain together with the discarded coats, shirts and trousers hanging in their dressing-room cupboards. His father would shed his stern authority, shining with boyish excitement which 'brought me closer to him than at any other time'.

But as the son grew beguiled by the mysterious glamour of the theatre, its giddy heights and darkened realms, his mother began to turn aside from it. Dolly was playing some of Ellen's old parts, playing them opposite Harry and before critics and audiences who held vivid memories of Henry Irving and Ellen Terry. Sometimes she felt like an impostor. Following the ghost of his father put an awful strain on Harry. His performances lacked warmth, as if he were being upstaged by a powerful unseen presence, grim, ironic, crafty. 'Filial piety is all very well', Max Beerbohm wrote in the *Saturday Review*, '. . . [but] Mr Irving's natural resemblance to his father is strong enough to rob him of any great credit.'

In 1907 Dolly had suffered a miscarriage – a sorrow that no amount of play-acting could heal. She grew absorbed in charitable work for the welfare of underprivileged children and, elected as one of the St Pancras Board of Guardians, she would eventually become recognised as a pioneer in social reform.

Harry was not much interested in the changes that were taking place in the Edwardian theatre – the vogue for dance ranging from the Tiller Girls and the new rhythms of ragtime and the tango to the Imperial Russian Ballet, or the intimate revues and popular musical comedies, and even the medieval miracle play which Max Reinhardt staged as a pageant and his production of *Oedipus Rex* where the actors, mingling with the audience, crowded in upon the stage from the auditorium. Harry's company made most of its money abroad. The syndicate investors insisted that he take his company to some of the British colonies which had never seen Henry Irving onstage, in particular Australia and New Zealand.

The prospect of leaving her children for so long filled Dolly with panic. 'I am a very domestic sort of person', she protested. And there was another reason for her panic. Among several plays that had been added to the repertoire was a dramatisation of R.L. Stevenson's *The Strange Case of Dr Jekyll and Mr Hyde.* The dramatic rights in the novel had interested Henry Irving but he never produced it and it was later adapted by his old friend and agent of destruction, Joe Comyns Carr, who changed Dr Jekyll from a sly bachelor conscious of the good and evil that coexisted within him into a much-loved physician married to a beautiful blind woman. This austere and altruistic stage-doctor suited Harry's deportment as an actor very well; but his awful transformation into the sinister shape of Mr Hyde could not help but bring to everyone's mind the terrifying spectre of Henry Irving: a bloodless, dry presence speaking through 'narrowed teeth and lips in a hard, thin supercaustic tone'. As Jekyll gave way each night to the diabolical Hyde, it seemed as if the unearthly spirit of Henry Irving had indeed returned from the dead and was devouring his son. The horror of this melodrama haunted the imagination of audiences who came to see it again and again. But the cumulative effect on the other actors was baleful and, although Harry himself seemed unaware of any psychological implications, Dolly grew terrified by what appeared to her as a possession rather than a performance – one that she was condemned each night to witness and yet, as the blind wife, never to see and powerless to control. This was a play which the syndicate insisted they must act in together and take with them to Australia and New Zealand. With great reluctance, Dolly agreed.

For Harry this year-long tour was to be a unique success. At last he was acting beyond the territory of his father and free to create the familiar characters as well as some new ones without comparisons. But Dolly suffered a nervous breakdown in Australia, which ended her acting career. Feeling miserable at leaving her children and obscurely guilty over her miscarriage, she lost confidence. In every role, she behaved like a blind woman, unable to leave the walls of the sets, overcome by terror whenever, led by the action of the play, she was compelled to edge, arms outstretched before her, towards the centre of the stage. Her trance-like manoeuvres were greeted with derision by the Australian audiences – except when she played the unseeing wife of Jekyll-and-Hyde and the mad Ophelia in *Hamlet*. Outside the theatre she appeared to forget her malaise. Harry protected her as best he could short of breaking his contract with the syndicate, replacing her with understudies and adding one of Wills's old warhorses to the repertoire in which she played another blind woman. But when Harry's company toured South Africa the following year, Dolly stayed at home.

She occupied herself, while he was abroad, making a new home for her family at 7 Gordon Square in Bloomsbury. Having also bought a derelict windmill and miller's cottage near Whitstable in Kent, she began spending her summers there gardening, giving the deprived children in London glorious holidays, and regaining her natural composure.

Harry too began a new phase of his career when, in 1913, he bought a twenty-one-year lease of the Savoy Theatre in the Strand. But he could not gauge the mood of the public and the new play which opened his season failed. Abandoning his plans, he let the Savoy to Harley Granville-Barker whose brilliant productions of *Twelfth Night* and *A Midsummer Night's Dream* seemed to place Harry deeper in the past. The hazards he was encountering as an actor-manager were more severe than he had bargained for, and what seemed his greatest asset – the theatrical legacy of his father – was also his heaviest burden. One success when escaping from this legacy was as 'Mr Nobody' in a modern morality play. Noticing his silent moods followed by dreadful eruptions of temper, his son sensed that he was 'heading for danger'.

He also noticed how very different his father looked from his uncle

Laurence. Harry was still from head to toe the Edwardian actor-manager with his 'curvilinear silk hat, the well-cut velvet-trimmed overcoat, the black-satin stock and suit of sober serge'. But Laurence, for all the trouble his wife Mabel took to spruce him up, holding a dress parade each morning to check his tie, socks and handkerchiefs, remained a dishevelled figure in his well-worn tweed suit with a fedora crammed on his head.

The two brothers seldom acted the same characters onstage, but when they did so they offered very different interpretations. 'Harry saw Iago as a subtle, Machiavellian villain, revelling in his devilment and relishing his power', Hesketh Pearson remembered. 'Laurence saw him as a bluff soldier, who has become jealous, resentful and malignant.' Harry's performance was the more dramatically entertaining, Laurence's the more disturbing since it suggested that all of us were susceptible to extremes of jealousy and revenge.

Laurence did not envy Harry the task he had set himself of resurrecting those spectres from the Lyceum – he insisted on his own 'strangeness'. Harry was of course the elder son, but he sometimes behaved as if he were Henry Irving's only son – despite the fact that Laurence had been at the Lyceum longer. Unlike Dolly, Mabel had no children. She was the businesswoman of the matrimonial partnership, noted for her common sense in contrast to Laurence's impish and sardonic personality. She learnt typewriting, managed their tours, continued acting and loyally promoting Laurence's career. Harry's was the more dominant presence, though Mrs Aria still saw him as 'a child' – someone who never quite attained his own adult identity. Critics would inevitably compare both his and Laurence's performances with those of their father – there was no escape from this. But Laurence was in perpetual search of an escape, taking his inspiration from foreign writers and exotic places beyond the frontiers of his father's experience.

Austin Brereton suggested that Laurence had wasted his talent 'on what his father would have called unwholesome plays'. Fond as Sir Henry Irving was of 'Fussie', the dog that Ellen Terry had given him, he would never have taken the liberty of parading the animal onstage. But Laurence, who had become as fierce an anti-vivisectionist as his sister-in-law Dolly was a children's welfare campaigner, trained his dog 'Lop' to be an accomplished performer and composed a one-act touring play, *The Dog Between*, in which Lop admirably upstaged both Mabel and himself.

Less eccentric perhaps was Laurence's devotion to the works of Ibsen. He played the romantic rake, Eilert Lövborg, in Mrs Patrick Campbell's production of *Hedda Gabler* at the Court Theatre in 1907, and six years later at the Haymarket Theatre 'a very fine part' – the tragic warrior-statesman Earl Skule in *The Pretenders*. 'All is going prosperously for me', he assured his mother during the rehearsals. But though *The Pretenders* was acclaimed by the critics, 'the ruder public had no appetite for it'.

Laurence must have hoped that this public would have a greater appetite for the plays of Eugène Brieux. They covered such rude subjects – from venereal disease to legalised birth-control – that they were seldom granted licences by the Lord Chamberlain. Under the pseudonym 'H.M. Clark', he translated Brieux's *Les Hannetons*, billing it as *The Incubus* for a performance by the Stage Society. Then, still chaffing at the English censorship laws, he took the play to the United States in the spring of 1909. *Les Hannetons* (meaning figuratively 'The Dizzy Ones') was the most readily enjoyable of Brieux's works. But the comedy bristled with moral difficulties: not one of the couples in the play was legally married. The Strindbergian theme appeared to label women as domestic tyrants and reveal as a delusion the freedom that sensual men habitually sought through not marrying their mistresses. American audiences were affronted. After nine weeks on tour, Laurence and Mabel came back noticeably poorer. But Laurence returned at the beginning of 1910, staging the same play with a more innocuous English title, *The Affinity*. To this, however, he incautiously added Brieux's most outrageous drama *The Three Daughters of M. Dupont*, a 'socially useful' work weighing the economics of prostitution against marriage and demonstrating how women can be condemned to slavery within wedlock. This time the American critics treated Laurence and Mabel as messengers of vice, peddling 'an odious spectacle of vulgarity'. One attack in particular, by the critic Alan Dale, was so abusive that Laurence insisted something must be done. He did not mind so much being called 'as immobile as a wooden Indian sign outside a tobacco shop' but he hated having Mabel described as 'ludicrous . . . with as much whimsicality as an oyster' and good for nothing beyond 'selling ribbons in a department store'. At the end of the play, Laurence came before the curtain and, stalking the footlights, striding back and forward in agitation, delivered a passionate counter-attack against Dale's slanders of his wife – to great applause from the New York audience.

But this outburst gave his adversary enormous publicity. The offensive review was reprinted everywhere and Laurence was rebuffed for having attacked the liberty of the press.

Back in England he was growing equally controversial following an ambitious adaptation of Dostoevsky's *Crime and Punishment.* He played the dissipated student Raskolnikov 'like one in ecstasy', according to the *Sunday Times* reviewer, giving a performance that was in the opinion of another reviewer 'quite deliciously ghastly'. *The Unwritten Law*, as it was called, was a bold experiment that succeeded unexpectedly as tragic melodrama – recalling, with its homicidal dreams and trances, the tortured world of *The Bells*. 'Laurence Irving . . . is now coming *rapidly* to a high position', Ellen Terry wrote in a letter to Mrs Rumball, '. . . he had great talent – so much more like his Father than H[arry]'.

Laurence also experimented with a more obscure European writer, Melchior Lengyel, whose 'Japanese drama' set in Paris he adapted, directed and brought to London. *Typhoon* presented a conflict between Japanese and western cultures. Laurence played Tukerumo, an intellectual dedicated to the occidental style of life, whose affaire with a heartless Parisian cocotte provides the action of the tragedy which leads to the murder of the girl and a European court trial that convicts an innocent man, and concludes with a Japanese finale – Tukerumo's suicide by hara-kari which Laurence performed with horrifying violence.

'*Typhoon* is & will be a success', Laurence assured his mother. This time he was right. The play ran for more than 200 performances. In 1913 Laurence planned another crossing of the Atlantic, not to the United States this time but to Canada, taking his two tragedies, *The Unwritten Law* and *Typhoon*, and rather surprisingly adding to his repertoire *The Importance of Being Earnest*, in which he acted the role of the foundling John Worthing who grows in earnest need of a fictional rebirth to gain his married happiness. What, in their very different fashions, these plays had in common was the questioning of a previous generation's moral authority.

He had found Canadian audiences more warmly disposed to his productions than their American counterparts. The Canadians, anxious not to be swamped by American culture, were forming a British Canadian Theatrical Organisation to strengthen their ties with Britain and were eager for actor-managers from London to tour their country. Laurence, along with

Forbes-Robertson and Martin-Harvey, were among the first of those invited to journey from the Atlantic to the Pacific and back entirely on Canadian territory – expeditions that 'would do more to tighten the bonds of Empire', Martin-Harvey wrote, 'than all the utilitarian and political schemes put together'.

Laurence and Mabel travelled with a company of some twenty actors. They embarked at Liverpool in the last week of January 1914 and endured 'five days of continuous rain', before landing at Saint John. The tour was to last almost four months, ending at Winnipeg in late May. Canadian audiences had looked forward to being shocked. But their interests were shifting, moved by an instinctive awareness of changes that were soon to overtake the world, and they regarded Laurence as a prophetic 'Leader of the Intellectuals', as the Canadian critic Hector Charlesworth was to call him.

The company was booked to sail back to England on the *Teutonic* in the last days of May. But eager to get home and finish a comedy he was writing about Napoleon, Laurence exchanged tickets with Martin-Harvey who was due to return on *The Empress of Ireland* three days earlier but who needed extra time to visit New York. So Laurence and Mabel boarded a train to Quebec City, leaving the company to pack up the costumes and sets and follow them as originally planned on the *Teutonic.*

It had been a happy tour and they had 'played the smalls' as well as the cities: crossing the prairies, travelling through the boondocks, visiting such one-horse towns as Moose Jaw in Saskatchewan, Medicine Hat in Alberta and Kamloops in British Columbia. As Laurence stood before the curtain after his final performance at the Walker Theatre in Winnipeg, he told his audience that he 'hoped in the near future to revisit Canada'.

To the sounds of an army band playing 'God Be With You Till We Meet Again', they sailed from Quebec City in the late afternoon of 28 May. That night, in dense fog, *The Empress of Ireland* was rammed between her two funnels by a heavily loaded Norwegian collier, SS *Storstad.* What then happened, the worst disaster in Canadian maritime history, has been described by the Canadian scholar Denis Salter:

> Huge volumes of water poured into both boiler-rooms; within minutes, the weight of the water pulled the *Empress* down on her starboard side and flooded the engine dynamos, shutting off the lights. People in cabins on the lower decks were either

killed outright by the blow of the *Storstad* or drowned almost immediately . . . those higher up tried to leave their rooms but many were trapped in them or in the corridors and drowned; those who succeeded in leaving their cabins started climbing up the sides of the ship to the top railings for safety.

. . . The captain and other officers remained at the bridge until the vessel sank. There were several hundred souls swimming about in the water, screaming for help and shrieking as they felt themselves being carried under, and uttering strange, weird moans of terror . . . Within an extraordinarily short period of fourteen minutes, the entire ship sank at 2.09am and finally came to rest on her starboard side 150 feet below at the bottom of the St Lawrence River.

There had been no time to launch more than a few of the forty-two lifeboats as the ship canted steeply over to starboard before sinking. Some 1,027 men and women drowned (840 of them passengers) and only 465 people were saved (of whom 29 were first-class passengers).

Back in London, Harry's seventeen-year-old son was sent down to the Canadian Pacific Railway offices in Cockspur Street to find out what had happened. Rumours flew around the crowds and at first it was believed that almost everyone had been rescued. But as the bulletins began arriving and messages were posted in the windows, the extent of the tragedy became clear.

Laurence and Mabel died a hundred deaths that night. One passenger saw him 'kissing his wife, and as the ship went down they were clasped in each other's arms'. Someone else thought that 'Mabel may have fainted before the final plunge and been torn from her husband's arms in the whelm of the sea that battered and engulfed them'. Having lost his wife, Laurence was reported to have 'vanished into the night to consummate his marriage to the sea'. But he was also described heroically swimming in the icy waters trying to help others before his strength gave out. And then there was another story in which Mabel, hysterical with fear, refused to leave her cabin, so that Laurence was forced to return with a lifebelt for her and, as the ship again listed sharply, he was flung against the cabin door. His face covered with blood, he was still attempting to lift his paralysed wife to safety when the sea closed over them. It was this last version that Florence accepted – to some extent it enabled her to assuage her grief by blaming Mabel for her son's death.

Two days later, the *Teutonic*, sailing from Montreal to Liverpool with Laurence's company on board, halted over the submerged vessel, everyone standing on deck as a bugler sounded the Last Post. That night, at the Oxford University Opera House, Harry made a short speech. 'I should not have been here to-night had I not thought that an actor is a servant of the public . . . Of my personal loss by my dear brother's death this is not the place to speak.' Of Laurence's loss to the stage, the newspapers were eloquent. No player's death since that of Henry Irving himself nine years earlier, it was said, had been 'mourned with such heavy headlines and deep obituary columns'. His memorial service at St Margaret's, Westminster, in the summer of 1914 was attended by 1,300 people – though his nephew thought he might have preferred the simple ceremony at the Walker Theatre in Winnipeg, where Johnston Forbes-Robertson unveiled a tablet to both Laurence and Mabel, recording their last performance together.

When the war came, Harry found he was in an unexpectedly strong position. This was an uncertain time for theatre managers throughout the country and no one knew what the public might want to see – or indeed whether people would want to go to theatres at all. Looking through the Lyceum repertoire, Harry picked out Conan Doyle's *Waterloo,* which was rapturously received by audiences.

Harry was more fortunate than most other actor-managers in London, paying a rent of £80 a week for a theatre with a capacity of £300 per performance (by the end of the war he was worth some £40,000 – Laurence's estate had been assessed as 'nil'). After Granville-Barker's season at the Savoy had ended, Harry reopened the theatre at the beginning of 1915 with a new play by H.A. Vachell. *Searchlights* was described by Harry's son as a 'conflict between a stern father, a wastrel son and his doting mother'. The young man discerned his own father re-establishing peace with him as the wastrel son 'in whom the war had awakened a sense of purpose'. Speaking of his own productive years at Marlborough, Harry had repeatedly urged his son to make something of himself at Wellington. Now, joining the Royal Flying Corps and then being awarded the Croix de Guerre, his son was upstaging him.

In some ways, life appeared to go on very much as it had before the war. Harry was still dressed each evening by the diminutive old Walter Collinson, and would prepare himself for his performances with a grilled cutlet, half a pint of champagne, then a nap. He realised that audiences wanted to be entertained with comedies in time of war, and in giving them what they wanted, he released in himself a bizarre comic talent that seemed to free him from the long shadow of his father – the comedian who had come to dread comedy.

'Books and books and books again absorbed most of his affection', remembered Mrs Aria. Watching Harry at work on his latest publications, *A Book of Remarkable Criminals* and *Last Studies in Criminology*, which reveal the seeds of criminality in even the most respectable citizens, she could not help remembering his drives out into the country with his father, Harry so upright, Henry sunk deep in a corner of the carriage, both addicted to their tales of ingenious murders 'the bloodier the better'. Harry often referred to one of Goethe's directives which his father used: 'Self-possession is the art of life'. But which self possessed him? When Harry burst into paroxysms of rage at what seemed no provocation, it was as if two contending selves within him had violently clashed, frightening his son and daughter and reducing Dolly to tears. But he never lost his temper with Mrs Aria. She felt for him what she had felt for Sir Henry and ventured to think that he felt the same for her: in short 'we loved each other', she wrote, '. . . he gave me a dear and tender consideration quite unmeet for the printed word' – though she hastily added he was 'never the philanderer'. He made her understand that she held a unique place in his life and that he recognised in her his truest living connection with those past days where so much of life now lay. In one of his letters he had spelt it out for her: 'There is no one who seems to understand me and sympathise with me as you do, and it is perhaps because you loved and felt with father, and know how he would have regarded things.' Mrs Aria was sure that Dolly would not mind. He was, she testified, 'the sweetest prince that ever stepped in the dominion of domesticity'. She went on seeing Harry continually at Upper Woburn Place and then in Gordon Square until Dolly spirited him and his books off to the slopes of Sudbury Hill in Harrow – away from her and the German Zeppelins.

Seeing him only at rare intervals when he was on leave, Harry's son was shocked by the marks of illness gathering on his father's face. His fellow actors too were becoming embarrassed by moments of nervous confusion. At the Savoy Theatre his last two roles were Hamlet and Mathias in *The Bells*. They were to be his farewell to the stage.

In the last year of the war, when Harry was forty-seven, his age group was called up for military service and he joined the Department of Naval Intelligence. Mrs Aria would secretly meet him at the railway station where he caught his train back home to Sudbury Hill (he was, she admitted, 'not exactly a saint'). In wartime 'the world of play-acting was too trivial for his best devotions', she believed, and though he could not tell her what precisely he was doing, she felt certain that with his forensic skills he was well cast for important work in 'the Secret Investigation Department'. But in truth he regarded this 'civil servitude' in the Admiralty as a mere interval in his career. Though amused by the smoky hush-hush atmosphere of his office, he grew impatient with its circumlocutions.

In 1918 he suffered what his daughter Elizabeth described as 'a nervous breakdown from overwork' and spent some convalescent weeks at home ('I can tell you', Elizabeth wrote to her brother, 'it's not an awfully happy household'). Harry, however, took an optimistic view of his health. 'I am getting better', he wrote to his mother, '. . . rest and good air ought to get me up.'

But he did not get better. No one knew that he had a progressive and eventually fatal anaemia for which there was no cure. On 11 November 1918, the sirens and church bells rang out over the country celebrating the end of war. Harry got up and went into town. A solitary gaunt figure, immaculately dressed and tapping an ivory-handled cane against the pavement, he walked slowly along the Strand to his club, the jubilant crowds making way for him.

He was in no pain, but his dejection spread a melancholy through the family. Some of that winter he spent in Whitstable before Dolly bought the lease of a corner house in Cumberland Terrace, overlooking Regent's Park, where Harry's friends could more easily visit him. As the weeks dragged by and his vitality ebbed, he passed much of the time dozing in his armchair or lying half-asleep in bed. His appetite for life declined so imperceptibly that he gave no obvious sign of apprehension, though his son noticed 'a glitter of disquiet in his dark eyes'.

On the morning of 16 October 1919 he looked much the same, but by the evening he appeared weaker. Dolly telephoned the doctor and then, on being told that this might be the beginning of the end, summoned her son and daughter. Harry roused himself to greet them 'with a shadow of a smile' then lapsed into unconsciousness. They sat by his bed through much of the night. 'He lay in peace, scarcely moving: now and again he stirred and whispered fragments of Hamlet's speeches.' At dawn the next morning he died. 'I looked for the last time upon my father', wrote his son. In the mask of death, he caught a semblance of the young man he had not seen since his own childhood. The scars of anxiety and anger, imprinted by the weight of being Sir Henry Irving's son, had vanished. This was simply the boy's father.

PART SIX

42
Family Affairs

The lines of people had begun forming outside the Drury Lane Theatre for Ellen Terry's grand jubilee, celebrating fifty years onstage, on 12 June 1906 early in the afternoon of the previous day. 'It must have been one of the earliest instances of an all-night theatre queue', wrote a young actor, Basil Dean. By midnight the streets were crowded and by noon the next day they stormed inside. But 'many of those who had waited confidently all night found themselves jammed tightly into standing rows at the back. Late comers were sent away in hundreds.'

Duse travelled from Italy and Réjane from France. Coquelin and his son performed a scene from Molière's *Le Mariage Forcé*; W.S. Gilbert produced one from *Trial by Jury* with a chorus of beautiful maidens and a jury of celebrated actors and writers. Gertie Millar came over from the music halls to sing for Ellen; Enrico Caruso, accompanied by Paolo Tosti, also sang; and there was an entertainment given by the 'Leading Comedians of London'. Mrs Patrick Campbell delivered a reverberating recitation, Lillie Langtry appeared as Cleopatra, and Charles Wyndham, a specialist in high comedy, put on a sparkling scene from *The School for Scandal*. It was, in Ellen's words, a 'mammoth matinée'.

Attired in a dazzling red dress ('*comme une flamme*',Duse described it), she made her appearance as Beatrice, playing opposite Beerbohm Tree's Benedick, with Forbes-Robertson as Claudio in a scene from *Much Ado About Nothing*. This brought on to the stage twenty-two members of the Terry family – Ellen's sisters Kate and Marion and her brother Fred and some of Kate's and Fred's children as well as Edy and a scattering of Ellen's grandchildren (May's daughter Rosemary and two of her sons, Philip and Peter), all these younger Terrys appearing as pages, dancers and torch-bearers. Only her son was absent. In letter after letter she had implored him to 'come over for just 2 or 3 days for this *exceptional* event in my life'. But he would not come. 'You travel everywhere except to England', she scolded him. '. . . I cannot believe you're not coming . . . you are unkind to me . . . or are you planning to surprise me?' But after the failure of *The Vikings* how could he return to the country of his rejection, having as yet no continental successes to parade? Ellen assured him that she had been confident of his success for years. But it was not enough. Fearing that gossip would fill up the empty space he left, she pretended to 'see' him in the crowds.

Ellen had appeared at times to take little interest in her jubilee. 'Why jubilee me?' she asked Audrey Campbell. She could remember Irving telling her that the theatrical profession intended to celebrate both their jubilees together. But after he died any interest in the commemoration had died too. 'There is nothing left remarkable / Beneath the visiting moon': Cleopatra's words, after the death of Antony, came to her when she thought of Henry. It was strange to think that he 'will have been away a whole year', she reminded her son on 13 October 1906. '. . . It only seems to me as if he had left the stage to go into "the Office" for an hour . . . and that it is all rather boring and useless until he comes back.'

But it was impossible not to grow excited as the day came near. 'How can I *help* but be *glad*.' She was overtaken by an exhausted gratitude and at the end 'I nearly dropped – my heart thumped in my head, my heels were all blistered, my eyes (or rather my eye) in torture & I would have been grateful if they drowned me – & all the while I felt overflowing with joyful palpitations'.

Grieving over Henry's death, feeling incomplete without him, she had been under medical care the previous autumn. A jubilee that did not somehow include him struck her as another painful reminder of his absence, her loss. So, in her speech at the conclusion of the celebrations, she accepted the long affectionate applause of the audience and the wild demonstration of the crowds outside as tributes to their partnership. 'I never forgot for a moment that they were not there for me alone,' she was to write towards the end of her memoirs, 'and that many were anxious to show me honour because I had worked with Henry Irving for a quarter of a century. I represented a chapter in the history of the English theatre, of which they were proud.' Then she hurried off to the Court Theatre and 'went through my part of Lady Cicely [Waynflete] . . . making them laugh – & feeling awful'.

At a banquet in Ellen's honour at the Hotel Cecil five days later, Winston Churchill described her as a great actress who had 'elevated and sustained the quality and distinction of theatrical art in England during long years when it had been discreditably neglected by the state'. She had been informed that King Edward's representative at the feast, the Duke of Fife, was to confer on her the Order of Merit that evening and she noted with some satisfaction that 'it was the only thing Mrs Watts wd accept on his [G.F. Watts's] work'. The granting of this honour was a secret and a mystery. 'I'm not supposed to know officially yet', she told her son, '& need scarcely say I shd be horrified if the chickens are counted before they were hatched!! Humpty Dumpty might fall down – & I shd be humiliated.' Perhaps she was the victim of a practical joke. In any event the Duke of Fife ate his dinner and left without conferring any honour.

There was one further chapter to these celebrations. Beerbohm Tree staged a special performance of *The Merry Wives of Windsor* with Ellen again playing Mistress Page, as part of the Shakespeare Festival. At the conclusion of the play, Tree delivered some twenty-four additional lines of verse:

> Stand here, dear sister-artist, England's pride,
> The Genius of her stage personified
> Queenlike, pathetic, tragic, tender, merry –
> Oh rare, O sweet, O wondrous Ellen Terry.

A modestly confused Ellen Terry then stepped forward and uttered the line: 'Oh Mr Tree I cannot find a word' – at which moment a well-trained white dove fluttered down with a document which an attendant fairy handed to her.

Miss Terry (greatly relieved): Thank you. Can I trust myself to read?
You know how much indulgence I must need . . .

And so on for a dozen lines, one of which alone ('Silence were better than a puny rhyme') spoke the literal truth. But this performance, in which Tree seemed to be inadequately hiding a lifelong passion for Ellen, conveyed a sadder truth. In her sixtieth year Ellen was an actress with a glorious past and almost no future. 'I will not say good bye', she had said during her jubilee speech. 'It is one of my chief joys that I *need* not say good bye – *just yet* – but can still speak to you as one who is still among you on the active list.'

But there were few roles for elderly women on the stage. Besides she had passed much of the winter 'frantic from pain in eyes and head' and was having increasing difficulty in remembering her words. All this was spelt out between Tree's lines. She needed her fellow actors' indulgence. Despite having been so well paid by Irving, she had little money in the bank. The matinée and banquet raised £5,784 for her, and a testimonial fund organised by the Liberal newspaper *The Tribune* at the instigation of William Archer, together with an American fund, added another £3,000 (together equivalent a hundred years later to almost half a million). The theatrical profession had done her proud.

At the beginning of her Shakespearean career Ellen had played the child Mamillius in *The Winter's Tale*. Now in the autumn of 1906, at what was almost the end of her Shakespearean career, she became Mamillius's mother Hermione at His Majesty's Theatre. Already the critics were treating her as a legendary figure above criticism. 'Hermione is the supreme triumph of Ellen Terry's age, as Ophelia was the supreme triumph of her youth', wrote Christopher St John. During the winter Ellen had felt irredeemably old. But now she revived. The change was extraordinary.

But it was not the money. It was love again.

Within six months of Irving's death, Ellen had finally assumed the character of Lady Cicely Waynflete in *Captain Brassbound's Conversion*. This 'adventure', as Shaw subtitled it, pitted what he saw as Ellen Terry's character and values against the style and habits, as he had witnessed them, of Henry Irving. In his stage directions, he described the intrepid Lady Cicely as being 'between thirty and forty, very good-looking and sympathetic, intelligent . . . A woman of great vitality and humanity.' Captain Brassbound, a saturnine character etched around Irving, is 'of handsome features, but joyless . . . a face set to one tragic purpose . . . interesting, and even attractive, but not friendly'. Lady Cicely, who ruthlessly embraces everyone with her motherly geniality and insists on their childlike good intentions, embodies the Muse of Comedy; Brassbound, who has been wronged and seeks revenge, represents Tragedy. Insofar as it had been designed as a Trojan horse, a heroically shaped animal full of concealed comic characters, to be wheeled into the Lyceum Theatre, its twelve-week run of performances at the Court Theatre during the spring and summer of 1906 was out of time and in the wrong place. Ellen was a good twenty years too old for the part and felt, as she confessed to Shaw, 'a mighty tame cat nowadays'. The play had many cunning contrivances – for example, at the court of inquiry before which Brassbound is brought, Ellen's barrister-like performance echoes that of her Portia in *The Merchant of Venice*. But her loving struggle was no longer with Irving – it was with Edy and Ted who both believed that Shaw had misrepresented her. In their experience she was less tender, less humorous and humane than Lady Cicely, less independent-minded but more dangerous. At her jubilee, *The Times* described her as a 'creature of rudimentary, full-blooded, naïve emotions' and this they could recognise.

Virginia Woolf saw *Captain Brassbound's Conversion* at the Court Theatre and remembered that when Ellen Terry made her entrance the stage collapsed 'like a house of cards'. And when she spoke 'it was as if someone drew a bow over a ripe, richly seasoned 'cello; it grated, it glowed, and it grumbled. Then she stopped speaking. She put on her glasses. She gazed intently at the back of the settee. She had forgotten her part. But did it matter?'

Ellen herself thought it did matter and apologised to Shaw for going astray. 'You are a faithful heroic DEAR! You try to keep your illusions about me, about my acting', she wrote to him. '. . . I am going to "try, try again" at Lady Cicely.' Shaw advised her to 'behave as if you were more precious than many plays, which is the truth'. Eventually she took his advice and improvised as she went along. Then she was 'magnificent', he told Forbes-Robertson. '. . . She simply lives through Lady Cicely's adventures and says whatever comes into her head, which by the way is now much better than what I wrote.'

Setting out to rescue his mother from Shaw's play-world, Gordon Craig suggested that his mother's lapses of memory were instinctive objections to an inadequate text, and her improvisations invariably improvements to work by second-rate dramatists. She was faithful to Shakespeare and never improved the speeches of Ophelia, Beatrice or Imogen. It was a nice argument but not true. Then again, did it matter?

'Shakespeare could not fit her, not Ibsen; nor Shaw', Virginia Woolf concluded. 'But there is, after all, a greater dramatist than Shakespeare, Ibsen, or Shaw. There is Nature . . . now and again Nature creates a new part, an original part. The actors who act that part always defy our attempts to name them . . . And thus while other actors are remembered because they were Hamlet, Phedre, or Cleopatra, Ellen Terry is remembered because she was Ellen Terry.'

They had still met only once, Bernard Shaw and Ellen Terry, during fourteen years of correspondence – until they began meeting almost every day during the rehearsals of his play. By this time Ellen was in 'that middle phase, so trying to handsome women, of matronly amplitude', Shaw observed, adding that her 'heart was for the moment vacant'.

Had she really resembled the lady in the play, who is rescued from conventional marriage to Brassbound by the happy music of gunfire (echoing a warning in herself), her heart would have remained sublimely vacant. But Ellen could not reconcile herself to the crowded loneliness of old age – not yet and possibly never. So when she noticed the young American actor James Carew, who had been engaged to play Hamlin Kearney, the 'robustly built' naval commander, she 'sailed across the room' to introduce herself. A few days later, Shaw was writing to her: 'you look 25; and I love you; and I am furiously jealous of Carew, with whom you fell in love at first sight.'

James Carew had been born in Indiana in 1876 and was almost thirty years younger than Ellen. According to Christopher St John, his striking features somewhat resembled those of 'Red Indians', as they were called. His forebears were German Jews and his actual name was Usselman (which was considered disadvantageous for an actor). He had seen Ellen Terry and Henry Irving onstage in Chicago, been inspired to take up acting himself and, coming over to London, joined the Vedrenne-Barker management at the Court Theatre. In 1905 he played the young Hector Malone in Shaw's *Man and Superman*, a secretly married, neatly built American 'not at all ashamed of his nationality'.

After *Captain Brassbound's Conversion* had completed its run, James Carew passed much of his time at Ellen's house in the King's Road. 'She was mad about me', he said. A straightforward man, he spoke the simple truth. Ellen held on to him as if to a witness of her reacquired youthfulness. They planned to go off together that winter on a tour of North America.

The 'Napoleon of Drama' in New York, Charles Frohman, had invited Ellen to make her first visit to America without Henry Irving. She agreed providing she could take Carew as her leading man. Making sure there would be no new lines to learn, she offered Frohman Shaw's *Captain Brassbound's Conversion*, Charles Reade's romantic comedy *Nance Oldfield* and Christopher St John's translation of Herman Heijermans's tragedy *The Good Hope.*

She embarked shortly before Christmas accompanied by 'my old Edy . . . [who] is so able and such a Duck', by Edy's inseparable companion Chris and by James Carew who 'goes on striving and acts better and better every week'. It was a highly unstable group, and though Ellen was optimistic she also felt anxious: optimistic about the others, anxious over herself. They were to visit what she called '*all* the best Cities'. But she trusted Frohman 'not to overwork me'.

Good hope seemed to animate Ellen's team. 'It refreshes me to come to America', she wrote to her son who was contemplating travelling there himself. 'It is a backward-forward place – heavenly hellish people in it, but I like most of them . . . Full houses is the order of the day & old Edy is very busy *enjoying herself* – Oh & working very hard. Only she is a conscienceless devil as you know – or bluffs at being one! She does tempt God tho' by rushing about day & night.'

Carew had been promoted to play the vengeful character of Brassbound and though the character did not fit him well, he appeared more easygoing as he travelled around the United States. But Edy thought him an 'unsuitable' escort for her mother. He was so brash, so commonplace and of such modest talent whatever part he played. Nevertheless she acknowledged that he put her mother in a better humour. So she extended him a modest friendliness. And Chris kept watch.

The enthusiasm of American audiences persuaded Ellen that the game was not yet over. 'If I was coldly received, in other words plainly told I was too old and ugly to remain upon the stage, I had determined to give up . . . and leave the stage quietly at the end of the tour', she wrote. 'But they opened their arms to me, flattered and spoiled me delightfully to the top of my bent . . .' So she resolved to continue with her new leading man. 'And I was married', she added, astonishingly.

They were married in Pittsburgh on 22 March 1907 – and for several weeks they kept it a secret. Writing to Shaw from Montreal a fortnight later, she seemed about to let go her secret – but just managed to hold it back. 'Pittsburg[h], of all places in the world, is lovely! Surely there never was more beautiful sunshine . . . a sort of day when one finds oneself blessing everything, to oneself of course!'

Only to her son, Gordon Craig, safely in Florence, did she reveal what she had done. 'This is Jim & me – we are married', she wrote on a postcard from Niagara Falls. '. . . You don't mind much, do you? You are happy and I'm happy, aren't you? . . . We had to keep it secret until we left off acting before American audiences – not caring to be a kind of circus. James Carew is an American – only 32 & a half but as old as the hills. I love him very dearly. I neglect no responsibilities.' Gordon Craig seemed delighted: 'how wonderful,' he exclaimed, '. . . we are a queer family.' As for Carew, 'a jollier, betterfellow I do not know', he added, realising how this would irritate his sister.

Ellen was relieved by her son's response (he claimed that as James Carew's stepson he had instantly shed ten years). 'I knew you wd understand', she replied, 'but it was good to get your p.c.'

Her friend Stephen Coleridge, however, did not understand – James Carew 'was as young as our own son', he objected, 'and the public & her best friends were grieved by such an act'. For almost thirty years he had been her financial adviser, her broker and loyal protector. He had saved her from some bizarre excesses, though not from a number of 'grimly humorous' situations such as her son's divorce where she paid his costs, her daughter-in-law's costs and the costs of the co-respondent. He could not prevent her giving money to all sorts of people – to pay, over several years, a nephew's school fees, or the travel expenses of a remote relation of Godwin's who wished to live in Canada, and a weekly allowance for the sister of Charles Kelly's first wife: it was never-ending. Coleridge particularly disapproved of the loans she had made to Henry Irving, which she tried to hide from him by saying they were for her solicitor. 'The name of my solicitor I really forget', she prevaricated when he questioned her. But worst of all was her chaotic treatment of Edy and Ted. 'My difficulties with dear Nellie & her worthless children were endless but I continued tirelessly to do my best to protect her without securing for myself her children's enmity', Coleridge recorded in the margin of one of her letters. 'Nellie never really remembered what she had given them – often she gave them money not meaning me to know it. This with her transparent nature landed her in contradictions.' All this was perhaps understandable, but not her disreputable marriage to Carew which threw a cold shadow over the romance on which her relationship with Stephen Coleridge had been based. She appealed to him to continue as her guide through the mysterious *terra incognita* of her financial affairs of which her husband 'knows nothing'. But eventually 'I stepped down-and-out', Coleridge wrote. It was to be the end – except for memories that were best left in the past. 'I only wanted to kiss the tip of your nose & say farewell', Ellen wrote to him in 1910. 'However, now farewell & goodbye, my dear friend.'

Edy too was 'strangely intolerant'. To have a new stepfather who was younger than she was, someone less convincing as a husband than the men – Sidney Valentine and Martin Shaw – Ellen had banished from her daughter's life, was infuriating. Here, all over again, was the story of her mother's marriage to Charles Kelly – only this time it was worse because Carew's coming disrupted that trinity of female happiness which had formed between Ellen, Edy and Chris after Ted had left the country. The three women had enjoyed what Chris called 'a lovely pleasant carefree existence'. They were making a garden at Smallhythe, would take themselves on drives to Bodiam in the moonlight and sometimes go off for excursions to Bruges on a pleasure steamer. 'This was perhaps the happiest period in my long friendship with Edy', Chris remembered. And now Ellen was ruining it. Why had she handcuffed herself to this banal American? Ellen's emphatic answer was, as she explained to her friend Graham Robertson: '*I couldn't be alone any longer* . . . Jim loved me – ! Told me so – & *meant it! – it is true!!* A Miracle! I have always believed in miracles = I love *him*.' Once the secret was out, Ellen could not help inviting her friends to celebrate her happiness. 'I just *had* to marry him', she wrote to Katherine Lewis. 'Hitherto I have ever given more love than I have received. Now I mean to try all I can to be a good companion & good friend to the man who loves me – he is a man & a half! No inexperienced boy – & I am very proud of him & feel I would like to share him with my friends.'

After returning from North America, they went 'rushing about in damp old England' still playing *Captain Brassbound's Conversion*. Indeed, as Ellen Terry's biographer Tom Prideaux comments, '*Brassbound* became their career'. But it was not a happy career. 'Oh my Jim, my Jim. I hope he will soar a bit soon', Ellen confided in a letter to her son. 'He is his own enemy – but people don't understand him . . . he is much to me – but I do miss Edy. She *evades* me all the while!!!' Part of the difficulty lay in the destructive power of Ellen's own acting. She filled the stage and, as Virginia Woolf observed, 'all the other actors were put out, as electric lights are put out'. And none of them was put out more dramatically than her leading man. 'Jim's brain is visibly half gone', Bernard Shaw observed: 'he holds on to the part as if nothing but the grimmest determination could save him from going mad on the spot.'

All this time Ellen besieged Shaw to find what she called 'a good engagement' for her husband and herself in one of his plays. 'We *must* work . . . I'd like you (for he loves you) to make him an offer. Oh, do be quick and ask him to play a fine part with a fair salary, or a mere good part with an unfair salary! . . . *It would do me such a good turn.*' But since Carew was regarded as a monotonous and Ellen, in her early sixties, a forgetful performer, neither Shaw nor anyone else could find new work for them. Apart from a short-lived attempt at a historical drama, Gladys Ungar's *Henry of Lancaster* ('a ghastly failure', Ellen called it), they were condemned to repeat their provincial tours of *Captain Brassbound's Conversion* with James Carew forever playing Brassbound, a character he grew to hate.

In the summer of 1908, however, Shaw did find a role for Edy at the Haymarket Theatre. It was a curious piece of casting – one of the most extreme examples of his theory of wishful thinking. Mrs Bridgenorth is a placid and humorous grey-haired woman who, in Shaw's disquisitory play *Getting Married*, patiently steers a difficult engagement within her family to a late but successful marriage. The message of the play – that very different sexual partnerships can coexist within a family without destroying it – was far from being Edy's opinion just then. While they were sailing back from America, Chris had gone to Ellen's cabin and upbraided her for treating her daughter so insensitively. In a letter to her son, Ellen explained that Edy and Chris (whom she insisted on calling 'Christabel Marshall') had 'simply sent me to Coventry in the ship coming over, & after 3 days & 4 nights of weeping, weeping . . . I plucked up a little spirit . . . Jim is all right about her [Edy] but C. M. makes Edy impossible for us.' Ellen was revising her memoirs ('this beastly book of mine') on the vessel, having 'left it frightfully too much to C[hris]' because of being 'in love with Jim & wanting to be with him'. Now she was on guard lest 'things creep in that must not go in for fear it is done on purpose by C. M. (but oh I can't think that of her)'. But she could not help it. 'My marriage was my own affair', she wrote, 'but very few people seemed to think so, and I was overwhelmed with enquiries, kind and otherwise.' All the same, she adds, she was feeling young and happy again – though this happiness was to be eliminated by Chris from a second edition of the memoirs.

'Other people have been poisoned by C. M. about Jim', Ellen confided to her son. Chris had sent Gordon Craig a letter enlisting his support of Edy against their mother and her husband. 'You at any rate have the good luck not to know the man', she pointed out. 'His only chance is for you to take him & train him for the stage. Who knows – he might become an actor . . . The conventional thing to say is that we hope she [Ellen] will be happy – but I don't join in my voice to the chorus. If she could be happy long with such a dull oaf I should think very ill of her. What I think matters very little, but as it makes Edy peculiarly solitary, I want you to be nice & remind her that there is one other person in the world of her own blood.' But though this invitation came with a message from Edy ('How do you like having a step-father younger than you are?') and was sugared with blandishments (including an offer from Chris to add a chapter celebrating his achievements to his mother's memoirs), Gordon Craig thought 'these girls are ignorant and intolerable' and wrote to tell Ellen so. 'C. M. is a slanderer & mischief-maker', Ellen answered. '. . . It has been rather terrible . . . it seems to me that Edy made Chris her mouthpiece . . . But what have I done? – my Jim & me – to arouse such wrath in these girls! . . . C[hris] & I are wider apart each day . . . I'd not care except for Edy . . . [She] is quiet – Chris is always virtuously indignant & bursting – & keeps it up all the while – oh it is tiring.' Ellen thought that Edy was 'by far the stronger' of the two girls. Why then was she so influenced by Chris?

Ellen had known that there would have to be a fight with Edy over her marriage – that was natural: they had fought and loved each other most of their lives, and their fighting was part of their love. But this battle was different. She strongly resented Chris's interference in what she thought should have been a simple contest between mother and daughter – a family affair. But Chris was one of the family now – more so than James Carew. It was as if Chris no longer recognised Mrs Carew as the Ellen Terry she had once worshipped, and treated her like one of those stupid women who go through life as if it were a romantic comedy. Idolised by men and lacking any tragic sense, such women had little understanding of how others struggled through their lives. But those who struggled were coming together and making their voices heard.

Little of this militant chorus reached the quiet Kentish marshlands of Smallhythe where the battle was more private. Ellen had given Edy a sixteenth-century, half-timbered house next to the red-brick village chapel, St John the Baptist (after whom Christabel Marshall had renamed herself). 'I gave it her. I *didn't* give her the Deeds & Papers!!' Ellen confided to Shaw. 'Which makes her *wild*. Poor kid – she knows about gardens. She knows much but she don't know that I safeguard her now & again. I love her – I don't know if she knows that.' Priest's House, with its upper storey overhanging the front, was little more than a hundred yards from Ellen's Smallhythe farmhouse. In past times, when the sea came to the very edge of the village and tall ships sailed across what were now green fields with grazing sheep, Smallhythe had been a harbour and Ellen's home the port officer's house.

Whenever James Carew came to Smallhythe, Edy locked the gate between the two properties and when James went out, Edy came in. 'I hope it is not we are keeping you away from the cottage!' Ellen wrote to her daughter in June 1908. 'It wd be too absurd – if you don't want to see us, there is *space* between the houses you know!' But Edy and Chris did not want to catch sight of Ellen's husband and even when Ellen fell and bruised herself, still Edy did not visit her. Separate delivery services had to be arranged for the adjacent farm and cottage in case they were accidentally brought together by the local tradesmen which 'wd never do', Ellen wrote sarcastically, signing herself nevertheless 'your most loving old mother'. Eventually it was Ellen who kept away from Smallhythe. 'I don't go to the cottage because I can't go anywhere where Jim can't go – and is not welcomed – never mind.'

Even at Ellen's home in the King's Road, Carew felt a stranger among his wife's grandchildren and old theatre friends. He said later that he might have remained with Ellen provided they did not 'live in the same house'. Certainly this is what Edy wanted. 'I give it two years', she predicted. In fact it was nearer three years before husband and wife finally separated. Carew had become as frustrated as Kelly had been and on one occasion kicked Ellen's dog which appeared to be receiving preferential treatment to him. But the two of them were never divorced and Ellen remembered Carew with far more affection than she did Kelly. 'Jim looks after *himself* thank goodness', Ellen later wrote to Mrs Rumball. '. . . [He] is all right. I scarcely ever see him.'

Ellen tried to be angry with Edy. 'I consider you are a very badly behaved young person', she scolded her, '. . . [but] I love you most dearly and trust you will see your way to leave off being a cruel and belligerent young woman as soon as you conveniently can.' But in an essay on Edy written soon after her death, Christopher St John maintained that 'Edy was blamed for the estrangement from her mother . . . could the whole story be told, she would be vindicated by an impartial judge'.

At Somerville College in the 1890s, Chris had not been permitted to receive her degree. If women were admitted to the Bachelor of Arts degree, they would automatically have been entitled to proceed to a Master of Arts degree and then to vote for the university candidate in Parliament – an anomaly that was not permitted by the government. 'This is the first time I remember having my attention drawn to women's suffrage', she later wrote, 'which was not to become a burning question until the next decade.'

It did not present itself to her again until Henry Irving's memorial service at Westminster Abbey in the autumn of 1905. Chris had written a eulogy of Irving, over 3,000 words, many of which were directed against critics who had been insufficiently appreciative of him – particularly Bernard Shaw. But in her verse epigraph to the essay two lines stood out, testifying to her sense of gratitude to Irving:

> O let me thank thee for the riches given
> By thy great spirit to my barren youth.

In her sensational novel *Hungerheart*, Chris was to explore her feelings for Irving. 'I had admired him living,' she wrote, 'I loved him dead.' She had of course admired his acting skills. 'He could not disappoint you . . . If he acted a rogue, he was a great rogue; if a saint, he was a great saint.' But what she truly loved was the tragedy of his career when 'during the last few years of his life he had lost his hold on the public'. She liked the idea that he had died poor. 'He should have died poor', she calculated. He had risked much, been brought low and finally, exiled from London, become like Chris herself, an outsider. 'I regard it as the crown to his existence, the seal on his greatness.' And this was not the end of it. 'By a man's enemies you may know him', she declared. 'It is a bad sign when the whole world is his friend.'

The whole world nevertheless appeared to be at Irving's memorial service. Beside them stood lines of policemen and beyond them arose a sound of commotion and the shuddering of flags. When she enquired of the police why they were in such great numbers, she was told that it was 'because of these women who want the vote'.

Chris and Edy were precipitated into active feminism at the time of Ellen Terry's jubilee. Not a single woman had been invited to join the committees which were organising the Drury Lane celebrations. The stage was to be swamped by men – women for the most part serving as programme sellers. When she discovered this, Ellen laughed out loud and proposed that she too should not appear onstage. But Chris was palpably angry. Recognised as 'a trouble maker', Edy had not been invited to help plan the commemoration – and since Ellen Terry's daughter was to be excluded, all other women had to be excluded too. But at the last moment Edy was invited to superintend a series of *tableaux vivants*. Under her direction, they presented a mute pictorial history of female power – from the Madonna and Joan of Arc to Cleopatra and Queen Victoria: 'a quiet call to arms', Ellen Terry's biographer Nina Auerbach calls it. Edy was soon to develop these stage pictures into female pageants as part of a political theatre that would raise money for the suffrage movement.

Edy was a natural suffragist. She did not have to think very deeply about it and never believed that the world would be transformed by the election of women as Members of Parliament. For her it was simply a matter of justice. 'I certainly grew up quite firmly certain that no self-respecting woman could be other than a Suffragist', she told a journalist in 1910. For the moment Chris lagged behind – the absence of the vote was not so important an injustice for her. 'I found it difficult to say whether I was for the Suffragists or against them', she wrote.

*

In 1906 Chris had begun composing a short book on Ellen Terry, the first in J.T. Grein's 'Stars of the Stage' series and published the following year by the Bodley Head. It is an outline of the great actress's career in which there is no mention of Edy or herself and only the odd barbed reference to Gordon Craig, whose production of *The Vikings* was 'crippled by the scenic experiments surrounding it'. There are several photographs of Ellen Terry's houses, but Christopher St John makes it clear that no reader will be invited within: 'the private life of a player is not the public's concern'. Chris's own passions, however, occasionally force their way on to the page as when she expresses regret that her translation of *The Good Hope* never reached London. 'Does no one realise what a monstrous state of unhappiness in ourselves the desire not to witness tragedy on the stage implies!'

It was while working on this book that Chris began helping Ellen Terry to organise her memoirs. Her job as what she called Ellen's 'literary henchman' was more that of a secretary than an editor – she would come to edit and add to the narrative only after Ellen's death. She was a far more professional writer than Ellen, though Ellen's best passages contain a peculiar vividness. Her book is 'a bundle of loose leaves upon each of which she has dashed off a sketch for a portrait – here a nose, here an arm, here a foot, and there a mere scribble in the margin', wrote Virginia Woolf. 'The sketches done in different moods, from different angles, sometimes contradict each other . . . It is difficult to assemble them. And there are blank pages, too . . . a gap she could not fill.'

Virginia Woolf, who later picked up bits and pieces of their history from her lover Vita Sackville-West, knew something of what might have appeared on those blank pages and why much that Ellen Terry had written was so contradictory. 'She hates the stage; she adores it. She worships the children; yet forsakes them . . . There is something in her that she did not understand; something that came surging up from the depths and swept her away in its clutches . . . She cannot sustain emotion . . . Is she a mother, wife, cook, critic, actress . . . Each part seems the right part until she throws it aside and plays another.'

Ellen's sudden marriage and quick separation belonged to one of those blank pages. She did not quite put James Carew 'in her pocket' as Bernard Shaw claimed, though that was where she later found him. What had come surging up was the sexual arousal at what she felt to be 'the half-wild thing' in him – 'that part of him I like best', as she wrote in a notebook. But as soon as she began to domesticate him, he gave himself up 'to overheated rooms, first-class railway carriages, hot water bottles, and eiderdown quilts'. As his ambitions were frustrated, the wild thing was reduced to his ill-tempered kicking of the dog. 'I hope you are very much in love', Gordon Craig had written to his mother. 'If not . . . poor James.' But neither mother nor son could sustain emotion.

James Carew blamed 'those bloody women' for the break-up of his marriage. And Gordon Craig agreed. His sister Edy was 'prejudiced in some odd way against the male sex', he believed, 'though always kind to me'. He blamed Chris. She defended herself by coming quickly to Edy's defence. 'I speak as a fighter', she had written in her eulogy of Henry Irving, and it was as a fighter that she spoke of Edy who was far from being the 'self-righteous and disagreeable prig' her brother portrayed. He did not understand that 'it was not of the marriage that Edith disapproved, but of the husband. She did not think he was worthy of her mother, and distrusted his ability to make her happy.'

Edy and Chris had left their apartment in Smith Square and in 1907 gone to live in a flat at Adelphi Terrace where Bernard Shaw also lived (it was, so the story goes, when hearing Edy call peremptorily up to Chris to 'throw down the latchkey', that he had decided to offer her the role of the bishop's wife, Mrs Bridgenorth, in *Getting Married*). Ellen had come to feel for Chris something of the same aversion that her daughter felt for James Carew. But again she could not sustain this feeling and when Chris provoked a crisis by leaving the country and making a religious pilgrimage to Rome (combined with an adventure in pursuit of 'a pretty woman who has run away from her husband'), Ellen relented. With James gone (he was given a small workroom for a time at the end of Ellen's garden in the King's Road), the problem for the three women was how to restore their relationship.

Most of Ellen's work onstage was now confined to benefits, galas, masques and matinées in aid of charities. She made appearances for the Prince of Wales's Holiday Homes for Governesses, the Church of England's Houses for Waifs, the International Physical Recreation Society, the Friends of the Poor and the Good Samaritans. Almost her only professional acting took place at His Majesty's Theatre in December 1908 when she played 'Aunt Imogen' in a musical entertainment for children. *Pinkie and the Fairies* had been written by her friend Graham Robertson for his god-daughter. Twenty years later, Robertson could still remember the terrific outburst of applause that met Ellen's entrance. 'She had not been seen for some time', he wrote in his autobiography, 'and when she stepped upon the stage a storm seemed to break. It crashed out suddenly, like a thunderclap directly overhead, pealed on for a few moments, then settled into a steady roar which rolled on and on with a rhythmic throb like the beating of great drums and seemed as though it would never cease.'

Despite the considerable funds she had received after her jubilee, within four years Ellen was again in need of money. Edy was busy making costumes, acting, and beginning her career as a director. But she earned little money, had no bank account and relied on her mother's regular hand-outs of cash. On top of all her other financial commitments, Ellen was also employing Chris. Because of her worsening health ('I think I have a skewer in my right eye'), there seemed little chance of being offered new roles in the commercial theatre. In the summer of 1910 she wrote to Bernard Shaw with an unusual appeal. 'A friend of mine – a courageous creature of 40, might have a very thorny path made less unendurable if she could get some work on a London Newspaper', she wrote. 'Do you think she writes well enough for that? . . . *do* glance through these newspaper cuttings and tell me what she ought to do.' In her edition of the Shaw–Ellen Terry correspondence, Christopher St John did not identify this 'courageous creature' as herself, and did not publish Shaw's answer, which seems to have been destroyed. 'I did not show her [Chris] your letter but told her bits of it as advice from a frightfully wise one who seemed to me to be always terribly right!' Ellen replied to Shaw. 'I fear she is beyond help. I have just bought a little play of hers (an all wrong, delicately wrong, one) for a little money . . . Great Scott, what a number of good people want things done for them . . . I'd rather like to murder now and again! Some of your imitators to begin with!'

In 1910 Christopher St John wrote three articles for *McClure's Magazine* under Ellen Terry's name, and the correspondence between the two women reveals Ellen's worry over this arrangement. In later years, when she was ill, she came to rely on Chris to write many of her letters. But 'to write to you by proxy wd be horrid', she told her old friend Bertha Bramley.

The little play that Ellen had bought was Christopher St John's one-act historical drama, *The First Actress*, which showed the sex discrimination of the Restoration theatre where men liked to assume the female as well as the male characters. The play gave Edy an opportunity to exhibit her talent as a costumier and presented Ellen herself in the final scene as Nell Gwyn. It was produced by Edy as part of a triple bill together with plays by Cicely Hamilton and Margaret Wynne Nevinson at the Kingsway Theatre in May 1911.

Chris's feminism differed from Edy's in so far as it was fuelled by what she described as 'an immense spiritual significance'. The principle for which she fought – 'the life-blood of the women's suffrage movement' – was the denial of men's superiority over women. She served as a committee member of the Catholic Women's Suffrage Society and carried banners for 'the most advanced "militant" organisations': the Women Writers' Suffrage League and the Women's Social and Political Union. 'No one will ever know what it cost me to take part in violence which was derided rather than feared', she was to write. '. . . I walked with downcast head . . . I never had a ready retort for the hard-featured women in smart clothes who abused me when I sold Suffragist "literature" in the streets.' In 1909 she was arrested for setting fire to a pillar box and 'stood in the felon's dock'. After the shock of her arrest, though she was not sent to prison, she changed the direction of her political career. 'I looked forward to returning to the theatre, to writing that one play which should pierce the deafness of the world.'

It was the political theatre that brought her and Edy closer together again. After Chris returned from Rome, the two of them had moved into 31 Bedford Street, a block of flats approached through a grilled iron gate leading to the actors' church, St Paul's, Covent Garden. On entering the building you were confronted by the complexities of its famous lift, an insecure-looking contraption with intimidating knobs inside and an arrangement of protesting pulleys and levers above, which, in response to cries of encouragement from the tenants, and after a haughty silence, would jerk you upwards and then judderingly stop dead at the third floor where, a little ashamed at having had such 'little faith in so excellent a vehicle', you emerged into Edy and Chris's headquarters.

It was a hive of perpetual activity – read-throughs and rehearsals, desperate commands and incessantly ringing telephones, and also the coming and going of excited actresses, of militant women on their way to or from jail, and law-abiding members of suffrage societies (one room had been lent to an international suffrage shop). Chris's small study was at the back where, since Edy never wrote, Chris wrote for her. Everywhere was scattered a confusion of scripts and costumes. 'The atmosphere was quite undomestic', wrote their friend Irene Cooper Willis. '. . . All the things that I had been brought up to believe should be done first, were done last, or, quite likely, not done at all. It was a revelation to me, born and bred in suburban propriety.'

Edy sold suffragist newspapers in the street with far more enjoyment than Chris. 'I love it,' she told a reporter from *Votes for Women*. 'But I'm always getting moved on.' She never broke the law, but would stand outside the Euston Miles Restaurant which advertised 'the best light and sustaining meals for brain-workers', and offer leaflets and papers to every passing pedestrian. 'If they refuse, I say something to them. Most of them reply, others come up, and we collect a little crowd until I'm told to move the people into the restaurant, and move on. Then I begin all over again.'

Edy also joined many suffrage societies: 'one cannot belong to too many', she said, '. . . I belong to ten now [April 1910] but don't seem able to remember more than seven . . . I organise for every society I belong to, not for any one in particular.'

The first play she directed for the Actresses' Franchise League, in the spring of 1909, was *How the Vote was Won*, a one-act comedy by Christopher St John and the actress-playwright Cicely Hamilton. But the great success came later that year with Cicely Hamilton's *A Pageant of Great Women*. This ambitious presentation, which involved over fifty women grouped into six categories (scholars, artists, saints, heroines, rulers, warriors), was set in a court of justice where, the production evolving from a pageant into a play, some of the women were released from their silence to plead their case against anti-suffrage prejudice (Prejudice was usually played by a man). Edy's nationwide productions of this pageant became 'major events in the Suffragists' calendar', wrote the feminist scholar Katharine Cockin, '. . . [and] one of the most profound responses to the crisis of gender staged by the women's suffrage movement'. At the opening in the Scala Theatre on 12 November 1909, Ellen Terry appeared as the eighteenth-century Drury Lane actress Nance Oldfield, Marion Terry as Florence Nightingale and

Edy herself as the popular French painter of animals, Rosa Bonheur (whom Ellen had met on her first visit to Paris). For the next two years, Edy would enlist members of the local suffrage societies to join her company and enact this alternative history.

Her talent for combining pictorial and dramatic effects, her knowledge of costumes and experience at lighting scenes and arranging music for them, made her an indispensable theatre director for the suffrage movement and she was described by one paper as 'the first woman stage manager on record'. Her bruising methods of direction quelled the schisms and jealousies. Even 'her suggestion was more like an order', Cicely Hamilton remembered.

Cicely Hamilton dedicated this famous pageant to Edy 'whose ideas these lines were written to illustrate'. But Christopher St John, who had been given the role of a female warrior at the Scala Theatre, could sometimes be heard complaining how her fellow performers were 'consumed by vanity'. She herself went through an uncomfortably jealous passage over her friend Cicely Hamilton's collaboration with Edy. When Edy passed this story on to her mother, Ellen innocently replied: 'I am sorry C[hris] thinks Cicely H[amilton] a humbug. I thought she liked her.' She did like her: but she loved Edy.

In 1909 the literary agency Curtis Brown had suggested that Ellen deliver some Shakespeare lectures in the United States. She was not accustomed to lecturing – the very word lecture intimidated her. But back in 1903 she had given a charming talk in Glasgow on what she called 'an unfrequented corner' of Shakespeare's world. 'The Letters in Shakespeare's Plays' was based on the dramatic use to which the playwright had put his characters' correspondence – letters written, read or paraphrased out loud; false, genuine and pseudonymous letters composed in verse or prose and ranging from Falstaff's brief warning to Prince Hal as read by Poins in *Henry IV* Part 2 to the outpourings of the 'madly-used Malvolio' addressed to Olivia in *Twelfth Night*. These letters were not as familiar as Shakespeare's songs and Ellen surprised some scholars with her calculation that there were thirty-four of them. But the question was: could she compose more Shakespeare talks to fill a touring programme?

'She applied to me as her literary henchman for advice', Christopher St

John recorded. 'She invoked my services.' The two of them began work on 'The Triumphant Women' (including Beatrice, Portia, Volumnia, Mistress Page and Rosalind), 'The Pathetic Women' (Viola, Ophelia, Juliet, Desdemona, Cordelia and Lady Macbeth) and 'The Children in Shakespeare's Plays' (from Ellen's early role as Mamillius in *The Winter's Tale* to the young princes in *Richard III*).

Sometimes Chris had to 'control my self-esteem when it threatened to become troublesome', and often she 'played the part of the devil's advocate'. At other times she was as obsequious as Uriah Heep: 'I was the apprentice and she the master craftsman.' But her job was not easy. She would sit opposite Ellen as she leafed through her Globe edition of Shakespeare, reading favourite passages, remembering particular productions, coming up with anecdotes. Then Chris would attempt to draft her notes into 'something answering to the description of a lecture'. But reading her script Edy would protest: 'That's not a bit like mother!' And Ellen would come out with all sorts of impromptu corrections. So Chris would go back with a mass of cuts, additions and transpositions and begin another draft. So they progressed . . .

. . . and what came through were a series of informal and loosely structured talks devised more for speaking and hearing than for reading, with plenty of quotations that enabled Ellen to travel back to her great days in the theatre. Her familiarity with these plays lent an ease and intimacy to her delivery, and the need she felt to re-enter Shakespeare's world gave audiences the sense of witnessing a whole season of Shakespeare productions.

Ellen had not been able to 'enlarge my prospect' with Shaw, but she recovered something of her position with Shakespeare. John Gielgud heard one of these readings and remembered Ellen starting off rather hesitantly, like a professor, spectacles on nose, eyes fixed to the enlarged text, careful and serious. Then Shakespeare's words 'seemed to catch her by the throat . . . and she began to act', he wrote in his autobiography. '. . . There was nothing frail about her now, no hesitation in her sweeping generous movements and the strong expressive movements of her hands, now at her lips, now darting to her lap to bunch up her skirts as if she were poised for flight.' Only her first lecture, 'The Letters in Shakespeare's Plays', was published in her lifetime, but Chris was pleased to note that the three others, which they had assembled together, were the more popular – the most popular of all being 'The Triumphant Women'. When all four lectures were brought out as a book after Ellen's death, Christopher St John supervised the texts and contributed an introduction in which she transferred one or two of her own experiences to Ellen, making her tell Henry Irving that Shakespeare was the only man she loved. 'When I was about sixteen or seventeen, and very unhappy, I forswore the society of men . . . Yet I was lonely all the same. I wanted a sweetheart. Well, Shakespeare became my sweetheart!'

After an encouraging experiment in London, Ellen set out for the United States and Canada in October 1910. 'The first time I am to make the journey *alone*', she wrote apprehensively to Stephen Coleridge. These Shakespeare lectures revived her career. Many of them were delivered in clubs, pavilions, assembly rooms and not theatres and they gave her a new audience. It was 'marvellous' to see these places so 'full of people, crowds of working people too, some quite rough & to note how they hung on to the words & how enthusiastic they were'. But it was 'far more exhausting work than playing a part', she discovered, 'for I have to sustain the burden of the whole entertainment for nearly two hours. And then there is the travelling.' It was the prospect of this continual travelling that made her nervous. 'I am about to live (!) day & night in a beastly jolting overheated railway car – for 2 whole months on end – always going going until I shall be *gone* . . .' she wrote to Bernard Shaw on 29 September 1910. 'It's enough to kill a horse.'

She opened with a matinée on 3 November at the Hudson Theatre in New York – and the audience loved her. So began a spectacular tour. Though Henry Irving's friend, the veteran theatre critic William Winter, thought she should have retired gracefully when Irving died, the public throughout the United States and Canada were delighted by this pendant to her career, treating her, when she spoke to them in that special veiled voice of hers, as if she were in some strange way one of Shakespeare's very own women. 'My hair has turned white already', she wrote to Gordon Craig. '. . . As to my lectures, the only fashion in which I can make them pay (& that they must do) is by moving from place to place without *impedimenta*.' She was astonished by the excess of everything wherever she went: 'too much money, too much pleasure . . . having heaps to do is the secret of happiness'. The actress Lena Ashwell remembered her 'almost blind', dancing into her dressing-room, 'stripped of all the luxury and care which had for so long been hers; courageous, undefeated, young, she hugged me and said: "What do you think of me Lena? Sixty-three, and on one-night stands".'

Back at the Hudson Theatre in New York in February 1911, she made ten recordings from Shakespeare (five of which, including 'The Death of Falstaff' from *Henry V*, were destroyed). But her voice can still be heard giving 'The Mercy Speech' from *The Merchant of Venice*, Ophelia's mad scene from *Hamlet*, the potion scene from *Romeo and Juliet* and speeches from *Much Ado About Nothing* and *The Winter's Tale*.

She returned to England in the spring of 1911 with a new reputation as a Shakespearean performer. She had lost her matronly amplitude and was again 'slender, with a new delicacy and intensity in her saddened expression', remembered Shaw. She continued working on these discourses, revising and improving them, reproducing them in huge type, heavily orchestrated with stage directions: 'Take time', 'Keep still', 'Horror, *not* loud', 'Dark, fierce, violent'.

She continued performing variations of this Shakespeare programme for ten years. The climax came in 1914 when she was invited to take it on a world tour beginning in Australia and New Zealand. Both her doctor and her lawyer warned her against such arduous travel. She had spent part of the year 1912 in a nursing home at 50 Weymouth Street under the name Mrs James Carew, suffering from what she called a 'ditheration of the brain'. She was allowed only two letters a week 'or I'll never get well. I'm ill enough God knows but there's life in the old Cat yet!' After a few weeks she was driven back home in an ambulance wearing an oxygen mask. 'Time was pushing her into retirement', Christopher St John wrote. She needed to keep Time in its place, to prove to herself, and show others, that she could still do such things.

On the voyage out, when her boat docked at Naples, Gordon Craig came on board, and the two of them, mother and son, went off on a happy drive together. 'Red Letter Day', Ellen wrote in her diary.

She was welcomed in Australia as if she were royalty, 'a queen of tears and laughter'. *The Sun* praised her for owning up to her age (though she had in fact miscalculated it) and the *Melbourne Age* let it be known that 'Miss Terry has been brought up in the grand school of manners'. Australian readers were informed that although her hair was grey, 'her eyes are bright and forever twinkling and her cheeks are clear and rosy as a child's'.

She appeared ageless. 'I'm both modern and old-fashioned', she was quoted as saying.

But her opening performance in Melbourne early that May was disconcerting. 'First lecture in Australia', she noted in her diary. 'Very ill, very nervous, but I let myself go!' After the first part of her recitation she was presented with flowers, the band struck up 'God Save the King', and the audience, thinking the entertainment over, left the theatre. When Ellen emerged from her dressing-room after the interval, the place was empty.

After this, 'houses good, notices splendid', Ellen wrote to Edy. She wished she had come to Australia earlier in her career. But towards the end of June, her heart beating like a 'kicking donkey', she fell worryingly ill again and put up in a nursing home instead of a hotel. 'My beloved old Edy,' she wrote from New Zealand, 'how hard I've been trying to keep going at my work, you'll never know, but it was no use trying, and at the conclusion of my last performance in Sydney, the doctor flatly told me I must not appear for a fortnight at least.' She arrived in Auckland feeling 'worse than ever', but was nursed by 'a kind landlady' and early in July resumed her tour.

She was back in Australia, staying with the Australian soprano Nellie Melba at her home in Coldstream, Victoria, when war was declared on 4 August. 'Are they insane?' Ellen had asked Stephen Coleridge during the Boer War. Over the next dozen years she became convinced that there was 'an increase in mad people around the world' – and the Great War seemed to prove her right. 'All engagements are being cancelled', she wrote – though she put on some performances for the Red Cross. Ellen admired Nellie Melba – 'strong in body and character – a *splendid* woman, a magnetic one'. Like many entertainers, Melba soon began giving charity performances to raise morale for the war, and Ellen sometimes accompanied her, though she herself thought 'the war is a nightmare' and its horrors ('thousands of lives lost . . . to gain ten yards in a little field') made her 'crazy'. As for Australia, it was 'a Garden. Heaps of lovely people, and heaps of uninteresting ones too!' she told Shaw.

She took every opportunity while in Australia to praise the women's suffrage movement back in Britain. 'Of course you know I'm a suffragette,' she told *The Sun*. 'Of course I am and so is my daughter Edith Craig.' But, she added, 'I don't believe in all their militancy'. Though Edy came to regret never having been sent to prison for the cause, Ellen feared for her safety. She had resented too the time and energy her daughter gave to 'those rotten suffragettes . . . it grieves me the lengths she goes to'. It was something Edy shared with Chris and it 'makes me sling the ink about', she admitted. As for herself she would refuse to vote because 'it was a dangerous thing to do without knowledge. I see this way & that way – & a wobbler like that does mischief.' But this terrible war redirected her anxieties and she prayed that 'no harm comes near you', she wrote to Edy, 'and that somehow or other we meet at home before Christmas'.

She was advised for her safety not to sail from Australia to Britain, but return instead by way of Canada. 'It will not be safe', she explained to Edy. '. . . I should hate to be blown up by a mine.' She sailed back in the RMS *Makura*, 'our lights turned down & all the port holes brown-papered so as to avoid if we can the Germans popping at us with their big guns'. It was a ghostly voyage and 'we are in God's hands'. They disembarked at Vancouver where Ellen took the train on her long journey to New York, arriving there early in 1915.

Her eyes were giving her so much pain that she decided to consult an 'eye-smith' before returning home. 'I have been quite blinded the last four days with *extreme pain in my head*', she told Gordon Craig. The specialist decided that an immediate operation was needed to remove a cataract in her left eye. 'I asked if it would hurt', and she was told 'very little'. But 'it hurt like hell . . . he prised up something, and then he cut, and my eye was all wet, and then my head seemed to be cut open at the top of my spine, and then torture for a *month*'. She went to bed but not to sleep, knowing if she moved 'it would cost me my eye'. After four days her vitality began to seep back and she 'slept a little without hallucinations'. On 27 February, her sixty-eighth birthday, a letter from Edy arrived and she had it read to her.

When at last she did get up, 'the tons of depression that have weighed on me, and anguished me, since the operation, are rolling away', she wrote. But the world to which she returned seemed to have been made insane by the war. 'Everyone speaks, nobody listens – a mad world and a stupid', she wrote to her son in Italy. '. . . This is a moment, it seems to me, when individuals like you & me shd *mind our own business*, & not trouble our heads about a place in the sun.' She longed to be home and to see familiar faces 'which are the only faces I *understand* – it takes so long to read the truth in new faces'.

'I don't think of *Death* myself with any terror', she had told Mrs Rumball. Watts's death back in 1904 had not really moved her: he belonged to a past that was itself dead. The deaths of Irving's loyal lieutenants, Loveday and Stoker, in 1910 and 1912 were closer to her and she sent wreaths to their funerals. But the death that affected her most was that of her 'Irving boy' Laurence on the *Empress of Ireland*. 'Remember thee!' she wrote in her diary, quoting Hamlet's vow to the spirit of his father. 'Ay, thou poor ghost, while memory holds a seat in this distracted globe.'

While in New York she read that Sarah Bernhardt was having her leg amputated. 'The mere idea seems grotesque', she wrote. The news was confirmed but by then she knew of Bernhardt's determination to continue acting and cabled her in Paris: 'Fine little Queen. Beloved woman. You frightened me, but you are ever young and ever triumphant. Congratulations. Devotedly, E.T.'

On 23 April 1915, Shakespeare's birthday, she gave her last performance on the American stage at the Neighborhood Theater in New York, delivering extracts from her Shakespeare lectures. She felt weak and nervous after her operation, and at one moment took off a long string of amber beads (the ones perhaps Stephen Coleridge had secretly given her all those years ago), saying with a laugh: 'The burden of my riches hangs heavy on me.'

She had booked her passage back on an American liner, the *New York*, and when Charles Frohman offered her a suite on the faster, more luxurious *Lusitania*, she refused partly because Edy had made her promise not to travel on a British vessel. The *New York* was certainly not luxurious, but 'I suppose on the whole I prefer *this* bed to the Ocean Bed!' Also on board was Diana Wilson, a young pupil of Isadora Duncan's, a grave and beautiful girl who read to her, packed for her, and made the voyage home enjoyable. Ellen was met at Liverpool by Edy, having learnt shortly before disembarking that the *Lusitania*, with Frohman on board, had been sunk.

43
Masks and Faces

It was at Florence in the spring of 1908 that Gordon Craig began to bring out his long-cherished theatre magazine *The Mask*. With diverse and unpredictable contents from past and present yet always pointing to the future, it was to last (with an interval for the war) until 1929. Containing woodcuts, etchings and drawings of designs for costumes and stage sets, *The Mask* was, unlike *The Page*, principally a magazine of words rather than illustrations – despite its championing of the 'old power of our eyes' that had been dimmed by the tyranny of language. 'I believe in the time when we shall be able to create works of art in the Theatre without the use of the written play, without the use of actors', he prophesied. But until this time arrived words were an awkward necessity.

His first need was to find someone in Florence who could help him conjure forth these words and take care of the surrounding labour they gave rise to: choosing the paper on which to print them, for example, and dealing with all those wretched business matters, such as money, which stood as obstacles in the path of free creative thinking. In Berlin he had found Maurice Magnus; in Florence he came across Dorothy Nevile Lees – or 'DNL' as she was identified in his alphabet of women.

Dorothy Nevile Lees was a Christian Scientist of unquenchable optimism, severely good-natured and practical, yet with a highly charged romantic temperament. She had been brought up at a large house in the gentle hills along the border of Staffordshire and Shropshire and educated at Cheltenham Ladies' College. In 1903, when the family fortunes went into decline, she set out in her early twenties for Italy (where her mother had been born). Arriving in 'the enchanted land of my childish imaginings, the Mecca of my dreams', and sensing she had reached in Florence 'the goal of a thousand precious hopes', she began to seek her destiny there – and would never return to England. Finding small jobs teaching and translating, she had also taken a position of governess and companion to the daughters of 'the noble Pandolfini family'. She was a figure from an early E.M. Forster novel, her rather plain face framed by thick brown hair gathered into an aureole.

Early in 1907 she met Gordon Craig at the hotel where he was living. He was ill in bed at the time and, though by now in his mid-thirties, appeared to her 'almost incredibly young . . . a mere boy'. But 'I had', she later reflected, 'very much to learn'. Nevertheless, it was true that, as Craig verified, 'I remained young for a very long time.' He knew she had written two books in English, mostly on the food, customs and culture of Tuscany (she had been commissioned to write two more books but was never to complete them). Her spare time was passed in painting water-colour landscapes and writing poetry celebrating her love of Italy (though expressing her wish never to be disloyal to the lanes and lawns, the swallows and larks, of her homeland). All this was very fine, but the question was: would she surrender all these bits and pieces and give herself over to Craig's interests? He hesitated a little before demanding this – and in that delicate moment of hesitation, it appears, she stepped forward and volunteered to devote 'everything to his work'. Indeed, she *insisted* on it. Her decision, she knew, would lead to 'an unknown future, hard and hazardous'. But it also meant she would 'be with him and for him'. And so: 'I made my choice.' In addition to her artistic interests she was a rapid and efficient typist, had learnt shorthand, and spoke fluent Italian. She was exactly what he needed. For more than twenty years she became what Christopher St John was becoming for Ellen Terry and Edy Craig: a factotum, secretary, literary assistant and more, much more. She typed and translated for him, negotiated with printers and publishers on his behalf, using a small allowance from her family, together with her payments for contributions to the *Christian Science Monitor* and the *Italian Gazette* as well as the proceeds from a sale of her jewellery and what she inherited after her mother's death, to pay off his creditors. It was essential that Craig and his magazine be 'kept afloat'.

The Mask developed into the equivalent of Gordon Craig's theatre. Open

THE MASK

A QUARTERLY JOURNAL OF THE ART OF THE THEATRE. ILLUSTRATED.

EDITOR, John Semar.

ARTISTIC ADVISER. Gordon Craig.

its pages and you enter his dramatic world. He peopled it with almost a hundred characters: 'John Semar' (of Javanese extraction), 'Jan van Holt' (who appeared to write from Holland), 'Adolf Furst' (the Berlin correspondent), 'Allen Carric' (who specialised in early Italian literature) and others such as 'Yoo-no-hoo' and 'Stanislas Lodochowskowski' from more exotic regions. To some of these pseudonyms he attached character sketches; for others he invented signatures and scissored out cardboard figures to stand along his bookshelves, a silent audience that appeared to watch him working at the centre of a magic puppet show. But 'Anthony Scarlett', 'Patrick Nevile', 'Conrad Tower', 'Fenella Ford', 'Lois Lincoln' and 'Pierre Rames' (Semar in reverse) were all noms-de-plume of Dorothy Nevile Lees. They wanted to make everything as 'mysterious' as possible, to put scholars off their tracks and keep them guessing – 'and it was good fun too', DNL wrote. One hot summer they spent by the sea, carrying on their work, each in a bathing hut, having one meal a day at a local *pensione* and sleeping on the sands at night. It was all an adventure, a marvellous game.

The Mask's contributors were a symbolic army with which Craig fought against the degradation of modern playhouses – illusory spirits guiding him on his quest to rekindle the sacred fires of an ancient art. He stood upon a crowded stage, a battlefield, where he was nevertheless the sole performer – as he imagined Hamlet to have been, the other characters merely visions and automatons seen through his mind's eye. In this fabulous theatre there were no tedious practicalities to restrict him, no vainglorious actors or commercial managers. Here at last 'I am a free man'.

But freedom was a hard taskmaster. He would lie in bed thinking, thinking, and his thoughts rose up – but the words remained below. Then eventually some letters and sounds, vowels and consonants maybe, seemed to cluster round and declare themselves. He would leap up, hurriedly put on one of his white tropical suits and, before these elusive words could get away, dash excitedly up and down the terrace like a lepidopterist chasing invisible creatures fluttering from the pages of his thesaurus. And all the time he would be dictating to DNL, trying to communicate everything he caught, anything that flew into his head.

All morning, as he hunted inspiration, he felt elated; every afternoon, when he read what DNL had taken down, he fell into despair. He would examine her script, his cardboard characters standing sentinel around him, and improve it to the very frontiers of illegibility. Then the process would renew itself. 'I *will* teach myself to write – I WILL,' he declared. So they struggled on: he thinking, walking, declaiming and soliloquising; she sitting, listening, writing and rewriting. Then one night they became lovers.

DNL had been brought up in a conventional family where divorce was regarded with horror. And that was why, as Craig explained, he could not marry her. Not only had he been married but he was also divorced: and he regarded the process with the same contaminating horror as her parents did. So there was no alternative for them both but free love. This was unfamiliar territory for such a politely tutored young girl. Still, she recognised Craig's boldness in this enterprise and was determined to match it with what she described as 'the immensely protective caution which even young and inexperienced women manifest regarding anyone to whom they are attached'. She was bound by something stronger than an attachment. 'I loved him passionately, whole-heartedly', she was to tell Craig's son Edward many years later. '. . . I only wish he had not had quite so much devotion from so many.' In the spring of 1907 however she knew only of Craig's ex-wife May on whom a door had been shut and bolted. Throughout the many shocks and hardships that awaited her she 'kept on as best I could', despite the fact that he did not appear to value her superhuman loyalty. Indeed, there were times when he seemed almost indifferent to her. So what was the justification for her 'life of complete self-suppression and abnegation'? It was simple. She counted herself fortunate to be experiencing such profound emotion. It brought her alive as she had never been before – people who pitied her never understood this. Nothing else mattered. She was to look back with pride at this 'great adventure'. It was 'as if, as in the old legends, a god had come down to earth'. She worshipped him not just sexually, but also for the visionary ideals of his great work in which she was allowed to clothe herself and carry some of the burden. To nurse his words into print, to punctuate and proof-correct them, and type lists, file letters, address envelopes, dispatch parcels became parts of a sacred task. So, despite her poverty and long periods of loneliness, these were fruitful years – and 'maybe someone writing of it all in future, when I'm no longer here, will give it a word of recognition'.

The multitude of pen names Gordon Craig employed in his magazine were all masks for himself, and the mask – 'the only right medium of portraying the expressions of the soul as shown through the expressions of the face' – became a symbol of the non-realistic theatre which, he prophesied, would emerge in time. The ultimate destination of realism was the cliché.

His writings in *The Mask* steer an ingenious course between the great theatre figures in his life. Godwin, it was, who had seen what prevented the English from restoring 'our ancient and honourable art' of the theatre to its rightful place. It was their eternal triviality, which they took pride in calling their sense of humour (though it was actually a fear of being ridiculed), which forbade them from doing anything bold and original. Had he not used his archaeological scholarship to bring past and present together? Might he not have carried this experiment into the future had he been given encouragement? Craig honoured his father, promoting his role significantly from that of an archaeological assistant and publishing in *The Mask* the twenty essays on 'The Architecture and Costume of Shakespeare's Plays' which had originally appeared in *The Architect*. These were introduced by 'John Semar', who quoted Beerbohm Tree's opinion that Godwin's work for *The Merchant of Venice* had made this the first production 'in which the modern spirit of Stage Management asserted itself'. It was Godwin, John Semar claimed, who 'in a sense not yet fully realised, fathered the new movement in the European theatre and founded that race of theatrical artists of whom the theatre of the Future shall be born'.

These articles were illustrated with Godwin's original drawings which Ellen (enclosing a cheque) had sent him. He even invited his sister Edy to contribute 'occasional notes about violently stupid or careless things you see' – adding hurriedly 'or rather promising things'. Ellen Terry's theatrical career he put to use as a cautionary tale. Her memoirs were a valuable publication, he thought, insofar as they revealed 'the narrowness of the theatrical brain, the limitations of the theatrical outlook' that prevailed among the stolid burly inhabitants of England. Any artist reading her pages would feel 'more insistently than before the imperative need of escaping from the triviality of the stage world, from the artificiality of its atmosphere'. Seen in this light, Ellen Terry's conventionally romantic career became a prelude to change since this must inevitably spread discontent with existing conditions. 'It is in arousing this discontent in the younger workers in the theatre that Miss Terry's memoirs will be of service to the Art.'

Ellen Terry was a mirror of the age from which Godwin is depicted impotently struggling to escape. As for Henry Irving, he stands between them, fixed in the impossible past but enigmatically staring into a visionary future. Craig warns us all to read nothing about Irving because we would read lies. Instead we must study his face to find the truth. 'To begin with you will find a mask, and the significance of this is most important . . . The face of Irving was the connecting link between that ridiculous expression of the human face as used by the theatres of the last few centuries, and the masks which will be used in place of the human face in the near future.'

Craig then confronted Isadora Duncan. In a series of sweeping statements, he had stripped his ideal theatre of actor-managers, commercial businessmen and playwrights – even Shakespeare was better read than acted, indeed 'the plays of Shakespeare are unactable'. Then he went further. 'Let me repeat again that it is not only the writer whose work is useless in the theatre. It is the musician's work which is useless there, and it is the painter's work which is useless there. All three are utterly useless. Let them keep to their preserves, let them keep to their kingdoms, and let those of the theatre return to theirs.' So what was left? 'I like to remember that all things spring from movement, even music,' he wrote, 'and I like to think that it is to be our supreme honour to be the ministers of that supreme force – movement.' But movement meant dance, and dance meant Isadora. He did not wish to be in servitude to her. She was a divine accident, he believed, not so much an artist as an inspiration of artists – and with rather too much ambition for a woman. As for himself, he was independent of his contemporaries, a messenger from the distant past heralding the future. So what should take the place of the dancer in his scheme of things to come? What he called a 'way out' or 'loop-hole' lay in replacing the movement of dance with the movement of symbolic gesture, and the photographic miming of human beings (whether dancers or actors) with the impersonal magic of abstraction. 'For me the human body in movement seemed to signify less and less', he told Adolphe Appia. '. . . The true and sole *Material* for the Art of the Theatre, light – and through light Movement.' As for moving objects, 'I have a greater feeling of admiration and fitness when I see a machine which is made to fly than when I see a man attaching to himself the wings of a bird'. Such a vision took its place along with Wyndham Lewis's Vorticist movement in Britain (Lewis, Craig believed, was an artist 'packed with signs of genius' – though his prose 'bores me'). Also standing with Craig's work was that of the symbolist painter Odilon Redon in France, and in Italy Marinetti's Futurist manifesto published in 1909 (a translation of which, by DNL, was published in *The Mask*). But Craig made it clear that 'there are never *two* best leaders. There is only one best . . . [and] the Readers of *The Mask* may rest assured that your leader is a long way in advance of [Marinetti].'

He was experimenting with marionettes. 'There is something more than a flash of genius in the marionette', he wrote in *The Mask*. '. . . The marionette appears to me to be the last echo of some noble and beautiful art of a past civilization. But as with all art which passed into fat or vulgar hands, the puppet has become a reproach. All puppets are now but low comedians . . . [But] they are the descendants of a great and noble family of Images . . . We must study to remake these images . . . we must create an Über-Marionette.' The Über-Marionette was more than a marionette, more than an actor, having 'the virtues of both & the vices of neither'. It occupied the same territory as the Wagnerian superman: 'the actor plus fire, minus egoism: the fire of the gods and demons, without the smoke and steam of mortality'.

In 1911 Craig published a book with the confusing title *On the Art of the Theatre*. He had intended to reprint the two dialogues from *The Art of the Theatre* published six years earlier, adding a few pages from *The Mask*. But as he went about preparing the volume, these pages from *The Mask* accumulated until they formed two thirds of his new publication.

On the Art of the Theatre, which conveys his ideas of stage design in all their poetic mystery, was to become a seminal work throughout Europe and America during the twentieth century. In the opinion of Alexander Hevesi, the dramaturge-*régisseur* of the Budapest State Theatre, who contributed a short introduction to the book, it was written with 'the soul of a child, with the knowledge of a student, and with the constancy of a lover' – though a pedantic biographer might query this last attribute. Students especially loved this book. Craig became their Leonardo da Vinci. As his prophetic prose enveloped them, they were carried away from the classroom and off to a metaphorical theatre where the author was talking to them urgently, intimately, charmingly. 'I'm going to give you all sorts of things to cheer yourself up with', he promised them, 'and you may with courage and complete good spirits throw what you will to the winds and yet lose nothing . . .' He introduced them to the hustling duties of the director, the proprietor, the stage-manager, chief actors, playwrights and other fifth-rate people, touched on the technicalities of lighting and the principles of costume, and advised them that their apprenticeship should last from six to ten years. Only then could they afford to forget it all and in this fashion they would gain experience and remain young. Above all they must not use their brains (which rob people of vitality) but rely instead on instinct and avoid all theatrical tricks and customs. He welcomed his student-readers like a band of disciples, rousing them as to a grand chivalric cause. 'Remember we are attacking a monster; a very powerful and subtle enemy . . . Alone and unaided I can reach no final results. It will need the force of the whole race to discover all the beauties which are in this great source, this new race of artists to which you belong . . . I claim the Theatre for those born in the Theatre, and we will have it!' His influence sprang from the very incompleteness of his work. 'My wishes seldom flower', he admitted to Kessler. But these wishes were widely scattered, offering a biblical prospect: a place of rhetoric with miraculous horizons.

His words were read as a revelation. Illumined by a divine, vibrating light, he appeared to stand like a companion spirit to 'the ever living genius of the greatest of English artists', William Blake (the man who had no mask according to Samuel Palmer), to whom this book was dedicated. What he wrote was enriched with echoes from Nietzsche and quotations from Whitman, Plato, Dante, Hazlitt and others – and orchestrated with the broad sweep of generalities ('The whole nature of man tends towards freedom'; 'Emotion is the cause which first of all creates, and secondly destroys'). He throws out questions in all directions – but gives few answers. 'I do not think the time has arrived when I can give you a hint of how to break this spell which lies over the European Theatre; besides, my purpose here is to put a question to you, not to answer one.' There were to be no short-cuts: 'we look for the truth to emerge in due time'. And this was good because 'I shall not remove from you the very difficulty which will be the source of your pleasure'.

There was a reason for this prevarication: his fear of misappropriation. 'I am afraid that if I were to commit my method to writing I should write something down which would prove not so much useless as bad. For it might be very dangerous for many people to imitate my method.'

In his preface to the book, Craig placed himself among a select few who belonged to the theatrical avant-garde. There were no Englishmen among them. No Albert Rutherston (whose work he considered pictorial rather than dramatic – useful perhaps for ballet). No Granville-Barker (a 'high-intentioned, orthodox idealist'). And no William Poel who, being so much of an antiquarian, 'did not understand the living theatre'. Craig invoked the names of Stanislavski and Meyerhold from Russia and the Swiss designer Adolphe Appia; from France he chose among others the actor and director André Antoine, founder of the Théâtre Libre, Paul Fort, the poet and founder of the Théâtre Mixte, which replaced descriptive scenery with evocative modernist sets, and Yvette Guilbert, '*la diseuse fin-de-siècle*', who communicated her songs not by words so much as by marvellous sounds that suggested meaning. Her emaciated figure, hennaed hair, long black gloves and white masklike face with its vivid red gash of a mouth, made posthumously famous by Toulouse-Lautrec, greatly excited Craig who claimed her as an inspiration. From Poland he picked out the recently deceased poet, playwright and director, Stanisław Wyspiański, whose 'total theatre' had been marked by classical symbolism and who had made the Ghost the chief character in his production of *Hamlet*. There were a few others invited to be his allies from Berlin, Munich and Amsterdam, but the only English-speaking member of this select company was 'our great poet' W.B. Yeats, to whom Craig gave a model stage complete with screens which worked better for the acting version of his morality play, *The Hour-Glass*, at the Abbey Theatre than for the Russian *Hamlet*. It was a pity, he thought, that Yeats later went off the rails 'looking at the moon'.

During these seven years in Florence, Craig attracted a miscellaneous group of assistants. Besides the ever-loyal Dorothy Nevile Lees, there was Gino Ducci, a postman who lent Craig his small printing press and helped with producing letter-headings, bookplates and pamphlets until his arrears of wages grew unsustainable. Michael Carr, a painter and carpenter who was to construct Craig's model stages with their moving screens, arrived from California with his wife. Extracts from her translation of an enormous work in Dutch on the Javanese shadow theatre became (along with DNL's Italian translations and Godwin's reprints) of use as 'fillers' for *The Mask*. Also from California came Sam Hume, a self-elected pupil whose amiability was sometimes interrupted by tremendous fighting fits following a few glasses of Italian wine, but who took over the sober business of making model stages after Michael Carr and his wife had been driven away by exhaustion and bankruptcy. Elena Meo's brother Nino also came out to join them. The only new arrival who spoke Italian, he was gifted with a fine singing voice and a talent for mime and improvisation. There was a musician too, Leigh Henry, well versed in the onomatopoeic possibilities of eastern musical instruments; an artist, Geoffrey Nelson, who was put to work drawing elevations; also a man who had given up medicine for his love of the theatre and another young man who came from Manchester and looked like a schoolmaster; and someone named Brown, reputed to be the son of a bishop, whose duties were unspecified. Besides these there was an accountant of whose skills there was often urgent need; and several others including local wood-engravers, carpenters and an electrician devoted to batteries and wires: altogether 'a body of earnest and thorough workers' drawn by Craig's advertisements for a school that would do 'what is left undone by the Modern Theatre'.

He had already seen the ideal place. The Arena Goldoni was a disused, open-air, early-nineteenth-century classical theatre in the Via dei Serragli, near an apartment in the Lung' Arno Acciauoli where, by 1909, after many changes of address, Craig was living. As he stood among the multifarious weeds of its dilapidated auditorium declaiming the words of Shakespeare with the sunlight flooding around him, he hardly seemed to notice its cracked walls with occasional trees leaning out towards him like an attentive audience. For him this was a 'lovely' place, a silent, light-filled arena which he was already calling 'my theatre' – though he had merely begun negotiating its annual lease of 840 lire (a little under £35).

In the seasons that followed, trees seeded themselves and grew up among the grey stones. Easy-growing flowers such as hollyhocks and convolvulus appeared too, and a line of tall straight plants which resembled a bright curtain whenever they came out with quantities of purple flowers. So the Arena grew more attractive. From a discarded stone arose a splendid peach tree bearing an amazing crop of fruit which seemed a good omen. Here Craig's band of workers was joined by a visiting horse and a smoky grey kitten called Pedrolino Goldoni which grew into a magisterial cat – and then there was the bear. Some prince (perhaps a friend of Maurice Magnus) had presented Craig with a bear cub, an engaging little creature, fat and woolly, which they called Giorgio. He would give people his paw to hold as he walked unsteadily around the arena and take milk from a bottle. But then something unexpected happened. Giorgio grew larger and visitors became frightened of him. So, to everyone's regret, he went off to a circus.

Craig's work with Ellen and Edy, with Duse and Stanislavski, reinforced his wish to have his own theatre where, as he had foreseen in his book, there would be one man 'who is a master in himself'. He called the place a school in his fund-raising prospectus, but what he actually had in mind was a fabulous workshop where he could 'conduct researches into every aspect of the three elements – Sound, Light and Movement – of which the Art of the Theatre is composed'.

He needed to recruit new enthusiasts, but how could he be certain they would not make off with his ideas? To prevent such treachery he began drafting strict monastic rules governing the conduct of all members of his future school. They must not join any other school; they must not communicate with anyone outside the school. They must give themselves over to silence and attention to their work. Only dedicated people would be accepted – and even them he suspected. 'My rule of no lady workers at the school must be kept to precisely', he reminded Dorothy Nevile Lees.

The delay in setting up this establishment was prolonged by his many journeys abroad. Because he was obliged to pass so much of his time in Russia, Craig soon made what he believed to be a bold business arrangement with his colleague Maurice Magnus, selling him the proprietorship of *The Mask* – along with its backlog of debts. Magnus, who dreamt one day of writing Gordon Craig's life, eagerly accepted. Undoubtedly he would have liked to be in a position to pay everyone handsomely. Unfortunately his mysterious business partner, whom no one seems to have met, would not countenance such extravagance. So he paid no one. Instead he issued a circular claiming for the magazine a distribution of 10,000 copies – for what harm could there be in adding a mere nought, just a zero, really nothing at all? But far from promoting cheerfulness, this spread turmoil among the unpaid workers and much distress to Dorothy Nevile Lees who, attempting to unravel his entanglements, came to see him as an 'evil genius'. At last, to her great relief, the agreement was torn up amid a parley of lawyers and Craig reacquired the ownership.

Wherever he went, Craig felt haunted by Isadora Duncan. On an early visit to St Petersburg in the spring of 1909, after eighteen months' separation, the two of them had met again for supper in Isadora's suite at the Grand Hotel d'Europe. Also present were Stanislavski and a woman – possibly an American or maybe a Scotswoman (it was difficult for Craig to be certain) – whom he guessed was Isadora's secretary. What then happened was dramatically unclear, like an out-of-focus film rerun at ten times its normal speed.

Stanislavski was always praising Isadora's qualities as an artist. But he never treated her as a woman – and no woman could rest content with this. He was a handsome man, no doubt of that, broad-shouldered, his black hair now streaked attractively with grey at the temples. Something, Isadora seems to have felt, should be done to advance matters – and what better occasion could there be on which to make this advance than now, following a few bottles of champagne and in front of the man whom she had loved as no other. 'I placed my hands on his [Stanislavski's] shoulders and entwined them about his strong neck, then, pulling his head down to mine, I kissed him on the mouth', she wrote in her autobiography. '. . . He wore a look of extreme astonishment.'

To Craig it was obvious that this scene was being conducted for his discomfort. Isadora had always been a flirt, always drunk too much champagne and enjoyed trying to arouse his jealousy. He recorded what he saw in his 'Book Topsy' in what amounted to a stage design for 'this rotten performance': the contours of the rooms, the placement at table, Isadora's arms encircling Stanislavski's neck as she kissed him – 'he objecting most politely all the time – and she refusing to accept his objections'. But Craig did not record what Stanislavski said to Isadora as she grappled to draw him closer to her. 'He started back,' Isadora revealed in her autobiography, 'and, looking at me with consternation, exclaimed, "but what should we do with the child?" "What child?" I asked. "Why, our child, of course. What should we do with it?" ' He then continued 'in a ponderous manner' to explain that he could never approve of any son or daughter of his being brought up outside Russia: 'my jurisdiction'.

Stanislavski knew of course that Isadora's and Gordon Craig's daughter, Deirdre (who was in France), was being raised beyond her father's jurisdiction. The child was in a position very similar to that in which Craig felt himself to have been, although he tried to suppress this knowledge.

Also half-buried within Craig, much denied and perhaps feared, lay the still-glowing embers of his love for Isadora. In his writings he was to accuse her of 'paganism', by which he meant confusing lust with love. He seemed unaware of the pain he had inflicted on her – 'her reason for offending me in this way I could not & still cannot fathom', he later wrote. He did not know that she had been told 'all the actresses of the Stanislavski troupe were in love with him'. Despite everything she too was still in love with him.

Gordon Craig's response lacked something of Stanislavski's polite (if ponderous) manners. By his own account he took the arm of Isadora's young secretary, manoeuvred her into an adjoining room 'with a bed in it' and persuaded her to lie down next to him 'with my arms around her', while the 'door handles twisted & knockings on the door went on'. He heard Stanislavski leave, irritably, and imagined Isadora lying alone in her own bedroom 'in a quiet bad temper'. Then he invited her secretary for a drive in the snow – 'an exciting cold hot drive' that mimicked his drive with Isadora in Berlin. They spent the night together in 'a nice room' at the hotel and, though he never verified her nationality, he could clearly remember her 'very white body'. Every so often 'a fearful twinge or wrench came to me', he acknowledged. But his fury with Isadora over her 'beastly behaviour' overcame these twinges. Accounts were to differ as to how 'Miss S.' reattached herself to Isadora. In any event they were together at Kiev a few days later. When Isadora asked her, looking 'rather pale and somewhat shaken', whether she 'did not want to stay in Russia with Craig, she said emphatically that she did not' – a feeling that Craig reciprocated: '*alone*, I thanked the Gods', he wrote.

'So we returned to Paris', Isadora continued. It was a pun as well as a statement of fact. For Isadora was returning to her new lover Paris Singer – 'my millionaire' as she called him, for whom she had 'sent my brainwaves seeking'. Singer was a 'strange silent man' who had inherited a good part of his father's vast Singer Sewing Machine wealth. He had recently parted from his Australian wife (by whom he had five children) and entered Isadora's life, putting her in mind of one of the Knights of the Holy Grail – in her autobiography she was to call him Lohengrin. Tall, blond, with curling hair and beard, his life crowded with elopements and infatuations, he set himself up as a quixotic patron of the arts. He appeared eternally busy, but what he actually did Isadora never found out. The secret at the centre of all this activity, his strangeness and the silence, was a powerful lack of talent. As a celebrated 'Renaissance King', he was expected to be an artist, scholar, scientist, architect, musician and doctor at the very least. He had no wish to disappoint people and it was true that he entertained many grandiose projects. He was an industrious dilettante, though, with little interest in the arts – 'I simply cannot comprehend how little he understood me and my work', Isadora complained. He was also a hypochondriac who made himself ill trying to invent a magic lozenge that would cure all diseases. He stands before us as someone, needing to be patted and flattered, who burst into rages or sank into sulks whenever he suspected his desire to please was being undervalued.

On his very first meeting with Isadora, early in 1909, Singer had frankly declared his wish to please her. Brimming with admiration, he had come round to her dressing-room at the Gaité-Lyrique after one of her concert performances and announced: 'I have come to help you. What can I do?'

Meeting Gordon Craig by chance in Paris before their encounter in St Petersburg, Isadora had gone for a walk with him in the Bois de Boulogne to discuss 'the wonderful things Singer might be about to do for her & her school'. This was hardly a pleasing discourse for Craig. Where was the justice when his own school in Florence still remained unfunded? Her attitude struck him as 'mean'.

By the time Isadora and Craig met in Russia, she and Singer were lovers. She 'made no secret of love', and this must have tightened the tension between her and Craig. Much later, when she asked Singer what had kept him attracted to her for so long, he answered thoughtfully: 'You've got a good skin, and you've *never* bored me.' In St Petersburg she would have been able to tell Craig that Singer was 'an expert voluptuary . . . his kisses grazed over my body . . . I felt a thousand mouths devouring me'.

Nevertheless to her dismay she found herself still vulnerable to Craig. 'I was on the verge of believing that nothing [else] mattered, neither the school, nor Lohengrin, nor anything – but just the joy of seeing him again.' But with this joy returned the old intolerable pain. The scene she made with Stanislavski was an attempt to anaesthetise it.

But it also showed a shocking change that was beginning to overtake her. In Paris she was leading the life of a *demi-mondaine*. This was what Singer had done for her. Craig, seeing her a couple of years later while seeking a French publisher for *The Mask*, wrote that the Topsy of whom he had been so fond was now 'horrific'. Paris life 'cooked her & dressed her up – absolute murder of the girl'. For Stanislavski, the one bright star in Isadora's life was her daughter Deirdre, who was always dancing and laughing, altogether 'a charming child. Craig's temperament and Duncan's grace.' He liked her so much that he fancifully arranged with Isadora 'to let me have her if she (Isadora) should die . . .' Deirdre was then aged three. Craig himself was to postpone meeting her for another three years.

At the beginning of May 1910, Isadora gave birth to a son, Patrick Augustus Duncan, at Beaulieu-sur-Mer, in a villa where she and Singer had first made love. Though frequently proposing to her, he was still married to his Australian wife and his name does not appear on the birth certificate – Patrick was officially the son solely of 'Isadora Duncan, *artiste*'. But Singer was delighted. And the birth had been comparatively easy.

They appeared, in the words of Isadora's friend Kathleen Bruce, to be 'more married than the most married people' or, as Isadora herself described their life, 'always quarrelling, always loving'. Singer's unstable temperament in some ways resembled Craig's. Her unfaithfulness and disloyalty to him seem at times to be enacted as a form of displaced revenge for what she had suffered over Craig – and she later regretted her treatment of Singer. By 1911 audiences had begun to notice that under the pouting baby face Isadora's body looked swollen and she had grown stout of leg.

In 1912, Paris Singer finally decided how he could help her. He would build a theatre for her, Le Théâtre du Beau, on some land he had bought just off the Champs-Elysées, in the rue de Berri. And to please her he offered Gordon Craig 50,000 francs to design it. The two men met for the first time that summer and discussed the construction, equipment and lighting of the place. 'This is exciting work', Craig wrote. He strongly advised Singer to let him 'frame the programme' of the theatre and 'exclude from your counsels all and every performer'. Only by the autumn did he come to his senses and realise that the programme would inevitably be framed by Isadora, whose dance pupils were to form a chorus for the Greek tragedies she intended to stage in what the newspapers reported as 'a vivid and artistic manner'. He at once sent in his notice. 'Although anyone might be honoured to build a theatre for Miss Duncan,' he wrote, 'I have made it one of my rules lately to work for no performer however highly gifted or eminent, & I cannot break it.' As for the theatre itself, the police persuaded Singer to abandon anything artistic in such a 'quiet, bourgeois neighbourhood'.

In Gordon Craig's letters and day books, Isadora appears as a dangerous apparition. As early as the summer of 1908, when she went to perform in London and met Ellen Terry, an alarm sounded in him. 'Meeting your mother has been a great thing', Isadora had written. 'She is marvellous – so Beautiful so kind . . . and the two nights she came to the Theatre I danced as in a dream.' Over this letter, in red ink, Craig scored the words 'lies' and 'all lies'. Everything about Isadora struck him as false – even her dancing which he called 'a direct case of piracy'. As for the meeting with his mother, 'you are merely an atom in the life of this lady', he wrote.

But Ellen liked Isadora and wrote to her sympathetically about her son. 'My heart goes out to him wherever he is', Isadora replied from New York, '– I long for him just as I long always to see his Baby [Deirdre], but I don't dare to think of it – or I shouldn't be able to live at all . . . He always looks wonderful – All the light and beauty of the World . . . *You* are the only one who understands how I love him – it will come right some day.' And Ellen did feel she understood Isadora's love. But she did not believe it would come right because 'Isadora [is] too temperamental . . . and what is more no woman should fall in love with a perfectionist – ever'.

The last time the two women saw each other was in June 1921 when Isadora performed her 'Revolutionary Dance' at Queen's Hall. Afterwards she stood before the curtain, and asked the audience to applaud Ellen Terry, a greater artist than she was – and everyone turned and cheered. But Ellen took away a sombre experience: 'I never saw *true* tragedy before', she said.

While in London that first summer of 1908, Isadora had taken Craig's eldest sons and daughter – May's children who were staying with Ellen – around the zoo and to *Peter Pan* and *The Pirates of Penzance*. She dreamed of returning to England, seeing Ellen and these children again, and 'perhaps Ted might be there too'. It was to guard against such a collision that Craig brought back Elena Meo and their two children (little Teddy and Nelly) into his life. She was the one woman he could trust – she had been 'longing I was with you and that we could be together'. And he agreed it should be so. He promised to escort them on this, their first visit to Florence. Travelling back briefly to England in 1908, he telegraphed DNL to meet him at Florence railway station on his return. She was surprised to be casually introduced to Elena and her two children about whom she had known nothing; and she was mortified to be left alone on the platform as they drove away in the carriage she had got. 'It was a deathly blow', she wrote, but 'I said nothing.' She said nothing the next day too when she was forbidden entrance to Craig's home. Falling ill, she lay in bed for days until Craig took the trouble to climb the 114 steps to her apartment, her 'tower with a view' by the Ponte Vecchio, and explain that her illness was becoming a source of gossip that might do him harm. So she returned to her work at the Arena Goldoni despite the agony of witnessing Craig escort his family around the place.

Fortunately for Dorothy he soon took Elena back to England, which he was to revisit irregularly until the beginning of the war. He liked the idea of travelling down to see his mother in the country and would have done so more often, he claimed, had he not been awkwardly poised between 'too much & not enough' work. His absorption made him solitary though never lonely even when 'I yearn to hear news & living things'. Out of the blue, 'on the wings of [a] dove', he would arrive at Smallhythe. And so, shortly after Edy and Chris had banished James Carew, they found themselves confronted by Ted.

What made Gordon Craig's visits to Smallhythe so objectionable to his sister was their mother's sudden worshipful attitude towards him. He became her prodigal son. However badly he behaved, she treated him as if he alone carried her life's blood, and Edy was a mere 'scamp' who 'forgets me' because 'she's busy helping all the other females!' In a letter to Bernard Shaw, she described Gordon Craig as 'my son [who] all along has been my sun. Without the warmth of him many a time I would have died and died, I know.'

Ellen still dreamed of finding some dramatic enterprise to bring her son back into her life. Early in 1913 she published a short book, *The Russian Ballet*, which celebrated 'a country which has no nationality and no barriers, the kingdom of dreams' that was formed by the coming together of Diaghilev, Nijinski, Pavlova and others. Christopher St John helped to draft the 5,000-word narrative which accompanied some rather crude illustrations by Pamela Colman Smith from *Les Sylphides*, *Le Carnaval* and *Spectre de la Rose*. 'Pixie' Smith was a young, elderly-looking American artist and folklorist, long associated with Edy's theatre productions and well known for her chanting performances of Yeats's poetry ('a savant with a *child's* heart', Yeats's father described her). Ellen liked to recommend her to Gordon Craig as an example of how he might successfully manage his career. 'She is extraordinarily industrious', she wrote, '& is everlastingly making (& selling as fast as she makes) lamp shades, candle shades. Paints wee boxes, cards, a dozen a day – trots them around. A funny little creature.'

Throughout the text of *The Russian Ballet* there are signs of Ellen reaching out to embrace her son's ideas. She points to the religious origins of dance ('the parent of my own art'), describes ballet as a dance poem and praises the Russians for their 'endeavour to restore the dance to some of its primal nobility'. She uses Nijinski as a unifying symbol for this agenda, comparing him with Henry Irving, suggesting that he was 'much affected' by Isadora Duncan, and even quoting a religious exposition of his genius by Christopher St John. But this was an ill-composed gift. Though Gordon Craig had been enchanted by Nijinski – more by his small gestures than by his magnificent dancing – he hated Benois's painted scenery, decided that Pavlova's vision (like that of so many women) was clouded with 'weakness & meanness', and distrusted Diaghilev's bag of virtuoso stage tricks – he was simply 'too afraid of failure' (something Craig was well qualified to recognise – an idea that he might stage *Cupid and Psyche* for Diaghilev came to nothing). He liked to believe that these Russians belonged to the past and complained that it was 'torture' for him to witness the theatre 'so vilely misused'. His mother's book fell into this waste-ground.

Edy and Ted had no wish to be tied together by their mother: but both needed her continually to invest in their careers. In May 1911, Edy formed the Pioneer Players and appointed Ellen its president – with Edy herself in control as managing director and stage director, and Chris a translator-adapter and dramatist. The Pioneer Players would borrow theatres, such as Harry Irving's Savoy, usually on Sundays for a single performance of a play that, between the rocks of commerce and censorship, would otherwise have no chance of reaching the stage. In the journal *Votes for Women*, Christopher St John complained that 'there is not one play on the London stage at the present time which takes account of women except on the level of house-keeping machines or bridge players – the actual or potential property of some man valuable or worthless as the case may be. It is strange to go out of the world where women are fighting for freedom . . . into the theatre where the dramatist appears unaffected by this new Renaissance.'

Women's campaign for freedom became part of the Pioneer Players' agenda, but they had a wider brief than the suffrage, and specialised in 'plays of ideas' which gave dramatic form to wide-ranging social, political and moral issues of the times – everything from food reform and the provision of housing, to censorship and prostitution. One of their productions, attacked for being 'a brief for bastardy', arose from Lloyd George's Insurance Act 1912 which offered welfare payment to married mothers the limitations of which were dramatically exposed by the story of a pregnant woman who refuses to marry the father of her child. The play was called *The Surprise of His Life* and would certainly have surprised Gordon Craig, being written by Jess Dorynne, the mother of his daughter Kitty. 'I have been waiting all this time for you to ask me to play with you in *Hamlet*!' she had told him when they were lovers. Shortly after their love affair finally ended in 1902 she wrote in her anguish and anger: 'I was an undeveloped & very sensitive girl – brought up to regard any familiarity between men and women as "shocking" – did you, whom I chose to be my lover and initiate [me] into the mysteries of love, expect this sensitiveness – & set to guide my narrow views into wider aspects gently? No, dear! . . . It was all violent – & I was tossed . . . here and there without any assistance from you . . . I chafe at the degrading injustice of it!' But against all her impulses she could not throw off the remembrance of her love for him. In 1913 she published a book, *The True Ophelia and Other Studies of Shakespeare's Women by an Actress*, in which she revisits her love affair with Craig through Hamlet's relationship with Ophelia – the 'most virginal of Shakespeare's heroines' who reveals 'an unsuspected depth of nature . . . as the tragedy unfolds'. The book is dedicated to 'My Belovedest' (probably Kitty) and several of the pages have that autobiographical urgency which is a recognised ingredient of Shakespeare scholarship. 'He treated her infamously, never giving her a chance of explaining matters, and now it is too late . . . And is the real Ophelia, loving and intelligent, that Shakespeare has drawn, not a worthy love for Hamlet the Dane, even if she were too young and inexperienced for the "Prince of Denmark"?'

Before the war there was inevitably a feminist emphasis to Edy Craig's productions. 'It is obviously quite impossible nowadays to produce thoughtful plays by thoughtful people who do not bear some traces of the influence of the feminist movement', the society's first annual report stated. 'But [we] . . . have never had either the wish or the intention of narrowing their choice to works dealing with one phase only of modern thought . . . if many of those who have sent us plays have found inspiration in various aspects of the feminist movement, we must conclude that it is because the feminist movement is, in itself, not without dramatic interest.'

To raise funds, Edy continued to run pageants, organised fancy dress balls and costume dinners which were advertised in the fashionable pages of newspapers and magazines. At some of these gatherings the Pioneers danced tangos and mazurkas, and they and their guests were photographed sometimes in astonishing Futurist uniforms. Otherwise they dressed up as historical figures – Cicely Hamilton appearing as George Eliot and Christopher St John as George Sand (on another occasion she was transformed into an impressive King Herod). To Edy's relief, the Pioneer Players made a small profit over its first three years. 'We face the fourth season with confidence.'

And then the war came.

When asked why she did not write about the theatre, Edy answered that 'the stage is too much a part of my very tissue for me to theorize'. She ruled the Pioneer Players in a manner not unlike Irving's rule at the Lyceum. Both she and her brother rejected the tepid description of themselves as reformers. Edy set out to *transform* the theatre, if need be on a shoestring, so that it changed the mind of the country; Ted, crowning himself a once-and-future king at a court that was yet to be created, dreamed of carrying out a Utopian revolution from beyond the contemporary horizon. Edy, with no theatre of her own, was responsible for staging 150 plays – many of them one-act events – over a decade. Her brother, though producing no plays with his platoon of marionettes in a crumbling arena, brought about a lasting change in theatre production.

In earlier days, he had thought of their doing 'big work together'. Edy had the knowledge to compile 'an Encyclopedia of costume . . . a thundering big work' which would stand on the same shelf as his own prophetic works. But she had become tied to a Fabian agenda. 'Edy had a success last night – but I detest turning *performances* into an excuse for delivering attacks on Censors & things', he complained to Ellen. And now Edy was luring their mother into her pioneering world of little theatres when the great Ellen Terry should be performing in a national theatre playing Chekhov's *The Cherry Orchard*. Chekhov's work 'is all so prettily sad, so whispered . . . and it can be exceedingly beautiful', Craig believed. 'But it won't do out of Russia.' His mother should travel with him to Moscow and see how Stanislavski had made that play 'as much his own as Irving made *The Bells*'.

Gordon Craig himself was still experimenting with his movable screens which could be used when the coloured light was projected onto them to paint a stage and introduce shifting areas of shade. He demonstrated their effect to his mother on a model stage and she ordered a set of them. Could her family be drawn together around these magical screens? Later she was persuaded that they were unmanageable: they were put into store and broken up.

But Craig's prospects shone more brightly now. Elena accompanied him to Paris and spent more time with him in London where, in the summer of 1911, a number of admiring artists and writers, including Roger Fry, Lady Gregory, Augustus John, James Pryde and W.B. Yeats, attended a dinner in his honour given by William Rothenstein and others at the Café Royal. After seven years of wandering abroad, England appeared ready to receive him: a prophet returning with honour to his country. The letter of invitation drafted by Martin Shaw reminded them all of Craig's 'inspiring and dignified vision of the stage'. It would be 'a fitting thing', this letter concluded, 'that some definite acknowledgement be made to Craig for his unfaltering devotion and high aims through almost insuperable difficulties'.

The word 'difficulties' awoke some agitation in Craig's mind. Might the whole affair be compromised through what had been an oversight on his part? It was really no more than a simple lapse of memory, a piece of parenthetical absent-mindedness (the failure to marry Elena). Nevertheless it might be open to misinterpretation. So he decided that they should be married 'without a fuss' in June, the month before his dinner, in order not to spoil the occasion.

Then he was gripped by a more dramatic apprehension. 'I don't want the purpose of this dinner to be changed by any *one* person who might take it into their heads to annex the whole affair', he warned Martin Shaw. The person who, in all her plurality, he had in mind was Isadora Duncan. Would she burst in and disrupt everything? Assured that there would be no trouble of any kind, he laid aside his marriage plans.

There were 180 guests at the Café Royal on 16 July 1911. James Carew came, and so did Frank Harris, H.G. Wells and Albert Rutherston, who designed a charming menu for the occasion. 'It was a grand gathering', remembered William Rothenstein. 'I had Ellen Terry as my neighbour, and Mrs Patrick Campbell sat by Craig. It was touching to see Ellen Terry's pride in her son; tears were in her eyes during some of the speeches.'

In a letter to Rothenstein from Moscow the previous year, Gordon Craig had written: 'I am in my first HOME here in Russia.' Triumphs abroad were of course admirable, but Ellen was not a cosmopolitan actress like Duse, and her interests lay mainly in the English-speaking world. She had hoped that her son might strike up a partnership with Beerbohm Tree, have his genius recognised at His Majesty's Theatre in London, and go on to make the British theatre his home. 'If you could arrange something good for me with Tree or any other good London theatre I should be very glad', Craig had encouraged her. '. . . no one could be more eager to do a cautious but courageous piece of work in the theatre than I am.' But she must also make it clear that genius such as his 'never get[s] on a step without a free hand'. Unfortunately Tree was to describe one of his models as 'L'art nouveau', after which Craig decided that Tree 'was suffering under the crippling effects of brain poison' and the two of them floundered into 'the solemn farce' of a legal battle. Now Ellen had another dream. According to Rothenstein, Craig had been 'delighted with this public acknowledgement of his work', and let it be known that he 'wished to found a school for the theatre in London'.

DINNER TO MR. EDWARD GORDON CRAIG
CAFÉ ROYAL, SUNDAY, JULY 16, 1911
MR. WILLIAM ROTHENSTEIN IN THE CHAIR

Craig's facial expression during Rothenstein's stream of oratory had been, in Paul Nash's view, 'baffling'. He was obviously pleased to see Elena accepted by everyone as his wife without having to go through the tedious fuss of a marriage. But as for the 'great gathering' itself, what did it signify? 'They gave me a high tea and then they all went home, feeling they had done their bit', he wrote. He had hoped for something infinitely better, something he dared not mention but hid under a facile smile: the conquest of England. He was all imagination after rereading *Peer Gynt*, a play that like *Hamlet* had cast its spell on him (his copy of the play is unmarked except for one word on the title page: 'Masterpiece'). As an illusionist in a world of make-believe, he dreamed of transforming the bleakness of reality into miraculous fantasy. Sometimes, as Emperor of Himself, he really seemed able to create whatever he wanted – everyone agreed he looked a 'magnificent being' at the dinner, with 'the countenance of a dreamer, of a genius perhaps . . .'. What he wanted to see rise up after these years of exile, after this dinner, was a Gordon Craig Centre in London: a place of absolute power. But the polite world was a severe disappointment to him. Feeling suffocated by the claustrophobic pettiness of it all he returned to Florence where the Arena Goldoni stood waiting in all weathers for his dreams to materialise.

But Elena was not downcast. She struck out on her own, lunching with Asquith, the Prime Minister, interviewing Sir Edgar Speyer, a baronet-banker with philanthropic leanings towards music, and pursuing various writers including the popular novelist Hall Caine (a great admirer of Henry Irving) and the newly affluent J.M. Barrie. Eventually she cornered a famous patron of the arts, Lord Howard de Walden, over a cup of tea. He surrendered handsomely, giving her £5,000 with which Gordon Craig could start his school in Florence, and promising three further payments of £2,500 over the following years to help with its running costs.

Craig announced the birth of his theatre school on 27 February 1913, his mother's sixty-sixth birthday. 'Whatever I am, or may be, I owe to the inspiring influence of my mother', he declared. 'I bring it to her as a birthday offering, fully recognising that I owe its fulfilment largely to her unwavering and helpful encouragement.' Whatever was good, whatever was bad, he attributed ultimately to Ellen.

It was the best of times for him but not for Ellen. 'Teddy is afloat now', she wrote despondently to Bernard Shaw. He was to be followed 'by a troop of some 15 young men his pupils', W.B. Yeats told Lady Gregory on 5 March. 'In Florence they are to master every detail of the craft of the theatre . . . They must accept a course of three years. He claims that he can get for almost nothing what in London would cost £5000 a year.' Once his project had developed, Yeats wrote, 'there is a possibility of a big scheme of poetic drama emerging with myself as literary adviser'.

The possibilities suggested by this school crowded around Craig so abundantly that he was obliged to employ as his 'personal secretary' Anna Tremayne Lark. She was a young girl with literary aspirations who had written stories for *The British Girl's Annual* and recently arrived in Florence with her parents. She went to work in a room next to Craig's studio, controlling the counterfoils, circulating advertisements, translating and indexing while Dorothy Nevile Lees gave her attention to *The Mask*. It was happy work. 'The wind drops and the sun comes out and all is calm', he wrote that April. Then, out of that calm sky, came tragedy.

On the afternoon of 19 April, Isadora's two children, Deirdre and Patrick, were being driven from her rehearsal studio at Neuilly back home to Versailles. At an intersection of the rue Chauveau and the boulevard Bourdon which ran parallel to the Seine and where the embankment had no parapet, the car stalled. The chauffeur got out to crank the engine, leaving the two children in the car with their nurse. But he must have left it in gear and failed to secure the parking brake, for as soon as the engine started, the car shot forward and skimmed down the grassy embankment into the river. Some workmen, who were drinking on a café terrace nearby, heard shrieks from the two children and their nurse, and one of them dived into the water, but could not reach the submerged car. The police and fire brigade arrived, and then a motor boat, but an hour and a half passed before the car was at last hauled by an anchor and ropes up the bank. 'There was a heart-rending scene', *The Times* reported the following day, 'when the door of the car was opened and the children were found clinging to their nurse.' As soon as she heard what had happened, Isadora telegraphed Craig in Florence.

OUR LITTLE GIRL DEIRDRE WAS TAKEN FROM US TODAY WITHOUT SUFFERING MY BOY PATRICK IS TAKEN WITH HER THIS SORROW IS BEYOND ANY WORDS I SEND YOU MY ETERNAL UNDYING LOVE = ISADORA

Over these words Craig wrote: 'always Have courage. THEY are happy & eternal too to be sure.' These were probably the words he sent her and which, she told him, brought her what comfort she could find. Two days later he wrote her a letter. 'Isadora my dear – not I alone but all of us feel we claim some share of your sorrow . . . You are bearing all the grief which would have been theirs – then dry your eyes for them . . . To say I love you would not cover the whole . . .' But his own unhappiness showed and was due, he told Dorothy Nevile Lees, to 'news of great sorrow of an old friend'.

Ellen assumed that he would go to Paris. But Craig did not go. He had sent out his best ambassadors, those words of solace, and could not follow them himself. As for his mother and Elena, they 'don't understand what she [Isadora] & I were always & always will be'. If they did not understand, this was because he had never told them what was locked up in his private world. He hated having these secret compartments of his life broken into. 'Why should I go to Paris?' he answered his mother. '. . . I made up my mind not to actually go.' He could not face the grief, the guilt.

Count Harry Kessler, who was preparing a monumental edition of Craig's *Hamlet* at the Cranach Press in Weimar (it would not be ready for publication until 1929), did go to the children's funeral. 'There was a most beautiful, moving ceremony in the studio, *the most moving ceremony I have ever been to*', he wrote. 'Nothing but exquisite music, Grieg's "Death of Aase", then a piece of Mozart, that seemed to embody the tripping of light children's feet on soft grass & flowers, and a wailing, infinitely moving melody of Bach. I thought my heart would break. Poor Isadora behaved splendidly . . . she is really *heroic*, *encouraging* the others, saying *there is no death*, really great in her terrible grief . . . Everybody in Paris is moved to the very depths of their heart by this tragedy.'

Craig forwarded this letter on to his mother. To Isadora herself, he wrote: 'My life as yours has been *strange* – you are *strange – but not to me*. And my darling I know how you can suffer & not show more than a smile.' Once he had exalted his own strength as being greater than hers. But now, he confided: 'My heart has often shaken with *terror* to see your strength. For my heart and your heart are one heart and an utterly incomprehensible thing it is. *I want to be with you* . . . And as I am with you, being you, what more is to be said. Let us not be sorry for anything – or where should we begin. You and I are lonely – only that . . . you & I must be lonely.' It was the same

Gordon Craig, the European, 1911

Elena Meo in England (*far left*), Isadora Duncan in Belgium (*left*) Gordon Craig at work, photographed by Isadora Duncan, Holland, 1906 (*below left*)

Daphne Woodward, Paris, 1943 (*right*); Olga Knipper as Queen Gertrude, Russia, 1921 (*below left*); Dorothy Nevile Lees, Florence, *c.*1920 (*below right*)

Wives and Husbands: Dolly Baird and Harry Irving as Henrietta Maria and Charles I, 1906 (*above*); Mabel Hackney and Laurence Irving in *Typhoon*, 1913 (*below*)

The Trouts: Edy Craig (*above left*), Clare Atwood (*above right*), Christopher St John (*below*)

Elena with Gordon Craig and their children, Nelly and Edward, Smallhythe, 1910 (*above*); Wedlock: Mrs James Carew, Winchester, 1907 (*below left*); Edith Craig, Feminist, London, *c.*1908 (*below right*)

Two funeral cortèges: Deirdre, Paris, April 1913 (*above*); Ellen, Smallhythe, July 1928 (*below*) (Edy and Gordon Craig leading the procession, followed by Olive Chaplin and James Carew, and behind them Fred Terry)

Gordon Craig at Vence, *c.*1960 (*above*) and Tourette sur Loup, France, 1950 (*below*)

solitude that had marked the 'dear lonely personality' of Henry Irving, an isolation that joined their hands in intimacy.

Elena wrote Isadora two letters early that summer, enclosing photographs of her own children, and expressing sadness over 'a trouble so great that words become almost foolish – Poor little Deirdre – do not for one moment think that I am so narrow or so small that I could not love her – & little Patrick too – dear babes . . . Your sorrow is the saddest thing I know.'

'Yes I take the hand you hold out to me so sweetly', Isadora responded. But there was nothing anyone could do to ease the pain. 'As for me – I feel as if *I* had died with them – what is here left seems such a poor shadow – what shall I do with it – all my life gone – and my works too – for how shall I ever *dance* again – how stretch out my arms except in desolation.' She and Craig continued writing to each other, weaving other people's letters into their own. 'All my life seems like a fine ship on the rocks and no hope of ever going another voyage', she told him. '. . . You are creating the only real world worth living in – *The Imagination* – This so-called *real* world is a refinement of Torture – and if it weren't for the escape the Imagination offers it would be Hell indeed.'

Early in September Isadora arrived at Smallhythe. While pregnant with Deirdre, she had dreamed of Ellen Terry, and now, as she explained to Craig, 'I wanted to feel your Mother's arms about me.'

In a letter to her son, Ellen wrote that 'I. D. is in the next room fast asleep . . . I pray that great tenderness will be shown by all – it might keep her from going mad . . . It was strange to watch the effect of the news upon [Elena].' According to Isadora, Elena (whose elder daughter by Gordon Craig, we should remember, had died in infancy) came to hate her. And although Ellen tried to reason Isadora out of this belief, she could not help noticing Elena's strange mood. '[She] was rather rough & hard.' But then a terrible thought struck Elena: suppose it had been Teddy and Nelly who had been killed? But that was impossible. Her children were not like other children. They breathed a rarer oxygen and were, thanks be to God, immortal. Elena distrusted other children and did not allow Teddy and Nelly to have friends of their own age. Ellen, who greatly admired her courage and brightness, deplored this peculiar elitism ('there must be some children of worth besides ours!'). Such exclusiveness protected Elena. She was suspicious of Isadora and had 'no place in her heart except her all-absorbing ferocious &

jealous love for you', Isadora told Craig. Everything Isadora told Elena of their relationship contradicted what Craig had written to her – but Elena had to believe him.

The emotional conflict between the two women provoked a crisis in Craig. He was the one person who could help Isadora and she wanted to see him – it was not enough to be told that they were the same person and he was always with her. But he could not risk seeing her. His instinct had told him even before the Café Royal dinner that Isadora would somehow cast a spell on him – and now this was happening. While negotiating with Paris Singer over the Théâtre du Beau, Craig had been, as Isadora Duncan's biographer Peter Kurth writes, 'unable to avoid a reunion with Deirdre, whom he met as a virtual stranger in Neuilly . . . [and] professed to be shocked that she had not run joyfully into his arms: "With all my children, especially the dear little girls, *all understanding* has ever been between us – always – and somehow little Deirdre seemed frozen . . . no tender leap towards me – no eager smile . . ." ' The guilt he suppressed under this naïve surprise now rose intolerably to the surface and he beat it off by castigating Isadora for Deirdre's death.

He had already told Elena that Isadora was an absentee mother who failed to protect her children (he made melodramatic references to fire and suffocation). The two women meeting had been 'a very silly business' and he reassured Elena that 'you did your part well and you are a dear good Nelly'. If her character was similar to Dickens's inestimably loyal Mrs Micawber, Isadora appeared a counterpart to the sinister siren Estella.

That autumn he travelled to Paris and saw where his daughter had drowned. 'The place still has tragic signs', he told Elena. He did not call on Isadora, but towards the end of the year she came and saw him in Florence. 'I am in a strange state beyond anything human I think', she wrote from the Grand Hotel in Florence. '. . . My Spirit feels some *healing & light* since seeing you.'

Craig does not seem to have revealed this brief encounter to Elena. Where did his loyalties lie? Elena 'stands as an example of the grandest type of woman', he had written in 1910. '. . . I was in love with her in Hampstead, and am in love with her still' – she 'who brought me my School in her hands'. Even so, he was 'not mad at all' to love Isadora. In his various writings over the years, he returned again and again to Isadora, accusing her of vainly trying to win a place in Elena's heart 'by pushing me out' and of having drowned her children 'like puppies in a sack'. Had she really loved them they would have surely lived. 'Never could they have died as they did die with their MOTHER watching . . . it was her own fault.'

This tragedy foreshadowed another one some ten years later when his and May's son Peter, a shell-shocked casualty of the war, drowned while attempting to rescue a woman from the sea off the south coast of England. May was an altogether different mother from Isadora. She watched over Peter, their youngest son, watched over him until he went off to the war. But Craig did not know him. So how could he grieve over this stranger – especially when he had never loved May? Peter's drowning finds no place in Craig's biography written by Elena's son. But it did involve Ellen herself who knew May's children better and for whom Peter had been 'the best of the lot'. She wrote to her son presenting the most optimistic gloss on this dreadful news. '*All is as it should be* – for the sweet young fellow could *never* have recovered from the war ghastliness, and it is just the sweet mercy of God that he should 'scape from suffering & be at rest.' But this was not how she actually felt. 'I am down & down about the sweet young fellow my poor Peter', she wrote to a friend. '. . . [I] cannot but feel much comfort in the knowledge that he has been saved the *terrors* of years to come.'

For the feelings which rose up in him over Deirdre's death, feelings from which he could not rid himself, Craig would later ask Isadora's forgiveness. 'Can you forgive me for all the bad things? & can you forgive me for trying to live without you? You see I can't', he wrote. '. . . If ever I have hurt you I have hurt myself far more – you have never hurt me . . . I have nothing to forgive & everything to remember.'

'A glimpse of myself – if I dared to lift the veil – might kill me', he had written to Isadora early in 1913. By the beginning of 1914, he absorbed himself again in the work of rediscovering 'some of those magic and elemental principles of beauty, simplicity, and grace' among which he could take sanctuary. 'My hands are full here', he had told Isadora. '. . . I have the task of Hercules to get through.' He began to form a library and build up a museum at the Arena Goldoni. By giving his time to the surrounding crew of carpenters, musicians, translators, a solitary figure at the centre of it all, he was 'trying to forget'. He bought a black-and-yellow stagecoach and, hiring four black horses, travelled through the Tuscan hills, valleys and vineyards which Dorothy Nevile Lees had celebrated in her books. Equipped with compasses, measuring lines and a 'proper photo machine', he came across village fiestas, watched religious processions, entered old theatres 'which are enough to warm the spirits'. He followed travelling companies of actors and acrobats – or simply studied the ever-changing light from sunrise to evening on the towers and pinnacles. 'I do not wish a man to be free from grief', he had written to Martin Shaw. But for a time, accompanied by Dorothy Nevile Lees and Anna Tremayne Lark, he could leave grief behind.

With their help, he also published an illustrated eighty-page brochure, *A Living Theatre*, setting out the aims and objects of the Arena Goldoni. But the school did not materialise as Yeats had thought it would. It remained a vision. 'I don't take "pupils" anymore', Craig wrote shortly after its opening. 'I am the sole pupil.'

And then the war came.

For Edy Craig's Pioneer Players the war meant business as usual. Refusing to be 'submerged by the high tide of that most violent of human activities which men call war', they confronted the jingoistic mood of the times with a series of uncompromising foreign plays forming a counter-attack on war by men themselves. They offered the public a drama of social evil translated from the Latin; a story of revenge by the Spanish playwright José Echegaray; a complex Japanese drama, *Kanawa*, by Torahiko Kori. They produced Christopher St John's translation of Herman Heijermans's *The Hired Girl*; Leonid Andreyev's 'grim comedy' *The Dear Departing* (in which a man hangs from a cliff-face attracting a crowd which waits for him to fall to his death – a crowd from which he hopes to collect money); and Nikolai Evreinov's expressionist monodrama *The Theatre of the Soul*, a challenging work showing the effect of war on a man in the process of psychological disintegration. One of their major productions was the French Catholic dramatist Paul Claudel's ambitious four-hour epic *The Tidings Brought to Mary* – an audacious choice wrote a reviewer in the *Westminster Gazette*, though 'I almost wish they had the audacity to cut it a little'.

Membership of the Pioneer Players decreased as actors were called up for military service and the Little Theatre, where they held many of their productions, was converted into a hostel for soldiers. Yet the company struggled on, helped financially in one crucial year by Christopher St John's old employer, Lady Randolph Churchill. They produced what no other theatre company dared or wanted to produce, and gained the reputation of being a uniquely 'brave society', as a writer in *The Sketch* described them. Somehow they managed to survive the war with an agenda that seldom failed to warn audiences that 'we are not going to enjoy ourselves', Virginia Woolf wrote, '. . . we are going to be scraped and harrowed and precipitated into some surprising outburst of bitterness'.

But the war took Gordon Craig by surprise. He wondered for a while whether he might ignore it. His mind had been fixed on a model for Bach's *St Matthew Passion*. The barely imperceptible opening to the music, like the rising of the sun, then the splendid rigidity of its advance followed by a superb expansion, flourishing like green shoots on a tree bursting into blossom in the moisture of the air, all this fascinated him. Could he arrange a sympathetic accompaniment using one of his theatre models to show life arising from an empty space, a void?

Elena was still trying to raise funds for his school, while he sent reminders to Lord Howard de Walden about the additional money he had promised. 'I am afraid that all the arts must go short for a while now', Lord Howard de Walden eventually answered, '. . . I don't know whether you are still endeavouring to carry on the school during the frenzy, but I am afraid it will be a difficult business.' He was persuaded, however, to send a couple of hundred pounds to meet Craig's 'heavy obligations'.

The war, Craig had been told, would cost millions of pounds, whereas his 'own Theatre war' could survive on a few thousand. Without this money everything was impossible – and he was obliged that August to shut the school and discontinue *The Mask*. 'I never dreamed that a little war could add so to the numerous disturbances that one's work already *had* before it begun', he wrote to Elena.

Italy was still neutral and, in the late summer sunlight of Florence, this business of war seemed unreal. Without Elena the disturbances in Craig's life multiplied. For example, he was seeing 'a hungry, savage, young sensualist', Constance (known as 'Stan') Krayl, whom in his alphabet of women he called KKK. She was unlike any other woman in this alphabet and she absorbed him.

Stan Krayl was a travelling woman, small, fast and beautiful, who followed the sun and wintered in Florence. She had made a marriage of convenience with Dr Krayl, a German specialist in hygiene who advocated nudity. From time to time Mrs Krayl, who was still in her young thirties and something of an artist, hibernated in her glass rooftop studio in the Piazza Santa Maria Novella. It was here one late October that a wandering Old Etonian, an aspiring actor called James Strachey Barnes, caught up with her and found himself treated to an emotional outpouring on Gordon Craig. He was apparently 'a nuisance', and worse than that 'a megalomaniac'. He insisted on an absolute monopoly of her. It was 'intolerable', Mrs Krayl complained. 'Gordon Craig for breakfast, luncheon, tea and dinner . . .' She invited Barnes to lend himself to a plot – which is to say, take her out to dinner on two consecutive nights. That, she reckoned, should do the trick. At the end of their second dinner Craig suddenly appeared carrying a glove which he conspicuously cast at his rival's feet, signalling a duel. Then with his other hand he seized Mrs Krayl by the wrist. Biting herself free, she rushed out and on to a victoria and was drawn slowly away by a decrepit-looking horse. Craig, meanwhile, looking like a magnificent lion, had barely time to raise the table at which they had been sitting into the air and hurl it on the floor before rushing across the Piazza Signoria in pursuit of his lady – and pursued by Barnes. The cab arrived at Mrs Krayl's apartment house with Craig on top and Barnes attached to one side. But neither of them was able to catch Mrs Krayl as she flew up the innumerable steps to her apartment like a swallow. Next day Mrs Krayl congratulated Barnes on his success. But there was a further problem: the absence of Gordon Craig. It was so tedious without him. Breakfast, luncheon, tea and dinner were intolerable. Would Barnes write him a disarming letter? From the safety of the country he did so and it was most handsomely received, Craig later inviting him to the Arena Goldoni. It was a school, he saw, of puppets, masks and models, but without opportunities for an aspiring actor like himself. 'I left his lovely little open-air theatre with regrets', Barnes wrote in his autobiography, *Half a Life*. 'The memory of it is like a glade of chequered light and dancing shadows . . . its high priest . . . a great mystic.'

Craig had developed a method of inking one side of the wood and producing a print 'resembling a brass-rubbing for a church floor'. He called

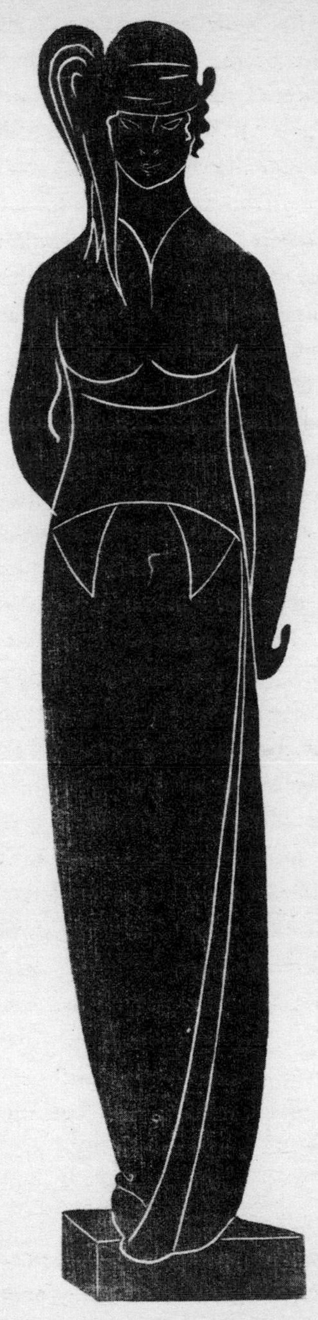

them his 'Black Figures'* ('sometimes a little black, sometimes more grey'). He had started on these Black Figures by accident and, while working on some of them for *Hamlet*, he made one of KKK as Eve. 'It represents the mother of all troubles', he told Kessler, '– add of most joys & there we are.' She also inspired the figure of 'Beauty' to which he added a companion figure 'The Beast'. His notebooks show her inevitably moving from beauty into beastliness and becoming 'a nuisance', especially when she turned up at Smallhythe. Such invasions were kindling in Elena a jealous hatred of 'a few people'. It was 'always the influence of one cat or another – and I am damn tired of these various cats'.

Mrs Krayl reflected life in Florence after Italy had entered the war in the summer of 1915 and had become 'a village full of petty intriguing foreigners'. Craig found it hard to go on living there. He moved from one inexpensive room to another less expensive one and for a time camped at the Arena Goldoni, spending his nights in a two-storey model structure made of wood with sliding panels filled with opaque paper which was perched on the stage. But the dampness made him ill and he suffered 'a breakdown of sorts'. The war was still confined to Europe, and he contemplated going to live in the United States or Samoa.

Towards the end of 1916, he moved to Rome where he received a large cheque from J.D. Rockefeller's daughter (a dedicated invalid called Mrs McCormick) for a complete set of his beautiful 'Black Figures'. Perhaps, when the time was right, he might reopen his school in Rome.

It was good to escape from Florence where Anna Lark, his young secretary, had given birth to a son (his son). The rumours that rose around her name and the financial demands she made had worried Dorothy Nevile Lees. Determined to struggle free from the endless galley sheets of Craig's proofs and indices, Anna had gone to Bologna, made plans after the war for a new life in Australia – and 'so far as I know', Dorothy Nevile Lees wrote, 'was

* L.M. Newman writes that 'the wood used for the Black Figures is a soft wood, e.g. pear, which is cut from the tree lengthwise and is described as plank. Normally softwood is cut with a knife, hence the results are called woodcuts.' But a knife was used for only a few of Craig's Black Figures, and he usually employed engraving tools to indicate costumes. 'Boxwood is cut from the tree in rounds and is endgrain. It gives more possibilities for tone than woodcuts and because it is worked with engraving tools the results are called wood-engravings. The Black Figures are therefore hybrids.'

never heard of again'. It was no loss to *The Mask*. With irritation and relief Craig checked into the Hotel de Russe where, at the bar one evening, he came across his old friend Maurice Magnus. He too had just reached Rome, having deserted from the Foreign Legion, escaped out of Algiers and travelled through France into Italy. He was shocked to find Gordon Craig putting up in a hotel which was 'not the right background for you'. In a few days, he had lodged him in a large studio flat belonging to Prince Wolkonsky, arranged for visiting cards to be printed, and secured him an introduction to the King of Italy's tailor – for all of which Craig appointed him his special agent. But he was aware of the ridiculousness of his position. 'This week I have entertained 2 Princesses, 1 Prince, 1 Ambassador, 1 Ambassadress and suite, 1 Legate to the Pope, 3 Countesses, 1 Marquis, 8 Artists, 7 ordinaries, 1 Count – and a gentleman', he wrote to Elena on 12 May 1917. Soon afterwards, with Magnus's guidance, he 'found 2 assistants – one business – one literary', he told his mother. These were probably the Countess Lovatelli (born Adelaide Keen) and Margherita Caetani, Principessa di Bassiano, an American who was to found two magazines. They were so sympathetic and obliging that life became 'more satisfactory than usual'.

Back in Florence, Dorothy Nevile Lees was shoring up as best she could the ruins of Craig's past. She brought his lights, marionettes, masks, screens and most of his library to Rome where she helped to arrange his large new studio in the Via Margutta, an artists' quarter near the Piazza del Popolo. Back in Florence, she negotiated a contractual release from paying rent for the Arena Goldoni and, when the authorities decided to requisition the place for 'military purposes' (a 'monstrous injustice' Craig called it – a 'knock-out blow' in her words), she cleared the premises of his equipment, folding away the model for Bach's *St Matthew Passion* and lodging it with a frame-maker. Everything else she stored away in the bulging offices of *The Mask*. 'Nothing, absolutely nothing, had been lost, injured or destroyed', she noted. It was an extraordinary achievement which would enable him to resume his work after the war. And there was something extra: she was expecting his child.

Her son – Davidino (later David Lees) – was born on 21 September 1917 in Pisa. Craig recommended discretion ('Veiled is best'). Anxious that she should not register in the hospital under his name, he went there with her. Before leaving he sent for Elena and their children to join him in Rome as quickly as possible.

44
Not Quite Alone

'For the last four years,' Ellen Terry wrote in one of her Smallhythe notebooks shortly before the war, 'Elena and her two wonderful children, my most beloved grandchildren, have lived with me and I am most happy, and not alone. Ted comes and goes from his work in Italy, and this must soon fix them all here. Meanwhile, they are my joys.'

They were like dream children, Teddy and Nelly. When she looked at them, Ellen could see her own Edy and Ted from the early days at Gustard Wood Common. Sometimes she would absent-mindedly call her granddaughter Edy (and little Ted, having the same name as her son, added to the happy confusion). As for Elena, she was never a rival for Ted's love. But Ellen could not help noticing that her son wrote far more constantly to Elena than to herself, thinking perhaps she shared his letters between them – though this was not so. She said little about him and looked far from well. 'I don't think she is very happy – although never *unhappy*', Ellen confided. The temperaments of the two women were very different. 'I am obliged to be very quiet & childish', Ellen explained. '. . . This climate which suits me is quite uncongenial to her.' Italy was the only country that Elena really liked, and England the country she had come to like least of all. But she would go anywhere to be with the father of her children. 'If you get your work in China . . . I'd go willingly', she wrote to him. '. . . I don't write much, love, because nothing to say except "I love you."' Before Italy entered the war, he was always about to appear, it seemed, or had just gone away, leaving photographs of them all grouped together in the garden or seated around one of the tables at Smallhythe. As for Ellen herself, 'I had fully intended going over to Florence alone to have a peep at you at home in the early spring', she wrote to him in 1915, '. . . but treachery on the seas bids me pause.'

Edy did not often appear in these photographs. Her brother was the kind of man you could more easily like while he was abroad – their letters from one country to another ('Dear old boy', 'Dear old girl') show their long affection. But he was a disconcerting presence at Smallhythe, disrupting the protective regime she was forming around their mother. She could not ban him from visiting them as she had banned James Carew. She was obliged to endure his presence until the war put an end to his visits – which was a blessing. But she liked her nephew and niece ('2 of the rosiest big apples' Ellen described them). They remembered all their lives Edy's eager sparkling eyes, so piercing but still kind. She was outspoken, but never really frightening – she treated Teddy like a younger brother, calling him 'old man' as she had called his father when they were young. She never let him or Nelly call her 'Aunt'. Sitting in her rocking chair, swaying fiercely back and forward, she would listen to Teddy spill out his troubles and help him solve them.

Teddy sometimes wondered why it was not possible for his father and Edy to be 'more openly the good friends they were at heart'. But 'they seemed to grow more apart', he noticed, believing (like children themselves) the stories 'that showed each other in an unfavourable light'. Theirs was a confusing family. But Teddy and Nelly felt 'very proud' of meeting their half-brothers – May's children – at Smallhythe – especially when they turned up during the war in uniform. As for their half-sister Rosie (whom William Nicholson had painted exquisitely as a child), everybody loved her.

Some of the children's most exciting days were passed at their grandmother's London house, with its oddly creaking staircase, in the King's Road. She would take them across the street to the Chelsea Palace Music Hall where the theatre manager, in his splendid top hat, white tie and tails, his glittering watch-chain suspended in a loop across his waistcoat, would escort them to a private box. They were allowed to walk on with her in several charity matinées, such as the ballet-pantomime *The Princess and the Pea* at the Haymarket Theatre where they took the final curtain. They also appeared in the great Chelsea Review in 1917 when their grandmother represented 'the Spirit of Chelsea' and they themselves were specially fitted up with some lines to speak by the author E.V. Lucas – even their mother joined a 'beauty chorus' there. Ellen believed that Nelly, with her flaxen hair and dark voice, so secretive and sickly (she struck Christopher St John as a 'dull, rather apathetic child'), might be a natural actress who came alive onstage. As for the enchanting Teddy, so much the image of his father she believed (though to other eyes resembling his Italian grandfather), he could do anything he wished. Both children 'lack discipline sadly', Ellen admitted to their father, 'but they lack nothing else'.

As part of their theatre education (they suffered little ordinary schooling), she arranged for them to join the Christmas seasons of children's theatre started by Jean Sterling Mackinlay at the beginning of the war. She also took them to the Savoy Theatre where Harry Irving was producing some of the melodramas and tragedies Ellen had performed with his father. Then, late at night, she would steal into Teddy's bedroom, wake him up and together they would go through the plays together – until Edy came storming in, scolding her mother and insisting that the boy get his sleep.

It was said of Ellen that she was a far better grandmother than mother. Such sentimental rumours irritated Christopher St John. 'Ellen Terry had not been a foolish-fond mother,' she wrote in the posthumous edition of Ellen's *Memoirs*, 'and in these days she was not a foolish-fond grandmother.' But she did, Chris saw, have one monumental weakness. 'She was indeed far more daft about Elena, whose single-hearted devotion to her son and his work won her heart, than about Elena's offspring' – those so-called 'wonderful children' who were, Chris reminded herself, 'dumped' on them by their father. She could not forget the adoration on these women's faces when he had suddenly appeared wrapped up in his cloak, his long hair spilling from beneath a wide-brimmed hat. She could still hear their laughter as he came out with his latest mad scheme and seduced his mother into paying for it. To see such irresponsibility prized above his sister's achievements was insufferable.

According to her friend, Una Troubridge, Chris had a 'violent' temperament and was 'incapable of compromise'. During the war, with mounting difficulties confronting the Pioneer Players, all the frustrations of the suffrage battles and then the Zeppelin raids over London, Chris often felt violent. To bring stability to their relationship, Edy introduced a new figure into the ménage. Clare Atwood, whom they were to call 'Tony', was in many ways an unexceptional person. Essentially she was an unexceptional painter of portraits and still lives, landscapes, interiors and decorative flower subjects which she exhibited at the Royal Academy and the New English Art Club. But she was also unexceptional in the sense that she took no exception to anything, seeing all points of view, never speaking of herself and, like the waiter in Shaw's comedy *You Never Can Tell*, spreading a stubborn truce all around her. Into whichever room she walked, peace would break out like a plague. Vita Sackville-West was to describe her as small and brave – and she needed some small bravery to stand between Edy and Chris at their most formidable. 'She has a gift for drollery . . . she restores the balance', Vita Sackville-West explained. There were two other qualities in her armoury: stamina and modesty. It was almost impossible to upset her. In 1915, when she joined Edy and Chris, Tony Atwood was in her fiftieth year – a little older than they were. She was a Roman Catholic, which inclined Chris in her favour, and she was not a writer – another good point. For thirty years she was to paint their lives together: their portraits, their houses and theatres, their cats, all in such an unexceptional way as to suggest that they lived lives of unexampled tranquillity. She did nothing to which Chris could object and everything which Edy demanded (taking on secretarial duties, performing minor roles in several plays and designing props – the most extravagant of which was a sixteen-foot-high crucifix for a production of Paul Claudel's *The Hostage*).

From the start Edy made very clear the terms on which Tony was to join them. 'I must warn you that if Chris does not like your being here and feels you are interfering with our friendship, out you go!' So Tony never interfered. She had another life in her studio even though, as Chris observed, 'we belonged to the same world, the artist's world'. In her trousers, jacket and Panama hat, Tony was pressed into service as the third musketeer in what became known as 'Edy and the Boys'.

The coming of Tony, so reticent and elusive, strengthened the bond between Edy and Chris. There was room for all: and all for one. 'Tony!' Chris was to acknowledge after Edy's death. 'I cannot write that name without giving thanks to the divinity that shapes our ends for having brought Tony into our lives.'

They needed to work well together looking after Ellen. She seemed to lose heart after the grandchildren went off to Rome in 1917. They 'melted out of my life . . . & I confess I feel rather lonely without them', she wrote to a friend. 'Thank God I have children – altho' I find 2 quite enough.' There was nothing for it but to 'try for some cinema work in Italy & go to my family there for awhile!' What fun it would be – and what fun it had been lying back-to-back on the hard surface of the ground floor in the King's Road with 'the chix' during the nightly Zeppelin raids. In fact Teddy and Nelly had been frightened of the loud explosions and looked forward to the adventure of travelling to Italy with their mother. And Elena was supremely happy to be with 'Big Ted' again.

The absence of these children weakened Ellen's resistance to the advance of time, Christopher St John observed, and 'from 1917 she began to lose ground'. She still loved going to the theatre – it was her main reason for staying in London. In the winter of 1916–17, at a school production of *Julius Caesar*, she had seen 'a wonderful little Brutus' played by a nine-year-old boy whose performance in 1921 as Katharina in *The Taming of the Shrew* 'gives us', she wrote, 'an idea of what the boy-actors in Shakespeare's time were like'. She marked his name – Laurence Olivier – as being 'already a great actor'.

Three great actresses in Europe, Bernhardt, Duse and Ellen Terry, were all making their final appearances onstage during these post-war years. At the Prince's Theatre in London in 1923, Sarah Bernhardt impersonated a young crippled man confined to a wheelchair. Afterwards Ellen went to her dressing-room full of enthusiasm for a courageous tour-de-force. The following year, after Bernhardt's death in Paris, she attended a Requiem Mass for her at Westminster Cathedral. Though bowed by age – she was in her seventy-ninth year – she straightened her back, held up her head, and moved with solitary grace to her seat near the catafalque, giving her own performance in homage to this gallant actress.

She also went that year to see a tragically frail Eleonora Duse, who had come out of retirement to give some performances at the New Oxford Theatre. She was 'superb' in *Ghosts*, Ellen wrote, and in *The Lady from the Sea* 'she was perfection. There is none like her, none!' Ellen had brought some flowers to Duse's dressing-room (Duse would use them in the play), observing that she was 'even nobler now than when she was young . . . [and] warmly affectionate to me and to my Edy'. Shortly afterwards, while touring with these plays in the United States, Duse caught pneumonia and died.

Trying to keep busy, Ellen had begun experimenting in silent films. In *Her Greatest Performance*, which was released at the beginning of 1917, she played a retired actress whose son, himself a well-known actor, is falsely accused of murder. The identity of the real murderer, however, is known to the actress's dresser, played by Edy, who surrenders the information on her death bed – after which the old actress plays 'her greatest performance' impersonating the dead woman and forcing the real murderer to confess. It was, her biographer Roger Manvell writes, 'a sad debut to the screen'.

She did not enjoy film-acting. But early in 1918, she was persuaded to make a 'guest appearance' in *The Invasion of Britain*, a propaganda film written by Hall Caine at the request of Lloyd George for the Ministry of Information. It took so long to produce, however, that the war was over before it was completed and, despite a new title, *Victory and Peace*, the film was never shown. But a two-minute sequence was preserved which illustrates Ellen's power for communicating pathos as she receives the news that her son has been killed in action. 'It matches for these brief moments', Roger Manvell adds, 'the screen achievement of Duse' who, in her one film *Canere* (Ashes), gave a touch of distinction to undistinguished material.

Ellen was to make three more films in the early 1920s. According to Christopher St John she was best as Widow Bernick in the prologue to *The Pillars of Society* (1920). But she seldom seemed to know when the camera was recording her or another actor, and was never well directed – in the view of a director of *Potter's Clay* (1922) 'she's just past taking direction'. In her last film, *The Bohemian Girl* (1922), acting with Gladys Cooper and Ivor Novello, she gave an unremarkable performance as a nurse.

It was as the Nurse in *Romeo and Juliet* that she made her last appearance in a Shakespeare play. 'I'm keeping all the rude bits in', she wrote to Marguerite Steen. But could she remember them all? Her sister Kate's grandson, John Gielgud, recalled that when she forgot her lines she pretended to be deaf and that the actors whispered the words to her. 'I am the Nurse I think S[hakespeare] wrote to a certain point', she told Gordon Craig, 'but I can't "*waddle*" – & am not deep-breasted – & Nurse is.' Yet her stage presence was so powerful that it threatened to eclipse the young Doris Keane's Juliet ('She is very *meek* under all the crushing abuse she has had showered upon her pretty head', Ellen confided to her son. 'At least her reading of the part *is her own* . . . myself I think she is very pathetic in the part . . . [and] never commonplace'). Ellen enjoyed playing the Nurse, conveying the tiredness of an old lady by yawning discreetly when saying: 'O Lord, I could have stayed here all night, to hear good counsel.' One of the highlights of the performance was her fierce indignation with Mercutio.

'After his exit she breaks off what she is saying to Romeo to interject "Scurvy knave!" ' remembered the biographer Elizabeth Jenkins.

> She does this twice in the text, but Ellen Terry did it three times, if not more, taking a step or two in the direction in which Mercutio had disappeared, rapping angrily with her stick. The audience were laughing their heads off. The other high point was when she came to wake Juliet on the bridal morning, exclaiming: 'Why, lamb! Why, lady! Fie, you slugabed! Why, bride!' This last word was such a peal of encouragement and congratulation and love, it made the discovery even more piteous.

From the surge of applause that greeted her first entry and the cries of 'Ellen Terry!' during the interval; from the enjoyment of her ranting against old Capulet and, in a tender key, her wonderful delivery of how, as a child, Juliet had fallen on her face and raised a bump on her forehead ('Thou wilt fall backward when thou hast more wit'), Ellen realised that she was coming to dominate the play and so damped down her performance – insisting that Romeo and Juliet join her for the ovation at the end. 'I do so hope you will love these young people as much as I do,' she said.

And that perhaps should have been the end. But she needed to keep occupied and was increasingly troubled about money. In 1921, her seventy-fifth year, she travelled up to the Gaiety Theatre in Manchester to give excerpts from her repertoire for a fee of £100 – twice-daily performances over a week. There was a protest by her friends who knew how physically unequal Ellen was to such an engagement. 'Her stubborn rejoinder was, "Edy needs a hundred pounds",' Marguerite Steen recorded. Seldom was £100 harder earned – it was 'a nightmare'. Afterwards Ellen stayed 'two weeks in bed'.

Other engagements kept her name before the public. She was a new character created for her by James Barrie in *The Admirable Crichton*, an old housekeeper called 'Darling'; and a 'Lady of the Manor' in *The Homecoming*, a one-act comedy by John Drinkwater; and the Bennets' neighbour Mrs Long in a dramatisation of *Pride and Prejudice*: all short manageable roles. She took part in Shakespeare festivals and went on a tour with a young actress called Edith Evans. She also continued to take part in charity events, gave recitals, delivered the prologue to a nativity play, unveiled a memorial tablet to Sarah Siddons, presented a national tribute to the famous music-hall impersonator of male characters, Vesta Tilley, and went onstage with a new generation of singers, dancers and comedians – Jack

Buchanan, Harry Lauder and others. At the Empire and Palace Theatres, both crammed to the roof, she gave performances for ex-prisoners of war, for American soldiers still billeted in England and for those who had been wounded or were, like her grandson Peter, mentally afflicted by the shock of war. 'I'm a great favourite . . . *Quite a success* in a different way, now I'm so old. They love me to come & meet them.' But she was horrified by what she saw, revealing a truth previously camouflaged by patriotic propaganda. 'I'm not sure that *Peace* does not seem worse than war', she wrote. '. . . During the war I often felt like tearing myself to pieces, and now . . . I'm all relaxed to bits.'

Her last drama, a musical fantasy for children, was produced at the Lyric Theatre, Hammersmith, at the end of 1925 when, approaching her eightieth year, she appeared as the Ghost of Susan Wildersham in Walter de la Mare's masque *Crossings*. This 'Midwinter Night's Dream', as it was called, involved a butcher, a baker and a mysterious candlestick-maker in addition to several children, miscellaneous fairies and some mice. They were accompanied by flute, strings and piano, though the apparition of Miss Wildersham was mercifully a silent part (except for Ellen's loud whispers to one of the children, asking where the exit was). 'I went to see *Crossings*', Graham Robertson wrote to a friend. '. . . In spite of its eerie charm as a book, it is one of the world's worst plays . . . it is a pity that such a good idea and so much good work and beautiful thought should be wasted.' He reported Ellen Terry as being 'very vexed and sore' at being dragged into such a sorry business.

It sometimes annoyed Ellen to hear herself described as 'a natural actress', as if she did not have to work hard preparing her roles. She had a way of 'floating' across the stage that appeared almost supernatural, but which depended on a technique she had developed of moving her leg fractionally backwards before her foot touched the boards. Never was this illusion of floating more magically conveyed than when she played the ghostly spirit-woman in de la Mare's *Crossings*. Christopher St John remembered how the 'vision of this fragile creature, far advanced in years, yet somehow not old, tremulously gliding across the stage with loving arms outstretched, all earthiness purged away by time, the spirit of beauty, rather than beauty itself, filled the spectators with a strange awe. A long sighing "Oh!" arose from them all, and the sound was a more wonderful tribute than any applause I have ever heard.'

45
The Long Game of Patience

Shortly after Elena and her two children joined Gordon Craig in Rome, all four of them moved on to a villa within sight of Max Beerbohm's Villino Chiaro in the fishing village of Rapallo. Here, among the orange trees and olives of the Italian Riviera, they were beyond the war zone with its bureaucracy of special passes, its mêlée of refugees and congregations of wounded soldiers which made the contemporary world so hostile – especially for Elena whose brother Nino had been killed in battle.

The Villa Raggio at Sant' Ambrogio belonged to a more peaceful time. Outside lay a wisteria-covered terrace and garden full of fruit trees and exotic plants. Set by a sandy road some 300 feet above sea level, the house looked across the mountainous outline of Portofino Bay down to the distant glitter of the Mediterranean. The annual rent was equivalent (at the beginning of the twenty-first century) to some £250 – a sum which Craig reckoned he could raise by selling a few woodcuts each year.

Sometimes Ellen despaired of 'good fortune coming to my wonderful son before I leave them all – or even during his own life'. He was so talented, yet 'he appears to me to *blunder* foolishly . . . & not be able to *retrieve* his mistakes'. In the past she had chided him for laziness: now she saw that 'his *industry is prodigious* & I love him for that – surely surely he must come into his own before long'. But her heart failed her whenever she thought that he might have laboured in vain, and 'I go slightly crazy'. There was 'no one else like him', she told Katherine Lewis, choosing the words she had previously used for Godwin, '– a man of *great ideas*, his own & no one else's . . . the *courage* of him! To go on, & on with no sign of proper recognition.'

In fact Gordon Craig was gaining considerable recognition in the academic world. A book published in 1931 by Enid Rose, recording and interpreting his ideas, lists many publications with significant references to his work: his conception of dramatic action as movement rather than story-development; the flat, neutrally tinted screen he had invented which could convey every mood in a scene; the emphasis he placed on the emotional value of lighting; his inspiration as an artist setting perpetually shifting 'theatre-puzzles'; his influence on the design of playhouses. This was a world of which his mother had little knowledge, though something may have reached her by the 1920s when she appears to have settled her anxieties. 'He will come late to his own, late but not *too late*', she wrote to Portia Knight, '& that, to my mind, is as it shd be . . . *He has never swerved from the highest purpose in his work* . . . all his weaknesses are merely *strengths* gone wrong.'

During 'that long game of patience' between the wars there was to be a revival of interest in wood-engraving. Craig was a founder member of the newly formed Society of Wood Engravers in London and became a regular exhibitor there. Orders arrived from all over the world for his dramatic Black Figures, his boxwood engravings and bookplates. 'I sometimes worked well into the night making prints so that they would be dry enough in the morning for him to sign', his son remembered, '. . . it was quite a job keeping the galleries and collectors supplied.'

But Craig's first task at Rapallo was to create a new magazine devoted to puppets and shadow-figures. *The Marionnette* appeared to be edited by 'Tom Fool' (sometimes referred to as 'Tom Fool of Europe') who raised the curtain on his 'motions for marionettes' presented as 'interludes in the drama for fools' (one of them, 'an interlude of assassination', hinting at a darker mood beneath the patina of eccentricity).

The Marionnette was to last approximately fifteen months, coming out at random intervals and bearing haphazard dates (the opening issue was marked 1 April 1918, the second 15 March, and the final volume, which was actually published in July 1919, was recorded as appearing in August 1918). This deliberate chaos was to confront bibliographical scholars with many complexities, and to baffle, tease and sometimes amuse specialist book collectors. It was, in effect, a satire on scholarship with a crazy agenda of theatrical anarchy. In an opening statement, Craig explained: 'Having lost our offices owing to an unforeseen burst of enthusiasm on the part of nobody, we are reduced to a box: a private box; Box 444 . . . it only remains to thank nobody for his burst of enthusiasm which caused us to skedaddle.'

Box 444 was the postal address of Dorothy Nevile Lees who continued from her flat in Florence to bring out *The Mask* as a monthly leaflet which was distributed with *The Marionnette* – before regaining its momentum in the 1920s as an illustrated quarterly journal.

Though he hid behind his many pseudonyms, Craig's presence was everywhere. *The Theatre Advancing*, first published in the United States by Little, Brown and Company in 1919, was made up from a medley of articles and interviews in *The Mask* and elsewhere, and was later issued with a monumental foreword, raised like a shield against those who would accuse him of having manufactured an illusory reputation. His integrity, he protested, was no illusion. Had he not been invited by Max Reinhardt and Beerbohm Tree to work in their theatres? Of course he had. But 'I will do no such thing . . . I will do it only in my own theatre. Is that clear?'

'I am at work on three books', he told his mother. In 1924 he published a charming, partly autobiographical volume, *Woodcuts and Some Words*. Most of the wood-engravings came from the turn of the century or between the years 1907 and 1909, and the words recalled his happy days with Nicholson and Pryde, as well as his launching of *The Page*. Also recollected from those pre-war years, and containing coloured prints, was *Nothing or the Bookplate* – fifty-one trifles on small pieces of paper (less small in the limited edition) serving to harness the book to its owner ('what a collar is to the dog'). Some were commissioned, others gifts. The owners included Isadora and Elena and Ellen and Edy and Jess and pretty Lucy Wilson and Dorothy Nevile Lees and the mysterious K and his son Robin and his daughter Rosie. It was published in 1924 – the year before his last trawl of scattered essays, *Books and Theatres*, which touched on everything from candlelight and magic to mules and idleness. But there was little time for idleness – 'the dynamic force within him kept us all going,' his son wrote. Then suddenly he would stop work, set off for a music hall or circus to see the clowns 'and we'd all go mad . . . having a sumptuous meal at the most expensive restaurant in the nearest town – Rome, Genoa, Venice . . . what the hell! Sometimes we all pack up and go and spend a week at some fabulous hotel, or take a sailing boat across the Gulf of Tigulio.' Then, all their money gone, it was back to work. Writing books might 'sound a pleasing sort of occupation', Craig told one of his daughters, 'but it's as pleasant as cooking chips & peeling potatoes & boiling & being ready by 1 o'clock sharp'.

Occasionally Craig would go walking in the hills with Max Beerbohm. They liked wandering off to a ravine down which the two of them would drop glasses and sit discussing the sound they made shattering on the rocks below. With such amusements as these, the cost of living was cheap. All the same Max, fearful he might be persuaded to hand over never-to-be-returned loans, preferred to watch his neighbour from a distance: a radiant picturesque phenomenon wonderfully unlike himself. Max's wife Florence, nervous of Craig's fecklessness (he was seen parading the streets with holes in his trousers), guarded her teenage niece 'Dody' from his company. The two of them, Max and Florence, would often speak of calling in on the Craigs' helter-skelter household during the evenings, enjoying these conversations so intensely that an actual visit eventually seemed unnecessary. But 'Dody' could not keep away – not so much from the lost-looking Nelly, with her pitifully thin hair and 'rather beautiful plain face', as from Nelly's clever, pale-faced, enormously blue-eyed brother Teddy who, knowing 'the most amazing things' and ignorant of 'the most ordinary ones', fascinated her and made her laugh. Their mother Elena, 'rather small and very Latinish looking' with prominent, uncared-for teeth, cooked strange meals for them: lunches with indecipherable, almost raw, pieces of meat served with warm baked potatoes and followed by curiously tepid puddings. Teas consisted of a cup of coffee, a game of draughts, and some books to read. Gordon Craig himself, with his amazingly long now-white hair and wearing a straw hat 'the size of an umbrella', some fuzzy white pyjamas and a once-upon-a-time white scarf, impressed 'Dody' as a peculiarly 'beautiful creature – his profile is simply marvellous'. But she noticed how fiercely he protected his daughter against 'any traitorous ideas of freedom'. His son he trusted absolutely.

The Victoria and Albert Museum in London had paid Craig £250 for some drawings and two plaster models of his *Hamlet*; and early in 1922, at the Stedelijk Museum in Amsterdam, he and Adolphe Appia were given the place of honour in a large international theatre exhibition (which later toured Britain) – Craig himself being invited to preside at its opening in the Netherlands. He was also commissioned by the British Drama League in London to build a model of one of his scenes for the British Empire

Exhibition in 1924. For this he chose his most popular wood-engraving, *King Lear in the Storm*. Here, strong diagonal lines collide with great curves and sweeps to convey the stylised impression of a whirlwind, while the small grouped silhouettes of dark figures at the centre seem to magnify the drama of nature. On the model itself, Craig thought that the driving rain might be suggested by stretching lengths of wire against an indigo backcloth – wire that would respond to the slightest movement of the paraphernalia which hurled around the thunder and lightning. But Teddy found that the wire was out of scale and 'painted a sheet of tin with midnight blue, scored it with a pin and got the same effect'.

Craig might not have a theatre of his own, but the Villa Raggio became his theatre workshop and a school where his son was the solitary pupil-assistant. Now in his late teens, the boy was no longer 'little Ted', but Edward. From

1924 onwards he would carry a new name, Edward Carrick (the Irish equivalent of the Scots Craig), into his professional career as film designer, art director and artist. While his sister Nelly went about helping their mother in the house, Edward was pulled into the vortex of his father's self-intoxicated labours, preparing prints, taking photographs of old illustrations, translating essays from the Italian, making lists and then more lists and acting as Craig's secretary, clerk and sorcerer's apprentice. 'I had to live a very unnatural life for a growing lad', he remembered. Most mornings he rose between half past four and five o'clock – sometimes as early as three o'clock – so that he could bicycle through the night to fish or go on smuggling adventures with the local boys or see a peasant girl to whom he had lost his heart. But he was always careful to be back for breakfast at half past seven. 'Father thought that anything that was not related to his work was time wasted', he wrote. After breakfast 'I would go up to father's room, dust everything, pick up papers, put away books, and fill all the fountain pens', he wrote. There were seven of these pens, each with a different width of nib, each with a special task to perform from proof-correcting to letter-writing. After the pens came the pipes. 'Like the pens, the pipes were of different sizes and weights to fit different moods', Edward wrote. Once they had been filled with their various tobaccos, the 'papers on the desk all had to be placed at right angles, in several piles . . . and one would be clever and foresee the sort of reference books he would require, and put them near by . . .'

Craig himself lay in bed thinking – lay in bed elaborating his thoughts. Then he would suddenly rise up, enter his room, and stay there for hours, writing, engraving and drawing. And the house fell silent. He enjoyed experimenting with his great model stage with its screens and lights and projectors – enjoyed it when all went well. If he captured an idea, he would shout out in triumph and summon Elena, Nelly and Edward. But there were also moods of terrible tension, exploding fits of temper.

Edward's job was to record all that his father did, showing how one scene of a play developed into another scene, how the lights were positioned and the colours of the gelatines chosen. Craig would afterwards study these technical notes – and suddenly alter a colour or change the title of a play (*Romeo and Juliet* into *An Italian Comedy*), explaining in a stage whisper that he was doing it 'to confuse the enemy'.

The enemy lay everywhere. At moments of extreme restlessness he would stand in the middle of his room and, gyrating his arms, hurl invisible curses at the four corners of the world where they lurked. According to the artist Paul Nash, though Craig was a man of extraordinary imagination, he was also (like the sculptor Jacob Epstein) the subject of many scandalous rumours. Gilbert Cannan had lampooned him as the scene designer Charles Mann in his novel *Mummery* and Humbert Wolfe ridiculed his work in an *A.B.C. of the Theatre*:

> S is for scenery. Gordon Craig and the rest
> just hang up a duster and hope for the best.

To the British edition of *The Theatre Advancing*, brought out in 1921, Craig added a dedication: 'To the Enemy, with a prayer that they will be stronger, more malicious and, anyhow, funnier than they have been in the past'. Judging from the awful sense of strain that on some days filled the Villa Raggio, the Enemy had answered this prayer. He could trust no one – even his friends had the most distorted understanding of his ideas.

His son tells a poignant story showing a sense of persecution closing in on him. Responding to the interest shown in his etchings at the Amsterdam exhibition, Craig had prepared a volume called *Scene*, writing the text within a month and illustrating it with some etchings from his pre-war portfolios. He used this book to explore the history of theatre architecture and then connect it with a record of his experiments, demonstrating how his visionary ideals were prevailing. 'By the interplay of forms and the distribution of shadows and oblique shafts of light,' the French critic Denis Bablet wrote, 'he conveyed the impression of fleeting movement and evanescent atmosphere caught in passing.' He could conjure up a thousand scenes from nothing, and create profound sensations, similar to music, with a harmony of colours and equilibrium of lights.

Realising that 'each etching was a piece of arrested action within a great symphony of movement', Edward decided to test its progression. He had converted the wine cellar at the Villa Raggio into a large carpenter's shop where he began experimenting with a wooden model, devising a remote control mechanism that could make the cubes which formed the stage magically rise and fall. 'Overjoyed by my achievement, I rushed to fetch Father', Edward wrote: 'his excitement was as intense as mine. As he worked the simple pulleys, the cubes, illuminated by two small lights, slowly began to ascend . . . he seemed to be in a trance. For a moment he had glimpsed the materialization of his dreams. Again and again he came back to the carpenter's shop to handle my rough model . . . he was hardly aware of my presence.'

Here, in miniature, was the evidence that his scene could begin to take on as many expressions as the human face. Eager to ensure that it would have practical development on an actual stage, Edward discussed it with an Italian friend who was studying hydraulics at the University of Genoa, and was able to report to his father that the device could easily be installed in a theatre. On hearing this, Craig's whole being changed. ' "How do you know that?" he roared. "Who gave you permission to mention it outside these walls? You fool. You fool!" He shouted and raged, then collapsed, spent with emotion.' The ingenious model, which had given him so much brief happiness, was hidden away at the back of the cellar and never seen again.

Until recently Gordon Craig had focused his mind on a theatre of the future. Now, as he sat bent over histories of ancient theatres, this focus seemed to be leaving him. 'To be pent up too long is not good', he had acknowledged in a letter to Kessler who warned him against turning his back on imperfect opportunities if only because, after a certain time, 'things that have been talked about get stale'. He began to feel imprisoned by this scholarship. Besides, he was too impatient to be a true scholar. He would seize upon a few pages of a book, pounce on something that caught his eye, make use of it then cast the book aside. He had no aptitude for the slow methodology of academic disciplines. 'His tide seemed far out', wrote Colin Franklin, the editor of his *Paris Diary*. It was a time of waiting, a time walled in by many books. 'I want *response*. I put out my hand. I want hands put out to grasp quickly & that is what I want advocated big & strongly', he appealed to Enid Rose while she was writing her book about his work. She had been a part-time teacher at the Royal Academy of Dramatic Art and, one of his most infatuated disciples, became a literary agent dedicated to making his name known throughout the world. At first Craig nursed hopes of her advocacy – there was something comforting about her adulation. But unlike dedicated scholars of his work – Sheldon Cheney in the United States and perhaps Janet Leeper who was to write a King Penguin volume on his work in Britain – Enid Rose had no gift for words. She struggled for accuracy but even when achieving it, especially when achieving it, reduced it to banality.

Her letters, brimming with devotion, are scored with his exasperated comments. It was as if she carried a caption around her neck: 'Please walk over me'. So he did: taking advantage of her lovesickness and transforming her from a part-time schoolmistress into his part-time mistress – and despising her for this weakness. Eventually he could not bear to see her. When she invites herself 'not to work, but just for the pleasure of society and the hope of cheering you with mine', he confesses that 'nothing would depress me more at the moment'. Near the end, dying of cancer, she was still writing to him, still hoping that he would grant her, and she be allowed to give him, some miracle of happiness. It seemed his fate was to be tortured by those who loved him even more than by his enemies.

But he consoled himself: 'One could do worse and one could do less.' Then another thought came to him: time 'spent in bookshops or any shops is rather a waste'. He was being overwhelmed by books – not their contents so much as the paper and bindings, their shape, the character of their type-setting, the creak of their hinges. And yet he loved all this paraphernalia. Such alchemy protected him from people and he presented his own books to the reigning monarch in Britain so that they could find their places in the Royal Library at Windsor Castle. He felt out of touch with the post-war world and his sense of isolation was reinforced by the actual solitude of his life at Rapallo. Besides the Beerbohms and their visitors, he saw few people beyond his own family. 'Isn't Rapallo too small a place for a man like you?' his mother had enquired. He had asked Elena (whom he now called 'Mama') to guard him – yet something was not right. Perhaps she was guarding him too well. Looking at her he realised how exhausted she had become.

In the mid-1920s they decided to leave Rapallo and by 1926 had settled into a new home, 17 Via Costa di Serretto, at San Martino d'Albaro, just outside Genoa – 'the most lavish house we ever had', his son Edward remembered. He had resumed working as his father's assistant, while Dorothy Nevile Lees continued bringing out *The Mask* in Florence. Craig had a magnificent library and the comfort of central heating throughout the house. Outside there lay a beautiful garden surrounded by orange trees for him to walk in. But instead of using the library and enjoying the garden, he locked himself into his bedroom convinced that someone was plotting to poison him. It seemed he had everything and nothing. In *Books and Theatres* he described himself as 'an unemployed artist of the theatre', who could merely 'dip a finger into the icy waters of history'. It was not enough.

He closed the shutters and turned out the lights in his bedroom. 'I had to knock in a special way before he would open the door and let me in', Edward remembered. His condition was obviously worsening – until Elena hit on a theatrical trick from the world of farce. She summoned the family doctor, who slipped into the darkened room behind Edward. Then, sitting at the end of Craig's bed, he asked him a question about dramaturgy. Craig could not help venting his fury in a devastating answer. The doctor then flung open the shutters and, letting in the sunlight, changed the scene into a miracle play. 'You are not ill,' he said. 'Get up!' And like Lazarus rising from the grave, Craig stood up murmuring, 'I think you are right' – for which he was rewarded with 'a marvellous tonic'.

But the best tonic came a month later. In August 1926, he received a letter from the Royal Danish Theatre in Copenhagen inviting him to 'draw the decorations and the costumes' for a jubilee production of Ibsen's *The Pretenders*. Over the past half-dozen years he had been asked to put on a play by Francesco Malipiero in Italy and a ballet in Paris; to produce *Pelléas et Mélisande* at La Scala in Milan and *Macbeth* in London with Sybil Thorndike playing Lady Macbeth. Each time he had begun negotiations and then found reasons to back away. He was emerging in the public mind as a man whose brilliant ideas were being purloined by others. The European theatre and even American films were earning money from his concepts while he went on walking the streets with empty pockets. But now he had found 'a dear friend' in the chief actor of the Royal Danish Theatre, Johannes Poulsen. What appealed to him about Poulsen's letter was that it seemed to come from a fellow worker asking for his help. 'You will have a free hand in every respect', Poulsen assured him. 'You will have at your disposal a big theatre – bigger than His Majesty's in London . . . a complete staff of actors and actresses, and besides an opera staff and an Orchestra, numbering 80 men . . .' The letter set out the exact dimensions of the stage, the mechanism by which it could be wheeled in a circle displaying a round horizon, as well as 'the best and newest lighting systems in Europe'.

'Your letter made me very proud', Craig replied. '. . . There are not many ancient theatrical families who have held their own as yours has done, so I am very happy and touched by your words.' It would be 'a delight', he added, 'for me to come to Copenhagen and work in the ancient and honourable theatre'. Such was his eagerness to embrace theatre work again that he asked for no money beyond his expenses for sketching some scenery and a few costumes – though by the end he provided an almost complete set of scenes and costumes and organised the production. It was an opportunity to prove he was an easier man to work with than his reputation suggested. 'I was charmed with everything – the absence of effort – the absence of pretension', he told Johannes Poulsen. '. . . You are a delight – I fancy that Garrick was not unlike you.'

The struggle between claimants to the throne in thirteenth-century Norway was a remote affair to Craig, who found Ibsen's play long and complex. But there was an internal theme – the drama between single-minded self-belief and the vacillation of self-doubt – that reflected something of Craig's own predicament. It was perhaps to this that he was alluding when, in his book of the production, he gave as the reason for breaking out of the historical framework his need to re-create a more poetic work – what he called the theatrical rather than the historical architecture of the play.

Craig made the Hôtel d'Angleterre, opposite the theatre, his headquarters. The rehearsals during the early autumn of 1926 provoked grave misgivings. 'We are going too fast', he warned the cast – and the opening night slipped back a couple of weeks to 14 November. Poulsen and Craig, however, got on well, their discussions sometimes continuing long past midnight. 'I find him one of the most charming and genial of men', Poulsen wrote to Janet Leeper. '. . . His mind is that of a great philosopher . . . He has a sixth sense for that which is true, genuine and beautiful in art which is given to only a few persons in each century.'

When the opening night came, Craig was so apprehensive that he could not stay in the theatre, but had to wander the streets of Copenhagen. The reviews (which he did not read) were mixed but his imaginative use of the theatre technology was much praised. Before he left, the artists presented him with an address paying tribute to his 'clear mind . . . rich imagination . . . and sublime genius'. In a letter to Kessler he wrote that, although using only a quarter of the material he had prepared, 'I did a terrific amount of work in Copenhagen . . . the actors and staff were perfect angels to me – nothing I wanted was found difficult'.

He was 'a happy man again'. And he had good news too for Elena.

Remembering how tired she had been looking, he was bringing back from Copenhagen a little servant girl to help her in their home, 'something rather special – 22 – daughter of peasant – but refined – smile nice'. She was, he added, 'very reserved'.

His happiness was still fragile and he was vulnerable not only to malign fantasies, but to the natural tragedies of life which had seemed to be piling up as he grew older. Not long after moving to Rapallo, he had met Maurice Magnus again during a visit to Rome. No longer the pink-faced pomaded comedian of the pre-war years, he looked a bleached and hunted figure, forever on the run, trying desperately to sell his memoirs and talking wildly of entering a monastery. The young men of golden promise to whom he had attached himself seemed to have faded away with the war. 'I am tired. I want to be quiet & sit still & just go on writing in my own little way.' Craig could sympathise with this – indeed, it was not so different from what he wanted. But despite his aura of optimism, Magnus was too servile, almost provoking Craig to behave oppressively. In any event he could no longer help his friend. So, begging £5 from D.H. Lawrence, Magnus fled to Malta where the police caught up with him. They waited below at his hotel while Magnus lay down on his bed and swallowed a glass of prussic acid. '*Et voilà tout.*' This dreadful story haunted Craig.

While in Rome he had also seen Isadora. One night they walked, arms linked, through the dark streets – 'a walk of a lifetime'. For him it was a walk into the past; for her a walk through eternity. 'Our hearts SANG – we were weeping as we walked . . . and ended smiling.' Nevertheless, this encounter came as a 'terrible trial for me', Craig later wrote, '– for she made the attempt to . . . rebuild our shattered dreams'. To follow this illusion further would have taken him past endurance. He had to escape.

They met briefly once more in the spring of 1920 in Paris where Craig had gone for the publication of a new French edition of *On the Art of the Theatre*. She was suffering from incurable heartbreak. 'I rush about trying to find a remedy,' she said, '. . . dreams are more important than so-called day life – only you need a good income to appreciate this theory.' Craig agreed. It puzzled him sometimes that 'I have never yet been bankrupt'.

Their last meeting seems to have been at Rapallo where she appeared 'sad and disillusioned'. They were a part of each other, these two, yet he could not bear to be with her. 'Dear dear dear Isadora', he wrote once she had gone. '. . . All the days & years with their sorrows of regret dance with me at this moment with LOVE.' Then the moment passed.

In the autumn of 1927 he learnt of her sudden death in a racing car, her neck broken by a scarf floating through the air and catching in the spokes of a wheel. He was convinced she had been murdered and dismissed her autobiography, published the following year, as a forgery. The facts and fantasies of her life were indivisible to him and followed his moods and tempers. Sometimes he had almost wanted to murder her himself, at least wanted her dead or never born. Yet even in his mid-fifties he feared not being able to live without her. She had given him such intensity of life that her spirit continued to possess him as he sat writing into old age, page after page, reliving his dreams, their love, the moments of happiness, and the pain, the rage, the guilt and finally the justification for it all. She had been 'the only one whose Genius was akin to mine' – though possibly Yvette Guilbert might have been another: 'a personality of genius,' he called her, 'to be ranked with Bernhardt & Duse & Ellen Terry' who 'in some particulars surpassed them' (though he could never be certain because she was protected by 'a nuisance in [the] shape of a manager-husband').

When asked one day whether the Beerbohms enjoyed a happy marriage, Craig had answered that Max 'had been a good son; and good sons make good husbands'. He believed that he too had a good marriage in all but name. He knew that Elena was above all the woman he needed, yet no single woman could be everything – it was unfair to make such a demand. In 1927, the rather reserved young peasant girl, with the nice smile, who had come from Copenhagen to help Elena in the house, told them she was expecting Craig's child. But he had a simple solution. He proposed that the girl continue living with them and in due course (with her child) become part of the family. But Elena, her faith in Craig badly bruised, insisted that the girl must leave.

In the early summer of 1927 he returned with the pregnant girl to Copenhagen. He longed to do something more for the Royal Danish Theatre. *The Pretenders*, he confided to his daughter Rosie, was 'the most difficult play god ever allowed an idiot poet to write . . . without a scrap of glee or sparkle in it'. Even so the production had been 'a big *success*' and might lead to a new chapter in his life. He had recently begun something of a new chapter by corresponding with Rosie in South Africa – 'please only write when you feel you love me', he advised her. 'Give me a kiss & say I've begun well for this is a beginning . . . I don't plan the future but I do assuredly slam the door on the non-future.' He was petitioning Johannes Poulsen to shape his future. 'I am terribly alone. I ache for my theatre', he wrote. '. . . I want somehow to work with you . . . I don't say that ever to people . . . I suggest . . . that you join me and together we form a company of clever beings . . . I work with no one as willingly as with you in future.'

One reason why Craig persisted with Poulsen was that he needed a second home in Copenhagen – a home for the Danish mother of his newest daughter and some money for them. In a letter to Rosie from Copenhagen, he writes some punning sentences that give a clue perhaps to the girl's name. 'I am a little in love – her name is Gold. I would possess gold. Too much gold, I think, I could not have . . . I came here in search of a goldmine – or rather mein gold.' But Johannes Poulsen could offer him no new work (though he was influential in having him made a knight of the Order of Dannebrog). By March 1929 Craig is writing to Poulsen: 'Some one I am trying to help – a Danish girl – is in need of a letter from me and I've failed to get into communication with her though I have her letters and her address. As she is quite poor but a real nice good girl I want you to help me about it . . . I am anxious – and I begin to think someone is keeping these [letters] from her . . . she is waiting to hear from me and is troubled – She is such a dear hearted being . . . I want my enclosed letter to get into her hands and to have a pencilled line *from her* to say it has reached her . . . *Don't trust the people of her house* to deliver the letter, she herself must be seen for a moment.' But there is no further mention of this 'little servant girl' who, with her daughter, passes nameless from the story.

In this heightened atmosphere, Craig became subject to more delusions. Believing that he was being blackmailed by someone very sinister in London, he sent his son Edward to England to uncover the plot (it turned out to be a mild practical joke). Unfortunately Edward, who was now twenty-two, fell in love with a young girl and wrote home telling his parents that he had become engaged and would be staying in England. Craig was furious. This was hardly the letter of a good son and therefore could not lead to a good marriage. He rebuked him strongly, accusing him of desertion and forbidding the marriage. Father and son met in Germany where Kessler was finally printing his edition of Craig's *Hamlet*. This was not a record of his

Moscow production, but a book which reveals his uncompromising vision of the play – 'one of the great books', William Rothenstein was to call it in a letter to Kessler at the beginning of 1930; '. . . certainly Craig's masterpiece as artist, & yrs as printer; to my mind easily the most important book since Morris's Chaucer'. But Craig knew he could not have completed it, and much else besides, without the help of his son who had been his assistant, fellow conspirator and keeper of his secrets. Alone, his confidence in the future faded. Edward had got a job as an art director in a film company and, longing 'for a life of my own', had set a date for his wedding. He was surprised when saying goodbye to see that his father was in tears. 'He seemed a broken man.'

46
An Occasion

On his return to Genoa, Craig heard that the stage-designer he most admired – his 'almost brother' Adolphe Appia – had died. They had first met at Zurich railway station (their work was being shown in Zurich at the largest exhibition of theatre arts ever held in Europe). Although unable to speak each other's language, they had communicated ecstatically. Appia was 'a fine creature', Craig thought, someone doing similar work to himself. How divine Appia's rage was when he heard Craig say that Wagner 'hated the theatre and used it as a Prostitute is used'. Of course, with the language obstacle, it was impossible for Craig to know how many of his own ideas Appia had made off with. But when Appia experienced reverses over his designs for some opera productions, Craig warmed to him wholeheartedly. 'You, my dear, are the very noblest expression in the modern theatre', he wrote.

Then from England came the news he dreaded most, news he could not accept. Edward had been down to see his grandmother Ellen at Smallhythe and wrote that he did not think she had long to live. Craig had seen his mother only two or three times since the end of the war. It was not that he no longer loved her – quite the contrary. But age was unnecessary. He could not bear to witness any ill come near her. Yet everything he heard from Edy and others disturbed him.

He remembered seeing her in 1922 when he came to London and opened the international theatre exhibition at the Victoria and Albert Museum. How proud she was of him! And how well she looked in a wonderful broad hat overlaid with ostrich plumes. But he had been surprised to find that she had recently moved from her splendid Georgian house in Chelsea to a dismal block of flats, Burleigh Mansions, in St Martin's Lane. Into these limited quarters – 'like a goods lift on a railway station' – had been piled remnants of her belongings (pictures by Watts, Burne-Jones and Sargent, a table, chairs and sideboard of Godwin's, some blue-and-white bone china Whistler had given her). Everything else had been sold along with the house, including, Gordon Craig was horrified to learn, 'some drawings of mine and rare copies of "The Page" '.

In the opinion of Marguerite Steen, Ellen 'had the least money sense of anyone I have ever known'. But Edy was her equal. It was Tony Atwood who discovered how things really stood. Among her many qualities was the possession of a modest fortune, nothing excessive but enough to have no difficulty paying Edy rent after she made up the *ménage-à-trois*. It was to her one day that Ellen showed her bank statement. She had a question. Did the figure on the last page mean that she was £1,600 to the good or to the bad? The answer was that she owed what was the equivalent, at the beginning of the twenty-first century, to £50,000.

To Christopher St John's mind, what had been wrong for many years was that Ellen Terry's financial affairs had been managed by men. It was refreshing to see the world turned upside down and Ellen rescued by a woman. Tony Atwood recommended the sale of the house in London and much else besides, and saw to it that Ellen's many allowances and annuities were cancelled. Edy agreed to all this and refused to take further handouts of money from her mother.

34 Burleigh Mansions, though airless and without light, was conveniently near Edy in Bedford Street and beneath James Carew's apartment in the same building (Ellen still saw him occasionally). It was also close to the theatres Ellen loved (among the best dramas she saw in the early 1920s were J.M. Barrie's fantasy *Dear Brutus* and John Drinkwater's chronicle play *Abraham Lincoln*). She was also near various cinemas and particularly enjoyed Rudolph Valentino's *Blood and Sand*, Conrad Veidt's *The Cabinet of Dr Caligari*, and Charlie Chaplin's *The Kid*. Tony and Chris spent days making the flat more 'Terrylike' by painting the walls in colours she liked. She had asked for 'a nice little flat near the theatres' and, in a manner of speaking, chosen it herself. 'Yes. I ought to have great peace in this dear little place,' she said when moving in. But she could not keep tumult out of the place. Frail yet still restless, she had become rather deaf and her eyes were so 'dim' some days that she could 'write only in scraps'. Her mind wandered as she moved hesitantly around the unaccustomed rooms and her

head felt 'like (Butter) Pudding & Mint Sauce'. She disliked using a stick and sometimes stumbled and fell – it was fortunate she had learnt as an actress how to relax her muscles when falling. 'I am unhinged (*not* unhappy) and uncomfortable', she wrote. 'I wonder where everything is . . . All is changed . . . I live in puzzledom.'

A funereal atmosphere hung around the place and she seemed for ever to be hearing the bell of St Paul's, Covent Garden, tolling nearby. To the writer Clemence Dane, the apartment was a cell in which Ellen's swift and radiant spirit had been caged. And it was clear to Marguerite Steen that following this move 'she panicked'.

'My soul is not my own', she had written to Gordon Craig, '& altogether I think I can stand it no longer . . . Things are not right with me – but it's no use talking. One cd die of worry at times – & up & kill at times.' He felt outraged on her behalf. Who did these guardians of her liberty think Ellen Terry was? Naturally she was what people called 'difficult' in her old age. Many old people were difficult – it was possible that he too might one day become difficult. But she was a genius. Time was not the same for her as for other people. Her spirit was eternally young.

Until now Ellen had always said what came into her mind and done what she wished. Now she was being told how she should feel and instructed what she must do. These orders continually rang out: 'Now you must have dinner', 'No, you must *not* go out', 'Pull yourself together', 'Now sleep'. She was seldom permitted to see her male friends in case they overexcited her. But she needed an audience. Her pack of carers seemed delighted with her performance until, chafing under their directions, she recovered something of her natural self and rebelled. Then they told her she was losing her mind.

That was how it appeared to Gordon Craig. 'Am I an old hag, Ted?' she asked him – and they laughed together at the absurdity, turning old age itself for a moment into farce. And it was true that her white hair was almost blonde, the texture of her skin, unobtrusively dusted with French chalk, remarkably smooth. Her figure had grown slender, her features regained their delicacy. Her lips too were touched with a coloured salve that came in small ornamental jars from Paris. She would get out these jars and bottles, ointments and powders, before her son arrived and she looked 'astonishingly beautiful' while he was with her.

But the new regime oppressed her. 'The days are so short – I wake in the morning – I meet a little misery – I meet a little happiness – I fight with one – I greet the other – the day is gone.' Though she hated staying indoors, her own room, it appeared, was where she gave least trouble. Bad temper seemed to rule Smallhythe and Burleigh Mansions. 'My friends nearly all quarrel with one another', she observed and this made her question the value of their friendship. She was impatient and worst of all she was frightened. 'It left me with an impression that the roof, floors, staircase, doors, furniture, and every person in the house were in some way preparing to do her harm', her son wrote. So he asked her what he might do to help and she made him promise he would do nothing in case she was punished by those who were looking after her. Was she really that apprehensive or was this another piece of acting? 'I never knew when the acting began or left off', Craig admitted, '. . . it was as well not to enquire too curiously.' He quickly decided that he could do no more. 'I would have tried to release her from this paradise, but I knew it was useless – it would have meant dragging her to pieces.' So he went back to Italy. He did invite her there, but they told her she was not strong enough.

In the spring of 1922 Ellen was persuaded to make a will. It was a simple document: appointing the Public Trustee as her executor; bequeathing £200 to her husband, James Carew, and £100 to her granddaughter, Nelly (though nothing to Nelly's brother Edward). She left Smallhythe to Edy and divided her financial estate equally between her daughter and son. But she felt troubled that she had so little to leave them. Even after selling her jewellery at Christie's she still owed money to 'my Banker'. She blamed the war which had ruined everyone. 'I was never so poor', she complained early in the 1920s. Her worries over Ted and Edy brought on 'a horrid nervous condition' and in a letter to Ted she confessed that 'I seem unable to do anything . . . I can't help myself.'

But there were others ready to step forward and help her. Howell Arthur Gwynne was the London editor of the *Morning Post*, a man it was said devoted to 'the dignity of journalism'. He was often described as being someone 'of note' and he knew many other men of note: Joseph Chamberlain and Cecil Rhodes, Kipling and Kitchener, Earl Haig and Lord Roberts – and not forgetting the eminently noteworthy King of Romania. How did such a well-connected personage from the world of politics suddenly appear as Ellen Terry's executor and trustee?

In his early forties Gwynne had married Edith Lane, a close schoolfriend of Edy Craig's. Ellen had treated this other Edith 'like a daughter' and the two girls were almost inseparable until 1907 when their friendship was abruptly broken off by Edith Lane's marriage. According to Ellen, Edith was 'solid kindness itself' – although, she added, 'I don't like her friends.' And there was a further ominous difficulty: although 'she was a dear *fierce* friend', she is 'too fond of me'. As Edith Gwynne, the childless wife of this important businessman, she re-entered their lives and presented Edy with a peace offering in the shape of her husband's services over this tedious matter of prematurely tidying up Ellen Terry's estate.

Edie Gwynne quickly made herself indispensable – 'a remarkably nice person . . . the faithfullest of creatures', Ellen described her, '& sometimes almost unbearable'. She was so 'jealous' and of such a 'queer temper' that Ellen came to dread her ghostly white face reminding her of benefits received, uttering threats of more to come, and generally making Ellen wish she 'had never been born'. Appalling arguments rang around Smallhythe whenever Edie Gwynne collided with other friends of Ellen's whom she suspected of harbouring similar designs to her own. 'I am sorry to say I had an awful row with Edie Gwynne', Ellen complained to Ted. 'She was *trying* to be kind but bossed me to death . . . She is of course so capable . . . but one cannot sell one's soul.' She spread a sense of incompetence among everyone. She would engage a taxi to meet a better train than the one Ellen had booked or recommend that she travel north when she wanted to go south – and then insist with much vulgar abuse that she had been right and everybody else wrong. 'Oh it is not to be endured,' Ellen burst out after one chaotic scene. 'She won't do it again!' But she did do it again. There was no stopping her. And Ellen could not send her away because her presence enabled her daughter Edy to travel the country and pursue her career. But what neither mother nor daughter realised was that Edie Gwynne was plotting to usurp Edy's place, using her husband to accomplish this.

'Taffy' Gwynne, as he was called, was noted for 'his tact and good humour', having built up his career working as a war correspondent. This was just as well, for he was entering what soon became a bitter war of wills and would need all his tact and good humour to come through. The campaign lasted for more than two years during which, having replaced the Public Trustee with her husband as Ellen's executor, Edith Gwynne made a bid to gain power of attorney. In the battle that developed, she accused Edy of viciously exploiting her mother's frailties. The solicitors, however, were unpersuaded and, at the beginning of 1925, drafted a new codicil. This revoked Howell Gwynne's appointment as executor and trustee, and put Edy herself in his place, together with the solicitors. 'Why we have put up so long with her [Edith Gwynne's] extraordinary temper is a puzzle', Ellen wrote. '. . . I *hate* being *out* with an old friend but in some ways a great deal of irritation is removed.' Three weeks later a third and final codicil was added to the bulging file of legal documents. This gave Smallhythe Farm to Edy, and divided the whole estate equally in two trusts for her benefit and that of her brother – Edy's part going on her death to Elena and her two children. Gordon Craig was entitled to the income from his trust fund which, on his death, was also to be passed on to Nelly and Edward.

People sometimes blamed Edy for leaving her mother for what Ellen called 'her Pageantry and Pioneering'. In 1920, after her production at the Kingsway Theatre of Saint-Georges de Bouhélier's *Le Carnaval des Enfants* (in which the living and the dead – attired as skeletons – shared the stage), the Pioneer Players were laid to rest: though they were briefly to be revived in 1925 for a single staging of the American playwright Susan Glaspell's experimental feminist drama *The Verge* – 'a wonderful play', Edy called it, 'completely mad'. Edy took a job at the Everyman Theatre in Hampstead under the management of Norman MacDermott who, during its early seasons, specialised in the still-controversial plays of Bernard Shaw. Her work there as assistant producer during 1921 went well. 'She avoided the worn-out formulae, the too consciously over-drilled effect of expertness,' the actor Ernest Milton wrote, 'and gave to her productions an element of surprise.' Among her successes was another attempt at Laurence Irving's strange play *Godefroi and Yolande* – 'an exciting jumble of a production' Ernest Milton called it. At the end of the season, Norman MacDermott paid her a handsome tribute which nevertheless read like the reference for a job elsewhere. But Edy could find almost no work in London. 'I do not remember any great rush to make use of her great skill and knowledge', wrote the actor and play-reader Allan Wade. The very nature of her talent seemed to present an obstacle. For all her attention to detail in the making of costumes, her productions gave the impression of being under-rehearsed – which made some actors nervous.

'To meet Edy for the first time could be disconcerting', Ernest Milton acknowledged. 'Her manner was so direct, her handclasp so athletic.' Her voice too seemed gruff and her face was curiously troubling, both 'an enigma and a revelation,' like some counterfeit reminder of Ellen Terry, the image seen through a chipped mirror – rough-hewn as it were and not quite true.

Watching her direct rehearsals at the Kingsway Theatre in the spring of 1922, Virginia Woolf saw a 'rosy, rugged "personage" ' dressed for the occasion in a white waistcoat with 'black bow tie & gold chain loosely knotted'. Wanting to catch the atmosphere of supple, free-and-easy, theatre manners, with Edy's military presence centre-stage (useful, perhaps, for a novel one day), Virginia Woolf noted down what she heard. So we too can hear Edy's voice:

Stop those monkey tricks, do Saunders – & let us have some light . . . Now all of you, listen *carefully* to the music. Make the movements that suggest themselves to you. Beautiful lady, you go up to the balcony . . . Young man, Dunlop, you walk straight – straight I say – straight – Can't you move the table? No? Well then to the right. Miss Potter (this with some acerbity) you needn't dance.

Consigned to the provinces, Edy began putting on nativity plays around Yorkshire and accepted the post of stage-director at the Leeds Art Theatre. She also travelled the country visiting day schools for the British Drama League and adjudicating plays at festivals for the British Empire Shakespeare Society. Whenever possible she returned to London to work for various clubs and guilds – producing, besides contemporary drama, John Fletcher's *The Faithfull Shepherdess* for the Phoenix Society and John Webster's *The White Devil* for the Renaissance Theatre Society. She still acted minor roles onstage and even took on some film work– most notably as Miss Adams, a character part in *Fires of Fate*, a Conan Doyle adventure that carried her off to Egypt for seven weeks and placed her on a camel.

The theatre manager Lilian Baylis was to oppose Edy's being appointed as stage-director at the Old Vic Theatre. 'We don't want another woman here', she was reported as saying. 'And anyhow we don't want Edy. She would upset the staff.' It was not only men who kept women out of institutions that were legally open to them. The male culture exploited the self-interest of a few women who did gain advancement and made them accomplices in gender discrimination. In Lady Rhondda's new feminist weekly magazine *Time and Tide*, where she had been given the job of music critic, Christopher St John argued that Edy's absence from the London stage, like the current exclusion of Margaret Bondfield, the trade unionist, from the Labour Cabinet, was a result of this discrimination. She urged women playgoers (who outnumbered men) to bestir themselves 'and give Edith Craig an opportunity before it is too late, of showing how many plays can reach and delight audiences, when handled by a genuine artist of the theatre'. Were they to do this 'it is conceivable that the whole history of the English stage might be changed'.

Had she worked in London, Edy would have been able to see more of her mother. Ellen missed her dreadfully when Edy went to Egypt, describing herself as being 'in the depths'. In a letter to Marguerite Steen she complained: 'I do nothing from day to day, and it is an AWFUL waste of time – and of course I am *bored* . . . I feel rather like *hating* everything.' But it was not simply Edy's absence that provoked these ill-thoughts, it was old age itself which made her wonder sometimes what point there was in being half-alive like this. On what she called her 'blind days' she slept all the time, which was 'abominably wrong'. To Ted she wrote apologising for her inability to write. 'The whole jumble of my thoughts wheels round & round me, & it's of no use trying to say things – just my love – my love – to you . . . I love you – I love you all . . . I love you Mama.' All this was immensely frustrating and she could not help contemplating how to bring her fitful existence to an end. 'Of course I'm just wicked to say I've had enough of it – but – well for one thing all my usefulness is over & to be of *no use* to anyone . . . that is *Hell* it seems to me.'

But there were good days. There were treats. Early in May 1922, Edy took her to Scotland where, along with Squire Bancroft, John Galsworthy, Earl Haig and others, she was presented with an honorary degree by St Andrews University. J.M. Barrie, who was then rector of the university, had proposed Ellen in response to the public dismay shown the previous year when the American-born actress, Genevieve Ward, became the first woman in the theatre to be appointed a Dame of the British Empire. Ellen's name had never appeared on the honours list because, it was supposed, she had led so wild a life: two illegitimate children, three husbands and dubious relationships with Henry Irving and other actors were altogether too much for the honours committee to overlook. But the public clamoured for her extraordinary career to receive official recognition and eventually the government gave way. On the New Year's Honours List of 1925 she was appointed 'Dame Grand Cross of the Most Excellent Order of the British Empire' (one class higher in the order than Genevieve Ward, who had been made a Dame Commander). In February 1926, a few days short of her eightieth year, she went with Edy to Buckingham Palace. Because of her frailty she was wheeled, not to the Throne Room, but through the long corridors to a private room where King George was waiting to receive her. The doors opened and Ellen, rising from her vehicle, 'made a most wonderful curtsey on entering – slow, stately, very expressive', Edy remembered. The doors then closed and Edy waited outside. A few minutes later the doors opened again and she saw her mother, 'now decorated with the Cross, groping for the door, assisted by an equerry. When she reached it, she became conscious of something amiss. "Oh dear! I quite forgot to walk out backwards!"' Everyone laughed and Ellen went off for an informal meeting with Queen Mary, who in the old days had often gone with her parents to the Lyceum.

Outside the palace, Ellen had a few words ready for the reporters, telling them how delighted she was with this 'honour to my profession, an honour to women, and very pleasant for me'. This short speech, prepared by Christopher St John, modestly combined the collective precedent set by Henry Irving with her own feminist message. 'A lovely time', Ellen noted in her diary. It had been a day out, a release from her prison. And it was indeed 'very pleasant' being honoured, though it meant much less to her than it had to Henry. In one of her diaries, she wrote: 'I want no appreciation or thanks for anything I have done in life. No. Let them thank me, if they must, by employing the outstanding talents of my children, who rather "lack advancement".'

Chris was severely critical of Gordon Craig for not allowing his daughter to come back to England. Nelly had little to do in Italy and would have made an ideal deputy for Edy. Ellen felt 'terribly in want' of such company. 'I long for the sight of all your faces . . . Would you like to send Nelly over to me for awhile and wouldn't she like to come', she had asked her son. But Nelly did not come.

In earlier times Ellen had been 'fortunate to have very nice people about me'. But now she was not so fortunate. Over four or five years, Edy employed twenty-seven personal attendants – what Chris called 'body-maids' – to cook and clean, read to her and keep her company. But Ellen treated them like incompetent understudies and was so fractious that one by one they all left. Chris could not help being amused at the irony of this greatly loved actress being blacklisted by the employment agencies. On the whole she believed that her friends and Tony Atwood's were more fitting female companions until, at the beginning of 1925, the twenty-eighth professional carer arrived – a sensible, good-humoured Yorkshire woman named Hilda Barnes. Ellen liked 'Barney' as she called her. 'She could keep her temper in the most trying circumstances', Chris admitted. '. . . She could turn her hand to anything . . . housekeeper, cook, maid, secretary, companion and nurse at one time or another.' But she was not popular with some of their women friends and not welcomed by those men who thought Ellen should be allowed more liberty – liberty, as Chris put it, 'to walk into the pond, or burn herself to death, if she liked'.

Every year Ellen would go to stay with her old friend Graham Robertson at Sandhills, his house near Chiddingfold in Surrey, and often prolonged her holiday with a visit to his near-neighbour, the poet Lady Alix Egerton who is 'simply the *Spirit* of Peace'. 'Being a long way off makes one see things so clearly', Ellen told Graham Robertson. But what she saw was not pleasant. She had known Graham Robertson for so long now that it did not matter what she said to him ('I always had a talent for holding my tongue'). She told him that she felt 'foredoomed' since leaving her Chelsea house, and he came to realise that she needed protection from her protectors – 'those terrible beings, the Ellen Terry Lunatics' who insisted that she was 'one of us', by which they meant a lesbian: the queen of their hive. She always felt much happier after these holidays at Sandhills, and giving her this escape was the best he could do for her.

Chris and Tony saw it differently. What these men did not understand was the peculiar nature of love between a mother and her daughter. They seemed to believe that Edy had shut Ellen away in a box. But Chris was convinced that Edy was sometimes made ill by her mother's predatory old age.

Across the battlefield of these men and women lay a scattering of Ellen's family. She saw little of her easygoing brother Charlie (whose pink face reminded her of their father Ben's) and almost nothing of George since his dull marriage in Wimbledon. But her big, blond brother Fred, who perpetually played the Scarlet Pimpernel and Henry of Navarre opposite his wife Julia Neilson, did come to see her. Reputed to be a lazy actor, he was actually struggling with ailments unmentionable in polite society which required him to seek treatment abroad. Marion too would come to see her. An exquisite actress within her narrow range – very handsome (except perhaps for her mouth, sometimes likened to 'a Japanese anemone in the rain') and very dignified (despite her habit of crying in the theatre during comedies) – her magnificent straight back was now twisted and bent by arthritis which had obliged her to leave the run of Somerset Maugham's *Our Betters* in 1923, never returning to the stage. She was shrunk and withered, but Ellen could not help mocking her sister's worship of the aristocracy, and invented for her various disreputable love-affairs which, when news of them reached her, made Marion shudder. (This was all the more naughty because Ellen knew that her sister, when younger, had been the mistress of Sir Squire Bancroft – until Lady Bancroft caught them on a sofa in his study at Berkley Square. Marion never got over this affair and steadfastly refused to marry Sir Frederick Haines, a military gentleman who, never relinquishing hope, sent her a yellow rose every day until his death.) Then, in 1924, Ellen's elder sister Kate died of senile pneumonia. Once the Terry of the age, though without Ellen's imagination, she lay in her coffin a forgotten figure and few people attended her funeral – 'a shocking house', one of them remarked.

That year Ellen suffered a minor stroke, and her doctor urged the importance of a quiet life. She drifted into a shadowy world where nothing was real and people had no names. 'Put your left hand tightly over your left eyelid – & then make your right hand into a fist, & peep through', she wrote to a friend. 'Try to read or write or look at the dear faces of your beloved ones. That is a measure of my eyesight now.' One day, suddenly recognising her husband, James Carew, she asked: 'Tell me, Jim, I can't quite remember – did I kick you out or did you kick me out?'

'Well, dear,' he replied, 'I think we arranged it between us, didn't we?'

'Yes, we did,' she agreed. Then after a pause she added: 'Dam' fools, weren't we?'

Vague yet still strong-willed, she would put a bed-sock on her head or take off her clothes in front of visitors. When there were more than two or three people in a room with her she grew agitated. She would speak of giving her captors the slip one night and joining her sister Marion in Monte Carlo, 'a delightful place' – had she been there once with Henry? (She had gone there shortly after he died when his presence was still very potent.) It was difficult to stop her wandering off into the London traffic or across the water-meadows and marshlands in search of the moon above Smallhythe ('I'll run out for a little walk in the amazing moonlight', she had written to Gordon Craig, '& shall be soothed & strengthened, & then I'll go to bed'). Some nights she refused to go to bed and would make a terrible hurly-burly, filling the room with flying objects.

Finally Chris and Tony decided that she must be moved to a 'mental institution'. This was shortly before Hilda Barnes arrived, while the battle over Ellen's wills was at its most intense. Marguerite Steen argued that shutting her away in an asylum would kill her. Why not sell the apartment in London, she suggested, settle Ellen in the farmhouse at Smallhythe and move Edy in there too? If Edy slept in the farm 'within hearing distance of Ellen' her anxieties would be quietened. This proposal was furiously resisted by Chris. To abandon her theatre work and devote herself entirely to Ellen would make Edy ill – and Edy was her prime concern. The love between mother and daughter was a coin that seemed to show a life-enhancing picture on one side and mutual destruction on the other. So how should it be spun into the air?

Such opposition to the asylum was mounted by Fred Terry, Gordon Craig and others (none of whom would contribute to the scheme) that it had to be abandoned. But the apartment at Burleigh Mansions was sold and Hilda Barnes arrived at Smallhythe where, during emergencies, she would be joined by a nurse. Barney experienced 'every sort of obstruction from Priest's House', Marguerite Steen observed, and was aware of 'something or someone like an enemy in the camp'. She followed the advice of Florence Terry's daughter Olive 'to be fond of Edy'. But mysteriously not all her letters reached Edy. Those that did get through, describing Ellen's 'stunts' and 'naughtinesses', also carefully recorded her expressions of love. This was just as well for Edy sometimes felt jealous of her mother's devotion to this unlikely companion with her corncrake voice and uncompromising exterior. In the revised edition of Ellen Terry's memoirs, Chris writes of

Ellen suddenly reviving before her death and calling out 'Edy!' But others heard her call 'Barney!'

Ellen spent Christmas 1925 at Edy's apartment in Bedford Street. One of the guests there was an American journalist, Velona Pilcher, who was to describe their Christmas Day party in the *Theatre Arts Monthly*. After dinner, Ellen retired to bed while the women played records on the gramophone and, still wearing their coloured paper hats, began dancing. Ellen must have heard this dance music from her bedroom, for she suddenly appeared in the doorway, 'a silver figure, wrapped in a long loose cloak of snow-white fur. The head was high, flung back defiantly from the bent body.' As the group of female dancers fell back, she began to dance, drawn by the rhythm of the music as if in a dream. 'Silently once around the table she danced – slowly, stately, delicately . . . and then silently passed again out at the door.'

On Christmas Day 1926 Ellen was too ill for dancing. Unlike her brother, Edy 'could always tell the difference between what was real and what was feigned', Chris claimed. Fearing their mother might be dying, she summoned him from Italy.

Gordon Craig was puzzled by the news. It was true that over recent years his mother had complained of being 'doddery'. But she had always been something of a hypochondriac. So he knew there was not much wrong with her. '*Nothing matters*', she reassured him and then: '*Everything matters.*' He took comfort from this paradox for was he not *everything to her*? Nevertheless he came over and 'found her pretending to be far more ill than she would in secret allow'. He did not need to speak to the doctor and nurses – he knew his mother's 'secret self'. She was, he conceded, 'just a little crestfallen'. He came near and spoke to her: 'how she sprang up! – lash! went her arm around my neck – she became twenty-three – such a kiss! – and subsided again . . .' It was a demonstration of the healing power of fantasy. Even though she was to break her arm in a fall later that year, her strong constitution carried her through. And she lived on.

According to Chris, Ellen 'set her heart' on spending another Christmas in Bedford Street. Edy 'got four ambulance men from a hospital nearby to carry her up the three long flights of steps. Our party of the lonely ones was much smaller . . . Ellen Terry was gay but more restless than I had ever seen her . . . She could not concentrate on anything now.'

Smallhythe Farm was so damp in winter that central heating had been installed. But something had gone wrong with the pipes and arrangements were made for Ellen to visit friends. That January she went to stay with the two Casella sisters, Ella and Marie, who lived near Maidstone in Kent.

'I had a foreboding of disaster', Chris remembered. When Graham Robertson visited Ellen there, he found her 'comfortable and happy . . . on the whole very well . . . Edy came in for a bit after tea . . .' Then disaster. There was 'a tragic scene, perhaps the most tragic in the whole drama', Chris wrote. She could not bring herself to describe what happened beyond using the words 'horrid scuffle in the dark'.

Graham Robertson had noticed that Ellen was having difficulty recognising one of the Casella sisters. Later on Alix Egerton and her sister Mabel came to stay in the house, and Robertson learnt that they 'were having the hell of a time with Edy'. Some act of madness had occurred, some struggle in bringing Ellen back to Smallhythe. For Chris to have been so distressed, that scene in the dark probably involved a clash between Edy and Ellen. Johnston Forbes-Robertson felt angry at what he heard and it may have been he who appealed to Ellen's husband, James Carew, to intervene. He promised to 'take a hand if it becomes necessary'.

On 27 February 1928, the British Broadcasting Corporation fixed up some equipment at Smallhythe so that, as part of a celebratory programme for what people believed to be her eightieth birthday, Ellen could broadcast a message on the radio. But she was incapable of delivering the words Chris had drafted for her – words taken from happier days, words borrowed from Henry Irving, words that Edy unsteadily read for her mother and which, as they travelled through the airwaves sounded uncannily like Ellen's own voice, though she lay upstairs in a terrible dementia.

It seems to me very wonderful that I should still be remembered, and that all this delightful fuss should have been made simply because I am eighty. I know I have to thank Shakespeare . . . This tribute to me is a tribute to Shakespeare, and so, to England . . . This celebration of my birthday has bereft me of words. Only 'my blood speaks to you in my veins' . . . I was always more proud of making an audience laugh, than of making it weep. This is . . . perhaps, who knows, a real farewell performance. Let the curtain come down on a smile.

She appeared more peaceful during the summer at Smallhythe. 'This is my house,' she told her doctor, 'bought with my own money.' She drew comfort from this fact. In the opinion of her nurse 'all was well with her'. All would be well if she could end it well.

Gordon Craig was in London that summer to open an exhibition of his designs for *The Pretenders* at the St George's Gallery in Hanover Square. Meeting Edy at a luncheon party in mid-July he had been 'awfully glad' to hear that their mother was 'pretty well'. He was so busy that he had not yet found time to visit Smallhythe. On 17 July Edy telephoned to say that Ellen had suffered a paralysing stroke that morning. 'This seemed to me one of those impossible things', her brother wrote, '– inconceivable.' What should he do? It was Edy who decided. She gathered him up and took him to join their cousin Olive Terry who had a car. Olive was 'a driver of Brooklands calibre' and she rushed them down in record time to Smallhythe.

They found Ellen lying on her bed, a crumpled figure, eyes closed, her face drawn to one side, making sounds no one could decipher. 'It was no longer her voice but rather the voice of some man', Gordon Craig thought, '– more like that of Irving, when murmuring in the last act of *Louis XI*. She was very fallen – all but the hands, which shone clearly for me, and seemed to speak.' He was fascinated by these hands, the largeness of which had embarrassed her when young, but which now seemed 'so alive and so expressive'.

The day before, a warm sunny day, Ellen had insisted on being taken out – she had not been outdoors for four months. Barney and one of the nurses pushed her heavy wheelchair through the orchard and then out towards the toll-gate and over the little bridge that crossed a narrow stream. They pushed her along the river-like road under a blue sky, and parked her wheelchair overlooking a bank of irises and with a view of the open marshlands covered with sheep. Then Barney and the nurse walked back a little towards a gate into one of the fields where they began talking with the crippled toll-gate keeper. But Ellen did not like to be 'left out of things'. She could hear the murmur of their voices and resented being stranded there. She called out but they did not hear her – or did not want to hear. She was bored. She was impatient. Bending down, she took off both her shoes and flung them angrily into the road – and Barney came running back to her. That night she slept like a child – nearly eight hours she slept. But she refused breakfast next morning and at a quarter past ten she had a stroke.

For four days she lay on her bed, silent except for the rattling of her breath, while the house filled up with her family. Her brother Fred arrived and Charlie, his pink face now white and anxious, and also some of the younger Terrys and Craigs. Marion came, though she was too contorted with arthritis to sit for long at her sister's bedside. James Carew, however, felt 'I could sit by her side for ever.' Edy watched and recited nursery rhymes, as if she were now the mother and Ellen her child. But only Barney could interpret the strange noises Ellen made. 'She wants to be moved', Barney would tell the others. 'She wants something cool on her forehead.' Gordon Craig was one of those who obeyed these instructions.

> I was on one side, with my hands held under her, the nurses on the other; and on the word 'up' we all raised her, the sheet was drawn away and a new sheet put in its place – then, on the word 'down' we lowered her . . . she took up the two words – and played see-saw with them: 'Up and down . . . up and down . . .' she growled in a semi-comic, true Terry way. The word *up* went with a sharp jerk . . . and the word *down* like a heap falling, and lengthened out into dowwwn . . . Twice she said it, and then 'Up to the skies . . . dowwwwn to the' – and it tailed away into rumblings . . . these were the last words I heard.

The news that Ellen Terry was sinking spread through the country. 'Messages came and went over the telephone day and night', Chris remembered. 'The King and Queen were among the first to express their concern . . .' Edy converted a room in the gardener's cottage into a news bureau which, assisted by several of her friends, she ran like a stage-manager's office in a theatre. By the toll-gate the journalists were assembling in their cars 'like black beasts of prey' waiting for the death, their headlamps levelled each night at the farmhouse. After one of these reporters crawled through the hedge and tried to reach Ellen Terry's bedroom, the police came from Tenterden to guard the house.

Chris, kneeling in prayer, became convinced that Ellen's spirit was wonderfully active; Tony and Olive stood ready to perform any errand that might be needed; the nurses came and went, checking pulse, temperature, blood-pressure; and Edy sat holding her mother's hand.

At half past eight on the morning of 21 July 1928, Ellen died. 'She can't be dead!' cried Olive. But there was a feeling of relief, an atmosphere almost of exaltation in the house. 'Mother looked 30 years old when she had ceased breathing the thin air of this small earth', Gordon Craig remembered. She had thrown off all signs of her difficult years, and 'a young beautiful woman lay on the bed, like Juliet on her bier'. But there was no Romeo, no man there, at the moment of her death. Chris was adamant about this. The women went out into the garden, leaving Edy alone. 'I heard her crying like a child', Chris wrote.

The obituaries recalled Ellen Terry's extraordinary partnership with Henry Irving. His had been the death of a tragedian marked by public grief. Hers was seen as the passing of a comedian, an occasion for celebrating a life of brilliance and gaiety. 'I do not like to cry,' she had once said, though tears came readily to her. She had the gift of making people happy, lighting up any room she entered. And if that light was now extinguished, it had 'burned long and brightly', Granville-Barker testified, 'and had given everything it came near brightness'. Those who had known her well, who had seen that brightness overtaken by a sadness which had always lain behind it, were glad she had finally been released into remembered light. 'Let us not burthen our remembrance with / A heaviness that's gone.' Prospero's words expressed Ellen's own wishes. She had copied down a poem by William Allingham with the line: 'No funeral gloom, my dears, when I am gone', adding: 'I should wish my children, relatives and friends to observe that when I die.' This they did, filling her bedroom that day with flowers.

Gordon Craig went straight up to London to make arrangements for Ellen's cremation at Golders Green and a memorial service that would take place in the actors' church, St Paul's, Covent Garden. Edy planned the funeral at Smallhythe. Chris saw to it that Ellen's body was framed by continuously burning candles, the flickering light caught by flowers in the dim corners of her room: light and colour everywhere. Gordon Craig designed a coffin in the shape of a canoe, a slender carpentered vessel, both ends delicately pointed, one arched like a prow, into which Ellen's body was moved on the last day.

Cars gathered for miles around Smallhythe on 24 July, the day of the funeral. The coffin, covered by a golden pall, was carried to the church, now carpeted with rosemary and lavender. Copies of William Allingham's poem forbidding 'black raiment, graveyard grimness' had been pinned up around the village, and the men in the cortège all wore coloured ties, the women summer dresses. All, that is, but one. Mrs Aria, a figure from the enigmatic past, wore black, grieving that Ellen would be reaching Henry

Irving before herself (she was to die three years later in a box at the Adelphi Theatre).

Before the entrance to the church an impromptu guard of honour had been formed by the haymakers, shepherds and farmers with their rakes and pitchforks. In the fields too, lined up against the hedges, stood other farmworkers, silent, their caps removed, facing the church, their dogs beside them. The congregation sang songs of praise. 'All Things Bright and Beautiful' floated over the cemetery and fields. And at the end the church bells rang out cheerfully.

The convoy of cars then moved off towards London. At Tenterden the shops had closed, the sun shining on drawn blinds. People lined the streets, motionless and quiet. News of Ellen Terry's death had passed through the country and become a national event in which everyone wished to take part. They saw her as 'the sweetheart of England', a sublime actress able to make everyone, the simple as well as the sophisticated, rejoice or suffer with her. For she 'made us realize', Sybil Thorndike wrote, 'we are at the same moment separate individuals, yet joined to the rest of humanity by subtle bonds'. Her audiences had not been mere onlookers, but participants in dramas of the human condition.

At all the villages they drove through people threw flowers before the cars. Huge crowds, 'all classes, all ages', had assembled at Golders Green. Photographers were everywhere. Again the songs of praise were sung, again 'All Things Bright and Beautiful' rang out as Ellen's body moved into the flames. Then the white dust was poured into a silver casket for the final service at Covent Garden.

Ellen's death brought her son and daughter together, uniting them as they had seldom been since childhood. Clutching Edy's arm as they led the procession from the church in Smallhythe, Gordon Craig had whispered to his sister in a voice that carried clearly to the mourners: 'We must have more occasions like this.'

PART SEVEN

47
For Friendship's Sake

She was dead but never absent. 'What you say about mother being very near is true', Edy wrote to her brother, '– so true down here [Smallhythe]. She is always light. Bright light.'

To Christopher St John it seemed a miracle that the stage goddess whom she had once so fervently worshipped and at whose feet she had vainly poured out her dreams should be the mother of the girl she came to love. But she could not pretend that their coming-together had been blessed with peace. Chris had discovered early on that Ellen 'did not understand me in the least'; and as for Edy, 'I had not the faintest notion of what was going on in her mind and heart and soul'. Love was beyond understanding. Did parents understand their children? Chris longed for faith which passed understanding, a prayer 'which pierces so that it assaults / mercy itself and frees all faults'.

Edy and her brother brought the silver casket containing Ellen's ashes to Bedford Street and this gave Chris an opportunity for making good whatever had been lacking in Ellen's last tormented days. She converted a small room overlooking St Paul's churchyard into an oratory and had it blessed. There she erected an altar, placed the casket on it and lit a sanctuary lamp. This lamp went on burning night and day for over a year while ecclesiastical negotiations were conducted over the casket's final destination.

The public expected Ellen's ashes to be laid to rest beside those of Henry Irving in Westminster Abbey. A petition, signed by distinguished people in the arts and sciences was prepared – and then suddenly withdrawn after official opposition was made known to the lying together of this ever-diverse pair in Poets' Corner (Florence Irving being still alive). A niche was then cut into the wall at St Paul's, Covent Garden, and the silver casket designed by

Gordon Craig's friend the silversmith Paul Cooper was brought there from Bedford Street. Sir John Martin-Harvey unveiled a tablet on 29 August 1929.

'No one could ever say no to Edy', one of her friends remarked. But Ellen had frequently said no. Their love for each other was strong, but it had not been a polite love and their embrace often took the shape of a struggle. Now Edy needed to make peace with Ellen. The best way of doing this, she believed, would be to create a permanent memorial to her at Smallhythe. She planned to convert the old timbered farmhouse into a museum with rooms displaying her mother's theatre treasures (relics of her years with Irving and a library for the use of scholars) while the bedroom would be kept exactly as it had been during her life. Edy's ambitions did not stop there. She was determined to transform the large barn adjacent to the farmhouse into a theatre. Here, on the date of Ellen's death, she would put on miracle plays, pageants, nativity plays, scenes from Shakespeare, poetry readings, recitations – ' a little bit of everything', in Virginia Woolf's words.

Ellen's estate had been valued at almost £20,000. This sum was divided into two trusts of equal value, but because the Smallhythe property was included in Edy's half of the estate she received fewer dividends (her brother and Elena Meo together had approximately £700 a year). She was told that some £15,000 would be needed as an endowment to acquire Smallhythe for the nation. Early in 1929 she launched a public appeal.

But Ellen Terry's legendary partnership with Henry Irving belonged to the previous century and there were not many people under fifty who remembered her performances at the Lyceum. There was hostility too from those friends who did not want to see her enshrined in a museum watched over by Edy and her comrades – Ellen herself, they protested, would never have wanted Smallhythe made into a place of pilgrimage.

Edy was soon engulfed by the convoluted process of fund-raising. A 'Preliminary Committee' came into being whose job was to appoint a 'General Committee' which was intended to encourage others by the sheer lustre of its names upon the writing paper. The actual work was delegated to an 'Executive Committee', a few members of which issued a private prospectus and then went their ways. Between Edy and the Memorial Trustees an agreement was eventually drafted requiring her to keep up the farmhouse as a museum at her own expense, but giving them the option to buy it from her within ten years and establish it permanently as an Ellen

Terry memorial. This turned out to be something of a phantom document since the Memorial Trust never seems to have completed its full journey into legal existence.

The appeal attracted less than £2,000. Chris felt furious with everyone. But watching Edy battling through her disappointment as she prepared everything for the first anniversary of Ellen's death, this anger gave way to admiration. How gallant she was! Her speciality lay in the art of the impossible, in succeeding at what no one else would attempt (her quixotic achievements with the Pioneer Players had been a fine example of this). During 1929 she gave up all other work in order to make the farmhouse 'a living shrine' and open the barn as a memorial theatre. She sold some of her mother's effects at auction and organised a fund-raising matinée at the Palace Theatre in London involving almost every actor who had appeared onstage with Ellen Terry – so many that they had to use the dressing-rooms of other theatres nearby and were seen dashing through the streets to catch their entrances. By 21 July Edy had filled the farmhouse with exhibits, opened it to the public and put on the first anniversary performance at the Barn Theatre. There were still holes in the thatched roof and gaps in the timbered walls. Detached car lights placed inside biscuit tins gave the stage its lighting. The audience, sitting on rough benches lined across the earthen floor, were invited to join in the songs and tributes. 'The programme had been hastily arranged, but it was of rare quality', Chris wrote.

Besides the Smallhythe estate itself, Edy also laid claim to what lawyers called 'the chattels' there. These included many letters and postcards. Examining them, Edy considered bringing out an edition of her mother's correspondence and suggested to Bernard Shaw that he write a foreword to this volume. But Shaw had over a hundred letters Ellen had written to him and brought them, neatly arranged in chronological order, to Bedford Street. 'It was then that the possibility of publishing the complete Shaw–Terry correspondence was first discussed', Christopher St John records.

Such a book would command a far larger sale than any miscellaneous correspondence. And Shaw being such a public figure, it would not reveal, Chris reasoned, 'those intimate secrets of the emotional life which ought to be protected from the public gaze'. There was only one indigestible ingredient: Shaw's persistent disparagement of Henry Irving. Ellen's love for Irving had been the reason for her omitting several of Shaw's letters from the first edition of her memoirs. But that had been soon after Irving's death. Besides, Ellen's answers to Shaw amounted to a vindication of Irving's character and genius, and gave proof of her loyalty to him. Nevertheless the two women were awkwardly placed. Edy had mistrusted Shaw's relationship with her mother, and Chris had contemptuously attacked him in her memorial essay on Irving. Now both of them were obliged to rely on his generosity. It was a peculiarly Shavian situation.

Shaw would have preferred to put the correspondence to rest in a manuscript library with instructions that it should not be dug up 'until we are all dead' – by which he meant Edy and Gordon Craig as well as himself and his wife Charlotte Shaw. But in view of Edy's circumstances (to say nothing of Gordon Craig's) and the undersubscribed Ellen Terry Memorial (for which he cared very little), he suggested licensing the publication of a limited collectors' edition of the letters from which he would take no royalties himself. But on moral rather than legal grounds, he insisted that the approval of Gordon Craig be obtained. So Edy spoke to her brother and he said that she could do whatever she liked. But afterwards he sent Shaw a less than candid letter ('the letter of a cockatrice', Shaw noted) questioning whether the letters were not in parts (those parts written by his mother) 'too fine' and too private for publication.

'Cockatrice' was also the word Craig used for Shaw, deploring that his mother should have spent so much time corresponding with such a pernicious windbag. Nothing could remove from Craig the 'objectionableness' of GBS and when he read his letters there rose up in him a 'faint desire to be sick'. He had given his permission to Edy to publish, but now begged her not to do so. '*For Mother's sake* & for H.I's sake & for the Theatre's sake [I] would willingly see them burnt.' To make money from such a publication would be 'a bad mark against you and me'.

Then everything changed. A wealthy American lawyer and publisher, Elbridge Adams, offered Edy £3,000 for Shaw's letters to Ellen Terry – and Shaw encouraged her to accept this offer. Adams went on to pay James Carew a further £400 for a batch of sixteen more of Shaw's letters in his possession. 'It is therefore no longer possible to pretend that we are under any pecuniary pressure to publish the letters', Shaw wrote to Gordon Craig. Had it merely been pretence? Inevitably, Shaw believed, this correspondence would one day be published. He therefore took the trouble to compose a 10,000-word preface and to have a dozen copies of it printed. As an interim 'solution' to the problem, he proposed lodging Ellen Terry's correspondence together with this substantial preface in the safety of the British Museum. But before doing this, he circulated the preface to various people to find out what they thought. T.E. Lawrence and the Abbess of Stanbrook thought it a pity to disturb the Ellen Terry legend with immediate publication. But Edy and Chris damned the legend and welcomed 'the truth about her'. Shaw then invited Gordon Craig to tell him whether he agreed with his sister.

Had Shaw ended his letter there, warfare between them might not have broken out. But for several years Gordon Craig had been using *The Mask* to stick pins into GBS. In the January issue of 1926, for example, he had deplored the false stage effects with which Shaw had swamped modern drama. He was little more than a pantomime giant, a-puffing and a-blowing as he plodded the world in his twenty-league boots, searching for something to say. In the guise of a 'Colossus', he had stormed the English-speaking theatre and shut its doors against authentic playwrights. In an open letter he sent to *The Mask*, Shaw signed off as being not seriously damaged but 'a little the worse for wear'.

Gordon Craig too was feeling a little worse for wear – 'not down you know', he told Edy, '. . . but just . . . you know . . .' He was fifty-six: not old enough to be really old, not young enough to be youthful. 'A new phase of life begins', he had written in one of his day books after his mother's death. But for a time it merely seemed as if a familiar phase of life was ending. In the autumn of 1929, at Box 444, the final edition of *The Mask* was steered through the press. He made several false starts elsewhere. An American director had invited him to provide sketches and models for a touring production of *Macbeth*, one in a series of 'famous masterpieces', which had its premiere at the Knickerbocker Theater on Broadway. Craig refused to travel there but, knowing the play so well, he spent three weeks plagiarising his own work and making a pile of striking sketches which he signed 'C.pb', indicating 'Craig-potboiler'. It was a 'distracting and stupid' interval though the money was useful. 'At times I am very unhappy about my work', he told Edy '– the time & sacrifices seem to have been useless because it has been given to people who really do not care.'

Edy was to adopt one of her brother's granddaughters, known as Ruby

Chelta Craig (following the divorce of his and May's eldest son – Ruby's father – Robert) and make her the principal beneficiary of a trust fund. 'I haven't made a will', Gordon Craig informed Edy in 1929, '– I ought to make it – but haven't decided whether to sell my collection of books . . .' His son Edward noticed how the gap between his aunt and his father was widening again. 'Father was a visionary with a strange veneration for tradition', he was to write. '. . . [His] tradition had little room for women. Edy was a fighter for their cause.' It was Bernard Shaw who would widen this gap between them.

Meanwhile Gordon Craig urgently needed someone to replace Edward as an amanuensis in this new phase of his life. From London he began restlessly wandering around Europe: to Weimar, Genoa, Heidelberg, Grenoble, Lyons, Paris and then back again to London, like a Don Quixote searching for his Sancho Panza – or possibly his Dulcinea. 'Cities seem to be like individuals', he had written to his mother when first travelling through Europe, '– awfully different & with nerves – moods & fads like people – hearts I hope too.' Which city would have the heart to give him what he needed? Several secretaries journeyed out from England, but they were all too timid or uninspiring – one of them a 'lady-like whore'. In Paris he accidentally came across his son Robin and wondered whether he might qualify: but there was the danger that he might communicate his secrets to May – she had probably 'twisted' him. He began exploring the ranks of his other children. His daughter Nelly was not really up to the job, though she had copied some seventeenth- and eighteenth-century manuscripts for him. Who else was there?

He had recently heard from Dorothy Nevile Lees – a letter accusing him of having done nothing since the war 'to show me any kindness or justice in either my personal or work relations with you, or in regard to Davidino'. He never saw her now. Had he looked upon her sad and serious face, dignified and without a trace of self-pity, yet haunted, almost permanently shocked in its expression, he would have seen a living rebuke as terrifying as the Gorgon's head. She missed him, missed him fiercely, missed the daily tasks he set her before the war – the verifying of dates and the spelling of names and especially her collaboration in his writing. She missed too his constant attentions: his rules for speaking, his lectures on the virtue of silence and the length of time she was allowed to visit him; also his advice to be 'always laughing' and 'a very good girl' by learning how to 'act with policy and grace and not give me further trouble'. Without this guidance it was hard to avoid trouble.

She often heard about him: how he was travelling through many countries, staying with rich friends, being given exhibitions, publishing books, attending parties and going to theatres. 'All this evidence of plenty forms a curious and rather bitter contrast to the plight in which I have been left, as sole return for 24 years of utterly devoted service and friendship', she wrote.

Davidino and I are often so poor that sometimes I have to pretend to him that I am out to meals because there is not enough for two. We never have anything but necessities . . . I wonder whether deserting me as you have, as woman, friend and worker, you have forgotten *everything* in the past? The adoration and faithful love I gave you; the sieges held for you; the battles fought . . . I gave the last soldo I had, or could raise at the Monte di Pieta, to ease things for *you*, and I did it all for love . . . yet you have quite forgotten me . . . Dearest Signor, is it to *end* like this?

How was he to answer this? DNL's fate 'depends on yourself', he advised her. She had picked up, doubtless from his enemies, quite a false picture of his life. He was still working and still poor – and DNL was frankly too old and too preoccupied with her son to resume working with him. Yet the truth was that she 'wanted nothing but to spend my whole life in his service'. There would be no end to that. Though Craig's son Edward had been assisting him, there was still much for DNL to do. From time to time they wrote to each other: but Craig never wrote to their son Davidino. 'I always taught him that he must never judge or criticize his father, only love him, & revere him for the great artist he is', DNL remembered. His Papa was 'different' she explained and must not be expected to behave as other people did. But during these early days Davidino would still question his mother: 'When will Papa come and see me?' And she answered that he was very busy but, like a god, 'one day he will come'. But, like a human being, Craig needed encouragement. Recovering herself, regaining her Christian optimism, DNL wrote again cheerfully, describing the many ways in which her life had improved since the birth of Davidino. But Craig returned this letter to her, scored with editorial comments showing that there were far too many words in it. She had forgotten his instructions to 'leave out all & any feminine feeling'. So she appealed to him once more, not on her own behalf but simply for his son 'who loves you, and whom . . . I am sure in your heart you love'. Now that Craig's other sons were married or dead, their splendid young boy 'might be such a joy to you, [and] if you could train him, such a *help* to you'. To know that father and son were together, she added, would be 'the dearest reward I could have for any good I may ever have done you'. Then at last Craig began writing affectionately to Davidino: 'Love me . . . I send a kiss . . . Papa.' These were sweet simple letters and DNL described the child's 'amazed rapture, his touching joy, the painstaking eagerness & love with which he wrote back'.

But she had also tried to get 'a regular sum' from Craig to help her bring up Davidino – almost as if she believed he lived a regular financial life. 'She [DNL] & May & the like are really at bottom private blackmailers', Elena warned him. 'I am sure she wanted the child to get hold of you.' To save him this 'pestilence', Elena offered privately to pay DNL £25 a year. But would she take legal advantage of such generosity? Craig sometimes felt angry with DNL's 'methods of communication with me'. For example, she dared to suggest that he loan *The Mask* some of the money he had inherited from his mother. No wonder, under such provocation, he had put an end to it – and to her. She used a tone which, however much she might try to disguise it, 'makes it clear to me that you consider I am at fault. I cannot have that.' Therefore she could not have the allowance. And Davidino would have no further letters – though his mother received some formal correspondence from Craig's lawyers about his ownership of *The Mask* archive. 'It was a very sad time, and quite inexplicable', she recalled, and she felt 'pretty well shattered'.

The truth was that DNL no longer held a significant place in Craig's life. Back in London by the summer of 1929, he had met her successor. Daphne Woodward was an intelligent, good-looking young woman who seemed to

'understand his loneliness and frustration' better than anyone. She had many admirable qualities: she spoke French, was learning Italian (something he had never really done) and was to become 'the best secretary I ever had'. DNL had addressed him as 'Signor' as people once addressed G.F. Watts, but young Daphne Woodward called him 'Pookie'.

When she took dictation he liked her to strip off her clothes, he told one of his sons – though she protested that she felt 'silly' sitting naked with a notebook on her lap. Her fascination with his theatre stories, stretching back into childhood, guided him towards that new phase in his life for which he had been searching – a new phase planted in memories of the past.

Long ago, on leaving England, he had planned to write about Henry Irving. 'Already I was preparing for the day when this great person would be with us no longer', he wrote in a chronology of his career. But he had moved away from Irving, though occasionally glancing over his shoulder to catch sight again of this revered figure. 'I have for long attempted to postpone, and postpone indefinitely, making any record of my master', he declared. With Daphne Woodward's enthusiasm, he went back and started again. 'I abandon myself to the old joy,' he wrote, 'and become once more a spectator and whole-hearted admirer of this exceptional actor, Irving.'

Gordon Craig's book on Henry Irving became the magic carpet on which he took flight from an embattled present and arrived back at a place of enchantment. 'These Lyceum days were *exciting days*', he tells us. 'They were positively worth living, if you chanced to be a member of Irving's company.' The mysterious glamour of that privileged company, its forests of wooden machinery, the tremendous bustle of its scene-shifters and stage-carpenters climbing and burrowing like elves and monkeys, furtive creatures living high up in the shadows – all this took his imagination captive. Why, having gained his place there, had he walked off into exile? The answer he gives is that once he had seen Irving performing at the Lyceum, he knew that he could never be more than 'a feeble imitation of him'. He found this knowledge dismaying for he had grown ambitious. Irving, he writes, 'suffered keenly whenever he found actors taking things easily, and considering too lightly this thing which to him was really a sacred trust'. Craig knew he had betrayed this trust.

He writes well on Irving's acting in *The Bells*, giving a brilliant impression of the mesmeric power with which he controlled the atmosphere even while taking off his boots, then pulling on and buckling up his shoes. What Craig is giving us is the portrait of a genius: a man who, despite his physical deficiencies, became a *dancer* on the stage. 'He was quite a simple man – he picked up a cup of tea just the same as you or I . . . he ate his toast without quoting Shakespeare.' Yet he was single-mindedly dedicated to his art. 'If he sat in a garden, the garden became a stage . . . If someone showed him a picture Irving saw in it only what he could use.' And when he played tragedy, 'the whole of nature seems to suffer'.

The book is uneven, sometimes moving easily, sometimes creaking. 'Writing is not my craft', Craig excuses himself. But through what he calls 'the cloud of language', the context of his craft emerges. Irving was the prophet; Craig his pupil: this was their sacred connection. 'Irving told me the way I was to go . . . [He] had expressed in a new way – his own way – and I, his pupil, followed his lead.'

Never was there a better-conducted theatre than the Lyceum. But 'I am of the irrational kind', Craig told Christopher St John. He was all imagination. Yet there is no doubt that he 'loved Henry Irving's theatre', Peter Brook was to write, '– its painted forests, its thunder sheets, its naïve melodrama – but at the same time he dreamed of another theatre where all the elements would be harmonious and whose art would be a religion'. This theatre produced effects as spectacular as Irving's by minimalist devices. 'Henry Irving was the full stop to a period in a long chapter of the stage – we have begun a new chapter.' Craig argues that there need never have been such a full stop between their careers but for the disgraceful snatching-away of the Lyceum which prevented Irving from founding 'the school of which the dramatic art of England still stands in the utmost need' – that school which he himself had also been prevented from founding. He also connects them symbolically through the language of masks and marionettes. Early in his book, he calls Irving 'the masked angel' and explains that he knew 'it was his mask that was to be the great actor – a mask which could be a hundred faces in one – and he had to design, cut out, polish, and perfect that mask'. He claims that when Irving measured himself for a suit of mail from head to toe, he became 'the nearest thing ever known to what I have called the Über-Marionette'. Craig's conclusion is that Irving must have been 'a great believer in puppets' and come to regret that 'in his theatre they had to be made of flesh and blood'. He concedes that Irving 'never expressed this', but confidently adds that 'he never failed to feel it'.

It was while Gordon Craig was busy discovering signs of his own theatre in Irving's Lyceum that he heard from Bernard Shaw, offering his help in a most bruising manner. 'I wanted you as an actor and not as the heir of your father, who was a very Victorian Piranesi', he explained. '. . . I saw that you cared nothing about the drama, and could not feel your art in dramatic terms . . . you were trying to make a picture of the proscenium, to replace actors by figures, and drive the dramatic poet out of the theatre. And as I was doing precisely the reverse, and the Zeitgeist carried me to success, you felt that I was the arch enemy.'

Shaw's purpose was to persuade Craig to give up his book on Irving ('of whom you can never know much that is worth recording because you were not acting-struck and he was nothing else'). But Craig's loyalty to Irving had grown so intense while writing his book that their identities seemed to merge. His reply to Shaw – pointing out that his book contained almost nothing about him because his relations with Irving were almost non-existent – was very much in Irving's style. The book is in fact scattered with asides that tell of Shaw's deficiencies: his irritating stage-directions, his awful horse-play and the theatrical business that was 'as old as the hills, and as dusty'. Each was marginalising the other in the history of modern theatre. But the real rivalry between them was for the heart and mind of Ellen Terry.

It was not a simple duel because it involved Edy. She had been pleased with the sale of Shaw's letters – and there was more money to come after Gilbert Samuel & Co. negotiated a further £3,000 for the copyright of Ellen Terry's letters. But though Elbridge Adams had by now paid out a great deal of money, he was still unable to publish both sides of the correspondence because he did not own Shaw's copyright. 'Certainly I won't give permission', Shaw told a reporter from the *Daily Express*. He had already explained to Adams that his 'desire to do Miss Craig a substantial service' had been assuaged by these sales. But Edy was dismayed. Why else had Shaw brought her these letters? No one could fathom his motives – certainly not the solicitors. Legally there was no need to consult Gordon Craig at all, but they invited him to sign a statement they had drafted. 'He [the solicitor] wants to do something that you and Edith both wish to have done,' the statement read, 'so I will not stand in the way and you may rest assured that having said this I shall stick to it; and when the book containing my Mother's letters is published you can rely on me not to write about it in the papers or give interviews.'

Shaw promised that all royalties from the publication would be paid to the Terry trustees: 'I take nothing.' He went further, paying half the costs

($5,541.85) of the limited edition of the book which was published by Elbridge Adams's Fountain Press. He also released Gordon Craig from the undertaking that had been forced on him not to write about the book. All this was extraordinarily generous. But then he spelt out what he believed Gordon Craig had done. 'Edy and Christopher, who, as strong Feminists, want justice done to the great woman E.T. sacrificed to the egotistical man H.I. which is the moral of the whole correspondence.' This was the dagger, forged by misrepresenting Edy's and Chris's views, which he plunged into Gordon Craig. Had not Craig sold Henry Irving's reputation for thirty pieces of silver which he claimed not to want?

By the autumn of 1930, battle lines were drawn up. On one side Christopher St John and Shaw (whose name does not appear on the editorial line of the title page) were coediting more than 300 letters and postcards that were to form *Ellen Terry and Bernard Shaw: A Correspondence*. Shaw silently revised many of the texts so as to avoid offending living people, but added his trenchant 10,000-word preface. On the other side, returning to England for the contest, stood Gordon Craig, loyally supported by his young assistant Daphne Woodward, as they prepared a companion volume to *Henry Irving* and a competitor to the correspondence. He would dedicate this new book to 'MY FATHER' and call it *Ellen Terry and her Secret Self*. Both books came out late in 1931.

Craig and Daphne Woodward put up in the well-named Hotel Burden at Weymouth. Here the wind 'sounded like the female side of hell let loose', he told Kessler, and the drizzling rain was 'suggestive of the worst phases of the British Drama'. This book about his mother was 'a weight on my heart because I don't know how to do it – as yet – and I very much doubt whether I shall please anybody with it'. He begged Kessler not to tell him he would make the book charming – 'that would throw me into the depths of misery!'

'I had not wished to write this book.' These were Gordon Craig's opening words and they led to his first salvo against Shaw. He was rescuing his mother's memory from Shaw's 'blind vanity and jealousy'. Craig 'loved and adored his Mother'. He could remember how 'she would dress up and do things and say things to conjure back the impression which she knew I wished to receive'. With this book he recreated these memories which Shaw threatened to obliterate by transforming his dear little mother into a wholly public person. But Shaw never knew her. No one knew her except himself.

'I knew her heart better than anyone else', Craig wrote. 'For I knew that life of hers which can be called her secret life.' Edy had never really been his rival for their mother's love because, like Shaw, 'my sister never knew her'. It was true that when very young 'she had but to say "Won't" for the greatest actress of the age to cry "marvellous!" ' which was annoying when 'I wanted my mother all to myself'. When they were in their twenties, Gordon Craig had written to Edy: 'Mother seems very depressed – I suppose it's one of us – or both . . . altogether we possess the cause of all her worries & can produce no remedy.' But Edy had grown up too 'inexperienced' for a close knowledge of their mother and it was through this inexperience that she had become Shaw's ally. 'The fault here does not lie with my sister – it cannot', he declared.

As with his book on Irving, the most radiant passages come from the theatre rather than from life. He paints an entrancing picture of the half-set stage with its red oaken boards, a stage which is not yet a public place belonging to audiences, but more of a playground for his mother and himself, a surreal warm private place filled with an assortment of marvellous toys. There was

> a painted rock, flat, and casting a long, thin shadow on the floor; a couple of cathedral doors leaning against one of the stage walls; by the side of these doors, three pine trees leaning, and in front of them a large gondola, in two pieces, with a big black stove of the eighteenth century close to it . . . Half a street is standing upright towards the centre of the stage, held in place . . . by little cables attached to ropes going far up into the flies . . . on all sides one sees piled-up pieces, of strange shapes and strangely coloured pattern . . . all standing rigidly eccentric, their inappropriate juxtaposition rendering each piece ridiculous, and yet appearing to us quite natural.

This is the secret world he and his mother inhabited. Craig acknowledged his mother's genius had absorbed two thirds of her life at his expense. But whenever he writes of his mother's genius, he is thinking of his own. Had they not both 'felt the call to work greater than the call of life . . . [and] that seeming indifference to other people's feelings when working'? All that he resented in his mother's career he presents as his own alibi for abandoning women and children. 'Genius has to fly free – talent chooses to go on rails: talent arrives at its destination, and within scheduled time.' Bernard Shaw's talent 'is able to move to a fixed rhythm, and makes for a given spot, and does things: genius is for ever changing its rhythm, goes nowhere, and *is* something'.

Ellen Terry and her Secret Self is like Craig's half-set stage, an incomplete place without structure yet teeming with possibilities. It is an amoeba of a book, changing its rhythm, leaving places, floating on a haphazard current of emotion. But then Craig adds a postscript. His target is Shaw's 10,000-word preface to *Ellen Terry and Bernard Shaw: A Correspondence*, which described his book on Irving as an 'idolatrous memoir'. Craig's postscript entitled 'A Plea for GBS' is dedicated to Henry Irving and was published as an annexe, a bound pamphlet of twenty-six pages tucked into a folder at the end of his Ellen Terry memoir.

Shaw had recorded that in the old days 'actors, like Jews, were a race apart; and like all segregated races they preserved manners and customs peculiar to themselves'. Their profession 'freed them from many of the inhibitions to which people outside that profession have to submit'. Ellen Terry was a woman of 'very exceptional virtue without having the smallest respect for the law'. She did not 'fight prejudices', Shaw wrote. 'She walked through them as if they were not there, as indeed for her they were not.' Her marriages were adventures and her friendships had the character of innocent love-affairs – like that with Shaw. Theirs were comedians' letters written to please and amuse each other and 'without ulterior motives or what matchmaking mothers call intentions'.

This was a different Ellen Terry from the one who appears in Gordon Craig's book. 'In every being who lives, there is a second self', he had written, '– sometimes three selves.' Shaw almost agreed. 'The stage is not one fairyland but two', he wrote: 'one for the public when the curtain rises, and another, which the public never discovers, for the theatre folk when the curtain falls. In that secret paradise genius excites a flush of adoration . . . I adored Ellen Terry.' Where Craig had set a rehearsal stage for his adored mother, Shaw prepared a backstage between performances.

GBS was a notoriously difficult man to fight. He was what Craig called 'the possessor of a gigantically card-indexed intellectual energy'. Whereas Craig could merely report on what someone had told him about one of his father's productions, Shaw had actually seen the production and implied that Godwin's craze for 'pageantry' had more in common with Edy's work than with her brother's. Shaw had also seen more of Henry Irving's acting than Craig had done, especially his early performances in Ireland. He was 'utterly unlike anyone else', Shaw granted. But because he 'could give importance and noble melancholy to any sort of drivel', dramatic drivel became a speciality at the Lyceum where Ellen Terry's genius was smothered.

In 'A Plea for GBS', Craig caricatured Shaw as 'a very large malicious, poke-nose old woman . . . with an idle and vindictive tongue'. But Shaw cheerfully accepted that 'to many people I am a repellent person with an odious character . . . a sort of literary gangster'. What his opponents learnt to fear most was his praise. When he described Craig's book as 'tragically moving . . . a poignant human document', it is as the prelude to a devastating analysis of Craig's immaturity. He was someone who, feeling he had never received enough love from his mother, remained a needy child all his life: an emotional inadequacy he diverted into the fantasy of being a thwarted genius. In fact he had become little more than a theatre antiquarian with a career, better described perhaps as a hobby, planted in the forgotten past.

But though Shaw probed the hidden roots from which Craig's anger sprang, he did not examine his own motivations. He puts something of the relations with his own mother into what he believed to have been Edy's attitude to Ellen Terry. 'Edy was unsympathetic to her mother in her early years because she was developing her powers of resistance to this domestic tornado. Edy finally got the upper hand, and so lost her fear of her mother, and with it her hatred of her. The word is a hard one, but children really do hate their parents in their struggle for independence.' Shaw gained his independence by eliminating the painful love he had felt for an unloving mother. Hatred is not a bad word to describe his reaction to his mother. But it was accompanied by a need to find motherly love in a woman such as Ellen Terry.

It was not surprising that Shaw's Ellen Terry 'was always getting in the way of my mother', as Craig complained, '. . . although one and the same person, they were leagues apart'. When pitting his anguish against the manufactured triumphalism of GBS, he scored some palpable hits. Casting Shaw as a jealous 'Iago, ever kindling himself to mischief', Craig describes the stabs of pain he inflicted. He 'has chosen to write about someone I love

. . . all that he writes only awakens care and grief of heart . . . this flower he has picked to pieces, ticketing each petal . . . he is jealous of sons and daughters, because loved by their mothers. He has an elbowing way.'

The quarrel spread into newspapers around the world, and Edy wrote to Shaw apologising for her brother's 'spluttered spleen'. He was a tormented soul. But she did not regret publishing their mother's correspondence. It contributed to the memorial through which she hoped to gain her own peace of mind.

Gordon Craig soon found himself fighting on two fronts: against GBS, the usurper who could not control his pen; and against Edy's army of supporters who could not control their rage. 'King of Cads – Prince of Hypocrites – Lord of Cowardly Assassins', one of their letters read. 'I salute you with a holy smack in the face which is now the mirror of a mean, spiteful, jealous soul! Your mother weeps in heaven at the spectacle of your degradation. To this can jealousy and vanity bring a man – the public traducing of his mother, the public slander of his sister.'

The correspondence outsold the memoir in Britain and America, and was to be followed in 1933 by a new edition of *Ellen Terry's Memoirs*, edited by Christopher St John. She reorganised the earlier chapters and wrote five additional chapters taking the story up to, and then a little beyond, Ellen Terry's death. Edy was credited as being co-author and co-editor, but her contribution was mainly confined to the notes, preface and general guidance. In a letter to John Gielgud, Harley Granville-Barker was to call this book of memoirs 'the best of its sort I know'. He was reading Christopher St John's version which makes Ellen Terry's writing more grammatically stable and chronologically coherent. By omitting what Pinero had called 'thoughtless passages', she slightly alters the tone of the writing, though Ellen Terry's charm still pervades the narrative. In her book *Actresses on the Victorian Stage*, Gail Marshall argues that the cumulative effect of Christopher St John's solicitous interference had been to distort the text, giving greater prominence to Godwin, almost eradicating Charles Kelly, and ironing out Ellen Terry's eccentricities. It is also true that Christopher St John ignored the annotated revisions which Ellen herself made to her story after publication. But she used a number of Ellen's letters, some of which Edy had bought at auction, and these letters are probably a better guide to what she actually thought than her diplomatic revisions.

The last five chapters have a peculiar tension of their own. 'My collaborator, his [Gordon Craig's] sister, has asked me to refrain from any vindication', Christopher St John writes. Yet her whole being palpitates with the need to vindicate the woman she had adored and to exact punishment on that monstrous regiment of men whom Edy somehow 'stopped short of murdering'. Gordon Craig does not benefit from these additional chapters, though Christopher St John took credit for not showing us all his many warts and pimples. 'After all, he did no harm.'

But by this time Gordon Craig had been driven from the country by another woman: his ex-wife May. Left to bring up their four children alone and accept an allowance each month from Ellen Terry who, she knew, disliked her, May had developed into a hard-headed business woman. With her mother-in-law's financial help and under the name Mary Grey, she made a career for herself as a theatrical costumier at a shop in Baker Street. But she was still entitled to alimony as the innocent party in her divorce. Now aged sixty, she had never wholly recovered from the bitter disappointment of her marriage or overcome her anger at seeing her ex-husband protected by his mother. He appeared to float through life exempt from all the consequences of his actions. Her allowance from Ellen Terry had ceased in 1917. 'I'm very sorry (now) for May – she looked haggard & ill', Ellen had reported to Craig the following year. But after Ellen Terry died and Craig was receiving an income from her estate, he seemed vulnerable at last. May was earning £300 a year but her job could be terminated on one month's notice. She had not been named in Ellen Terry's will and knew that it would be impossible to get money directly from Craig himself. But in 1929 she proceeded with a petition for alimony and then, in 1931, while he was in England, obtained a garnishee order in the High Court, sequestering royalties from his United Kingdom publishers and seizing money from the Ellen Terry estate. Craig was incredulous. May was no better than a blackmailer who had been extracting 'money from me ever since' the beginning of the century. Having read that he was going into partnership with the celebrated promoter C.B. Cochran,* she had scented more money. 'She pursues the coin as though I could grow it', he complained in his diary. He

* At a dinner in 1926, Cochran had invited Craig to stage Shakespeare's *Henry V* with the famous actor-aviator Robert Loraine (who was also at the dinner) as King Henry. After several years of reflection, Craig told Cochran that the play did not appeal to him.

broke off negotiations with Cochran and refused to publish another book for twenty-five years, by which time May was dead. Having been advised by his lawyer that she had 'no chance while I don't make money in England', he decided to earn 'no more money than I can live on'. He was to pass the rest of his life in exile.

48

Good Night Unto You All

'I noticed a change in Edy after her mother's death.' In earlier days Chris believed she had resembled her father – judging from what she had been told was a portrait of him in Ford Madox Brown's picture, *The Last of England*. But during the 1930s her physical resemblance to her mother grew more apparent. She fell into some of her mother's ways too. Because of her rheumatism she took to using a stick and, though her sight was good, would sometimes falter and feel her way forwards as Ellen had done on her blind days.

'You are a bit alone I feel', her brother wrote. But Edy was gaining in authority. Looking like an eccentric eighteenth-century lady with brilliant white hair, she presided at the head of the table during meals. In the garden at Smallhythe, extending herself on a chaise longue, dressed in her flowing red linen smock and blue scarf, she had the air of a yacht at anchor. Though frail she was still active – never more so than when galloping around in her old bathchair. About ordinary matters – what day of the week it might be – she was vague, but would focus considerable concentration on details of her work: a button, a feather, the fold in a quilt or curtain.

In the wardrobe room upstairs she hung many of her mother's stage dresses, including the glittering green beetle-wing costume Ellen wore as Lady Macbeth, in which Sargent painted his famous portrait of her; and the 'merry pink' dress Edy had made to outshine Madge Kendal in Beerbohm Tree's production of *The Merry Wives of Windsor*. To these she added Henry Irving's scarlet robes of Cardinal Wolsey and a striking collage of him as Becket by the Beggarstaff Brothers. Along the corridor, in Ellen's bedroom, she placed the two school desks she and her brother had used when children. Downstairs she assembled all sorts of memorabilia from Ellen's contemporaries and predecessors – David Garrick and Edmund Kean, Sarah Bernhardt and Peg Woffington, a memorable picture of Eleonora Duse, and some turquoise earrings worn by Sarah Siddons, which had been given to Ellen by Marie Corelli. The library, full of theatre books and containing Irving's acting editions of Shakespeare, would become a place where visitors could 'study drama and the history of drama'. By the late 1930s Edy had made the farmhouse a perfect small museum – though Chris never overcame her dislike of visitors.

At the same time Edy took charge of the Elizabethan barn and in 1931 formed the Barn Theatre Society, largely financed by subscriptions. She believed that drama needed to escape from the traditional picture-frame stage and could involve an audience more directly when played in churches and priories, within parks, on pavements, even from the backs of carts or lorries. The Barn held a crowded 120 people, and Edy's productions there, with nosegays hanging from the rafters, rushes spread across the floor, the red fire buckets lined against the walls, swallows and swifts circling and swooping overhead, and harpsichord music playing in the intervals, had an air of improvisation. Here was the true spirit of theatre – 'the real thing', as the actress May Whitty called it. The actors dressed in the cottage, walked across the garden and spoke Shakespeare's lines on the intimate stage. 'In its strange mixture of professional and amateur, of gaiety and sadness – the ease of a country garden party and the solemnity of a tribute to a great artist, whose work was done in cities – it is amazingly fitting and right,' John Gielgud wrote to Edy in the mid-1930s, 'and I believe that Nell would have loved it as much as you and I do.' Edy used anything and everything – beads, spangles, suede, feathers, cheesecloth, flannel, clever paintwork on simple sacking – to create her effects. 'She'd turn over a lot of old junk in the theatrical clothes basket,' Sybil Thorndike remembered, 'pick out bits here

– bits there' and transform them into costumes and scenery. She knew how a costume should be worn – the turn of a collar, the cut of a coat, the fall of a skirt. She had a flair too for marshalling crowds of villagers and teaching children in her nativity plays how to be Holy Innocents. 'She never failed to pack a little dynamite among her luggage', the actress Margaret Webster wrote. During rehearsals she was sharp, outspoken, sometimes scathing. But Margaret Webster remembered 'being pulled out, made a little taller' during these rehearsals. 'There is something in the air – a positiveness. It makes you feel you want to do things – it makes you believe you really can.'

'You made me feel I could have played . . . Cleopatra!' says old Mrs Swithin to Miss La Trobe, the sturdy play-producer, in Virginia Woolf's *Between the Acts*. Though there is 'nothing private; no strict biographical facts' in the novel, Miss La Trobe owes her imaginative existence mainly to Edy Craig (though in a passage where she fixes black side-whiskers to a man and makes him look like King Arthur she momentarily brings to mind Julia Margaret Cameron). Miss La Trobe has the ability to awaken people's unacted parts. For 'we all act all parts'. Virginia Woolf, who applied to join the Barn Theatre Society in 1933, shows us a woman of wonderful energy, 'all agog to get things up'. She achieves much with very little, spreading a sheet on the lawn to represent a lake, preferring an old dishcloth to fine silk – finding it more useful. We see her striding around the fields like a commander pacing his deck. From scraps and fragments she creates her illusions. When these illusions succeed she glows; when they fail she despairs. She growls, beckons, bosses, shouts, crushing her play-manuscript as she battles with the elements, suffering triumph, humiliation, ecstasy, dejection. She is comical, tragic, ludicrous, heroic.

Alongside these productions at the Barn ran the drama of Edy's life with Chris and Tony. The sets against which this drama was played – a scattering of cottages, the small church, farm buildings and the Toll House, like upturned vessels stationed on the edge of land, crooked, tottering with age, built with ships' timbers, the oak iron-hard against the salt gales – had a fairy-tale atmosphere, as if they had all risen from the sea and might drift away one night on a centuries-old tide. It was the very place of places. In summer there were often children running around, Terry and Craig grandchildren, playing with the 'dear but not good' dog, the plethora of multicoloured cats and the fleet of thorny hedgehogs that had taken a fancy to

Chris. They would play hide-and-seek among the wagons, make themselves useful winding up buckets of precious water from the fascinating well and gather crab-apples in an orchard bright with tremulous sunlight flooding through the branches of the fruit trees. To these children, Smallhythe seemed a green and spectral place where the grown-ups wore sandals and bright smocks, drove around in a pony-and-cart, and sometimes slept on beds of hay.

Most of the people who camped there and joined Edy's band of supernumeraries were women. But there were also men. Many were homosexual, though there were bisexual men and women too, and even a few marriages among them – *mariages blancs* for the sake of friendship or convenience, and marriages by women who wanted children. Other women and some of the men too treated younger members of the community as the children they never had. Much teasing and gossip went on and there were moments of malice and uncertainty. But what helped to give stability to this milieu was the hostility and incomprehension of the world around them. At Smallhythe, they could breathe more easily. Here it was the conformist who felt an outsider.

The garden at Smallhythe, worked up from a potato patch, thrown down like an embroidered cloth on the edge of the marshlands, reflected this heterodoxy and charmed that great creator of gardens, Vita Sackville-West. 'Sometimes the crab-trees, rounded like great umbrellas, dripped with heavy violet fruit', she remembered; 'indeed they greatly resembled umbrellas, so perfectly shaped, with the fruit hanging all along the branches which were the ribs . . . sometimes the red-hot pokers speared a patch of shade; sometimes the lilies flanked the pathway like surpliced choristers down the church's nave; but whatever the season the garden held that particularity of character which made anything possible.'

'If ever I encountered in real life a character made for Shakespeare it was Christopher St John', wrote Vita. '. . . There is violence in this noble nature. It is as easy to imagine her raging battle-axe in hand against false idols, as to imagine her in a medieval monastery, scrupulously bent over the illuminated capitals of a manuscript.' This boisterous scholar was now a massive character 'with a huge posterior kept together by very tight corduroy trousers straining at the seams', remembered the architectural historian James Lees-Milne. By contrast, Tony Atwood appeared 'pretty and slight' though completely disguised by men's clothes – usually a duck jacket and curry-coloured tweed trousers shaded by an enormous panama hat. She would potter around the garden like an illustration of some tropical tea-planter who had wandered into the wrong book.

All of them had nicknames, many nicknames. Chris was 'Master Baby' and Tony 'the Brat' and the two of them collectively were known as 'the serfs' and sometimes 'the Matka's Boys', Edy herself being 'the Matka' and occasionally 'Boney'. In later years another companion joined the encampment, a 'rather terrifying' woman called Mrs Seal and known as 'Bruce', who occupied the Toll House. She lived there rent-free in return for domestic services at Priest's House. 'I remember her wearing on her big head a minute beret Basque and leaning over the lower section of the stable-like door of Toll Cottage, brawny arms akimbo, in a very defiant attitude, to all the world resembling a bull ruminating whether to emerge and charge the spectator', James Lees-Milne nervously observed. She always called her neighbours Mr Chris and Mr Tony, and despite her aggressive posture, 'her status in the colony was relatively subordinate'.

The only person without a nickname – virtually without a name – was the handyman who was called on to confront emergencies. For a brief period when Edy owned a motor-car (called Belinda), this generic man performed as chauffeur, Edy climbing into the front seat beside him, 'the serfs' ganging up at the back, and a sprinkling of miscellaneous guests perched swaying in the dickey. But Belinda rapidly aged and latterly Edy relied on her niece Olive, that motorist of Brooklands calibre, to whirl her around the Kent countryside.

In the summer of 1931 two new friends began visiting Smallhythe, the novelist Radclyffe Hall (originally called Marguerite but now known as John) and her companion Una Troubridge, a sculptor separated from the admiral, her husband, who had infected her with venereal disease. The two of them lived six or seven miles away across the county border in Rye. A flamboyant character who smoked small green cigars, Radclyffe Hall had gained notoriety after her lesbian novel *The Well of Loneliness*, described by the *Sunday Express* as 'unutterable putrefaction', had successfully been prosecuted under the 1857 Obscene Publications Act.

Meeting 'the famous trio' at Smallhythe 'immediately roused her spirits', Radclyffe Hall's biographer Sally Cline writes. She liked the way they 'outraged everyone's expectations', and she enjoyed the sheer chaos of the entertainments there – everything from marvellous Shakespeare scenes played by John Gielgud, Peggy Ashcroft and Edith Evans (the only actress with the moral courage, Edy believed, to have stood up to her mother) to curious jumble sales featuring Chris's shrunken vests and 'things of unthinkable dilapidation . . . ready for decent cremation'. She also liked Edy's friends: the noisy Vera 'Jack' Holme, once an imprisoned suffragette, who came to help with the Barn theatricals; and the ex-Slade School student Winifred Ashton who, turning to novels and playwriting, used the pen-name Clemence Dane.

Their many names appeared to give them the lives of shape-shifters and changelings. Like 'the mechanicals' in *A Midsummer Night's Dream* (which was performed at the Barn Theatre in 1929) they appeared free to choose their gender, change their character, alter their very identities. And so transform the Barn Theatre into the Palace of Theseus, as King Oberon might do, let the trumpets flourish, and Edy will enter as Peter Quince, the carpenter, who delivers the prologue and allots the parts. Snout, the tinker's part, is obviously Tony's: she will make an irreproachable Wall when the others come to blows. And Bottom, the weaver, crowned with his ass's head, is inevitably Chris, who will play the part of Pyramus and wants to play all the other parts too, including Moonshine and the Lion. And finally, as the deus ex machina, step forward Vita Sackville-West, to take the role of Titania, Queen of the Fairies, who for one incredible moment will find herself infatuated by Bottom and will play Thisbe in Quince's play.

Vita Sackville-West came to Smallhythe in September 1932. Attired in her breeches, she read her poem *The Land* from the stage of the Barn Theatre. Her husband, the diplomat man of letters Harold Nicolson, thought the performance 'very enjoyable', though some younger members of the audience (among them Stephen Spender and William Plomer) were 'overcome by giggles', having read the recent parody of Vita's poem in Roy Campbell's *The Georgiad*:

> Write with your spade and garden with your pen.
> Shovel your couplets to their long repose
> And type your turnips down the field in rows.

A prologue to the melodrama should tell us that Vita had recently been abandoned by her great love, Evelyn Irons (a graduate, like Chris, of Somerville College), who had left her for another woman. Adept at concealment, Vita hid her unhappiness from those around her – even from her husband and Virginia Woolf. Only one person saw through her cheerful mask, and this was Christopher St John.

The drama opened when, shortly after her recitation of *The Land*, Vita invited Edy, Chris and Tony over to Sissinghurst Castle. She and her husband Harold were restoring this romantic pile, renovating its Gothic tower, its library, the Priest's House and the cottages, and integrating them all into the famous gardens they were laying out: the rose garden, the white garden and the herb garden; the yew walk, the lime walk and the moat walk; the nuttery and orchard. But standing amid this great archaeological re-creation, Vita appeared to Chris 'a tragic figure . . . All this beauty of environment, and she is not happy.'

Vita took the three of them around the castle and to her bedroom. Contemplating a worn piece of green velvet on her dressing-table, 'I felt my whole being dissolve in love', Chris declared. '*I have never ceased to love her from that moment.*' The more she contemplated Vita, the more confident Chris felt that here was a frightened woman. She could tell from the very irises of her eyes that Vita was not normal. Normal people – those insensitive ones – made such narrow rules for happiness. Vita was altogether different. Wherever she went, she let in light and passion, opening up all sorts of possibilities. That day she took Chris over to the Long Barn at Sissinghurst and, walking together, she let her hold her hand, consoling her for the loss of Evelyn Irons. 'I can see her now lying on the straw in her flame-coloured coat', Chris wrote in her love-journal for Vita. '. . . There was a moment when she came near me, knelt by my side & supported her arms on my lap. It was as if a wave had swept over me . . . Yes, I did think intermittently from that day, that I had kindled a spark of love in her.' Then Vita gave her a string of blue Persian beads which Chris accepted as a token of her love, keeping it in her pocket by day and placing it beside her bed at night. 'I acknowledged her as my lord. I wanted to be her faithful servant.'

Early that November, Vita came to visit Edy's flat in Bedford Street and, her biographer Victoria Glendinning tells us, she 'allowed Christopher to come with her in the car all the way to Tonbridge, where she was put on a train back to London'. Travelling over Westminster Bridge, she had confided that 'the list of those whom she really loved was a short one, and now I was on it'. Then, stretching out her hand and touching her, Vita said: 'I do love you – for all you give me.' At the end of their car journey, she parked in a dusky side-street near Tonbridge station and 'gave me a lover's kiss', Chris wrote. 'In all my dreams of her I never dreamed of that . . .'

A day or two later Chris wrote her first love letter. 'I can never think of your sex, only of your humanity. I could love you in breeches, or in skirts, or in any other garments, or in none . . . I don't think of you as a woman, or as a man either. Perhaps as someone who is both, the complete human being who transcends both.' This was how Virginia Woolf presented Vita in her recently published novel *Orlando* – and why Chris was to address her letters to 'My Lord Orlando'.

Shortly before Christmas, Vita allowed Chris a single night of love. Then she set off with her husband on a three-month lecture tour of the United States. Probably she intended this night together to be no more than a mark of gratitude for the comfort Chris had brought her. But the effect was devastating – all the more so because it came at a time when, having published the Shaw correspondence with Ellen Terry and completed the new edition of Ellen Terry's memoirs, Chris's work as 'literary henchman' to the Terry family had come to an end. Although Edy still adjudicated plays, directed one or two charity performances and gave a few talks at universities around the country during the 1930s, she increasingly confined herself to Smallhythe – and Chris wrote no new plays for her. She had ceased writing for *Time and Tide* in the early 1930s, but in 1935 she did publish a short biography of Christine Murrell, an ardent feminist and distinguished doctor who succeeded in storming 'the apparently impregnable male fortress' of the medical profession. She was, Chris wrote, 'a woman of massive frame, a virile woman, whose irreproachable feminine clothes seemed incongruous' and who never married 'because she was not the sort of woman who has a natural chemical affinity with a man'. This was a good subject for her, but the book did not command large sales. So 'I am hoping the Lord will provide'. Much of her career had been passed 'writing what I've been asked to write', but now 'I long to burn my boats – give up pot-boiling', she told a friend. She wanted to write fiction again – something more radical than *Hungerheart*, something bolder than *The Crimson Weed* and even braver than Radclyffe Hall's *The Well of Loneliness* – something that would destroy for ever the nonsense about it 'being impossible for any woman to deny her nature which is to love a man. I must before I die write on this subject.' But she never did. 'Writing of any kind – even a letter – is a terrible effort at the present time', she told one of her friends in the autumn of 1936. 'Feel mentally *chained*. Some "inhibition" I suppose.'

Her writings over the previous quarter of a century – the monographs on Henry Irving and Ellen Terry and the Shakespeare lectures she drafted for Ellen – had brought a patina of calm to her life. Writing 'forbids me to hate', she said. 'Or, rather . . . takes away the power and possibility of hating.' Nevertheless she was aware of a volcanic anger within her. 'I choose the evil so often,' she confessed, 'so very often.'

What carried her through in the past had been the beneficent power of her religion and the good fortune of knowing Edy. In 1911, after her return from Rome, she had composed a love-journal for Edy – 'The Golden Book' she called it. 'I shall write in it only what I want her to know and say no word of the many things I had rather keep hidden', she wrote on the opening page. '. . . The instinct that bids us not to force our small uglinesses upon others is so deep-rooted that it seems as if Nature herself must have planted it. So I do not say everything, even to Edy.'

'The Golden Book' reveals the immense gratitude Chris had come to feel for Edy. 'She gives me so much & I can give her nothing but black word on white paper', she wrote. 'I pray very earnestly that I may bring nothing but good in her life – nothing ugly, or mean, or selfish.' But undeniably she felt 'a little coarser, a little lower, a good deal more earthy'. The difference between them could be purged, Chris believed, by her religion and eventually eliminated by age itself which would extinguish her unsatisfied desires. In the meantime there were tremors of wickedness when, feeling herself agonisingly unfulfilled, she would hurt Edy 'with all my strength'. In 'The Golden Book' she sought to atone for such episodes. 'More than once I have made the tears come to my darling's brown eyes because of what I have said or done to her. When I think of this I am ashamed; & I am also ashamed when I think how wonderfully she loves me . . . [But] I feel sometimes as if I was waiting for something.'

She was waiting for Vita. She had never known 'unalloyed bliss' before that lover's kiss in the car. And after their 'night of love' she looked forward to an enduring physical passion that had been absent from her relationship with Edy. 'You do love me, don't you?' Vita had asked. And Chris replied: 'More than words can say.' But, as Victoria Glendinning writes: 'Vita did not love Christopher.'

Chris had expected Vita to seek her out swiftly after she and Harold returned from the United States. They did come to Smallhythe, the husband and the wife, that 'well-graced pair', and gave one of their practised performances, 'Impressions of America', at the Barn Theatre, Harold strolling around the stage, Vita seated at a desk, the two of them speaking as naturally as if they were at home. Chris sat there in torment. 'Don't say you are disappointed in me', Vita had written from the boat on her return voyage from America. 'I couldn't bear that. There is no one in whose estimation I would rather stand high than in yours.' Chris copied this down in her love-journal for Vita. Such compliments were all very well, though 'I wasn't disappointed in *her*,' she noted, 'but in the development of our relationship'.

It might have been better had she been disappointed. But Vita's aristocratic place in society miraculously raised her above such feelings. For as Edy observed, Chris was a romantically inclined conservative with deeply planted loyalties in the glamorous past as well as a radical agenda for the future. Vita can have had no idea of the passion she had let loose the previous year. All the inhibitions and discretions that had been ingredients of Chris's life with Edy were discarded. 'I have ceased to be young and to look on the world with eyes that are young', Chris had concluded. She had recognised this without ever quite accepting it. For it was not true. With Vita she seemed to regain the passion of her youth.

Reading the amorous letters Chris sent her (she claimed to have written 200 of them), Vita realised that something must be done to bring a resolution to their relationship. So one June day in the summer of 1933 she took her for a drive in the car – that car with its memories. 'I loved you so dearly that day', Chris wrote in her love-journal. 'Shall we ever have another night together?' she had asked. Vita's courage must have failed her – or else she thought an offhand answer would convey the truth less brutally. 'Why not?' she said. So they drove on, Chris 'longing to reach through her body to her innermost heart'.

Vita had probably been told of Chris's previous attempts at suicide and was seeking a safe arrangement. She invited her to make regular visits to Sissinghurst Castle that autumn to teach her son Ben calligraphy. What she did not say was that she would be careful never to find herself alone with Chris again – though she would continue to invite her over with Edy and Tony, and remain loyal to the three of them.

Despite these precautions, Chris grew more demanding. By the end of 1933 it became clear to her that everything was over. Vita wrote to explain that she was 'deeply in love' with her sister-in-law Gwen St Aubyn, who had recently had a bad car accident. This 'dread letter' showed that Vita 'gave me her body without her heart', Chris wrote. Both Edy and Tony were alarmed by her state of mind. There were 'terrible scenes' between the three of them at Smallhythe – scenes that horrified their friends. Radclyffe Hall and Una Troubridge did what they could to alleviate Chris's 'atrocious suffering' and protect the others from its disastrous effects. But entering this emotional war zone was a perilous business. They had been thinking of building a house near their friends until they heard the usually mild-mannered Tony – that diplomatic Wall so extensively battered between Chris and Edy – firmly reject them: 'We can't possibly have a house out here!'

Edy had never admired Vita – she couldn't even be trusted to sharpen a pencil properly. Among their friends it was the composer Ethel Smyth who helped Chris to recover, gallantly assailing Vita as a Pharaoh who had hardened her heart. Gradually the turmoil subsided, though 'I haven't known what it is to be happy for nearly two years', Chris told her friend Mary Eversley ('Mary Query' as she was nicknamed) in the summer of 1935. As late as 1936, in her love-journal, Chris was to condemn Vita's book, *Saint Joan of Arc*, as 'insufferably patronising' – and then go on to publish a bitter attack on it in the *New Statesman*. Vita was simply 'weak and wavering', full of 'feeble jocularity', and her book had obviously been corrupted by that 'dissolute child' Gwen St Aubyn. But she still loved Vita. Over twenty years later, when making her will, she was to appoint 'the Hon. Lady Nicolson (Hon. V. Sackville-West)' her literary executor, leave her 'my Caroline Chair and Black Mirror' and pass on that time bomb, her love-journal.

What finally re-established stability at Smallhythe was a crisis in Edy's life. She had kept events going at the Barn Theatre through these most awkward and demanding times. On her visits to London, she also found time to organise a pilgrimage of more than fifty members of the Lyceum Company to Henry Irving's tomb in Westminster Abbey to commemorate the centenary of his birth; and at Stratford-upon-Avon she presented a death mask and cast of Ellen Terry's hands to the Shakespeare Memorial Theatre. She directed several revivals of *The Shoe*, her play for children made up from nursery rhymes and set to music (in one of which Lady Diana Cooper made her first appearance onstage). She could be seen at these performances bent acutely sideways in much pain and shaking with tears of laughter. Working in the theatre brought back her strength. Her pencil beat the air with its accustomed ferocity; her commanding voice rang out across the fields with its old tyrannical insistence. More taxing for her were the talks she was invited to give: on 'the performance of plays' at Liverpool, and on 'the theatre as a building' at Cheltenham. She had fallen quite seriously ill late in 1932 when Chris first became infatuated with Vita. Then, early in 1937, shortly after giving a speech at Glasgow on her suffrage work, she caught pneumonia and came near to dying. The thought of Edy's death 'has frozen my blood', Chris wrote. Edy was the 'beloved person' who 'has been the partner in my life since I was 23 – all to me that is meant by home and family – a never-failing refuge in trouble'. Chris and Tony sat by Edy's bed until 'she is now out of danger and making what the doctors call "satisfactory progress" ', Chris wrote on 10 March – describing herself as 'joyfully relieved from terrible anxiety'.

Edy had paid tributes to many of her predecessors and it was now time, her friends realised, for them to pay tribute to her. In the autumn of 1938, a few weeks short of her seventieth year, she was given a celebratory dinner at the Savoy Hotel in recognition of fifty years' work in the theatre. Sybil Thorndike read out a congratulatory message from Queen Mary, and among the ten speakers – costumiers, actors, playwrights, directors – Cicely Hamilton recalled how Edy loved thrusting her into 'impossible situations' such as suddenly conducting an orchestra; and another speaker remembered a young assistant at one of Edy's pageants declare: 'Oh! I *liked* her. She's rude!' At the end of the dinner, Violet Vanbrugh presented Edy with a cheque and a scroll signed by 200 of her colleagues.

But it was obvious that she could not manage the museum and theatrical work at Smallhythe much longer. It was Vita who advised her to contact the National Trust through the person of James Lees-Milne, 'who deals with houses'. This she did in March 1938 with a letter written by her solicitor-friend, Irene Cooper Willis. Unfortunately, as was its custom, the National

Trust had no money. But when explaining this, James Lees-Milne added that he would nevertheless very much like to visit the property. He was invited down that May by Chris representing herself as 'the normal intermediary between Miss Craig and the outside world'.

He drove through Appledore along the narrow hedgerows and across the Levels between the Isle of Oxney and the heights of Tenterden until he saw the tiny hamlet with its 'cluster of half-timbered buildings and a crow-stepped church of red brick'. He already knew that this had been a small landing-place or inland harbour during the sixteenth century when the Rother was still navigable as far as Smallhythe. Now, in the early summer, the river was scarcely more than a trickle, though another strip of water known as the Dock lay to the south of the house. 'With its dappled russet roof, walls of packed timber beams, an upper storey overhanging the lower, the house had been a yeoman's dwelling for centuries', he wrote, '. . . built probably early in Henry VIII's reign, as the headquarters of the harbour-master.' He looked around all the adjacent buildings Ellen Terry had acquired: Priest's House beside the church; the Barn, the Toll House and Yew Tree Cottage, coeval with the farm and immediately facing it on the opposite side of the road.

'I was wholly captivated by the seclusion of the place,' he wrote, 'the picturesqueness of the buildings and setting, the fascination of the shrine, the charm of the elderly ladies, and the casual happy-go-lucky spirit that prevailed. I have seldom walked through rooms more nostalgic of a particular owner.' When the time came to leave, he felt the unlikely sensation of being almost 'in love' with the three 'trouts' (the name coined for them by Vita Sackville-West). Had they put a potion in his coffee? Later he came to realise that he had possibly made a mistake in describing the 'formidable and rather rebarbative' Edy, the 'frankly ugly' Chris, and the obstinately mute Tony as 'dear old souls'.

He was to send in a very favourable report on Smallhythe. 'In Ellen Terry's little house one feels she might walk past one at any minute, and in her bedroom that she might appear before her dressing-table brushing her hair.' But he did not believe the National Trust could possibly accept such a property. The outgoings exceeded the income from visitors each year, some of the buildings were in urgent need of repair and no endowment was being offered. Moreover, in the event of Edy's death, Priest's House was still to remain the home of Chris and Tony, not passing to the Trust until they too had died. There were simply too many disadvantages. Yet the National Trust did accept Smallhythe with all Edy's conditions (none of her mother's belongings was to be moved one inch). The gift was formally made in 1939 and there was to have been a ceremony which had to be postponed because of the war.

Edy was determined that this war should not interfere with her theatrical projects in the Barn – certainly not with the most significant of them on her mother's birthday. It was, of course, more difficult to recruit actors – so many of them seemed to be abroad. 'I went there many times during the war years, when bombs and incendiaries were falling night after night and there were so many shattered farms on the marshes', remembered Irene Cooper Willis. Edy sometimes thought of moving into the farm itself to guard its treasures from the bombs. At other times she got out an old perambulator packed with essentials and prepared to scoot down the road with it ahead of the enemy. The bangs and crashes all around them occasionally grew so loud, so near, that the three of them ate their supper under the table. Between meals, Tony would patrol the streets carrying out mild fire duties; Chris would position herself in the garden armed with a spade; while indoors Edy continued with her work, creating marvels with pieces of string, strips of elastic, pins and paste. There was no petrol now, but people came by bicycle and on foot, with their horses, farm carts and pony-traps. Her letters to them, full of orders and errands, were written in her director's style: 'Send down all the curtains you can find . . . Where is the Chinese Robe? And don't forget the beefsteak. I want my green Woolworth case with note paper in it . . . Jumble sale next Wednesday – where is your jumble? I want a pair of silky pyjamas large size for Chris . . . Ask Tony to bring down my coloured inks.' When the messengers arrived, Edy's voice would ring out telling them all what to do and not to do. This was her loyal army of amateurs on whom she worked her magic. Even in the darkest days of the war, 'the Memorial kept its doors open', recorded Allan Wade.

It was difficult for Edy not to blame the National Trust for the war. Using Chris as her notary, provisioning her with a bottle of red ink, she laid all the wartime inconveniences at the Trust's door – the ration books, bombs and so on. The bundles of documents that were sent to her by way of reply provoked fresh outbursts of panic. She wondered what the National Trust planned to do about the noise of those guns at Dover and the 'high-flying air army over Kent'. She welcomed the guard of seven men posted at the bridge over the Rother, which she assumed was their personal staff. But the complaints mounted. What about the rats – the ones that were undermining the stone foundations of the house and making it rock? Also, would the National Trust intercept the Black Maria that was probably coming to take Edy to prison for the non-payment of her rates – or was it her insurance? They must insist, too, that the officers of the Trust protect them from any allied troops who might be billeted on them – perhaps it would be best if the Trust bought up the surrounding land. And what seemed so extraordinary was that Edy won her battles with the National Trust, which paid out money here and money there for repairs and services for which it was not liable, Vita Sackville-West having arranged for financial help to be given anonymously. All this was done under the belief that the three of them were destitute, whereas Edy would leave almost £15,000 when she died in the late 1940s and Tony more than £30,000 in the early 1960s.

James Lees-Milne did not open his arms to everyone. But however naughtily Edy and her friends behaved, he could not help liking them. 'Left for Smallhythe', his diary entry for 26 March 1942 reads. 'Miss Edith Craig was in bed, but the other two old ladies were about . . . Their grey locks were hacked short and both wore tam o'shanters. They were charming to me . . .'

Chris was being taken under the wing of her recent champion, the vehement and rebellious composer Ethel Smyth, then in her young eighties. They had first met at Bedford Street in 1911 when Chris was obliged to listen to her condemnation of Ellen Terry's acting and of all Catholics – 'a feeble lot, especially if they are converts'. Ethel had nearly been converted to Catholicism herself but, she informed Chris, writing her Mass in D had 'sweated it out of me'.

'I did not take to Ethel at this first meeting', Chris remembered. The daughter of a soldier, Ethel Smyth had been a terrific battler all her life. Her battle to win a career for herself in music was soon caught up in a larger battle for the political emancipation of women. During the suffrage campaign, many militant suffragettes had paraded the streets to the beat of her 'March of the Women'. It was impossible not to warm to an inveterate crusader who conducted this march with her toothbrush from a window in Holloway jail. Chris did not meet her again until the 1920s when, as music critic for *Time and Tide*, she wrote 'some flattering notices of Ethel's compositions'. After that she was accepted as a friend, though their friendship did not become close until 1934 when Ethel, 'like the Assyrian wolf', had come down on an astonished Vita Sackville-West 'and spent the afternoon savaging the culprit' for ill-treating Chris. Then in the early 1940s, when Ethel was drafting her will, she asked Chris to be her literary executor. 'I am leaving you everything', she declared, pointing to rows of uninviting files on a shelf above her mantelpiece. She offered Chris £30 to bring some sort of order to these papers after her death. Chris hesitated while Ethel stood waiting for her answer. But how could she refuse this lonely old woman, 'cut off by her deafness and her infirmity' from her friends? So she stammered out a not very enthusiastic consent and 'got the only embrace she ever gave me'.

Ethel Smyth died in May 1944 at the age of eighty-six. Not long afterwards, Chris went over by train to her house in Woking to make a list of what she had been left – a surprisingly large quantity of letters, articles, notebooks and diaries. 'It required some pluck to make the journey', she remembered, '. . . as this was the time when the "doodle-bugs" were rampant. Several people had been killed by one of these bombs the day before at the Waterloo ticket office.' She arranged for the archive to be taken to Priest's House and, assisted by Edy, settled down to sort the papers. It was good to be working again, though the work was often interrupted by Edy's ill-health. Many of Chris's letters have the same refrain: 'Edy not at all well – I am worried about her.'

Edy had celebrated the end of the war with a parade of Ellen Terry's stage costumes on Shakespeare's birthday. During the spring and early summer of 1946 she staged several small plays in Tenterden and directed a pageant at Chilham. But, suffering from a weak heart and being in continual pain from arthritis, she could do nothing more that year. At the end of February 1947, disobeying her doctor's orders and feeling far from well, she left her bed and with Chris and Tony made her last journey to London to celebrate the centenary of Ellen Terry's birth at St Paul's, Covent Garden. 'Although a bitterly cold and foggy day it was a joyful occasion', James Lees-Milne remembered. 'The three trouts were prominent in the front pew, Chris St John "wearing a fawn teddy-bear coat, a man's pork-pie hat, and waving a gigantic bunch of golden daffodils at her friends in the rear". The church was crammed with stage celebrities, some of whom read lessons, while others recited from Shakespeare.'

On her return to Smallhythe Edy began having fits of giddiness. 'We kept her in bed during the spell of cold weather as her bedroom was the only room we could keep warm', Chris wrote. By March her doctor ominously pronounced her to be 'much better'. She was full of plans for a summer event at the Barn Theatre, something really splendid celebrating the centenary of Ellen Terry's birth. They would do such things, Shakespearean things . . . she looked positively well as she spoke of them. On the morning of 27 March she was particularly cheerful. Then, suddenly, she died.

It was 'without pain', Tony wrote – indeed, it was a relief from pain. She had been discussing a Shakespeare event for the Barn Theatre when she broke off, murmuring: 'It's all dark. Who put out the light?' Tony and Chris hurried to her bedside and held her hands while a neighbour tried to pour some brandy down her throat. She breathed twice, it seemed – and then the light went out. The doctor arrived and assured them that there was nothing he could have done. Olive, Edy's cousin who lived at Tenterden, was the witness on the death certificate.

'The others will miss her sadly', John Gielgud told his mother. In a letter to Gordon Craig, Chris wrote the following day: 'I will not speak of my own grief . . . I would like to assure you that it was solely from love of Edy that I got angry with you when you seemed to me not to appreciate her character and gifts – & failed to show her brotherly affection.' Over the last year, however, while working on his memoirs, he had been sending charming letters to his sister as he sought to recover their childhood years together. Edy would look up dates and chase after facts for him – and this, Chris acknowledged, 'made her happy . . . I doubt if anyone in the world had a warmer appreciation of your genius.' Though she did not wish to write of her grief, Chris could not hold back. 'It is as if half myself had been torn away, and that I shall have to live now with the other and worser half. We have been together for 47 years – Tony who joined us in 1916 – cemented rather than loosened the bonds of our friendship', she continued her letter. '. . . The fact is I still find it incredible that Edy has gone – it may be a mercy for her that she was cut down with such appalling suddenness, but [this] does make it worse for the living who loved her, to whom she was the dearest thing in life.'

Craig answered with one of his imaginative letters. 'Don't get dim,' he urged her. 'The longer I live the more my thoughts turn with young joy towards ET, EWG, EDY – *each night* last thing these three names, Mother, Father & old Edy as we called her (as I called her when a schoolboy), these 3 names are sounded in the dark. And then I feel light – gay – nothing dim at all. So (I feel) you may very soon begin to revive – I may say that may I not?' He also petitioned her as a 'WRITER and friend' on 'how to tackle certain themes in my memoirs: for I have to face up to them . . . "Respectability" – "Love – children" & I ought to be a clearer, *clearer*, clearer writer as you are.'

Edy was cremated on the last day of March and her funeral held at the little brick church, St John the Baptist, where almost twenty years before, her mother's funeral had taken place. The congregation of 'stage celebrities' which had so recently attended Ellen Terry's centenary at St Paul's, Covent Garden, travelled down for this sadder ceremony. 'The two surviving old ladies were extremely upset', James Lees-Milne wrote. Tony had told him that they needed no help since they were being looked after by Olive. Nevertheless he felt drawn back to Smallhythe that spring and reported that they 'are infinitely pathetic and, if possible, worse off than they were in Miss Craig's lifetime'. They begged him to let the National Trust manage everything 'as though they were already dead'. The farmhouse was in a chaotic state, Yew Tree Cottage lay empty, the Toll House was soon to be burnt to the ground, the timbers of Priest's House were rotting away and the Barn itself had become dangerously insecure. Like a discreet army of occupation, the National Trust moved in its builders and decorators, adding a bathroom, water-closet and a switchboard to the farmhouse, driving away more rats, renovating all the properties and making a generous donation for the restoration of the Barn Theatre. By 10 August the Barn stood ready. Three women were celebrated at the first festival since Edy's death: Ellen Terry, Edy herself and Virginia Woolf, whose essay on Ellen Terry (written shortly before her own death in 1941) was read aloud by Vita Sackville-West. Sybil Thorndike's address that day, which paid tribute to Chris and Tony as well as to Ellen and Edy, was later to be published in a volume of recollections with the simple title *Edy*. 'I am sure you will like Vita's contribution', Chris wrote to her friend Mary Doncaster. 'I fear mine is too poignant. I was grief-stricken when I wrote it . . . I have never got over the loss of her. She was certainly my better-half.'

On 24 July 1949, at a ceremony long delayed by the war and many post-war complications, the contents of the museum were formally accepted by Vita Sackville-West on behalf of the National Trust. An Ellen Terry Fellowship had been created and everything, it seemed, placed on a firm foundation for the future. Chris looked around her, saw how everything had been made, and behold, it was really very bad. And Tony agreed with her. Whatever the National Trust did, they opposed it, like children quarrelling with their parents. 'They never ceased to complain to all and sundry, especially at Sissinghurst, how the Trust did nothing for them', James Lees-Milne discovered. But they were old and full of grief. In 'The Golden Book' Chris had speculated over what might happen when one of them died before the other.

> My dream is of a place where the silence is like velvet; where I shall come first, and where I shall be allowed to lie for a while with my eyes shut, very tired. Those who see me so lying will pass me by gently; except one or two who have loved me, who will sit by me, waiting; so that when at the last, I shall open my eyes, they shall rest on the known & the desired.

Smallhythe itself appeared to become that velvet place. It had grown 'oppressive', Marguerite Steen wrote, 'a theatrical Lourdes jealously policed by Christopher St John and Clare Atwood, self-appointed temple virgins, whose unauthorised interference reduced curators to despair'. The first curator, a charming woman engaged with Chris and Tony's approval, was soon driven away by their hostility. They were rude to her simply because she was not Edy and this made them angry.

To everyone's relief the position was taken by Olive. She was not a woman to be easily intimidated. As Florence Terry's rebellious child she had been expelled from her boarding school at Lausanne and, at the age of eighteen, begun an acting career touring with her aunt Marion Terry. But during a performance of Laurence Irving's version of Brieux's *Les Hannetons*, she fell in love with the actor-manager Sir Charles Hawtrey. He was almost three times her age, a master of comedy blessed with wonderfully immobile features that were especially effective, it was said, when playing errant husbands. He himself married twice and, though producing no children with either of his wives, did in 1906 have a son by Olive – the pale, spectacularly good-looking Anthony Hawtrey whose birth is overlooked in Charles

Hawtrey's posthumous autobiography, *The Truth at Last.* After several hopeless years pursuing this errant comedian with writs, Olive had married a man called Charles Chaplin by whom she had 'a nice little black baby, dark and curly, with a delicate heart'. Latterly she had taken up with a new inamorata – a young woman artist described by Chris as looking 'like a nice little Eton boy'.

Olive knew Smallhythe well. She was not Edy herself, of course, but a blood relative whom Edy had admired – and someone with whom Chris could not quarrel without doing violence to Edy's memory. Cataloguing the library, restructuring the farmhouse, letting light into the rooms, she was, in the opinion of James Lees-Milne, a perfect custodian. 'It probably contains more personal associations with a great figure of the past than any museum in the land', he wrote. 'And of course it is not really a museum at all but a home.'

The visitors who came to this home sometimes felt they were in the presence of Ellen Terry. Over the years Olive appeared to become her living image. 'Draped in one of her aunt's Tyrian robes, one would say it is Ellen, moving through the mottled sunlight', Marguerite Steen observed. '. . . Ellen with her smile full of amusement moves in her niece's shadow, prompting her with a nudge or a wink when Olive's memory gives out under the barrage of questions she is called upon to answer. "Go on: make something up!" '

Chris soon vacated the battlefield and retreated deep into Priest's House. 'I need the sun', she had written when younger. 'Summer has all too short a date.' But now she lived in winter shadows. Locking the door, she gathered Ethel Smyth's papers around her and began writing her Life. Ethel Smyth had not asked her to write a biography – she had written a good half-dozen autobiographical volumes herself. But one or two people had mentioned the possibility and Chris felt it might be helpful. Writing had often steered her through difficult times.

It was to be fifteen years since the day she had dodged the 'doodle-bugs' and begun to make an inventory of Ethel Smyth's archive that her book was finally published. 'One of the worst trials of old age is that one gets slower & slower as the time passes quicker & quicker', she explained to a bookseller. The book is partly an anthology with quotations from Ethel Smyth's diaries, partly a composite biography with contributions from other writers.

Several figures from Chris's past make their appearance – one of them her early love, the harpsichordist Violet Gordon Woodhouse, with whom Ethel had also become infatuated. The book is dedicated to Clare Nielson, an exhilarating companion who had once occupied Yew Tree Cottage and was valuable for rather more than 'the faultless typing' noted in the acknowledgements. Among the personal recollections are six pages contributed by Vita Sackville-West, ostensibly on Ethel Smyth's writings about which, she protests, Chris knew more than herself. For she must have entered 'the overcrowded attics of Ethel's mind', Vita reasoned. 'I imagine Christopher, like some enchanted child given the free run of the galleries under the roof, turning over the extraordinary assemblage of lumber, the accumulation of a lifetime, and a very long life at that; miscellaneous objects as in a theatrical storeroom, but all authentic and human.'

This description of the book fitted all too literally the awful accumulation of lumber within Priest's House during Chris and Tony's last years there. A pungent smell pervaded the rooms – neither woman risked a bath. 'Baths indeed!' Chris exclaimed. 'I can do without 'em. A towel & a bottle of eau de cologne are excellent substitutes.' The spirit of Edy seemed to float upon this thick atmosphere – 'she often gives us advice and guidance.' In her will, Chris bequeathed all her money to the Ellen Terry Fellowship – whatever else she possessed, beyond a few specific items destined for Vita, being passed on to Tony. She must have regretted that Edy had been cremated, particularly since Olive mislaid her ashes which lay for years in a tin box with a request that they be scattered on her two friends' graves (Chris herself had shown little patience with James Carew's ashes when they arrived at Smallhythe in 'a nasty little box', putting them quickly on the rubbish dump – and Olive was to burn his correspondence with Ellen).

Tony 'has been my ALL since Edy left us – my joy & my solace', Chris declared. In 1951 Tony went into hospital to have a hysterectomy. 'Thank God she got through,' Chris wrote, 'thanks to her splendid constitution and her calm courage.' In November 1955 it was Chris's turn to go into hospital after a bad fall and though 'this makes things difficult' and 'I am never as well as before', she too came through. What they both minded most was being unable to paint or write. In the summer of 1960, suffering from senility, Chris was moved to the West View Hospital at Tenterden where she gained a fearsome reputation for throwing her lunch trays at the nurses (though she became a different person, coherent, happy and talkative, when the actor Donald Sinden came to visit her). She was to die there of pneumonia on 20 October 1960, four days short of her ninetieth year. Tony, who died almost two years later at the age of ninety-six, had bought a small plot in a corner of the churchyard at Smallhythe where she and Chris were to be buried in graves next to each other, Chris having made a request for her stone Madonna to be placed between them. It is no longer there.

49
White Candle, Aged Face

'I don't grieve – but I shall grieve', Gordon Craig wrote after he heard of his sister's death. He could hardly believe that Edy had been in her late seventies. 'Our friendship (E & I) was an ideal thing from year 1 to year 20 or so,' he told his son Edward, ' – then a large gap – and it became ideal again about two months ago – and we both looked forward to ending as we began.' They ended as 'Dear old boy' and 'Dear old girl' without ever having grown old in their knowledge and experience of each other. 'She was a dream', he concluded.

When he looked back at his sister he saw 'the same preference for being lost as I had', though never lost when alone. She needed plenty of noise from the next room to remind her she still belonged to the world – and perhaps she needed a friend or two as he did. She struggled to do what she wanted and what she believed her mother wanted. But when she played a piece of music, she hesitated; and when she went onstage, her heart seemed to leave her. Once she had dreamed of being 'a great beauty' and this awakened in her 'an unnecessary sorrow' for ugliness. Onstage she failed to live up to Ellen Terry's standards just as her brother failed to live up to Henry Irving's standards. Then they both went off in their own directions which were 'far more valuable'.

He had not seen his sister for the last twenty years of her life – twenty restless years moving around Europe oscillating between illusions of poverty and wealth. As a poor man in the early 1930s, he had put up at a cheap *pension* in Paris with his devoted secretary Daphne Woodward. Being poor meant that he could no longer pay her wages, but she had a small income of her own which came in useful. During these years he reviewed books for all sorts of journals from the *Times Literary Supplement* to the *Architectural Review*.

Reviewing somewhat increased his annual income, but its main attraction were the books themselves. Books had become his friends. In his library lay his wealth.

A young bookseller called Ifan Kyrle Fletcher had recently begun what would be more than thirty years' intermittent work on a Gordon Craig bibliography. He was 'a good fellow' and 'has high ideas as to the prices of books'. Craig returned in 1934 to Genoa where Elena and their daughter Nelly, assisted by the ever-present Daphne, helped him sort out his archive for the bookseller's inspection. He came and at the end of his examination was able to give them exciting news. The collection might be worth 'something like £40,000'. In short: Craig was wealthy.

He knew instinctively how to deploy this mythical fortune. He would present it as credit to whomsoever promised to create his School of Theatre (where the books and papers might be housed). This dream, which he had carried within him for more than quarter of a century, led him on and he began negotiating with a group of bankers and scholars in Holland.

A little later that year, after refusing an invitation to the Volta Congress in Rome which he nevertheless attended, he began to think his dream might be better realised in Italy. After all, what more theatrical leader was there in the political world than Mussolini? He impressed Craig as being what the world most needed: 'a born Hotel Manager . . . who is far greater than all Prime Ministers, Diplomats and other Dictators'. He welcomed the coming of the Italian fascists. 'Exit humbug – enter men who are serious', he wrote. '. . . To know what it feels like one must be in Italy. It's a touch or a wave of the ancient grandeur coming out of the skies.' He did not believe Mussolini wanted war. Neither, it seemed, did Hitler. Under Hitler's leadership Germany was achieving salvation. It was impossible not to welcome the news of Max Reinhardt being 'driven from the German theatre, as its Jews are not much wanted', he noted in his diary in April 1933. Craig enjoyed the vitality of the Jewish Theatre and of course individual Jews such as Will Rothenstein had been generous to him. But collectively, he told his daughter Rosie, they 'only allow their own success to be boomed'. Hence Reinhardt owned many theatres and Craig none. But soon there would be a change. 'Thank God, you artists of to-morrow, for the courage of Mussolini, Hitler, Lenin and the awakening of Italy, Russia, Germany, Spain . . .'

By the beginning of 1935 he had completed the sorting-out of his collection and was bargaining with Harvard University in the United States and also with Genoa itself, as well as with Vienna and London too. But Russia, he thought, might be the best place of all. While everything was poised in the middle of what seemed an international auction, he left with Daphne for Moscow.

Craig was much fêted during his two months there. He found the communists 'delightful people'. Although he had gone to Russia 'as an honoured guest and . . . was welcomed as a loved master,' he wrote, 'I really went there to learn'. He saw the delightful Olga Knipper again, still merry and erect, her spirit unflagging; and also the ailing Stanislaviski, now confined to his bed. He met Bertolt Brecht and also 'the very best of the Moscovites', Sergei Eisenstein, 'the uncrowned King of the Cinema world, a world I have hated for the rubbish it belches out . . . but now for the liking I have for Eisenstein I am raising my opinion of Cinema'. He was taken to a wonderful production by the Moscow State Jewish Theatre of *King Lear*, directed by Alexei Gravoski, invited to produce *Macbeth* and promised a new experimental workshop. They would pay him well too. Then he learnt that he was not permitted to take this money out of the country: and the whole pack of cards collapsed.

He and Daphne returned by way of Vienna. Here, on the morning of 22 May 1935, Daphne mentioned that she was not feeling well and went off to see a doctor while Craig made his way to the Nationalbibliothek to discuss his archive with the theatre historian Joseph Gregor. That afternoon a message was brought to him saying that Daphne had given birth to a daughter and that he was a father again. He went across to the hospital in the evening and suggested that, bearing in mind the date of their daughter's birth, they should call her 'Two Two'. Then, having made arrangements for the baby to be looked after in Vienna, they completed their journey back to Genoa.

Craig had not forgotten how upset Elena had been after the episode with the little servant girl from Copenhagen. 'I will try not to be depressed – or depress you less', she had written to him. '. . . Lots of funny things have passed & we have lived on, but now I do feel as they say you have had a good fling my pet – I only beg of you now to think of my feelings.' While sorting through his archive, Craig had come across a day book written during their early years together: 'She [Elena] has brought me new life, new trust . . . she is so beautiful always – so tender so strong and so true . . . the sun sees me, the earth hears me, shall I lie?' But he had lied again and again and 'I do not know what to do'.

Elena did not like the presence in their house of a young secretary so palpably in love with Craig. And when, in due course, she learnt of 'Two Two's' birth, she finally lost her temper. 'I'll be very clear', she wrote to him. 'I will not live in the same house as Miss Woodward . . . I'd not trust myself too near her because at first sign, in spite of religion, I'd strangle her . . . she is a dirty sneaking middle-class thief . . . Miss Woodward has spoilt everything for me, even part of my faith in you – because, dear heart, you treat me ugly to please her.' Unable to bear her mother's unhappiness, Nelly also confronted her father, though by then Daphne had moved to Paris. Once he sold his archive, Craig explained, they could live in a castle and all would be well.

Towards the end of 1935, somewhat upsetting these plans, Italy invaded Abyssinia. Like Beethoven turning away from Napoleon, Gordon Craig felt disillusioned with Mussolini. Once he had thought him a genius among political leaders. Now the serene climate of the country Craig loved above all was being destroyed and he decided: 'I must go.'

He travelled back to Paris, back to the same cheap *pension*, in the summer of 1936. He was accompanied by an entourage of trunks and boxes and packages and portfolios containing his invaluable cargo of books and papers – and was joined by Daphne. This bulky collection, the work of a lifetime, obsessed him. It was like a miraculous child which must be lovingly cared for and looked after like no other child. One day soon it would bring him wealth and immortality. And while its final destination was being charted, he would continue to enrich it, feed it with manuscripts retrieved from the dead and with fresh writings: records of his recent wanderings, correspondence with his most loyal friends such as Max Beerbohm and Martin Shaw (and of course Elena) as well as younger allies like Harry Irving's son Laurence. Upstairs in her small room Daphne was kept busy typing new diaries and old day books which Craig would soon use as sources for his autobiography.

'What dull days – what dull pages', he wrote towards the end of 1937. Navigating through these foggy days, steering by whatever beacons he could pick out, he was calculating a course for the Utopian land where he could lay down the heavy burden of his work. He had agents posted in several countries – secret agents, he thought of them, believing that none knew of the others. The *pension* meanwhile was bursting with his possessions, an unwieldy vessel made top-heavy after Elena had forwarded from Genoa between sixty and seventy more boxes of annotated first editions. But as his collection swelled, growing ever more prosperous, Craig himself sank deeper into debt. He waited for the expected miracle – then suddenly found himself in a nightmare: 'War is declared after endless attempts to keep this man Hitler peaceful.'

Craig's son Edward urged him to hurry back to England. But how could he do so while his archive, these very pieces of himself, had come to rest in France? To abandon it would be a fatal amputation – and there was no chance of getting safe passage home with such a convoy while people were lining up with minimal baggage for the boats. It was his duty to stand guard and wait for a solution to occur – maybe this war would precipitate matters.

Elena and Nelly did return to England, having dinner with Craig in Paris on their way back. And 'Two Two', now aged five, joined him and Daphne at their *pension*. This was the first time Craig, now almost seventy, had seen his daughter since leaving Vienna in 1935. They got on 'grandly', especially over meringues and cream, though he seemed to forget sometimes that daphne (whose name he now spelt with a lower case d) was the child's mother. He particularly admired Two Two's indifference to the war – if only he could put it out of his mind so well. But already France was 'a little upside down'. Sometimes he would liken himself to that 'lonely gent' Robinson Crusoe, shipwrecked by Hitler, and attempting to make his solitary existence secure with what stamina and ingenuity he could summon – a grimmer and more sophisticated metaphor for his life than the adventures of *Treasure Island*. He had been enchanted when, in his early twenties, he first read Defoe's novel. Among 'the babble of things and people', this 'beloved book' became his special friend on whose make-believe island he could leave behind his troubles. During the mid-1920s and late 1930s he prepared some sixty wood-engravings – scenes, masks and historiated or decorated initials – for these 'strange and surprising adventures' and in 1944 was to engrave another twelve blocks – all of which would be

published posthumously.* Among these pictures there is no Man Friday, for the book itself had become his companion – a solace for loneliness and an enjoyment within the loneliness that was creeping around him. 'In the silence of the reading he entered the silence of the island . . . [and] achieved a kind of peace', his son Edward wrote in a foreword to the book.

At the end of 1940, together with other British citizens in Paris, he and Daphne and 'Two Two' were rounded up and taken to a prison camp at Besançon. The men were separated from the women and children, and all of them placed in cold damp huts. By the standards of war, conditions were not bad. But for Craig it was like entering Dante's *Inferno*: 'All hope abandon, ye who enter here.' His hands began to shake, he grew dreadfully thin, and it did not seem that he could long continue to stay alive.

But then, rekindling hope, an image of his astonishing archive appeared like a mirage in the desert. A German lawyer, Heinrich Heim, who was attached to Hitler's headquarters, came across his books in 'Shakespeare and Company', Sylvia Beach's bookshop in Paris, and decided that Craig's inspiring works were what Germany needed to rebuild her national theatres after winning the war.† Early in 1941, Craig was released from Stalag 142 and allowed to return to his Paris *pension*, where he was joined again by Daphne Woodward and 'Two Two'. There were no conditions – he was never asked to 'do any German propaganda'. Heinrich Heim arrived and handed him 10,000 francs for a set of *The Mask* to be delivered 'at the end of the war'. He also persuaded the director of the National Gallery of Dresden to offer Craig 2,389,000 francs for the Gordon Craig Collection which they planned to exhibit very gloriously at Linz. At the beginning of November, Craig signed a contract and received his first instalment of 400,000 francs.

This odd contract with the enemy brought Dorothy Nevile Lees back into the story. The death of *The Mask* in 1929 had been like a shadow of her own death. 'I hadn't much heart for anything after such a break', she

* By the Basilisk Press, London, in 1979. It is a disappointing publication. Craig found it difficult to maintain consistency in width and style. 'However visionary, witty or detailed each individual image and however inspired its cutting,' writes L.M. Newman, 'they do not make up a whole within the long text. Kessler's firm guidance was clearly needed.'

† It has been suggested that in his youth Hitler was an admirer of Craig. It seems more likely, however, that Heinrich Heim, the compiler of *Hitler's Table Talk*, whose job in Paris was to 'find theatres', introduced Hitler to Craig's theatre work. Heim was certainly under the impression that he had done so.

confessed. Nevertheless there were even now ways in which she could be of use: assembling and sorting 'old copies, stacks of clichés . . . files of correspondence, surplus paper'. She sent Craig bulletins of desiderata: faded leaflets, clippings, old bookplates, index cards, offprints, spine labels, errata slips, notes on the bindings of rare volumes, booksellers' catalogues containing items on popular Italian comedy and the conventions of the Chinese stage, as well as complimentary references to his work – anything, in short and at length, that might quicken the pulse of 'the one outstanding English artist of world celebrity in the theatre'. And eventually she tempted him back into a piecemeal correspondence with her. 'It is such a pleasure to get your letters', she told him, '– like finding a flower in the letter box . . . It would be heavenly if I could see you.' So he ceased writing to her. 'Dear Signor, do write: your letters are so much to me.' But he would not and, in the silence, she turned back to his letters of past years. 'It is almost inconceivably noble to act as you have done', he had once written. And then she opened one of his books in which he had inscribed a few words to her as 'the most faithful of all'. She cherished these tributes as if they were her medals and set about annotating with pride his many scathing criticisms of her.

At the beginning of the war 'it looked very unlikely that I should survive events'. She was arrested together with other English inhabitants, but then sent home. She kept steadily at work, writing a little journalism, making translations, and giving unobtrusive English lessons to various families. She was almost destitute, but her chief anxiety circled around *The Mask* archives. With the help of an old rag-and-bone man who had a handcart, she moved the papers from place to place, seeking security and finally settling everything in a dungeon below her new apartment in the Via Foscolo. Here she continued to verify and catalogue the contents of her many box-files and cupboards, listing typographical errors in prospectuses, noting the density of inks, the quality of paper samples and printing plates. And at last it was all in perfect order.

In secret, DNL was also doing work for British intelligence. 'We were all living in danger', she remembered. So when, on the morning of 8 May 1944, a pink-skinned, hatchet-faced German officer from the SS arrived, she expected to be carried off to prison – perhaps even shot. But it was worse. The Nazi officer demanded to inspect *The Mask* papers, informing her that Craig had sold everything which survived to Germany. It seemed hardly possible to her that there had been such a transaction. With great ingenuity she delayed the surrender of these documents, staying out of her apartment all day, rearranging the collection at night (eliminating anything that was 'sacred', hiding what was most valuable) and all the time writing to Craig to find out what she should do – though never hearing from him. Then, at midday on Friday, 23 June, a German truck stopped outside. It was full of German soldiers who came swarming in, racing up and down the cellar steps, manhandling everything they saw with 'the indiscriminate violence and haste of a looting or a rape'. They snatched, they tore and they dropped armfuls of her memories into the muddy gutter as if they were 'bales of coke or firewood'. Surrounded by her emptying shelves, DNL watched like a drowning woman. Her archive was 'dear to me as a child whose every moment and move I had watched over since birth'; and 'I never heard anything about it all & its ultimate destination'. But she had saved what was dearest to her.

The battle for Craig's archive in the middle of a world war grew ever more bizarre. A cheque for £100 arrived in Paris from Harvard University – sent in the hope that he could arrange safe passage for his papers across the Atlantic. The Nationalbibliothek in Vienna too re-entered negotiations – Craig selling fifty or sixty designs from his collection. The perpetual air-raids and crowded convoys of military vehicles between France and Germany made transportation extremely difficult and by the beginning of 1945 Craig had managed to send a mere fourteen boxes of his treasure to Linz. But then some improbable news reached him: dozens of cases of 'the Craig Archive' had been discovered in a salt mine near Munich – all those magazines and manuscripts that had been plundered from Dorothy Nevile Lees's dungeon in Florence. They were transported to Daphne Woodward who filled in the complex forms needed to complete their passage from Germany (other boxes from Craig himself travelling meanwhile in the opposite direction). It must have seemed to him that he was selling this magical archive many times and that however many times he sold it, there it lay around him still, growing more plentiful, waiting to be sold again (even the boxes he had sent to Germany were to be returned to him after the war).

In June 1942 he had moved from the *pension* to a large studio apartment at 85 rue Ampère, near the Place Pereire, taking with him his innumerable cases of prints and publications (as well as Daphne and 'Two Two'). He paid off his debts to restaurants, shopkeepers and booksellers; he had money in his pocket and life again was very pleasant. He was writing his memoirs and in 1943 saw a new French edition of *On the Art of the Theatre* hailed by Jean-Louis Barrault as his 'Catéchisme' and 'the true artist's guide to the Theatre'. Later on 'Two Two' would join Barrault's Théâtre Marigny before marrying and, as 'Daphne de Padron', going to live in Venezuela.

With no restrictions imposed on him, Craig was 'living as fully as ever'. After all 'I am not old yet', he reflected, merely 'aged'. He had inherited his mother's 'bright spirit, light step and vivid presence', wrote Janet Leeper who, seeing him for the first time in his mid-seventies, was impressed by 'his calm dignity in a sea of troubles'. The art historian Virginia Surtees, meeting him shortly after the war, observed 'a tall man, his large frame reduced by age, enveloped in black corduroys . . . Around his neck a white silk or twisted coloured scarf. His fair skin was traversed with lines; a long thin narrow mouth, the short-sighted eyes "scrutinising intensely, peering myopically," as Paul Nash observed many years earlier, set close to the thin prominent nose . . . The eyes would lighten with merriment at a newly devised tease or with enthusiasm when expounding the lighting for his theatre models but they would assume a different intensity when ridiculing something or someone whom he felt had used him, or a theatre he had known, basely. A mass of white hair swept back from a wide brow fell almost to his shoulders.'

He was 'in love with life' and also with a 'black-haired poetess' called Elinor, 'a truthful creature – & a handsome one – & a lot more', who worked for the Red Cross. They exchanged letters, long loving letters, almost daily; they went for walks together in the Bois de Boulogne and the Luxembourg Gardens; they ate in secluded restaurants . . . until one day her husband in Germany read his letters and everything had to end. It had been a happy episode and Craig was temporarily broken-hearted. 'Sadness – only a little is enough', he noted. Approaching his mid-seventies, and suffering from a troubling hernia, he quickly fell in love again, this time with an 'adorable' Spanish actress called Maria Casarès. This was to be his last passionate involvement, 'insane and wise of us both'. An hour with her 'is like no hour I ever dreamed of or experienced', he told her. '. . . I love you & I cannot remain silent – my poor senses are my only friends.' Of course it could not last and he would soon encounter the 'folly & sorrow that come on the very heels of love'. He 'mourned secretly for Maria'. But 'we had a blessed time'.

Craig described the advance of British and American troops on Paris as 'disastrously successful' (250,000 people were reported to have been killed, wounded or taken prisoner). 'Let's hope Paris won't be bombarded,' he wrote in one of his diaries, 'for it is a nice place – & the people the most intelligent in Europe I should say.' Why, he wondered, did Hitler 'keep it up'? He wished the allies could congratulate him on having fought a good fight and then call a truce – was this any less idiotic than all the terrible fighting? 'What can I do?' he asked himself. And his answer was the same as his mother's had been in the First World War. 'The most & best I can do is to mind my own business.'

It was sad to see the Germans leave Paris 'in carts & on bicycles, the carts garlanded, departing slowly . . . so many depressed people'. But the end of the war meant more international post – and he welcomed the arrival of foreign visitors. In his exile, letters had become his lifeline and he depended on them in much the same way, L.M. Newman suggests, as sailors at sea did. He received letters from Elena, Nelly and Ted, from Martin Shaw and Laurence Irving ('I love hearing from Laurence'). He heard too from Dorothy Nevile Lees. These had been difficult years for her, years of poverty and danger, working for allied intelligence while her son David, an Italian citizen who became a corporal in the Italian army, was away on military service. 'I record only the sunny hours' had been the title of her journalistic column, and this she struggled to keep up in her correspondence with Craig. She also began to communicate with his son Edward, pouring forth pages in honour of Craig's genius and the happiness she derived from her own life of 'incessant work, little profit, in complete obscurity'. Her stoicism was bound with 'many hurts and humiliations' and had to contend with an irrepressible resentment at his callous and, in someone so sensitive, inexplicable lack of feeling. Looking back she sometimes wished 'I could have done more & better'. But this was what she set about doing. 'The joy of work which one loves heals everything', Craig told her and she knew this to be true. For the last twenty years of her life she gave herself over to three noble enterprises. First she developed her fine collection of Craigiana, many shelves of publications which she donated to the British Institute in Florence, 'a safe and dignified place' in the city he had loved and which students could visit from around the world. She made some duplicates of this material to enrich her second project – an archive, built around the correspondence between her and Craig (she had destroyed the most intimate exchanges but kept the dried flowers and leaves and a poem – all memorabilia of their son's birth) which she left to David.* Finally she bombarded the British government with appeals to grant Craig a civil list pension – a mission that was still unaccomplished by the time of her death in 1966, the same year as his.

In Paris after the war, the theatres had opened again and Craig saw Laurence Olivier who came over with the Old Vic Company to play *Richard III* for the Comédie Française. In a letter to Olivier, he wrote: 'You entered – you drew the door to – the lock snapped . . . You began to talk in a voice that compelled . . . Immediately I began to listen with care – & as my eyes were open I saw a number of things being done by you & done neatly & slowly there ceased to be any fear in me that you might fail . . . Very sure of yourself – bienissimo! . . . At the end I went away haunted by Gloucester.' After seeing him in *King Lear*, he noted: 'Admirable . . . Olivier *is* an actor' – one of the few who carried on Irving's tradition. But no one was 'so dangerously good as Irving', he told Kenneth Tynan. 'The Terrys were always a slapdash sort of family. The Irvings were precision instruments.' Next to Irving and his company, Granville-Barker looked a small man among giants, while the director William Poel was simply 'a clinking master of the dry and dusty theatre of archaeology'. As for John Gielgud, who claimed Irving as 'a great idol', he seemed as poor an actor as Matisse was a painter. 'Nothing he did gave me delight . . . I gape when I think of him.'

Daphne had by now found a job as a translator with UNESCO and could pay the rent for herself and 'Two Two' at the studio building. Craig accused her of 'deserting' him – which meant that he was about to desert them. After many arguments, he left her in charge of his collection, travelling in search of sun, air and health. Suddenly the weight of his mountainous archive lifted and he felt free. 'I am here in Corbeil which for several reasons seems to be a fairly good copy of Heaven', he wrote that year to his son Edward, '. . . a circus was here one evening – 3 children 3 men and 1 goat performed the entire thing – no tent – one lamp – on the river side – 800 spectators on benches and soap boxes – band i.e. 1 drum 1 bassoon . . . I never was present

* David Lees, who was a professional photographer, sold part of this archive to Harvard University and the rest to the Archivio Contemporaneo del Gabinetto Vieusseux in Florence.

at such a perfect spectacle – never saw such a scene – nor heard such persuasive music – and left the ring in a state of enchantment.' It was the sort of spectacle Edy might have enjoyed.

While at Corbeil he saw Elena, who was travelling back to Genoa to retrieve whatever she could from their house for her future life in England with Nelly. 'They walked about the countryside', their son records, '– and when she left it was as though he had been awakened from a dream.'

Soon he was pressing on south to Le Cannet, Camassade, Tourettes, Vence. Each place held some special quality: but it was the ancient town of Vence, small, rocky, surrounded by great walls high in the hills above Nice, that he finally chose. 'Cakes and Sweets here', he wrote, and that would certainly have appealed to him in his boyhood (a period he was then revisiting in his memoirs). These memoirs were to reach just beyond 1906, the year he had first visited Vence, making his initial etching there for *Scene*. Forty years later he was alone again. 'Alone' was to be the last printed word of his memoirs.

> Alone, & warming his five wits
> The white owl in the belfry sits.

Craig was to inscribe these lines of Tennyson's at the end of his book. But it was to take him two years in hotels, inns, *pensions* throughout Vence to alight on his own belfry. Le Mas André, its thick walls of rough-hewn stone under a pantiled roof, was 'a really delightful place' on the outskirts of Vence, along an unfrequented road, the Corniche du Malvan. He occupied half the villa, settled down among the umbrella pines and olive trees, and waited for some woman to do 'the odd jobs that women always did'.

'Of course I dislike visitors', he wrote to someone who proposed visiting him. Yet he realised that he was 'far too much alone'. Visitors in any case did not greatly affect his solitude – what he called 'that aloneness of the in-between hours'. Whether he was living 'on the earth or in another world', he could not always tell. But he knew that Vence 'has marvel in it' and 'all is real peace'. He suspected that he was 'jollier' than people with crowded lives like Winston Churchill with his motor-cars and secretaries and cigars. All the same, he could not help resenting that 'I have next to nothing'.

From time to time he would ask Daphne to send him books and tobacco he needed from Paris. The cases from the Munich salt mines had finally arrived there and so had the contents of *The Mask* offices in Florence. The studio was crowded with such an enormous gathering of these books and papers that the landlords implored Craig to take them away so that they could rent the rooms to tenants. But from his deckchair at Le Mas André, just below the derelict chapel of St Anne and looking over the Côte d'Azur, Craig could see no urgency for decisions. He had hopes of selling everything to the Victoria and Albert Museum in London, or possibly the Old Vic Theatre archive, but they were quenched by May's outstanding High Court order against him – even though she agreed to accept no more than 10 per cent of the price. In any event he preferred having a private deposit in Paris with an unpaid librarian. But he was pleased by the interest people were showing once more in his collection – the University of Southern California in Los Angeles, the Appia Foundation in Berne and the Bibliothèque Nationale in Paris were all in contact with him. He had become adept at encouraging these enquiries and then finding difficulties that prevented them from reaching a conclusion – it was as good in its way as a game of Patience. Decisions were so unsubtle, conclusions so final – a sort of death. He felt something similar about his memoirs on which he had been intermittently at work for fifteen years. 'To write an autobiography, how difficult this must be', he had written in the mid-1930s, and he had been right.

It was the need for money that in 1957 decided him to sell the archive and publish his book. He used newspapers and some well-directed letters to bring attention to his predicament. The *News Chronicle* in London described him as 'a lonely and penniless man' who 'does his own washing, his own darning and sewing'. The *Observer* reminded its readers that he had anticipated Brecht and was 'still several lengths ahead of the theatrical *avant-garde*'. Was it not shocking that this genius of the modern theatre, whom Isadora Duncan had likened to Shelley, 'a creature of fire and lightning', could no longer afford to visit England? Not that he had even received 'a scrap of help from England', Craig added. 'What a swindling world it is nowadays.' These tactics worked well. For 'lo and behold [I] was offered a sum of money for my Collection by the Bibliothèque Nationale de France', he informed Marguerite Steen. He also arranged with the curator André Veinstein, a most cultured and civilised man, to retain any items of sentimental value as well as some material he might need for a second volume of memoirs. For what he did sell, he received approximately £13,000

– which he placed in his bank account at Nice. It was 'enough in all conscience'. Enough at least for the present. Also 'I discover over £19,000 worth still with me . . . I blink! I rub my eyes and quietly marvel that luck was with me still.'

Index to the Story of my Days, the title he gave his memoirs, was published in Britain and the United States in 1957, appearing in a French translation (*Ma Vie d'homme de Théâtre*) five years later. It is a book of immense charm that shows the reader why, despite all the difficulties he presented, the sheer impossibilities, men and women were so romantically drawn to him. Here is a person of mysterious gifts, sensitive and vulnerable, who needs someone special – a parent, a lover, a champion – to lead him to the success he deserves. On the inside back flap of the cover was printed a tribute by Max Beerbohm, describing him as 'a man of genius', famous and honoured in Russia, Germany, Italy, France – but 'less laurelled' in England, though 'a great English artist Craig assuredly is'. The following year he was appointed a Companion of Honour and, his doctor advising him against travelling to Buckingham Palace for the investiture, it was presented to him at a ceremony in Nice. 'I was very honoured when our Queen made me . . . whatever it was', he used to say.

He sent an early copy of his book to Elena, drawing her attention to two pages covering the year 1900 when they met. 'We both undertook to do what we liked doing and could do', he had written. '. . . Elena and I had that capacity, and we have it still.' In an accompanying letter he promised her that 'our life in Florence with our two [children], begins volume II; it will make some of 'em open their eyes'.

Over three years earlier Elena had gone with her daughter Nelly to live in an eighteenth-century thatched cottage at Long Crendon in Buckinghamshire, near Bedlow where her son Edward and his wife lived. It was a happy arrangement enabling her to see her two grandchildren, a boy and a girl. But on 24 December 1957, after a short illness in her late seventies, she died. When Craig heard the news he was overcome with even greater incredulity than he had been over Edy's death. 'I can't believe it', he kept saying. But once he acknowledged her death, 'I doubt I shall write down more'. He instructed their son Edward to return his letters to Elena and was angry that not all of them could be found. He began to speak disparagingly of *Index*, a silly book crowded with worrying people – dead people. He longed for something abstract, a land of non-being where there was no dying, and where his 'theatre of silence', full of eternal light and movement, could occupy his dreams. Then suddenly he found this dream. 'I have had rather a curious experience', he wrote to Evald Junge. 'I have been reading a book signed by the name I pass under . . . a very good book on a rather difficult subject . . . wonderful ideas.' These pages from *On the Art of the Theatre* lived on while the cast of *Index* passed away.

He would sometimes take a taxi down to Nice and walk along the Promenade des Anglais, where Isadora had been killed in that racing car, hoping to find her living spirit – after all, 'Who knows?' Almost as sad had been the death of his German champion, 'the only man who helped me . . . never failed me', Harry Kessler. He had last seen him at the Café de la Paix in Paris shortly before the war, ill and impoverished by his habit of spending like a millionaire, 'so altered as to be almost unrecognisable, his life had been disintegrating around him' as the shadow of Hitler obliterated his life at Weimar. Shortly after the war the man who had introduced him to Kessler, William Rothenstein, had died; and then ('the one I miss most') his generous neighbour at Rapallo, Max Beerbohm, and after that 'dear old' Martin Shaw with whom he had begun his career. It was as if he had been writing his memoirs all those years to keep them alive. These lights that had illumined his youth were now put out. But it was only after Elena had died that his defences momentarily broke down and grief overtook him. His refusal to acknowledge death had been like that of a child who believes he is immortal. But Elena's death gave him a sense of his mortality and he wrote to their daughter Nelly that he did not expect to live much longer.

Nelly's life had been devoted to her parents. She suffered from anaemia and was easily tired. She had wanted to be an actress like her grandmother and had taken on a few small roles before Craig summoned her, along with Teddy and Elena, to Italy. For the next ten years she had helped her mother at Rapallo and Genoa and done work for her father in the Italian archives. Then, after her brother's marriage in 1928, she went to stay with him in London and joined the Old Vic Company. But again her father summoned her back. In 1939 when she and Elena returned to England, Nelly took on voluntary work and, after the war, worked as a temporary assistant at Gabrielle Enthoven's theatre collection at the Victoria and Albert Museum and also at David Low's bookshop in Cecil Court. The illness which would eventually kill her was gradually creeping forward in these post-war years, but when she read her father's letter from Vence she shut up the cottage at Long Crendon and travelled out to him.

'I only hope poor Nelly is not disillusioned', her brother Edward wrote to Janet Leeper. 'She has had such a bad time with father in the past and time & distance have helped make her forget.' She found him in excellent health – remarkable for someone aged eighty-six. 'Papa has been extremely good and kind to me', she told her brother. '. . . When he dies – he says that he wants to be shipped to England and buried with Mummy [Elena].' Meanwhile she would have to stay in Vence longer than she had expected.

Her duties were oddly demanding. She was required to open her father's curtains at twenty minutes to eight each morning so that he could have coffee, milk and *biscottes* at eight o'clock. 'I will now have a nap,' he would say when he had finished. He rose a second time at half past nine and, still in his dressing-gown, went to the 'Book Room' where everything lay ready for him. He locked the door and windows and, spreading out across the table a piece of folded pink blotting-paper, began counting his money, the notes and coins, very carefully, recording everything in a little book. This he did each day. After the money had been reckoned, he might add a paragraph to an article or write some notes in one of his opuscules (paper booklets), paste in an engraving, put on a cover and make up one of his 'Doubles' – books enriched with marginalia which he could sell again. Then he had a bath and dressed. Most days a woman came to clean the villa and prepare lunch – usually some fish, cheese and white wine – after which he retired for another nap and rose again, a third time, for tea, the writing of letters, and the reading of books.

'I am feeling in need', he wrote. He needed Nelly to speed into Vence four or five times a day ('like a madman') for things he had not known he needed half an hour earlier (he bought her a bicycle with a little motor attached at the front). He needed her to make supper in the evenings or to escort him to Nice and other places for dinner and to discuss Shakespeare over these meals (was the Dark Lady really a black cat?). He needed her to understand that he could do everything for himself and yet be ready to help him whenever he couldn't, to welcome guests one day and to guard the door against them another day (she could tell which it was to be when she drew his curtains in the morning). Above all he needed her to steer him safely, late into the night, between the rocks of boredom and anxiety. 'I sit – I puzzle – I end doing small nothings', he wrote to Nelly's brother, Edward. '. . . I *smoke*, I play cards – Patience – daily. That quiets me . . . I enjoy the warm days . . . I dread the cold ones.'

On those cold days, steering perilously close to one of the awful rocks, he would sometimes erupt in anger. When Nelly told him he was not giving her enough money for household expenses and she was using her own small capital for buying his food and medicines, paying the cleaner and doctor, he 'began shouting and telling me I was a thief – a bitch etc., and I said "O.K. – I go" ', she wrote to her brother. 'You know one gets tired and fed up with this everlasting shouting and he would not look at the Account book, and wanted to start fighting me with his fists – he gets blind with rage and as he gets older he gets worse . . . I cannot fight an old man . . . I will expire one of these times.'

Reading Marguerite Steen's *A Pride of Terrys*, Nelly recognised these flashes of 'the Terry temper' and wondered how her mother had 'put up for so long with Papa's temper and his changes of mood'. Nelly herself, at the age of sixty, did not have her father's stamina at the age of ninety and would occasionally give him supper in bed simply to save them 'the trouble and pain of having to look at the other'. Often she did not get to bed until one or two o'clock the next morning. 'My life now is just dead – no friends . . . nothing', she wrote. 'Sometimes the doctor would call round to examine the combatants, giving Nelly injections for what he believed was arthritis but which were early symptoms of muscular dystrophy. He would congratulate her father (who despite being toothless 'eats like a lion and drinks too') on his capital appetite. He was 'a very strong healthy man at heart . . . nothing the matter with you'. Craig always felt better for these visits. 'It was good he came.' The counting of money was now his reckoning of life, and when the money ran out, Death would come for her final payment. The local doctor was the only man for whom he had respect – he was never rude about Dr Peyregne. It was not *intelligent*, he reasoned, for his friends to go and die, and as for himself it was out of the question: 'I have so much to put straight.' But he was haunted by this fear, seeing shadows moving about the place, messengers of death, and suspecting his daughter of trying to poison him. 'I wish you would die,' he shouted at her when, having toothache one day, his terror rose, '– drop dead in front of me now!'

His games of Patience were rituals that kept the spectre of death waiting. In moments when his memory lapsed, Elena and Edy would return, and he still had the power to summon back that dear solitary man, Henry Irving. 'My Master – the Guv'nor – very kind – firm – cutting at times but wonderful to me'. When some of his visitors enquired after the secret of his long and fruitful life, he would reply: 'Don't worry. Let the others do that for you.' It was a philosophy to which he clung tightly. He had been a Mr Micawber when young: in old age he was Harold Skimpole, the sprightly epicurean egotist in *Bleak House*. If, for a moment, some problem approached, he seemed to grow frail until, assuring himself that Nelly had it in hand, he would give a deep sigh and say: 'That's good – I must not worry at all.' And with that sigh the wrinkles left his face and 'he was calm as if nothing had happened', Nelly observed, '– like a shaggy dog who shakes off the rain'.

There must have been moments when he noticed how lonely his daughter had become. He pined for a new secretary – someone top-grade who would devote herself to him and be happy to work for nothing – 'and she must be pretty'. But this was now beyond him.

He had set himself an impossible conundrum. The more death was delayed, the more terrifying it appeared. 'It's taking so long – so long,' he complained. After his ninetieth birthday however he felt confident of reaching a hundred. And yet 'Oh Lord how old *old age* is. One doesn't (one *cannot*) conceive *how* old and awful old age is, till one is up to the eyes.' To feel the pulse of life again, he needed treats – to take taxis all over the place and make them wait all day, all night if necessary, until he felt like returning. He needed money to eat in good restaurants, to enjoy three weeks' holiday in a good hotel: in short, to regain some of the habits of youth. But the more money he spent, the less there was in the bank and the nearer he felt to death.

Not long after she settled into Le Mas André, Nelly was dispatched to Genoa to recover eighteen large boxes of theatre material, nailed down by a carpenter, which Craig had secretly lodged with the Italian comedian Petrolini. 'Papa is up to I know not what', she wrote, '. . . I am afraid that he is intending to sell a lot of things to USA etc which should belong to France.' He was rereading his correspondence with Isadora and in 1962, after burning some ten letters that struck him as being too painful, he sold the rest, together with other Isadora Duncan documents, to the Dance Collection of the New York Public Library for the Performing Arts. At the same time, he went on exchanging his treasures for bundles of banknotes from visitors all over the world – banknotes which he could count next day.

These visitors included, sometimes to his bewilderment, members of his extended family: his eldest daughter Rosie (now living in South Africa), his eldest son Robert and his youngest son David Lees, who photographed him in bed and at work – also his youngest daughter 'Two Two', whose carefree spirit reminded him of himself when young, and his cousin John Gielgud who was impressed by his long white silky hair, his prodigious vitality and the surgeon's overall he wore, that enabled him in his eighties to 'adjust his truss at mealtimes with discretion'.

Though he was still Ted to his family, he preferred to be known as 'EGC' in public. There seemed to be a regiment of scholars perpetually advancing upon Vence. Despite a crippling illness, the American collector and bibliographer Arnold Rood ('jolly nice fellow, very kind') would turn up with armfuls of presents and then sit staring in silent admiration ('Can't you take him away somewhere', Craig appealed to Nelly, '– he makes me feel nervous.'). The theatre critic Kenneth Tynan arrived from London and found him full of mischief and conspiratorial glee, like a very ancient schoolboy playing truant. From Rome came Ferruccio Marotti, who 'makes up for the thirty-seven young hopefuls who have, in the last thirty-seven years, buzzed around me', and whose book, published in 1961, Craig relished having read aloud to him. He also liked the book (or 'thesis' as he called it) by the French critic, Denis Bablet, translated by Daphne Woodward and published a year later when Bablet and his family finally left Vence. Evald Junge, a 'confidential secretary' who later styled himself as another of Craig's sons, pleased him by arranging a limited edition of recordings from some talks Craig had made for the British Broadcasting Corporation in the early 1950s. To Harvey Grossman, a teenager from the United States who burrowed into the cellar of an abandoned hostel in Vence for a year, Craig explained that his ideas had been obscured. Only a poet could disentangle the superficial contradictions of his writings on space and stillness, see how his lights were connected to the principle of evolution, and explain how he had reintroduced architecture into the theatre. A poet could understand the supple dynamics of his vision and transform his thoughts into revelations. Perhaps Harvey Grossman was that poet . . .

Craig valued the work of an enthusiast like Janet Leeper. But best of all he warmed to men such as Bernard Miles, men of the theatre, men of pluck and genius like himself, who bought his books and designs, and with whom he had fun 'pulling the modern theatre apart and putting it together again . . . differently'. Another legendary figure of the theatre, Peter Brook, also came to see him. Brook had been excited by the purity of indignation in this 'hermit visionary', by 'the beauty of harmonious form, the suggestive power of lighting' on which the geometry of an effective stage depended. He regarded Craig as a mentor, his biographer Michael Kustow notes, but classed him as 'both an inspiration and a warning'.

Peter Brook, Bernard Miles and Laurence Irving were among more than sixty people who, as 'The Friends of Gordon Craig', raised funds to ensure that, from the early 1960s onwards, he would be paid £100 a month for the rest of his life. These generous benefactors included many actors (Peggy Ashcroft, Edith Evans, Douglas Fairbanks, Vivien Leigh, Laurence Olivier, Michael Redgrave and Peter Ustinov) and others connected with the theatre: the painter John Piper, the stage designer Tanya Moiseiwitsch, the choreographer Wendy Toye and directors Peter Hall and Glyn Byam Shaw. The last name on this alphabetical list of well-wishers was Daphne Woodward. She had come to see Craig in Vence, staying nearby at a hotel, and Nelly observed how her father, drinking cognac with her, became 'highly nervous'. Daphne confided that she was suffering from cancer and had only a couple of years to live – following which he must keep a fatherly eye on 'Two Two'. This was the sort of news he had to be careful 'not to worry' about. And to those who saw him strolling along the streets of Vence and Tourettes 'dressed in his Arab burnous, his eyes shaded from the glare of the sun by a local straw hat with an enormous brim', and carrying an old attaché case full of papers, pens and pencils ready to trap any ideas that might suddenly alight on him, he appeared a carefree figure. He would raise his walking-stick, Henry Irving's Malacca cane with its silver-gilt head, and salute pedestrians with a familiar three-note cry, 'Ha-ha-haa', signifying that all was well.

Two or three times he went into hospital – the Hôpital Anglais at Cannes where the matron was 'like a dear kind mother to me' and the English-American Hospital in Nice where Nelly found him drinking champagne with the nurses. Though he became very deaf, he refused a hearing-aid and when Nelly rented a television set he sat in front of it every day for a week and then gave his verdict: 'I never want to have one – it mesmerised me so. Take it away.' He absorbed more pleasure from a lucky white cat that had adopted him. 'My white pussy cat is a joy', he wrote. 'Never a harsh word – always loving – and *looks* at me!' Purring with admiration, this white cat, he thought, was the spirit of his mother, behaving at last how he always wished her to behave.

His melancholy evaporated whenever he was brought evidence of the public esteem in which his work was held. There was a large exhibition of 'the Gordon Craig Collection' at the Bibliothèque Nationale which was later shown, together with work by Adolphe Appia, at the Venice Biennale, and also a good small show put on at the Mermaid Theatre in London by Bernard Miles.

In the autumn of 1965 he had a fall and Nelly wired her brother that it was 'touch and go' whether he would live. Edward arrived and so did David Lees and also 'Two Two' whose mother Daphne had just died. 'Father lay on his bed with closed eyes, his long arms moving in the air above his head, the first finger and thumb of his right hand continually moving as though he was holding a needle and embroidering some complicated pattern in an imaginary tapestry, while with his other hand he seemed to be searching for something in the air', Edward wrote. Embroidering the air, uttering strange sounds, he seemed 'lost between a real and imaginary world'. He had suffered a stroke, but his tenacity carried him back to the real world and by Christmas Nelly reported him as being 'just a bit weak' and Dr Peyregne announced: '*C'est un miracle!*'

On 16 January 1966 he celebrated his ninety-fourth birthday with a party of fifty guests. He was often very rude about the presents people brought him, but such were the privileges of age that his insults were greeted as witticisms. In his slippers and dressing-gown, his hair uncombed as he upbraided the British Consul, he 'looked just like Edy did at times', Nelly observed. 'Not a smile anywhere, a sharp crafty look.' A three-tier birthday cake with a single candle was carried in and everyone shouted: 'Blow out the candle!' When he had blown out candles in his young days with May Gibson, Jess Dorynne, Elena Meo and others it had always led to a birth.

G is for Gordon – though he never guessed right,
Continued like Goethe to call for more light.

But he stepped back from this small flame like a man fearing extinction. Darkness 'is horrible to me'. When he spoke, like a man who is already dead and does not know it, 'there was awe in his voice', Nelly heard, 'and he looked frightened'.

Each week that spring and summer she noticed some small change in him 'not for the better'. He still wanted to see people, but most of the day he slept and saw imaginary people. In mid-May he had another fall, but would not go into hospital. An artist, Walter Hodges, who visited him that month, saw emerging through the lines of his old white face 'the lineaments of the very handsome man one sees in his early photographs'.

In July he had a second stroke. The doctor sat him up in bed, his chin resting on his chest, but he did not speak or open his eyes. Nelly put eau de Cologne on his forehead and later told her brother that the last words he whispered to her, gentle and low, had been 'I love you and Teddy'. On the evening of 28 July, while she was washing him, she heard him give a deep sigh, like the sigh he had given when telling her he 'must not worry at all' but let others do the worrying. Next morning the doctor came and told her he was dead. He looked calm as if nothing had happened.

On 1 August his body was cremated at the Marseilles Crematorium. The urn containing his ashes was taken to England to be buried next to Elena's at Thame Churchyard in Oxfordshire. 'The ashes are with me,' his son Edward had written that autumn to Janet Leeper, '& strangely I find them great company.'

An Outline of Sources

The standard biography of Sir Henry Irving was written by his grandson Laurence Irving in the late 1940s and published in 1951 by Faber & Faber. Two further volumes of his family history, *The Successors* (Rupert-Hart Davis [*sic*] Chatto & Windus, 1967) and *The Precarious Crust* (Chatto & Windus, 1971), contain many interesting glimpses of Henry Irving's two sons, the actor-manager H.B. (Harry) Irving and the playwright-actor Laurence Irving (the author's uncle) about whom Austin Brereton published *'H.B.' and Laurence Irving* (Grant Richards, 1922). I have found several volumes on Henry Irving that were brought out shortly after his death very useful, especially Bram Stoker's *Personal Reminiscences of Henry Irving* (William Heinemann 1907, revised edition) and Austin Brereton's prodigious *Life of Henry Irving* (Longmans, 1908). Among recent studies, I have used are Madeleine Bingham's *Henry Irving* (Allen & Unwin, 1978), Alan Hughes's *Henry Irving, Shakespearean* (Cambridge University Press, 1981), Jeffrey Richards's edition of Irving's essays, addresses and lectures in *Sir Henry Irving, Theatre, Culture and Society* (Ryburn Publishing, Keele University Press, 1994) and his socio-cultural analysis of Irving's theatre career, *Sir Henry Irving: A Victorian Actor and his World* (Hambledon & London, 2005). I have also immersed myself in the publications of the Irving Society (www.theirvingsociety.org.uk): its excellent magazine *First Knight* and newsletter *The Irvingite*. Henry Irving makes an appearance too in several works of fiction, from George and Weedon Grossmith's *The Diary of a Nobody* (which first came out in *Punch* in 1892) to Pamela Hansford Johnson's *Catherine Carter* (Knopf, 1952) and Ngaio Marsh's *Final Curtain* (Collins, 1947) in which Sir Henry Ancred 'the celebrated Shakespearean actor' is having his portrait painted in the character of Macbeth – before being mysteriously murdered. (Ngaio Marsh has some fun with this retired 'Grand Old Man of the British stage' by association. She makes him speak of his Norman ancestors 'as if they'd been chosen from the dramatic personae in a Lyceum production', have a son (deceased) named Henry Irving Ancred and calls one of the bedrooms in his ancestral home 'Ellen Terry'.) The story of Ellen Terry, Godwin and Watts forms the basis of 'Hebe Elsna's' (Dorothy Phoebe Ansle's) historical novel *The Sweet Lost Years* (Hale, 1955).

Ellen Terry's autobiography *The Story of my Life* (Hutchinson & Co) was dedicated to her daughter Edy and first published in 1908. It was reprinted in 1933 in a much-revised edition, the title page of which reads: '*Ellen Terry's Memoirs* with a Preface, Notes and Additional Biographical Chapters by Edith Craig & Christopher St John' (Victor Gollancz). As Ellen Terry's 'literary henchman' Christopher St John produced her *Four Lectures on Shakespeare* (Martin Hopkinson, 1932) and also edited *Ellen Terry and Bernard Shaw: A Correspondence* (limited issue, the Fountain Press, distributed by G. P. Putnam's Sons, and trade issue, Constable, 1931). This contains 191 letters from Terry to Shaw and 118 letters and postcards by Shaw, who edited and revised many of the texts. Twenty-six of Ellen Terry's letters written between 1878 and 1917 to Stephen Coleridge, which he selected to illustrate her 'purity of mind' (his name suggestively omitted from its pages), were published in the year of her death by Mills & Boon with the title *The Heart of Ellen Terry*. The first full-length biography of her, Roger Manvell's *Ellen Terry* (Heinemann, 1968), has generally been regarded as the standard Life, though it has been succeeded by several later biographies, the most noteworthy of them being Tom Prideaux's *Love or Nothing: The Life and Times of Ellen Terry* (Millington Books, 1975), Nina Auerbach's *Ellen Terry: Player in her Time* (Phoenix House / J.M. Dent, 1987) and most recently a short well-illustrated Life by Joy Melville (Haus Publishing, 2006). *Ellen Terry and her Sisters* by T. Edgar Pemberton (C. Arthur Pearson) appeared in 1902 while the sisters were alive and *A Pride of Terrys* (Longmans), a very readable family saga written by Marguerite Steen 'in fulfilment of a promise' to Ellen Terry and dedicated to the memory of her mother Sarah Ballard Terry, was published in 1962.

Edy: Recollections of Edith Craig, edited by Eleanor Adlard (Frederick Muller, 1949), contains seventeen essays about Ellen Terry's daughter, one of them by her brother Edward Gordon Craig, another by Christopher St

John, who also contributed a biographical note. Her career has been closely examined in two academic studies by Katharine Cockin: *Edith Craig* (Cassell, 1998) and *Women and Theatre in the Age of Suffrage: The Pioneer Players 1911–1925* (Palgrave, 2001). An agreeable short biography of mother and daughter, *Ellen and Edy*, has been written by Joy Melville (Pandora, 1987).

'I am very doubtful whether the public realizes that I have (since 1899) *worked* exceedingly hard most of the time', Gordon Craig wrote in a chronology he was preparing for Janet Leeper (see Select Bibliography). This is borne out by the many hammock-shaped shelves of publications by and about him. *Gordon Craig: The Story of His Life* (Victor Gollancz, 1968) remains the standard biography – a difficult and courageous task undertaken by his and Elena Meo's son Edward Craig. Equally agonising in its fashion is *Edward Gordon Craig: The Last Eight Years 1958–1966* (Whittington Press) containing Nelly Craig's letters to her brother Edward, who published it in a limited edition of 345 copies in 1983 shortly after her death. Gordon Craig's *Paris Diary 1932–33*, edited and with a Prologue by Colin Franklin (who perhaps wisely cut the original diary by about one third), was published by the Bird & Bull Press in 1982. The *Correspondence of Edward Gordon Craig and Count Harry Kessler*, meticulously edited by L.M. Newman, was published in 1995 (W.S. Maney & Son). Thirty-six of Craig's letters to Johannes Poulsen, edited and with an introduction by Svend Kragh-Jacobsen, are printed as an English-language appendix to Ulla Poulsen Skou's *Genier er som Tordenvejr* ['Genius is like a Tempest'] (Selskabet for dansk Teaterhistorie, 1973), and his correspondence with Olga Knipper-Tchekhovna appears in the two-volume edition of Knipper's letters, published in Moscow in 1972. Extracts from Craig's letters and diaries are reproduced in Francis Steegmuller's *Your Isadora: The Love Story of Isadora Duncan & Gordon Craig* (Macmillan, 1974) and there are quotations from his correspondence in volumes of memoirs and criticism too vast to be recorded here. Enid Rose's hagiographical volume *Gordon Craig and the Theatre: A Record and an Interpretation* (Sampson Low, Marston, 1931) contains lists of his publications between 1898 and 1930, his international and group exhibition catalogues between 1904 and 1929, and books by other writers with references to his work between 1896 and 1931.

Craig appears as Sherwood Saville, 'the Maker of Masks', in John Cournos's novel *Babel* (Heinemann, 1923), as the scene designer Charles

Mann in Gilbert Cannan's novel *Mummery* (Collins, 1918) and as the nameless 'figure in a great black cloak and a wide-brimmed high-crowned hat' in 'Gooseberry', published in Sylvia Lynd's *The Mulberry Bush and Other Stories* (Macmillan, 1925).

The Gordon Craig catalogue of books assembled by Dorothy Nevile Lees is in the Harold Acton Library at the British Institute in Florence (and can be accessed through archivio@britishinstitute.it). Part of Dorothy Nevile Lees's archive, well described by Beth Carroll-Horrocks in *Theatre Survey*, vol. 46, no. 1 (May, 2005), pp. 103–13, was sold by her son David Lees (Davidino) in the 1980s to the Harvard University Theater Collection at the Houghton Library, which also houses other Craig items (there is a finding aid at <http://oasis.lib.harvard.edu/oasis/deliver/advancedsearch?_collection=oasis. or alternatively the contents can be reached through Hollis). A collection of Dorothy Nevile Lees's papers is held at the Archivo Contemporaneo of the Gabinetto Vieusseux in Florence, catalogued by Ilaria Sborgi (<http://www.vieusseux.fi.it/archivio/fondi_acb.html).

The best published guide to Craig's prolific output – his books and contributions (including reproductions) to books, the texts of plays which he produced, the periodicals which he edited and for which he wrote, his one-man and group exhibitions, and the programmes of plays which he designed, produced or dreamed of producing, is still the bibliography prepared by Ifan Kyrle Fletcher and Arnold Rood and published by the Society for Theatre Research in 1967 (though this publication omits some articles that can be found in Craig's press-cutting books in Paris). The bibliography does not of course include his posthumous publications. Of these the most significant are the rather uneven edition of Defoe's *The Life and Strange Adventures of Robinson Crusoe,* which had been originally commissioned by Craig's patron, Count Kessler, and was eventually published with some typographical eccentricities by the Basilisk Press in 1979, with a Foreword by his son Edward Craig; and his *Black Figures* (originally intended for Craig's model stage) of which a limited edition (500 copies containing 105 reproductions and an unpublished essay written by Gordon Craig in 1945, together with an introduction and scholarly apparatus provided by L. M. Newman) was published by Christopher Skelton in 1989. In my opinion the latter volume exhibits his wood-engraved work as well as anything produced during his life – with the spectacular exception of the Cranach Press

Hamlet (German edition, 1929, English edition, 1930) which incorporated work first done for his model stage in Florence, then transferred on cardboard figures to Moscow, and which reveals more clearly than anything else how vividly Craig interprets Shakespeare's text. Among those books published in his lifetime, Craig's *Henry Irving* (J.M. Dent, 1930), *Ellen Terry and her Secret Self* (Sampson Low, Marston, 1931) – its provocative annexe loaded into a pocket at the back and aimed at Bernard Shaw – and his memoirs, *Index to the Story of my Days 1872–1907* (Hulton Press, 1957), have been particularly relevant to the interweaving stories I have attempted to reconstruct.

The accumulation of writings (in memoirs and autobiographies, volumes of critical analysis, collected and uncollected newspaper reviews, theatre magazines and learned journals) about Henry Irving and his two sons, and about Ellen Terry and her daughter and son, is far more extensive than I had expected. But it was not until I came to explore the unpublished material engulfing these six characters that I was made aware of the foolhardiness of embarking on such a wide-ranging and complex group biography. A comprehensive inventory of these archives – a veritable marathon of scholarly travail – would consume more years than I have at my command and absorb more philanthropic sponsorship than my publishers, in their darkest nightmares, could contemplate. I happily resign myself therefore to a succinct description of these archives supplemented by a select bibliography of publications I have consulted.

In 1959, Laurence Irving's family archive, which he selectively used as research papers for his volumes of biography and autobiography, was anonymously purchased and donated to the Theatre Museum Association before being passed on to the British Theatre Museum in London (becoming one of the principal collections which, brought together in 1974, were to form the museum itself). This collection, now at the deposit in Blythe Road, West Kensington, includes both printed books and manuscript material ranging through speeches, pamphlets, souvenirs, programmes, menus, account books, photographs, drawings, scrapbooks as well as the manuscript of Laurence Irving's biography of his grandfather. In addition to some fifty-seven files of related documents there are a further forty-six files of correspondence (more than 2,000 letters to and from Henry Irving covering the years 1870 to 1905). Heroic labours have been undertaken by Helen Smith assisted by Frances Hughes to catalogue this material which Helen Smith has entered on a website, <http://www.henryirving.co.uk.>

I must add here that Henry Irving not only had poor eyesight but what initially appeared to me as indecipherable handwriting. Fortunately his great-grandson, John Irving, provided me with a secret formula for unlocking the meaning of the written texts. For the benefit of future Irving scholars, I can reveal that it entails holding the pages at an acute and curious angle, and then examining in a strong light the foreshortened lettering that emerges. Among the correspondence in this collection is a letter inviting Henry Irving to judge some students' diction. On the back of the page he has scrawled: 'Can't read the beggar's name.' Using John Irving's special method I can confirm that the word is definitely 'beggar's' – and that the letter is from the Prince of Wales. Of particular interest in this collection is the sombre correspondence between Harry and Laurence Irving and their mother Florence, as well as her letters and diaries over quarter of a century.

Although the Theatre Museum in London (to which Arnold Rood's collection of Gordon Craig papers, books and periodicals has been transferred from New York) is the chief repository of the Irving papers, there are several other significant collections in Britain. The Bram Stoker Collection at the Shakespeare Centre Library at Stratford-upon-Avon holds many boxes of ephemera relating to the Lyceum Theatre during Stoker's term there as manager (including a receipt for Irving's kangaroo from London Zoo in 1890). The Russell-Cotes Art Gallery and Museum at Bournemouth contains a rich hoard of Irving memorabilia originally brought together by his friends Sir Merton and Lady Russell-Cotes who dedicated a room of their home in Bournemouth to his memory. Among the relics in the museum are snuff boxes and inkstands, belts and pipes, knee-buckles and meat-skewers, statuettes and busts, prints and water-colours and plaques and medals. There are also approximately a thousand portfolios containing albums, articles, leaflets, fliers, playbills, posters, newspaper cuttings, together with a lock of Irving's hair and the text of Merton Russell-Cotes's oeuvre *Henry Irving: Home and Abroad*. In 1927 the curator, Richard Quick, printed an illustrated souvenir of this Irving Collection and in 2005 the museum mounted an exhibition, *A Life on Stage*, marking the centenary of Henry Irving's death in the preparation of which additional material was discovered. Elsewhere there is a gentle scattering of Irving memorabilia around Britain (the British Library owns a few letters from Henry Irving to Bernard Shaw and a small amount of correspondence from Florence Irving, her son Laurence and daughter-in-law Dorothea). Among provincial centres a significant collection of Henry Irving's correspondence and miscellaneous papers is held by the Brotherton Library at the University of Leeds.

At the end of 2005 the Irving family donated the bulk of its own collection of documents to the Drama Department of Bristol University. This gift includes 123 items in Henry Irving's deed box, discovered in the cellar of a London solicitor and rescued by John Irving from a dumpbin in 1996, and copies of Gordon Craig's correspondence with the biographer Laurence Irving (John Irving's and his sister Elizabeth Brunner's father). Also included in this donation is the inventory which John Irving completed in 1997 of Henry Irving papers at manuscript libraries in the United States (some 560 items). Among this index of material are listed Henry Irving's letters to the American theatre critic William Winter and the British publisher William Heinemann, in addition to approximately eighty other correspondents, held by the Folger Shakespeare Library, Washington DC; his correspondence with Clement Scott at the Huntington Library, San Marino, California; his letters to Joseph Hatton and others (including a letter by Irving to Gordon Craig written for his twenty-first birthday and several to Irving from the Dean of Canterbury, F.W. Farrar, fixing a date for a reading of *Becket* at Canterbury Cathedral on 3 May 1897) in the Harry Ransom Humanities Research Center at the University of Texas at Austin; letters to Bram Stoker, Henry Loveday, Lady Dorothy Nevill and others in the Special Collections of the Harold Mudd Library at Claremont, California; documents relating to tours of North America, together with some Laurence Irving correspondence in the Special Collections of the Rush Rhees Library at Rochester, New York; the Austin Brereton papers, including Henry Irving's and Ellen Terry's correspondence to Brereton, in the Harvard Theater Collection at Cambridge, Massachusetts, which also holds Gordon Craig's heavily annotated biography of Irving. Kristan Tetens of Michigan State University has compiled an extensive website of Henry Irving material: <http://www.msu.edu/~tetenskr/IrvingArchive.htm>

Those who are lured to Austin, Texas, by the prospect of seeing the patent leather shoes Ellen Terry wore as Portia should be warned before they set out that she 'never wears "Patent Leather Shoes" ' – and also that the false shoes are not actually there. But at the Russell-Cotes Art Gallery and Museum at Bournemouth you may see duelling swords, daggers and pistols, stomachers and cloaks and tankards and girdles and suits of armour made of blued steel. A casket from *The Merchant of Venice* is there and so is the black costume Henry Irving wore in *Hamlet*. Other elaborate costumes, reproductions of sets and theatre material from Lyceum productions are owned by the Bram Stoker Collection at Stratford-upon-Avon, the Theatre Museum in Covent Garden, the London Museum (where the Royal Shakespeare Theatre collection of Lyceum properties is on loan) and Ellen Terry's and Edy Craig's home at Smallhythe in Kent, now owned by the National Trust. Millais's portrait of Henry Irving is owned by the Garrick Club in London and Whistler's painting of him as Philip II of Spain hangs in the Metropolitan Museum of Art in New York. Watts's portrait of Ellen Terry, entitled *Choosing*, belongs to the National Portrait Gallery in London and Sargent's painting of her as Lady Macbeth is in the Tate Britain Gallery on Millbank. Watts's painting of Kate and Ellen Terry, entitled *The Sisters*, hangs in the Octagon Room at Eastnor Castle, Ledbury, Herefordshire. His painting of Ellen as *Wife of Pluto* is in the Walker Gallery, Liverpool; and paintings of her as Ophelia and as Francesca in his *Paolo and Francesca* are both at the Watts Gallery, Compton, near Guildford.

In his *Portrait of Ellen Terry* (Amber Lane Press, 1989) David F. Cheshire noted that the 'principal repository of Ellen Terry memorabilia and associated papers is the Ellen Terry Memorial Museum, Smallhythe Place' and that the house with its contents was 'presented to the National Trust by Edy Craig in 1939'. The National Trust has done an excellent job renovating the farmhouse, Barn Theatre and Priest's House on the estate, but the condition of the written archive, which included Edy's papers and well as her mother's (over 20,000 items), remained haphazardly inaccessible for over fifty years. Occasionally disturbed by curators from their repose and given well-intentioned if rather idiosyncratic treatment, many of these papers have over recent years been heroically listed and arranged by Katharine Cockin, working in the unheated rooms of Smallhythe during the winter months. She has continued sorting, copying and cataloguing these papers at the University of Hull and is setting up a web-based catalogue (currently available via the university website: http://ellenterryarchive.hull.ac.uk) describing in detail the papers of both Ellen Terry and Edy Craig which are owned by the

National Trust (and which will be available at the British Library in 2009). Her project, when complete, will be accompanied by a printout from the database published in book format. Concurrently, as judges say when handing down sentences, Dr Cockin is committed to the hard labour of preparing the multi-volume *Collected Letters of Ellen Terry* (for publication by Pickering & Chatto).

Wherever Henry Irving papers are lodged in Britain there is inevitably some associated material of Ellen Terry's and often Edy Craig's letters too. The correspondence between Bernard Shaw and Ellen Terry is held by the British Library (43800–43802, 46172 ff 39–49, 46505 f 33, 71068) in which there are also a few Edy Craig and Gordon Craig letters. There is an interesting series of more than seventy letters from Ellen Terry to Elizabeth, Lady Lewis, covering the period 1889–1923 (Dep. C.837, ff 85–168, ff 1–61) and to her daughter Katherine Lewis 1892-1923 (Dep. C. 845, ff 34–97) in the Lewis family papers at the Bodleian Library, University of Oxford. The letters Ellen Terry wrote to Stephen Coleridge, now among the boxes of Coleridge correspondence from those who in his *Memories* (John Lane 1913) he called the 'good and famous', are lodged at the Garrick Club, London. In the United States Ellen Terry's papers are widely dispersed and can be found in the Fales Collection, Bobst Library, New York University; the Folger Library, Washington DC; the Furness Collection and the Rare Books Room, Van Pelt Library, both at the University of Pennsylvania; the Houghton Library, Harvard University; the Huntington Library (which has some of her letters to Graham Robertson); the Players Club, New York City; the Tucker–Coleman Papers in the Swem Library at the College of William and Mary; and the Department of Special Collections, University of California, Los Angeles, which owns Ellen Terry's letters to Audrey Campbell and also two boxes of Edy Craig material together with Christopher St John's manuscript, 'The Golden Book' (58 leaves in a black leather journal). Much Ellen Terry correspondence lies within various collections at the Harry Ransom Humanities Research Center, University of Texas at Austin. In the Edward Gordon Craig Collection alone there are 325 letters from her to her son, 29 from him to her, and 134 from him to his sister Edy.

At first glance, a list of Edward Gordon Craig papers generously, almost randomly, distributed around the world seems to suggest that there is no major archive connected with the arts that does not hold examples of his work. L.M. Newman's international survey of his archives, published by the Malkin Press in 1976 (with addenda inserted in 1996), contains more than a hundred repositories in some seventeen countries – and this has increased over the last thirty years (Nelly Craig's collection, for example, was subsequently acquired by the Ohtani Women's College, Osaka, Japan, adding a new country as well as a new scholarly, if somewhat daunting, host). The collection that Gordon Craig sold to the Bibliothèque nationale de France in 1957 (now transferred to the Departement des arts du spectacle, Paris) is described as 'a portion' of the archive by the curator of the Edward Gordon Craig Collection at the Harry Ransom Humanities Research Center in Texas. The former does indeed have the largest Craig collection in the world: 10,000 books, 1,000 manuscripts, 1,000 original drawings, 6,000 letters as well as diaries and notebooks (see *Gordon Craig et le renouvellement du théâtre*, Bibliothèque nationale). But then the Harry Ransom Humanities Research Center, which purchased many of Edward Craig's papers in 1969, has some 3,000 Gordon Craig letters, as well as many of his day books, manuscript notebooks and folders of printed material. The situation has been growing more complex as the years pass. For a Gordon Craig scholar it appears possible to study texts of the very same letters in various countries and collections. At Eton College Library, the librarian Michael Meredith, a Browning scholar waylaid by his enthusiasm for Craig's work, has built up a magnificent attic roomful of Craig's books and other publications as well as acquiring from the Craig family over the years what has been for me an extraordinarily interesting collection of his letters in various forms. So, apart from adding the Craig–[Isadora] Duncan Collection which Gordon Craig himself sold to the New York Public Library at the Lincoln Center in 1962 (of which a register and a transcription were made by Nicki Nowlin Ostrom; see *Bulletin of the New York Public Library* 76 [1972]), the most useful compass for finding these archives remains L.M. Newman's international survey, supported by the *Location Register of Twentieth-Century English Literary Manuscripts and Letters*, volume 1, A–J, pp. 215–16 (the British Library 1988) which is updated through the Reading University website (www.locationregister.com).

Finally I should add that my work has benefited from exploring one or two privately owned collections, the owners of which wish to remain private.

Select Bibliography

Adlard, Eleanor (ed.). *Edy: Recollections of Edith Craig* (1949)
Anon. *Letters of an Unsuccessful Actor* (1923)
Archer, William. *Henry Irving, Actor and Manager: A Critical Study* (1883)
Archer, William. *The Theatrical World* (vols for 1893 to 1897)
Aria, Mrs. *My Sentimental Self* (1922)
Asche, Oscar. *Oscar Ashe: By Himself* (1929)
Ashwell, Lena. *Myself a Player* (1936)
Asquith, Lady Cynthia. *Diaries 1915–18* (1968)
Auerbach, Nina. *Women and the Demon: The Life of a Victorian Myth* (1982)
Auerbach, Nina. *Ellen Terry: Player in her Time* (1987)
Bablet, Denis. *Edward Gordon Craig*, trans. Daphne Woodward (1966)
Baker, Michael. *The Rise of the Victorian Actor* (1978)
Baker, Michael. *Our Three Selves: A Life of Radclyffe Hall* (1985)
Bancroft, Marie and Bancroft, Squire. *Recollections of Sixty Years* (1909)
Barnes, James Strachey. *Half a Life* (1933)
Beerbohm, Max. *Around Theatres* (1969)
Beerbohm, Max. *More Theatres: 1898–1903* (1969)
Beerbohm, Max. *Last Theatres 1904–1910* (1970)
Benson, Frank. *My Memoirs* (1930)
Bentley, Eric. *The Theory of the Modern Stage* (1968)
Bernhardt, Sarah. *Memories of My Life* (1908)
Bingham, Madeleine. *Henry Irving and the Victorian Theatre* (1978)
Blatchly, John. *The Bookplates of Edward Gordon Craig* (1997)
Blunt, Wilfrid. *'England's Michaelangelo': A Biography of George F. Watts, O.M., R.A.* (1975)
Booth, Michael R. 'Pictorial Acting and Ellen Terry' in *Shakespeare and the Victorian Stage*, ed. Richard Foulkes (1986)
Brereton, Austin. *Life of Henry Irving* (1908)
Brereton, Austin. *'H.B.' and Laurence Irving* (1922)
Bruce, Kathleen. See Kennet

Bryant, Barbara. *G.F. Watts: Portraits* (2004)

Calmour, Alfred C. *The Amber Heart: A Poetic Fancy in Three Acts* (1888)

Carr, Alice Comyns. *Reminiscences*, ed. Eve Adam (1926)

Carroll, Lewis. 'Stage Children', *The Theatre* (2 September 1889)

Carroll, Lewis. *The Diaries of Lewis Carroll*, two vols, ed. Roger Lancelyn Green (1953)

Carroll, Lewis. *The Letters of Lewis Carroll*, two vols, ed. N. Norton Cohen with the assistance of Roger Lancelyn Green (1979)

Chapman, Ronald. *The Laurel and the Thorn: A Study of G.F. Watts* (1945)

Cheshire, David F. *Portrait of Ellen Terry* (1989)

Chesterton, G.K. *G.F. Watts* (1901)

Cline, Sally. *Radclyffe Hall: A Woman called John* (1997)

Cockin, Katharine. *Edith Craig* (1998)

Cockin, Katharine. *Women and Theatre in the Age of Suffrage: The Pioneer Players 1911–1925* (2001)

Coleridge, Stephen. *The Heart of Ellen Terry* (1908)

Coleridge, Stephen. *Memories* (1913)

Cook, Duncan. *Nights at the Play* (1883)

Coquelin, C. *The Art of the Actor*, trans. Elsie Fogerty (1932)

Craig, Edward Anthony. *Gordon Craig: The Story of His Life* (1968)

Craig, Edward Anthony (ed.). *Edward Gordon Craig: The Last Eight Years 1958–1966: Letters from Ellen Gordon Craig* (1983)

Craig, Edward Gordon. *Gordon Craig's Book of Penny Toys* (1899)

Craig, Edward Gordon. *Bookplates* (1900)

Craig, Edward Gordon. *The Art of the Theatre* (1905)

Craig, Edward Gordon. 'A Letter to Ellen Terry from her Son', *The Mask* (1908)

Craig, Edward Gordon. *On the Art of the Theatre* (1911)

Craig, Edward Gordon. *The Theatre Advancing* (1919)

Craig, Edward Gordon. *Scene* (1923)

Craig, Edward Gordon. *Nothing or the Bookplate* (1924)

Craig, Edward Gordon. *Woodcuts and Some Words* (1924)

Craig, Edward Gordon. *Books and Theatres* (1925)

Craig, Edward Gordon. *Henry Irving* (1930)

Craig, Edward Gordon. *The Pretenders of Henrik Ibsen* (1930)

Craig, Edward Gordon. *The Tragedie of Hamlet Prince of Denmark* by William Shakespeare, illus. Edward Gordon Craig (1930)

Craig, Edward Gordon. *Ellen Terry and her Secret Self* (1931)

Craig, Edward Gordon. *Index to the Story of my Days 1872–1907* (1957)

Craig, Edward Gordon. *Black Figures* (1989)

Craig, Edward Gordon. *Gordon Craig on Movement and Dance*, ed. Arnold Rood (1978)

Craig, Edward Gordon. *Paris Diary 1932–1933*, ed. Colin Franklin (1982)
Craig, Edward Gordon and Hevesi, Sàndor. *The Correspondence of Edward Gordon Craig and Sàndor Hevesi 1908–1933*, ed. György Székely (1991)
Craig, Edward Gordon and Kessler, Count Harry. *The Correspondence of Edward Gordon Craig and Count Harry Kessler*, ed. L.M. Newman (1995)
Dane, Clemence. *Eighty in the Shade* (1959)
Dawick, John. *Pinero: A Theatrical Life* (1993)
Charles, Dickens. *The Dickens Theatrical Reader*, ed. Edgar and Eleanor Johnson (1961)
Disher, Maurice Wilson. *The Last Romantic* (n.d.)
Donaldson, Frances. *The Actor-Managers* (1970)
Douglas-Home, Jessica. *Violet: The Life and Loves of Violet Gordon Woodhouse* (1996)
Du Cann, C.G.L. *The Loves of Bernard Shaw* (1963)
Dunbar, Janet. *The Early Victorian Woman* (1953)
Duncan, Isadora. *My Life* (1928)
Fecker, Constance. *Bright Star: A Portrait of Ellen Terry* (1971)
Forbes-Robertson, Johnston. *A Player under Three Reigns* (1925)
Ford, Colin. *Julia Margaret Cameron* (2003)
Forshaw, Charles (ed.). *Tributes to the Memory of the Late Sir Henry Irving* (1905)
Gielgud, Sir John. *Distinguished Company* (1972)
Gielgud, John. *Gielgud's Letters*, with an introduction and ed. Richard Mangan (2004)
Gielgud, Kate Terry. *An Autobiography* (1953)
Glendinning, Victoria. *Vita: The Life of V. Sackville-West* (1983)
Godwin, Edward W. 'The Architecture and Costume of "*The Merchant of Venice*"' 1875, *The Mask* I (1908–9)
Gorelik, Mordecai. *New Theatre for Old* (1940)
Gross, John. *Shylock: Four Hundred Years in the Life of a Legend* (1992)
Hamilton, Cicely. *Marriage As a Trade* (1905)
Hamilton, Cicely. *Life Errant* (1935)
Harbron, Dudley. *The Conscious Stone: The Life of Edward William Godwin* (1949)
Harker, Joseph. *Studio and Stage* (1924)
Hatton, Joseph. *Henry Irving's Impressions of America* (1884)
Hiatt, Charles. *Ellen Terry and her Impersonations: An Appreciation* (1898)
Hughes, Alan. *Henry Irving, Shakespearean* (1981)
Ibsen, Henrik. *The Vikings at Helgeland* (1858)
Innes, Christopher. *Edward Gordon Craig* (1983)
Irving, Sir Henry. *Theatre, Culture and Society*, ed. Jeffrey Richards (1994)
Irving, Laurence. *Godefroi and Yolande* (1898)
Irving, Laurence. *Henry Irving: The Actor and his World* (1951)

Irving, Laurence. *The Successors* (1967)

Irving, Laurence. *The Precarious Crust* (1971)

James, Henry. *Summersoft* (1895; manuscript, Harry Ransom Humanities Research Center)

James, Henry. *The Scenic Art* (1949)

James, Henry. *The Scenic Art: Notes on Acting & Drama: 1872–1901*, ed. Allen Wade (1957)

Johnson, Pamela Hansford. *Catherine Carter* (1952)

Jones, Henry Arthur. *The Shadow of Henry Irving* (1931)

Kennet, Kathleen, Lady. *Self-Portrait of an Artist* (1949)

Kessler, Count Harry. *The Diaries of a Cosmopolitan: Count Harry Kessler 1918–1837*, trans. Charles Kessler (1971)

Knight, Joseph. *Theatrical Notes* (1893)

Kurth, Peter. *Isadora. The Sensational Life of Isadora Duncan* (2001)

Kustow, Michael. *Peter Brook: A Biography* (2005)

Laver, James. *Whistler* (1942)

Leeper, Janet. *Edward Gordon Craig: Designs for the Theatre*, with a chronology compiled by Edward Gordon Craig (1948)

Lees, Dorothy Nevile. *I Record Only the Sunny Hours*, ed. David Lees (1986)

Lees-Milne, James. *Caves of Ice* (1983)

Lees-Milne, James. *People and Places* (1992)

Loshak, David. 'G.F. Watts and Ellen Terry', *Burlington Magazine* 105 (November 1963)

Lucas, E.V. *Prologue to Ellen Terry's Bouquet*, illus. Laura Knight (1917)

Manvell, Roger. *Ellen Terry* (1968)

Marshall, Beatrice. *Emma Marshall: A Biographical Sketch* (1900)

Martin-Harvey, Sir John. *Autobiography* (1933)

Meisel, Martin. *Shaw and the Nineteenth-Century Theatre* (1963)

Melville, Joy. *Ellen and Edy* (1987)

Melville, Joy. *Ellen Terry* (2006)

Murray, Paul. *From the Shadow of Dracula: A Life of Bram Stoker* (2004)

Nash, Paul. *Outline* (1949)

Newman, L.M. *Gordon Craig Archives: International Survey* (1976)

Nicoll, Allardyce. *A History of Late Nineteenth-Century Drama*, two vols (1949)

Olivier, Laurence. *Confessions of an Actor: An Autobiography* (1982)

Olsen, Victoria. *Julia Margaret Cameron & Victorian Photography* (2003)

Ormond, Leonée. *George Du Maurier* (1969)

Pearson, Hesketh. *Bernard Shaw* (1942)

Pearson, Hesketh. *The Life of Oscar Wilde* (1946)

Pearson, Hesketh. *The Last Actor Managers* (1950)

Pearson, Hesketh. *Beerbohm Tree* (1956)

Pemberton, T. Edgar. *Ellen Terry and her Sisters* (1902)
Perry, Edward. *Remembering Ellen Terry and Edith Craig* (1948)
Peters, Margot. *Bernard Shaw and the Actresses* (1980)
Peters, Margot. *Mrs Pat: The Life of Mrs Patrick Campbell* (1984)
Pollock, Walter H. *Impressions of Henry Irving* (1908)
Prideaux, Tom. *Love or Nothing: The Life and Times of Ellen Terry* (1975)
Reade, Charles. *Peg Woffington* (1853)
Reade, Charles. *The Wandering Heir* (1873)
Reade, Charles, and Reade, the Revd Compton. *Reade: A Memoir*, two vols (1887)
Richards, Jeffrey. *Sir Henry Irving: A Victorian Actor and his World* (2005)
Richardson, Joanna. *Sarah Bernhardt* (1959)
Robertson, W. Graham. *Time Was* (1931)
Robertson, W. Graham. *Letters from Graham Robertson*, ed. Kerrison Preston (1953)
Rose, Enid. *Gordon Craig and the Theatre: A Record and an Interpretation* (1931)
Rothenstein, William. *Men and Memories 1900–1922* (1931)
Saintsbury, H.A. and Palmer, Cecil. *We Saw Him Act: A Symposium on the Art of Sir Henry Irving* (1939)
Sanderson, Michael. *From Irving to Olivier: A Social History of the Acting Profession 1880–1983* (1984)
Scott, Clement. *The Drama of Yesterday and Today* (1899)
Shaw, Bernard. *Captain Brassbound's Conversion* (1899)
Shaw, Bernard. *Dramatic Opinions and Essays* (1913)
Shaw, Bernard. *Pen Portraits and Reviews* (1932)
Shaw, Bernard. *Sixteen Self-Sketches* (1949)
Shaw, Bernard. *The Drama Observed*, four vols, ed. Bernard F. Dukore (1993)
Shaw, Martin. *Up to Now* (1929)
Shearer, Moira. *Ellen Terry* (1998)
Sheridan, Alan. *Time and Place* (2003)
Skou, Ulla Poulsen. *Genier som Tordenvejr* ['Genius is like a Tempest'] (1973)
Souhami, Diana. *The Trials of Radclyffe Hall* (1998)
St John, Christopher. *The Crimson Weed* (1900)
St John, Christopher. *Henry Irving* (1905)
St John, Christopher. *Ellen Terry* (1907)
[St John, Christopher.] *Hungerheart: The Story of a Soul* (1915)
St John, Christopher. *Christine Murrell, M.D.: Her Life and Work* (1935)
St John, Christopher. *Ethel Smyth: A Biography*, with additional chapters by V. Sackville-West and Kathleen Dale (1959)
Sinden, Donald. *A Touch of the Memoirs* (1982)
Sinden, Donald. *Laughter in the Second Act* (1985)
Stanislavsky, Constantin. *My Life in Art*, trans. J.J. Robins (1924)

Steegmuller, Francis (ed.). *'Your Isadora': The Love Story of Isadora Duncan & Gordon Craig* (1974)
Steen, Marguerite. *A Pride of Terrys* (1962)
Steen, Marguerite. *Looking Glass: An Autobiography* (1966)
Stoker, Bram. *Personal Reminiscences of Henry Irving*, two vols (1906, revised edition 1907)
Tennyson, Alfred, Lord. *The Cup* (1881)
Tennyson, Charles. *Alfred Tennyson* (1949)
Terry, Ellen. 'Stray Memories', *The New Review* 23 (1891)
Terry, Ellen. *The Story of My Life* (1908)
Terry, Ellen. *The Russian Ballet*, illus. Pamela Colman Smith (1913)
Terry, Ellen. *The Heart of Ellen Terry* (1928)
Terry, Ellen. *Ellen Terry's Memoirs*, with a preface, notes, and additional biographical chapters by Edith Craig and Christopher St John (1933)
Terry, Ellen. *Four Lectures on Shakespeare*, ed. Christopher St John (1932)
Terry, Ellen and Shaw, Bernard. *Ellen Terry and Bernard Shaw: A Correspondence*, ed. Christopher St John (1931)
Trewin, J.C. *Mr. Macready* (1955)
Tynan, Kenneth. 'Visit to the Past' (1936), in *Curtains* (1961)
Woolf, Virginia. *Orlando* (1928)
Woolf, Virginia. *Between the Acts* (1941)
Woolf, Virginia. 'Ellen Terry', in *Collected Essays*, vol. IV (1967)
Woolf, Virginia. *Freshwater*, ed. Lucio P. Ruotolo (1976)
Webster, Margaret. *The Same Only Different: Five Generations of a Great Theatre Family* (1969)
Williams, Harcourt. *Four Years at the Old Vic* (1955)
Wills, Freeman. *W.G. Wills: Dramatist and Painter* (1898)
Wilson, A.E. *The Lyceum* (1952)
Winwar, Frances. *Wings of Fire* (1957)

Index